THE
DMK
YEARS

'In *The DMK Years: Ascent, Descent, Survival*, R. Kannan masterfully chronicles the evolution of the Dravidian movement from an emancipatory crusade to a seasoned political venture navigating the grim realities of realpolitik. Delving into the vicissitudes of fortune of Annadurai, Karunanidhi, MGR and Jayalalithaa—the loftiest lights of *Thamizhunarvu*, or Tamil affinity—Kannan, who empathizes with his protagonists without deifying them, brings to life the saga of Tamil Nadu in this magisterial account. In so doing, he also reminds us of the need to wield power scrupulously and only for effecting meaningful change, whose pursuit must always galvanize a leader. Rigorously researched and remarkably narrated, *The DMK Years* is an essential read for all those interested in the fascinating tale of one of India's most dynamic states!'—Shashi Tharoor, author and member of Parliament (Lok Sabha)

'As the DMK celebrates seventy-five years of its existence with a second consecutive sweep in the parliamentary elections, R. Kannan completes his Dravidian trilogy with a flourish. Structured as a comprehensive narrative of the DMK's history revolving around the figure of Muthuvel Karunanidhi, *The DMK Years: Ascent, Descent, Survival* is an indispensable compendium for anyone interested in the history of the Dravidian movement and Tamil politics'—A.R. Venkatachalapathy, author of *Swadeshi Steam: V.O. Chidambaram Pillai and the Battle against the British Maritime Empire*

'The so-called North–South divide within India, of which Tamil Nadu is the epicentre, has caused considerable—and unnecessary—acrimony in recent times. Much of this is because most people, especially in the North, do not know enough about the tempestuous yet ideologically stirring politics of Tamil Nadu. R. Kannan, one of the most perceptive chroniclers of the evolution of recent Tamil Nadu politics, has now written a masterly, highly readable and well-researched book, *The DMK Years*, which is a must-read for all those who wish to understand the current and past genesis of the state's ruling party'—Pavan K. Varma, author, former diplomat and former member of Parliament (Rajya Sabha)

'A definitive work on the DMK's formation and growth, this book provides an insight into how Tamil Nadu's politics is intertwined with the evolution of the DMK as a party. Through meticulous research and interesting anecdotes, R. Kannan gives a rare account of the party's ideology and changing strategies from the time of Independence to the current years. It is an essential read, especially for those interested in Tamil Nadu politics'—Nidhi Sharma, senior journalist and author

'*The DMK Years* by R. Kannan offers an exhaustive overview of the history of the Dravida Munnetra Kazhagam (DMK) and its significant role in the political landscape of India. For anyone outside Tamil Nadu looking to understand the DMK, this book is an essential read. Kannan takes readers through the various ups and downs of the DMK, providing a comprehensive narrative that spans from its founding by C.N. Annadurai in 1949 to its contemporary presence under M.K. Stalin. This meticulously researched book gives a fantastic peek into the minds of many DMK leaders, helping readers understand their idiosyncrasies and motivations. Through detailed accounts of key events, such as the 1972 split with M.G. Ramachandran, the Emergency of 1975–77 and the party's recent resurgence in 2021, Kannan illustrates the resilience and adaptability of the DMK. Moreover, the book delves into the DMK's pioneering welfare policies and its "Dravidian Model" of development, highlighting its impact on other states, while also adding to the criticism the party deserves. *The DMK Years* stands out as a critical resource for anyone seeking to grasp the complexities of Tamil Nadu politics and the DMK's enduring influence'—Dhanya Rajendran, editor-in-chief, News Minute

THE
DMK
YEARS

ASCENT
DESCENT
SURVIVAL

R. KANNAN

PENGUIN
VIKING

An imprint of Penguin Random House

VIKING

Viking is an imprint of the Penguin Random House group of companies
whose addresses can be found at global.penguinrandomhouse.com

Published by Penguin Random House India Pvt. Ltd
4th Floor, Capital Tower 1, MG Road,
Gurugram 122 002, Haryana, India

Penguin
Random House
India

First published in Viking by Penguin Random House India 2024

ISBN 9780670097890

Typeset in Adobe Caslon Pro by Manipal Technologies Limited, Manipal
Printed at Thomson Press India Ltd, New Delhi

www.penguin.co.in

Contents

Preface

I was born in the north of Madras, as Chennai was known till 1996, only a short walk from where the Dravida Munnetra Kazhagam (DMK) was publicly launched on 18 September 1949 and grew up in a politically surcharged milieu where political meetings and rallies were the order of the day. For weeks before the elections, the place resembled a festival venue with boisterous rallies, campaigns and fiery speeches. I grew up listening to political speakers of all hues and shades but the speakers of the Dravidian movement held me in thrall. It was difficult not to be affected. The movement grew on me.

My childhood coincided with the DMK's innocent phase. When the party split in 1972, I was in high school. During my adult years, the DMK was no more in power. In 1989 briefly, in 1995–96 and again between 2016 and 2019, I had the opportunity to see the party from close quarters.

My writings on the party began during the aught years. The political biography of the DMK's founder leader Conjeevaram Natarajan or C.N. Annadurai (Anna) was followed by one on the All India Anna Dravida Munnetra Kazhagam (AIADMK) founder leader M.G. Ramachandran (MGR). Both were brought out to mark the centenary years of the leaders. They were the first comprehensive English biographies of these colossuses.

This book, in conjunction with *Anna: The Life and Times of C.N. Annadurai* and *MGR: A Life*, my earlier books, could be said to constitute a trilogy on the Kazhagam of Tamil Nadu and its charismatic leaders.* Together, they recount the story of Tamil Nadu since Independence. Anna told the story up to 1969, and MGR took it up to 1987. This work takes it to the summer of 2024, only months short of the DMK's seventy-fifth birthday.

When I initially pitched this theme, it failed to gain traction with Penguin Random House India. Author Pavan Varma connected me with Sudha Sadanand of Westland Publications, and they were interested. However, it was not to be. The previous iteration of Westland folded in the spring of 2022, and my search for a publisher began anew. I remain grateful to Pavan and Westland.

It was then that my former editor, Kamini Mahadevan, suggested I approach Meru Gokhale, who set the ball rolling. Executive Editor Karthik Venkatesh perused the early chapters and signalled we were on.

The DMK's identity politics remains unique. The state's public distribution system and welfare populism have been a model for other states. Today, thanks to its human resources and development indices, Tamil Nadu is India's second-largest economy after Maharashtra.[1] An estimated thirty-five lakh migrant workers from mostly the Hindi heartland have chosen the state to better their lives.[2]

It was the Congress's Kumaraswamy Kamaraj who, as chief minister from 1954 to 1963, laid the agricultural, educational and industrial foundations of modern Tamil Nadu. His Dravidian epigones have stood on his shoulders.

A sixth-grade school dropout, the young Kamaraj was consumed by the independence struggle. Married to the Congress movement, he spent nearly nine years in British jails, stayed single and led a

---

* By this, I mean the DMK, All India Anna DMK and the Marumalarchi DMK. Of course, Periyar (the revered) E.V. Ramasamy's Dravidar Kazhagam (DK) too is a part of the story, especially prior to the founding of the DMK and, to some extent, even after that, till the passing of Periyar.

bohemian lifestyle. His rustic charm and plain-speaking endeared him to the masses. Kamaraj rose through the Congress ranks to head the party in his home state and later India. However, he was no match for the DMK and its cultural nationalism.

The DMK began as a separatist party. Anna's mentor, Periyar E.V. Ramasamy, had, in 1939, advocated a separate Tamil Nadu to ward off the teaching of Hindi in the state's schools, seeing it as a northern cultural assault on the Tamils and their language. The demand soon morphed into Dravida Nadu or a separate south. Periyar reverted to his original demand after the 1953 reorganization of the states.

Periyar's thoughts and advocacy were radical and unpopular. Prizing his freedom of expression, Periyar had eschewed political power. His *fidus Achates* C.N. Annadurai (Anna) sought political power as an instrument of change. Using as an excuse the seventy-year-old Periyar's marriage to his much younger aide Maniammai, whom Periyar had named heir to the movement, Anna bolted. For fourteen years, the duo had braved formidable odds to spread the message of self-respect to Tamils. But now they were estranged.

In 1949, Anna founded his party, the Dravida Munnetra Kazhagam (DMK). Unlike his utilitarian mentor, he began to peddle a serious brand of identity politics where *Thamizhunarvu* (Tamil affinity) was the guiding light. The DMK spread slowly but surely. Anna and his *thambi*s (younger brothers, also a term of endearment) spoke and wrote mesmerizingly, promising an independent Dravida Nadu free of being under Delhi's thumb. His thambis thundered, 'Dravida Nadu or death!' But, non-Tamils cold-shouldered the idea. Even Tamils had rallied behind Anna and not the ideal. So when Anna dropped the demand in 1962 after the Indo-China War—in the wake of an impending ban on secessionist advocacy—it mattered little to the DMK cadre.

The party prided itself on being left-of-centre, emphasizing cultural nationalism, state autonomy and parity for all regional languages alongside Hindi. Periyar undercut the DMK's identity politics, calling Kamaraj a pure Tamil, or *Pachai Thamizhan*, and throwing his weight behind him.

His former disciple, on the other hand, moved closer to the erstwhile Congress leader and chief minister of Madras State Chakravarthi Rajagopalachari, or Rajaji, whom he once considered a 'wily fox', and his rightist Swatantra Party (1959–74). The scarcity of rice and the 1965 anti-Hindi agitations had primed the DMK to take power in 1967. Stitching a rainbow alliance with the Left and the Right and promising three measures of rice for a rupee, Anna rode to power that year. However, fifty-eight years old and more seasoned, Anna rightly feared they were not yet ready. His brief tenure is known for symbolic wins, such as renaming Madras State, Tamil Nadu, legalizing self-respect marriages sans priests, and declaring Hindi off-limits in government and aided schools. It was a high time for the party.

Kalaignar M. Karunanidhi succeeded Anna as chief minister and party head, thanks to M.G. Ramachandran, or MGR.

In 1971, the party won by a brute majority. Power appeared almost 'absolute' now. Much as Periyar had feared, the DMK comprising those from modest backgrounds had begun to move closer to Lord Acton's dictum, 'Power corrupts, and absolute power corrupts absolutely.'

Karunanidhi began to consolidate his hold on the party and government and passionately peddled state autonomy even as his more vocal *udanpirappugal*, or siblings, saw him as akin to Bangladesh's Sheikh Mujibur Rahman. Hitherto an ally, Indira Gandhi followed the advice of her Tamil chieftains, who felt the need to cut Karunanidhi down to size. MGR, who felt he was being sidelined, became an instrument in their hand.

In 1972, MGR founded his Anna DMK, later called the All India Anna DMK. While Karunanidhi insinuated that MGR was a Malayalee, MGR called him a 'dark force'. The fight between a scriptwriter and his hero became the state's politics from then on. In the process, Kamaraj, who had hoped for his Congress to return to power, died a dejected man.

The dismissal of his government in 1976 during the Emergency, followed by the Sarkaria Commission of Inquiry, was a dark period for Karunanidhi. However, only three years later, in 1980, Karunanidhi joined forces with Indira Gandhi to take on MGR. 'Nehru's daughter, welcome! Give us a stable government,' he sloganeered alliteratively in Tamil. The Emergency, which jailed his son, nephew and 417 others, and took two lives, was treated as something from the past. In the aftermath of the dismal Janata Party performance at the Centre, the alliance won massively in the parliamentary elections but failed to unseat MGR only months later in the assembly elections.

After MGR's death and with a divided AIADMK, Karunanidhi was back in power in 1989. He reserved 33 per cent for women in local bodies and enabled the inheritance of ancestral property for women the same as their male siblings.

But his Sri Lankan Tamil brethren militants ran amok in Tamil Nadu's backyard. Only two years into his term, they had provided the pretext to get rid of his government. Further, Rajiv Gandhi's assassination raised existential questions for the party. But Karunanidhi was back in power in 1996. His opponent, Jayalalithaa Jayaram, who had inherited MGR's mantle, had sunk herself in the quicksand of graft and ostentation. But she resurfaced in 1998 as the Bharatiya Janata Party's (BJP) biggest coalition partner in the government. The 1998 Coimbatore bombings by Islamic radicals had played a key role in her victory.

Jayalalithaa and the radicals had changed the narrative, giving a foothold to the Hindutva-peddling BJP in 'Periyar's land'. But in a year, the nation was back to the polls. Dissatisfied with the BJP's efforts to bail her out from the criminal cases, Jayalalithaa pulled the plug. That election, Karunanidhi again did the unthinkable when he chose the BJP to fight Jayalalithaa, driving his earlier ally,

G.K. Moopanar, into her arms. He justified that he had to run a political party and famously declared Jayalalithaa's 'corruption was more dangerous than communalism'.

The 2001 elections were a major comedown for Karunanidhi. With his allies deserting him, Karunanidhi, the fierce champion of a casteless 'Tamil race' was in bed with all the caste outfits.

Thanks to Moopanar, the Congress (I) and other allies, Jayalalithaa was back in power in 2001. From then, Karunanidhi and Jayalalithaa began to alternate in power until she won a successive term in 2016 when Karunanidhi was an old horse.

Anna had felt a national role for the DMK was distant. But with the sclerosis of the Congress (I) and the emergence of a third alternative, the DMK found itself in the front and centre of governments in Delhi in 1989–91, 1996–98 and 1999–2013.

During the first United Progressive Alliance (UPA) government (2004–09), the DMK was known for presiding over the communications revolution but was also bogged down by family disputes and the 2G scam. In 2017, a Central Bureau of Investigation (CBI) court acquitted all the 2G accused. The CBI appeal is pending.

In 2011, the bungling of the law and order and power fronts saw Karunanidhi lose. He never returned to power.

In 2016, Jayalalithaa passed away and then in 2018, Karunanidhi did, ending the era of mass leaders in the state. In 2021, Karunanidhi's son, M.K. Stalin, came to power. His government has continued the welfare path, announcing a monthly stipend to women and girls in government schools. Women could ride city buses for free.

Today, the DMK is the third-largest parliamentary party. Importantly, it has been peddling a staunch anti-BJP/Narendra Modi narrative in the name of secularism and federalism.

But the BJP is unlike any other opponent. Its brand of Hindutva has yet to strike a chord, but it has already changed the political discourse in the state and put the DMK on the defensive, challenging its brand of secularism and non-belief.

Furthermore, the Dravidian narrative of inclusiveness has yet to be translated fully. Affirmative action programmes have yet to reach everyone evenly. Thus, the DMK, or the Kazhagams, already face the unenviable task of winning back those having voted with their feet for caste outfits that masquerade as political parties. Ultra-Tamil nationalists and film actor arrivals are other challenges.

It is unclear if cultural nationalism, social justice and secularism alone could continue to deliver for the DMK, or the Kazhagams. Good governance, jobs, sustainable development, water and the environment will likely assume more political heft in the years ahead.

The road to M.K. Stalin's trillion-dollar economy would also require such deliverables. It cannot be politics as usual or should not be.

Despite the endnotes, this book should not be considered academic. The attempt here is to tell the story of the last seventy-five years of Tamil Nadu with an emphasis on the DMK. In the process, the colossuses are discussed, and their major moves and decisions are interpreted.

In writing this book, I have relied mostly on original sources.

I am indebted to many for their kindness and assistance. I am grateful to Gerry Bennet, a former UN colleague, for his editorial suggestions on the first draft. I am grateful to Sithanai for his research support and to the late G. Elavazhagan for introducing him to me. I especially thank Sachi Sri Kantha who, from Japan, provided me with some rare material and articles for this work. I wish to record my thanks to Sadagopan Raveendran, Iniyan Sampath, T.K.S. Villalan, V. Jayaprakash, Seethai Pathippagam's B. Rajasekaran, Arul Natarajan, *The Hindu*'s Vibha Sudarsan, S.K. Subrramanya, K. Arun Kumar, Anna Peravai's Sembian, N. Moorthy, Pranav Moorthy, R. Subramaniya Bharathi, V. Karthik Kumar, Richard Franklin, S. Kirubakaran, 'Stills' E. Gnanam and Wideangle Ravi Shankaran, K.S. Radhakrishnan, D. Mahalakshmi, N. Manickam, DK's V. Kumaresan, Kavitha Muralitharan, K. Muralitharan,

S. Puviarasan, Dr S. Mohan Raj, S. Rajaram, Dr Sundeep Kumar S., T. Chitrarasu, T.K.S. Manivannan, Thaenpaavai Kannan and Anna Arivalayam library assistant T. Padmanabhan for their help. I wish to thank Shashi Tharoor, A.R. Venkatachalapathy, Pavan K. Varma, Nidhi Sharma and Dhanya Rajendran for their blurbs. I am grateful to Karthik, my editor, who patiently shepherded this project. Similarly, I wish to record my appreciation to Ralph Rebello for his patient and meticulous copy-editing. My thanks go to Meru Gokhale, former publisher and editor-in-chief at Penguin Random House India, and the others instrumental in the making of this book. This book would have not been possible without my wife Usha's understanding and support. My special thanks to her.

A note on the usage of names: I have settled on Tamil Nadu instead of Tamilnadu since the former seems more commonly used; I have used Adi Dravida and Dalit and Periyar and EVR, and initials and full names interchangeably. Tamils use a patronymic system and take their father's given name as initials before their name. I have used traditional spellings for names such as Kannadasan and Nedunchezhian but have chosen the changed spellings for places. Thus, Trichy is Tiruchi and Tuticorin Thoothukudi; also, in cases where the Tamil words are not that commonly known, for example, *Manavasam* or Pari, I have followed the transliteration *Manavaasam* and Paari for the ease of the non-Tamil reader.

Chennai   R. Kannan
1 May 2024

1

Muthuvel Karunanidhi aka Kalaignar
The End of an Epoch

Just once, at least now, shall I call you 'Appa' (father)?

My beloved leader, wherever you left for, you let us know before going. This time, why did you depart without informing us?

O Leader, who has become one with my feelings, body, blood, thoughts, and heart! Where have you gone, leaving us behind?

As early as thirty-three years ago, you wrote that these words—'He who worked without rest, rests here'—be inscribed on your memorial. Have you departed, content that you worked ceaselessly for this Tamil society?

Having declared a contest, are you in hiding to find out 'who would surpass the heights you have crossed at ninety-five after eighty years in public life'?

On your ninety-fifth birthday,* on 3 June, on the soil of Thiruvarur. I asked: 'Give me half your strength.' I beg you for that strength and the heart you borrowed from Arignar Anna.

Will you give them to me, O Leader?

---

* In contemporary Tamil political tradition, the ongoing year is considered the age. Karunanidhi was actually ninety-four when he passed away.

1

With that gift, we will fulfil your unrealized dreams and ideals!

From the hearts of crores of party men and women, a request . . . just once . . .

Please utter: 'My fellow party men, whom I consider dearer than my own life!' once more, O Leader! It will make us go on for a hundred years with a sense of nation and language!

Rather than calling you 'Appa, Appa', I have mostly called you 'Leader, leader'.

So now, just once, may I call you 'Appa', my leader?[1]

—M.K. Stalin's 8 August 2018 eulogy for his

father and DMK patriarch 'Kalaignar' (maestro)

Muthuvel Karunanidhi

On 27 July 1969, at forty-five, Muthuvel Karunanidhi succeeded Anna as party leader. From then on, he would be referred to as *Thalaivar* or leader. The movement consumed him. As a young man addressing rallies, he could not be near his wife when she breathed her last. The movement came first, and his time was mostly spent with the cadres; the family had long come to accept that he was larger than just a family head, and his calling was to lead his people and the state. He had become Thalaivar to them from the beginning.

Karunanidhi, the Dravidian movement's last titan, passed away at 6.10 p.m. on 7 August 2018. Together, the man and the movement exemplified the centuries-old struggle for the emancipation of the Tamil lands. In his rise lay the story of the rise of the backward and humble.

Born on 3 June 1924 in Thirukuvalai, a village 74 km east of Thanjavur, the hotbed of caste consciousness, Karunanidhi was the only son of Ayyadurai Muthuvel and Anjugam. His elder sisters, Periyanayagam and Shanmugasundaram, were sure their little brother was destined for glory. His success, however, did not come easily and was achieved with unparalleled industry and talent. Hailing from a modest, backward Isai Vellalar farming family, Karunanidhi, like the movement, had to battle his way forward constantly. Till the end and even after scaling enviable heights in public life, he frequently attributed criticism from Brahmin commentators to his Shudra or lowly caste status.

The Social Context

Unlike Karunanidhi, his parents were religious. His father, a farmer, was also the village doctor, a poet and a raconteur. Known for its temples and the cultural dominance of the Brahmin community, Thanjavur and its environs were fertile ground for not just paddy but also for the stirrings of the non-Brahmins. Not surprisingly, Erode Venkatappa Ramasamy (EVR) 'Periyar's' non Brahmin Dravidar Kazhagam (DK, founded in 1944) commanded a sizeable following in Tiruchi and Thanjavur districts. Even as a schoolboy, Karunanidhi came under its influence.

Periyar's DK was the culmination of two parallel movements, one political that had commenced with the advent of the Justice Party, and the other its parent, the cultural. The cultural movement began with the colonials and the missionaries, with their interest in Tamil, their ideas about Tamil and the caste structure, the spread of education, the historical finds and the rediscovery of Sangam literature in the field of letters. Revisionists argue that the interest was propelled mainly by proselytization. Nevertheless, led by revivalists, the cultural movement, the first, sought to correct social inequality wrought by the accident of caste, believed to be alien to Tamil civilization. The Justice Party, the second movement, provided the context and helped emphasize Tamil genius, egalitarianism and a rich, luxuriant past. The forces unleashed by the two would coalesce into the DMK.

For more than a millennium, Tamil nationalism was considered passé. Secular Tamil literature extolling valour, giving and grace had taken a back seat with the Bhakti movement of the Nayanmars and the Alwars (sixth to twelfth centuries CE). Medieval Muslim incursions turned the political narrative again into a religious one, this time as Muslims versus Hindus. The Nayaks and the Marathas, who replaced the Muslims, created space for Hindu spiritual revival, and religious works such as *Tiruppugal*, *Villibharatham* and *Kanthapuranam*, and literary commentaries became the order of the day. Ramalinga Adigal's (Vallalar) life, teaching and his *Tiruvarutpa* profoundly influenced a section of the Tamil Hindus in the nineteenth century. With colonization, the Tamil cultural nationalist space would be subsumed, this time by the independence movement.

Tamil and Tamil Nationalism in the Twentieth Century

The twentieth century was marked by Subramanya Bharathi's patriotic poetry that fanned the flames of the independence movement.[*] Dominated by Brahmins in the south, the independence movement positioned Tamils energetically within the Indian mainstream. Religion, arts, culture, the political and social discourse had predominantly fallen into the hands of elites who considered Sanskrit divine, Telugu musical and English practical. Sanskrit remained sacred in temples, while Telugu was ensconced as the language of Carnatic music in the Tamil lands. Dance forms like Bharatanatyam became the upper classes' domain, and English was the lingua franca of the elites and government. In short, there was little need for Tamil beyond the confines of one's home. Tamil stood relegated to the households of the great majority of the subaltern masses who had neither the imagination nor knowledge of their Tamil nation's erstwhile glory, much less political independence,

---

[*] Sundaranar's *Manonmaniam*, from where the Tamil invocation song 'Neeraarum Kadaludutha' is excerpted, was also scripted during this period. Again, its impact was limited to the Tamil literary circles, failing to reach the masses.

as even the great empires of the north had failed to encompass the Tamil lands. The non-Brahmin Dravidian movement would challenge this status quo with mixed results.

Non-Brahmin Identity and Assertion

The Presentation Sisters wanted the pupil's name changed from Stalin if he was to be admitted to their renowned Church Park Convent, then a co-ed school. The Catholic sisters' aversion to the Soviet dictator was understandable. His father made it clear that the name of the boy, born four days before the Soviet leader's death, was non-negotiable. 'We should be ourselves,' he told his son and found him another school.* The father was Karunanidhi.

This was typical Karunanidhi, a contrarian who swam upstream for the cause of Tamils and Tamil Nadu. Almost till the end, an octogenarian Karunanidhi pushed the limits of human endeavour, much like his early mentor, EVR. Until he fell critically ill in 2017, the nonagenarian leader continued his five-decade-old practice of writing a missive, instructing or exhorting his *nanba* or friend initially and *udanpirappugal* or siblings later.[2] From 22 October 1968, he wrote more than 4000 such letters in the party organ *Murasoli* (Drumbeat). Not a week passed without a well-argued statement from him on political and social issues. A man who transcended generations through his speech and reach, he had a 4.8 lakh following on Facebook.

Early Successes

Karunanidhi showcased his talent for writing and organization early on. He edited a handwritten journal, headed a student organization

---

* Stalin was to have been named Ayyadurai, combining the diminutive 'Ayya' for Periyar and Durai of Annadurai. But hearing of Stalin's death at a rally, his father Karunanidhi immediately announced that his son would be called Stalin.

and led processions against Hindi imposition in 1938. While in high school, EVR's weekly, *Kudiarasu* (Republic) interested him much more than school lessons. The result: he failed his intermediate exams all the three times he was allowed to take them. Furthermore, his self-respect precepts upended his marriage to the girl he had fallen in love with from a conservative family. Heartbroken, he dabbled in playwriting and acting and in 1945, on EVR's invite, Karunanidhi joined *Kudiarasu* in Erode as an assistant editor. It would be the best apprenticeship he could have ever had.

A year later, with EVR's permission, he relocated to Salem to pen the script for *Rajakumari* (Princess, 1947), where he met Marudur Gopala Ramachandran (MGR), its hero. It was a runaway success. *Mandhirikumari* (Minister's Daughter, 1950) that followed was also a huge hit. A string of successes would make them household names by 1950. The two would begin a friendship and journey that helped each other scale newer heights in films and public life.

Karunanidhi penned stories and scripts for seventy-five movies and innumerable propagandist plays such as *Udayasuryian* or the Rising Sun, which helped popularize the DMK's symbol, the rising sun. His commentaries for *Thirukkural*, Sangam literature, displayed his ceaseless pen, which poured out rich, elegant Tamil with often sharp social reform messaging. *Parasakthi* (1952) with Sivaji Ganesan remains his most popular film, with the hero's five-minute court monologue being the jewel among the immortal lines in the film.

In the 1949 split between EVR and Anna, Karunanidhi stood by Anna. His commitment, drive and talent would soon give him an early start. He presided over the party's Kovilpatti conference in 1951, which had chalked out visions of a drawn-out struggle for an independent Dravida Nadu or south India. Not surprisingly, in less than two years, he led the party's now famous Kallakudi agitation in 1953—displaying imagination and leadership when he lay on the rail tracks, exceeding the party mandate and cementing Anna's confidence in him. That year, he also enticed MGR into the party.

Karunanidhi began to command an individual following in the party early on. As the third treasurer of the party from 1959 till Anna's death, he proved a consummate fundraiser. His influence was such that, in 1961, E.V.K. Sampath demanded that the function be entrusted to no one individual. He was far-sighted. In 1972, MGR, now treasurer, took exception to how Karunanidhi played favourites with the election funds in the 1971 elections without his knowledge. But earlier, in the 1967 elections, Karunanidhi's money-raising skills exceeded Anna's expectations and the Rs 10 lakh limit set by the party, prompting Anna to give him the moniker 'Mr Eleven Lakhs'.

Anna increasingly relied on Karunanidhi to deal with intra-party issues. On Anna's behalf, he negotiated political alliances and, in 1967, stitched together the rainbow alliance that brought the DMK to power that year. Felicitating him on his birthday on 3 June 1968, Anna said:

Karunanidhi is someone who, whether asked to lie on the rails or take up the minister of public works position, would take the command as the same and would harness all his talent to complete it—the country knows that I for sure have a great deal of affection and respect for him.[3]

As Anna's Successor

On 6 March 1969, Karunanidhi succeeded Anna as chief minister. In his first and second innings that lasted until 31 January 1976, he took the social revolution engineered by the DMK forward with his left-of-centre agenda, social justice, populist schemes like eye camps, Tamil cultural renaissance and clamour for state autonomy. He proved an able administrator in touch with the ground. He nationalized buses, expanded the public distribution system, increased food subsidies and promoted industries.[4] His ambition, operation and political strategy catapulted the DMK to a national role. Prime Minister Indira Gandhi banked on his support for her reformist agenda and to break free of K. Kamaraj, the regional boss.

In 1971, the DMK was re-elected with a brute majority, and Karunanidhi emerged out of Anna's shadow. The young chief minister's combative spirit and ideological assertiveness grated on Indira Gandhi's lieutenants in Tamil Nadu. Relations with Delhi began to sour. In 1971, when he was at the zenith of his second political innings, his followers compared him to Sheikh Mujibur Rahman of Bangladesh. However, his worst nightmare also began in October 1972, when ally-turned-rival MGR broke away, levelling charges of nepotism and corruption that dogged his political career until his end. Similarly, he lived through the charge of introducing a whole new generation to alcohol when he lifted prohibition in 1972, citing financial reasons.

In the Doldrums

A new low between the Centre and the DMK was reached when Karunanidhi fiercely opposed the Emergency. His bête noire MGR's craven rollover to Indira Gandhi may have left Karunanidhi with little choice. Karunanidhi, nonetheless, prided himself as a valiant fighter. On 31 January 1976, his government was dismissed for corruption and planning violence. A witch-hunt of DMK men followed with 419 party workers, including Stalin and nephew Murasoli Maran, jailed under the Maintenance of Internal Security Act (MISA). In this dark period, he refused to yield.

Shaken by the dismissal and the repressive Emergency measures, some frontline leaders feared Karunanidhi was taking the party down with him and advocated disbanding the DMK and turning it into a social welfare outfit. At this point, echoing their sentiments, Pulavar Govindan, the Assembly Speaker, wrote Karunanidhi a letter, requesting him to step down. In his lengthy reply, Karunanidhi said they could have given him poison instead and that a good politician was akin to a captain who would not desert his ship even if it were to sink.

The 'captain' was friendless and alone. Those who owed their place to him were now asking him to quit. With the Emergency censors banning political activity or writing, Karunanidhi resorted to allegory. On 19 July 1976, he wrote about himself and his situation poignantly using the selfless palm tree as a metaphor. The best of his letters, this deals with the palm's humble beginnings, how it grew on its own without anyone watering or tending it, and its self-effacing sacrifice and service to others who proved ingrates. It was his story:

Sibling,

Today a tree is narrating its tale. It is a sad story yet interesting. Poor thing: don't ignore it because it is just a tree. Open your ears to the tree that is baring its heart out today.

I am called a palmyra . . .

The palm went on to say that it had given its leaves to make fans, its splints for toys and mats, despite its lips being scalded with lime, its juice and flowers for rice flour rolls, and its flesh to eat. And then? Let us hear it in his own words:

It then rained suddenly—lightning and thunder! For a couple of days, they [the men] never came to me. I heard the town was flooded now. The rains did cool the parched lands, but the water bodies were flooded!

There was a canal at the boundary of my town, and I was told the canal was overflowing. Soon as the message reached me, those men came. They had axes and hacksaws. Without even looking up, they began to cut me. I endured the pain, for I know this would serve some purpose.

Soon as I came down, they carried me across the overflowing canal. What else could they do? They couldn't swim across the canal. They now walked on me and reached the other side. In a few days, the place came to be called Palmyra Bridge. The floods subsided in a couple of weeks, and normalcy was restored. The men came back again and discussed among themselves.

'This palm was useful till now to cross the canal. Now we can cut it into two and make a sturdy ladder,' said one. Another approved.

Then more people came marching towards the few men. They were angry at the few men.

'Do you have a heart? You cut off the palm tree that was of many uses. Like a light at the tunnel, the tree served as a bridge for the people. Now you want to make a ladder of it? Is this just? Leave this place!'

Once the people scorned them, the men slipped off without speaking a word. Now I continue to serve the people as a bridge considering myself lucky for having them step on me. This is my story!

With love,
M.K.[5]

Devotee-like Followers

Despite what those cowering leaders thought of him, Karunanidhi had long become the party.

Notwithstanding the Emergency, men and women travelled to Chennai in buses and vans to meet their Thalaivar (leader), get photographed with him and contribute to the party's legal defence fund against the Sarkaria Commission. To avoid the regime's restrictions, they dressed as pilgrims and tonsured their heads, except that their shrine was their Thalaivar's abode. While party elders were so stricken with the fear of associating with him, droves of families came daily to hold his hand, shed tears and assure him that they were with him. It was then, on 20 August 1976, to be precise, that Karunanidhi said in Tirupur:

> Whether it is going to be criminal proceedings against me, or life imprisonment, or gallows, or any altar where I may be tortured or killed, I have this great confidence that I have a place in the altar of your hearts. Hence I continue to speak to you and write to you.[6]

Ups and Downs

Yet, his personalized style saw the Navalar Era. Nedunchezhian, in 1977, lead several senior leaders like K. Rajaram and S. Madhavan into MGR's AIADMK. They had concluded he was finished. They were wrong.

The post-Emergency phase consigned Karunanidhi to the political opposition for thirteen years. In the Opposition, he worked even harder (he is said to have worked eighteen hours and seen at least 100 people daily) and devised new strategies to keep himself and the party relevant.

In 1989, he returned to power thanks to a divided AIADMK, only to be dismissed again, this time on charges of close ties with the Liberation Tigers of Tamil Eelam (LTTE). In the 1991 elections, he faced his second major challenge when a suicide bomber killed Rajiv Gandhi, and all except him lost as the DMK was considered sympathetic to the Tigers. It was the DMK's worst performance, and with the Jain Commission's interim report pointing an accusing finger at the DMK, it appeared that the DMK's political future was in doubt.

The crippling Emergency, the Sarkaria Commission, political wilderness, allegations of a nexus with the LTTE, the discrediting campaign in the wake of Rajiv Gandhi's assassination and the

hugely debilitating charges of family rule and scandals in the UPA-
II government are only some troughs that Karunanidhi faced. To
bounce back, he did the politically unthinkable at times: allying with
Indira Gandhi in 1980 and the BJP in 1999, actions construed as
unabashed political opportunism by his detractors and as political
astuteness by his followers.

Similarly, under his leadership, the DMK saw unprecedented
highs and lows. Though only five feet five inches in height, the
politically consummate, charismatic and never-tiring regional
chieftain frequently punched above his weight (and height)
nationally, not the least in 1999 and 2004 when the DMK's support
proved crucial to the government formation in Delhi and he donned
the role of kingmaker.

None could better Karunanidhi's enviable record of sixty years of
a legislative career and twenty more in public life or his film-writing
career.

The Record

During his fifty years of stewardship, the party has been out of power
for twenty-seven years in the state. And in 1993, the party split again,
this time for stifling organic leadership—V. Gopalsamy or Vaiko
who was emerging as the most popular leader after Karunanidhi was
shown the door. The party was emaciated but Karunanidhi held it
together during the lean years. In June 1980, in the wake of the
DMK's unexpected defeat in the Tamil Nadu assembly elections,
Karunanidhi had said:

> Oh Tamils, if you throw me into the seas, I will float as a
> catamaran for you to use me to sail; if you throw me into the fire,
> I will become firewood so that you could cook and eat. I will not
> shatter into smithereens if you strike me against a rock. I would
> become like the coconut thrown against the ground and become

smaller pieces, becoming an eatable for you. Oh, Tamils. You can
do whatever to me; I will always serve you.[7]

Until the end, his followers desired his service, making him the
longest-serving head of a party. Their adulation and reverence
appeared to grow with his age. In the 2016 assembly elections,
despite his infirm speech delivery at times, cadres waited on cue to
be electrified by his customary salutation to them as 'my dearer than
life siblings'. On his birthdays, thousands queued up for the singular
experience of getting a close glimpse, touching and wishing him
well. Their pure and simple affection for their leader had to be seen
to be believed.

In the Tamil literary tradition, *Aram Paaduthal* is when an
intended or unintended poetic uttering comes true. Karunanidhi, a
poet, among other things, may have done just that, albeit in prose,
when on 10 May 2016, he declared he would retire 'only if nature does
something to me'. Only months later, age-related illnesses would turn
the nonagenarian leader—whose life until then had been characterized
by prolific writing, speech-making and intense political activity—into
a figurehead of the party he had led for forty-eight years.

Until nature overcame him, Karunanidhi was known for his
phoenix-like ability to rise from his political ashes. He never lost
an election since he was first elected in 1957, and twelve times after
that to the assembly and once to the now-defunct legislative council.
Tamil Nadu's political history was intertwined with Karunanidhi for
six decades.

As Rajiv Gandhi's death cast a long shadow over the man and
his party, a reunited AIADMK under Jayalalithaa succeeded the late
MGR in 1991. In 1996, thanks to Jayalalithaa's ostentatiousness and
venality, Karunanidhi sprang back only to lose power in 2001, return
in 2006 and remain out of power from 2011 till his end.

His last two innings were marked by progressive legislation and
social welfare measures such as 33 per cent reservation for women

in local bodies and 30 per cent in government, equal inheritance of ancestral property for women, the medical insurance scheme and the recognition of the third gender. They will also be equally remembered for his joining the freebie race with rivals MGR and Jayalalithaa, the scandals that rocked the nation and the fall in public life standards.

Karunanidhi proved agile to the changes around him. Despite his atheist moorings, he was pragmatic regarding secular projects, as when he took financial assistance from godman Saibaba on the Krishna waters or when, early on as chief minister, he played a role in reviving the Thiruvarur temple car run. Nevertheless, he remained closer to EVR than Anna when he wondered in 2007 if the Hindu god Ram was an engineer when the Sethusamudram project ran aground because of the natural Adam's Bridge or Rama's Bridge (Ram Setu).

He found himself equally helpless during the final Eelam war. On 22 April 2009, as reports of civilian casualties mounted, he wrote:

> I don't know the way—I am in a responsible position—yet in a hapless state to save our race . . . I don't know what to do . . .[8]

Karunanidhi missed the opportunity to live up to his claim of the leader of the world's Tamils 'Thamizhinath Thalaivar'—by clinging to his office. He said he would have lost the little leverage he had as chief minister. It was self-deception of the worst kind.

Time helped the Tamils of Tamil Nadu to forgive him. They have celebrated him and deserted him in equal measure throughout his career. With his political warts and all, Karunanidhi remains one of independent India's tallest sons and the sole torchbearer of the Dravidian movement in the post-Anna era.

2

DMK aka 'Teardrops'

On 9 July 1949, the seventy-two-year-old EVR wed his thirty-two-year-old trusted aide Gandhimathi, rechristened Arasiyal Mani and later Maniammai, causing outrage in the Dravidar Kazhagam (DK). 'She entered as a storm,' Anna described the development later.[1] He and his cohorts were itching for political power, and 'the storm' had felled Anna's hopes of succeeding EVR. EVR had upstaged them with Maniammai as his political heir. The DK was now safe as a social movement.

A hugely disillusioned Anna had retreated to Kanchipuram, choosing to quit public life. Periyar's nephew E.V.K. Sampath followed him, and so did others, to persuade a reclusive Anna to return to active politics. Writer 'Kalki' Krishnamurthy sent emissaries and openly exhorted Anna to join the Socialist Party. Anna lent his ears but said nothing. His quiescence led to murmurs and protests, prompting an anxious Rama Arangannal to rue that inaction could chase away those who had come to them. Anna explained his procrastination as constructive inaction to discern those who would stay the course with them. 'Patience is always imperative in politics!' he told Arangannal.[2] Nine weeks later, thanks to Sampath and others, the DMK was born. But Anna kept his political ambition under check for seven years. In 1956, the party opted for electoral politics.

The DMK Is Born

K.K. Neelamegam led the 17 September 1949 founding meeting at 7 Coral Merchant Street, George Town in Chennai (then Madras). Nedunchezhian read out Anna's lengthy statement where Anna warned that 'enmity will only grow' if they laid claim to the DK and suggested the DMK.[3]

Anna said:

> When we say Dravidar Munnetra Kazhagam [Progressive Association for Dravidians], it introduces the prohibition that only Dravidians can be its members. I don't think this is apt for today's global context and period. Our party's ideal is to maintain Dravida Nadu as a prosperous land. To add the proviso that only Dravidians can live on such a Dravidian soil is narrow-mindedness and also that which cannot be achieved. Our party's ideal should be to work towards a problem-free and happy sustenance for those who are grateful to this soil regardless of race. We should work with the broad perspective that Dravidam can live here. So too Aryam, Christians and Muslims . . . Unlike the Dravidar Kazhagam, which fought only for racial welfare, we have to struggle based on geography for the good of the entire 'Dravidam'. I humbly believe that instead of 'Dravidar Munnetra Kazhagam', it would be appropriate in all respects for our party to have the name 'Dravida Munnetra Kazhagam'.[4]

In grounding the movement in territorial terms, Anna had made it inclusive, thus avoiding the pitfalls of the inchoate parent Kazhagam's scheme.

Initially, the acronym DPK for the Dravidian Progressive Federation denoted the party in English. During the 1953 'Three Fronts Agitation', *The Hindu* coined the acronym DMK, which stuck.[5]

On 18 September at 7 a.m., the seven-member organization committee met under K.K. Neelamegam's leadership to request Anna to serve as the DMK's general secretary.[6] But a grateful Anna would pronounce Periyar as the party's 'titular' president that evening at the party's launch.

At 10 a.m., Anna, Nedunchezhian, Neelamegam, A. Sithaiyan, N.V. Natarajan, K. Govindasamy, Kanchi Manimozhi, K.A. Mathiazhagan, K.V.K. Samy, Madurai Muthu and G. Parangusam met to decide a 110-member general council.

A thirty-member propaganda committee with Nedunchezhian as secretary as well as a twelve-member organization committee with N.V. Natarajan, a six-member rules and regulations committee with K.A. Mathiazhagan and E.V.K. Sampath, an eighteen-member finance committee with Kanchi Manimozhi and a five-member headquarters committee with A. Govindasamy as secretaries were also established.[7]

The Hindu reported as follows:

MADRAS, Sept. 17: The Working Committee of the Dravidian Federation met this morning at No. 7, Coral Merchant Street, George Town, and passed a no-confidence resolution in their leader, Mr E. V. Ramaswami Naicker. The Committee further resolved to form a new party called the Dravidian Progressive Federation, with Mr C. N. Annadurai as General Secretary.[8]

Tamilarasu Kazhagam leader M.P. Sivagnanam (Ma.Po.Si.) records that the press gave much importance to the revolt against Periyar, with the Congress circles concluding that the Dravidian movement was finished.[9] They could not have been more wrong.

The public launch of the DMK was scheduled for the following evening at Robinson Park, Royapuram, a low-income neighbourhood. The founding meeting and the public launch are often conflated. Karunanidhi and poet Kannadasan record that both took place on 17 September. Kannadasan, however, adds that on 18 September, he and Karunanidhi left by the 6.30 a.m. train to Salem, where Karunanidhi's family awaited him.[10]

On 18 September, *Maalaimani*, the DMK mouthpiece, announced the public launch thus:

DRAVIDAR MOVEMENT PUBLIC MEETING
ON DRAVIDAM'S FUTURE PLAN
PETHAMPALAYAM PALANISAMY PRESIDING
COMRADES:

1.	Bharatidasan	15.	N. Jeevarathinam
2.	C.N. Annadurai	16.	C.P. Chinnaraju
3.	A.V.P. Asaithambi	17.	Thangapazham
4.	K.V.K. Samy	18.	E.V.A. Vallimuthu
5.	A. Sithaiyan	19.	Madurai Muthu
6.	Parangusam	20.	N.M. Subramaniam
7.	K.K. Neelamegam	21.	C.D.T. Arasu
8.	E.V.K. Sampath	22.	Manimozhiaar
9.	S.R. Subramaniam	23.	Sathyavanimuthu
10.	N.V. Natarajan	24.	K.A. Mathiazhagan
11.	Kanchi Kalyanasundaram	25.	Murugu Subramaniam
13.	M.K.T. Subramaniam	27.	K. Anbazhagan
14.	T.K. Srinivasan	28.	M. Karunanidhi

will address
Venue: Chennai Royapuram Robinson Park
Time: 18.9.49 Sunday 4 p.m.[11]

For the first time, DMK flags with a black upper half and a red lower half fluttered at the venue, the black denoting darkness and the red light.

'Disgrace'

The meeting began at 5 p.m. amidst a slight drizzle. A. Sithaiyan, N.V. Natarajan, Sampath, S.R. Subramaniam, A.V.P. Asaithambi, Nedunchezhian, Madurai Muthu, K.K. Neelamegam and S. Sathyavanimuthu spoke. As Anna took the floor, the drizzle turned to a downpour, but the crowd stayed put. Anna compared the DMK's predicament to his audience's inconvenience.[12]

While extolling Periyar, Anna said his leader had brought disgrace upon them:

> Periyar is conducting himself against democracy and ideology . . .
> He has slipped from the path he had set and stumbled. We pointed
> out that it was wrong! Is it only us? All the people [did so]. The
> movement is great, movement's ideals are greater. We will not
> compromise our ideology. We will not allow disgrace.

Asking how a child would feel if a family head were to constantly chide it as a 'lazy, useless, wastrel', Anna said they were like such children under him and were now embarking on a 'separate family, a separate camp, a separate party, Dravida Munnetra Kazhagam'.[13]

Wishing Periyar a long life, he emphasized that their goals were the same and not in competition:

> This is not a competitive Kazhagam . . . There is no difference or
> change in the ideas. Social and economic reforms, egalitarianism,
> and freedom from northern domination are the tenets of Dravida
> Munnetra Kazhagam . . .
>
>   From two directions, the two Kazhagams should destroy
> northern imperialism, destroy the conservative woods, create the
> socialist garden and help Dravidam bloom. It does not matter
> which Kazhagam forms the garden, for the flowers, unripe fruit,
> and fruits will showcase Dravidam's resurgence. Both gardens are

necessary. No need for antagonism . . . The thinking should be
that whichever blossoms will be a garland for Dravidam . . .[14]

He said they were 'untrustworthy' and 'worthless' to Periyar, and
they had left graciously.

> In all these years, he has been the only leader I know, understood
> and have seen. I have never worked under any other leader. I have
> not felt like doing so, and I won't. That is why we did not create
> a president for the Dravida Munnetra Kazhagam. [I] did not
> consider it essential now . . .
>
> Dravida Munnetra Kazhagam is surely a graft mango plant . . .
> the graft mango plant is not inimical to the mango tree. It is not
> contradictory to the Dravidar Kazhagam. The graft mango plant
> has concurrent ideas . . . [15]

He hoped that they would reconcile as they had done once before.
That change took eighteen years. Anna's longanimity tolerated
Periyar's vicious opposition to him and his DMK even as DMK
journals like *Murasoli* responded in kind.

In an exemplary gesture only a few days after the 1967 election
results, on 28 February 1967, Anna repaired to Tiruchi with
Nedunchezhian, Karunanidhi and Anbil Dharmalingam to call on
EVR. Someone pointed out that Swatantra leader and ally Rajaji
could take offence. A grateful Anna brushed aside the suggestion,
saying, 'He was the one who introduced me to this country. It would
not be human if I didn't call on him after becoming chief minister.'[16]

The entourage reached Periyar's abode at 6 p.m. A supplicant
Anna said their success was because of Periyar and sought his
blessings. 'You must guide us,' he said.[17] A contrite eighty-seven-
year-old Periyar was stricken with shame. 'Anna walked in like the
groom. I had my head down like the bride out of embarrassment',[18]
and 'I was in a situation where I would have had to sacrifice my

dignity. Graciously Anna did not put me in that situation and acted most magnanimously,' EVR said later.[19]

The men were colossuses. How did it come to this?

The Political Father

EVR's rendezvous on 20–21 May 1935, with a twenty-five-year-old Anna at Tirupur at a Sengunthar (Anna's caste) conference, would change the future of the Tamil lands. Anna was awaiting his BA (Hons) degree results. Probing further, EVR learnt to his delight, that he desired a public career, not employment. Periyar became his 'leader' and Anna his 'adopted son' from that day. Periyar had earlier been part of the Congress but left it after his attempts for the party to accept the principle of communal representation came unstuck. In 1925, EVR founded the Self-Respect movement, a radical anti-Brahminical front that sought to restore honour to the Tamils. The thirty-year older EVR was thus at permanent war with caste, Hindu gods, myths, scriptures, Brahmins, Gandhi and the Congress. It was not the most promising camp to be in.

A maverick, the radical EVR was fatherly and authoritarian, and the relationship was full of ups and downs. Anna's reverence and gratitude for Periyar kept the relationship going. He would later describe the fourteen years with his guru as his 'spring'. The duo travelled the nooks and crannies of Tamil Nadu to spread the message of self-respect.

With Anna, Periyar's decade-old Self-Respect movement had gained a stellar disciple and its first master's degree holder. Till then, the more educated and urbane shunned the radical EVR and his movement. EVR, proud of his acquisition, flaunted both Anna and his degree, but he also opened doors for him. The young disciple proved worthy of the fuss. He sugar-coated Periyar's stinging messages. Consequently, in a first, Periyar's views were heard in colleges and universities. But equally, Anna's attributes marked him out as a leader in waiting.

EVR was the only other rationalist who could command a following like Gautama Buddha. Reposing his faith in science, invention and technology, he worked tirelessly to create an egalitarian society that would reach the apogee of human potential. Taking on caste, he threw the baby out with the bathwater, singling out Hinduism and the Brahmin as the malaise. He explained:

> Although I may have spoken falsehood in business, I would not have said falsehood or knowingly a disingenuous idea in public life. Why should I, [who is] like this, bear enmity or hate? I desire to bring my land and people on par with the West's level of civilization. I rightly or wrongly consider that the Brahmin community is a stumbling block.
>
> Shouldn't the Brahmins exhibit that they are not so? In truth, if only I had the support of the Brahmins, I would have brought our land a great deal forward.[20]

On the gods, EVR posited: 'Till the stones of the temple, the temple and its gods exist, our lowliness and degradation will be permanent.'[21] Despite this, he considered conversion 'a very disgraceful thing' but rooted for Islam, sympathetic to its apparent egalitarianism. He would have been equally disgusted with any form of radicalism today, for he began his speeches thus:

> He who created God is a fool
> He who propagates God is a scoundrel
> He who worships God is a barbarian

In his rationalist crusade, EVR often proved offensive and personal. There is plenty to pick and choose from his eighty-year public career to paint him as hateful or high-minded. Pandit Nehru considered EVR's methods 'primitive' and 'most barbarous' and his advocacy of violence against Brahmins as 'criminal or lunatic'. On 5 November

1957, Nehru suggested to Kamaraj that Periyar be confined in a 'lunatic asylum and his perverted mind treated there'.[22]

EVR was no avatar. But he braved indignities, revulsion and even violence to take his lofty message to a people unprepared for him. It was a hugely thankless task.

While his atheism failed to take off, the revolution he sowed— self-respect, equality, education, affirmative action—has borne rich fruits, enabling upward mobility for millions of men and women. Periyar dismissed meritocracy as a fraud.* Time has mostly vindicated him. But he would have also agreed that endless reservations were counterproductive. It is no surprise that profanity notwithstanding, he commanded followers, who, much like the kamikaze, were willing to give their life for their leader.

Periyar believed that the Britisher and his work 'have reduced the hegemony of Aryan culture'.[23] It has, to some extent. Yet, the inability of the Dravidian revolution to equally touch all the subalterns is clear with the Dalits and the Vanniyars. Equally clear is the power of economic mobility to confer social acceptability over a period on castes that hovered on the periphery.

'Teardrops'

The 1938 anti-Hindi agitation, the first of the three (1948–50 and 1965) led by EVR, saw 1200 court arrests till Hindi was withdrawn in 1940. Anna got his first prison term of four months.

In the winter of 1938, during the height of the struggle, Periyar had proposed 'Tamil Nadu for Tamils' in response to the 'Aryan' Hindi in schools, and later an independent Dravida Nadu made up of the southern states. Dravida and Tamil were interchangeable to

---

* He was positive that Adi Dravida leaders like M.C. Rajah and R. Veeraiyan were as qualified as C.P. Ramasamy Iyer and reservations would help them reach such high positions as the Brahmins. *Kudiarasu*, 22 November 1925.

him.[*] Periyar's Dravida Nadu was a racial project—to expel Brahmins and north Indian banias (merchants) while welcoming the Dalits, backwards and minorities from the north as their kin.[24]

In 1944, Anna seminally changed the name of the moribund Justice Party that EVR had come to lead in 1939 to Dravidar Kazhagam. The first major break in 1945–46 was caused when Periyar dictated black shirts for the Kazhagam. Anna demurred, fearing the optics of being painted as fascist. Independence was the next flashpoint. Anxious about history's judgement, Anna differed with Periyar that it was a day of mourning. But these tensions only betrayed their fundamental difference: EVR was a social reformer and averse to political power as corrupting. Anna saw power as a tool for reform. He needed to be politically correct.

In July 1948, they briefly buried the hatchet and came together to fight Hindi. That autumn, an effusive Periyar famously declared in Erode that he would pass on the baton to Anna. But he instead chose Maniammai, his newlywed wife, to be his political heir. As a shrewd Anna painted the act as an 'inappropriate marriage' to decamp, Periyar launched a vicious campaign against the 'disingenuous', 'ingrates' and 'power seekers'. Anna's *Dravida Nadu* weekly began to publish the names of those who lamented Periyar's action as 'Teardrops'. Periyar promptly seized on the phrase, and 'Teardrops' became his shorthand for the DMK.

The teardrops were growing, and to undercut them, Periyar threw his weight behind Congress leader K. Kamaraj, who symbolized the arrival of the lower backward classes. He dubbed him as *Pachai Thamizhan* or 'pure Tamil'.

This would see Anna slowly gravitate towards Rajaji whom he had once called 'Kulluka Bhatta',[†] and the 'Machiavelli of Mambalam'[‡].[25]

---

[*] In 1944, while rechristening the Justice Party as Dravidar Kazhagam, Periyar admitted 'Dravida' was to accommodate the non-Tamil leaders in the party. R. Kannan, *Anna*, 88.

[†] The commentator of the *Manusmriti* that prescribes caste by birth.

[‡] Rajaji's residence was in Mambalam, Chennai.

Rajaji, whom Kamaraj had eased out as chief minister in 1954, floated the Swatantra Party in 1959. He would go to any lengths to bring Kamaraj and the Congress down. For all their greatness, Rajaji and EVR were humans.

On 22 February 1962, sharing the dais in Kanchipuram with Rajaji, his new protege, Anna, poured his heart out:

> Rajagopalachariar is a genius. It is only because Annadurai had not gotten close to him that he had learned nothing about him . . .
>
> They criticize it as an undesirable friendship. I wish to tell Rajagopalachariar: Rajaji *avargalae* (the equivalent of sir or *ji* as a suffix), I had given my best to a leader. I had even lost my heart to him. I had been a true follower. But the good wishes I failed to receive from him, the goodwill that he did not show me, I get from you—whom I have all along opposed.
>
> I consider this indeed a very strange thing in the whole world. You are, therefore, involved in this endeavour where there is no gain [for you]. If I refer to the Gita, do not look surprised, wondering if I also know Gita. I wish to say clearly and categorically that this *nishta karma* (path of right action) you are engaged in would not be in vain.[26]

Compassionate but 'Indecisive'

Teardrops was the mildest of Periyar's bristly attacks. Despite what Periyar thought of him, to the brethren, he was their *Arignar* or scholar. Actor K.R. Ramasamy's (KRR) mother worried that her son was spending all his time with Anna to the point of neglecting his promising career. 'Mother . . . he will rise as a tall leader. He is a genius. Those who speak ill now will speak highly of their association with him in the future,' KRR tried to reassure her. KRR's mother would not be convinced.[27] But her son was right.

To his thambis or younger brothers, Anna remained a transformational figure. He was their Robert Ingersoll, Kemal Pasha, Garibaldi, Socrates and Lenin all rolled into one.[28]

Anna's hold over the Tamil masses was ethereal. He exulted in referring to himself as a 'commoner' but traversed the world of the learned and the unlettered with equal ease; he practised a rare leadership of 'family affection'—a first and last in the history of political organization.

True to the other meaning of his name's diminutive 'Anna', he towered as the 'elder brother', building a rare kinship and family bond between the cadres. The DMK under him resembled a large family where Anna, the elder brother, provided leadership and direction with compassion, empathy and understanding. Incapable of exerting authority, his humanity brought devotion from his siblings. He exercised this aura sparingly. While agreeing to solemnize his wedding, he instructed M.S. Venkatachalam, Anna's English publication *Homeland's* assistant editor, that he prostrate at his father's feet as the groom and not his.[29] His mantra 'duty, dignity and discipline' rang hollow as the party grew and failed to eschew the lumpen. After his exit from the DMK in 1961, Sampath described 'family affection' as a cover-up for Anna's slipshod leadership.

Frustrated with Anna's leadership style, A.V.P. Asaithambi's *Thani Arasu* (Independent) brought out an issue with Anna's picture upside down on its cover. Anna refused to act. He pointed out that Asaithambi, a close relative of Kamaraj, had cast his lot with them and suffered many a privation.[30]

Anna's expansiveness was not limited to party men. P. Ramasamy, the Mylapore DMK secretary, penned an editorial in his *Nathigam* (Atheism) weekly calling the Rs 10,000 contribution from Annamalai University students in 1959 for Anna's *Homeland* 'shameful'. Anna ignored it, but Ramaswamy's continued criticisms got him expelled. When *Homeland* went into a hiatus, a Heidelberg printing machine fell into disuse. Ramaswamy needed one but was reluctant to approach Anna. His agent did. As the price came up, Anna wondered who the buyer was. The agent hesitantly revealed the buyer's identity. A gracious Anna said Ramasamy could pay whatever he could afford.[31]

Similarly, Bharatidasan's was among the ten statues erected at the Second World Tamil Conference in 1968. In January 1958, Bharatidasan's ad hominem attacks doubted the modesty of the women of Anna's household and mentioned Anna as an accomplice.

With his persona and gifts, Anna could have cut his teeth in national politics. He chose instead a political trajectory limited to the Tamil-speaking areas aspiring for a different emancipation— from the vestiges of Sanskritization and social divisions that had compelled the Tamils to submit.

Many believed the DMK was a 'liberation movement'.[32] But Kannadasan, a convert turned rebel, concluded, 'The DMK was a curse to Tamil Nadu like the Nazis were to Germany.'[33]

By 1949, Anna was an eminent speaker, author, essayist, leader, writer and dramatist. That year, he stormed the cinemas with his play *Velaikaari* (Servant Maid). The script showcased a fine pen, spewing memorable lines such as '*Kathiyai theethathe thambi buthiyai theetu* (don't sharpen the knife, sharpen your intellect).' Some DMK cadres tried to embarrass Periyar. At a public meeting when one pointed out, 'Our leader Anna exhorts us to sharpen our intelligence, whereas you ask to sharpen the knife', Periyar effortlessly responded: 'One has to sharpen what is wanting.'[34]

But writing, speech and stage were the DMK's soft power. The soft power threatened to dislodge the traditional political forces that the Tamil nationalist party Tamilarasu Kazhagam's Ma.Po. Si. asked, 'Can actors govern the country?' Kamaraj and others had similar doubts.[35]

The hard power came from agitations harnessing the cadres. Although they spawned violence and sometimes death, they seized the people's imagination and helped build a south versus north narrative, propelling the DMK centre stage. Nehru described the DMK's methods as 'ridiculous nonsense' and 'foolish', the DMK as 'tribal folks' and 'degenerates' and the separatist Dravida Nadu claim as 'mad'.[36] The DMK would not flinch.

Dravida Nadu

Nehru need not have worried. The Dravida Nadu project did not enjoy popular backing. Periyar wanted the British to give him his Dravida Nadu. Periyar, who once broke Ganesh's idols, appeared akin to Ganesh. In a competition for a mango with Karthikeya, his younger brother, Ganesh had once circumambulated his parents instead of the universe and was rewarded with the mango. Like Ganesh, Periyar had chosen the short route. But, he was no Ganesh.

In April 1965, Periyar revealed that the British had told him that they knew only Hindus and Muslims and were unaware of the Brahmin and the non-Brahmin. After this, Periyar met Muslim League leader Mohammed Ali Jinnah in Bombay, where Jinnah promised that they would jointly table the subject on his visit to Chennai. P. Balasubramanian, who translated for Periyar, said that when Jinnah asked Periyar if he could rally the people of the south, a flabbergasted Periyar could not articulate a proper response.[37]

Again in Chennai, to Jinnah's query about the Justice Party, Periyar said there were nine leaders, they were of different castes but non-Brahmins. 'What is the idea behind such a party? It is a good cot, of course, but it happens to be without legs,' Jinnah had 'mocked', records Periyar.[38]

Anna must have realized the conceptual muddle and, importantly, the futility of Periyar's Dravida Nadu project. Still, he held on to it dearly, even after quitting the DK, lest his guru accuse him of having gone soft for power. Anna's separatist project enunciated territory rather than 'race'. The DMK's Dravida Nadu was a confederation of the Tamil, Telugu, Kannada and Malayalam areas knit together through English, with the right to secede. Nationality was open to all. But Dravida Nadu was cold turkey with non-Tamils, who viewed it as a Trojan horse for Tamil domination.* In 1956, ironically, Anna, fearing being reduced to a minor player, opposed the Centre-mooted Dakshin Pradesh, mirroring his Dravida Nadu sans independence.

By 1958, a flip-flop Periyar compared the project to an 'onion' (nothing inside when peeled), wisely shrinking his claim to Tamil Nadu. Anna could not emulate Periyar. Much human and intellectual capital had been invested in marketing the promised land. Size was important. Nedunchezhian mocked small-sized countries like Belgium as *keerai paathi naadugal*, nations the size of a spinach patch, and yet independent. Tamil Nadu, without the rest of the south, would have been another *keerai paathi* country.

Dravida Nadu never existed. But no amount of debunking deterred Anna. He asked if political India existed before.

Anna regularly argued that Pakistan became a reality despite fierce opposition from Gandhi and Nehru.[39] The difference was that Pakistan had the backing of a substantial majority of its future nationals.[40] He outlandishly claimed that the 'just of the world'— Pakistan, Hindustan and the UN—would come to Dravida Nadu's defence.[41] But who were Dravida Nadu's enemies?

Anna expected many freedom fighters such as Bhagat Singhs, Tirupur Kumarans and V.O. Chidambarams to redeem the 'motherland'.[42] 'Sacrifice does not mean it is the monopoly of one party; [neither] does it mean that it is for a certain period alone. Sacrifice is a continuum without an end! In that continuum, one chapter was written by the Congress—we should write the next chapter,' he said in 1957.[43]

---

* Even as early as 1950, he had to disabuse the charge that Tamils would suppress Malayalis as 'not only wrong but a dangerous scam'. *Dravida Nadu*, 7 January 1951, 5.

Despite this tall talk, Kannadasan suggests troublingly that even within the DMK, no one seriously believed in the idea. He described a typical meeting:

> As the speaker said, 'We will attain Dravida Nadu', C.P. Chitrarasu on the dais would flippantly remark to the neighbour, 'Give him the hoe right now. He is going to set off to mark the boundary! Those listening to this have nothing better to do; we too have nothing better to do; get him down quickly.'[44]

No wonder writer Jayakanthan accused Anna, the 'Kemal Pasha of the Tamils', of perpetrating a 'political stupidity' or 'political fraud'.[45] It was 'stupid' as the Telugus demanded their state with Chennai as the capital. But caught in his own snare, Anna remained relatively cool to the Telugu and Tamil boundary claims with Andhra and Kerala. It helped that Periyar and Kamaraj were more indifferent. He did not have to fear the Tamilarasu Kazhagam made up of the Tamil intelligentsia, which was at the forefront of the boundary struggle. They could never steal his thunder.

Even under pressure to drop the Dravida Nadu demand, the eternal procrastinator waited for an organic moment. In October 1962, the Chinese gifted it to him when they moved into Indian territory. As the Sixteenth Amendment proscribed any secessionist advocacy the following year, Anna gave up the demand for good only to see Kamaraj pronounce him a 'coward'. His thambis could not have cared less. *Ananda Vikatan* rightly observed in its tribute: 'They had not come together because of Dravida Nadu; they were there because of Anna. This alone is proof that he was an individual force transcending politics."

---

* *Dravida Nadu*, 7 January 1951, 6.

'One Humanity, One Almighty'

Similarly, a politically ambitious Anna had declared Saint Thirumoolar's 'One Humanity, One Almighty' as his credo at Prophet Mohammed's birthday celebrations even while in the DK. With EVR's belief that non-idol worship was elevated, his disciple was a regular at the prophet's birthday celebrations as a speaker. In 1954, Anna's movie *Sorgavasal* (Heaven's Entrance) ended with Thirumoolar's line.

Muslims found the DK and DMK leaders' praise of their prophet and familiarity with their beliefs exhilarating. This would build an early alliance between them. But Anna and his cohorts were not Nehruvian secularists—equidistant from all faiths. They were not even EVR. EVR was partial to Islam, but deep within, he saw all faiths as enslaving mankind.

DMK leaders shied away from temples and eschewed Hindu symbols. Actor S.S. Rajendran (SSR) refused to play religious or mythical characters and, therefore, gained the moniker 'Latchiya Nadigar' (Idealistic Actor). In 1956, the DMK renegade Sivaji Ganesan was greeted, 'Tirupathi Ganesa, Govinda' (finished!) for visiting Tirupati. He left the party. The brightest star in the DMK firmament, MGR initially had to turn down roles that he considered 'irrational'.

Even in conjuring up visions of a glorious Tamil past, Anna and his thambis used Karikal Chola and Cheran Chenkuttuvan as tropes. They carefully avoided the later Cholas, Raja Raja and his son Rajendra. The piety of the later Cholas, not to mention their patronage of Sanskrit and Brahmins, made them non-kosher.

But the DMK script was inexorably shifting. In 1952, Karunanidhi's hero in *Parasakthi* declared the now immortal lines: 'I caused trouble in the temple; not because the temple should not exist; [but] because it should not be the haven of the cruel.' The following year, on 27 May 1953, while Periyar gave the call to break

Ganesh idols to 'eradicate' the Brahmin-perpetrated idea of Ganesh
as the first and foremost god,[46] Anna famously made it plain, 'I would
neither break the Pillayar (Ganesh) nor the coconut' (the offering).
In the autumn of 1965, he denied to *Illustrated Weekly*'s A.S. Raman
that he was an atheist:

> No. But I don't believe in institutional religion. It is, however, my
> conviction that man cannot live without religion, because it alone
> can build up his character. I am against idol-worship, I am also
> against iconoclasm. Breaking idols is as bad as worshipping them.
> I am a rationalist.[47]

By 1966, MGR would play Murugan, albeit in a dream sequence, and
Jayalalithaa, his consort Valli in *Thanipiravi* (A Special Creature).

3

Building the DMK

The party's growth came to rest on the tripod of organization, propaganda and agitprop. Fifty propagandists were pressed into service from 16 October 1949 to eighty-five hamlets and cities, including Thiruvananthapuram.[1] As a result, 300 units sprang up in a month. District conferences scouted for interest and talent at the district, sub-district and village levels, built a cadre base and groomed local leadership. The conferences necessitated feeding thousands and extensive transport and communications arrangements. No party could match these mass contacts and organizational efforts.

The first district conference on 1 January 1950, in Tiruchi, was followed by the Chennai, Coimbatore, Madurai, Tirunelveli, Chengalpattu and Kanniyakumari conferences in the second year. A thematic women's conference and another for students were also held in Chennai. Additionally, these frequent interactions helped first-tier leaders obtain exposure and leadership. Thus, if a twenty-four-year-old Sampath was president of the Madurai district conference held on 10 June 1950, twenty-six-year-old Karunanidhi got the presidency of the Kovilpatti conference held on 26–27 August 1950. A twenty-eight-year-old Adi Dravida (Dalit) woman, Sathyavanimuthu, opened the 5–6 May 1951 Salem conference.

Propaganda

Plays and concerts were a regular feature at conferences. Well-known artists N.S. Krishnan (NSK) and K.R. Ramasamy (KRR) performed at these events. However, there were also lesser-known performers such as the early tenor Nagoor Hanifa whose 'Anna beckons the common public to join him to wipe precious Dravidam's suffering today' tugged the heartstrings of party men.[2] Hanifa's services saw him make it to the legislative council. Some propaganda songs were cut into gramophone records and repeatedly played before an event.

Public meetings were the mainstay of the party. With the leader himself being an extraordinary speaker and writer, it was no surprise that speech and writing became seminal. Almost every leader in the DMK was a speaker and a writer. To some, public speaking became a livelihood.

Fruit vendors, cart pullers, daily wagers and the like from the unorganized sector were enticed by the DMK. Why? Kannadasan felt the DMK speakers were banal and catered to the primordial sentiments of the unlettered masses and he mockingly wrote that the speeches were considered 'wonderful'. DMK flags began to sprout, and other than Brahmin establishments, the DMK was able to breach others, such as tea stalls and barber shops—so much so that even in Mumbai and Myanmar, the Tamils were 'converting' to the DMK, said Kannadasan.

Kannadasan wryly observed, 'The things that become popular in this country are the DMK, *Daily Thanthi* and *ilandhai pazham* (jujube fruit) song! Our taste was only this level.'[3] The mass circulation *Daily Thanthi* was read by those with basic education. The street fruit cart vendor's song in *Panama Paasama* (Money or Affection, 1968) catered to the not-so-lettered.

But it was not easy to recruit members. Salem's Veerapandi Arumugham writes that even in 1956, people were 'very reluctant' to enlist as members and would join only to retract the following day, saying they were 'afraid'. This happened so regularly that it took three months for Arumugham to enlist twenty-five members, a minimum requirement for a branch.[4]

Party Journals

DMK's major writers and leaders brought out a weekly or a monthly as a norm.* Founded in 1942, Anna's *Dravida Nadu* weekly had a good readership. Karunanidhi's *Murasoli* (Drumbeat), Nedunchezhian's *Mandram* (Association), Kannadasan's *Thendral* (Southerly Breeze), Mathiazhagan's *Thennagam* (The South), N.V. Natarajan's (NVN) *Dravidan*, Anbazhagan's *Pudhuvazhvu* (New Life), T.K. Srinivasan's *Gnaiyiru* (Sun), Chitrarasu's *Theepori* (Spark) and Asaithambi's *Thaniarasu* (Independent Nation) were some of the better known. The Dravida Pannai publishing house pioneered the publication of

---

* M. Karunanidhi's *Murasoli* (Drumbeat), Nedunchezhian's *Mandram* (Association), K. Anbazhagan's *Pudhuvazhvu* (New Life), C.P. Chitrarasu's *Theepori* (Spark), *Inamuzhakkam* (Nation's Voice), *Tamil Mandram* (Tamil Association), *Theechudar* (Flame), NVN's *Dravidan*, T.K. Srinivasan and A.K. Velan's *Gyaiyiru* (Sun), M.S. Sivasamy and Thangapazham's *Kilarchi* (Revolt), P. Ganesan's *Nilavu* (Moon), Mathiazhagan's *Thennagam* (The South), Arangannal's *Arapor* (Just War), Thillai Villalan's *Thambi* (Younger Brother), K. Rajaram's *Thiruvilakku* (Sacred Lamp), P. Kannan's *Pagutharivu* (Rationalism), A.P. Janarthanam's *Thozhan* (Comrade), A.V.P. Asaithambi's *Thaniarasu* (Independent Nation), Paalvannan's *Kalaimandram* (Art Association), Murugu. Subramaniam's *Ponni*, K. Appadurai's *Virundhu* (Feast), S.S. Thennarasu's *Thennarasu* (Kingdom of the south), A.K. Vilvam's *Thannatchi* (Self-Rule), Bharatidasan's *Kuyil* (Cuckoo), M. Thangavelar's *Poompuhar*, K. Kothandapani's *Thaninadu* (Independent Nation), *Anna*, C. Chittibabu's *Dravidastan*, *Thiruvidam* (Sacred Place), Karunanidhi's *Muthaaram* (Pearl Garland), Murasoli Maran's *Maravan Madal* (The Warrior's Letter), T.K. Srinivasan's *Thaainadu* (Motherland), V. Thirunavukarasu's *Poonthotam* (Flower Garden), M. Masilamani's *Kattupadu* (Discipline), Thirumalaisamy's *Nagarathoothan* (City Messenger), Thoppur Thiruvengadam's *Thenpulam* (South), Kannadasan's *Thendral* (Southerly Breeze), Kaatoor Gopal's *Uzhaippali* (The Worker), Annal Thango's *Thamizhnilam* (Tamil Land), A. Krishnasamy's *Engal Nadu* (Our Country), Erode Chinnasamy's *Samaneedhi* (Equal Justice), S.S. Marisamy's *Gandeepam* (Bow) and P.C. Ganesan's *Madhavi* were the more regular of the movement's publications. *DMK Mupperum Vizha Malar*, 1974, 61–62.

Anna's speeches and writings, and at least forty other publications churned out DMK literature.[5]

In the battle for hearts and minds, Periyar, a Class IV dropout, had demonstrated the power of the pen. As early as 1929, his flagship *Kudiarasu* sold 13,000 copies.[6] But Anna and his *thambis* were in desperate need of a daily.

The Search for a 'Daily'

On 10 August 1949, the party's first mouthpiece, T.M. Parthasarathy's *Maalaimani*, hit the stands with Anna as editor and Nedunchezhian as chief deputy editor.[7] It sputtered and folded on 20 July 1950, before its reappearance in January 1951 with Karunanidhi as editor, only to cease publication again two years later.[8] In October 1950, Anna formally applied to turn his *Dravida Nadu* weekly into a daily and run *Vanguard*, an English journal. A company was registered. Only Rs 13,500 of the planned Rs 1,00,000 as a corpus was collected. On 11 March 1951, Anna threw in the towel at the Kanchipuram general council, admitting, 'I can't run a daily.'[9] However, the need for a daily was acute, and there could be no let-up in the efforts towards it.

The 17–18 November 1951 Madurai general council asked DMK units to purchase a yearly subscription of Rs 24 and to send Rs 5 for every event. On 15 June 1953, *Namnadu* (Our Land), with Anna as editor, Nedunchezhian as chief deputy, Kanchi Kalyanasundaram as executive editor and A.S. Venu, R.S. Pandian and Sivaprakasam as deputy editors, was launched.[10] Kalyanasundaram and, at times, Anna penned the leader. Priced at an anna, the daily had a circulation of 16,000–17,000 copies at its peak. Two years later, Nedunchezhian took over as editor. *Namnadu* ceased publication on 2 December 1972.[11]

The new force wove a web of equality and Tamil pride like never before. Party mobilization took place in simple and unexpected ways. At meetings and functions, Anna mentioned every DMK worker who had played a role in organizing, the names of local functionaries, etc. Also, he would throw a shawl around their neck, and in turn, they would fete their leader similarly. A sense of equality was instantly established.

The local tea shop, bicycle rentals, hairdressing saloons and the *padippagams* or reading rooms became the DMK's propaganda and recruiting ground. Hairdressing salons with radio and newspapers organically provided a place for DMK aficionados to congregate for political gossip and to read party journals. Bicycle rentals peddled the party fare. Tea stalls in the pre-television era sold hot tea even as the radio dished out news. The state's politics, DMK's moves, Anna's speeches, writing and agitations were hotly debated over tea.

Thambikku Letters

It was Anna's writing that essentially rallied the cadres. In 1955, Anna's famous *Thambikku* (to the younger brother) letter series in *Dravida Nadu* would set the standards for political communication on the nation, language, society and party affairs at such a personal level to the cadres. The 288 letters were written from 8 May 1955 to 21 January 1969—over a period of almost fourteen years—an average of twenty-one letters a year. The letters sounded as though Anna was physically next to the reader. Anna aimed to write weekly but often failed. Here is a sample letter penned after a hiatus:

> Younger brother!
> Why are you wearing a frown?
> Why do you ignore my calls?
> You are angry with me! Isn't that the reason behind your silence?
> Are you that angry? Even as I keep beckoning, you don't respond or turn in my direction! It is fair that you are angry! Yes. I have erred. But should you carry so much anger?

'Why not Anna? How many days since you have spoken to
me? What was important that kept you busy without time to talk
to me? Did you set off to see new lands? Or did you get on to a
vessel to see the sea's beauty?' [so you ask.] Will one search for coal
pieces when golden nuggets are in the lap? Here I am, to rejoice
in listening to you . . .[12]

But not all writing and speech were erudite or kosher. Anna's
Romapuri Ranigal (Roman Queens) or *Kambarasam* (The Essence
of Kamban) gave ample scope to venture into steamy territory.
Listing Kamban's verses on Sita's private parts, Anna launched a
frontal attack, accusing the poet of sensuousness. Anna teased out
such elements for his younger audience even as the word remained
disputed.* Anna's homey analogies, short stories and references often
touched on the sensual. While exhorting students to be aware but not
dabble, he compared politics to the aunt's daughter (consanguineous
relationships/marriages are not unusual among Tamils), advising:
'You can dote on her but not touch her.' He compared the DMK's
decision to contest polls on Kamaraj's challenge to an ascetic's
unexpected 'yes' to the flower vendor's regular tease to marry her.
Not all DMK leaders were as nuanced or proper. Over the years, a
genre of lewd speech and writing came to haunt the movement.

Stage and Films

More than the writing and speeches, the stage and cinema set the
party on an exponential growth trajectory. But the party would pay
the price for this fast-track growth, and the tail would begin to wag
the dog, leading to splits in 1961 and 1972. Anna's *Chandramohan*
and *Needhi Devan Mayakkam* (The Justice God's Predicament) were

---

* For a debate on the Tamil word in question, see Jonas Buchholz, 'Countering Pin C.N.
Annadurai's Critique of the Rāmāyaṇa', in *Zeitschrift für Indologie und Südasienstudien*
32/33 (2015–16), 203–232.

part of the repertoire of plays staged initially for fundraisers. Anna, Karunanidhi, Anbazhagan, C.V. Rajagopal, Rama Arangannal and Sampath donned roles when the plays were staged in their home towns.[13] The movement's plays were progressive and didactic.* K.R. Ramasamy was the first to stage the party's plays. S.S. Rajendran (SSR) and D.V. Narayanasamy followed. MGR's *Inba Kanavu* (Sweet Dream) from 1953 proved popular.

Films took propaganda and the party to the next stage, projecting the DMK into the audience even as a vigilant censor frowned on these attempts. Karunanidhi began the trend of acronyms, homonyms and double entendres positioning Anna in the movies. No one was fooled when his *Parasakthi* (1952) heroine spoke of her reformist elder brother—Anna (the Tamil word for older brother is Anna and it was the short form of Anna(durai)'s name as well). Similarly, when the movement's sympathizer N.S. Krishnan sang *Theenaa Moonaa Kaanaa,* as the acronyms for Thirukural Munnetra Kazhagam in *Panam* (Money, 1952), it was clear the acronyms were that of the DMK.

From 1953, MGR fan clubs became a major vehicle, promoting the DMK with womenfolk and fans. After *Rajakumari* (Princess, 1947), a string of successes with *Mandhirikumari* (Minister's Daughter, 1950) and *Marudha Naatu Ilavarasi* (Princess of Marudha, 1950) saw MGR and Karunanidhi partner to produce *Naam* (Us, 1953), which did not fare well. *Malaikallan* (Mountain

---

* *En Kaanikkai* (My Offering) spoke to the harsh life of labour, *Andaman Kaidhi* (Andaman Prisoner) and *Naam Iruvar* (The Two of Us) campaigned against old men taking young wives, *Imayathil Naam* (Us in the Himalayas) evoked Tamil pride with Cheran Chenguttuvan humbling the north's Kanaka and Vijaya; *Paithiyakkaran* (Madman) delved on widows' plight, Karunanidhi's *Orae Mutham* (One Kiss) romanced a princess and a nobody, his *Thookumedai* (Gallows) peddled self-respect. At the same time, *Mandhirikumari* (Minister's Daughter), later a cult film with MGR, was rife with political equivoque, *Kaviyin Kanavu* (Poet's Dream) featured an immigrant who brings ruin to the land of his refuge and *Puyalukkupin* (After the Storm) revealed a fake ascetic's misdeeds. *Chandrodayam* (Moonrise) was about fake pontiffs and *Porvaal* (Battle Sword) peddled social themes and self-respect. *Dravida Nadu*, Pongal Issue, January 1950, 38–41.

Thief, 1954) proved a hit though. Their friendship, collaboration and later feuding would make history in films and politics.

During *Malaikallan*'s making, Karunanidhi conferred the hyperbolic title *Puratchi Nadigar*, or revolutionary actor, on MGR. MGR was surely a trailblazer. From 1958, with his *Nadodi Mannan* (Vagabond King), where MGR wore the DMK's black and red, spoke and, in the latter movies, sang Anna's paeans and exhibited pictures of his leader. *Nadodi Mannan* nearly dished out the DMK's manifesto. By 1962, MGR and the DMK, a party full of promise, had become interchangeable. Anna had to occasionally defer to the crowds' craze for his star disciple and halt his speech. While Anna was confident and indifferent, others were not.

Agitprop

Agitprop was the third leg on which the party stood. The reintroduction of Hindi in Classes I to VI from 2 May 1950 and the Supreme Court upholding reservations as unfair saw the party joining forces with others, including the parent DK.[14] Still, the state administration's ban on plays and writings was a windfall for the party, hungry for agitations. The DMK charged the Congress, which had once fought for free speech, as behaving exactly like the British. The Congress was the foreign power, and the DMK was the freedom movement. Anna would copy the Congress's independence struggle in countering these government moves.

With their testimonies, DMK writers turned their status as the 'accused' facing prosecution for objectionable writing into a bully pulpit for propaganda. Party workers congregated to celebrate the twists and turns in the hearings. Jail sentences came as manna to the DMK. Leaders and workers wore them on their sleeves as marks of sacrifice and were rendered heroes.

Overzealous officials compounded the administration's faux pas. On 22 July 1950, A.V.P. Asaithambi and two others were tonsured, despite posting bail for publishing objectionable material. Publishing their tonsured pictures, *Dravida Nadu* alliteratively called attention to the 'Ahimsa' government's 'atrocities', and Anna made a huge fuss over the incident.[15] A legal defence fund was set up, and lawyers were hired even as the prosecution sustained the attention on the DMK. This became a regular course of action for the DMK, and the legal battles were an issue to mobilize cadres.[16]

Some eight weeks later, on 18 September 1950, Anna was found guilty of inciting communal hate in his *Arya Maayai* (Aryan Illusion) and slapped with a Rs 700 penalty and a six-month simple sentence. Anna told the assembled crowd:

> The jail sentence is not the first in my public life.
>
> I was in Chennai prison for four months during Acharya's [Rajagopalachari] time when the anti-Hindi protest happened. I was confined in the Saidapet sub-jail for a week. When Acharya became governor general, I was in prison for a few days. I have rubbed shoulders with Periyar, whose heart has been steeled by his prison record. Therefore, prison will not ruin me . . .
>
> We have sung at thousands of events
> The flower garden where the cuckoo sings
> Is the prison that aims at us
> That is where I am heading . . . Au revoir. Greetings.[17]

The jail term sparked protest meetings in several places.* In a knee-jerk reaction, the administration slapped ban orders in Adirampattinam, Thiruvarur, Thanjavur and Kunrathoor. In Thiruvarur, police with batons charged the crowd.[18]

---

* Some of these bans continued well into the late 1950s. Karunanidhi's *Thookumedai* (Gallows) was banned on 25 April 1959 as 'it deliberately intended to outrage the religious feelings of a class of citizens of India and also on the grounds that it is indecent, scurrilous and obscene.' (1962) 2 MLJ 520.

Periyar had also been jailed for his earlier work, *Ponmozhigal* (Adages). Placed in adjacent cells, the mentor and the mentee avoided each other. A tender word, Anna said, would have made him reconsider his DMK. On 28 October 1950, they were released prematurely. 'Success! Success! Total Success!' a triumphant *Dravida Nadu* declared.[19] That evening, Anna claimed, 'In this country, Periyar and I are the last "moderates". Others in our party are all extremists . . . who will rise fiercely seeing a wrong!' and said the two provided insurance from them. He said:

> You threw us into prison. What happened? . . . In many places, the
> Hindi names in railway stations were erased . . . In Kumbakonam
> they had erased the word Brahmin in 'Brahmin Coffee Hotel'
> . . . This is a 'sample' of what might happen if we go in![20]

The DMK turned every event into a propaganda exercise. On 6 October 1950, when Anna reached Egmore Railway Station after jail for *Arya Maayai,* he was given a hero's welcome.[21] Months later, on 1 March 1951, hundreds of DMK volunteers defied the ban, reading excerpts from the book, and the DMK pilloried the government for not proceeding against them.[22]

Charting a Militant Course

At the 26–27 August 1950 Kovilpatti Tirunelveli district conference's plenary, Anna announced black flags against central government officials to protest 'Delhi domination' and outlined a slew of protest ideas to be considered. Claiming Rs 10 crore were lost as fares to the north, he suggested boycotting or ticketless train travel, shunning mill cloth from the north, patronizing handloom and protesting against Hindi and Marwari pawn shops. Neither the train boycott nor the protest against Marwari shops would come to pass.[23] Borrowing from the Tamil classic *Manonmaniam,* Anna said,

'If this army were to fail, who else can succeed?' Black flags would remain an important symbol in the hands of the DMK, though.

Secondly, Kovilpatti saw Karunanidhi and Sampath—two powerful claimants to Anna's affection—openly locking horns. Karunanidhi had suggested faster communication means between the headquarters and the field to grow the party. Sampath, however, felt that 'Those who came only yesterday or today are suggesting programmes for the party.'[24] Anna's balancing act began early on when on 7 September 1949, Anna, Sampath and Karunanidhi addressed a meeting at Chepauk, explaining the Kovilpatti resolutions in a show of unity.

On 9 September, the day of the first black flag demo, KRR, Nedunchezhian, Karunanidhi, NVN, Sampath, Mathiazhagan, poet Kannadasan and others filed into a line on both sides of the street where the Hindi Prachar Sabha stood. At 3.45 p.m., Anna arrived to inspect the formation. R.R. Diwakar, the minister of state for information and broadcasting, arrived to the chant of 'Diwakar, go back!' and some women thrust a black flag into his hand. At the second venue in Chennai, the crowds were larger. The following day, Diwakar was again accosted by black flags in Kanchipuram, Mamallapuram and Thirukazhukundram. *Dravida Nadu* called it the 'First Phase of the Freedom Struggle'.[25]

On 24 October 1950, minister without portfolio Rajaji faced black flags at Fort St. George and later at Royapettah.[26] Mounted policemen swung into action, charging the protesters with batons. In the event, the protesters and Rajaji did not come into contact. Eighty-three were injured and thirty-four were charged. 'Ram Raj in Madras', *Dravida Nadu* jeered later. The magistrate offered to excuse the thirty-four if they promised not to participate again, which was rejected. 'What is this north and south? Who teaches you such things?' asked the magistrate. 'Dravida Munnetra Kazhagam. Our own Kazhagam,' was the response. They were sentenced to two weeks.[27]

The administration played further into the DMK's hands. For two months, Kunrathoor had been under a ban. On 26 October 1950, the day of a DMK meeting, police fired eight rounds, injuring three people severely.[28] Kunrathoor had forced the authorities' hand to open fire.[29] Anna described it as another Jallianwallah Bagh. The DMK was pushing the envelope.[30]

In his 28 October 1950 statement on the events, Anna, appropriating Byron's 'A heart for every fate' from *Ulysses,* asked for an *Edhayum thaangum idhayam.* '[Protestors] I congratulate you. I honour their bravery and sacrifice . . . Oh, bloodied warriors! Long live your glory! May your numbers rise!' he said.[31]

From 7 January to 17 July 1951, black flags were shown to central ministers Harekrushna Mahatab, K.M. Munshi, Gopalsamy Iyengar and Jagjivan Ram. On 6 April, President Rajendra Prasad faced black flags, as did Prime Minister Nehru on 16 July at the Kolar Gold Fields.[32]

Pledgors for Dravida Nadu

The 17–18 November Madurai general council saw forty-five of the 112 members participate in the seventeen-hour discussion that decided against participation in the first general elections to protest the Constitution.[33] Earlier, on 26 January 1950, as India turned into a Republic, Anna lamented that they had not fought hard enough to stave off the mishap of the unitary Constitution. He wrote then:

> The train had left, and the Indian subcontinent's Constitution had begun to rule us . . . Our legs are chained [and] our hands cuffed . . .
>
> Our land that even emperors Harsha, Kanishka, Akbar, Ashoka, Chandragupta and Aurangzeb could not conquer has been reduced to kowtowing to the Delhi crown . . .

Then, in an epiphany, he prophesied that 'The Congress party has none to "fill in" the shoes of first-rung leaders like Nehru and Patel. Whoever reaches that place would not enjoy . . . [their] influence and aura.' But he had not considered the power of democracy. For all its flaws, India's democracy has proven resilient, the disaffected won over by the charm of electoral office or brutal repression.

Anna analysed that the Congress 'greatly banked' on the Opposition's disunity. While the DMK's chances were bright, they stayed away from the electoral race as the public ought to think of them as 'honest'.[34] More than the public, Anna feared validating EVR that they were after power. Instead, the party decided to back communists and progressive non-Congress candidates in return for their pledge as follows:

> I support the Dravida independence issue. If I become a member
> of the assembly or Parliament, I will work on the above issue and
> gather support for the DMK's policies. I promise that I will work
> to lobby support for the DMK's plans to get rid of exploitation
> and imperialism.

Periyar, who never lost an opportunity to take a jibe at the DMK, rightly termed the DMK's pledge 'meaningless', wondering what could be done if the pledgors resiled.[35] EVR's words would ring true. More than 150, including a Brahmin, had signed the pledge.[36]

Doctrinaire Communists

Following communist leader A.K. Gopalan's proposal of a united front with the DK and the DMK, P. Jeevanandam (Jeeva) met Anna four times. But Periyar wanted nothing to do with the DMK.[37] Besides, the communists disapproved of the separatist DMK plank. Dogmatic, they called self-determination a 'capitalist national plan' and, in Stalinist polemic, argued that the Tamils, Telugus,

Kannadigas and Malayalis had become nations, making Dravida Nadu redundant.[38] 'I am seeking the heart. Not world history!' responded Anna to his presumptive fellow travellers stuck in their doctrinaire corner.[39] If they feared the DMK as 'reactionary', they also rightly understood its threat to their constituency.[40]

The DMK peddled democratic socialism. Anna would famously utter that the 'DMK is the true communist party' and he 'would go to Moscow and tell (Gyorgy) Malenkov' this.[41] At the first state conference, he said he could spread communism within the Dravida Nadu's borders and hoped for a time when Periyar, the communists and his DMK would be in one camp but with the adjective Dravida in it.[42] The relationship between the three would remain troubled till 1967. In 1957, the communists withdrew their candidate at the last minute to ensure Nedunchezhian's defeat in Salem. A left-of-centre party, the DMK was faulted as having no serious economic policy. In 1965, Anna told the *Illustrated Weekly* that, 'Federalism, full autonomy for the States and egalitarianism' were the party's principles, too broad a sweep for a student of economics.[43]

But the first year had ended well. On 2 December 1951, V.M. John declared open the party headquarters *Arivagam* (the abode of knowledge) at 24 S.N. Street, Royapuram, bought with donations from KRR and others.* The party boasted 35,000 members, 505 units, twelve district units and 2035 public meetings. It said eleven books were banned. It counted the removal of Hindi, favourable court verdicts and the black flag demos among its victories. It would soon count the successful independent pledgees for Dravida Nadu amongst its victories. But this would prove ephemeral.[44]

---

* W.K. Devarajan and Nedunchezhian had identified the property for purchase. Navalar Nedunchezhian, *Vaazhvil Naan Kandathum Ketathum*. (Chennai: Navalar Nedunchezhian Pathippagam, 2000), 214. KRR's benefit performances were critical to raise the purchase sum. Arangannal says the Mathiazhagan family's gift of Rs 5000 was also used to purchase the property. K.M. Selvaraj, *Maamanidhar Mathiazhagan*. (Chennai, Kaniur Pathippagam, 2004), 10.

4

Election, Kallakudi, Kamaraj

First State Conference—1951

The party's first state conference on 21–22 January 1951 at the Island Grounds, Chennai, proved a huge success. Three consulates had initially indicated that they would set up stalls but didn't follow through. It would have amounted to a diplomatic faux pas.[1] The conference had maps showing the mineral and agricultural wealth of the Tamil areas.[2]

In the plenary, Anna outlined a course of action to achieve Dravida Nadu that never came to pass: a referendum in 1954, appealing to the United Nations if the results were unheeded, contesting from jail if interned, and a resolution declaring independence in power; dismissed, they would run on the same plank and 'win again and again'. The political choreography, in retrospect, was, at best, a grand dream and, at worst, mere bluster.

Anna also foresaw political turmoil in 1960 and the DMK offering civil disobedience. He asked followers to be ready to make brave sacrifices, to treat prison no different from their homes.[3] On 2 March, he wrote: 'We are seeking an independent country, comrades, independent country!—how many members support it— is what the political world would ask.'[4]

In his presidential address, Anna announced a list of sixty-nine candidates for the assembly and nine for Parliament who were pledgees of the DMK's stipulation to work for Dravida Nadu. In the event, forty-three were elected to the assembly and five to Parliament. The DMK had conducted 1300 campaign meetings.[5] M.A. Manickavel Naicker's Commonwealth Party and S.S. Ramasamy Padayachi's Toilers Party were the prominent winners, with six and twenty-four seats, respectively.[6] But they did not belong to the DMK and caused the most grief, pushing the party to reconsider its decision to stay off the electoral arena and enter the 1957 elections.

A.N. Sattanathan, who headed the first Backward Classes Commission, identifies Brahmins, Vellalas, Naidus and Reddiars as the traditional land-owning classes. He places the Vanniyars above the Adi Dravidas in the north in the social hierarchy and equal or more in numbers to them. Their 'low level of educational achievement and the absence of a sizeable upper crust, there being very few big landlords, merchants or moneyed people' had prevented them from emerging as a dominant caste, says Sattanathan, which is also the reason for them being pioneers at caste politicization.[7] He places the Kallars and Maravars in the southern districts and Kongu Vellalars in Salem and Coimbatore as the predominant communities. He speaks of Yadavas, weavers, and Nadars as spread across the state.[8] Today, Sattanathan would have included the Pallars or the Devendra Kula Vellars as a sizeable community in the south, the Arunthathiyars in the west and the Parayars, all Dalits in the north.

On 4 March 1952, at the DMK felicitation at St Mary's Hall, Anna said that the elected independents considered a cross-over to the Congress akin to 'embracing a leper', and people considered such individuals worse than lepers. Power, however, took care of any fear of contracting the dreaded disease. Although, the United Democratic Party, an alliance of the communists and the Kisan

Mazdoor Praja Party (KMPP), commanded a majority in the assembly, the governor nominated Rajaji to the legislative council as an eminent writer and swore him in as chief minister. Rajaji announced that he would seek fresh elections if he could not prove his majority. It was a threat and it worked.[9] Soon after that, on 10 April, much to the DMK's chagrin, Manickavel Naicker was sworn in as one of the fifteen ministers of the Rajaji cabinet in return for his support.[10] DK's *Viduthalai* published a cartoon depicting him as Vibishana.[11] S.S. Ramasamy extended support soon and 'did a Manickavel' two years later, joining the Kamaraj ministry on 13 April 1954.

Paatali Makkal Katchi (PMK) founder Dr Ramadoss observes that after the two Vanniyar leaders joined the Congress, the community was divided, and many had moved to the DMK.[12]

Striking with Kid Gloves

On 27 April 1952, as minister Manickavel motored to Walajapet to declare open the municipal library, DMK cadres with black flags lined the Trunk Road for 'a mile', shouting 'Traitor go back'.[13] In a missive, Anna said they had suffered the 'agony' of staging the protest because of a 'dangerous man', as he described Rajaji who had caged the Vanniyar 'lion' with an office.

Manickavel himself justified his crossover as a representation of his community. Inclusion did not mean representation, argued Anna, citing a disillusioned Ambedkar leaving Nehru's cabinet. Manickavel had also argued that his promise was for an assembly resolution on Dravida Nadu, which was never tabled. Releasing his letter, which said, 'I support the formation of Dravidasthan', Anna termed the argument 'clever' but not 'just'.[14] Not to antagonize the Vanniyars, Anna had handled Manickavel with kid gloves. Two years later, the DMK would not even take note of Ramasamy Padayachi. But these developments greatly pushed it towards electoral politics.

The 1 August 1952 Defacing Hindi Campaign provided a distraction from Manickavel's reneging. Periyar had called for it, and Anna chose to emulate him, noting that the two Kazhagams would attack the common foe as a 'double barrel gun'.[15]

Amid shouts of 'Hindi down, down!', Anna defaced the Hindi letters 'Erode Junction'. Periyar did the same in Tiruchi. After defacing the board at the Tiruchi post office, Karunanidhi headed for the railway station, where a board was kept for Periyar and him. The zealous Kazhagam men had defaced the rest.[16] In several places, the two Kazhagams had engaged jointly.[17] But this would never be repeated, and in 1965, at the height of the anti-Hindi agitation, EVR would reiterate his call to ban the DMK. Nedunchezhian in Madurai, Sampath in Coimbatore, KRR and Mathiazhagan at Cuddalore defaced Hindi letters.

Humanitarian Work

Nature's fury provided the party opportunities to showcase service, too. On 30 November 1952, a storm wrought havoc in Thanjavur and Tiruchi districts, killing 370 people and thousands of livestock, uprooting thousands of houses and trees and destroying crops. The loss was estimated at Rs 5 crore. On 14 December, in a massive public meeting in Thanjavur, Anna offered the DMK's help to remove trees and bury the dead and suggested an additional tax of a rupee for every ten rupees of property or land tax in the two districts and diverting funds meant for religious festivals. He termed the suggestion as 'humanitarian'.[18]

On 1 and 2 January 1953, Anna, Karunanidhi, Mathiazhagan and Nedunchezhian performed in *Chandrodayam* and KRR, Sivaji Ganesan and SSR in *Chandramohan*, the first of the benefit plays staged at Sir Theagaraya College that netted Rs 7736.[19] The relief fund distribution was held at Thanjavur on 28 April.[20]

Hands-Loom Large

Handloom weavers were the next focus. With cloth from northern mills flooding the market, weavers had no work. From a weaving family himself, Anna designated 4 January as Weavers Day, when DMK leaders would sell handlooms. Anna in Tiruchi, Karunanidhi in Chennai, KRR in Kanchipuram, Sampath in Coimbatore, Chitrarasu in Madurai, Asaithambi in Virudhunagar and Nedunchezhian and Kannadasan in Karaikudi hawked handlooms that day, bringing in a whopping Rs 1 lakh.[21]

Tiruchi wore a festive look, with streets adorned with welcome arches bearing banana trees and wall messages. Many had gathered as early as 7 a.m. before *Dravida Pannai*, the house where Anna stayed. Dressed like a trader, Anna called out movingly: 'Purchase handloom cloth' even as the cart moved on to the accompaniment of Nagoor Hanifa's songs. The response was overwhelming. 'Anna! I asked you at Chinthamani. You asked me to come over to Rockfort. I came to Rockfort. You had left for the big bazaar. Here too, without selling to me, you ask that I come to another place! Please give me just one shawl, an eight anna towel,' cried a buyer. But that towel was already sold out. No replenishments had been planned, and many went away disappointed.[22] Anna had sold handlooms worth Rs 5000.[23]

Although the target was Rs 25,000, Rs 27,500 were collected from plays and donations, including from Tamils in Bihar, Ceylon and Indochina. Speaking at the Pongal fete at Pachaiyappa's College, Madras, Anna asked cadres to buy only handloom henceforth. He exhorted women to wear handloom, saying that it was 'equal to killing ten weavers' if they bought a yard of mill cloth.[24] From 7–13 January 1955, the DMK would mark Handloom Weavers Support Week for some years. Handlooms became the DMK symbol, much like homespun (khadi) for the Congress.[25]

Three Fronts

The 25–26 April Lalgudi meeting was a sea of people, and the marquee burst at the seams. Here, MGR pledged that he 'from the Keralite part, will do my best' for the party's work, and Sivaji Ganesan that he would tear up film agreements for the party. However, outshone by MGR, a Ganesan torn within would leave the party in 1956.

But another star was emerging in a surefooted way, and he was no pushover like Sivaji Ganesan. It was Karunanidhi. Lalgudi had authorized an agitation to demand that Dalmiapuram, renamed after industrialist Dalmia who had established a cement plant there, go back to its original name, Kallakudi.[26] 'This name stands as a symbol of shame in Tamil Nadu,' said Anna, tasking Karunanidhi to lead the Kallakudi front in July, as one part of the party's signature Three Front Agitation.

Karunanidhi addressed meetings for a month and said that holding Anna in his heart, he had set out to the battlefield! His hyperbole continued:

> On the battlefield, the northerner's rage could be at us. Could . . .
> take my life. If I am felled, a team of warriors is ready to continue
> the struggle! . . . In this good Tamil Nadu a foreigner's name? A
> place named after a man who grows fat exploiting [us]? No! No!
> We will change this name . . . this crusade will only be through
> peaceful means. But we will take it if they can't stomach this and
> unleash force! Let blood drop, our blood flow. No worry! We will
> gather the blood spilt and will use that to erase the 'Dalmiapuram'
> name from the board![27]

A Tiruchi labourer who asked Karunanidhi, 'Instead of eradicating poverty, isn't the Dalmiapuram agitation an empty pomp?' had perhaps spoken for a majority and the rest of the parties.[28] Karunanidhi explained that with a Rs three-crore investment, Dalmia was taking away Rs 25 lakh annually, which was the sweat of 2000 Tamil workers. 'Dalmiapuram agitation is laying the foundation stone to end this injustice,' he concluded.[29]

The second front was against Rajaji's caste-based education scheme. Sampath was to head it. Rajaji's scheme reduced school time for children and envisaged apprenticeship in their father's vocation for the rest of the day. EVR dubbed it the *Kulakalvi* or hereditary educational system, and that the wily Rajaji wanted a cobbler's son to remain a cobbler. On 8 July, DMK workers marched to the residence of the DMK-supported legislators, urging them to oppose the scheme. Outlining the agitation at the Chennai district conference on 11–12 July, Anna said: 'I have asked comrade Sampath to picket Acharya's (Rajaji) residence with colleagues [on 14 July]. Let Acharya order an attack on Sampath and his colleagues, spill their blood and wear it as his *thilak* to sit in the legislature,' Anna said in another melodramatic speech.[30] Sampath was pre-emptively arrested on 13 July.

The third front was against Nehru's remark—'nonsense'[31]—to characterize the Tamilarasu Kazhagam's stopping of the Mumbai Mail at Walajah in July 1953 as part of the boundary agitation. Nehru had earlier termed the Hindi defacing campaign 'childish nonsense', 'extreme immaturity' and 'no greater folly',[32] and Anna had famously said: 'Let us forgive and forget.' This time, however, forgetting his advice to 'forget', Anna refused to let it go: 'On 15 July, all day trains should stop . . .' he instructed.[33] At the 4–5 July Chidambaram conference, he reasoned, 'Only if the fifteenth stop trains agitation is successful and the news reaches Nehru will he understand Dravidam's surge. How else can he learn of this? Is he going to see these conferences on television! . . . Therefore, we need to make Pandit know the situation here.'[34] The Pandit would learn of it, but it would only harden his views about the DMK.

On 13 July, around 7.15 p.m., after the DMK executive concluded its session, deputy commissioner of police F.V. Arul (later inspector general of police) arrested Anna, Mathiazhagan, Sampath, Nedunchezhian and NVN at *Arivagam*. The following day, newspapers came up with the sobriquet—the DMK's 'Big Five Leaders'—for them. In retrospect, it is clear that only three fit the bill: Anna, Karunanidhi and MGR. The agitation, however, would proceed as planned.

The stop-trains agitation on 15 July resulted in eleven protesters being shot dead, hundreds injured and more than 3000 placed in custody. On 17 July, Nehru, speaking at Lakshmanapuri, said he shuddered to think what would happen if such people came to power.[35] It was not just Nehru. *The Hindu, Swadesamitran, Dinamani* and *Kalki* saw it as 'wanton' and 'communal hate'.[36] *Dinamani* published a picture of an ass on the rails at Kandamangalam under the caption 'Stop trains—Donkey too participated.'[37] But, the DMK had been noticed even far away. *The New York Times* reported the protest on 17 July.

> The dissident Dravidians of Madras state in South India, descendants of the race that occupied most of India before the Aryan invasion about 3,000 years ago, are in the third day of violent demonstrations against the Government which have cost at least six lives and seriously disrupted railway service throughout the lower part of the peninsula.

The paper said that Nehru had dubbed the interruption as 'nonsense' a week prior and '[t]he Dravidian group answered yesterday [15 July] with a new campaign of railway sabotage more fierce than before.'[38] Anna wrote exultantly, 'Look, if America's *New York Times* published it as news, then imagine, younger brother, how intense the protest must have been'.[39]

Kallakudi

Karunanidhi had exceeded his mandate of pasting the poster bearing Kallakudi on Dalmiapuram, turning it into another stop-trains agitation. In his granular account, Kannadasan says Karunanidhi wondered how to get arrested and, as the train pulled over, chose to lay on the tracks and was arrested. It was 9.45 a.m. By now, incoming trains had brought in DMK men and onlookers, numbering 'thousands'. The third batch was scheduled for 1.30 p.m. Its leader, Kannadasan, had not slept the previous night or eaten anything in the morning. T.K. Srinivasan brought him a couple of vadas and tea. The station appeared like a festive site, but the police, in their hundreds, were on edge. They were also hungry. The deputy collector, who was also Ariyalur magistrate, arrived.

As the train arrived, Kannadasan and others ran to lie on the tracks but got pushed behind the goods train by the police baton charge. The train began to leave the station. T.K. Srinivasan now advised, 'Go, go. Lie down before the running train.' Kannadasan retorted: 'You too join me. Let us both die'. Alas, the train paused after a furlong. Kannadasan saw '5000 people' squatting on the rails now. Charged by the sight, he ran the whole stretch towards the train to the lusty cheers of the crowd. As the armoured policemen charged, he was struck but noticed that it did not hurt. Some policemen were DMK sympathizers. The inspector struck his head, kicking him out of the rails, at which an incensed crowd began to throw stones. 'Fire', shouted the deputy collector. Kannadasan walked through the firing. His left elbow had been dislocated. At the Lalgudi hospital, as the injured cadres, indifferent to their pain, inquired about his injury, Kannadasan felt ashamed that he was the least hurt.

Kannadasan broke down when C.P. Chitrarasu and T.K. Srinivasan visited him the next day at the Lalgudi sub-jail. The trial lasted four hellish months. Kannadasan writes that the funds raised were stuck somewhere. The lawyer, unpaid, did not show up for some hearings. Kannadasan wrote that 'since the real warriors had gone hiding,' others unconnected to the agitation were charged. He and twenty-four others were sentenced to eighteen months of rigorous imprisonment. But none of the 'big leaders' came to see them off. Kannadasan made bail after two months.[40]

There was more violence that day in Thoothukudi, where DMK men stopped the Coimbatore passenger train in four places. In Melur, 150 squatted on the tracks with a 1000-strong crowd on the platform. Three were killed on the spot, while a fourth died at the hospital as the police opened fire. The crowd engaged in arson, snatched a woman's jewellery and 'there was even an attempt to murder a Brahmin child', Chief Presidency Magistrate Venkataramana Naidu said. In Chennai, DMK volunteers stopped the Grand Trunk Express.[41] At Kallakudi, the police had fired sixty-four rounds and two men, a tailor from Lalgudi and a weaver from Tiruchi, had become collateral damage.

In his testimony, Anna termed the agitation a watershed moment for the party. He expressed surprise that his calls were so effective that '5000 people had courted imprisonment'. He could have added that six were dead; one had lost a hand and another a leg. The magistrate characterized Anna's statement and that of the others as 'propagandistic' and 'much of it irrelevant'. Observing that the accused 'are held in high esteem by a vast section of the public,' he condemned their 'methods', took note that they were 'most anxious to see that their men behaved in a peaceful, nonviolent and dignified manner' and slapped a Rs 500 fine and, in case of default, three months' simple imprisonment.[42] The five chose jail. The party lost no time creating a Kallakudi and Thoothukudi legal fund, and on 3 October, MGR debuted his *Inba Kanavu* (Sweet Dream) for the benefit performance in Tiruchi.[43]

After the first day, the authorities backed off, and the poster-pasting ritual continued for some months peacefully.[44] Karunanidhi records that Anna would not talk to him for some time. But the agitation had made national headlines, and Karunanidhi himself would be called *Kallakudi Kondaan*, or the Conqueror of Kallakudi. A propaganda song sang paeans to Karunanidhi thus:

Kallakudi konda Karunanidhi vazhgave!
(Long live the true maestro who had won the hearts of the people!)

On 21 November, Karunanidhi and his team were released.[45] A hero's welcome awaited them at Egmore Railway Station, where NSK, MGR and others received them. Like in the movies, MGR carried Karunanidhi through the vast crowd, losing his expensive watch.[46]

But Nehru was furious. He had damned the stoppage of trains as 'ridiculous nonsense', noting rightly, 'Because I referred to some of their doings as foolish, they said, "We will indulge in them all the more." It is a little difficult to argue with them.'[47] Nehru added, 'There should be no toleration of such stupid, nonsensical and foolish acts . . . These are petty matters, which will pass, but we have big issues to consider.'[48] But the DMK would become a 'big issue' in a decade.

The Sampath-led protest against Rajaji's caste-based education would never come to fruition. Sampath had been taken into custody earlier. On 14 July, police foiled a procession led by Sathyavanimuthu that day and twenty-one other attempts, including the last on 30 July 1953, arresting and charging protesters.[49]

Rajaji refused to yield. An indignant EVR disastrously advised on 9 March 1954 at Athur, Salem, 'Identify the Brahmin house, keep a knife of fewer than six inches. When I instruct, shove the Brahmin with the knife.'[50] Thankfully, no one followed through, and the silent churning against Rajaji would see to his exit in the next weeks.

Kamaraj

On 14 April 1954, Kamaraj became chief minister, the first non-Brahmin Tamil from a most backward community (Nadar). Periyar, who had vowed to destroy the Congress, now threw his full weight behind Kamaraj, calling him *Pachai Thamizhan* or a pure Tamil.[51] Kamaraj stood for election from Gudiyatham against a communist candidate. Both the DMK and the DK lent their support to Kamaraj. Anna feted Kamaraj as *Gunala kula kozhunde* (the paragon of virtue and the life-sapling of the community). Jayakanthan found the DMK advocacy for Kamaraj 'obscene' and full of the 'most crude Brahmin hate slogans'. He felt Kamaraj should have disallowed it.[52] Jayakanthan need not have feared. Competitive politics would see the DMK soon become a bitter Kamaraj critic.

Few have scaled the heights or plumbed the political depths of India as much as Kamaraj. Gifted with the easy grace of a country parson, Kamaraj symbolized an era of selfless altruism, public service, political chutzpah, far-sightedness and stellar leadership. As chief minister from 1954 to 1963, he laid the state's educational, agricultural and industrial foundations. His epigones have stood on his shoulders to build on those foundations. Famous for his noncommittal 'Yes. Let us see' remark, Kamaraj was not a man of words but of action and his modus operandi, simple—to be around people and learn from them.

Kamaraj rose further to become the kingmaker, naming Lal Bahadur Shastri and Indira Gandhi as prime ministers. However, closer home, Kamaraj was blindsided by the DMK. Substantial but wooden, the *Pachai Thamizhan* greatly underestimated the force of identity politics, symbolism and cinema. His derisive *koothaadigal* (mountebanks) were making strides under his very nose. Even in 1957, when the DMK debuted with fifteen members, he felt the communists were more 'dangerous'.[53]

By November 1955, Anna had concluded that Kamaraj 'is not the least interested in the rights of Tamils or Thamizhagam. We are the ones who praise him as a pure Tamil—he does not have the habit of entertaining language, race and nationhood sentiments in his heart—the one thing that gives him briskness and strength is "hunting votes".'[54] Still, the following month, as a huge cyclone struck havoc in Thanjavur and Kamaraj rushed there, Anna praised him wholeheartedly:

It is the place where a responsible chief minister should be! Yes! He is with senior officials around him. He is seriously involved in wiping the tears of the people subjected to this great destruction . . . He sees our tears and sheds his. He offers abundant consolation in havoc-stricken places. He is not the chief minister who sits in the fort and 'orders'. He is not a priest who explains this as the Almighty's wrath! People are duty bound to praise him for coming flying unto them to offer back their lives—himself greatly distressed that this havoc had struck during his term. Younger brother! I must mention. We are proud of Chief Minister Kamaraj's sense of responsibility . . . no one can forget, cannot forever, that the chief minister's heart is pure, and his interest in the poor and the lowly is pure on this occasion.[55]

But this was a rare occasion, and the DMK of symbolism and Kamaraj of substance could only be adversaries.

Sivaji Ganesan Leaves

In the same missive, Anna had also asked the artists to go in person to collect relief aid.[56] The following week, he singled out MGR for walking the streets of Madurai, 'stretching his hand out' for contributions and expressing pride that he had a 'friend' with such a heart who was also a Kazhagam person.[57] MGR's may have been the most demonstrable act of charity, but Sivaji Ganesan claims he collected the most, yet 'elder brother' MGR was feted. A hugely disappointed Ganesan joined film director Bhimsingh on a visit to Tirupati only to face posters obscenely proclaiming—'Tirupati Ganesa Govinda!' on his return. Kannadasan was at the forefront of this pillorying effort. Those were heady times when the party took its rational credentials seriously, with Nedunchezhian serving A.K. Velan notice for scriptwriting *Nallathangaal* (1955) where Lord Shiva resurrects Nallathangaal, the wretch, and her children. Fearing the party's diktat, MGR asked for a doppelganger in *Madurai Veeran* (1956) on his ascent to heaven.[58] As calls for Ganesan's expulsion grew, the party discovered he was never a member.[59]

As Sivaji Ganesan's producers avoided Kannadasan, MGR sought him out. Kannadasan wrote for *Madurai Veeran* followed by *Nadodi Mannan*, *Raja Desingu* (1960) and *Mannaadhi Mannan* (Emperor, 1960), movies that took MGR to the next level.[60] Ganesan was just the first casualty of Anna's style of condoning natural selection.

Piggybacking on Tamilarasu Kazhagam

Earlier, we saw that the DMK had opposed Dakshin Pradesh, a province within India comprising the southern states. Dakshin Pradesh would have given the Telugus an electoral advantage over the rest. Anna cleverly criticized the idea as a 'mixture' in a melting pot. He said the DMK wanted to 'divide linguistically, unite racially and form a Dravida Republic Federation' to thwart northern dominance.[61] His Dravida Nadu envisaged separate linguistic entities and legislature, each uniting as a federation. Still, it would have required enormous constitutional imagination to maintain the political balance, and even with political parity, the project could have ended up like Yugoslavia. However, the DMK was in good company. In a telegram on 1 February 1956, Kamaraj's benefactor,

Periyar, urged Kamaraj, who was in discussions with Nehru and others in Bengaluru at the Congress executive meet then, against it.[62] That Rajaji sponsored it made Dakshin Pradesh even more unpalatable. In his telegram, Periyar said: 'Dakshin Pradesh will first finish you; then me. I will begin an unprecedented and shocking agitation.'[63]

The DMK was now part of Ma.Po.Si.'s Tamilarasu Kazhagam-led efforts at opposition to Dakshin Pradesh, demand for including Tamil areas in Madras State and renaming it Tamil Nadu.

Following the 19 February 1956 all-party meeting on the Marina Beach in Madras and the closure the next day to press the above demands, Anna wrote about the unprecedented one-lakh-strong procession that day: 'But *thambi*, I am a "shorty", right? I have never felt bad about it till now. On 20 February, alas! I felt bad that I am "short" like this and not "tall". Do you ask why?'[64] Anna said that he wanted to look over his shoulders to savour the crowd but could not.[65]

Often, history keeps an unfair account. The DMK's role was marginal in the issue of Chennai for Tamils and the boundary agitation. Only a third of the 6000 sq. km of the Keralite Tamil areas were incorporated into the reorganized Madras State. Devikulam and Peermedu remained with Kerala. Kamaraj's emotional quotient on these issues was dismal. His flippant remark '*Kulamavadhu medaavadhu?*' (pond or hillock, what does it matter if it is here or there?), gave Anna a stick to beat him with. His apologist Periyar explained that the Tamils in those areas were not indigenous and had gone there for work.

In January 1961, Ma.Po.Si. conducted a civil disobedience campaign for naming Madras State, Tamil Nadu.[66] Although the DMK belatedly joined the name change bandwagon, Anna could pummel Kamaraj as insufficiently Tamil. Anna's DMK equally owes 'state autonomy'—its post-separation mantra—to the Tamilarasu Kazhagam. But from 1956, the DMK would become the most vocal advocate of the Sri Lankan Tamil cause.[67]

5

In Pursuit of Power

General Secretary Navalar Nedunchezhian

The 17–20 May 1956 second state conference at Tiruchi opted for electoral politics, marking a decisive shift in the party's course. On 19 May, uttering his now famous invite, 'Younger brother, come! Do lead! We will submit to your command; come!' Anna welcomed a thirty-six-year-old Nedunchezhian as general secretary. He wrote later: 'The Kazhagam he has is not ordinary! More than 1000 units! Ceaseless public contacts. Numerous tested youngsters, warriors with scars from sacrifice, and those who preserve dignity.'[1]

Thirteen months earlier, on 24 April 1955, at Anna's request, Sampath had proposed Nedunchezhian. Karunanidhi and others had seconded it. This process was, however, not as easy as it seemed. Anna said a 'storm' had confronted him, and no one would hear of him stepping down. The idea had germinated two years prior, and Anna took residence at Nedunchezhian's place and 'tolerated' his house's vegetarianism to loosen the 'little shy' younger brother and for Nedunchezhian to get to know him better.[2]

Was Nedunchezhian the apt commander? Sampath had his misgivings, and Anna had to assuage him, saying that Nedunchezhian was only a nominal head and that he would still be in charge.[3]

Nedunchezhian was no polymath like Anna or Karunanidhi or a man of overpowering charisma like MGR. But a ranking senior with a genial disposition and a master's degree, Nedunchezhian was respected. Unlike Karunanidhi or Sampath, he had no independent following. Both had eyed the position, forcing Anna to settle on Nedunchezhian to preempt a contest. N.V. Natarajan served as his deputy.

That Sunday, the party passed thirty-three resolutions—the last and most pivotal authorized the party's electoral participation. In the morning's poll, 56,942 had voted for DMK's participation in elections and 4203 against it.* Anna said the naysayers were interested in seeing that 'no danger comes our way'.[4]

Emphasizing that sinecure ministerships did not bring greatness, he said the country had to be reclaimed. In his speech on 20 May, Anna pointed out to chief ministers Omandur Ramasamy Reddiar, Kumaraswamy Raja, Rajaji and a host of other personalities to argue how they were once powerful but how time had passed them by:

> Would we desire a ministership after seeing [their fate]? If it so happens that we are seized by desire, there is our drama company where if we donned the role for four days, the desire would be sated. What is wrong about it? Therefore we are not in this for ministership(s).[5]

The burden of reclaiming their country had fallen on them—the 'commoners', and he asserted that the decision was planted on them:

> Like repeatedly telling a young man with no thought of marriage that he wishes to wed and he consequently acquires such desire . . .

---

* The ballots were to be dropped in a red or a black box symbolizing for and against, respectively. Nedunchezhian, *Vaazhvil*, 272.

saying that [the DMK] desires to contest elections, they have made us reach such a decision.[6]

The truth is that Anna had long understood the power of electoral representation. In a candid moment, he told his thambis:

> You assemble lakhs of people before me. You tie flags higher and higher. Your praise reaches the skies. The garlands touch the gopuram. If I show these to the Delhi folks, will they climb down?[7]

Anna needed legislators, parliamentarians and power. Yet, Anna feared power, if acquired early, would sully the party. Sampath advised inducting 'action-oriented idealists, and the selfless' to avert the danger.[8] In four years, Anna would choose power over Sampath. Unlike Periyar, Anna felt they could 'season' themselves from power's forbidden fruits. He could not have been more naïve about his siblings. As a first step towards elections, an election committee with Anna, Sampath and Asaithambi was set up.[9]

The conference had been a massive success, with Anna alluding to a four-lakh attendance. A week later, Anna wrote:

> Thambi, you have overwhelmed me—I am searching for words in elegant Tamil—for the word, success is inadequate to explain our achievement . . . [I] did not feel like talking or writing about its huge success, greatness, and reasons. I wish to be in this deep state of quietude . . .
>
> Tiruchi state conference has given us this brave emotion. All [this is] the result of your intelligence! The fruits of your work! All owing to the feeling springing from your heart. Thambi! Let your ability grow—fame glow—I congratulate you.[10]

Kamaraj now wondered about the 'sacrifice' of the DMK, which had no role in India's independence, caricaturing it as a party of public speakers and artists. The initial rapport between Kamaraj and the DMK had long ceased. If Kamaraj aimed at the DMK's soft underbelly of a party divorced from the independence struggle, the DMK hit at his woodenness as anti-Tamil. Kamaraj had taken a larger view, letting go of Peermedu and Devikulam to Kerala after putting up a fight. Besides, his administration baulked at the clamour for renaming Madras State to Tamil Nadu. In 1956, as the Sinhala Only Act in Sri Lanka led to ethnic violence there, Kamaraj's usual reticence saw the DMK putting up posters across the state that July and August, which read:

Murder! Murder.
Horrible Murder.
What is Kamaraj doing?
What is Nehru saying?[11]

As Periyar defended Kamaraj, Anna said Periyar's support for Kamaraj was built on the circularity of logic: 'Kamaraj is ours. Therefore, he is good. Kamaraj is good; therefore, he is ours.'[12] On 5 August 1956, quoting a devotee's hymn to the Lord that said: 'Whether you strike or embrace [me] I am your worshipper', Anna said Periyar justified Kamaraj's every unjustifiable anti-Tamil act.[13] In September, Periyar simply said he could not find fault with Kamaraj as he was beholden to Delhi, insisting that 'He is a friend of the Tamils. He is waiting to do more good for the Tamils.'[14]

Electoral Debut

The first casualty of the party's decision to take the electoral route was its Tirunelveli district secretary, K.V.K. Samy, whose murder on 30 September 1956 by suspected political foes showed that the road to power would be bloody. Anna wrote, 'Not a day passes without me asking for a heart to bear anything (inspired by Byron's *To*

Thomas Moore). A great fire that the heart cannot take has entered and is burning . . . Torment, torment I have never experienced so far . . .' Samy was just thirty-two.[15] The DMK considered Samy its first martyr who had made the 'supreme sacrifice'.[16] Violence and thuggery remain the integral twins of political life in most parts of the developing world. In retrospect, the party appeared more than ready.

At the 16 December 1956 Vellore Election Fund meeting, where entry was by tickets, Anna painted the Congress's greatest strength as Nehru, a 'leader without equals' but not 'ours', who was akin to the Dalai Lama, Bulganin, Khrushchev, the Abyssinian king, Queen Elizabeth and Eisenhower. Like them, he said he could be welcomed as a guest. He asserted that with the DMK, the buck stopped in Chennai. Besides, petty shopkeepers, mill labourers, beedi workers, handcart pullers, load bearers, wood splitters and sweepers comprised the DMK. They should send someone like themselves to the legislature and be accountable to the voters. On the other hand, the Congress was a party of mill owners, bus owners, major merchants, traders and landlords, he claimed.

Campaign

On 10 January 1957, Nedunchezhian announced 142 candidates for the 205-strong assembly and sixteen for the forty-one parliamentary seats at the Coimbatore election conference.[17] A search committee headed by Nedunchezhian, with NVN, Sampath, Karunanidhi, Mathiazhagan, Asaithambi and Madurai Muthu had travelled the state for twelve days to identify candidates.[18]

With the DMK not a recognized party yet, those like Nedunchezhian had to settle for other symbols like the rooster.

The DMK came up with catchy slogans on the issues of the time, like inflation and the 23 November 1956 Ariyalur train tragedy, which left 142 dead. O.V. Alagesan, the minister of state for railways, offered to resign like the minister Lal Bahadur Shastri.

But his resignation was not accepted.[19] It was a field day for the DMK.

Ariyalur Alagesanaare
Neer aandadhu podhadhaa?
Palar maandadhu podhadhaa?

Ariyalur Mr Alagesan
Isn't your rule enough?
Aren't the deaths of many enough?* asked the DMK.

The manifesto emphasized Tamil cultural nationalist themes and price control, among other things. *Murasoli* ran cartoons conveying the manifesto in visual and simple terms. The paper also superimposed Anna on to the famous Lord Horatio Kitchener cover, from 5 September 1914, published by *London Opinion* for recruiting men for the First World War effort. Anna, instead of Kitchener, was seen calling on his thambis to join in the task to 'save Tamil, Tamils and Tamil culture.' Anna said it would take fifty years of inspired work to create the state for Tamils to hold their heads high worldwide. He asked thambis to be part of the efforts to realize that ideal.

This was its first election, and the DMK made a virtue out of necessity when it came to caste, one of the two Cs in the Tamil Nadu elections, the other C being cash. In Veerapandi village, for instance, Vanniyar, Mudaliar, Vellala Gounders and Adi Dravidas were the major communities, but Anna had chosen a minority Devanga Chettiar candidate. Even as the majority leaders and notables were with the Congress, a younger generation slowly gravitated towards the DMK.

---

* Ariyalur is where Alagesan hailed from.

Thus, Veerapandi Arumugham and his friends worked for the DMK candidate even as his dad and the village bigwigs stood by the Congress. The party had no funds, and they scraped the bottom of the pot. But the DMK candidate's easy manners and approach drew the voters to him, forcing Arumugham's father to change tack, paying the voters to vote for the Congress. Although the DMK candidate lost the elections, in Veerapandi, he had pulled ahead.[20] The following year, Arumugham and his team won 75 per cent of the votes in the local body polls.[21] The DMK was making steady inroads.

Besides, the self-styled Congress Reform Committee (CRC) dissidents headed by K.S. Venkatakrishna Reddiar opposed to Kamaraj's dominance, would set up candidates against the official candidates. The fiery Forward Bloc leader Pasumpon Muthuramalinga Thevar campaigned for them. A powerful orator and a staunch believer, Thevar bitterly opposed the Kazhagams.

Despite being its debut election, Anna's campaign drew crowds, eliciting the comment, 'Crowds for the DMK . . . votes for the Congress' from Kamaraj.[22] 'If that hand were to get strong, it would squeeze the Tamils' jugular and supplicate to the northerners. What is Kamaraj good at? In protecting or promoting Tamil—is he good? Has he been skilful in saving Tamil Nadu's boundaries? Not at all!' was Anna's refrain in return.[23]

Brickbats were common at DMK meetings. Showcasing a stone missile at his native Kanchipuram, Anna said: 'Look at this. Do you think it is an ordinary stone? No! It is the last relic of the teetering Congress edifice', auctioning it off for a handsome price. When a scurrilous handwritten poster on Anna's paternity showed up on an electric pole next to his residence, an unfazed Anna asked that a lamp be placed so that the degrading remarks could also be read in the evenings.[24]

On 21 February, Muthuramalinga Thevar launched a scathing attack in Kanchipuram on Anna and the DMK. Alluding to Tirumoolar's 'One humanity, one Almighty' credo that Anna made famous and the Kazhagams' rejection of worship of many gods, Thevar said that when a son points to his father's photographs as a boy, a groom and as a father, the viewer should not be asking, 'Do you have so many fathers?' Would such a person be considered intelligent?' Thevar asked and said that the Almighty was one but was worshipped in different forms, and wondered if having so many gods was a lowly thing. Thevar said the DMK's north-south divide accepted Mohammed Ali Jinnah and the British but not northern freedom fighters such as Lokmanya Thilak.

> In what way Jinnah is not a north Indian? How is the name of Jinnah and Robinson (Sir William Rose Robinson, a police chief of the 1870s, also officiated as governor, after whom the park in Royapuram where the DMK was launched was named) so sweet to you, sir? How is the name of poor Tilak so bitter to you, sir? I am not able to understand.

He said he would not allow the degradation of Tamil civilization in the name of Tamil affinity and rights and the growth of atheism through the Brahmin, non-Brahmin divide.

Thevar wondered how Anna's steamy *Romapuri Ranigal* could protect the non-Brahmins and came down heavily on him for his *Thangaiyin Kadhal* (Sisters Love) of incest.[25]

Anna and the DMK studiously avoided engaging the towering Thevar an icon for the Mukkulathor community. But Periyar's campaign against him and the DMK hurt. He called the DMK 'wastrels with no plan' and set about saying, 'Let us defeat the teardrops, Pancha Pandavas! Let's go!'[26]

In an election meeting with A. Ramasamy Mudaliar, in his hometown Kanchipuram, Anna, said:

> Periyar Ramasamy, for whom I have given so many years of my toil, is up against me with a determination to end my political

career. But this genius Ramasamy, for whom I have not done even
the littlest bit, has now come to my rescue . . .[27]

It would take Anna another ten years to dislodge the Congress. In
1962, he would repeat the words more forcefully in Rajaji's presence.
Yet perhaps the simple and accessible Anna and his thambis appeared
more like their own to the voter.

DMK candidates barely slept or ate. Indeed, Anna and
Karunanidhi didn't. At his Kulithalai constituency, Karunanidhi's
day began at 5 a.m. and stretched through the late evening. Unlike
Congressmen, he mingled easily with the working class and
the peasants, eating at their places.[28] Karunanidhi resourcefully
distributed printed handbills and recorded speeches. Bamboo-mat
advertisements and calendars proclaiming Karunanidhi as *enga veetu
pillai* (our son) abounded, making Karunanidhi ubiquitous in the
campaign.

Velliyanai, a backward rural area in his constituency, had
no major DMK presence. But the penny had dropped instantly
for the astute Karunanidhi. Some 10,000 agricultural labourers
were employed across 10,000 acres in the constituency under two
tenancies. *Maaterkaarargal* were given the oxen, seeds, fertilizers and
manure and the produce was shared 60:40. *Kaiyerukaarargal* were
mostly Adi Dravidas, tribes and farm labourers who worked for a
daily fee. But a court ruling rejecting their lessee status deprived
them of the protection of the law, and the landlords brought in
labourers from Mannargudi and Malabar.[29] Karunanidhi promised
to redress the situation if elected. He kept his promise.

The party won fifteen assembly and two parliamentary seats,
polling 16,53,494 or a third of the votes. It had finished second in
forty-seven seats. Congress's 49,16,375 votes, or three times that of
the DMK, had translated to 151 seats. Anna said that proportional
representation would have brought different results.[30] Indeed.
However, the DMK would not speak of proportional representation

when it began to reap the asymmetrical rewards of the first-past-the-post system.

Sampath and R. Dharmalingam were elected to Parliament. Anna, Karunanidhi, Anbazhagan, Asaithambi, A. Govindasamy, P.U. Shanmugam and M.P. Subramaniam were elected to the assembly. Kannadasan had lost. On 31 March 1957, Anna was chosen as head, Anbazhagan deputy, Karunanidhi whip, and M.P. Subramaniam and Govindasamy secretaries of the DMK legislature party.[31]

In keeping with its separatist credentials, the first decision that the DMK's legislature party took was on 28 April, when it chose to boycott the presidential election, protesting a second term for President Rajendra Prasad from the north and describing the two Opposition candidates as 'reactionary'.[32]

The Congress administration did not invite Anna and the other DMK MLAs (members of the Legislative Assembly) to any official event.

'A Strange Group'

On 29 April, felicitating speaker Krishna Rao, Anna described the DMK as a 'strange group' arising from a strange situation.[33] On 6 May, he interpreted the vote for the DMK as a vote for the 'freedom fighters' and asked that Congress seek more for the state, showcasing them to Delhi.[34] On 4 July, he remarked that they had not entered the assembly to remain in the Opposition. 'If not today, one day we will assume the responsibility to rule', he said.[35] Three days later, on 7 July, he noted that the government was not keen on land reform and the slogan, 'north shines, south declines' was not alliteration and that they should use them as 'sappers and miners' to get the state's due share.[36]

In his maiden speech on 4 May, Karunanidhi spoke about the 10,000 farmhands in Nangavaram and Dhimachipuram. In a twenty-day protest from 23 August to 9 September, peasants under his leadership defied a legal ban on entering the lands and began cultivation, courting arrest daily. [37] Ultimately, the Karunanidhi-spearheaded struggle would pay off, earning them the right to work the farms and an assured wage for the farm hands.[38]

The DMK boycotted the governor's address in keeping with its stand that the institution was redundant and cost Rs 10 lakh annually.[39] Later, while criticizing the 31 July 1959 dismissal of the E.M.S. Namboodiripad government in Kerala, Anna would make the earthy remark, '*Aatukku thaadium, naattukku governorum thevai illai* (A goat doesn't need a beard and a state doesn't need a governor).'[40]

Similarly, there were also some below-the-belt moments. On comparing the richness of Hindi and Tamil, Anna said,

> If we were to ask, 'What grammar is there in Hindi? What is its literary flourish?' after much effort, they would show us two epics—Tulsidas's Ramayana and the All-India Railway Guide. They offer these two as the best literary works in their language.[41]

The DMK would pitch for amending the Constitution for all languages to become official and, until then, for English to be retained.[42]

What Difference Did the DMK Make?

Anna first took the floor on 29 April 1957, and his last address was on 15 December 1961. The DMK was only one of the five Opposition parties in the legislature, but it shouldered the burden of being the most vocal. Its cultural nationalism and left-of-centre approach saw Anna put Tamil Nadu, its people and the language on top. *Vikatan* said DMK's entry made the assembly smell of 'Tamil fragrance'.

Anna and his colleagues spoke in good Tamil and used literary references. Every day, a member or two quoted the *Kural*. Finance Minister C. Subramaniam (CS) presented the budget in Tamil, and the budget booklet used the Tamil salutation 'Thiru' as opposed to the Sanskrit 'Sri' for his title. The DMK had introduced the Tamil equivalent, *nidhinilai arikai*, for 'budget'. The House was fuller than before, and the DMK members were an energetic team, most active during the question hour. Earlier, reporters considered covering the assembly, boredom; now, there was competition, mainly when Anna spoke. In replying to the debate on the budget, CS said that he had prepared himself reading Anna's *Panathoatam* (Money Garden) and *Ilatchiya Varalaaru* (The History of Ideals) and had a typed version of *Ilatchiya Varalaaru* on his table.[43]

But Anna's concern was more than Tamil. His major complaint was that the big-ticket infrastructure and industrial projects were with the Centre or private hands and that only palm and cactus fibre industries were in the state domain. Anna pointed out that there were people who could invest Rs 50 crore in the north while there were none to invest even Rs 5 crore in the south.[44] 'What was wrong in us saying "north shines, south declines"?' he wondered.[45]

It was a time before the liberalization that began in the late 1980s, after which chief ministers could canvass for foreign direct investment. While complimenting the Congress government as 'capable', Anna exposed its powerlessness awaiting sanction from the Centre, be it the Land Ceiling Act, independent food zone, state trading of grains or price rise of tamarind and chillies (as the state could not stop their export), the sanctioning of the Neyveli Lignite or Salem Steel plant, more sugar mills, paper plant, spinning mills and mills in general, rebate for handloom weavers—everything depended on the Centre.[46]

The DMK's specious argument began to take root. Kamaraj's stature had turned Tamil Nadu into a major source of central investment and industries and had put it clearly in the league of Maharashtra and Punjab. But Kamaraj and his colleagues did not counter the DMK refrain effectively. They either did not wish to dignify the charge, thought it was beneath them or were incapable, or felt that development would speak for itself. Whatever the reason, they were wrong.

The only one who could join issue was Periyar. Even as the DMK claimed it had changed things, in late July, Periyar said: 'Nothing can be done by going to the legislative assembly.'[47] Three months later, he said the DMK was on the payroll of Brahmins.[48] The bonhomie between Rajaji and the DMK had begun to irk Periyar.

But the DMK's focus remained on cultural nationalist issues. On 11 August, speaking in Madurai, Anna said they had only pressed for a vote on two issues: renaming Madras State to Tamil Nadu on 7 May and the plight of handloom weavers.

> Why did we want a vote on just this? We knew that we would lose. But should not the country see who is Tamil and who say[s] 'No' to Tamil Nadu?' While the entire Opposition stood up in support with pride, all the 150 Congress members were 'embarrassed' as they stood up in opposition.

Periyar nonetheless wondered what the vote had achieved. Anna said: 'We have not achieved just yet. What we have achieved is that we have written a new chapter in Tamil Nadu's history. It won't be visible now.' He said that when a grandchild studies history, it will be astonished that there were people who said 'No' to Tamil Nadu.[49]

Mudukulathur

In August 1957, Anna claimed that the three months in the legislature had given the ten-year growth of the previous years for the party, adding that the foreign press was taking note of them.[50]

But a legislative track was also a political minefield. Caste riots between the middling Maravars (Maravars, Kallars and Agamudayars are together called Mukkulathor or Thevars) and Pallars (Dalits) between 14 and 20 September led to many Dalit deaths, police firing, Maravar deaths and the arrest of the charismatic Forward Bloc leader Muthuramalinga Thevar, a member of Parliament. Periyar stood by Kamaraj. A deeply religious Muthuramalinga Thevar was neither a friend of the Congress nor of the DMK. His popularity amongst his people posed a serious threat to the ambitions of others.

The communists had moved a no-confidence motion against the Kamaraj-led administration. The DMK found itself on a sticky wicket. An aspiring party, it required both the middling Thevars and the Dalits. On 30 October, speaking on the motion, Anna said he had lamented that in his public career, he had yet to address a meeting beyond Paramakudi (in Ramnad, the Thevar bastion) as the DMK had no presence in those parts. He said he was somewhat happy that that was the case, as otherwise, the DMK would have been blamed as insinuators. Seeking a judicial inquiry, the party took the middle ground and abstained from the vote.[51] *Dravida Nadu* pointed out that many were eager to see how the DMK, new to the legislature, would act—if it would 'slip' or 'tilt'. Instead, it slithered. Since the judicial inquiry was not conceded, it staged a walkout.[52]

Defending the Mentor

The next test was fairly easy and was an opportunity to embarrass Kamaraj, whom Periyar recklessly supported. On 11 November, the Kamaraj government passed the Prevention of Insults to National Honour Act to pre-empt Periyar and his followers from burning the Constitution and, fifteen days later, pictures of Gandhi against the Indian state's not-so-commensurate efforts to eradicate caste first. On 3 November, the DK gave fifteen days' notice to delete the provisions of the Constitution dealing with religious freedom, which it said protected the caste system and the Brahmins.[53] The bill made insults to national symbols and Gandhi an offence. A week earlier, on 4 November, Nehru reiterated to Kamaraj that Periyar's intended act was 'the most barbarous thing' he had 'come across in any civilized country.'[54] Nonetheless, on 26 November, some 3000 DK party men burnt copies of the Constitution and were arrested. Periyar was taken into preventive custody one day prior, released on 29 November and sentenced to six months imprisonment on 14 December for the symbolic protest.[55]

Anna sarcastically lauded the effort to save Gandhi's portrait by a Congress administration that he said had failed to save Gandhi himself. Terming the bill 'bad, unnecessary and leading to cruelty', he pointed out that in 1953, the Congress had adopted a laissez-faire attitude, arguing that Ganesh's aura grew further as Periyar broke Ganesh's idols. However, Home Minister Bhaktavatsalam insinuates that Kamaraj may not have been fully for the measure against Periyar.[56] On a visit to the state, Nehru reiterated that Periyar was a 'lunatic' who belonged to a 'lunatic asylum'—words he had used in his 5 November letter to Kamaraj on Periyar's advocacy of violence against Brahmins and recommended that he be banished.[57]

Black Flag for Nehru

With his comments, Nehru had gifted the DMK another excuse to protest. The 27–28 December Nagercoil conference resolved to show Nehru black flags on 6 January 1958.[58] A day later on 29 December, Anna described Nehru's comments against Periyar as 'vehement, vindictive and violent' and *Dravida Nadu* said that Nehru set aside 'graciousness' on his visits.[59]

The protest saw two deaths from the stampede that resulted from the police's baton charge. Earlier, 4700 people were taken into preventive custody. Anna said there was never before a demonstration of such dimensions in the city, not even during the 1928 Simon Commission visit.[60]

Nehru appeared indifferent to the DMK's inane protest. Two years later, however, to pre-empt the DMK's protest against the President, Nehru reiterated his 1959 assurance made famous by the DMK that English would remain in use until the non-Hindi speakers wished it otherwise. In the meantime, the DMK was finding new allies in its struggle against Hindi steamrolling. Thus on 22 December, in a meeting convened by Rajaji at Gokhale Hall, the slogan 'English ever; Hindi never' coined by Professor Kothanda Rao of Karnataka was adopted and later popularized by Rajaji.[61] Piqued by Rajaji's closeness to the separatist DMK, the prime minister wrote:

In Madras State there are some people and a well, organized group who even talk about a separate independent State of Tamil Nad. Anything more foolish I cannot imagine. Any attempt to bring this about will not only create disruption but civil war, because I think that any further division of India will never be tolerated by the great majority of our people. We have had enough experience of partition. I know very well that you are not in favour of this separate independent State in South India. But I do not remember you raising your powerful voice against it in the way you have raised it about the Union language.[62]

On 28 March 1958, Rajaji responded that he had not raised his voice in public as he did not 'wish to give that recognition to it which my opposition would carry by implication'.[63] But it was equally clear that Rajaji and Anna were drawing close. Anna had once considered Rajaji wily. He now sang the paeans of his praise as *Mootharignar* or the wise scholar. *Mootharignar* could give an image makeover for the DMK, considered fringe and lumpen with an anti-Brahmin antecedent.

Meanwhile, *Viduthalai* published a list of thirty-three senior positions that had gone to non-Brahmins to explain Periyar's support for Kamaraj. Paraphrasing the DMK's criticism of Kamaraj and Periyar as 'fourth rate', it called them 'blockheads, miscreants, power-hungry dogs'. It rightly argued that Kamaraj could not be expected to support all of DK's ideals when those who had been 'soaked and got bloated' in the DK were saying 'God is one' and 'Brahmins are also Tamils'.[64] Periyar described the DMK as 'Non-Brahmin slaves'—subjugating themselves to the Brahmin in their desire for power.[65]

Rising Sun

On 2 March 1958, the Election Commission recognized the DMK as a regional party and allocated them the rising sun symbol. In the previous year, MGR's name in *Chakravarthi Thirumagal* (Emperor's Daughter, 1957) was *Udayasuryian* or rising sun. In 1948, A. Govindasamy had the rising sun symbol for his Vanniya Kula Kshatriya Party. He later became secretary of the Toilers Party with the rooster as its symbol. In 1954, when Ramasamy Padayachi merged his Toilers Party with the Congress, Govindasamy, on Anna's advice, revived the Toilers Party and, instead of the rooster, chose the rising sun. In 1957, Anna requested the Election Commission to allocate the symbol officially since Govindasamy was part of the DMK. In the 1959 Corporation elections, DMK candidates fought on the rising sun symbol.

Ripon Building Breached

The year 1959 had begun well for the DMK. Anna had complained earlier that the DMK was considered 'a horde', 'a stupid crowd' and a 'small party'. However, this would change with the DMK winning forty-five of the ninety seats contested of the total 100 seats in the Chennai Corporation.[66] Ripon Building, the seat of the city government, Anna wrote, was changing things for the DMK finally:

The biggest hurdle for those of us in the DMK is the continuing state of ignorance about us! . . . No newspaper is aware of us! No one knows us. Now after the Madras victory, Indira Madam is issuing a statement; the Congress working committee is to deliberate [on this development]. The hardships of showcasing our ideal . . . were not small! Many a time, we have held black flags to express our ideas, held protests, and defied bans; some lay down on the rails putting their lives at risk . . .[67]

Anna announced that the DMK would not stake a claim even if it had won another ten seats, prompting *The Mail* to criticize him as shirking his responsibility. On 15 January 1959, in a massive public meeting at the Marina, Anna got a resounding 'yes' from the audience to take over the Chennai Corporation.[68]

Karunanidhi had pushed a hesitant Anna to field candidates for eighty of the 100 seats, and Kannadasan, D.V. Narayanasamy, MGR and others had played a crucial role during the campaign.[69] Anna, who originally wanted the DMK to stand in thirty, singled out Karunanidhi as the architect of the victory and presented him a ring. As a disappointed Kannadasan confronted him, Anna told the poet to get a ring so that he could present it to him at the next meeting. Kannadasan was embittered.[70]

The party fell short by six councillors for the post of mayor. MGR's help was enlisted, and A.P. Arasu became the first DMK mayor. He became the first elected DMK official to boycott the Independence Day celebrations, in keeping with DMK's beliefs. On 9 October, Nehru, who disapproved of statues for the living, unveiled the DMK-sponsored statue for Kamaraj in Chennai. The DMK councillors had proposed to erect a statue for Anna, who demurred and suggested that they honour Kamaraj instead. It was Kamaraj's first and perhaps the state's first statue for a living person. The DMK had, in its way, established a precedent. Anna would have his statue in 1968 and Karunanidhi in 1975.[71]

The arrival of the 'commoners' in the Corporation's seat of power also led to reports of political interference and corruption. Yet, buoyed by its success, the DMK would announce that the Corporation Ripon Building* would become the gateway to Fort St George.[72]

The man who would play a critical role in making that happen had been making the right moves. In 1957–58, as unprecedented rains lashed Chennai after eighteen years, matinee idol MGR saw a rickshaw man at a railway crossing drenched in the showers. When he expressed pity to his brother, the latter wondered lightly if the rickshaw man would wear a raincoat. MGR latched on to the idea, and his ever-resourceful manager, R.M. Veerappan, got thousands of raincoats made at Rs 10 apiece. Anna distributed these at an event at Nungambakkam. Many of the rickshaws now began to sport MGR's image.[73]

After *Nadodi Mannan*, MGR became the party's mascot.[74] On 30 November 1958, Anna called MGR his *Idayakani* or his heart's fruit and said the fruit had 'fortunately fallen in my lap'. But strong headwinds were brewing for the party.

---

* It would also begin the use the term *Maanagaratchi* for the Corporation in Tamil.

6

First Split

Sampath–Anna differences

The gifted Sampath enjoyed a special relationship with Anna. Seventeen years younger, he was sharp, a wee extra principled and widely read. He had forsaken his uncle, Periyar, and his inheritance to follow Anna. Anna was fond of him. But Sampath also possessed a sense of entitlement. This and his exposure to Delhi saw Sampath exceed his remit, calling for a meeting at advocate V.P. Raman's (later advocate general) house on the issue of Dravida Nadu following his September 1958 tour to the Soviet Union. Nedunchezhian, Karunanidhi, N.V. Natarajan, Asaithambi and Mathiazhagan showed up. Sampath telephoned Anna, who was surprised but travelled from Kanchipuram to join them.

Sampath argued that Dravida Nadu was impossible and suggested they either seek a separate Tamil Nadu (like Periyar from April/May 1958) or the right to self-determination within a united India. Anna reportedly said, 'Sampath, you say this after going to Delhi Parliament and Russia; I knew this even from the beginning when your dad [Periyar] proposed this . . .!' Karunanidhi and the others appeared closer to Sampath's position, according to Sampath's sympathizers. However, eternally overcautious, Anna was not ready to administer the shock and reasoned that the cadres had to be prepared first. He assured Sampath, 'The time will come, and we should wait for the right time. When that juncture is reached, I will announce it myself at a conference. Until then, do not talk about this. Do not discuss it.'[1]

But Dravida Nadu was not the only issue, and Sampath was restive again soon. A year and some months later, on 20 February 1960, Sampath circulated an eight-page letter to the 120 general council members, arguing that everything in the party rested on one man—Anna. He charged that for Anna and some others (read Karunanidhi), politics was a subsidiary occupation—'like poultry farming was to farmers', and to entrust all responsibility in such people's hands would lead to 'great danger' and 'great humiliation'. Sampath wanted responsibility diversified. He said the party's initial idealist streak and selflessness had diminished. Instead, frontline leaders were focused on financial security, personal comfort, pleasures and the trappings of the high life, with a degradation in moral values.[2] Sampath had fired the first salvo.

The second salvo was more potent. The 19 June Kumarapalayam general council took up Sampath's resolution that the general secretary, deputy and district secretaries not hold electoral office. (The earlier 11–12 July 1959 Mayavaram general council saw a majority agree that the general secretary should not hold a dual position.) However, Anna persuaded the Kumarapalayam council that this be a convention rather than a rule. Meanwhile, it was resolved to protest the 27 April 1960 presidential order on the progressive use of Hindi.[3] Anna named Sampath to head the agitation committee with Karunanidhi and sixteen others.[4] Was it an olive branch?

But Anna and Sampath differed on many things. The 30 July party executive in Chennai had deliberated for four hours before settling on black flags as a protest to the President. A greatly hesitant Anna feared the protest would invite the army and the agitation would inconvenience the DMK actors, read MGR and SSR. When he finally relented, Anna wanted actors to be exempted. 'Is this the speech of the one who would lead [the Tamils] to freedom?' Sampath would ask later, pointing out to Tamilarasu Kazhagam's Tamil Nadu name change agitation in which its film personalities T.K. Shanmugham and G. Umapathy had courted arrest. In any case, the next day at the Kodambakkam anti-Hindi conference, Anna wished Sampath, 'Younger brother farewell! Fare well!' If Anna thought his expansive gesture of investing Sampath with the leadership of the seminal agitation would placate him, he was mistaken. The differences were too deep to be papered over by Anna's gestures.

Thankfully, the agitation never came to pass. On 3 August, on receipt of Sampath's letter on the impending protest, a furious Nehru sent for Sampath only to upbraid him. But in the end, he agreed to write to Sampath as requested: 'We hold fully by the assurances given' on the continuance of English even while expressing 'deep regret' at the DMK's protest plans 'which can only mean disrespect to our President.'[5] Earlier, on 7 August 1959, speaking in Parliament on Frank Anthony's resolution on the inclusion of English in the Eighth Schedule of the Constitution listing official languages, Nehru had expressly assured that for an indefinite period, English would continue as the 'associate additional language' until the non-Hindi speaking people desired otherwise.[6] Nehru was reiterating the 7 August 1959 assurance to Sampath.[*] Consequently, the DMK dropped its plan. On 7 August, at the Marina Beach, Anna sang paeans for Sampath, exulting, 'The hand that wrote the assurance to my younger brother is the hand that shook Eisenhower's hand. Truman, Stalin.'[7]

After this, at the 25 September general council at MGR's residence, Sampath acquiesced to Anna's wish to return as general

---

[*] The DMK had since insisted on constitutional protection for the assurance in vain.

secretary. According to Kannadasan, Sampath had approached Karunanidhi to take over, but Anna had talked him out of it. This appears implausible, but Sampath may have seen Karunanidhi as a tactical ally in offloading the Dravida Nadu baggage.

Nedunchezhian records that Mathiazhagan and Chitrarasu desired the position, and Chitrarasu, seen as a candidate backed by Karunanidhi, refused to yield. In the end, Anna had stepped in to prevent a contest and, in his acceptance speech, mentioned that he had 'greatly desired' Mathiazhagan to take over.[8] Sampath became the first decorative presidium chair and Karunanidhi treasurer.

But in its aftermath, on 30 October, a self-assured Anna began his five-part series 'All are this Country's King' in *Dravida Nadu*, a rendition of Shaw's *Apple Cart*, 'a comedy in which a king defeats an attempt by his popularly elected prime minister . . . to reduce him to a cipher.' Anna was King Magnus. Instead of Prime Minister Proteus, he had chosen the self-righteous Bill Boanerges, a minister but also a bit of a character, for Sampath. He called him *Puyalaar* (Mr Storm) after the Hebrew meaning of Boanerges, namely, 'sons of thunder', a surname given by Jesus to apostles James and John also meaning a vociferous preacher or orator. Wasn't Sampath the DMK's wordsmith?' After Kannadasan drew attention to Anna's nuanced attack on him, Sampath's 'Annavin Mannan' (Anna's King) response in Kannadasan's 21 January 1961 *Thendral* (Southerly Breeze) noted that Anna was perhaps disillusioned with republicanism and pointed out that Anna could have engaged in more important tasks that waited his attention.[9]

Sampath's essay saw that issue of *Thendral* sell the most in the weekly's history. However, Anna's supporters were far from thrilled. Earlier, in the *Inamuzhakkam* (Nation's Declaration) Pongal issue, Sampath had said that titles for politicians were 'vulgar', asking that he be simply referred to as comrade and not *Sollin Selvar* or wordsmith, his title in the party.

The Jinxed Vellore Executive

The Vellore party executive and general council on 21–22 January happened against this already sour background. As snide and disparaging references were made to him and his supporters who were not present, Sampath objected and Anbazhagan, Madurai Muthu and another member responded, leading to the 'two-minute tension' as Anna described the incidents later. Emotions had run high, threats were issued and MGR and SSR had shown up from the anteroom. Anna condoned their presence. SSR had figuratively pulled up Sampath's shirt and dealt a blow. Sampath noted in the minutes' book, 'I don't wish to preside over this Neanderthal council.' His amendments, however, continued to haunt the executive. Two were significant. One was that the general council should elect the presidium chair, general secretary, treasurer and eighteen executive members instead of the general secretary. Another amendment proposed that the presidium chair convene the bodies and chair the sessions, making the position substantial. NVN, part of the original rule-framing committee, complained that the amendments hurt 'our self-respect'. A troubled Anna said, 'If something happens to the party, I won't be alive.' However, describing himself as a conservative, Anna, punning on the word 'right', said, 'Rightists are always right, and leftists will be left out', and adjourned the meeting. Sampath was a leftist.

The next day's *Nava India* evening daily broke the news of the attack on Sampath and his resignation as presidium chair. *Namnadu* denied any untowardness and said that Sampath had resigned voluntarily. For his part, Sampath said he was pained that Anna had threatened to 'throw out' the few leftists. Anna now issued a lengthy statement saying the discussion in the executive had led to 'two minutes tension' and except for 'raised voices', there was no untowardness. He claimed that after this, everyone remained still for five to ten minutes, and their eyes were moist. And after lunch, when the executive reconvened, Sampath's *Thendral* rejoinder and argumentative behaviour came up for discussion. Sampath said he had spoken his mind, but since he was in the minority, he would resign as the chair. It was 5.30 p.m.

The executive continued till 8 p.m. Later, Anna, Mathiazhagan and Sampath went for a drive. Anna's entreaties in the car bore no result as Sampath refused to change his mind and handed over his resignation at 11 p.m. The three were emotional. The executive met the next morning without Sampath and referred the amendments to a committee. At 12.30 p.m., the general council began deliberations. Mathiazhagan did not attend. Since the proposers stayed away, the resolutions were rejected. Anna ended his statement by saying, 'There was no scene or scuffle.' But the damage had been done.[10]

The Reconciliation That Did Not Last

Chitrarasu, Mathiazhagan, Govindasamy and NVN now tried to reconcile the two leaders. Govindasamy got in touch with Kannadasan and, as agreed, brought Anna from Kanchipuram to a neutral place in T. Nagar. After tea, the talks began at 7 p.m. Govindasamy was around. A feeling of affection and bonding laced the talks, and Anna reportedly promised that at a later stage, he would create a situation where Sampath would lead the party.

In the end, Anna issued a statement in which he said that he was 'pained' by violence and the 'evil forces'. Sampath, for his part, regretted his essay and 'greatly appreciated and welcomed' Anna's statement. Anna had implicated the actors as the evil forces; they sent a telegram asking him to retract. To placate them, Anna issued another statement. In trying to please everyone, Anna failed, pleasing no one. Kannadasan's essay titled 'Confession', in the Catholic tradition, criticizing the troublemakers and the sycophants, saw that issue of *Thendral* register record sales.

A month later, on 20 February, a man tugged at Kannadasan's shirt and tried to beat him up with his footwear in a meeting in Tiruchi. On 21 February, Sampath implicated Karunanidhi and the actors in this action and began an indefinite fast from 22 February in Nungambakkam to 'eradicate the Kazhagam's pollution and cleanse the party'. Having failed to dissuade Sampath and describing the 20 February incident as 'the greatest blemish' in his life, Anna visited him daily, pleading with him to give up the fast. As Sampath's situation deteriorated on the third day, an alarmed Anna stopped eating. When a greatly emotional Anna pleaded this time, Sampath agreed to end his fast. In his 24 February statement, Anna reiterated the Tiruchi incident as the 'greatest blemish' in his life,[11] and called for the 26 February reconciliatory 'Guards Meeting' at Thiruvottriyur.

There he spoke sentimentally:

We are simple commoners. Believing in an ideal, we found this movement to dedicate ourselves. We bound this movement with family affection. Since one mother could not bear us all, different mothers gave birth to us. We took upon responsibilities like brothers . . . The people of Tamil Nadu treat us like their children and have reposed trust in us. If this party is destroyed, there is no salvation for another generation . . .

Anna threatened to quit public life if there was no unity. Both sides were moved at this, and Kannadasan ran over to Anna to hold his hand and apologize for any wrongdoing. Asaithambi expressed regret. There were other emotional scenes. Anna brought Sampath, Karunanidhi and Nedunchezhian next to him and embraced them together. The atmosphere was emotional and cathartic. SSR and Karunanidhi, who had resigned earlier, took back their resignations.[12]

In a meeting at Mylapore on 27 February, Sampath explicitly clarified that he had no issue with Karunanidhi, MGR, KRR and SSR, his 'dear friends' and that his actions were in the interests of the party. Anna himself vaunted that even siblings would fight over property. Still, the Kazhagam's children are twins bound to each other by affection more than biological siblings. He suggested a unity tour to all the districts of Sampath, Karunanidhi, Kannadasan and himself.[13] In his 4 March statement, propaganda secretary Nedunchezhian urged unity and discipline.[14]

The Congress exulted at the DMK's misery. CS, the Congress's protagonist, said that the DMK was a laughing stock as its dirty linen was being publicly washed. 'To peep into the neighbour's window is a lowly act,' Anna told CS, adding that CS did not know what it is to lead a party.[15] On 19 March, when the party appeared to be on the mend, Anna began his letter with Thomas Jefferson's quote, 'When angry, count to ten before you speak. If very angry, count to one hundred.' He said that he counted thousands, kept silent and desired a state of no anger. But he had reacted angrily in the assembly the earlier week to CS's derision of his Kazhagam. Anna explained:

> My anger was not because I was slighted. I am a piece of wood on those occasions. Thambi! Yes! But, minister Subramaniam spoke very insultingly about our Kazhagam in the assembly . . .
>
> He had said you are a laughingstock with your situation discussed in the streets! . . .
>
> If there is a blight, a setback [to the Kazhagam] it will be a great blow to the country . . .
>
> Is Kazhagam dust to fly away in the wind? [No. It signifies] the identity of minds! The fusion of hearts! A blend of colours! Therefore, the coming together has clarified that there is no difference.[16]

But Anna had spoken too soon. The post-Thiruvottriyur events boded ill for unity. In the first meeting at Mayiladuthurai, Karunanidhi spoke for a few minutes and left. The page had not been turned. The Kazhagam was now akin to a broken mirror. Anna, who had said that if someone left the party, he 'agonized like flesh tearing from the body',[17] retired that night with *Lady Chatterley's Lover*, according to Sampath, and postponed all the meetings from 9 to 19 April except the 9 April Chennai meeting.

Anna's heart leaned towards Sampath, but his head was cocked to Karunanidhi–MGR. On 7 April, Anna and Karunanidhi failed to attend T.M. Parthasarathy's book launch of *DMK's History*. Anna said his car had broken down. It was the party that was broken. The portents were clear.

On 9 April, the day of the Chennai meeting, Sampath, Kannadasan, and many others quit the party. That evening in the public meeting at the Marina Beach, Anna, in a rear-guard action, said,

> They may leave me in politics. They cannot exit my heart. There is no bigger heart in the world than mine. [You] can't find [a bigger heart] . . . I am most unfortunate. When I left Dravidar Kazhagam I lost a father. [Now] my younger brother[!] . . .
>
> I am hopeful that he will return.

Sampath Walks Out

But Anna's moving speech failed to touch Sampath. In his lengthy 12 April statement, Sampath said that he and his associates were taking all the 'truth and good' of the DMK with them. The DMK was a 'crowd of empty enthusiasts' and cinema, the tail was wagging the party dog, said Sampath. Anna's price for the 'public worship' by his associates was condoning their excesses. Anna wanted to be 'worshipped' and had become a pontiff, Sampath added.[18]

But, founding his Tamil Nationalist Party, Sampath would make claims that did not add up. Sampath had decamped calling the Dravida Nadu demand a 'mirage' even as his party advocated self-determination for Tamil Nadu within the Indian Union. Sampath's issue was not Dravida Nadu. His issue was that Anna was a hostage in the hands of Sampath's detractors. After a brief independent and disappointing performance in the 1962 general elections, Sampath ended up with Kamaraj.

In his 1969 tribute to Anna titled 'Astonishing Politician', Sampath suggested in so many words that Anna was 'indecisive' and yet had risen to capture the hearts of so many. Sampath had dealt a decisive blow to the indecisive Anna, at least in the short term. Sampath's attacks on Anna resembled the earlier attacks of Periyar on Anna.

In his 23 April letter, Anna listed his 'Guru's' [Periyar] choicest abuse showered on him: mountebanks, hawkers, illiterate people, vulgar speakers, money seekers, seekers of office, sensuous speakers, those who live off story-writing, the destitute and wanderers. He said that listening to Periyar's attacks on him, the Congress acquired the 'training' to denigrate him. He had not been able to repay his debt to Sampath. But now he had the peace of one who had cleared his debt. He bore Sampath's attacks, which he said copied Periyar and the Congress to a fault.

Anna said Sampath only joined a long list of those who rejected Dravida Nadu—Nehru, Kamaraj and Periyar. Dravida Nadu was not a hasty decision but a very considered one. He said that this attachment had made Sampath speak with conviction in the 1953 Lalgudi conference, inspiring Sivaji Ganesan to declare that he would tear up his film contracts to fight for Dravida Nadu if Anna were to command. In 1958, Sampath compared Anna to Mazzini and Dravida Nadu to Mazzini's Italy.

Anna ended his letter thus: 'For those who consider that taking me as an "elder brother" even politically as wrong or degrading,

Don't forget ideals!
Don't get angry!

Living together is a responsible act—understand
If you find fault, then no one will be next to you!"[19]

Anna wrote six letters from 23 April to 4 June to point out the
contradictions and inconsistencies in Sampath's stand and speeches.
He needn't have. The cadres were there for Anna, not Dravida Nadu.

7

Soldiering On

The split had left Anna saddened. But brooding was not an option. With elections in February 1962, Anna's work was cut out. As early as 1951, Anna had argued that Congress victories were made possible by a divided Opposition. On the first day of the 13–16 July 1961 third state conference at Thiruparankunram, Anna suggested a single Opposition front.[1]

Five months later, in the 16–17 December Coimbatore election conference, he spelt out the logic of seeking help from the ideologically diverse Right and the Left.

> If a thief suddenly enters my house, I will use any stick to beat him and chase him away. I won't be examining if the stick is Swatantra or communist . . .
>
> I am not saying that we should have an ideological truck with our friendly parties and contest elections. All that I am saying is that we should have seat adjustments. We intend that the opposition votes should not be dispersed.[2]

This was not to be. On 3 January 1962, Rajaji admitted that they could not overcome differences in the allocation of constituencies, describing the development as a 'new year gift' to the Congress.[3] CS said the alliance had not come about as it was 'abhorred by God'.[4] A decade earlier, Rajaji had considered the DK 'bed bugs' and the DMK 'ants' to be crushed and Anna, for his part, had described Rajaji as 'Kulluka Bhatta'.* However, Periyar's championship of Kamaraj and Rajaji's about turn on Hindi had brought synergy between the two. They had first met at publisher Subbiah Pillai's residence on the issue of Hindi opposition on 28 January 1956.†[5] Rajaji explained the congruence later as 'English unites and Hindi divides'.[6] As Rajaji threw his enormous prestige behind the DMK, the *Mootharignar* or wise scholar had a major influence on his new protégé.

On 28 January, Rajaji graciously asked his party workers to work for Anna and, on 22 February, addressed a joint rally in Kanchipuram with him.[7] Anna's speech there captures the distance he had travelled towards Rajaji and from Periyar.

Only a day earlier, Periyar called Rajaji and Anna 'pedestrian hawkers', criticizing the DMK's promise of three acres of wetland and five acres of dry land and Rajaji's promise to abolish the land tax.[8]

---

* On 6 October 1953 Rajaji said:

  Ants and bed bugs still exist. The likes of Dravidar Kazhagam soaked in hate and spreading communal hatred are these ants. Bed bugs bite hiding. These ants bite openly. When the bite is harsh it is only natural that the ants should be crushed. We have overcome the bed bugs. We need to eradicate these ants too. *Dravida Nadu*, 18 October 1953, 14.

† DMK advocate V.P. Raman's father, A.V. Raman, and Rajaji were friends, and at the junior Raman's urging, Anna would see Rajaji for a fifteen-minute courtesy meeting at their place in 1957. The meeting would be much talked about. K.S. Ramanujan, *The Big Change*, Higginbothams, Chennai, (1967), 84.

Campaign

To counter Periyar's campaign, *Murasoli*'s Pongal issue ran below-the-belt cartoons under the head 'Ask Periyar' with EVR's controversial responses to questions like 'Why did clothing prices increase?', 'Why did unemployment rise?', 'Why is rice costing more?' and paraphrasing his responses: 'Because Dalit women have started wearing blouses'; 'Because Dalits are applying for jobs'; 'Because those toddy drinkers have started eating rice'.[9]

The DMK manifesto described the party as a 'freedom movement' committing itself to Dravida Nadu without naming it as such. The ambitious manifesto saw the party take credit for Congress ministers obtaining more for the state, promised industrial growth, a custom-free port, the Sethusamudram project, Cauvery delta oil field, Salem Steel Plant, an atomic plant, solar electricity, desalination, linking the Buckingham and Vedaranyam canals, rubber from coir, paper plant, vegetable oil, the right to recall elected representatives, legalizing self-respect marriages and nationalization of bus routes and houses for Adi Dravidas among others.

It advocated that the Neyveli Lignite Plant come under state control and that Madras State be renamed Tamil Nadu. Catchy cartoons with sharp messages and simplified statistics compared the Tatas and their likes to the teeming millions in poverty, promising equality and socialism under the DMK. Periyar loomed large. Listing Periyar's earlier criticisms, the DMK asked voters to judge if his support for Kamaraj and the Congress was fair. Anna promised to reduce or remove indirect taxes if voted to power.[10]

The party fielded 143 candidates for the 206 assembly seats and eighteen candidates for the forty-one parliamentary seats. Resources were limited, and the party fought the elections with only Rs 4 lakh. While Karunanidhi performed his *Udayasuryian* (Rising Sun) play as part of the campaign, MGR drew large crowds. Anna campaigned round the clock, invariably running late. But the crowds stayed put. In Veerapandi Arumugham's Salem constituency, Anna was scheduled to speak at 4 p.m. but arrived twelve hours later to an audience that had fallen asleep in the open ground waiting for him. This was the case wherever Anna spoke. People waited to get a glimpse of this short man who was emerging as a phenomenon. Veerapandi Arumugham ended up winning the seat by 8700 votes. The wind was changing direction.[11]

The campaign also had lighter moments. Sampath contesting the South Madras parliamentary seat said he would beard the lion (the DMK) in its den. Anna smilingly admitted that it was fine to meet the lion, but as to who would exit the den—the lion or the visitor—was to be seen. The speech evoked much mirth even in the Opposition camp.[12]

The DMK won fifty assembly seats out of the total 206 and polled 34,35,633, or 27.10 per cent of the votes, while the Congress won 139 assembly seats, polling 58,48,974, or 46.14 per cent.[13] It contested eighteen and won seven of the forty-one Parliamentary seats.

1962 ASSEMBLY ELECTION

Party	Contested	Won	Votes	Percentage
INC	206	139	58,48,974	46.14%
DMK	143	50	34,35,633	27.10%
SWATANTRA	94	6	9,91,773	7.82%
AIFB	6	3	1,73,261	1.37%
CPI	68	2	9,78,806	7.72%
SOCIALIST PARTY	7	1	48,753	0.38%
INDEPENDENTS (IND)	206	5	6,76,892	5.34%

1962 PARLIAMENTARY ELECTION

Party	Contested	Won	Votes	Percentage
INC	41	31	56,23,013	45.26%
DMK	18	7	23,15,610	18.64%
SWATANTRA	16	0	13,00,526	10.47%
AIFB	1	1	1,75,772	1.41%
CPI	14	2	12,72,313	10.24%

The DMK strength was mainly concentrated in urban areas. In fifteen constituencies, it lost by a margin of fewer than 1000 votes and had expanded its base beyond the northern districts and cities.[14] Kamaraj's strategy to prevent re-election of the fifteen DMK legislators from the previous election ensured that only Karunanidhi was re-elected.

But the strategy had boomeranged. Instead of fifteen, there were fifty this time. 'They tried to get rid of fifteen and lost out on fifty', Anna noted and prophesied that they would aim at the fifty next time and lose another seventy-five.[15] Similarly, Nehru had ignored the DMK in his 6 February 1962 campaign speech at Madras Beach, choosing to criticize Rajaji. But ignoring the DMK was no more an option.[16]

The impressive performance was marred by Anna's defeat to a bus owner. 'What does it matter if one Annadurai does not enter the legislature? In my stead, I am sending fifty Annadurais,' said an unfazed Anna.[17]

Kamaraj said the separatist DMK's rise as the major Opposition party was not a 'sound development'.[18] Periyar explained the Congress performance as caused by 'enemies within' and the Congress's 'indifference'.[19] Kamaraj's biographer, V.K. Narasimhan, records that the DMK's 1962 ascent 'agitated Kamaraj so much', and the issue was discussed at the Congress Working Committee. The DMK's victory in the 13 August Tiruchengode parliamentary by-election after that further 'shocked' Kamaraj and Delhi. Kamaraj and his ministers had camped there for days.

The DMK's electoral successes made it appear that the Dravida Nadu challenge was no more polemics. The Centre's pushback saw the Sixteenth Amendment against secessionist advocacy passed on 18 January 1963. To take on the DMK politically, Kamaraj mooted his famous Kamaraj Plan or K-Plan, calling for senior officials to take up party work. J.B. Kripalani notes that Kamaraj had conceived the idea for him exclusively but Nehru 'took advantage . . . to get rid of . . . possible rivals and their supporters.' Kripalani even suspected Indira Gandhi as the originator of the idea and not Kamaraj.[20] Nevertheless, on 2 October, Kamaraj stepped down. Periyar presciently warned earlier: 'Either on your own accord or on the advice of others, your resignation of chief ministership will be suicidal to Tamilians, Tamil Nadu and yourself.'[21] On 9 October, Kamaraj rose to become the president of the Congress. However, back home in Tamil Nadu, his stars were on the decline.

'Call My State Tamil Nadu'

On 29 March, Anna was elected to the Rajya Sabha and MGR, the following day, to the legislative council; the latter only the second DMK actor after K.R. Ramasamy on 8 April 1960.[22] Earlier, on 27 March, MGR said he was a 'ball of emotions'.[23]

Rajaji had suggested that Anna consider the Rajya Sabha. K. Rajaram claims he mooted the idea publicly. Anna credits Thiruvannamalai MP, R. Dharmalingam, for persuading him to go to Delhi.[24] While Anna was exposed to national politics, the country took the measure of the man from the deep south and his DMK. Anna vindicated himself, turning the House into a bully pulpit for his vision of a plural and federal India. India's strides, aided by the retention of English, should be credited to him.*

Like Anna, the debate on renaming Madras Tamil Nadu had also moved to Delhi. It was not the DMK but CPI's Bhupesh Gupta who sponsored a private member's bill. Earlier attempts in the state had been in vain. The Congress feared the implication of 'Nadu', which meant land and country. So, on 19 August 1960, when Praja Socialist Party's S. Chinnadurai moved a resolution to rename Madras State 'Tamilnad', CS accepted the term 'Tamil Nadu' for internal use.[25] However, this half-measure would not please the DMK and the communists, who staged a walkout.

On 24 July 1964, DMK's Rama Arangannal unsuccessfully tabled a resolution for the name change.[26] Industries Minister R. Venkataraman said that 'Tamil Nadu makes everyone happy. Similarly, "Madras State" also makes everyone happy. Why should we destroy this now?'[27] The Congress never missed an opportunity to advocate cultural nationalist issues.

---

* Former foreign minister Dinesh Singh had once bitterly observed that Hindi would have triumphed but for Tamil Nadu. Swaminathan S Anklesaria Aiyar, 'How English survived in India,' *Times of India*, 13 March 2004. Accessed 21 March 2021, https://timesofindia.indiatimes.com/home/sunday-times/all-that-matters/How-English-survived-in-India/articleshow/558981.cms.

The likes of T.S. Pattabiraman further betrayed the Congress's deep-seated indifference to cultural nationalism when he claimed in the Rajya Sabha, 'About five hundred years ago, there was no united Tamil Nadu and only Chera, Chola and Pandya kingdoms. Such a demand cannot be historically justified.' Anna pointed out to the Sangam work *Paripadal's 'Thandamizh veli Thamizh Nattu akamellam'*, which means 'Tamil Nad which is surrounded by sweet Tamil on all the three sides' and other literary references in support of this. He said it was a sentimental issue and asked if the Congress was ready to refer it to the public. 'Are you prepared for that? That is what we ask. You are not prepared for that and that is why I say— call my State "Tamil Nadu",' he concluded.[28]

Price Rise Agitation

It was not just on the cultural nationalist front that the Congress bumbled. Rice was becoming scarce back home. The situation was so stark that a minister was designated exclusively for food. The DMK's price rise agitation blamed the Congress's inefficiency and held out the hope of three measures of rice per rupee. Protests before the assembly on 30 June, rallies on 1 July and picketing before government offices on 19 July led to 5000 arrests and two deaths in custody. On 19 July, Anna was arrested in Vellore for picketing.

On 5 August, Periyar called the arrested 'fools' and, on the promise of three measures of rice per rupee, said: 'Does anyone have the brains to think how it is possible to give three measures of rice per rupee? Did anyone think? Even if you mix two measures of sand with a measure of rice, it can't be done.'*[29]

---

* On 12 February 1961, *Dravida Nadu* published a poem on its front page titled 'Padiarisi Sollum Kudiarasu' or measure of rice that speaks of the state of the Republic. *Dravida Nadu*, 12 February 1961, 3.

Periyar had been trying to knock sense into the Tamils dazzled
by the DMK campaign. A year earlier, on 9 July 1961, speaking at
Devakottai, he had famously warned:

> Comrades! I am 82 years old. I may die at any time. But you would
> continue. Being aged let me tell you something akin to a dying
> declaration. One who must give a dying declaration does not have
> to lie. The development under Kamaraj had not occurred in two-
> three millenniums . . .
>
> Comrades! Trust me. If this country must redeem itself, you
> must hold on to Kamaraj firmly for at least another ten years.
> Benefit from his rule. If we don't hold to Kamaraj, the Tamils
> have no one else for redemption.[30]

The Chinese Excuse

Periyar would be proven right, but public memory is short-lived.
News of the Chinese incursion on 20 October 1962 had electrified
the country. Anna, the master strategist, lost no time in taking
advantage of the nationalist fervour to suspend his Dravida Nadu
campaign.[31] P.U. Shanmugam and other inmates with Anna at the
Vellore jail saw the incursion as an opportunity to take advantage of
vis-à-vis the Dravida Nadu issue. Anna too, except that he wished to
abandon the demand. 'Do you expect me to fish in troubled waters?'
he asked P.U. Shanmugam.

On the evening of 3 October, the day of his release, he suspended
the demand only to give it up later for good, justifying his decision
elegantly: 'If we don't like the one [northerners] in Delhi, will we
like the one far away in Peking?'[32] Facing a Hobson's choice, the
man who had built his career, reputation and party had chosen
discretion over valour. Arguing that their struggle and sacrifice will
not be remembered, he said:

Then what is the use of our sacrifice? And what will be the fate of our descendants? They will all become orphans! Fearing the government's wrath, even our friends and relatives would hesitate to meet us. When freedom fighter V.O. Chidambaram came out of prison, there were only two people to receive him! That was the fate of even such a stalwart! Can we think of rendering a higher sacrifice than that colossus?

But the talk of struggle and sacrifice was redundant. The DMK leader had consulted his colleagues to disappointing results. Except for Karunanidhi, no one was prepared for a life spent in jail. Nedunchezhian and student leader Aladi Aruna said they could spend three months in prison, while NVN said a year, but only after the wedding of his offspring.[33] This could not be a 'freedom movement'. In true DMK style, the party now went to the other extreme, painting the Chinese as demons, exalting India's resistance, singing Nehru's praise and making the highest contribution to the defence fund. MGR had auctioned the souvenir sword given at the *Nadodi Mannan* felicitation in Madurai as part of the contribution.[34]

The volte-face didn't stave off the danger that loomed large. On 5 November, the National Integration Committee recommended amending Article 19 on freedom of expression banning secessionist advocacy.[35] On 13 November, in the debate on national integration in the assembly, Anna rebutted the suggestion of an India under one umbrella, pointing out that the Gupta, Ashoka and Mughal empires did not extend below the Narmada River. Adding that those mighty empires did not last, he prophesied harshly that 'history will judge that [India] will be destroyed' for the same reasons. He said the DMK were very aware that they would incur abuse, blame and repression, but they were willing to shed blood—and wished that the Congress knife cause it. 'Therefore, if you have a knife, sharpen it. If you have a law, bring it expeditiously,' he said defiantly.[36]

But when the Sixteenth Amendment obliging candidates and the elected to swear to 'uphold the sovereignty and integrity of India' stared in his face, Anna proved a pragmatist but attributed the change to the 'Chinese menace'. On 25 January 1963, in the initial debate, he claimed, 'The unity of India has been taken to be a part and parcel of our philosophy; not because of your legislation but because of the Chinese menace. We felt that we should stand or fall together.'

When Bhupesh Gupta described him as a democratic 'pretender' as there was no support from the rest of the south for his separatist plank, the agile politician turned the disadvantage to his advantage:

> May I ask whether one solitary figure necessitates amendment to the Constitution? I want to know whether one solitary figure, unsupported by Andhra, Karnataka and Kerala, one solitary figure from Tamil Nad, necessitates the amendment of the Constitution?

Quoting Shakespeare's *Julius Caesar*, Bhupesh Gupta said that Anna had a 'lean and hungry look' like Cassius, who hankered for power. Thankfully, Gupta did not complete the quote: 'He thinks too much: such men are dangerous.' Praja Socialist Party's M.S. Gurupadasamy adequately made up for Gupta when he characterized the DMK as 'a pathological, politico-social phenomenon and just an aberration . . .'[37]

Anna pleaded for the government to try to understand him and his DMK 'before you try to ban'. Wondering if they were 'so debased . . . to be treated as untouchables' as the National Integration Committee had chosen not to meet them, he said although 'very small men', they represented 3.4 million voters against the Congress's five million and if the Congress were not to place any hurdles, the DMK would be the 'next ruling party in Madras'. He said the 'very mention of separation is not a danger to sovereignty', adding that the DMK should be won democratically.[38]

In the final debate on 9 May, Anna said the Congress were a majority and could easily pass legislation, and it was 'easier for me to go back to my people and say, "Well, I fought for you singly and all alone, and yet the Bill was passed. What shall I do?" And my people, naturally, will say, "All right; let us resist it."' Quoting the German saying, 'If you would not be my brother, I would break your head and make you one', he concluded with the plea, 'Please do not break the heads if you want concord.'

This time T.S. Pattabiraman poked a serious hole in Anna's argument, asking if Anna 'can hope to get even one single representative in a municipality elected in the other State[s]' of the south. He said Anna represented only 25–30 per cent of the electorate in Madras State or a fortieth of the 'population of the entire Dravida Nad'. Laying Anna's next move threadbare, he said, 'He will say that he did not give it up voluntarily . . . Therefore, I am sure Mr Annadurai will like to welcome this Bill.' The bill passed with 137 ayes. Anna was the only nay-sayer.[39]

The amendment had helped Anna untie the Gordian knot. On 24 October, Anna said the DMK would not commit suicide by violating the Constitution. Kamaraj termed it 'an act of a coward' saying there was no 'real change of heart'.[40] 'We had no intention of obliging the Congress by committing political hara-kiri,' Anna would say later.[41]

On 3 November, the DMK constitution dropped separation and opted for autonomy and a closer union of the Dravidian states.[42] *Malai Murasu* rightly commented that the DMK's new motto of state autonomy would bring Ma.Po.Si. to one's mind, who had mooted the idea as early as 1945.[43] Anna had ridiculed the demand as 'mouse hunting' compared to his DMK's 'tiger hunting'. On 20 October 1958, he said: 'What we need is independence. Not a few sharing of powers.'[44] State autonomy would henceforth take centre stage in the DMK's discourse. The 6 January 1973 Pudukottai general council further diluted the DMK's destination, emphasizing cultural unity instead of a political union between the southern states.

On 2 October 1963, M. Bhaktavatsalam succeeded Kamaraj. A prescient Periyar had warned Kamaraj against the idea in a telegram saying that it would it would be 'suicidal' to his political career and the interests of Tamils and Tamil Nadu.

MGR Resigns

Dravida Nadu was behind them. But there were other challenges. In March 1964, while Anna served in prison, MGR sprang an unpleasant surprise by resigning from the legislative council. T.R. Ramanna, a movie director, records that MGR's elder brother, M.G. Chakrapani, did not like party men frequently troubling MGR for funds and that the resignation was intended to be a 'shock treatment' over this issue.

A deeply troubled Anna said he could not envisage a DMK without MGR or vice versa. MGR's statement on 18 March 1964 would make Anna happy, however, putting to rest his anxieties. MGR clarified that his resignation was aimed at those in the party whose actions he did not comprehend and that he intended to continue to work for the party.[45]

On 15 November, eight months after the MGR affair, Anna wrote,

> Kazhagam's decisions are not based solely on my choice or likes or dislikes. Notwithstanding this, when I have a 'wish', some in the Kazhagam do not desire to fulfil it. I have felt this on many occasions. What is the use of lamenting or trying to analyze the reasons? The situation is such. That's it.

Anna had wished for his bosom friend C.V. Rajagopal to be fielded as a candidate for the legislative council, but the frontline leaders derided the idea. Rajagopal would eventually become a member of the legislative council in March 1966.[46]

The crowds for MGR's *En Kadamai* (My Duty), released on 13 March soon after, began to drop. Four months later, MGR made amends when he sang *Moondrezuthil en moochirukum* (My breath is in three letters) in *Deivathaai* (Mother God), referring to *Kadamai* (duty), a three-letter word in Tamil but understood as the DMK. The actor and the party were inseparable.

1965 Language Riots

Hindi would become the sole official language on 26 January 1965. English was to be dropped as an associate official language. This was what had been decided when the Constitution had been adopted in 1950. Nehru was no more. He died on 27 May 1964. Kamaraj would play kingmaker and facilitate a smooth transition, helping choose Lal Bahadur Shastri as prime minister. Nehru's absence would be sorely felt during the language riots. Shastri lacked Nehru's stature or alacrity. Bhaktavatsalam proved completely wooden.

Students announced 25 January as a day of mourning, while the DMK was to mark 26 January with rallies. Earlier on 19 January, in the Hindi Opposition Conference convened by K.A.P. Viswanatham in Tiruchi, Rajaji had famously remarked that the constitutional provision on Hindi should be 'thrown into the sea'. On 1 February, Periyar said that the DMK was 'shaking a dead snake', lamenting that there were 'ten fools even behind the DMK'.[47]

On the night of 25 January, Anna and 3000 others were taken into preventive custody and released on 2 February. Karunanidhi was picked up on 16 February at 10 p.m. and taken in a lorry from Madras to Palayamkottai prison, a 625-km ride. The first to be charged in Tamil Nadu under the Defence of India Rules, Karunanidhi was kept in solitary confinement from 18 February to 4 April 1965. After visiting Karunanidhi, Anna famously said, 'Palayamkottai has become my place of pilgrimage.' Emotions ran high, and equally pessimism about the anti-Hindi protests. A police officer asked

MLA M. Rajangam, 'Yaenda (why in singular) Rajangam, even if you fight for a hundred years, can you people get rid of Hindi?' To which Rajangam said, 'Even if it takes a thousand years, we will die opposing Hindi but not accepting it.'[48]

Without the DMK leadership, students were in control of the protests. Passions raged high, and Keezhapazhuvoor Chinnasamy, Virugambakkam Sivalingam, Triplicane Aranganathan, Ayyampalayam Veerappan, Sathyamangalam Muthu, Mayiladuthurai Sarangapani, Viralimalai Shanmugham, Keeranoor Muthu, Sivagangai Rajendran and Peelamedu Dhandapani took their lives, self-immolating or poisoning themselves or being killed in police firing, and becoming martyrs.

For eighteen days, the protests raged, turning the state into a civil war zone. On 10 February alone, police fired in seven locations, killing twenty-four. The next day CS and O.V. Alagesan resigned. On 12 February, another thirty-one died in police firing. Chief Minister Bhaktavatsalam said fifty-one were killed in police firing.[49] The Congress government had failed dismally, and Kamaraj was absent throughout. On 3 February, following Kamaraj's and others' advice to 'go slow' on Hindi, Shastri promised there would be 'no imposition'.[50]

On 4 March, Anna told the Rajya Sabha that the Congress government had treated it as a purely law and order issue and 'fifty or sixty men, seven-year-old girls, eight-year-old boys, eighty-year-old men, etc. [were] shot down dead on the streets of Madras'.[51] He took Home Minister Gulzarilal Nanda to task. Saying Nehru flew to Assam, toured the entire state and addressed four or five public meetings during the language riots there, he asked:

> What have you done? I put that question not in anger but with agony. When our men were being shot down dead, when our property was being destroyed, when our people were hunted like wild animals, you came to Kerala and yet you did not have the

courtesy to come to the State of Madras. You could have addressed through the AIR, asked the people to be calm . . . I am very sorry. I do not think we needed help in any other matter or at any other time except at that time.[52]

But terrible acts had been committed on both sides, and Periyar rightly wondered how someone could chase, gouge out the eyes and set fire to two sub-inspectors in Tirupur and beat to death two policemen in Gudalur. 'Did these policemen and sub-inspectors impose Hindi? Is this agitation? Is this the way to challenge the government?' He said that 'at least four boys should have been shot. Nothing was done!'[53]

The man who had lit the first fire of revolt against Hindi in 1938 foresaw the threat the passions held for the Congress and Kamaraj in the elections later. He suggested an iron hand, banning the Swatantra and the DMK and gagging the press.[54] On 10 February, he advised his friends and supporters to carry a knife, a bottle of petrol and a matchstick to set fire to the Tamil dailies as he had not seen such an unsafe atmosphere under a government in sixty years.

On 17 February, comparing Rajaji and the DMK to sham beggars faking disability for sympathy, Periyar said they were raising the bogey of Hindi, taxes and price rise for votes. 'This time with Brahmin, Muslim support, fifty [MLAs] have come. If our people were intelligent, so many would not have come.' He said if this government were to go, the next would surely be Brahmin or their 'slaves'.[55] On 18 March, as the protests ceased, he reasoned that fearing a ban, the DMK had ended the agitation and termed it 'cowardice'.[56]

Anna, however, repudiated any responsibility for the violence, pointing out in the Rajya Sabha 'that we have not written a single appeal, not written a single editorial, not written a single article, either welcoming or encouraging such agitation'. Anna questioned if the Hindi zealots wanted unity or uniformity and 'Is it language alone that stands as a handicap to that unity?'

He said he was not enamoured of English. Still, he wanted it as an equalizer until all regional languages were official and sufficiently developed and Hindi, 'due to the natural process' and without government backing, became the 'de facto link language' and then the 'de jure link language'. He noted that if 'Switzerland can make it practical to have four or five languages, I think arithmetically, we can have fourteen . . .' And then, tongue in cheek, he continued:

> Our Home Minister talking in this House the other day said: 'Oh, I am not a Hindiwalla. My mother-tongue is Punjabi and then I adopted Gujarati as my language. Now I am converted to Hindi.' Unfortunately, we do not have such experiences. It is a very good experience to have mother-tongue, to get another adopted tongue, and then to plead for a third tongue. You yourself have stated, that you are cut off from your moorings. Fortunately or unfortunately we are not cut off from our moorings. I can never forget that I have got a hoary language called Tamil. I will never be satisfied till that language in which my forefathers spoke, in which my poets have given sermons and scriptures, in which we have got classics and literature of inexhaustible knowledge, I will never be content till that day when Tamil takes its due place as one of the official languages in the Union.

He praised ministers CS and O.V. Alagesan for saving some of the good name of the Congress by their gesture of resignation.[57]

In an interview in November 1965 with the *Illustrated Weekly*, Anna listed his six main objections as Hindi being untenable for the south, that it represented the tyranny of the majority, would reduce southerners to second-class citizens, all Indian languages were as good or bad as the other, that domination of Hindi areas over the non-Hindi ones will 'hamper rather than promote integration' and lastly, Hindi was, for now, inadequate for modern science and technology. He said famously that if the principle of numerical superiority were the yardstick for the national bird, 'our choice would have fallen not on the peacock but on the common crow!'[58]

The DMK's views on the language issue had begun with the advocacy of retention of English alongside Hindi post 1965 when Hindi was to become the sole official language. Almost a decade earlier, on 31 July 1956, the Official Language Commission (7 June 1955), under the chairmanship of B.G. Kher had opined: 'The obvious linguistic medium for pan-Indian purposes is the Hindi language' and favoured a three-language formula of Hindi, the regional language and English.[59]

At the 10 December 1957 all-party meeting to discuss the Kamaraj government's views on the Kher recommendations, Anna concurred with the state's position that English should continue beyond 1965 and in the 30 June 1960 issue of *Namnadu*, said the DMK, too, had a role in shaping the Congress's two-language stance. However, on 29 April 1963 at a Marina meeting, Rajaji, Anna and other leaders took a maximalist position, calling for English to be the sole official language. Yet, in June 1963, the DMK general council called for all fourteen languages to be official.[60]

'Kamaraj, My Leader, Anna, My Guide'

On 8 August 1965, participating at Kamaraj's sixty-third birthday felicitation by *Tamil Cinema* editor Kareem at Periyar Thidal, MGR created another controversy by calling Kamaraj 'my leader' and Anna his 'guide'.[61] Madurai Muthu, SSR and an anonymous critic issued statements against MGR. Referring to the anonymous critic, MGR said: 'Who is this important person?' He had checked with Nedunchezhian and Mathiazhagan, and they did not know. No one seemed to know. A hero who feared the party and its diktat only a decade ago now wondered: 'How is praising Kamaraj praising a party? Is the DMK made up of workers who do not know the difference between the two!' It was a test of wills between MGR and the party. Both had come a long way together.

Journalist Tamilvanan noted in its aftermath, 'MGR is part of the DMK like the veshti's silk border. If the silk is ripped apart, can it be a silk veshti? Won't a silk-less veshti become a rag?'[62] Anna knew that silk was uncomfortable when it hit the skin, but then a veshti was nothing much without it. On 8 October 1972, in his famous Thirukazhukundram speech, where he asked that the DMK functionaries and elected officials submit accounts, MGR reiterated that there could be many leaders but only one guide. Like Gandhi was the Congress's guide, he said Anna was the DMK's guide.[63]

'Woven an Intricate Net'

The Mail reported that MGR was the 'biggest attraction' in the 11–12 June 1966 Tiruchi-Thanjavur conference in Tiruchi, and Anbazhagan 'tactfully handed the mike to MGR' as soon as the actor made his entry.[64] The conference had built consensus for a broad Opposition coalition, and Nedunchezhian, Karunanidhi and Mathiazhagan were named the first point of contact with the allies.[65]

Ma.Po.Si. desired a seat in Chennai. Anna requested D.V. Narayanasamy, councillor Sadagopan and former mayor S. Krishnamurthi to yield Thyagaraya Nagar to Ma.Po.Si. They obliged. If they had not, he said he had intended to shift Karunanidhi from Saidapet to his South Madras parliamentary seat, giving Saidapet to Ma.Po.Si. Anna would not have contested.[66]

Seat allocations could be sorted out, but Anna could not agree to a minimum programme sought by the CPI. In the event, the CPI stayed away from the DMK-led alliance. But the Marxists were in. Anna had brought together the Swatantra to the Marxists and remarked later, 'I have woven an intricate net. No one can escape it',[67] crediting Karunanidhi as 'fundamental' in stitching together the alliances.[68]

Rajaji played a decisive role, often penning letters to Ma.Po.Si. to tone down his criticism, contending that the DMK's 'patriotism' was purer than the Congress's. Why this change? Ma.Po.Si. testifies: 'The change in Rajaji was not because of any philosophy. His only motive was to defeat Congress rule—especially Kamaraj. He wanted to use the DMK for it . . . He was willing to do anything to defeat Mr Kamaraj and the Congress.'[69] In four years, a repentant Rajaji would join hands with Kamaraj to take on the DMK.

But then, Shastri died on 11 January 1966. Kamaraj threw his weight behind Indira Gandhi against Morarji Desai to succeed Shastri. The senior leadership known as the 'Syndicate' had offered the position to Kamaraj, who reportedly said: 'No English, no Hindi, how?' In three-plus decades, Deve Gowda would show him how. Indira Gandhi would assert herself, leading to a break-up of the Congress in 1969 into the Congress (Organization) and Congress (Requisition or R, later I for Indira). Kamaraj's political decline began in 1967 when he lost to an unknown DMK student in his hometown. Indira Gandhi would accelerate Kamaraj's fall. In 1971, she joined forces with the DMK against Kamaraj.

Tailwinds were favouring the DMK.

8

In Power

Virugambakkam Conference

The four-day election conference, from 29 December 1966 to 1 January 1967 at Virugambakkam, brought together alliance leaders Rajaji, Anna, Muhammad Ismail, Forward Bloc's Mookiah Thevar, Ma.Po.Si., Naam Tamilar (We Tamils) Party's Si.Pa. Adithanar and CPM's R. Venkataraman. This was a one-off event. The Swatantra and CPM would not share a campaign stage afterwards, revealing the ideological tensions in the rainbow alliance. The three-mile-long procession on the conference's opening day saw 300 buses and 12,000 cyclists as well as thousands of people walking the eight-mile stretch from Island Grounds to the conference venue. There were catchy slogans: *Kamaraj annachi milagaai vilai ennachu?* (Elder brother Kamaraj, what about the price of chillies?), *Aalunkatchi annachi, arisi vilai ennachu?* (Ruling party elder brother, what about the price of rice?)

In his inaugural address, Karunanidhi listed the resolutions the DMK had sponsored in the assembly and the achievements of the DMK's Chennai Corporation. Anna promised that people would have the right to recall their representatives and to hold referendums on major issues. These would never come to pass. Rajaji described the conference arrangements where the DMK excelled as 'magical'.[1] Taking a dig at Kamaraj's confident remark that 'Congress will win lying down', he said 'lying down for sure, but win, doubtful' and expressed his wish to see Anna and his thambis in power. Anna termed Rajaji's blessings as 'destined'.[2]

The DMK manifesto promised good governance, land to the tiller, a land army, 'Dravidam within India', civil service exams in regional languages and nationalization of banks, buses and cinemas. Committed to socialism, the party said, it had put the 'Country first and Kazhagam next' in the 1962 and 1965 wars. It listed forty-nine of its salient areas of work, including advocacy for the name change to Tamil Nadu, Salem Steel Plant and removal of land and allied taxes for farmers with less than five acres.[3] CPI's Kalyanasundaram charged that the DMK's manifesto reflected Rajaji's ideas.[4]

The catchiest of the promises was outside the manifesto and was the promise of three measures of rice. *Daily Thanthi* took the message energetically to the people.[5] Posters pitched pithy messages: 'Where is the Salem Steel Plant? Kalpakkam Thermal Plant? Cauvery Basin Oil? Sethusamudram?', 'Should those who devalued the currency rule the country?' 'Is your vote for those who created widows in the anti-Hindi agitation?'[6]

Meanwhile, Rajaji assured his followers that a DMK victory would not result in 'cutting the tuft of the head; if someone did that, they would send them to jail. Even Brahma can't destroy Brahmins. Therefore, no one needs to fear. Vote for the DMK men!'[7] Rajaji said, 'In Tamil Nadu, beat down the black crow (a disparaging remark on Kamaraj's dark complexion)! Congress would be destroyed all over India.'

When Periyar and others pointed out that the promise of the three measures of rice was an impossibility, Anna said on 24 October 1966 at Cuddalore, that instead of questioning these claims, they should give them a chance to rule and question him at the same Cuddalore grounds at the end of 1968—if they failed in their promise.[8]

On 1 January 1967, the last day of the conference, Anna, choosing to stand for a Parliament seat for South Madras, read out the names of the candidates. The mention of 'Mr Eleven Lakhs' for Saidapet—as Anna referred to Karunanidhi as treasurer exceeding the target set for election funds by a lakh—brought lusty cheers. Three years earlier, on 7 July 1963, at the victory celebrations of the Tiruvannamalai by-election, Karunanidhi had indicated that the DMK would need Rs 5000 for a constituency and should fight 200 seats and therefore required Rs 10 lakh.[9]

Anna asserted elsewhere that, 'We have not gotten a single contribution from any big industrialist'[10] and that 'Careerists and profiteers have no place in our organization'. He compared contributions from the rich to butter in a leper's hands.[11] The party was clearly in its most innocent phase. However, Nedunchezhian would admit, 'For many millions of our people, caste is still the only consideration. This is a hard fact. Hence, we can't ignore this though we are not wholly influenced by this alone.'[12] Fifty years later, caste has become more critical, and social justice, the Dravidian movement's central tenet, ironically remains a culprit in perpetuating caste consciousness.

On MGR's gift of a lakh, Anna said the money was as good as his and instead asked the matinee idol to give a month for the campaign, claiming famously that his 'face will fetch a lakh votes'. However, less than two weeks later, on 12 January 1967, screen villain M.R. Radha, who was in the Periyar-Kamaraj camp, shot MGR who had returned from his first round of campaigning. As the star lay immobilized, the ever-resourceful R.M. Veerappan brought out posters and adverts of a bandaged MGR appealing to voters from his hospital bed. 'I was to have come to your homes, but it could not be done. Now I am asking for your hearts', the advert in 14 February's *Daily Thanthi* said.[13] Radha had turned the demi-god into a god by his villainous off-screen act. The party milked the sympathy to its fullest, with Anna and Karunanidhi attributing the actor's survival to his philanthropy.

The party was nonetheless potent. With 4000 units, 5,00,000 members, party organ *Namnadu's* circulation of 25,000, *Daily Thanthi's* backing and the alliance, the party was poised for a good fight. Anna, however, left nothing to chance. 'After telling your wife, "Do you know how fond I am of you?", is it fair to be out of town for twenty days in a month?' The homey analogy was used to stress that their fondness for the Kazhagam should result 'in securing victory'.[14]

In the third week of January 1967, Anna asked his audience not to question the promise of the rice but to test them. 'Give us five years. I give you an undertaking if it is not achieved in five years, DMK will not contest polls! Write it down . . .'[15]

On 1 February, *The Hindu* predicted that Congress would 'get through' despite the 'stiff contest'.[16] But pollsters propose, and voters dispose. The first result broke with the Swatantra party candidate, H.V. Hande, defeating Congress stalwart T.N. Anandanayaki.[17] It was a deluge afterwards. Kamaraj and his ministers, save one, had been routed. The first-past-the-post system had rewarded the DMK with 40.69 per cent of the votes against the Congress's 41.10 per cent—138 seats for DMK and a mere forty-nine for the Congress. All twenty-five DMK candidates to Parliament had been elected. Kamaraj said that his defeat mattered little before the Congress's and noted that people had desired change.[18]

Even as news of Kamaraj's defeat reached him unofficially, Periyar lamented: 'Lost, all lost . . . I said [to Kamaraj] don't go to Delhi keeping your trust in this fellow [Bhaktavatsalam] here. He shot himself in the foot; he brought this upon himself.'[19] He called the DMK victory a tragedy.[20] The 'rainbow alliance' with little in common except Congress/Kamaraj hate had led to turning Aesop's story of the four bulls and the lion on its head.[21]

Anna, who had refrained from campaigning against Kamaraj, greatly regretted his defeat. He told the Swatantra's H.V. Hande, who visited him: 'If the voters of Tamil Nadu could defeat a stalwart like Kamaraj, who has done so much good to the state, how much time would it take for the electorate to do the same thing to us?'[22]

At midnight on 22 February, as the results made clear that he had made history, Anna remained grounded. When questioned, Anna, as was his wont, punning on the word 'Vaaimai' in Tamil, responded that *Vaaimai vendradhu*, or the truth won. Still, when separated into two words, *vaai* and *mai* meant mouth and ink, referring to the DMK's speeches and writing.[23]

Sattanathan mentioned the *Economist's* awe that 'for the first time, black men with un-pronounceable names were in the seats of power'. Sattanathan had also said that the age of Brahmin leadership in politics 'was over'.[24] In 1981, a year before Jayalalithaa's foray into Dravidian politics, he could have hardly visualized a Srirangam Iyengar woman, emerging as a leader.

At the Marina celebratory meeting four days later, Anna observed that the Congress's 'fall had come about in a second' and he would 'take it as a political lesson' for the DMK. As Anna was a Rajya Sabha member, Nedunchezhian, Karunanidhi and even Rajaji believed they had a shot at the chief ministership.[25] On 24 February, Anna ended speculation and revealed that he would head the government.[26] The DMK's victory would worry Indira Gandhi, who revealed years later that some things she had heard about the DMK's propaganda had caused her concern until she met Anna, who assured her that the DMK had no separatist ideology. She was 'convinced that he could control anyone in his party who said anything against the unity of our country'.[27]

1967 PARLIAMENTARY ELECTION

Party	Contested	Won	Votes	Percentage
DMK	25	24	5,524,514	35.78%
INC	39	3	6,436,710	41.69%
SWATANTRA	7	6	1,414,208	9.16%
CPM	6	4	1,057,542	6.85%
INDIAN UNION MUSLIM LEAGUE (IUML)	1	1	180,392	1.17%
INC	39	3	6,436,710	41.69%

1967 ASSEMBLY ELECTION

Party	Contested	Won	Votes	Percentage
DMK	174	137	6,230,552	40.69%
INC	232	51	6,293,378	41.10%
CPM	22	11	633,114	4.07%
PRAJA SOCIALIST PARTY (PSP)	4	4	136,188	0.89%
IUML	3	3	95,494	0.62%
SAMYUKTA SOCIALIST PARTY (SSP)	3	2	84,188	0.55%
DMK IND	2	2	70,665	0.46%

Anna's first port of call was Rajaji. As a grateful Anna credited their victory to Rajaji, 'You have popularized the rising sun like a god among people,' a magnanimous Rajaji said in return.[28] The meeting between Anna and Periyar happened on 2 March, after which the Dravidian patriarch would explain his about-turn on the DMK. 'Yes! I have now flipped the dosa to the other side! How long can I cook the same side? Shouldn't the other side too be done!'[29] Periyar had not reached the decision quickly, and his advisers were opposed to the shift.[30] Beholden to both leaders, Anna would remain deferential but prove early on that he was his own man.

Ministry Making

Success spawned difficulties. Anna received fifty to sixty telegrams every day recommending someone or the other to the cabinet. N.V. Natarajan and C.P. Chitrarasu were insistent on ministerships. They had sent their wives and children to Anna to plead on their behalf. Anna told poet Karunanandam that he was no Caesar to pose 'Et tu, Brute?' to Natarajan, Chinnaraj (Chitrarasu) and Dharmalingam.[31] On 26 February, addressing the DMK legislators, Anna revealed that aspirants had argued heatedly, abused him and cast mud standing outside his house to curse him in Tamil tradition. 'After some time, when we had all seasoned, this government could have come to us. It has come too soon,' Anna said in disappointment.

Chief Minister Anna retained the interior ministry, a practice his successors have followed. The number two, Nedunchezhian, was given industries and education, and Karunanidhi public works. Food took precedence, with Mathiazhagan designated as both food and revenue minister. Similarly, the Adi Dravida portfolio, earlier under the ministry of agriculture, was hived off to be made a separate ministry and Sathyavanimuthu, a Dalit and Buddhist, was appointed its first minister.

Earlier, Anna had dispatched Sezhian with the cabinet list to MGR. MGR recommended against Adithanar whose *Daily Thanthi* had consistently lampooned him. However, with a staggering 3,00,000 prints, the daily had played a decisive role, and Adithanar ended up as Speaker. MGR suggested that the pivotal industries portfolio—where money could be made, as he had understood it—be given to Nedunchezhian. Ironically, in 1972, Nedunchezhian would figure among those named by him as corrupt in his memorandum leading to the Sarkaria probe.

Anna and his cabinet were sworn in on 6 March at the Rajaji Hall. It was an apt venue. Rajaji had locked him up in jail but enabled him to reach the government, Anna recalled later.[32] Emulating

Charles Bradlaugh, Anna and his colleagues took their oaths as per their conscience. At Fort St George, the chief minister escorted each cabinet colleague to their seats before returning to his own.

Rajaji-Anna-Periyar Relations

Anna set the tone for his relationship with Rajaji at the outset. At the 26 February victory celebrations, the chief minister-designate refused to yield to Rajaji's wish to speak last, leading to Rajaji's open lament, 'If Anna would not listen to me now, how would he heed my words later?'[33] The 26 March *Ananda Vikatan* cartoon showed Rajaji saying that he did not like controls,* with Anna responding, 'That's why I am little by little getting rid of your control of me.'[34]

As he refused to accommodate the Swatantra's request for the Speakership, Rajaji commented that 'the honeymoon between the DMK and Swatantra is over'. Anna downplayed the rift, saying, 'The marriage had begun.' But the marriage was strained. Ma.Po. Si. records that Rajaji now wished for the DMK administration to fail. Seeing religion as the DMK's soft belly, he advised Ma.Po.Si. against accepting the Hindu Religious and Charitable Endowments ministry, as Anna had desired.[35] However, the personal warmth between the leaders was never under strain.

Anna's heart was more with his mentor, Periyar, although he revered both Rajaji and Periyar equally. On 20 June, in response to a question about whether Periyar would be given a freedom fighter's pension, Anna said in the assembly, 'I have dedicated this ministry itself.'[36] Equally, his respect for Rajaji made him stick to prohibition despite losing Rs 11 crore in revenue.[37] While Kamaraj patted Anna, Periyar saw a Brahmin plot. On 4 March, Periyar alleged that

---

* An allusion to Rajaji's 'licence-permit-quota raj' comment and position against government controls of the market and economy.

Rajaji used prohibition to shut down 2600 schools to deprive non-Brahmins of education. Still, liquor had become a 'cottage industry'. 'It is the Brahmin's dharma that our people should decay in all fields and perish. Brahmins will never show anyone the right path,' he said.[38]

At the 2 April Thanjavur general council, the chief minister made it clear to party men, who suggested a review, that while the cries of the womenfolk reverberated in his ears, he would remain steadfast on prohibition.[39]

Assertive Administration

Anna's major concern was to avoid mistakes, and 'hasten slowly' became the government's policy.[40] In a statement, he urged party men not to interfere and officials not to oblige them.[41] As chief minister, he quietly kept the slips with names recommended for medical seats—a great fad to this day—but did not act on them.[42]

The first challenge was the food front. The DMK government accelerated rice procurement, went after hoarders, prohibited interstate rice movement and encouraged food production with high-yield varieties and two crops.[43] Rajaji said the action against hoarders would lead to 'tyranny and corruption' even as the chief minister indicated that he had little latitude.[44] On 30 March, Anna lamented that he had no powers to import rice to keep his promise and said in another context that he would 'haul up [the Centre] to the stand if they were to obstruct', and this was the difference between his government and the Congress.[45] His speeches remain seminal to the debate on Centre-state relations.

The DMK chief minister was a leader and not a pleader. Anna's two years in power were marked by such plain speak, but he was ministerial and statesmanlike. When the Neyveli Lignite Corporation (NLC) wanted a higher tariff because of higher production costs, an official commented that it was unfair to expect NLC to perform differently when public undertakings like

Hindustan Steel were making a loss. Anna said one could speak in such a manner in a public meeting but not as a chief minister. It was only fair that the Centre expected just returns. The state electricity board agreed to the higher price.[46] Similarly, on the issue of Katchatheevu, an island claimed by both India and Sri Lanka, the chief minister revealed that the Centre had asked for a paper on the island's ownership but requested no further discussion in the interests of bilateral relations.[47]

No more just the DMK leader, the chief minister slept only four hours daily. The sea change that the DMK had brought about was unmistakable.[48] The unseen divide between the administration and those it served had suddenly snapped. From humble backgrounds, people from the rural hinterlands and peripheries entered the secretariat with familiarity and entitlement. It was as though they had come to power, and each one owned the administration. It was a true republic. District secretaries became key interlocutors with their district administrative counterparts, bringing a direct connection between the people and their public servants. Some would become alternate centres of power in the later DMK administrations. Interestingly, in the Three Front Agitation, when questioned by the superintendent of police to explain his party position as district secretary, Anbil Dharmalingam said it was akin to that of a district collector.[49] Further, with the advent of the DMK, backward, Dalit and rural representation began to grow in government services aligning the aspirations of the new government and this new breed of government servants.[50]

Form and Substance

On 8 April, Anna said in Delhi that it would be sufficient if the Centre retained only such powers necessary for preserving the unity and integrity of the country, leaving adequate powers to the states. He called for a 'High Power Commission' on the issue.[51]

The Anna-led DMK administration was high on symbolism.
Elegant Tamil terms took the place of English and Sanskrit. On 14
April, Anna unveiled a neon sign outside Fort St George, replacing
'Government of Madras' with *Thamizhaga Arasu*, and the motto
Satyameva Jayathe with *Vaaiymaiye Vellum*, in chaste Tamil. On
26 April, *Sri, Srimathi* and *Kumari* became *Thiru, Thirumathi* and
Selvi, respectively, and the secretariat became *Thalaimai Cheyalagam*.
Labour Day, 1 May, was declared a holiday.[52] In the fall of 1967,
Valluvar's kural couplets would be placed in buses. Later that year,
the DMK's efforts would finally bear fruit when in May 1967, All
India Radio dropped *Akashvani* to use *Vanoli* in its broadcasts.[53] In
his June 1967 budget speech, the chief minister indicated a plan
to beautify Cooum, a river flowing through Chennai, a Congress
government idea pending implementation.[54]

In the drive for a clean administration, legislators were not part
of the interview panel for medical and engineering seats, which were
greatly sought after and would become the mainstay of corruption in
the ensuing years.[55] As promised, 169 bus routes were nationalized at
Rs 1.12 crore and cess for dry lands removed, foregoing Rs 1.6 crore.[56]
The chief minister refused to remove the urban land tax as he said it
was fair to tax the propertied.[57] This sense of equity and egalitarianism
saw him offering all free education up to the pre-university level,
including forward caste families with less than a Rs 1500 annual
income. Describing the gesture as 'innovation' and 'revolution', the
chief minister said they were considered 'communalists', and this
would not have been expected of them.[58] To a question on choosing
staff based on reservations for government jobs, Anna said, 'Caste
differences are slowly disappearing. However, so long as benefits are
based on caste, such differences would exist.'[59]

On his former separatist stand, Anna said they had sought
Dravida Nadu for industries, to safeguard language, more power to
the states and to protect culture. These objectives remained. They
had given up Dravida Nadu, but that did not mean they would give

up opposition to Hindi or their advocacy for investments in Tamil Nadu. He rued the absence of heavy industries in the state's domain, which was limited to cottage industries, with all profit-making industries relegated to the private sector.[60] He said that electricity and irrigation were the biggest industries in the state domain. If they had employment-creating industries, states would get non-tax revenue, easing taxes on the poor.[61]

The DMK administration's industrial policy was harmony, equitable distribution of profits and seeing that most revenues went to the state.[62] In power, Anna's DMK administration strove to take a left-of-centre path. But Anna confided that his initial 'hate' for industrialists had turned into appreciation for their meticulous planning for the state's development and industrial growth.[63] Rajaji continued to oppose leftist measures and openly preached to the DMK that they should treat the communists as 'foes' waiting for 'anarchy' in the country.[64]

The Tamil Nadu Agricultural Lands Record of Tenancy Rights Rules, 1969, weighted in the lessee's favour, provided a forum to adjudicate disputes in proving lessee rights as most leases were oral.[65]

Politics of Rice

But Anna struggled to make good the promise on rice. The refrain now became: 'Moondru padi latchiyam oru padi nichayam—Three measures is the ideal; one measure a sure deal!'* Thus the DMK's flagship rice scheme was modified to a measure and launched in Chennai and Coimbatore in late May amidst misgivings from the civil service. The scheme, costing Rs 5 crore, reached 31 lakh

---

* In a pre-emptive strike, in early October 1966, the Tamil Nadu Congress Committee (TNCC) meeting at Karaikudi had hatched the idea of abolition of land tax and state trading of food grains, both populist measures to undercut the DMK. The DMK had advocated abolition of all taxes for farmers with five acres and less, and state trading to get rid of middlemen.

people, but soon folded for want of funds, and the chief minister said they would have received Rs 10 crore in subsidy if they were wheat eaters.[66] The Centre rejected Anna's request for assistance and suggested that he introduce new taxes. Anna instead suggested that defence spending be reduced to fund such programmes.

The Congress hung pots on trees with the words *Paanai inge! Padiarisi enge?*, meaning 'Pot here, where is the measure of rice?'[67] The Opposition gloated at his failure, but the public appeared largely forgiving of Anna. In the August 1968 by-election to fill the South Madras parliamentary seat vacated by him, Anna fielded Karunanidhi's nephew, Murasoli Maran. One of the Congress's posters read *Padhi poi, meedhi noi* (half of the DMK's promise was falsehood and the other half grits). Anna said that at least they had managed grits. 'Look at the women's crowd. Don't you still understand? You offered just lies,' he told the Congress. Maran won by a higher margin than Anna.[68]

Rice would take centre stage in Dravidian politics thenceforth. In 1972, Karunanidhi founded the Tamil Nadu Civil Supplies Corporation (TNCSC), a state variant of the Food Corporation of India (FCI), which would begin to procure and store rice. Two years later, ration cards were issued to families and public distribution outlets were opened. Later, when he became chief minister, MGR increased the number of public distribution outlets, extended them to the rural areas and ensured procurement from the market when the state's produce could not meet demand.

In 1996, Karunanidhi priced 20 kg of rice at Rs 40, which became Rs 20 under Jayalalithaa, then free in 2011, and was later expanded to 5 kg per head.[69] Today, Tamil Nadu remains the leader in the public distribution system. In retrospect, the paternalist populist politics and the freebie raj that followed, make Anna's difficulties, for a tiny fraction of the less than Rs 220-crore budget, look insane.[70] Liberalization had certainly empowered the states. Equally, his successors have excelled in fiscal irresponsibility.

The first crisis outside rice was the mysterious fires of 2–3 July in 600 slums. The slums were believed to have voted for the DMK. Anna did not engage in speculation. Neither did he approve of the vigilante attack on an Opposition legislative council member.[71] The fires would later spark the idea of fire-proof houses and the launch of the Slum Clearance Board. On Anna's request, donations poured in, with MGR's Rs 25,000 being the highest. Anna had wanted to collect a crore for reconstructing the huts into concrete houses.[72]

Self-Respect Marriages and 'Tamil Nadu'

Despite the fire and destruction, July proved to be a good month. On 18 July, Anna's two major undertakings—legalization of self-respect marriages and the name change from Madras to Tamil Nadu—were carried out. Earlier, on 7 June, speaking in Periyar's presence at an event, Anna had compared the legislation to a son who had travelled far, bringing his father his 'most desired' gift. The legislation legalized marriages without priests and the ceremony consisted of an exchange of garlands and a ring or thali.* To Hande's criticism that they were repeatedly targeting Hindus, Anna said, 'Muslims will endeavour to reform Muslims' and, citing Vivekananda, exhorted that a true Hindu should not resist change. He said that they had dreamt many days and nights for this day.[73]

On the name change to Tamil Nadu, the chief minister pointed out that it was not a victory of the Tamilarasu Kazhagam or the DMK but of all—Tamil, Tamils, Tamil history and Tamil Nadu. He recalled the sacrifice of Sankaralingam, who in 1956 had fasted unto death demanding the name change.[74] As Anna called out 'Tamil Nadu', 'Vazhga' or 'long live' rent the air. It was a moment of frisson.

---

* Periyar had surprised all when, while reviewing the final draft cleared by the law department, he suggested the word 'and' be replaced by 'or' on tying thali (nuptial chain) after the exchange of garlands.

'No' to Hindi

For once, the shoe was on the other foot on Hindi opposition. On 28 July 1967, 100 MPs wrote to table the amendment to the Official Languages Act of 1963 in the monsoon session as promised, enabling the continuance of English. Meanwhile, students announced a black flag protest during Indira Gandhi's 28 August visit.

The DMK, which had once thrived on black flag protests now urged the students against it. On 28 August, the students met the prime minister at the airport and demanded that all regional languages be made official. The prime minister advised that they keep their demands focused, and they asked that Tamil be made official. The prime minister now indicated that the others, too, would seek the same, to which the students said that their concern was Tamil and Tamil Nadu. Anna now intervened to say that the matter could not be resolved there, that the prime minister had heard them, and that he hoped she would do the best for Tamil Nadu. He then gently brought the meeting to an end.[75] But peace appeared elusive.

Two months later, on 13 December 1967, the Official Languages Amendment Bill was passed in Parliament. While providing for the continuance of English, the bill accorded primacy to Hindi. Maran said, 'the facade of giving English an associate status' on page 1 was 'nullified' on page 2. Fearing that a simple majority in Parliament could overturn the promise, Maran insisted on a constitutional amendment incorporating the Nehru and Shastri assurances.[76] Kamaraj expressed concern that Hindi speakers could now seek to join the civil service with just their mother tongue, while non-Hindi speakers would require either English or Hindi.[77]

Back home, anxious that their future was now pegged to Hindi, students took to the streets from 18 to 22 December. On 21 December, train coaches and effigies of Indira Gandhi and Morarji Desai were burnt. The DMK administration was, for once, on the other side.

On 22 December, as students blocked the Mumbai Express, a worried Karunanidhi rushed against police advice to stand next to the train and advise the students that they should leave it to the DMK government to safeguard their interests and let the Mumbai Express proceed. It was a daring act, but it worked.

On 18 January 1968, Parliament passed the Official Language Resolution reaffirming Hindi as the sole official language and emphasizing the three-language formula. In addition to Hindi or English, it said regional languages could be considered for civil service exams.[78] It was a half measure and the accent on Hindi made students greatly uneasy. Anna spent five nights with the twenty to twenty-five student leaders, who grilled him on the way forward. In the event, Anna played his last card—doing away with Hindi in state and aided schools. On 23 January, Nedunchezhian moved a resolution which said that 'the adoption of one of the regional languages [Hindi] alone as the Official Language' would 'result in the domination by a region of one language', demanded all regional languages be made official and until such time, English continue as the sole official language. The three-language formula posed a 'disadvantage and additional burden to the people in the non-Hindi regions'.[79] The resolution dispensed with Hindi in schools and Hindi command words in the National Cadet Corps (NCC). It assured Tamil as a medium in all the colleges and as a language of administration within five years. Anna said, 'I have done what I can; let Delhi do what it can'.[*,80]

To charges of stoking separation, Anna said he could declare separation and go down in history, but 'we are not at that juncture'.[81] When the Leader of the Opposition P.G. Karuthiruman asked that Anna give in a little, Anna said, 'Should we be the only ones to show flexibility? Is sacrifice limited to only us? We have given in all the time, did the others give in once?'[82] 'How do we make it clear that we have come to the brink of that patience?' In conclusion, he said, 'As those who had fought for it, who had pined for it, who had

---

[*] Command words were briefly in English.

suffered, today, as I read the resolution "No more Hindi lesson", the happiness that coursed through can only be felt by me and not those who had not suffered for it.'[83]

Second World Tamil Conference

It was appropriate for the 3–10 January 1968 Second World Tamil Conference, a commitment made by the earlier Congress administration in Malaysia at the first conference in 1966, to be hosted by the DMK administration. The DMK turned the academic exercise into a massively popular event, with hundreds of thousands soaking in the celebrations and imbibing Tamil pride and culture. Statues of ten Tamil savants were erected on that occasion.

On 1 January 1968, Arcot Ramasamy Mudaliar unveiled Anna's statue gifted by MGR on Mount Road, now Anna Salai. In his speech, Karunanidhi listed the various efforts to obtain Anna's consent, adding that Anna was not pleased.[84]

On 1 August 1968, a Kannadasan-led Congress procession saw protesters throw black cloth over Anna's statue as they crossed it. An upset Anna said, 'It is some happiness to know beforehand that when I die, these persons too will condole my death.'[85] Consequently, Rajaji termed the statue for Anna while in office as 'unwise'.[86] Meanwhile, Periyar would also propose a statue for Karunanidhi. Karunanidhi was being identified as the number two after Anna by no less than Periyar himself. His drive and energy had catapulted him to a de facto second place for long. But Jayakanthan was not impressed. Periyar was an iconoclast and Jayakanthan said it was 'shameful' that Periyar, who fought superstitions, supported it.[87]

Busmen-Student Clashes

The busmen-student clashes in March 1968 proved to be the next challenge. On 25 March, a fracas between a law college student on the one hand and the driver and conductor of the bus flared up, and a busman died later. As a larger confrontation loomed, Anna dispatched Karunanidhi, who met the busmen with his cabinet colleagues Govindasamy and Muthusamy at 3 a.m. As the conflict spread to the other campuses, tear gas and batons were used even as the chief minister sought the help of the CPM legislators to pacify the busmen. A judicial probe was ordered.[88] In all this, he urged the police to show restraint. But many in the party felt that the police should have dealt with the protests more firmly. An upset city police chief returned his paycheque and asked to be relieved of his post. Anna retained the cheque as a souvenir but advised against 'a hasty decision in a disturbed state of mind'.[89] The police chief stayed.

Goan Freedom Fighter Ranade's Release

On 15 April, Anna travelled to the US and Japan on invitations from those governments. On his way to the US, Anna visited Vatican City, Paris and the UNESCO.[90] En route in Mumbai, the committee for the release of Goan freedom fighter Mohan Ranade urged him to appeal for Pope Paul VI's intercession during his private audience with him.* Sending his aides away, the pope met Anna with just Reverend Jerome D'Souza, a constituent assembly member from Chennai. In that private setting, Anna appealed to the pope to use his good offices to free Ranade. Ranade was released on 26 January 1969, only a week before Anna's death. He travelled to Chennai to pay his respects to the departed leader.[91]

In the US, Anna noted that 'No party should be in power for more than ten years . . . As you stay longer in office, you grow conceited with power. I pray daily that such conceitedness from power does

---

* In 1955, Mohan Ranade was imprisoned in a Portuguese prison for an attack on a police station. His appeals and efforts to free him failed and Ranade spent another eight years in prison after Goa's liberation in 1961.

not go into my head.'[92] On a coalition government with the DMK in the Centre, Anna said: 'It is enchanting. But far distant.'[93] He would not have imagined that in three decades, his DMK would be part of a coalition at the Centre for seventeen years.

No-Confidence Vote

On 28 July 1968, speaking at the Tamilarasu Kazhagam's conference on state autonomy, Anna suggested that except for defence, the rest should be open for discussion and wanted the Centre to take what the states would willingly offer as they were linked to the people while the Centre was far removed.[94]

On 23 August, eighteen months into Anna's term, P.G. Karuthiruman tabled a no-confidence motion listing eleven charges—from lack of a steady industrial policy to illicit liquor. Karuthiruman charged that, under the DMK, the state had slipped to the tenth or eleventh place from the second in the industrial ranking. Anna intervened to ask if it was proper to compare the Congress's twenty-year record to his eighteen months in office.[95] The chief minister defended his administration passionately. He charged that Congress had never trusted their ability or the depth of their people's contacts. But there were also lighter moments.[96] When asked if Anna was talking about the prices of tamarind coming down, Anna responded, 'The price of tamarind came down because of the tamarind tree,' evoking much laughter.[97] The Congress described the chief minister as a good and honest man but expressed doubts about those around him.[98]

On 16 September, Anna underwent surgery at the Memorial Hospital in New York for cancer in his throat. As people prayed for him, the chief minister declared, 'No need to consider that I don't have faith in prayer. Prayers are of various kinds. I pray within, without others' knowledge. I am also aware that many pray for me. Equally, I am aware that those prayers would bear much fruit.'[99]

Anna confided to his host, India's permanent representative to the United Nations, G. Parthasarathy, that the conduct of his colleagues saddened him and Tamil Nadu, which he had wished to turn into a garden, had 'become a toxic field'.[100] Physically broken and greatly disillusioned, the chief minister would savour the fruits of his labour one last time against medical advice, participating in the 1 December official celebrations for the Tamil Nadu name change.

But this happiness was cruelly cut short. On Christmas Day, forty-four peasant worker families, Adi Dravida women and children, were burnt alive in their huts in Keezhvenmani, leaving the chief minister shattered. On 14 January 1969, in his last epistle to his thambis, Anna called his office the 'prisoner of circumstances'.[101] Operated again on 25 January 1969, Anna succumbed to his illness on 3 February.

After Anna Who?

Dinamani said a million people attended Anna's funeral, and the *Guinness Book of Records* registered it as the largest in numbers.[102] Karunanidhi's 300-plus line elegy for the departed leader would become immortal and would later be cut as a gramophone record. Jayakanthan however, said that the mourning, a social etiquette, had turned to 'social indecency' in Anna's case.[103] On 9 February, he lamented that 'Indira Gandhi's intelligence and honour had gone bad then that she went to perform circumambulation at Annadurai's tomb'.[104]

The choice of the Marina as Anna's resting place, taken by Karunanidhi in consultation with MGR, became controversial, with Karuthiruman complaining that the public objected, claiming that the Marina had been defiled. A pained Karunanidhi asked: 'Who are these public? Where are they?' He said he had 'wondered from which sky they had jumped and had searched and searched for those public' in vain. He asked if the Congress consulted other parties on cremating Gandhi and immersing his ashes in the rivers of the country.[105]

Anna had metamorphosed into one of modern India's most fascinating leaders. Steering the party of the 'modest', as a family head, to a political force, he had created history, ushering the 'commoner' to power. Premature death consolidated his status as a colossus. Rajaji wrote: 'Sadness will always be part of life. Warriors will not get confused seeing death. They will continue intrepidly to do their duties to realize the deceased's wishes. This is my wish for the DMK's thambis.'[106]

9

Chief Minister Karunanidhi

On 9 February 1969, Nedunchezhian made it clear that he expected the chief ministership as a matter of right. He said he was the acting chief minister and the number two in Anna's cabinet.

Nedunchezhian possessed none of Karunanidhi's industry, charisma or chutzpah required for the top job. On top of it, he was mulish. On one occasion, Anna recommended DMK student leader L. Ganesan's writer friend Pa. Jeyaprakasam to Nedunchezhian as 'our boy' with a master's degree in Tamil. The education minister, with clinical detachment, advised him to apply when lecturer positions opened up. Anna then suggested Jeyaprakasam's services for the Second World Tamil Conference, only to hear that someone else had been appointed. 'Keep reminding me,' Anna told L. Ganesan. Once they stepped out of Anna's abode, Ganesan told his friend, 'If Kalaignar [Karunanidhi] were in Navalar's [Nedunchezhian] place, he would have handed out the appointment order and gone over to inform Anna that he had "fixed a job for the younger sibling".'

Nedunchezhian, a man whose political career had been built on catchy oratory and gentlemanliness, was condemned to a permanent number two position. He suggests that Karunanidhi greatly desired to succeed Anna even as he was fighting for his life, and MGR, Si.Pa. Adithanar, Mathiazhagan, Sathyavanimuthu, P.U. Shanmugam,

Anbil Dharmalingam and Mannai Narayanasamy hatched a plan to make his rival the chief minister.

But it was MGR's support that mattered, and Karunanidhi duly credited him:

> My dear friend, the late MGR shouldered the huge responsibility of making me assume the chief minister's post, although everyone in my household deterred me from becoming chief minister. He came to my house, pacified them and resolved that '[I] will not cease until I take you and make you sit in the chief minister's chair.'[1]

On 10 February, at the DMK legislators meeting chaired by A. Govindasamy, Mathiazhagan proposed Karunanidhi, and Sathyavanimuthu seconded him. S.J. Ramasamy proposed Nedunchezhian and V.T. Annamalai seconded him, only to see Nedunchezhian withdraw from the contest.

Karunanidhi was sworn in as chief minister later that day. In his autobiography, Karunanidhi recalled the *Esquire* cartoon mocking Franklin Roosevelt in his second term as a bad word. 'Here too, some press barons, elites, mill owners, the landed gentry, the rich and aristocrats have discovered a bad word. Karunanidhi is a bad word in their view,' he alluded about his becoming the chief minister.[2]

Karunanidhi retained all of Anna's ministers. A disappointed Nedunchezhian opted out, saying he did not wish to work under the leadership of a 'fourth-rate person'.[3] That evening, Periyar, who had thrown his weight behind Karunanidhi on Kamaraj's advice, said that Nedunchezhian and others should 'blindly support' Karunanidhi.[4]

Only forty-four, Karunanidhi had reached the pinnacle quickly. But he was no Anna. At least not yet. Anna blossomed into an elder statesman in his final years. 1971–76 would prove turbulent for Karunanidhi.

Karunanidhi appeared gracious in his victory. On 11 February, as Nedunchezhian was clearing his office, Karunanidhi took his hands into his and pleaded that he join the cabinet or become the party's general secretary, only to see a sulking Nedunchezhian refuse his entreaties. Karunanidhi later recorded that although he was chief minister, he always stood up and received Nedunchezhian.[5]

On 15 February, Periyar preached 'obedience' to Nedunchezhian, who had reiterated that he would stay away from the ministry. Subsequently, that day, Karunanidhi expanded his cabinet, taking in P.U. Shanmugam, Adithanar, K.V. Subbiah and O.P. Raman. The next day, Nedunchezhian was conspicuous by his absence at the 16 February Memorial Day procession to Anna's mausoleum.[6] Karunanidhi revealed years later that Nedunchezhian wanted to be deputy chief minister as well as the party chief.

DMK President Karunanidhi

As speculation mounted that Karunanidhi would also head the party, on 9 March, in a felicitation meeting for the chief minister at Napier Park, DMK's parliamentary leader, K. Anbazhagan, had, with a homey example, expressed his doubts about Karunanidhi's ability to step into Anna's shoes as party leader.[7]

In April, Nedunchezhian unilaterally declared his candidacy. But days before the 27 July general council, Karunanidhi threw his hat into the ring. Expressing 'shock', Nedunchezhian said he was encouraged by Karunanidhi's mention of consensus, even until two days earlier and did not expect him to make a run. Karunanidhi countered that, though Nedunchezhian had spoken of his intent to the press 'not less than ten times', he had neither consulted him nor others. He noted that Nedunchezhian was aware, like the rest, that he had shouldered most of the responsibility in the party in the last few years, and Anna's letters to him would also make this clear. He asked Nedunchezhian to withdraw from the contest and rejoin the cabinet.

MGR now chimed in:

> Ninety-nine per cent of the DMK desire Kalaignar Karunanidhi
> as general secretary. Therefore, they are pressing him to
> contest . . . When Navalar [Nedunchezhian]—who does not
> enjoy a majority—insists that his view should be accepted, it is
> tantamount to coercion. The Congress party became decadent
> because the party leadership was with one while the administration
> rested with another. Because I do not want such an eventuality for
> the DMK, I suggest that both positions be vested in one person.

MGR's declaration, 'I do not want such an eventuality for the DMK',
showed that the man had become the supreme arbiter of power in
the party. His argument on duality was specious but it carried the
day. Periyar had also argued for the chief minister to be the party
head. On 11 January 2010, Karunanidhi said in the assembly that he
owed the presidency to MGR and was 'indebted for life'.[8]

The centre of gravity had shifted to Karunanidhi. Karunanidhi
again reached out to Nedunchezhian. Meanwhile, Madurai Muthu,
Anbil Dharmalingam, R. Dharmalingam, Mannai Narayanasamy
and M.S. Sivasamy hit upon a compromise formula under which
Karunanidhi would be president—the position in which Anna had
nominally placed their mentor, Periyar—except that the president
would wield all the powers. As Nedunchezhian demurred, the
president and the general secretary were made equally pivotal, with
the president making decisions in consultation with the general
secretary.* In retrospect, Karunanidhi, a born leader, would have led
the party with or without any statutory powers.

On 27 July, the two would meet one-on-one for ten minutes
before the general council, and Nedunchezhian would accept the

---

* Karunanidhi in a later letter included Arangannal, N.V. Natarajan and Anbazhagan
while excluding Sivasamy. *Kalaignarin Kadithangal*, 8: 193–94.

compromise.[9] That day, 320 of the 326 newly constituted general council members chose Karunanidhi as the party's first president, Nedunchezhian as general secretary and MGR as treasurer. Karunanidhi had repaid his debt to MGR, now the third-ranking leader in the party.[10] But he would not need MGR to govern and would steer an independent course.

On 12 August, a reconciled Nedunchezhian joined the cabinet as minister of education and health, apparently giving in to Periyar and others.[11]

First National Role

Karunanidhi began emulating his mentor even as he strove to emerge from his shadows. In a society where age was equated with maturity and wisdom and consequently accorded respect, Karunanidhi's youth, haste and leadership style seemed to come in his way. On 25 February 1969, as chief minister in the House, Karunanidhi acknowledged that he was 'a little hasty and anger prone'.[12]

Indira Gandhi had remarked, 'I have heard that he is a confrontationist.' Her misgivings would come true after 1971. Months later, when Indira Gandhi unveiled Anna's portraits at an event at Rajaji Hall, Karunanidhi disabused her 'fear and doubt', assuring her that 'We will extend a hand in friendship; lend voice for rights'. Between 1969 and 1971, he stood by Indira Gandhi in her fight against the Congress's old guard or Syndicate and threw her a political lifeboat when her political career appeared in peril. But the massive victory in 1971 would go to the heads of both leaders and seriously pit one against the other.

On 1 March 1969, speaking to the legislative council, Karunanidhi made it clear that cooperation was a two-way street with the Centre. Karunanidhi's first visit to Delhi as chief minister on 17 March saw him tell a well-attended press conference that 'Giving more powers to the states would not affect the unity of the country',

Photo credit: 'Stills' Gnanam

Indira Gandhi and Karunanidhi as allies

wishing that the issue of regional autonomy could be settled in a 'friendly manner'.[13] This would become his catnip. So consumed was Karunanidhi by the idea that he obsessed over it in the early years.

If he had already made a splash with his outspoken views, Karunanidhi made a mark at the 19–20 April 26th National Development Council (NDC) meeting when he called for, among others, the states to have a major share in shaping national policies, turning over loss-incurring public-sector undertakings on an experimental basis to the states to turn them around and effecting economies in defence expenditure. These were thoughtful, rational suggestions, yet they failed to gain traction even with fellow states. But Karunanidhi never gave up and, year after year came up with far-reaching suggestions that would have turned India into a model of fiscal and political federalism.

Hedging his bets carefully, he became the first chief minister to advocate bank nationalization at the NDC meeting.[14] It was a clever move. The June 1967 AICC session vetted Indira Gandhi's ten-point economic programme, including bank nationalization. But the Congress's conservative old guard opposed the radical idea, and the prime minister was not too sure about such a gamble yet. Karunanidhi could have sensed that Indira Gandhi would emerge victorious in the intra-Congress fight. Nationalization had been a long-standing DMK policy, and Karunanidhi had now taken it to Delhi. As he recalled in 1994, the DMK, with its feet firmly in Tamil Nadu, 'had extended its hands nationally'.[15] On 19 July, Indira Gandhi announced the nationalization of fourteen banks and insurance companies, upstaging the economically coy Syndicate.

'Confrontationist' Karunanidhi was proving to be an ally. This was just the beginning. Karunanidhi's centrality would again manifest itself with the 20 August presidential elections turning into the last battleground between the Syndicate and Indira Gandhi. The Syndicate snubbed Indira Gandhi, rejecting her proposal to nominate Jagjivan Ram, a Dalit, in Gandhi's centenary year. Instead, it chose Parliament Speaker Sanjiva Reddy. As the prime minister openly expressed her dismay, on 20 July, V.V. Giri, the vice president, resigned and set himself up as an independent candidate. The previous day, Giri had signed the ordinance on nationalization. As Congress president S. Nijalingappa fatefully reached out to the Swatantra and the Jan Sangh for support, Indira Gandhi seized the moment to advocate for Giri's call for a free 'conscience vote'.

How did Karunanidhi become instrumental? As early as May, Punjab chief minister Gurnam Singh, on a visit to Tamil Nadu, met Karunanidhi in his efforts towards Opposition consensus. Following this, in mid-July, as the fourth largest party in Parliament and with substantial votes in his kitty Karunanidhi shot off a letter to Opposition chief ministers to meet to discuss their stand in the presidential election.

Between 21 and 23 July, a host of leaders from the Jan Sangh to the Muslim League, the Swatantra to communists and the chief ministers of Punjab and West Bengal, conferred with Karunanidhi in Delhi. The Right's choice was either C.D. Deshmukh or Karunanidhi. Karunanidhi spurned the suggestion, explaining picturesquely that a farmer preferred to 'plough deep than to plough wide'. On 26 July, Karunanidhi announced in Chennai, CPI, Praja Socialist, Akali Dal, Muslim League and DMK support for Giri.

In the three-cornered contest (Reddy, Deshmukh and Giri), Giri was expected to lose. Indira Gandhi said: 'That may be the end. I may have to go.'[16] However, Giri won in the second count with just 14,500 votes. He had trailed until the vote count reached Tamil Nadu. The DMK's 35,448 votes had bailed him and Indira Gandhi out.[17]

That October, the party expelled her. The party split as the Syndicate's Opposition Congress (O) and the Ruling Congress (R) led by Indira Gandhi. As she headed a minority government, Karunanidhi, the Left and smaller parties held her afloat. Thanks to the tailwind provided by the DMK, Indira Gandhi never looked back till she fell in 1977.[18] Not all this help was prompted by altruism or 'socialist' ideals. In Karunanidhi's home turf, Kamaraj's Congress (O) remained the only Congress that mattered. From then on, Karunanidhi, to undercut Kamaraj, would help breathe life into the Congress (I) in the state.[*][19]

Karunanidhi on a Mission

It was an auspicious beginning. But Karunanidhi's focus remained Tamil Nadu. He embarked on a cultural nationalist and social justice agenda, reflecting his Tamil nationalist aspirations and wish

---

[*] The Congress R would, in 1978, undergo another split and the faction led by Indira Gandhi would now come to be known as Congress I, the I standing for Indira.

for a legacy. Like a modern Chola emperor, Karunanidhi left behind two monumental creations, the Valluvar Kottam and the 133-foot Valluvar statue at Vivekananda Rock in Kanniyakumari, which he was immensely proud of.* In 1969, a committee for the erection of a statue of Chola emperor Rajaraja within the Thanjavur Big (Brihadeeshwara) Temple was formed. However, in April 1970, Karunanidhi ended up opening it outside the temple precincts, as the Archaeological Survey of India (ASI) refused permission on the grounds of preserving the temple's original character.

Freedom fighter V.O. Chidambaram's oil press was exhibited permanently in Chennai; the monthly freedom fighter stipend of Rs 50 was raised to Rs 75 and given to 6002 freedom fighters instead of the extant 107 beneficiaries, while financial assistance was extended to the families of noted freedom fighters such as Vanchinathan. Memorials for Rajaji and Kamaraj were commissioned, and poet Bharati's and Kamaraj's houses were turned into memorials. Chieftain Kattabomman's fort was rebuilt and declared open on 18 August 1974. An art gallery came up at the ancient port town of Poompuhar that year.[20] Cooum clean-up and beautification were also attempted unsuccessfully. However, on 13 October 1974, *Kalki* said the money could have been spent creating jobs. It also said the party's 'standing' had a free fall after Anna's death.[21]

In January 1976, before dismissing the DMK government, Indira Gandhi took to task the spending on these ventures and faulted some social welfare schemes.[22] If these were symbolic, there were also substantive contributions that would speak of Karunanidhi's legacy.

The young chief minister seemed to be on a mission. The words of P. Sabanayagam, his chief secretary from 1971–76: 'The CM himself spared no efforts to improve the conditions of the poor,

---

* There were suggestions that this should have been done with private contributions and some government input. *Kalki*, 29 September 1974, 11; *Kalki*, 13 October 1974, 7.

formulated workable schemes—education, healthcare, shelter—also economic development; there was progress all round. Law and order was well-maintained.'[23]

In Anna's tradition, Karunanidhi described himself and his administration as 'one from a very modest' background.[24] Hailing from a numerically insignificant backward community, Karunanidhi remained acutely conscious of his social background and the struggle to reach his place. In his first speech to the House as chief minister, he said that as the one from the 'most backward community', he would strive to uplift the backward and downtrodden but also 'do my best to care for the interest of the forward communities'.[25]

On 1 April 1969, a separate backward classes (BCs) ministry was established, followed on 13 November by the first Backward Classes Commission headed by the erudite A.N. Sattanathan. On 7 June 1971, the Dalit and backward quotas were raised from 16 to 18 per cent and 25 to 31 per cent, respectively. The Commission had recommended the status quo for the Dalits and raising the ceiling to 33 per cent for BCs.[26]

Sattanathan had identified nine backward castes as benefiting disproportionately by their numbers, recommended enlarging the reservation pool and developing a most backward class list and economic criteria to mitigate what later came to be termed the 'creamy layer's' advantage. Karunanidhi only went for the first recommendation. On 16 August, the cabinet included nine new castes into the backward list. In all, fifteen castes were added by 1976, including the landowning Kongu Vellalas.[27*] However, in

---

* In 1980, MGR upped the 18 to 19 per cent for Dalits and 31 per cent to 50. On 28 March 1989, Karunanidhi, responding to the Vanniya demand for separate reservations, created the most backward category giving them compartmental reservation of 20 per cent within the 50 per cent. On 22 June 1990, following a court order, a percentile was earmarked for tribes.

trying to burnish his social justice credentials, the chief minister had not foreseen the Vanniyar challenge down the road.

Similarly, in a conscious effort to make the state's services more representative, in 1972, Karunanidhi pointed out that eighteen Adi Dravidas were chosen for the ninety-nine openings through the state public service commission to Group-1 posts, such as deputy collectors, deputy registrars, deputy superintendents, joint commercial tax officers, etc.

On 15 September 1969, the Manu Needhi scheme begun in 1968 in Chengalpattu district was extended to the entire state, under which district officials made weekly visits to the countryside to hear and resolve grievances. Karunanidhi said that 1500 villages were visited in a week. On 7 July 1971, responding to criticism that this was a 'show', he said the scheme had resulted in four lakh *pattas*, or title deeds, being given to the poor.[28] In August 1974, a Chief Minister's Special Wing was constituted to address people's grievances. By 1975, more than 1,10,000 petitions were received, and almost all were disposed of.[29]

Assertive and Benevolent Populism

An ardent Tamil nationalist, Karunanidhi designated the third day of the Tamil month of Thai in January as Thiruvalluvar Day and brought into vogue a Tamil year with Thiruvalluvar's birth as 31 BCE alongside the Gregorian year for use in the state.[30] The Thiruvalluvar year has come to stay, at least in wedding invitations and other formal invites. His effort on 1 February 2008 to designate Thai in January instead of Chithirai in April as Tamil New Year has, nonetheless, proven unpopular.[31] The chief minister's Tamil sense was so rich and deep that he suggested *Aavin*, meaning 'of the cow', for the state's commercial dairy products.[32] *Aavin* is a household name today.

Adopting part of the *Tamil Dheiva Vanakkam* of Manonmaniam Sundaranar's *Manonmaniam*, the Karanthai Tamil Sangam has sung it as the Tamil Thaai Vazhthu or the invocation song for Mother Tamil since 1914. The Sangam had appealed to Anna to declare it as the state song. On 11 March 1970, Karunanidhi declared its adoption. On 23 November 1970, a government order made select verses of the song into the official *Tamil Thaai Vazhthu*, forever placing the Tamils in his debt.[33] Tamil savant Ki.Va. Jaganathan considered Tamil a 'minor deity' and suggested a saint Thayumanavar song instead. Karunanidhi stood his ground with his secular choice. On 17 December 2021, M.K. Stalin's DMK government declared the song the state anthem, requiring all to rise when sung, following a high court decision that said it was a prayer song and not an anthem.[34]

In the fall of 1970, Karunanidhi floated the idea of a flag for the state. The Opposition, including Rajaji, was opposed to the idea.[35] Undeterred, Karunanidhi addressed a letter to the prime minister and, on 7 July 1971, revealed her acknowledgement of such a practice overseas.[36] On 27 August that year, in Delhi, Karunanidhi, inspired by a flag sent from Malaysia by a Tamil, unveiled a flag he had designed for Tamil Nadu with the Indian flag at the top left quarter and the Srivilliputhur Temple Gopuram, the state emblem, on the bottom right corner.[37] The friendly Punjab chief minister welcomed the proposal. Karunanidhi did not pursue this as he would his other Tamil nationalist goals.

In the summer of 1974, the DMK administration introduced Tamil *archanas*, or worship, alongside the Sanskrit archanas as an option which never really took off. Similarly, his sons-of-soil policy of 80 per cent of jobs for Tamils remained rhetorical.[38] Beginning 19 April 1974 and until 31 January 1976, the state extended pensions to 1471 'language martyrs' who participated in the anti-Hindi agitations.[39] The Supreme Court struck it down later as 'containing the vice of disintegration and fomenting fissiparous tendencies'.[40] Also, student leaders from the anti-Hindi agitation were placed as district public relations officers (PRO) and assistant PROs. In

February 1976, Indira Gandhi complained that the DMK had 'infiltrated' every level of the state administration.[41]

Karunanidhi wooed the Muslims by declaring Prophet Mohammed's birthday a paid holiday. On 16 October 1974, he renamed the Government Women's Arts College Quaid-E-Millath Women's Arts College after Muhammad Ismail, the Muslim League leader from Tamil Nadu. On 9 January 1974, the cabinet included Urdu-speaking Muslims on the backward list, and Karunanidhi said that a million would benefit.[42]

On 8 October 1971, Seven Wells in Chennai was renamed Vallalar Nagar after saint Ramalinga Adigal.[43] Earlier, the Hindu religious endowments had been upgraded to a ministry in 1970.[44] Until 1967, there were 9000 temples under the state administration and temple revenue stood at Rs 3 crore, which rose to Rs 12 crore in 1976. By 1975, the number of temples and institutions brought under the state rose to 41,306, with 2,01,343-acre temple lands added.[45] A family insurance scheme was also introduced if a temple staff member expired and a certain amount was paid.[46] Karunanidhi said that while 200 temples were renovated in 1967, in the five years of DMK rule, 1620 temples saw renovation.[47]

His attempt to reach out to Hindus saw his administration assist with renovating the Thiruvarur Thyagaraja Swamy Temple car and re-lay four streets at the cost of Rs 4 lakh. In 1969, as the car rolled out after twenty-two years, the DMK regional strongman Mannai Narayanasamy symbolically joined the car pulling. Two days later, Karunanidhi said in the presence of Periyar that the four streets would serve the public beyond the car festival.[48]

On 2 December 1970, in keeping with Periyar's views, the Tamil Nadu Hindu Religious and Charitable Endowments Act was amended to allow all, irrespective of caste, and those qualified to become priests. Karunanidhi said the move would 'remove the thorn in the heart' of Periyar. For the purpose of training non-Brahmins, two training schools were set up. Karunanidhi said twelve writ petitions were filed to challenge his move. On 14 March 1972, the Supreme Court ruled that under the constitutional scheme, the appointment of priests has to be from a specified denomination as per the Agamas. On 15 April 1974, the assembly passed a resolution seeking a constitutional amendment to overcome the obstacles*.[49] Two thousand Adi Dravidas were made trustees of temples. Karunanidhi also named a college after Dalit icon, Dr B.R. Ambedkar.

From 1971 to 1975, Karunanidhi marked his birthday with the launch of populist schemes. In 1971, the Lepers Rehabilitation Homes and Beggars Rehabilitation Homes were launched at Paranoor in 1974–75.[50]

In 1972, the most popular of the schemes, the eye camps for the poor, were conducted. By 1975, 262 camps had screened 6,07,727 people, cataract surgeries were performed and glasses given to 1,00,363 people. In 1973, the abolition of 1432 handheld rickshaws was done with great fanfare, and by 1975, from a fund collected for this purpose, 2155 cycle rickshaws were issued. In 1974, a rehab scheme for the differently-abled was launched, and Rs 1 crore was earmarked for wheelchairs, tricycles, aluminium walking sticks and hearing aids as assistance. The scheme intended to train 1000 differently-abled people, with a stipend of Rs 50 a month, and provide them with government jobs. Many of these schemes fell by the wayside in the following years and controversy about how contributions were forced abounded. A raffle prize of Rs 38 lakh was announced as part of fundraising for the beggars' homes.[51] In 1975, orphanages for more than 3000 orphans and destitute widows were launched, with the first declared open in Mylapore.[52]

Building on the Congress government's achievements in rural electrification, by 1972, only 3000 villages remained without power. Of the 23,000 Adi Dravida colonies, only 4354 were electrified until

---

* But a resolution was elusive until 2006 when Karunanidhi again passed an order and it was upheld by the Supreme Court in 2015. Ironically, the first non-Brahmin priest would be appointed by the AIADMK government in 2018.

1967 and in the five years of the DMK administration, 18,036 were added.[*][53]

A steady stream of leftist measures was mooted in a bullish manner. On 15 February 1970, the DMK administration brought down the land ceiling from thirty to fifteen standard acres and did away with the exceptions for sugarcane, grazing lands and dairies. Rajaji described it as a 'political fraud' and warned that the move would produce 'results worse than Joseph Stalin's moves produced' and that smaller landholdings were antithetical to modernized farming.[54] Karunanidhi said the Act could net 16,350 acres during the Congress administration. By 1975, he said, it had yielded 78,956 acres of surplus land, of which 58,536 were distributed to 35,482 landless.[†][55] A Tamil Nadu public information advertisement claimed 26,60,889 pump sets in India, of which 7,13,312 were in the state, and in the eight years of DMK rule, 4,23,490 were given power. Similarly, by 1975, five lakh housing pattas were issued to the backward and Dalit classes.

By 15 August 1972, those companies with more than fifty buses were nationalized, and in 1973, this was done for all buses. But its implementation ran into a legal challenge.[56] It took another ten years before the Supreme Court declared the measure valid. Karunanidhi considered the issuance of more than six lakh pattas, two lakh houses, a bill for workers to shareholders and part of the management and bonuses for busmen as 'achievements' on his birthdays.[57]

Karunanidhi drew up a seven-year plan to remove 1200 slums by 1978. The dynamic Rama Arangannal became the first chairman of the Slum Clearance Board. The Board aimed at building 25,080 units.

---

[*] Kamaraj pointed out that there was uninterrupted power during the Congress period as opposed to the fitful distribution during the DMK rule as connections were given indiscriminately without augmenting power production with new plants. *Kalki*, 11 May 1975, 28. Bhaktavatsalam said three-fourths of the villages had already been connected. M. Bhaktavatsalam, *Enadhu Ninaivugal*, 202–04.

[†] These figures are not consistent. See *Kalaignarin Kadithangal*, 2: 34–35.

Karunanidhi was a vocal advocate for more central allocations, investments and industries in the state. The Thoothukudi deep sea fishing harbour, Thoothukudi fertilizer plant, Kalpakkam second phase's capacity increase by 200 MW and three new sugar mills were achieved in these years.[58] Similarly, on Karnataka's intention to build the Hemawati, Kabini, Amarangi and Suvarnavathi dams on the Cauvery, the assembly passed a resolution on 8 July 1971 seeking to refer the dispute to a tribunal.[59]

But it was not all fragrance. Despite the apparently progressive land legislation and labour measures, the DMK's approach to the agrarian and labour issues showed the compulsions of a party in power and the newer and affluent constituents it wished to please. Farmers and workers began to agitate against power tariff raises and workers for better pay in 1970–71. Students would turn restive with the administration, according primacy to Tamil instruction over English in higher education. While Rajaji worried about national integration, Periyar was concerned that students would be confined to a narrow space with just Tamil.[60]

Nonetheless, 1971 was a particularly buoyant year as the DMK defied all predictions and beat its own electoral record. The DMK won 184 of the 234 seats. The Kamaraj–Rajaji 'Grand Alliance' which was favoured to win managed only twenty-one seats between them. Kripalani was convinced that the Congress had rigged the national election.[61] It was the DMK's best electoral performance ever. It led to a Karunanidhi who had arrived and, in a rush, would assert himself. Thus, the DMK would venture aggressively into trade unions long considered a communist preserve. In the districts, the DMK functionaries with DMK-bordered veshtis and shawls were becoming a law unto themselves. Kamaraj and Rajaji alleged that corrupt elements that had reared their head even during Anna's time felt freer now. Karunanidhi was to become a cult and Murasoli Maran became the eminence grise, fuelling tensions within.

Sycophancy assumed new heights within the Dravidian movement. Matinee idol MGR paid his dues, describing Karunanidhi as 'a second edition of Anna' and 'Anna's heir' by July 1970. In twenty-seven months, however, the very man who had helped him rise would now decide to strike, dealing a grievous blow to Karunanidhi's ambitions for thirteen years.

10

'Autonomy in the State and Federalism at the Centre'

Rajamannar Committee

On 19 August 1969, Karunanidhi announced the formation of a three-member committee on Centre-state relations, with Justice P.V. Rajamannar as chair and A.L. Mudaliar and P. Chandra Reddy as members. Six months later, at the 21–22 February 1970 Tiruchi district conference, the chief minister energetically floated the idea of *Maanilathile suyatchi, Mathiyile kootatchi* (autonomy in the state and federalism at the Centre) as part of his 'Five Great Declarations'. The other four were:

- To walk steadfast in Anna's path
- To create a non-hegemonic society
- To ever oppose Hindi imposition
- To eschew violence and to defeat poverty

A month later, on 21 March, while participating at the 21–22 March National Development Council meeting, Karunanidhi issued an ultimatum to the prime minister to announce the Salem Steel Plant in that meeting, failing which, he said, he would withhold consent to the Fourth Five-Year Plan. There were no precedents for such a strident style of advocacy, and CS expressed his displeasure later. However, on 17 April, the prime minister announced as demanded in Parliament and laid the foundation stone on 16 September that year. So far, so good.

Greatly influenced by Sheikh Mujibur Rahman's positions in East Pakistan, Karunanidhi now attempted to push the envelope.* On 29 March 1970, three days after Sheikh Mujibur declared Bangladesh independent, Karunanidhi declared, 'I believe no one in India would wish to create a Mujibur Rahman in each state.' Indira Gandhi appeared amused with the gawky comparison, but it also grated on her.†

Rajaji now compared Karunanidhi's clamour to Charles Lamb's *A Dissertation Upon Roast Pig*. In the story, swineherd Ho-ti's son Bo-bo accidentally burns their cottage and the nine piglets. Tempted by the smell of the burnt meat, the boy feels the meat, burns his fingers and, taking his fingers to his mouth to cool them, tastes the crumbs and discovers its deliciousness. Neighbours haul the father-son duo to court after realizing that the duo's cottage caught fire every time there was a farrow. The jury ends up tasting the roast meat and rendering a 'Not Guilty' verdict. But people burn their cottages to roast pigs until a wise man tells them there is no need to burn their houses down. Similarly, said Rajaji, some chief ministers reminded him of the above story. They welcomed Bangladesh's uprising, implying that Karunanidhi wanted to burn down the house (India) to roast the pig (autonomy).[1]

Sheikh Mujibur would manifest in his other references during that term.

---

* In 1970, Awami League leader Sheikh Mujibur Rahman won a majority on a six-point plan limiting the federal government to defence and foreign affairs.
† Beginning 28 March, Murasoli Maran penned a five-part essay in *Murasoli* titled 'Lion's Roar of Freedom in Bangla Country' to celebrate its birth.

Again, on 12 September 1970, Karunanidhi sponsored and presided over a State Autonomy Conference in Chennai in which Periyar, Muhammad Ismail, West Bengal chief minister Ajoy Mukherjee, Pranab Mukherjee, N. Srikandan Nair, Arangil Sridharan, S.M. Krishna, parliamentarians and leaders participated. The chief minister claimed the presence of the various leaders as support beyond the DMK for the demand and asked for the party volunteers to take the message to the people.[2]

Key Recommendations

On 27 May 1971, the Rajamannar Committee made recommendations that would have turned the Centre-state equation upside down. Echoing the Administrative Reforms Commission headed by Kengal Hanumanthiah, it suggested an Inter-State Council of chief ministers with the prime minister as its head as a forum for decisions of national importance or affecting state/states, recommended corporation tax, customs and export duties and capital value tax in the divisible pool, income tax and investments of less than Rs 100 crore in the state domain and shifting several subjects from the concurrent and central to the state list. It saw high courts as apex courts on civil and criminal matters and the Supreme Court as a constitutional court.

Pitifully, none except the Inter-State Council would happen in his lifetime. In time, Karunanidhi's chimera softened and was almost forgotten once he tasted power at the Centre. In the seventeen years that the DMK was part of the Union government, Karunanidhi did little to advance his agenda other than the Inter-State Council, owing more to his equation with Prime Minister V.P. Singh in 1990. The Council itself has proven a far cry from what the Rajamannar Committee intended it to be.

The Rajamannar Committee report was forwarded to the prime minister on 15 June 1971. The report was also sent to chief ministers and parliamentary party leaders.[3] On 22 June, the prime minister said, 'These are important issues and we intend to consult all the Chief Ministers.' This would take twelve years and ironically come on the heels of the 1983 southern chief ministers meeting in Bengaluru, where MGR participated. The shrill Akali Dal demands, not to mention Khalistan, finally saw Indira Gandhi deign to set up the Sarkaria Committee on Centre-state relations in 1983.

Karunanidhi, like his predecessor, felt heavily constricted. He wished to spruce up the ramparts of Fort St George but was told that it belonged to the Ministry of Defence, and he needed to seek approval from the ministry. The chief minister's heart sank. The government in the Centre was hanging in the balance with his support, but then his powers as the state's chief minister were supine. He promptly addressed a request to the defence ministry and later took deputy minister of defence, M.R. Krishna, to show him the shabby growth around the fort, after which permission was obtained for the clean-up.[4]

There were other issues. For instance, his wish to install a statue of Rajaraja Chola within the Big Temple, a UNESCO heritage site, was shot down by the ASI. Karunanidhi was so frustrated that he declared he would chase out the ASI from the state and even threatened to go on a procession with the statue to the Big Temple.[5] He also complained that chief ministers had no right to hoist the national flag on Independence or Republic Days. He said that this was a matter of 'self-respect'.[6] However, there were also substantive issues like the devolution of power, taxation and finances. But other than finances, his fellow chief ministers would not venture far. The idea of state autonomy was cold turkey.

Hitching Wagon to Indira Gandhi

On 5 September 1970, the bill on privy purses failed in the Rajya Sabha by one vote. The debacle was caused by DMK's

S.S. Rajendran, who stepped out when voting, claiming an upset stomach. While the circumstances remain unclear, the Congress regarded it as 'great acting' by the actor.[7] Probably, it was the hand of destiny guiding the course of events. Not deterred, a presidential ordinance 'derecognized' the rulers at midnight only to be struck down by the Supreme Court on 15 December. Twelve days after this rebuke, on 27 December, Indira Gandhi, deciding to take her case to the people, recommended mid-term elections.

Quickly sensing an opportunity, Karunanidhi hitched his wagon to Indira Gandhi's star.[8] As the Left and the Congress (I) warmed up to Karunanidhi, on 26 October 1970, the Swatantra ended the alliance with the DMK.[9]

Following talks on 19 January 1971 between Indira Gandhi and Karunanidhi, the latter told presspersons that the DMK had fought 170 seats in 1967 and intended to fight a higher number. The Congress (I) was offered five to seven parliamentary and ten to fifteen assembly seats. On 23 January, after CS said they would go it alone, he and Bhaktavatsalam returned to seek twenty parliamentary and eighty assembly seats. They were offered up to eight parliamentary and less than fifteen assembly seats this time. CS called it an insult and left.[10]

MGR hoisted the party flag at the 24 January election conference at Ashok Nagar, Madras, declared open by Nedunchezhian. That evening, Karunanidhi revealed that talks had failed. The DMK had offered up to thirteen assembly and eight parliamentary seats instead of the Congress (I) demand for eighty assembly and twenty parliamentary seats.[11] Karunanidhi had played hardball. It was working. At midnight, with G. Parthasarathy, Indira Gandhi telephoned Karunanidhi to pitch for twenty assembly and ten parliamentary seats. C. Subramaniam later explained, 'At the last moment, I think we felt a bit nervous.'[12]

The DMK withdrew five candidates to give Congress (I) nine parliamentary seats and the lone Puducherry seat but no assembly seats. Rajaji's *Swarajya* said that Indira Gandhi had 'mortgaged' her Tamil Nadu unit to the DMK.[13] H.V. Hande wrote that 'Indira Gandhi's eagerness to make Karunanidhi chief minister as opposed to Kamaraj' made her accept Karunanidhi's terms.[14] Leftist turned Congress (I)'s Mohan Kumaramangalam, who had made it clear he would not contest without the DMK, stood from Puducherry.

In its manifesto, the DMK took credit for, among others, the Salem Steel Plant, the East Coast Highway, Kalpakkam, Madras Metro Water, Thoothukudi deep seaport, banks and bus nationalization, removal of taxes for farmers, land ceiling to fifteen standard acres, a ministry for backward classes, slum clearance, more than ten dams, free education up to pre-university, a cement factory in Alangulam, Arakonam Cast Iron Factory, Nylon Fishnet Factory, renaming *Akashwani* to *Vanoli* and Dalmiapuram to Kallakudi. While recommending public-private partnerships in big and mid-sized industries, it said it would strive for a 'socialist society', a planning commission for each state and an agricultural productivity council. The manifesto declared that other than powers necessary 'to preserve the strength of India', the rest should be with states.

Periyar Unwittingly Helps Rajaji

Rajaji had joined hands with Kamaraj in a 'Grand Alliance'. On 25 February 1971, in a massive rally at the Marina Beach, Rajaji applied vermilion and blessed the twenty-five-year-younger Kamaraj. Describing the battle as between 'good and evil' and 'bigger' than against the British, Rajaji clairvoyantly warned that Indira Gandhi was a dictator-in-waiting and that both she and the DMK should be defeated.[15] Kamaraj said that those who wished to emancipate the poor should be straightforward. He implied that the DMK–Congress (I) alliance was not.[16]

Photo credit: Wideangle Ravi Shankaran

Kamaraj and Rajaji in a 'Grand Alliance' against the DMK and Congress (R)

Meanwhile, Periyar's anti-superstition procession on 21 January at Salem—with obscene pictures of Hindu deities and 'a 10-foot-long image of Lord Rama with people beating it with chappals'—created much controversy. A week later, the chief minister said he was unaware of the Salem incident and 'as far as Periyar is concerned, he has the right to think radically. But a government cannot be that powerful to execute all what he thinks'. Periyar joked that the chief minister had to 'assume ignorance and distance himself from it', adding that he 'understood their pickle'.[17]

On 15 February, the chief minister revealed that he had acted against 'two or three' police personnel. That week, comedian and critic Cho Ramaswamy's *Thuglak* published the rally's photographs and a cartoon on its cover showing Periyar beating Ram and Murugan idols with chappals and a grinning Karunanidhi in the company of policemen. The cartoon later showed up as a campaign poster from 'Salem devotees' asking, 'Are you going to vote for the disciple who unveiled the statue of Periyar who beat Ram and Murugan with chappals?' The posters were removed and confiscated, *Thuglak* was raided and copies seized, catapulting Cho Ramaswamy's stock, not to mention the sales of *Thuglak*.[18] The Madras High Court would later order the return of the posters.[19]

As the administration's bonafides in this instance became questionable,[20] on 17 January, *Murasoli* published a campaign advertisement asking how acting against such acts, namely *Thuglak*'s, unlike previous administrations, could be wrong.[21] Salem turned into a hot potato for Karunanidhi. Periyar said that the DMK was being made a 'scapegoat'; much to the DMK's relief, he stayed away from the campaign.[22] On 22 February, *Murasoli* published a full-page campaign advertisement taking credit for the *mahamagam*, the consecration of the Vaidheeswaran Temple, the desilting of Kapaleeshwarar Temple (in which Karunanidhi himself took part), the renovation of Srirangam Temple and the running of the Thiruvarur car under the heading, 'Who is atheist?'[23]

As Karunanidhi portrayed Rajaji and Kamaraj as reactionary and Indira Gandhi as progressive, Rajaji argued that no one questioned Winston Churchill about economic policies as they knew that the priority was to overcome the present danger—Hitler.[24] As Kamaraj hit out at the DMK administration as unprincipled and corrupt, Karunanidhi said that Kamaraj believed in 'caste politics' and, weeks after the polls, stated that Kamaraj had reduced himself to a 'Nadar leader'.

MGR and Karunanidhi were the star campaigners for the DMK. However, MGR's campaign almost did not happen. MGR initially said he was busy but then told R.M. Veerappan he had not received an invite. R.M. Veerappan shrewdly pointed out that talk about the elections being won without MGR had to be avoided. Karunanidhi disarmingly claimed that MGR did not need an invite. In the end, thanks to R.M. Veerappan, the communication gap was bridged, and MGR set off.

Few could match Karunanidhi's election campaigning. Until he turned into an old war horse, Karunanidhi never tired of travelling thousands of kilometres to meet people on the campaign trail. In the earlier days, there were no time restrictions to end the campaign by 10 p.m. Starting at Hosur in the evening, Karunanidhi would continue through the night and end at Krishnagiri the next morning with the words, 'There dawns the rising sun!' Similarly, beginning in Tiruchi, Karunanidhi would end in Kanniyakumari, having addressed some hundred meetings in between and snatching a few winks of sleep in his campaign vehicle. As the vehicle neared the venue, if he found someone dozing still, Karunanidhi would administer an affable knock saying, 'If we slept, the country would also go to sleep.'[25]

'DMK was the lamp for the house and the worker for the country', declared the advertisements, while manifestoes were explained through simple cartoons. *Murasoli* published these reductionist cartoons in a visually appealing manner.

Drawing large crowds, Kamaraj had confidently told pressmen, 'See me in Fort [St George] in the future.' In anticipation, chief secretary E.P. Royappah had called on Kamaraj. On 4 March, Rajaji confidently prophesied that the DMK's days in power were numbered.[26]

The results were stunning: contesting 201 seats, the DMK had won 183 with 76,10,766 votes or 46.5 per cent. The Congress had fought in 194 seats and won 15 with 54,05,856 votes or 33.1 per cent. The Swatantra had won six of the nineteen seats fought with 4,65,112 votes or 2.8 per cent. Rajaji described the victory as the 'by-product of the vulgar licence, permit raj's foul smell'.[27] However, it could not prevent Periyar's scorn as to 'Why could not those gods help Kamaraj get victory?'[28] Kamaraj was the sole winner in the parliamentary elections.

It was a massive victory that defied any rationale, except that time had passed by Kamaraj and Rajaji. Indira Gandhi's populist rhetoric of 'Garibi Hatao', or 'exit poverty', had resonated across the nation. CS later said, 'In my view, if they had not been with the Congress, they would have been completely routed. Unfortunately, we gave strength to the DMK at that time . . .'[29] The brute majority would go to Karunanidhi's and Indira Gandhi's heads, and Rajaji's words would come true in 1975.

1971 ASSEMBLY ELECTION

Party	Contested	Won	Votes	Percentage
DMK	203	184	76,54,935	48.58%
CPI	10	8	3,64,803	2.32%
AIFB	9	7	2,68,721	1.71%
PRAJA SOCIALIST PARTY (PSP)	4	4	1,47,985	0.94%
IUML	2	2	69,634	0.44%
INC (O)	201	15	55,13,894	34.99%
SWATANTRA	19	6	4,65,145	2.95%

1971 PARLIAMENTARY ELECTION

Party	Contested	Won	Votes	Percentage
DMK	24	23	56,22,758	35.25%
INC (I)	9	9	19,95,567	12.51%
CPI	4	4	8,66,399	5.43%
AIFB	1	1	2,08,431	1.31%
IUML	1	1	41,925	1.10%
INC (O)	29	1	48,53,534	30.43%

Land ceiling, land to the tiller, dividends for workers, removal of agricultural tax, houses for farm hands and Adi Dravidas and much Tamil cultural nationalist symbolism were some of the highlights of the 1971–76 administration.

Karunanidhi moved quickly. Decisive and dynamic, he carried the weight of his mandate with flair. A meeting of the district collectors was scheduled for 6 April. Royappah would have conducted the proceedings. Calling a press meeting at midnight, Karunanidhi announced that Royappah was posted as deputy chairman of the planning commission and P. Sabanayagam, a junior, was appointed chief secretary. The Supreme Court dismissed Royappah's claim of malafide as baseless later. But the charges from MGR the following year could not be shaken off that easily.

The 24–25 April 1971 Coimbatore general council formed two committees, one comprising seven members to study and report on ways to achieve egalitarianism and the second with twenty members to study the Rajamannar Committee report when published. Sezhian and Maran were appointed coordinators of the committees.[30]

Prohibition

We saw earlier that Anna had toyed with the idea of lifting prohibition. Unsurprisingly, a sprightly Karunanidhi was itching to embark on that road, the rationale being that the estimated Rs 26 crore in revenue could fund many welfare schemes. MGR, a health buff, avoided drinking even in movies. He was also acutely conscious of the stigma associated with drinking and drunkenness. Yet, as early as 13 September 1969, MGR issued a dissembling statement calling for a stop to liquor permits and alcohol. He did not stop there.

The DMK treasurer pointed out that the neighbouring states made a windfall from alcohol while Tamil Nadu suffered losses and that despite the loss in revenue, the ideal remained completely unfulfilled. 'Thamizhagam is like a deer surrounded by hunters,' he said. MGR urged help from the Centre. This may have resulted from some consultative work between the two leaders to test the waters on the dicey issue.

But then there was a long pause for twenty months. The cat was out of the bag when the 24–25 April 1971 Coimbatore general council regretted the Centre's unwillingness to compensate, claimed that prohibition hurt the poor and authorized the government to 'act accordingly'. *Murasoli* termed the resolution as 'guidance to the government'. Meanwhile, Karunanidhi said the review was also necessitated because of 'people's welfare'.[31]

On 19 June 1971, while presenting the 1971–72 budget, Karunanidhi rhetorically wondered how long Tamil Nadu could be like 'camphor amidst a raging ring of fire', protecting itself from the neighbouring states. He announced that he would lift prohibition from 30 August. Congress criticism was sharp: '*Kamaraj padika sonnaar; Karunanidhi kudika sonnaar!*' (Kamaraj said study; Karunanidhi said drink).[32] As Kamaraj announced a protest, Karunanidhi wondered if as much as a squeak came out of Kamaraj when Mysore relaxed prohibition, and Maharashtra made it possible to drink half day. 'Did he say let those picketing [against lifting prohibition] go do it then?' he asked.

On the rainy evening of 20 July, Rajaji, who had introduced prohibition and sales tax to offset the revenue loss somewhat, showed up at the chief minister's residence to plead for the continuance of prohibition only to hear him plead his inability to heed his plea. On 20 June 1985, Karunanidhi said that he had explained to Rajaji that the government was losing some Rs 200 crore, the treasury was bankrupt, and he had heard that the Centre was planning to dismiss his government because of this. He said the move was to stave off dismissal.[33]

Poetic Sparring

On 30 August, as 7395 toddy shops and 3512 arrack shops were thrown open, and liquor flowed after thirty-four years, MGR called it a 'sad day' while Rajaji poetically vented his grief under the heading *Saaraya Sagaptham* or Arrack Era:

15 August is not a festival
30 August is the Tamil Nadu fete

The lowly rose after prohibition was lifted;
For the fallen to suffer like before

Forgetting the profound Arignar Anna
Throwing to the winds, Valluvar's words
Karunaiyaar,* who, thanks to the boon, rose to his post
Has given toddy and arrack
Debuting shops in the thousands
Let us praise the chief minister's service! . . .

While there is a shortfall of food in poor homes
There is a great carnival at liquor stores!
Hail! The one who launched the liquor stores
The chief minister of Tamil Nadu!
The blessed Karunai Selvar (Mr Compassionate)![34]

Rajaji fretted that a whole new generation that had not known the evil of liquor was now 'completely sold to the liquor monster'.[35]

On 17 September, Karunanidhi used a poets' meeting on Periyar's birthday to respond. Titled 'Oh, Old Brahmin, Your Words Have Come True', he used Tamil wordplay and facts to pillory Rajaji. He said the country knew how the permit-holding Swatantra folks had hopped from bar to bar to drink. The almanack's (read Brahmin) new rule was that the rich could drink but not the poor, even if they died of spurious liquor, he said. Karunanidhi said the boon was not from Rajaji but from the people. If prohibition was national, he would also pitch in and remove permits and not issue permits on the ruse of heart disease.

Oh, Old Brahmin, Your Words Have Come True . . .

A poem on the liquor era
Emperor Rajaji was a great sage . . .

---

* Karuna is compassion, here Karunanidhi in irony.

In Odisha when their party [was] in power
It was a flood of wine! Then,
Why his heart went barren?

He blesses me as the son of mercy
Who obtained a boon! I bow.
But it was not him—The people—
It was them—who extended their boon!

Blessed with the boon—fortified with
The courage of Periyar and Anna
Even now I say,

Listen!
If a nationwide prohibition law
On liquor is enacted
Bowing down with folded hands
I would be the first to act on it

And even after one such law
There will not be any permit
To allow a select few
To booze in the name of heart disease.

In case full details be required
I shall list it out later.[36]

Rajaji could be easily silenced. He was in his nineties, his health
was frail and his following was limited to a section of the Brahmins
and the educated. The new difficulty was MGR, who took his
propaganda role seriously. Earlier, at the general council, MGR had
pointed out that lifting prohibition was 'temporary' and that the
party should conduct a campaign on the ills of drinking. Running

with the hares and hunting with the hounds, on 12 August, the chief minister announced a committee headed by MGR with legislative council member Nagoor Hanifa, Porselvi Ilamurugu, Tamilarasi and legislator and student leader Ganesan as members. *Murasoli,* in a rare editorial leader, said it was with 'great sadness' that the decision to lift prohibition was made, and the fact that MGR headed the committee was proof of its sincerity. But sincerity was the issue. The chief minister was to launch the committee on 15 August, Independence Day. The committee would not, however, even take off.

On 13 September, in a statement, MGR advocated for a nationwide referendum for adult women to decide on prohibition. Two days later, his Sathya Studios staff swore to abstain from drinking and convert others. MGR issued a public appeal at Anna's mausoleum the following week. MGR's actions were inconvenient to the administration, and tongues started to wag. As the mausoleum show faltered, MGR reproved the journals, which said that the DMK leadership had let him down and ridiculed Vellore Narayanan's *Alai Osai* daily for the detailed headcount of 150 at the mausoleum with him, and said that he did not need to prove his popularity.

On 21 September, MGR said that some had portrayed his efforts as divisive to the Kazhagam and that it was 'completely wrong'. He claimed the Kazhagam's leaders were fully supportive, refuting that he was angling for a ministership and that his efforts were aimed towards this goal. He made it clear that he had no such thought, that he would not quit films and that he was starring in a film written by P.U. Shanmugam on continence.[37]

However, some felt that MGR's actions were intended to distance himself from a policy that womenfolk seemingly disapproved of. If MGR felt let down by the party leadership, he did not show it. If Karunanidhi wished for MGR to soft-pedal the issue, he did not mention it. Clearly, something had gone amiss between them. Busybodies and the press widened this cleavage.

Cho Ramaswamy's *Thuglak* fortnightly carried a piece by party official and *Alai Osai* (The Sound of Waves) editor, Vellore Narayanan, who lamented that the party leadership had not proceeded against MGR for his views against the party's decision on prohibition, after he had supported it at the Coimbatore meet. Narayanan finally appeared to advise Karunanidhi to safeguard his position. MGR said that Karunanidhi was not in such a 'pitiable' situation that he would have to safeguard his position. But Narayanan was right.[38]

11

Second Split

On 1 January 1972, the hike in power tariff led to a major showdown with farmers. Karunanidhi threw 30,000 farmers into jail, and sixteen died in police action. On 9 July, Kamaraj, with a black shawl around his neck, led a silent march seeking the release of farmers and talks with them. Similar rallies were conducted in all major towns.[1] The DMK administration was on its knees, and Karunanidhi admitted later that he had 'learnt a few lessons'.

In August, Kamaraj prophesied that the DMK government would fall under the weight of its actions or that people would bring it down.[2] However, trouble came from an unexpected quarter in the guise of MGR, and the lessons would be dearer.

In his autobiography, Karunanidhi theorizes that Congress (I) schemed to divide the DMK, and MGR with his personal problems went along. 'The one who planted such a poisonous seed in Mrs Indira Gandhi's mind was central minister Mohan Kumaramangalam. Having become a member of Parliament thanks to the Kazhagam's support, he began to repay his debt thus,' Karunanidhi wrote in anguish.[3] MGR, 'was the man who, only a month before (*sic*), had declared at a DMK conference [in Madurai] that the Tamils would face Indira Gandhi's military if the state autonomy demand was not conceded. Instead, Indira

Gandhi made him meet her government's income tax authorities,'
he said.[4]

Photo courtesy: SAIL

DMK's nemesis and Minister for Iron and Steel Mohan Kumaramangalam

At the 5–6 August 1972 Madurai conference, MGR's last gasp
of loyalty was declared before he called out the DMK.[5] Karunanidhi
commented: 'Isn't it the case that those who choose to betray profess
themselves as absolutely loyal? Didn't Judas, who betrayed Jesus
Christ, act so even at the last minute?'[6]

But MGR was not the only man pretending all was smooth
between them. On 28 July, felicitating MGR for the Bharat or
national best actor award, the chief minister, in the last recognition
of his debt to MGR, read the following ode on him:

The hero who shines invincibly before and after!
An embodiment of character whose fame is akin to the mount
A full moon possessing the power that even kings did not possess
Your fame should live along with the south and the southerners!

So that the hearts of those like me who had risen because of you
exult at it!

Mohan Kumaramangalam's father, P. Subbarayan, had served as
premier of Madras. Educated at Eton and Cambridge, Mohan
Kumaramangalam, a leftist, later joined Congress (I). In the new
churning of Tamil politics, he was at the mercy of the DMK for
his public career. Maran recorded that the demure Mohan, 'the
scion of a zamindar!' regretted being reduced to seeking help from
parvenus and decided to 'finish' the DMK. A defiant Karunanidhi
played into his hands. But Mohan, in retrospect, appears a
whipping boy.

Karunanidhi reckons things began to go wrong with the labour
dispute at the 16,000-employee-strong Simpson group of companies
in early 1972. Simpson was but a symptom. The DMK's labour arm,
the Labour Progressive Federation (LPF)'s strong-arm tactics saw
it displace the independent union as the lead union in Simpson on
8 May 1971.[7] Kamaraj and the Left charged the DMK with union
busting.[8] Further, the management-allied DMK union's agreement
with the management led workers to call for industrial action.[9]
Simpson now turned into a headache. The Centre got involved and
Karunanidhi capitulated, asking his man to stand down, paving the
way for elections and a compromise claiming it as a goodwill gesture.
Yet, the CPI, which was strong among factory workers, would not
forget the ordeal.

Mohan Kumaramangalam and CS, reputedly allies, had turned
vocal critics. Karunanidhi was so fed up with them that the 17
January 1972 Thanjavur general council authorized the leadership to
review its ties with Congress (I) and CPI. Another resolution singled
out Mohan Kumaramangalam's 'indifferent' and 'cavalier' attitude,
naively appealing to Indira Gandhi to keep him under check.

Meanwhile, as CS explained later, the Congress (I) 'began to
think how to displace the DMK, which was becoming entrenched

by using various methods and felt a reunited Congress could take the DMK down'.[10] That was the overt response. The covert plot's hero was MGR.

Karunanidhi said that 'now almost inimical',' the Congress (I) unsuccessfully tried to 'infiltrate' press tycoon and minister Si.Pa. Adithanar and settled on MGR, having failed with him.

> After this, Delhi's gaze fell on [my] friend MGR. They needed someone who was a strength for the DMK but, at the same time, was weak and unable to face difficulties. MGR fitted the bill.

Director General of Police K. Mohandas wrote that MGR relented.[11] MGR disclaimed quid pro quo with Congress (I) as 'contrary to truth', adding that the DMK believed that if the charge was repeated, people would believe it.[12]

Personality Cult

The issue was that the two were no more the humble twenty-three-year-old scriptwriter who had discovered his hero in MGR, the handsome thirty-year-old, or the struggling actor who had found his muse in Karunanidhi after eleven years of an uneventful film career. They were now the two major political forces in a party, the DMK, that was too small to accommodate both men. The inevitable had to happen.

Anna, Karunanidhi, MGR and Jayalalithaa were all larger-than-life personalities. Some of this metamorphosis was organic and some engineered. Leaders had long become deities. Referring to them by their names and not their titles was almost a sin. Therefore, when Durga Stalin announced Nedunchezhian by name and not his honorific 'Navalar', M.K. Stalin, her husband, slapped her 'so hard and fast' that the new bride never forgot the new code of conduct.[13]

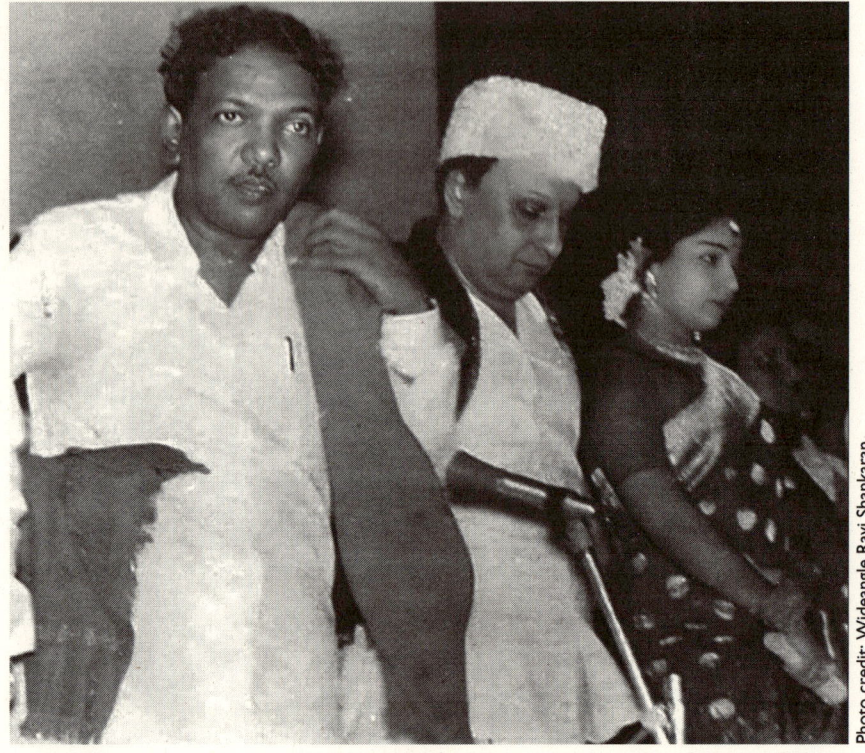

Three chief ministers in the making: Karunanidhi, MGR and Jayalalithaa in more harmonious times

Under the thrall of his new stature, Karunanidhi took a contemporary senior aside to suggest that he address him 'Kalaignar' now that he was chief minister. The intrepid contemporary, who was on a first-name basis, asked him, 'Isn't Karunanidhi your name?' The not-so-unctuous contemporary was kicked upstairs to the Rajya Sabha and made adequate amends by singing paeans to 'Kalaignar' later. In his second innings, an even more confident Karunanidhi sought recognition in ways that spawned much fawning but also fuelled criticism.

In 1971, as H.V. Hande accused Karunanidhi of promoting a 'personality cult', the chief minister shut him down with an Opposition member's comment to Rajaji that he would not be surprised 'if one day Rajaji claimed to be God Himself'.[14] Rajaji, of course, was Hande's leader. But Hande was not alone.

On 22 April 1971, Karunanidhi began addressing cadres as *Udanpirape*, or 'sibling', signifying his arrival politically. He had called himself *Maravan* (warrior) and had addressed cadres as 'Dearest comrade', or *Aruirthozha*, until then. As the aura around Karunanidhi began to be woven, on 9 June, MGR and Sathyavanimuthu declared open a housing unit called Karunanidhipuram at St Thomas Mount in his presence. On 15 July, Governor K.K. Shah, who once suggested his initials stood for 'Kalaignar Karunanidhi' Shah to show his bonhomie and compared Karunanidhi's poetic prowess to Walt Whitman's, inaugurated the Kalaignar Karunanidhi Trust for poor children.

On 14 August, Periyar breathed life into his 1968 idea of a statue for Karunanidhi. He said there were five or six statues for him, and nobody asked him if those could be erected. Similarly, one need not ask Karunanidhi, he opined, adding that when there were statues for the dead, why can't there be one for the living?[15] In 1975, the statue was declared open by Periyar's widow, making Karunanidhi only the second DMK leader after Anna with a statue in his lifetime.

The next day, an eleven-floor government building was named Karunanidhi Maaligai, or mansion. However, weeks earlier, when Annamalai University chose to confer an honorary doctorate on Karunanidhi, some felt things had gone a bit too far. Floored by the winds of change and considering Anna's erudition, Annamalai University had conferred an *honoris causa* on him, unwittingly fuelling a race amongst his successors for such recognition. Anbazhagan would have to wait another twenty years for the gesture.[16]

Calling Karunanidhi a 'man of letters,' the citation in part read:

At the comparatively young age of forty-seven he has been sky-rocketed into the position of one of India's leading political thinkers and leaders. Qualities that have helped him to achieve this are—purposive dynamism, constructive idealism, courageous thinking and daring action. He has gone all out to meet life's challenges, he fights the good fight with all his might.

Regretfully, not everyone thought so. On 22 July, a day before the award ceremony, a pamphlet purportedly issued by the state's 'Youth Congress' tastelessly described the awardee as a 'folklore writer' while another with a Marxist-Leninist bent said that only socialist societies could create jobs. Police had to quell the protest by those Karunanidhi termed 'radical students'. Later, even as students identified a body found as that of a fellow student, a judicial inquiry said it could be Udhayakumar, the dead student, adding that he may have drowned. Rajaji, however, pointed out that there was little trust in the state's judiciary, and Bhaktavatsalam claimed that the father was compelled to deny that the body was his son's.[17] Kamaraj later compared the police action to the excesses in East Pakistan.[18] However, on 26 July, Karunanidhi told the assembly that if not for the police action, they would be 'observing a moment of silence' for him.

On 1 August, CPI leader Tha. Pandian compared Karunanidhi to Maxim Gorky, who had no formal university education but whose works were texts at universities. Pandian concluded rightly that Karunanidhi richly deserved the honour. Nedunchezhian further said the university had 'elevated itself' by honouring Karunanidhi.[19] On 13 September, MGR, felicitating him, described Karunanidhi as the 'life of the four and a half crore Tamils', adding that many more doctorates awaited him.[20]

A little patience on the part of the chief minister would have pre-empted the need to justify the award. Humility and a deeper sense of self would not have led to such a situation in the first place. But the chief minister was in a hurry. Patriarchal populism had turned his birthdays into major public welfare exercises. Assertive populism saw him fetishizing state autonomy. The chief minister's regional autonomy refrain and hard-nosed style strained relations with the Centre.

As previously stated, on 26 March 1971, Sheikh Mujibur Rahman had already declared Bangladesh and the next day Maran penned a five-part essay on Bangladesh's rise. On 29 March, Karunanidhi hoped 'that no one would come forward to deny states their rights and thereby create [Mujibur] Rahmans in state after state [in India]'.[21] On 3 April and 6 December, the assembly passed resolutions condemning Pakistan and on 17 December, as India recognized Bangladesh, Karunanidhi moved a resolution felicitating the new nation.

Bangladesh and Sheikh Mujibur loomed large in Karunanidhi's mind. At the 12–13 February 1972 DMK conference at Rajapalayam, posters of the two leaders with lines on state autonomy were featured at the entrance. A booklet brought out was later destroyed 'on reflection'. In May, speaking at the Mannargudi Thanjavur district DMK conference, Periyar said that he disagreed with regional autonomy as he wished for a separate Tamil Nadu. The state government's *Tamilarasu* published the speech.[22] Rajaji, however, said regional autonomy was seeking a 'share of the booty of the licence-permit raj'.[23]

Indira Gandhi commented on the Rajapalayam conference posters as strange. On 21 May 1972, speaking at Madurai, she expressed surprise at comparisons made with Bangladesh and asked: 'What was it that moved 75 million people to such sacrifice and suffering? Can you compare it with conditions in Tamil Nadu? Can you say that this situation exists here?' The prime minister said that in the last two years, 'hardly a week has passed in Parliament when I am not blamed by the entire Opposition for favouring Tamil Nadu.' She asked, 'What would happen for instance to the market for the Coimbatore textiles or to the people from Tamil Nadu, who were employed in the public sector industries elsewhere in the country, if other States also asserted themselves likewise[?]'[24] In June, she again warned of the dangers of autonomy.[25] If the comparison to Bangladesh was silly, Indira Gandhi's concerns were also greatly exaggerated, although she appeared to believe in them.

Differences with MGR

But Karunanidhi was indifferent. The massive mandate of 1971 had set him free. Or so he thought. While Anna was coy in how he exercised power, a younger Karunanidhi was assertive. Party men with DMK veshtis and shawls as uniform were loud and ubiquitous in the corridors of power, and ministers appeared loose in dispensing favours. Kamaraj complained of corruption and the haughtiness that had come to embody the administration.

Anna had been politically deified with daily invocations and crude statues. Karunanidhi was on the path to Annahood, but there was a hitch—MGR. If Karunanidhi felt the chief ministership had taken him to another level, MGR appeared to be an independent spirit with a massive following. The party flag was often described as the 'MGR flag' and the DMK itself as the 'MGR party'. In many places, his fan clubs were the party's backbone. Anna was easy about it. Karunanidhi, like Sampath and Kannadasan, was ill at ease.

Some busybodies instigated an already stardom-conscious MGR that the party could not do without him. Even in 1960, R.M. Veerappan's intervention had staved off a fans' conference. MGR had then assured them that his actions would not cause 'anxiety' to Veerappan. But now, Karunanidhi appeared overcome with anxiety.

Karunanidhi records that MGR wished to be 'Medical Minister' (*sic*) or minister of health, and he had agreed but asked that he quit films.* 'Karunanidhi is a good story writer,' mocked MGR later.[26] R.M. Veerappan affirms that the twenty-three-year-old Jayalalithaa had put MGR up to it. MGR was 'greatly upset' when law minister Madhavan said that rules did not permit a dual role adding, 'Why do you have to be a minister? You can be above all of them. We will give you that stature and honour.'[27] But MGR had already reached that stature. When Karunanidhi pointed out that a minister-actor

---

* MGR would have the last laugh as in 2021, M.K. Stalin redesignated the health ministry as 'Medical'.

would have looked 'odd', MGR took it as a slight.[28] In retrospect, Karunanidhi could have taken the easy way out by calling the actor's bluff. However, as Karunanidhi often said, 'Hindsight is a perfect science.'

The bigger slight was Karunanidhi's eldest son, M.K. Muthu. Karunanidhi had become *Kalaignar* and *Thalaivar*. He wished to be his own man, but the masses went into raptures for one man like no other—MGR. The scriptwriter, therefore, had chosen to craft a new script with his son as the hero. On 21 September 1971, *Murasoli* officially broke the news of Muthu playing the lead role in *Pillayo Pillai* (Oh! The Son, 1972), produced by Karunanidhi's Anjugam Pictures.[29] On 21 October 1971, MGR declared the shoot open despite the underlying tensions.[30]

In March 1973, MGR dismissed talks of Muthu emerging as a competitor as 'ridiculous, silly'. No one has 'stayed on like him', and Muthu played his 'life on the stage'. 'Isn't that something? How can that be a rival to MGR?' he posed.[31]

Despite this bravado, Muthu had become an issue. Maran's brother Murasoli Selvam later alleged that MGR 'threatened' the producer who had initially intended to cast Muthu.[32] The film proved a dud.

Permissions came quickly for Muthu fan clubs from the parent organization, while those for MGR were put on hold. Further, at the DMK Madurai meeting kick-off on 4 August 1972, M.K. Muthu, dressed in military fatigues in a jeep, led a mammoth procession.[33] As tension simmered, Karunanidhi reached out to MGR through Chief Minister Farook Maricar of Puducherry, promising that the *mandrams* or fans' associations would not be an issue. However, an unsure MGR later agreed to the fateful Thirukazhukundram and Royapettah meetings, as shown below.[34]

On 9–10 August, Karunanidhi wrote two letters where he referred to his son Muthu at the rally, the praise Maran won for his speech from leaders and claimed that Madurai had never seen such a rally. But the conference had caused Karunanidhi much heartburn. He could speak for only twenty minutes, after which he 'fainted'. Kamaraj described it as the 'act's climax' while MGR reasoned later that the crowds had begun to disperse after his speech.[35] In his speech, Karunanidhi allegorically referred to Indira Gandhi as the cow and Mohan Kumaramangalam and C. Subramaniam as the calf—alluding to the Congress (I)'s symbol cow and calf. While the cow was quiet, the calves were jumping, he said.[36]

But MGR rankled more. By leaving early, the actor had dealt a serious slight in public. Each slight made the other wary, and Ma.Po.Si. records the incident as a major cause of the split.[37] The conference had begun on a bad note. Karunanidhi claimed that MGR desired an invite for Jayalalithaa, which he rejected as not befitting the Dravidian movement.[38] They chose to part company.

MGR Throws Down the Gauntlet

MGR fired the first salvo. On 8 October, at Thirukazhukundram and later that evening at Royapettah, MGR attacked the DMK head-on, asking DMK functionaries and elected representatives to disclose their assets, adding that he would bring a resolution to the general council and go to the people if he did not find support.[39] At Royapettah, MGR emphasized: 'MGR is DMK, and DMK is MGR.' Mathiazhagan, speaking earlier, had urged him to get politically more engaged. MGR said that even his little political involvement was not to the liking of some and that he pitied them. He reiterated his call for party and elected officials to account for their assets. Karunanidhi had been listening to the rebellious speech on police wireless in Madurai. MGR had crossed the Rubicon.[40]

Kannadasan now advised Karunanidhi to buy time, passing a resolution seeking accounts. Not the one to blink first, Karunanidhi indicated he would act decisively at the executive to 'finish' MGR, and there wouldn't be much trouble.[41]

Game of Chess

On 10 October, the thirty-three-member executive saw Manoharan, Sezhian, Maran and Arangannal wishing for an explanation from MGR, while a majority sought MGR's expulsion.[42] Karunanidhi said that he adopted a moderate position.[43] Consequently, the executive suspended MGR from his primary membership and other positions for discrediting the party. N.V. Natarajan briefed the press. After they fell out in 1978, Karunanidhi and Nedunchezhian blamed each other for the suspension. 'After most of the executive members and the general secretary had reached a decision, is it not my duty to acquiesce to it[?]' wrote Karunanidhi, who blamed Nedunchezhian for authorizing N.V. Natarajan to inform the press.

Nedunchezhian said that Karunanidhi was 'desperate' for action and that he had only noted the resolution and passed on the 'note' to Karunanidhi, who signed off on it.[*] When asked by N.V. Natarajan if this could be given to the press, Nedunchezhian said yes. Karunanidhi, according to him, misrepresented this singular 'yes' to depict him as the one behind MGR's suspension.[†] But all this was semantics. The situation had become inexorable. Karunanidhi had chosen to act decisively, and the executive had gone along.

MGR's fans ran amok, and lorries and buses could not ply if they did not sport MGR's image. Karunanidhi later rued that ministers could not address meetings and claimed 'hundreds of buses were set to fire'.[44] Kannadasan opined that the country had not witnessed such 'unrest' since Indira Gandhi's expulsion.[45]

MGR had become a rage. *Alai Osai* published the developments as headlines and saw the twelve-paisa paper fetch two to three rupees

---

[*] Nedunchezhian had actually recommended suspension. *Murasoli*, 9 July 1988, 3.

[†] K. Manoharan, who could not stand Nedunchezhian, writes that the resolution was crafted by Nedunchezhian. Nedunchezhian later told his friends that he had avenged himself by expelling MGR who had stood in the way of his becoming chief minister. K. Manoharan, *Thamizhagath Thalaivar Kalaignar* (Chennai: Poompuhar Pathippagam, 1988), 82–83.

in the black market.[46] Cho Ramaswamy lamented that Kamaraj was pushed to the last pages even in pro-Kamaraj dailies and journals.[47]

The next day, Karunanidhi said that MGR 'has been suspended from the party for saying publicly that there is corruption in the Kazhagam'. He added that MGR had 'neither written nor spoken to him' about the disclosure of assets. He pointed out that as early as 27 August 1969, he had moved a resolution in the assembly mandating for the first time in India that legislators, ministers and their families declare their assets, and this was happening. He said that the Kazhagam had 15 lakh members and 18,000 branches and asked if saving the party or his friend of twenty-seven years was important.

Indicating that the feud had been simmering for some time, Karunanidhi said there were reports of fan clubs removing his pictures and setting the DMK flag on fire in some places in the past weeks. The Madurai fan club had passed a resolution asking for his resignation, and Dharmapuri, Puducherry, Pandaravaadai, Madurai and other places issued pamphlets 'condemning' him and 'insulting the Kazhagam'.[48]

When the executive met again on 12 October, on Manoharan's suggestion Karunanidhi agreed to give a day for MGR to express regret. Meanwhile, there were other efforts at reconciliation. On the morning of 13 October, Periyar advised the chief minister to avoid a split. MGR had met Periyar two hours earlier at the latter's request and had complained of the corrupt legislators, the bad name for the party and him being kept in the dark on the party's financial dealings. Periyar had urged that he express regret. MGR remained noncommittal.

In a separate development that morning, Manoharan and Veerappan had indicated to Nedunchezhian and Karunanidhi that there was still room for possible reconciliation. On the afternoon of 13 October, while with MGR, Manoharan telephoned Maran to come over.[49] Listening to their exhortation, MGR almost relented but retracted after a telephone call, according to Karunanidhi.

Veerappan said MGR changed his mind after an attack on a cinema showing his film.[50]

The 13 October executive unanimously recommended expulsion. The coup de grace was achieved the following day, with E.R. Krishnan proposing the expulsion and Chittibabu seconding it, and 277 of the general council's 310 members present endorsing it. It was decided to hold meetings in 200 places to explain this action. Karunanidhi told the council:

> Everyday MGR runs prayer meetings at Sathya Studios, like Gandhi conducted prayer meetings at Sabarmati Ashram—every day, a crowd gathers—he offers advice—the papers publish it as news daily; how long will this happen—it can go on for ten days; the excitement could last for ten days; but those Opposition folks who wish for the Kazhagam to be divided are using this . . . Congress has girded its loins to repeat his (MGR's) charges; Indira Congress will use it; other parties will continue this.[51]

Even Homer sometimes nods. Karunanidhi could not have been more wrong about MGR.

MGR pointed out that he had fifteen days to respond but had been thrown out in four days. He invoked an age-old saying to ask, a 'lid could be placed on a boiling pot of rice, but could we shut up the public?' He said the executive, or some ministers, did not make up the Kazhagam, which had millions of workers. Mindful of what happened to him, his Anna DMK constitution stipulated that primary members choose the leadership.[52] That day, Karunanidhi lamented that MGR's followers were garlanding his picture with chappals, while in 1961, Anna's picture was broken only in one place.[53]

The next day, on 15 October, even as a youth at Udumalpet, unable to take MGR's expulsion, committed self-immolation, Karunanidhi addressed a public meeting at the Marina where he said:

My good friend, then and now, and I would always call him my good friend, revolutionary actor MGR has, through his unexpected criticism, caused anguish to lakhs of Kazhagam's cadres, pain to the 18,000 branch secretaries, hurt to the 135 circle secretaries, anxiety to the 14 district secretaries, and the executive and the general council . . .

If we were to present the accounts of the 18,000 branch secretaries, can you imagine how hard it would be? Is it humanly possible to scrutinise them all? Is it practical?

MGR, of course, is aware of this. Yet, he asked. Why? His motive was that he should exit or be expelled. He wished for one of the two.

The evidence is that when the 26 executive members petitioned for action against him, our eyes grew moist, and our voices trembled as we reached this decision. The decision saddened us. But MGR was happy when he learnt of it . . . He had *payasam* (sweet porridge) at the news . . .

MGR says that others entertained doubts and, therefore, he does too. This is like the Ramayana.

A washerman suspected her, so Ram sent Sita to the forest! Ram can do it! Can Ramachandran wish to drive the Kazhagam to the forest?[54]

MGR maintained:

I know the pain I suffered when I was expelled. It is because of the way they sent me out and the cause. How many elections and emergencies I would have involved myself [for the party]! When I consider that I had eaten from the same leaf,* they chased me away.[55]

---

* A Tamil expression to show the closeness between people.

In their best days of friendship, a DMK propaganda song by Nagoor
Hanifa went as follows:

Engal veetu pillai
Ezhaigalin thozhan
Thanga gunam ulla kalaimannan
Makkal thilagam engal MGR annan

He's our son
The friend of the poor
A gold-hearted king of art
'People's darling' MGR, our elder brother

Now Hanifa reflected his leader's evaluation of 'our son':
Valartha kadaa maarbil paindthathadaa
Vanjagar soozhichiyile veezhnthathadaa, saaindhadhadaa
Nandri marandhadhadaa, naanayathai izhandthadaa

Our pet 'ram' rammed our hearts*
And fell flat to traitors' plot
Forgetful of gratitude
Lost his integrity.

---

* Ram is used to signify the male sheep as well as Ramachandran.

12

Anna DMK

Pushed to the wall by his supporters, MGR floated his Anna DMK*
on 18 October 1972. With Anna's bust on the DMK flag and his
name as a prefix to the DMK, MGR laid claim to Anna's legacy.
At the DMK's urging, Anna's widow Rani sued the ADMK even
as their son Elangovan welcomed it. (She withdrew her suit later.)[1]
A sour Karunanidhi said, 'He has achieved what he wanted and
planned.'[2] Maybe. By expelling MGR, Karunanidhi had unwittingly
forced the metamorphosis of the actor-politician to a political leader.
MGR was no more his *Puratchi Nadigar*. He had catapulted him to
Puratchi Thalaivar (Revolutionary Leader).

But it was not an easy decision for MGR. Hitherto he had had
the best of both worlds—the real and the reel. And the DMK behind
him. Completely shaken by the expulsion, MGR thought he was
finished.[3] He had broken down hugging *Alai Osai's* Narayanan who
assured him that the whole of Tamil Nadu was behind him, and its
future was in MGR's hands.[4] Narayanan was not off the mark.

As Rajaji† compared MGR's expulsion to that of throwing Anna
himself out, the DMK leadership quickly dubbed MGR a Malayalee

---

* MGR's followers had renamed some units of the DMK after Anna a day earlier. The
prefix All India was added on 12 September 1976.
† Rajaji passed away on 25 December 1972.

and an 'enemy of Tamils'. On 1 December, MGR, in turn, called Karunanidhi a 'dark force', an epithet that Jayalalithaa would employ ad nauseam later.[5]

In six days, six DMK legislators had jumped ship. Karunanidhi claimed, 'If Karunanidhi's government is toppled, then only a Tamil such as Kamaraj's rule should follow. We will never allow the enemies of Tamil to succeed.'[6] As another two MLAs and an MP made their way to the ADMK, Karunanidhi said, 'In addition to MGR, even if more than 40 [MLAs] join the ADMK, I am not worried.'[7] Nedunchezhian said that 'the ADMK would disintegrate in three–four months. Its present strength is illusory.'[8]

Yet Karunanidhi employed both threat and persuasion to stanch the haemorrhage. Sivakasi legislator K. Kalimuthu heard an angry chief minister telephoning him to ask what 'mischief' he was up to as MGR's fans there had passed a resolution against the expulsion. Twice summoned to meet the chief minister, Kalimuthu, however, repaired to MGR's abode in Ramavaram instead of Gopalapuram where Karunanidhi lived. A surprised MGR said he had not expected him and if this was the 'dynamics, then we can finish them!'*[9] In contrast, Duraimurugan enjoyed a son-like relationship with the actor. Yet he told MGR that while he was 'worthy of worship', MGR was not 'a political leader', and his 'leader' was Karunanidhi.[10] Karunanidhi may not have had MGR's glamour. But he was a self-made leader of gravitas. Until he breathed his last, such diehard disciples and workers remained Karunanidhi's strength. Nonetheless, MGR was emerging as a force to reckon with.

The biggest catch for the ADMK was the articulate deputy leader of Parliament K. Manoharan, in mid-November, who called Karunanidhi a 'manic fascist'† and other names to please

---

* Karunanidhi said Kalimuthu left owing to local turf wars and on his departure had referred to him as 'God who dwells in the heart!' *Kalaignarin Kadithangal*, Vol. 7, 216.
† Karunanidhi said Manoharan was disappointed that he was not named the DMK's parliamentary head. *Murasoli*, 29 September 1980, 4.

his new leader.[11] Yet it was Mathiazhagan, feeling demoted as Assembly Speaker, who now used his perch to visit the most grief on Karunanidhi. * Karunanidhi dispatched S.D. Somasundaram thrice to dissuade him, but in the event, Somasundaram left him for MGR.[12] On 23 October, Mathiazhagan called on Rajaji, setting off a train of cataclysmic events.[13]

Periyar said: 'MGR is not ours nor is he our race' and two weeks later called to ban the ADMK.[14] Kamaraj saw no virtue in MGR, who was in cahoots with the DMK's excesses all along. He questioned his credibility.[15] The CPM took time to warm up to MGR. But it was revenge time for the CPI. M. Kalyanasundaram and Baladhandayutham, both MPs, turned MGR's self-appointed advisers so much so that Periyar commented that 'this mischief is caused by two Sat Shudras'.[16]

On 29 October, at the ADMK's public launch, the party's organizing secretary K.A. Krishnaswamy claimed 6000 branches and a million members for the new outfit.[17] Tamilvanan cynically characterized MGR's supporters as those who hated Karunanidhi and those who 'did not know' MGR.[18] On 7 December, Karunanidhi claimed that only twenty or twenty-five of the 18,000 units had switched to the ADMK.[19]

Murasoli now caricatured MGR as an old man with a hairpiece and as a buffoon and referred to the ADMK as an 'actor's party' with 'fans'. Karunanidhi tried to nip the ADMK in its bud. On 17 October, MGR formally complained to the governor of violence and repression against his followers.[20] By March 1973, Kamaraj said that it was the first time in his public career that he was witnessing the ruling party sponsoring 'an orgy of violence against the Opposition'.[21]

---

* Mathiazhagan formally joined the ADMK in March 1973 saying that it was the 'true DMK'. *Navamani*, 10 March 1973, 1. He returned to the DMK in November 1973 and on 25 April 1974 become the deputy chairman of the state Planning Commission. *Murasoli*, 26 April 1974, 1.

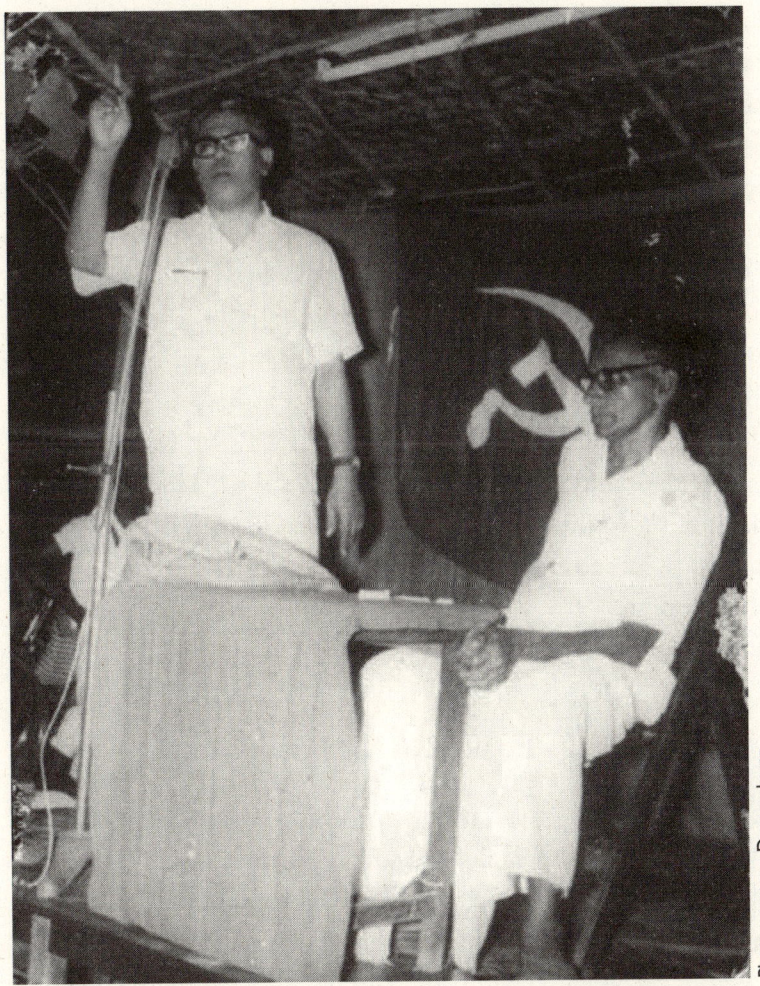

Photo courtesy: Devasankaran

The CPI's feisty Baladhandayutham addressing a meeting

To MGR, the DMK was the 'Karunanidhi party', and all except
Karunanidhi were clean.[22] Aided by the CPI, MGR systematically
threw dirt on Karunanidhi, strengthening Kamaraj's and Rajaji's
refrain on corruption and the precipitous fall in public standards.
On 4 November, MGR, accompanied by Kalyanasundaram, handed
over a memorandum of thirty-two charges to Governor Shah to
be forwarded to the President. Shah said he was constitutionally

required to first verify the facts with the state government.[23] On
7 November, MGR presented the memorandum to the President
seeking a commission of inquiry against the Tamil Nadu cabinet,
DMK district secretaries, officials named by him and officials and
persons abetting the 'corrupt ministers and officials'.[24] MGR said
later that he would not be surprised if the DMK ministry were to
fall, claiming that those who had crossed over to him were 'above
corruption' and no one could escape an inquiry by joining his party.[25]
But these moves to topple the Karunanidhi ministry came to naught.
MGR was still an unknown political commodity.

Dated 7 November and 20 December, CPI's M. Kalyanasundaram
and K. Baladhandayutham, legislators K.T.K. Thangamani, K.T.
Raju, and P. Manickam and M.V. Sundaram and S. Narayanan
addressed a memorandum with twenty charges to the President.[26]
On 1 December 1975, K. Manoharan and G. Viswanathan presented
the last charge.[27]

'Planks Soaked in the Same Puddle'

On 8 November at Thiruvathipuram, Kamaraj famously summed up
the two Kazhagams as 'planks soaked in the same puddle', making short
work of MGR's dissembling claims. On Karunanidhi's statements on
Kamaraj succeeding him, Kamaraj said the chief minister had hitherto
described him as 'an enemy of Tamils' and wondered, 'Why this
drama? To cheat whom?' He concluded that people realized there was
little difference between the DMK and the ADMK.[28]

Kamaraj was wrong. On 10 November, the ADMK and CPI
joint rally against the DMK administration was so well attended
that Rajaji saw 'proof' that the Karunanidhi government should go.[29]
Mathiazhagan was seen witnessing the rally. On 12 November, the
Congress (I) high command called the developments in the DMK
a 'purely internal matter' while observing that the Centre should
investigate the corruption charges.[30]

On 13 November, as the assembly convened, MGR said, 'Today's government has lost the confidence of its party and the people. In this situation, is it within the rules and code of conduct that this ministry continues?' Karunanidhi said he was silently watching the 'calf attacking its keeper'.[31] When MGR raised the issue again later, the Speaker commented, 'An extraordinary issue' that called for an extraordinary solution had been raised. 'Thus, MGR asks you if you will face the people today. Does the chief minister wish to respond to that?' he added gratuitously. As the chief minister waved 'no', Mathiazhagan said, 'that a majority of legislators are there is undeniable' however, since a 'tense, extraordinary situation prevailed', he advised that the chief minister 'magnanimously go to the people and seek a fresh mandate' and adjourned the assembly until 5 December 'to give time to the chief minister' to consider his 'suggestion'.[32]

A constitutional coup appeared afoot. The governor prorogued the House the next day. MGR called for a state-wide shutdown on 15 November and later claimed that 'people have spoken' and that the government should step down. On 16 November, Mathiazhagan challenged the governor's action as lacking good faith. MGR and CPI's K.T.K. Thangamani filed similar petitions. That day, DMK's N. Veerasamy and a few others gave notice of a motion to remove the Speaker. Additionally, the 183 members of the DMK and allies addressed a letter asking the Speaker to quit and forwarded it to the governor.

On 26 November, ADMK and CPI voters visited their MLAs to urge their resignation or withdrawal of support to the Karunanidhi ministry. Karunanidhi invited four representatives to his residence and sarcastically remarked later that 63,000 had voted for him, but only 500 had shown up. He said he was not sure how many of them were his constituents.[33]

On 28 November, the governor summoned the House for 2 December and, the following day, sent a message to the assembly listing the agenda and any other business, an indirect reference to the notice for the removal of the Speaker.

On 3 December, police entered the Clive Hostel of St Joseph's College in Tiruchi, leaving students in 'pools of blood' and one dead. A judicial inquiry pointed to police excess and busmen collaboration. The incidents came in handy for the Opposition to paint the DMK administration as repressive and high-handed. However, there were even more serious issues at stake.[34]

2 December 1972 Assembly Events

On the morning of 2 December, MGR had given notice of a censure motion. Acknowledging receipt of a no-confidence motion against himself, the Speaker said he would allow discussion the following day. The chief minister observed that Mathiazhagan had 'lost the confidence of the House long ago'. The Speaker replied that it was 'a matter of opinion'. As they continued to argue, the Speaker remarked that Karunanidhi was 'living in a land of fiction' and that the 'people will soon give their verdict'.

Meanwhile, Nedunchezhian wanted the no-confidence motion against the Speaker, who had 'lost the confidence of 184 members' to be given precedence. The Speaker, however, ruled that MGR's censure motion would take precedence and invited him to speak on it. Nedunchezhian now moved a resolution that the Deputy Speaker preside over the House. A separate chair was placed before the Speaker's rostrum for Deputy Speaker P. Srinivasan. Srinivasan allowed N. Veerasamy to move his motion, put it to vote and announced that it was carried.[35] Amidst the uproar, Karunanidhi presented the supplementary estimates for 1972–73.

Consequently, DMK members and the Opposition spoke on the respective motions. MGR spoke for over ninety minutes, waving some papers although his mike was switched off. At 1.30 p.m., both chairs extended the proceedings. After expunging each other's proceedings, the chairs adjourned the House to 4 December. Mathiazhagan left at 2 p.m. The Opposition left with him. Srinivasan left half an hour later.

Outside the House, a chappal thrown from the first floor landed close to MGR's car, leading to his famous statement that the 'assembly is dead'. Later, in a joint statement, Congress (O) and the Swatantra said that 'Mathiazhagan and Karunanidhi appear to have taken this *kudumba pasam* [family affection] to its logical and extreme end. They have, therefore, begun to feel that the assembly is their family property.'[36]

On 7 December, even as the Opposition boycotted the House,[37] Karunanidhi moved a confidence vote, which was carried out on 11 December. He wondered about the need for an inquest when there was no corruption. [38] That day, the Madras High Court held that the Speaker's removal was not 'illegal or unconstitutional'.[39] That month, Mathiazhagan called on Indira Gandhi in Delhi to press for an inquiry commission on the charges.

On 15 November, Indira Gandhi forwarded the charges to Karunanidhi. Projecting a picture of nonchalance, Karunanidhi mirthfully commented: 'Saw, enjoyed reading it (charges). There is nothing new there."[40] But the charges would come to haunt him. In his 286-page response dated 14 December with his statement of assets and that of his ministers, Karunanidhi described them as 'extremely frivolous, vexatious and false' and noted that the state cabinet was not accountable to the Centre and that it cannot be subject to inquiry. He said MGR had enacted a 'stunt' in Chennai and Delhi, and the "'political Machiavellism (*sic*) of the Communist Party" lent respectability to the gimmick'. He referred to the phrases 'it is believed', 'further believed', 'generally believed' and 'widely believed' in the document to show the loose nature of the charges. [41] Karunanidhi contended that if a government had to change because

---

* On 14 December, Karunanidhi provided comments to the charges. On 10 January and 5 February 1973, MGR and Kalyanasundaram respectively submitted rejoinders. Karunanidhi provided further comments on 28 May 1973. The DMK government published the memos, comments, rejoinders and answers as three booklets.

of defections, elections would have been held every five months and not five years.[42]

Following a meeting with the prime minister and ministers in Delhi in early January 1973, Karunanidhi claimed they had 'laughed' when he pointed out some of MGR's more 'absurd' charges.[43]

To take the wind out of the Opposition's sails, the Public Men's Conduct Enquiry bill was introduced on 12 February, providing for investigation against ministers and legislators and three years of jail if the charges were not proven.[44] MGR dubbed it the 'black act' even as Kamaraj described it a 'dangerous act'.[45] However, these gestures would endear Karunanidhi to Sarvodaya leader Jayaprakash Narayan (JP), who took them at face value.

On 25 December 1972, Rajaji would breathe his last.

Dindigul By-Election

The Dindigul by-election on 21 May 1973 was the first opportunity for MGR to prove he was the messiah in waiting, Karunanidhi that his strength was intact, and Kamaraj that MGR was the false messiah. On 11 May, MGR's fans celebrated the release of MGR's *Ulagam Sutrum Vaaliban* (Globe Trotting Youth), with a rally in Madurai with the slogan, 'Sari here; where is he?' Madurai Muthu had vowed to don a sari if the movie was released. The administration did all in its power to scupper its release but failed.[46]

Dindigul saw the ADMK's K. Mayathevar, fighting on the twin leaves symbol, secure 2,60,930 of a total of 5,05,253 votes. With 1,19,032 votes, Kamaraj's candidate V.C. Sithan claimed second place. The DMK finished a humiliating third with 93,496 votes, and the Congress (I) candidate lost his deposit. Karunanidhi recorded Dindigul as a 'great defeat in the DMK's history' and a speed breaker for all future victories. The mood in the DMK camp was sullen. CPM mouthpiece *Theekadhir* (Flame) published the trivia that Maran had stepped out during the counting and, to a query on the trends, responded irritably, 'In the next elections, Jayalalithaa will win.' Little could Maran have known then of his prescience.[47]

As MGR called for his immediate resignation and mid-term polls, Karunanidhi compared the defeat to the recent defeats of Sheikh Mujibur's Awami League in two parliamentary seats and claimed, 'Film glamour had temporarily eclipsed sacrifice, principle, industry, political heredity and achievements.'[48]

Kamaraj, however, suggested that MGR was a thief who stole the fruits of his work:

> We had galvanized all the Opposition sentiments for six years and prepared the people. We were the ones who worked, seeded, watered, and weeded. Someone else is rushing to harvest. That is thieving. He is stealing what we have saved. At least should not the people have sense?[49]

MGR had destroyed Congress (O)'s dreams of a comeback. On 14 August, Kamaraj met Indira Gandhi in Delhi, indicating a potential detente.

The echoes of Dindigul were soon heard within the DMK too. The general council meeting in June earlier had asked party members in nominated positions to make way for apolitical people not to approach authorities except for public causes and lessees to return government lands. It authorized the reintroduction of prohibition in stages.[50]

When ADMK members connected the reintroduction to the DMK's defeat, Karunanidhi said that if people were sober, they would mostly vote for the 'good people', which is why his administration had reconsidered it, implying that the vote for the ADMK had been done in a state of intoxication.[51]

Allahabad, Muster Roll, Katchatheevu

Close on the heels of Dindigul came the Opposition's 14 October social justice conference in Allahabad. Karunanidhi records that his participation was resented in Delhi. As posters in Hindi proclaiming, 'Ram's enemy Karunanidhi' greeted him, Karunanidhi said that Ram's enemy was Ravana and not him. Allegorically comparing states to a daughter-in-law unable to cook since the mother-in-law had provisions under lock and key, Karunanidhi pointed out that even digging on a national highway to install a water tap required the Centre's nod. He recommended reservations for the backward in education and jobs in central government institutions, sowing the seeds for the Mandal Commission.[52]

Back home, the Rs 2-crore Muster Roll Scandal of phantom workers at the Chennai Corporation in November added to Karunanidhi's woes.[53] As the DMK Mayor Munusamy was arrested, a furious Karunanidhi shouted to Chief Secretary Sabanayagam: 'Am I running the government or you!?' Sabanayagam explained that the vigilance inquiry had implicated the mayor and offered to resign. Karunanidhi explained that 'Munuswamy's wife and children had come crying, tearing their hair and clothes asking him what he had done to her husband—an old-timer, loyal DMK worker of his—and so Karunanidhi got worked up.'[54] The scandal saw the arrest and prosecution of two former mayors and thirty-seven others and Karunanidhi dissolving the Corporation and later citing these as impartiality on his part. *Kalki,* however, called for the Local Administration Minister Anbil Dharmalingam to step down owning moral responsibility*.[55]

Periyar's Death

On 24 December 1973, Periyar passed away. Karunanidhi records that he wanted state honours for the Dravidian patriarch. When Sabanayagam pointed out that Periyar had not held any office, Karunanidhi wondered if Gandhi had held any. Sabanayagam then argued that Gandhi was the father of the nation. Karunanidhi

---

* Dharmalingam had earlier resigned on 10 March 1972 and was re-inducted on 2 September 1972.

retorted: 'Periyar is the father of Tamil Nadu.' Rajaji and Periyar, the two colossuses who had straddled India, were no more.

Resolution on State Autonomy

On 29 January 1974, Karunanidhi complained that he was not consulted on the India–Sri Lanka communiqué on stateless persons that day, saying this was the 'respect' that the Centre accorded an Opposition-ruled state.[56] On 2 February, at the launch of Maran's *State Autonomy*, the chief minister said the inability of chief ministers to hoist the national flag on Independence and Republic Days showed how the Centre 'neglected' the states.[57]

In the 24 February Coimbatore assembly and Parliament by-elections, and the elections to the Puducherry assembly, the DMK faced a rout.[58] Despite the setback, Karunanidhi remained buoyant and combative. On 12 March, speaking at the legislative council, he threatened to go on a procession with the Rajaraja statue to the Big Temple and to expel the ASI from Mahabalipuram.[59] As previously stated, the ASI had disallowed the installation of the statue within the temple.

On 9 April, Karunanidhi said he would follow a 'sons of the soil' policy (which he announced on 15 July) and in an indirect reference to MGR's Keralite origins said that 'in south India, there can be only one Kerala; there is no room for two Keralas in India', and suggested 'those from other states live [with that consciousness in mind]'.[60]

The culmination of this assertiveness was the 16 April resolution on state autonomy, which sought to invert the balance of power towards the states on whose strong shoulders the Centre would come to rest.* Introducing the motion, Karunanidhi cited the DMK

---

* In April 1971 the Sezhian-Maran Committee on the Rajamannar Committee's observations was formed. Its 33-page report was endorsed on 8 January 1974 by the

giving up Dravida Nadu as 'ardent patriotism' and the Rs 6 crore National Defence Fund contribution to discourage 'unwarranted and unnecessary doubts' on the move. The Opposition nonetheless viewed it as a Trojan Horse for secession.

The resolution sought to 'effect immediate changes in the Constitution'.[61] However, Karunanidhi said the resolution was not brought forward because he thought the Centre would concede the demand 'the next day', terming it the beginning of the democratic revolution that India was to witness. Karunanidhi compared India to a man freed from prison, unable to embrace his child as his hands and legs were still bound as he had forgotten to remove the chains in the joy of freedom. Similarly, 'India has become free. Then, why should its limbs, namely the states, be kept bound by the chains of concentration of power in the Centre?' he posed. He pointed out that the Constitution was 'not immutable' and wondered if the 'domestic colony' situation should not be 'eradicated'. *Murasoli* said it was the 'first salvo fired' against the system.[62]

Constitutional Changes Sought

The DMK government suggested provisions empowering the Centre or Parliament vis-à-vis the states be removed, the removal of the institution of the governor and the chief justice to take charge during the interregnums between governments, an Inter-State Council, presidential assent for state bills to be omitted and precedence to the state law in the concurrent list; the finance commission to be a permanent body and members appointed in consultation with the Inter-State Council; a Federal Debt Commission to examine the debts of states and in time to function as a Federal Development Bank dispensing loans; a Relief Fund for

---

general council and was adopted on 20 April 1974 after a cabinet discussion. *Murasoli*, 9 January 1974, 1; *Murasoli*, 10 January 1974, 1; *Murasoli*, 18 February 1978, 1.

each state, a statutory independent experts' Planning Commission advising and recommending on state-formulated schemes for consideration by the Finance Commission; states to have the power to start and carry on new industries and foreign exchange provided by means of block grants; high courts as the highest court except in constitutional and inter-state issues; appointment of high court judges vested with the states; a federal and state civil service; Rajya Sabha with equal representation for all states like the US Senate; Parliamentary seats not to go below that decided in 1951; continuation of English; inter-water disputes referred to the Supreme Court by the Centre failing which the parties could refer and a bench of all judges to hear it; all ocean resources within the territorial waters adjacent vested in the state; and finally, amendments to the Constitution to be ratified by all state legislatures. The government paper proposed a new federal and state list and two lists on subjects to be transferred from the Union and concurrent lists to the state list. Unsurprisingly, archaeology was one of the subjects to be transferred from the concurrent to the state list.[63]

Debate

Manali Kandasamy's Tamil Nadu Communist Party, a DMK-aligned breakaway group from the CPI, IUML, Forward Bloc and Tamilarasu Kazhagam supported the resolution. The Congress and communist parties, and the ADMK opposed the resolution.

CPI's K.T.K. Thangamani called it an omnibus resolution wanting the 'entire Constitution to be recast'.[64] Congress (O)'s J. James and ADMK's P. Srinivasan cited the DMK's 1972 Rajapalayam conference, the refrain of Bangladesh and comparisons with Sheikh Mujibur as betraying the DMK's intentions. James said the resolution desired a weak Centre, wondered who would bear the responsibility to ensure the state's economies and worried that the proposed model would be harmful. James posed to the IUML the fate of the minorities if the Hindu majoritarian Jan Sangh was voted to power in a state, to which Karunanidhi posed, what if they were to be elected to power in the Centre? He would have scarcely imagined that his DMK would be part of such an arrangement in twenty-five years.[65]

ADMK's G.R. Edmund suggested granting the DMK demand would be akin to 'handing over a sharp sickle to a thief' and famously derided the Rajamannar recommendations as unfit for even a high schooler to learn anything from. Ponnappa Nadar of the Congress (O) said he did not see Tamil Nadu in fetters as portrayed by the chief minister. [66] Congress (I)'s T.N. Anandanayaki sarcastically wondered if hunger and famine would vanish if the DMK was granted its demand on a platter. [67]

Karunanidhi maintained that he sought state autonomy 'for all' and explained that even state autonomy 'won't be enough' to act on Katchatheevu, which the Centre was considering ceding to Sri Lanka. Desiring that the states decide their fiscal contribution rather than the Centre, he said that of the state's tax contribution of Rs 395.43 crore in 1974–75, only Rs 242 crore would be returned to it. He described the central government as 'illusory', seen only at the time of the budget, adding that the one intertwined with the common man was the state. After five days of discussions and his 110-minute reply, on 20 April, as the Congress (I) failed to empathize with him, an exasperated chief minister said, 'Exactly why the heck we ask for this.' In closing, he said the DMK's patriotism was second to none.[68] That day, the resolution was put to vote amidst the ADMK walkout and carried.[69]

The debate moved to the legislative council from 23 to 27 April, where a member again cited Rajapalayam. Deputy Chairman Ma.Po.Si. came to Karunanidhi's defence when he said, 'Even if four crore Tamils turned into Mujibur Rahman, Tamil Nadu would not become independent. If a single Indira Gandhi were to turn

into Yahya Khan, it would become an independent country!'*[70]
Karunanidhi himself told the legislative council:

> The banyan tree's base does not weaken when the props get
> strong. The banyan stands strong together with the props—
> similarly, states equipped with additional powers would only lead
> to strengthening the Centre. That is how it should be. Ambedkar
> has said that the word 'Union' has been used instead of 'federal'
> and notwithstanding this, our Constitution is federal in nature.
> To aspire for that federal principle and autonomy element to
> bloom fully and emit fragrance is not separatist advocacy.[71]

On Katchatheevu, Karunanidhi pointed to West Bengal Chief
Minister Dr B.C. Roy, who had moved the Supreme Court on the
transfer of Beru Bari to East Pakistan and obtained the ruling that the
transfer required a constitutional amendment. Karunanidhi said that
his government was the successor to B.C. Roy's 'feelings of affinity
for the state'.[72] But Karunanidhi was no Roy. Although he put up
a fierce façade of opposition, he told the prime minister's emissary
G. Ramachandran that 'to protect his political turf, he would take a
stand contrary to the Government of India, but she should go ahead
with the decision'.[73]

On 27 April, in his reply, Karunanidhi described the extant
powers to a shirt stitched for a four-year-old asked to be worn by an
adult.[74] The chief minister said a 'major duty' of his public life was
accomplished, and he looked forward to the moment to work 'without
regard for office' towards the ideal.[75] ADMK walked out. The motion
was put to vote and was passed with 161 for and 23 against.[76]

In retrospect, the resolution was, at best naïve or sunken cost
fallacy. Only seven months earlier, on 14 October, Karunanidhi

---

* On 26 April 1973, Karunanidhi elevated Ma.Po.Si. as deputy chairman of the
legislative council.

had claimed in Allahabad that Congressmen wanted to dismiss his government because of his demand.[77] On 17 October, the Anandpur Sahib resolution anchored in Sikh rights seeking a larger Punjab with its constitution and only perfunctorily mentioning federalism augured ill and may have permanently dented Karunanidhi's more reasonable demand.

Cabinet Changes and *Thamizhinath Thalaivar*

On 4 May 1974, Karunanidhi dropped Sathyavanimuthu from the cabinet for breach of collective responsibility and for criticizing the government, turning his ministry into an all-male one. N. Rajangam was inducted as Adi Dravida welfare minister in her place, and C.V.M. Annamalai was inducted as backward classes minister.[78] Earlier, on 1 March, the Adi Dravida Housing Welfare Corporation, aiming to build one lakh houses in 1975–76, was formed.[79]

Sathyavanimuthu maintained she had been axed for floating the Dalit League, of which, she said, Karunanidhi had made a 'big deal' at the executive.[80] She alleged discrimination in the administration, pointed out the absence of Adi Dravidas in the organization—not even a circle or a district secretary—and said that Adi Dravida legislators were not a concession from the party but were a result of reserved seats. She polled fewer votes in the general council race than Karunanidhi's third son, M.K. Stalin, and how could she 'stomach this?'[81] At twenty-one, Stalin may have been the youngest in the general council. That day, *Murasoli* began using the moniker *Thamizhinath Thalaivar* or the leader of the Tamil nation for Karunanidhi.[82]

Katchatheevu

On 28 June, India ceded Katchatheevu to Sri Lanka. An all-party meeting was called the next day to register protest. Karunanidhi said he had warned Indira Gandhi on her return from Sri Lanka on a hasty decision, adding, 'At least the day before the agreement, they could have said "come immediately" and I would have rushed.' He would not blame Indira Gandhi's government but the Constitution and said, 'the foundation of that constitutional edifice should be destroyed . . .'

> It is Katchatheevu today
> Rameshwaram could be tomorrow
> Dhanushkodi day after
> Perhaps Madurai after that . . .

he remarked at a public meeting.[83]

But Karunanidhi was only being partially truthful. MGR rightly wondered if Karunanidhi would reveal the details of the 19 June meeting in Madras with Foreign Secretary Kewal Singh and holding him 'fully responsible' for his 'failure to guide the Centre properly on the Katchatheevu issue', asked that he step down. MGR also advocated that the Tamil Nadu assembly resign en masse to protest the ceding of Katchatheevu. Karunanidhi, in return, wondered if MGR would ask Indira Gandhi to resign.[84]

On 19 June, Kewal Singh, accompanied by B.K. Basu, the director of the historical division, had obtained the chief minister's 'general acceptance' to the Centre's plans to cede Katchatheevu to Sri Lanka. But Karunanidhi had also indicated that 'for obvious political reasons, he could not be expected to take a public stand in favour of it', but promised to see that the backlash did not blow up. Kewal Singh asked that nothing be done to embarrass the Centre or turn it into a state vs Centre issue. The foreign secretary reminded him that the state had been kept informed 'throughout the negotiations'.

The meeting had lasted an hour; Chief Secretary Sabanayagam and later Home Secretary S.P. Ambrose were present with

Karunanidhi. The chief minister had wondered if the prime minister had taken the Opposition into confidence and was told that only one or two senior cabinet ministers were in the know. The prime minister wished to 'have Tamil Nadu's views before discussing it with Opposition leaders'. Karunanidhi had also wondered if the signing of the agreement could be deferred by another two years and was told of 'internal' and 'external constraints' and the 'urgency and need for a bilaterally negotiated compromise settlement.' The foreign secretary indicated that Sri Lanka had given concessions in return that it was unwilling to initially, and international arbitration or, for that matter, 'strong feelings prevalent in Tamil Nadu' would not be helpful to India in its dealings with Sri Lanka.[85] Karunanidhi seemed to understand. In his desire to rise to the occasion to become a statesman, he had not foreseen the difficulties ahead for the Indian fishermen and how the issue would come to haunt him.

Unaware of his leader's complicity, on 23 July 1974, the DMK's parliamentary leader Era. Sezhian called the agreement 'pure surrender' and the move 'an unholy and disgraceful act of statesmanship unworthy of any government'. The ADMK's K. Manoharan also termed it 'unholy' and dubbed it 'the worst agreement signed by any civilised country'. Both the DMK and ADMK members walked out. CPI's M. Kalyanasundaram welcomed the agreement but rightly foresaw that Indian fishermen would have problems fishing up to and beyond Katchatheevu after the agreement.[86]

Karunanidhi now engaged in damage control. The 7 July general council passed a resolution that the Centre reconsider its decision, and on 14 July, the DMK held a protest. But Karunanidhi was locking the stable after letting go of the horse. At the Marina that evening, he reiterated that a Tamil should rule the state and dubbed the call for resignation as the ADMK's 'mantra' for they had no other policy or ideal.[87] On 21 August, Karunanidhi moved a resolution on Katchatheevu that said his government was not consulted: 'I repeat.

This government was not given any signals . . . and wholeheartedly say it was not a party (to the decision).'[88]

Prohibition

Earlier, on 14 August, announcing that prohibition would be reintroduced in two stages, Karunanidhi said the 'thorn that had pierced the heart' had been removed.[89] On 15 August, Karunanidhi became the first chief minister to hoist the national flag at Fort St George, a symbolic concession.[90] The Congress (O) promptly wondered if the 'right' would bring the price of rice down. Karunanidhi retorted that it was a matter of self-respect and wondered if prices had come down in the last twenty years when the governor hoisted the flag.[91] From 15 September, arrack shops downed their shutters.

In December 1974, Karunanidhi effected a cabinet reshuffle, demoting Anbil Dharmalingam to information and moving Madhavan from industries to food. Mannai Narayanasamy was moved to municipal administration.[92] Chief Minister and party head Karunanidhi appeared to be in total control of the government and party. The Emergency was to test both.

13

EMERGENCY

The year 1975 had not begun well. Strikes began in early January in the Christian Medical College (CMC) hospital, and fifteen employees were fired for indiscipline. The issue had come to the fore much earlier, on 24 October 1974. In late February 1975, Karunanidhi suggested reinstatement of the employees to end the strike, but the management would not hear of it. On 16 March, Karunanidhi justified his suggestion by citing Simpsons and other instances where such a gesture had led to resolution. He denied power and water had been cut to the CMC, said the management had 'influential backing', and self-pityingly added that his only fault was 'going to the succour of Harijan workers' and the Christian hospital was unwilling 'to forgive', which was 'the cardinal principle of Christianity'. In the end, Karunanidhi said he would provide alternate jobs for the dismissed, including the eleven Dalit Christians.[1]

The previous day at a public meeting, CS spoke about the state's interference in the CMC issue, adding he would return after 20 March to review how relief funds for drought were spent before sanctioning further relief. On 17 March, a touchy Karunanidhi said Tamils were a 'people of honour', rejected central 'alms' and appealed for public contributions the following day, adding that CS viewed a state government as a 'slave'.[2, 3] From 21 March, *Murasoli* began publishing the contributions.[4] On 5 November, the chief minister indicated a special central grant of Rs 7 crore, of which 70 per cent was a loan and 30 per cent subsidy. Yet, the major burden of the Rs 58.8 crore relief works was accomplished by the state itself, he claimed later.[5]

Kamaraj's Dilemma

Meanwhile, in a major tour in the summer of 1975, his last, Kamaraj, compared MGR to Maricha, the golden deer (in the Ramayana) and exhorted womenfolk not to be ensnared by the 'illusion'. He noted he was the first to 'congratulate' Anna, but seeing the 'growing pain of the ordinary people and the corruption,' he said it would have amounted to 'betrayal' if he had kept silent. He asked that they not be deceived a third time.[6] Kamaraj warned that the Congress (I) was about to repeat the same mistake as in 1971, except this time it would go with the ADMK, earthily describing the move as 'leaving the ghost and embracing the vampire'.[7]

Worse still for Kamaraj, JP, spearheading a campaign against corruption, seemed to hold tight to the 'ghost'. On Karunanidhi's invitation, JP declared open the Rajaji Memorial on the evening of 5 May and the following day noted at the Marina meeting that unlike Congress (I) chief ministers H.N. Bahuguna and Abdul Gafoor, facing corruption charges, Karunanidhi had tabled his response in the assembly and ordered an open inquiry. JP rejected MGR's charges against the DMK as baseless and abusive.[8] MGR wondered why JP, who was critical of Indira Gandhi, was not critical of Karunanidhi. The next day, JP wanted Kamaraj to break the deadlock of Opposition unity—translation—work with the DMK. JP later recorded that Kamaraj was not pleased with his speeches on his tour. Kamaraj was in an unenviable position. His contemporary

Congress (O) leaders and JP saw Indira Gandhi as the principal evil. Kamaraj felt that in comparison to the Kazhagams, she was the lesser evil.

That day, heeding JP's request, Karunanidhi announced that the state's lottery scheme would end on 15 September 1975.[9] The personal relationship that Karunanidhi built with JP was such that he would later invite him to his son Stalin's wedding on 20 August 1975. JP, who was in jail, was touched.[10]

On 15 June 1975, the DMK marked a 'surge day' to press the long-standing demands such as the Salem Steel Plant, Kanniyakumari Railway Line, Neyveli Second Mine, Kalpakkam, Sethusamudram, Cauvery and the Krishna waters. Karunanidhi said those schemes were moving at the speed of a 'tortoise on an oily glass plate'.

Opposition to the Emergency

Close to midnight on 25 June, the President proclaimed an internal Emergency, suspending civil liberties and meetings in open spaces, and introducing press censorship. Hundreds of Opposition leaders, including JP and over 1,10,000 others, were detained under the Maintenance of Internal Security Act (MISA) and Defense and Security of India Rules.[11] Rajaji's words had come true. On 12 June, the Allahabad High Court struck down Indira Gandhi's election to Parliament for electoral irregularities.

On the 26th and well through the next morning, Karunanidhi was closeted with Nedunchezhian, Anbazhagan and a few others on the DMK's response. On 27 June, the executive took up the Karunanidhi-crafted resolution. Describing the Emergency as the 'inauguration of dictatorship', the resolution sought its immediate withdrawal, the release of leaders and the lifting of press censorship. It was adopted unanimously by sixty-three of the seventy-five members present.[12] *Murasoli* carried the headline 'Indira Gandhi becomes a dictator' in a cartoon depicting her transformation into the Nazi dictator.

There was no going back now. Later, in 1994, Karunanidhi claimed a Union minister (most likely CS) came home to advise that he retract the resolution and, in return, promised his government's extension, as in Kerala. Karunanidhi says he chose not to bend.[13] But the relationship was beyond mending, and the Emergency was just the last straw. That MGR and the CPI hastily welcomed the move further narrowed Karunanidhi's options. Cho Ramaswamy describes Karunanidhi as 'a reluctant opponent . . . [who] later on, . . . put on the mantle of a great fighter against the Emergency'.[14]

Karunanidhi took care to show that the opposition was not from his administration. Besides, he even used the Emergency and the dreaded MISA provisions to suppress opposition and blank out criticism.[15] The party and not the government had adopted the resolution. But these nuances were lost on Indira Gandhi, who was under a siege mentality. On 30 October, when ADMK's P. Srinivasan wondered why he had not moved an official resolution, Karunanidhi famously replied, 'A warrior would know which hand should hold the sword and which the shield.'[16] The speech issued as a booklet titled *Sword and Shield* was banned in February of the following year.

On 1 July, the prime minister announced the twenty-point programme to rein in prices, alleviate rural indebtedness and increase production. Karunanidhi promptly welcomed it, hoping for further 'progressive measures', including nationalizing major industries. However, on 4 July, Maran told the US consul general that the DMK was prepared for the long haul, that Indira Gandhi was wooing Kamaraj, for with him beside her, she would feel emboldened to strike at the DMK. On the other hand, if the DMK and Kamaraj were to join forces, she 'will not be able to control the situation in Tamil Nadu'.[17] That day, Kamaraj fretted to Karunanidhi and Nedunchezhian that 'The country is lost!' However, he counselled patience when Karunanidhi offered to quit and join the resistance under his leadership. Sanjiva Reddy, too, counselled patience. Karunanidhi recorded that both leaders had pointed out that the 'breeze of independence' still wafted in Tamil Nadu.

Marina Speech

Two days later, promoted only by their party titles, the DMK's top three addressed a gathering at the Marina where Karunanidhi clarified the rally's purpose was to 'safeguard democracy' and not to criticize Indira Gandhi.[18] However, carried away by the enormity of the moment, Karunanidhi's speech was laced with biting sarcasm and pluck. Pointing out that the 'great change' of 1969 would have gone astray if not for the DMK, Karunanidhi crowed: 'V.V. Giri was elected President! Indira madam could continue in office!' because of the DMK. If the DMK had chosen to hold back then, 'What would have happened to India?' he posed rhetorically. He meant Indira. 'The DMK is accused of treason. We gave six crores for the [1971] war fund. Is that treason?' he asked.

Karunanidhi said that his administration had launched and implemented fifteen items of the twenty-point programme years ago and sought funds for the rest. He noted that 30,000 houses for Adi Dravidas and plans for 5000 houses for fishermen were underway. He said the twenty-point programme fell short when compared to the vision of the DMK administration and its programmes.

> Where is all this in the twenty-point program? Should we not ask how many industries were nationalized following the banks? What happened to nationalization after that? Is there a scheme such as Tamil Nadu's housing scheme for Adi Dravidas elsewhere? [Is there a] Slum Clearance Board? . . .
>
> How long will this situation last?
>
> A week, a month, a year, or longer—it is not clear!

What is our situation—unclear!
But we are not stuck—nor concerned![19]

A year later, however, he would claim 'with heartfelt sincerity' that his party felt 'heartfelt love' for the twenty-point programme compared to other parties and 'no one could match the DMK to propagate' it.[20]

Then, Karunanidhi said he had asked his colleagues to walk to the podium, leaving behind their cars as a dress rehearsal for the day when they would no more be ministers. He said this was how they were once; hence, it would make no difference if they were out of power.

Nedunchezhian wondered who was in danger because of the Allahabad verdict: Indira Gandhi or democracy. In the end, Karunanidhi administered a solemn pledge in Anna's name to the assembled:

This gathering at the sands hereby pledges to protect Indian democracy under any circumstances and in any eventuality. We will see that nothing happens to Indian democracy. We endorse the DMK executive's resolution. We appeal to the prime minister to release the arrested leaders and to ensure reasonable freedom of the press. Long live Indian democracy.

The US consul general noted, 'They appeared to be deeply touched with this solemn ending.'[21] The Congress (I) expectedly found no solemnness and derided Karunanidhi's speech as the 'most disgraceful political perfunctoriness'.

'Walking Both Sides of the Road'

The speech led the Opposition to demand his government's dismissal, and Karunanidhi did not rule out his government being shown the door and leaders arrested.[22] On one occasion, Karunanidhi hoped those reporting his speeches to Indira Gandhi also reported the public's reaction. In their meetings, Anbazhagan and Maran found little justification for the Emergency. As paraphrased by the US consul general, Maran said, 'There was no threat to India, only to Indira.'[23]

Karunanidhi continued to adopt his dual stand of letting the party speak in strident tones while at the same time, in early July, his administration took into custody advocates of secession, thwarting their 10 July meeting.[24] Government advertisements claimed: 'Tamil Nadu has carried out numerous far-reaching, progressive economic measures', adding 'Tamil Nadu marches ahead to implement the rest of the economic programme of the Prime Minister'. Home Minister Brahmananda Reddy, however, said, 'But to say that we have already completed the programme will not be in the right spirit'.[25]

Karunanidhi was also accused of making use of the MISA against opponents. Furnishing statistics of criminals and anti-social elements, Karunanidhi said it was 'strange' and 'perverse' that the CPI argued that the arrested belonged to the Opposition.[26] MGR charged that MISA was used to wean away people from his ADMK and that supporters were harassed and humiliated, and police beat up students and stamped their faces with faeces-stamped boots, making them eat it.[27] MGR said people felt 'liberated' when the DMK ministry was dismissed.[28]

The irrepressible Karunanidhi also designed for himself a national good offices role. On 9 August, at the fifth Tirunelveli district conference, Anbazhagan proposed and Nedunchezhian seconded a resolution calling on Karunanidhi to undertake the necessary efforts to 'change the extraordinary situation' by engaging leaders and chief ministers and meeting the prime minister.[29]

Karunanidhi had extended an olive branch to Indira Gandhi in only six weeks. That month, he also termed the Emergency 'good'. On 13 September 1975, the US consul general noted the ambivalence:

> . . . The DMK has increasingly been walking both sides of the street. Karunanidhi termed the emergency 'good' last month. His recent trip to New Delhi, although still somewhat shrouded in mystery, represents further erosion of his early (in the emergency) stand against the prime minister's actions.[30]

Perhaps journalist Kuldip Nayar met Karunanidhi around this time. He recorded, 'When I met Karunanidhi to seek his support for anti-Emergency activity, he was afraid to do anything in public. He said he could at best help me start an underground newspaper which, he made very clear, should be distributed outside the state.'[31]

On 22 September, Periyar's widow, Maniammai, unveiled Karunanidhi's statue on Anna Salai. Two days later, Governor Shah opened the eleven-floor Karunanidhi Building. That day Karunanidhi dropped Anbil Dharmalingam on the grounds of 'indifferent health' and effected a minor reshuffle, adding revenue to Madhavan and moving S. Ramachandran from transport to local administration at his request. To the question that Dharmalingam could have resigned, Karunanidhi said, 'You are aware of everything. Please do not ask me further about this,' indicating their differences.[32]

Kamaraj Memorial

On 2 October 1975, Kamaraj breathed his last. A gracious Karunanidhi rose to the occasion. The Congress (O) planned to keep the body in state at the Teynampet Congress Grounds, cremate him and then build a memorial. Someone suggested Rajaji Hall for public viewing. Karunanidhi showed up as soon as he heard the news and, as though he had read their minds, suggested the body be moved to

Rajaji Hall as large crowds were expected to pay homage and soon thereafter turned up there.

Karunanidhi suggested that the final rites be held next to Gandhi Mandapam so that a memorial could be built there and tasked Rajaram to convey the same to the governor. That evening, in the pouring rain, Karunanidhi took Congress (O) leader Rajaram Naidu and others to the grounds along with the public works minister. The area was cleared of trees, and throughout the major operation, Karunanidhi oversaw the work. An emotional Rajaram Naidu later said that the chief minister guided them those two days when they were 'helpless' and said they were unsure how the debt could ever be repaid. On 4 October, Karunanidhi named the Marina Road after Kamaraj and announced that his birthplace at Virudhunagar would become a national memorial.[33]

Events Leading up to Dismissal

The sombre situation was only muted by reality. Karunanidhi increasingly suspected that elections would not be held on time. On 27 October, to a question, Karunanidhi replied with characteristic pluck that when the prime minister herself could not respond on the timing of elections—how could he, a mere chief minister? Later at Dindigul, Karunanidhi asked party men to be ready, regardless of elections happening on time.[34]

On 22 December, Karunanidhi called for elections in February 1976 after the expiry of the legislature's term.[35] At the party's fifth state conference at Coimbatore from 25 to 28 December, he reiterated his call for simultaneous elections to Parliament and the legislature. Karunanidhi proposed the first three of the eleven resolutions calling for the prime minister to convene a round table conference with the Opposition, and elections and stated that the fundamentals of democratic principles were unaffected by her constitutional changes. Karunanidhi urged cadres to send telegrams to the prime minister seeking elections.[36] But these fell on deaf ears, and on 29 December, the four-day Chandigarh Congress (I) meeting recommended extending the Emergency for six months and Parliament by a year.[37]

The Coimbatore conference was also the venue of defiant and crass speeches from second-rung leaders like A.V.P. Asaithambi that *Murasoli* chose not to report. Karunanidhi himself was restrained and resigned to the impending doom. On 27 December, he referred to the possibility of his government's dismissal as early as the following morning, indicating they were ready to leave then and there, adding that the party was bigger than the government.[38] Although the morrow came and went uneventfully, the echoes of Coimbatore were soon heard.

On 8 January 1976, Indira Gandhi described the Opposition-run states Gujarat and Tamil Nadu as 'two islands . . . where every effort is being made to destroy that discipline, where every encouragement is being given, who want to seek aid from outside to speak against India, who try and think of their interests before the national interests'.[39] Karunanidhi responded, 'People know the truth,' but refused to comment on the lack of order. Earlier, Minister of State for Home Om Mehta (nicknamed Home Mehta) had charged in Parliament that Karunanidhi was impeding the Congress (O) and Congress (I)'s unification efforts.[40]

On 29 January, two days before the dismissal, in a missive full of foreboding titled 'Let the cowards step aside. Let the brave follow', Karunanidhi reminded the DMK faithful that their fellow travellers were of many kinds: those who braved the odds but were unable to give up the comfort of the shade and therefore blamed the DMK's ideals; those who journeyed on others' shoulders only to speak ill of those shoulders later; and a third who could not complete the journey. 'History is clear. Those who are left at the end of the journey are not as many at the beginning', Karunanidhi said and pointing to the apostles deserting Jesus wondered: 'If such was his fate, who are we?' Internalizing the ordeal, he wrote:

Those who cut the hand that feeds; those that tear apart the arm that garlands them; those who break with a sledgehammer the arm that carried them; those who abuse the ones who had given them a life; if there is justice, let that take them into account.

Sibling,

You come along! Let us continue the journey.
Let us mouth, 'Cowards step aside; brave follow' and walk towards the ideal.[41]

The letters of this period stand out for the depth of emotions, pain, faith and resilience that Karunanidhi summoned from within.

Dismissal

On 31 January, Karunanidhi appeared to sense his government's impending fate. Having gone to address the Don Bosco High School, Egmore, Chennai, Karunanidhi, sensing his fate, indicated in his speech that it was probably his last event as chief minister and sent away his official car.[42] Earlier, that day's headline in Kannadasan's *Navasakthi* (New Force), 'Tomorrow will see a new dawn,' saw Karunanidhi calling him at 1.30 p.m. even as Rajaram, Maran and Marisamy disabused Karunanidhi of any such eventuality. Ninety minutes later, it had happened, wrote Kannadasan.[43] *All India Radio* announced the dismissal in its 6 p.m. bulletin. Yet, when Sabanayagam broke the news, Karunanidhi was 'taken aback' as he had probably not expected such 'drastic action', especially with his term expiring in a few weeks.[44] Summoned to Delhi the week of 25 January, Governor K.K. Shah had argued against central rule but was intercepted at Hyderabad and was asked to return to affix his signature on the dismissal report.

Shah's report charged the DMK administration with 'maladministration, corruption, and misuse of power' for partisan political ends.[45] Shah had praised Karunanidhi the previous day for providing 'Ram Rajya' in Tamil Nadu.[46] Some DMK leaders had held out the threat of revolution, and others had made 'sinister comparisons . . . in their public utterances with the events in Bangladesh and the fate of Mujibur Rahman', Shah added. He recommended a judicial inquiry. *India Today*'s cover story said of Karunanidhi, 'When some of his more foolish supporters began to describe him as another Mujibur Rahman, it was time to call his bluff.'

The 22–24 January 1976 DK conference at Thanjavur, where some Dravidar Kazhagam speakers advocated secession in the presence of Anbazhagan and Rajaram, appears to have clinched the issue. Advised against participation, Karunanidhi did not attend.[47]

Following his dismissal on 31 January, Karunanidhi noted that his 'only crime' was to ask for the Emergency's withdrawal. 'We must pay the price,' he added.

CS, however, claimed that 'There was a sense of relief [amongst the public] at elimination of DMK'.[48] *The Mail*'s headline 'Calm, peaceful Tamil Nadu welcomes President's rule', with sub-headings 'DMK wrongs have to be set right', 'Day of Deliverance', 'Freed from Tyranny', 'Sigh of Relief', etc., showed *The Mail*'s ire on Karunanidhi and his administration. In its haste to damn the DMK, *The Hindu* said that the dismissal 'will be endorsed by large sections of the public who have suffered under nine long years of such misrule', which included Anna's brief and fitful tenure. Pictures of Karunanidhi, including calendars with his images, were taken down from all government offices.[49] MGR termed the dismissal a 'courageous act' and supported Indira Gandhi's attempts at 'protecting democracy'.[50]

Central reserve police were flown to Tiruchi and the army alerted. Shah had cancelled his trip to Ooty, feigning illness. P.K. Dhave and R.V. Subramanian were appointed as advisers to the governor. Senior police officials V.R. Lakshminarayanan and K. Mohandas were transferred to Chennai and later joint secretary, home, C.V. Narasimhan, would move to Chennai to take over anti-corruption and surveillance. From Delhi, M.K. Narayanan monitored the progress of the inquiry to be announced. Central reserve police guarded all central installations.[51]

In a statement, Karunanidhi said the people of Tamil Nadu had much faith in Gandhi and Anna's path and urged them to maintain peace and non-violence in a spirit of duty, dignity and discipline.[52] He wrote the following day that the best honour and pride was being known as 'Anna's siblings' and that was enough for him.

Turncoats were not new for Karunanidhi. But now it felt like the ground under his feet was slipping away. He was yet unprepared for what lay ahead.

14

Suffering and Pain

MISA

Before long, 8000 men were rounded up.[1] While most were released a few weeks later, 419 were interned under MISA without a trial. Only a sub-district DMK official then, Vaiko was the first to be arrested. A.V.P. Asaithambi, an advocate for an independent Tamil state at Coimbatore, was picked up along with others. Soon enough, police knocked at the Gopalapuram residence for Stalin. Karunanidhi promised to send word on his son's return. However, Congress (O) sources believe that Karunanidhi requested Kannadasan to intercede with the Centre for moderation.

On 1 February, Stalin was arrested after Karunanidhi called the inspector general of police. Stalin was to stage his *Murase Muzhangu* (Oh! Drum Beat) play at Madurantakam, when the news of his father's promise reached him. Cheering him up when he turned up, Karunanidhi said: 'This imprisonment would be a stepping stone for your political career.' Indeed it was. Karunanidhi did the same with Murasoli Maran, who reached Chennai a day later.[2]

Taken to the central prison, Stalin was pushed inside a dark cell where he fell on Dravidar Kazhagam's K. Veeramani, who was shocked to see him there. The 8x8 cell meant for one already had eight people. The room reeked of urine as the pot was in a corner. The nine had to sleep brushing aside each other and with their breath on the other. Stalin would find out in the morning that the cotton balls he brushed against were the bandages of lepers housed there.

A hundred inmates in the ninth block were to perform their ablutions in the three or four toilets within half an hour. Further, neem oil and mud were thrown on to the food served. But the worst was yet to come. On 2 February, the second day, inmates of the ten cells in the block were drawn out and beaten by warders in the sight of the others. That night, Stalin was in the third cell with N. Veerasamy, Chittibabu, Neela Narayanan and V.S. Govindan. 'Come out, guys!' shouted a voice. As Chittibabu moved forward, he was received with a slap and baton charge. Veerasamy experienced the same fate. 'Come out, da (Tamil singular, here a term of abuse)! Oh! Are you Stalin? Karunanidhi's son?' said a convict who menacingly administered a blow on Stalin's face. Further, the baton landed on Stalin's right elbow, and he lost consciousness. Chittibabu fell on an unconscious Stalin to ward off the raining blows, taking them upon himself. Convict Suruli stamped Chittibabu with his boots so badly that Chittibabu's navel was torn, necessitating two surgeries to which he succumbed on 3 January 1977. A journal he kept in prison and produced before the Justice Ismail Commission confirmed that political prisoners were beaten up and tortured and officials were responsible.

Although the beatings stopped after two days, other forms of harassment continued. Stalin records that jail superintendent Vidyasagar's father had lost to DMK's N.V.N. Somu in the race for the chairmanship of the Pachaiyappa's College Trust, and MISA came in handy for Vidyasagar's vendetta. After Maran's letter on the excesses was sneaked out to a shocked home minister, the jailer was shifted to Vellore.[3] Vidyasagar and six others were suspended from 3 June 1978.[4]

On 31 March 1978, speaking on the Ismail Commission report in the legislative council, N. Veerasamy moistened the eyes of many a member.

> We would have understood if you punished the DMK if we had committed mistakes in our nine-year rule. But when Congress (O) and Marxist Communists and those like the seventy-year-old Nellai Jebamani, a seasoned politician and freedom fighter, is accosted by a twenty-five-year-old warden: *Yenda, Jebamani nee thaanaada?'* (Are you Jebamani? in singular) and kicks him, my heartstrings were tugged. He shed tears looking at us, for the blow on him was so hard. We, in turn, cried helplessly, looking at him. There was nothing else that we could do then.[5]

The DMK attributed Chittibabu's and Sathur Balakrishnan's deaths to the confinement. The party sent a stipend of Rs 200 each to 124 families and Rs 100 to twenty-three families, totalling Rs 1,88,000.

The Shah Commission noted that 1027 were arrested under MISA in Tamil Nadu. Shah reported:

> DMK had to bear the brunt of MISA onslaught followed by Dravidar Kazhagam. Majority of DMK and DK men were accused of having rowdy elements under their command, likely to indulge in prejudicial acts and critical of the Emergency and president's rule. Grounds of detention also mentioned anti-government or secessionist speeches but no place, date or time of the speech given. Interference in the district administration and amassing wealth by corrupt practices were other grounds.

Shah said that despite the absence of specific instructions from the government, the 'District authorities went about using MISA extensively against the members of DMK . . . simply by furnishing vague and general grounds in a stereotyped manner.'[6] It was clear that they probably avenged their hurt and humiliation at the hands of some of these functionaries. Tamilvanan commented, 'No one defeated Kalaignar Karunanidhi. He fell on his own. He fell because he did not submit to the central government and he did not discipline the Kazhagam men.'[7]

Sarkaria Inquiry Announced

On 2 February, *Murasoli* asked followers to go 'singly' to pay homage to Anna on his death anniversary on 3 February.[8] Rajaram, P.U. Shanmugam and Sadiq Pasha were seen with Karunanidhi and Nedunchezhian paying homage at Anna's mausoleum on the 3rd.[9] That day, Om Mehta announced the establishment of the Justice Sarkaria Commission of Inquiry. Om Mehta said fifty-four allegations by M.G. Ramachandran, Kalyanasundaram and others necessitated the move. Of these, twenty-seven pertained to Karunanidhi, thirteen against his ministers and fourteen related to abuse of authority.[10] Thirty-nine months later, on 7 January 1978, Karunanidhi said in the assembly that MGR had 'stabbed in their hearts' and perhaps even the memorialists would not have visualized the 'cruelty' it would spawn.[11]

On 3 February, Karunanidhi wrote to the home minister, assuring him of the DMK's belief in democratic processes and support for the Centre's efforts at law and order. The following day, he welcomed the inquiry as an opportunity to explain.[12]

On 6 February, for four days, Karunanidhi published a list of those unable to go to the Anna mausoleum—revealing those under custody in the era of strict censorship. The first list of sixty-five names included Neela Narayanan, V.S. Govindarajan, Thoppur Thiruvengadam, Pon. Muthuramalingam, K. Tirupathi, M.K. Stalin, Murasoli Maran, MP, S.S. Marisamy, MP, P.A. Saminathan, MP, S. Kandappan, R.D. Seethapathy, A.V.P. Asaithambi, Maduranthakam S. Arumugam, S.S. Thennarasu, R. Ganesan,

Duraimurugan, K. Veeramani, K. Subbu, S.M. Ramachandran, Saidai Sambandam, Chittibabu, MP, N. Veerasamy, Arivazhagan, M.R. Radha, Vezhavendhan, Neetolai Adiyar and others.[13] The second list included two women.[14]

Karunanidhi under Siege

Karunanidhi described the turn of events as a 'gift of the times' to discern the copper from the gold, as he had indicated days earlier, and that those ready to resolutely face suffering should follow him.[15] On 8 February, amidst the pall of gloom, Nedunchezhian issued the following statement:

> Even when a few birds that descended for the fish leave the lotus pond, the lotus stems would stay put through the pond's thick and thin. So are the true siblings raised by Arignar Anna. Some prosper, putting themselves first, leaving the Kazhagam behind. There is no need for surprise if they fly away because of their self-interest. Innumerable others perform their duty putting the Kazhagam above them. It is because of them that the DMK grew from strength to strength. In the future, too, it will grow because of them.[16]

The pressure on the DMK members was 'so intense' that members were directing their resignations to the district collectors, not the party leadership.[17]

Some began to see the writing on the wall with Karunanidhi at the helm. On 11 February, S. Ramachandran tried to separate the movement from the man, arguing that it was Karunanidhi, not the DMK on trial and suggesting that Karunanidhi and those facing charges step down until cleared 'to prevent the DMK from disintegrating', and that, if they did not, general secretary Nedunchezhian should boldly suspend them. 'No individual, however great he may be, can ever be more important than the

DMK, which had been built with the blood and tears of partymen,'
he concluded. Nedunchezhian said that the general council was the
right forum to raise and resolve these issues but could not meet since
many of its members had been arrested.[18] S. Ramachandran and S.S.
Rajendran fell prey to the Centre's scheme, and S. Ramachandran
had identified those to be taken into custody, alleged Karunanidhi
later.[19]

Even as others, who owed him their positions, shunned him
and Karunanidhi grew forlorn, an elderly man showed up to console
him. Nine days later, Karunanidhi wrote about the elder's visit and
his sage advice:

> At this very old age, he has come to my home. He blessed me.
> 'Even under the influence of overwhelming affection, befriending
> an elephant is a risk while befriending a dog is the best! as
> *Naaladiyar* puts it,' he said . . .[†]
>
> Wow! Even though I met this elderly man after a long time,
> he has made me realise life's unique and deep meaning. I sighed.[20]

Indira Gandhi's Marina Speech

Four days later, on 15 February, at a public meeting at the Marina,
Indira Gandhi alleged that the DMK had plans for violence in
February and, if left unchecked, would have carried out its plan and
later claimed martyrdom. She said, 'While one or two top people
may not be asking for separation, there are other members who were
speaking about it and making undisguised open threats to the rest
of the country.'

---

[*] *Naaladiyar* is an ancient Jain work on morality.
[†] Though the mahout takes care of the elephant for a long time, the elephant at times
kills the mahout. On the other hand, even when the owner kicks the dog, it returns
the pain with love and affection by wagging its tail—is the meaning of this song.
[Song 213]

The prime minister said that the DMK's tall claims on development and the twenty-point economic programme were 'hollow', mentioned the death of 'twenty farmers' in the farmers' agitation and a Dalit delegation's complaint that the Keezhvenmani accused had gone free. She said that central funds for Dalit welfare were underutilized, Dalits were kept segregated, and, despite the state's claim that there were no bonded labourers, some had come to see her. She said people would 'realize how much Tamil Nadu had been wronged by the former regime'. The present DMK was making irresponsible remarks on the Indo-Sri Lanka relationship and had deviated from Anna's path, she concluded.

Sabanayagam nonetheless told the US consul general that claims of plans for violence were simply wrong, that the administration's welfare programmes were well-known and that it was for the people and not Indira Gandhi to judge the DMK administration. Yet, weeks later, Sabanayagam also remarked that the DMK, from the top down, 'were too interested in money'.[21]

DMK—To Be or Not to Be

The following day, trying to burnish the DMK's patriotic credentials, Karunanidhi, in a poem, expressed his assurance that the DMK would place its 'resolution' and 'demands' in abeyance in case of 'harm' to India and fight for the country's honour.[22] That day, senior leaders met at Madhavan's place with Karunanidhi to discuss Karunanidhi stepping aside.[23] On 17 February, S.S. Rajendran joined the 'Dump Karunanidhi' campaign, asking Karunanidhi to step down.

Instead of stepping aside as his detractors wanted, Karunanidhi did everything he could to put off a ban on the DMK, as was feared.[*] On 17 February, he wrote again to Om Mehta to assure him that

---

[*] On a visit to Madras on 17 April, Brahmananda Reddy clarified that only those parties advocating secession were to be banned, giving a breather to the DMK. Accessed 21 March 2022, https://www.wikileaks.org/plusd/cables/1976NEWDE05685_b.html.

the DMK would 'approach all problems in a parliamentary and democratic manner".[24] On 18 February, Karunanidhi disclosed that he had dispatched Rajaram to meet the prime minister and the home minister to relay the same. Later, Madhavan met the President and central ministers while Karunanidhi—with Nedunchezhian, Rajaram and Madhavan—met Governor Mohanlal Sukhadia to reiterate the message.[25] Karunanidhi had attempted to meet Om Mehta during the prime minister's mid-February tour.[26]

Karunanidhi records that the inquiry brought much personal humiliation and grief. Searches were conducted in his houses, the *Murasoli* office, party offices and houses of relatives and cadres. One day, income-tax officials raided his second residence. As he entered his house, the officials, who knew him well, asked, 'Who are you, sir? What is your name?' He also recorded that his wife, Rajathi Ammal, was 'three-fourths rendered naked' and searched for diamonds or gold on her person.[27]

On 23 February, Karunanidhi reminded the siblings of Sangam poet Oreruvuzhuvar's poem about a deer caught in a hunter's net, wishing to run away. Unlike the deer, Karunanidhi said that his legs refused to move, for he lived for the sake of others. Karunanidhi also pointed out to Kaniyan Poongundran's lines that 'Death is not new' to be astonished about, and therefore, there was no need to fear death.[28] On 10 May 1979, speaking at Tiruchi, Karunanidhi revealed that, with all that was happening to him and his family, he had contemplated 'suicide'. But the outpouring of affection made him realize that, although he had lost power, he had a 'permanent place in their hearts', and such dark thoughts were untenable.[29]

On 24 February, echoing his 29 January letter, Karunanidhi again used the analogy of a long journey to indicate what was

---

* Replying to Karunanidhi, Om Mehta said that release of the arrested would be 'considered with due regard to the developing situation in the state'. On 3 March, Sabanayagam told the US consul general that 90 per cent of those detained had been released. 'Situation with the DMK,' 4 March 1976, US consul-general cable. Accessed 2 May 2022, https://wikileaks.org/plusd/cables/1976NEWDE03310_b.html.

happening to the Kazhagam and him.[30] A month after the arrests, as no kin was allowed to see the interned and the families came crying to him, Karunanidhi threatened that he would stage a protest to the inspector general of police if family members were denied visitation rights. He succeeded in obtaining permission for them.[31]

A hiatus in writing ensued from 26 February to 15 March. That Karunanidhi was under some pressure was clear when *Murasoli* published inane headings for two days during this interregnum. On 2 March, 'Okra good for the body: Russian returned Adhilakshmi's research' said *Murasoli*, and the following day blared, 'Castor oil cools the body: physician Vedanthaiya announces'.

On 2 March, Karunanidhi began answering questions as Karikalan, responding to an order against him writing as Karunanidhi.[32] But even this was not good enough for the censors. His recommendation to a reader, who had asked him about devils and ghosts, to read rationalist M. Singaravel's book was disallowed as the censors felt that he was obliquely referring to Indira Gandhi.[33] On 16 March, an apologetic and emotion-filled Karunanidhi said he had been remiss with the siblings.[34] This was also the time that Karunanidhi gave up his plans to travel to meet party men on the advice of Pulavar Govindan and C.P. Chitrarasu. They wanted him to keep a low profile.[35]

Meanwhile, the calls for his resignation had not abated. When Pulavar Govindan wrote, urging him to leave, Karunanidhi replied that they could have given him a little poison instead. He said a good politician was akin to a captain who would not desert his sinking ship and would rather consume poison than quit the party.[36]

On 20 March, responding to letters from the interned, Karunanidhi wrote movingly:

Can anyone say that the Ganges and the Cauvery had become dry because of the water that flows into the ocean? Let the water that drains into the ocean become part of it; let that which

flows into the fields bear fruit. Would the river become dry
just because some water drains into the ocean and turns salty?
Let us carry on our tasks with that faith. The few who run to
save themselves by condemning the Kazhagam, abusing the
Kazhagam's leadership, would have to one day answer to their
conscience.[37]

On 3 April, after two months, Karunanidhi set off to Tiruchi by
road to attend the funeral of Sathur Balakrishnan, the first MISA
casualty. The reception in Tiruchi and Madurai was heart-warming,
and throughout the trip, people were eager to see Karunanidhi and
exchange words with him.[38] Perhaps this unswerving affection from
cadres steeled him. The next day, Karunanidhi told presspersons
that he had volunteered to step down. Still, the general secretary
and the treasurer saw no need for it, and there was no support in
the executive or the general council. Karunanidhi also indicated
that following Rajaram's visit to Delhi, he had written to the prime
minister about the situation in the state.[39]

Valluvar Kottam

On 8 April, he wrote about the President opening the Valluvar
Kottam on 15 April. Karunanidhi was to have declared the Kottam
open on 22–23 February. But that was not to be. Karunanidhi
indicated that he had yearned for the moment since the idea was
conceived on a visit to the Valluvar Temple at Mylapore towards the
request for its renovation. Here, the wish for a structure for Valluvar
in the heart of the city sprang in his mind.

Discussions with Ganapathi Sthapathi, the head sculptor,
began soon afterwards. Sculptor S.K. Achar of Vivekananda Rock
Memorial (at Kanniyakumari) fame joined later. Karunanidhi had
created some amateur pictures to visually indicate the structure and
the seat of the Thiruvalluvar statue. Importantly, he desired a stone

car like the one in Thiruvarur. S.K. Achar recalled later that no one had ever thought of a stone car.

A second letter followed on 15 April, making the pain of not being invited evident.

Karunanidhi said he felt like the mother of a bride who could not witness the wedding standing beside the daughter at the altar, but his eyes were filled with tears like hers.[40]

Quoting from poetess Avvai of the river that had run dry yet gave water when dug, Karunanidhi said, similarly, even if his and his siblings' identity were to disappear, their ideals, industry, sacrifices and achievements would remain etched forever. 'Therefore, the place in history for us is not a concession! Whatever happens, it cannot be hidden!' he said. [41]

On 24 April, in the first indoor meeting at Saidapet,* Karunanidhi described the direct rule as a blessing in one way, adding that he was shorn of words to thank the prime minister for the opportunity to judge who his friends were and who were not. Karunanidhi said, 'Some branches of the twenty-seven-year-old DMK might have been cut off, but as long as the trunk and the main root are there, the party will live and grow strong. We want to build the DMK by constructive methods and not by agitation.'[42]

Here, Karunanidhi had called for contributions to the legal defence fund. Money orders poured into his residence and party office, as did party workers and their families. An overwhelmed Karunanidhi wrote two weeks later, on 11 May, to indicate that, except when he slept, he was always surrounded by workers and their families.[43] Karunanidhi had to be direct four days later, saying he could not spend the whole day receiving contributions. He then specified that he wouldn't meet them on Wednesday and gave time slots in the morning and evening.[44]

---

* Karunanidhi says that the first one was on 3 August 1976. *Nenjuku Needhi*, 2: 566.

Writing about this period later, Karunanidhi noted that except for Anbazhagan and himself, some others, once ministers, wore a 'face of despair and loss', and he feared that if he spent more time with them, he would contract 'cowardice'. Senior leaders suggested a name change; some even suggested turning the party into a cultural outfit. Karunanidhi cautioned against losing one's fundamentals. Word got around, and front rankers from the prison wrote against a name or leadership change. Reading the letter to others, Karunanidhi pledged emotionally, 'Let's live with the Kazhagam or let's fall with the Kazhagam'.[45]

Censorship, Executive, Comparison to Lenin

On 1 June, his letter with the salutation 'Oh elder brother' on Anna, to be published on his birthday on 3 June, was censored indiscriminately. Karunanidhi tried to point out that the deleted portions were not anti-national and approached the government in vain when that failed. His patience wearing thin, Karunanidhi handwrote a pamphlet on his dedication to safeguarding press freedoms, mentioned the censors not permitting the line about Anna's affection for him and the need for cadres to maintain peace.

Fearing intelligence might sniff out his plan, Karunanidhi prepared a thousand pamphlets secretly, with the help of his sons, Alagiri and Tamilarasu. Announcing his decision to conduct a protest walk to officials and sending a telegram to Indira Gandhi[46] on 2 June at 10 a.m., Karunanidhi exited his car after crossing the Thousand Lights area in Chennai and began walking towards Anna's statue with the DMK flag and distributing the pamphlets. At Anna's statue, he raised the slogan 'Dictatorship'. Porselvi and her husband Ilamurugu, Murasoli Selvam, Alagiri and Tamilarasu and the crowds that had joined chimed 'down, down'. Karunanidhi and some others were taken into custody to be released around 2 p.m., on instructions from Delhi, as it was his birthday the following day.[47]

Twenty-seven of the sixty members and twenty-four special invitees participated in the 3–4 July executive called to discuss the Swaran Singh committee's proposals on constitutional changes.[48] But the executive is better known for the revolt by Mathiazhagan and S.S. Rajendran. Mathiazhagan spoke of the 'extraordinary' situation and called for the resignation of the president, general secretary and treasurer. Rajendran supported him. As the executive demurred, both walked out. Rajendran was attacked outside and ended up bruised.[49] On 6 July, Mathiazhagan, Rajendran, D.V. Narayanasamy and S. Ramachandran were suspended from the party and expelled on 1 October.[50] The executive appointed a committee headed by Madhavan, with L. Ganesan as the organizer, to analyse and report on the Swaran Singh proposals.[51]

Karunanidhi appeared to be hemmed in from all sides. On 10 July, Karunanidhi penned the most poignant of his missives, comparing himself to the palm tree we saw in the first chapter.[52] By August, there were plans in place for Karunanidhi's arrest. Four days later, Assistant Solicitor General V.P. Raman indicated to the US consul general that he had advised the Centre against giving Karunanidhi an opportunity to claim victimhood and that the arrest should wait until criminal charges could be framed.[53] On 5 August, Karunanidhi said that even if the inquiry led to a ten-year sentence, he was only fifty-two and would be out at sixty-two. He asked cadres to remain calm even if he was sullied. He said Periyar and Kamaraj had been blamed, and such accusations were part of a 'trend'.[54]

But he need not have bothered. Cadres loved him, as was evident from his 20–22 August tour of Coimbatore, Tirupur, Thanjavur and Tiruchi. Mobbed wherever he went, Karunanidhi also encountered poignant scenes of men and women breaking down before him, moved by his situation. On 21 August, Karunanidhi said at Tirupur that he was not grieving for having lost power, and his heart was filled with pride and happiness that he had a permanent place at the altar of their hearts.

In the first display of reflection, Karunanidhi admitted 'few mistakes here and there' in his administration, claimed 'those few bosom friends were punished' and pointed out how he had acted in the Muster Roll scandal.[55] Stating that it was not possible to destroy the DMK, Karunanidhi said, 'Therefore, they can insult. They can insult Karunanidhi, disgrace Karunanidhi, turn Karunanidhi a low life, tarnish Karunanidhi, make Karunanidhi unclean . . . if they destroy Karunanidhi, they think they can destroy the Kazhagam.'[56]

On 6 September, speaking at Salem, he said they feared the impending constitutional changes to introduce socialist measures might destroy fundamental rights and snatch states' rights. The DMK had suggested adding the word 'federal' to the Swaran Singh Committee's proposal to call India a socialist, democratic and secular republic.

From 13–15 September, Indira Gandhi visited the drought-hit areas in Tamil Nadu for three days. She indirectly criticized the DMK as divisive, termed its slogans on caste, language, autonomy and separatism 'ridiculous', and urged the state's people to make up for lost time. Om Mehta said that besides the Sarkaria Commission, the Central Bureau of Investigation (CBI) was also involved in unravelling the DMK's misdeeds.[57]

On 15 September, addressing meetings to mark Anna's 68th birth anniversary, Karunanidhi continued to speak of the DMK's journey and his record of public service, adding that his every action was 'aimed at the welfare of the Tamils' and not his own.[58]

Two days later, Karunanidhi chose to respond to the prime minister. Admitting that some in the DMK had made speeches 'reflecting' separation, Karunanidhi reminded her that MGR had once defied the army, and such extremists were not in the DMK but in the AIADMK. On the prime minister's call on countering secessionism with propaganda, Karunanidhi asked that the Kazhagam be included as part of that propaganda force and that together they would endeavour to defeat separatist and anti-nationalist forces, adding that they would take such a pledge on Anna's birth anniversary.[59] He regretted that Tamil Nadu Congress Committee and police intelligence officials had fed the prime minister false and malicious reports about him. Referring to a book on Lenin and the anti-Lenin campaign that led to some followers deserting him, Karunanidhi said that Lenin eventually triumphed, and the Russian Revolution happened. Karunanidhi said he did not want anyone to think he was equating himself with Lenin. In the end, Karunanidhi said several other Karunanidhis would emerge in his place even if he was finished.[60]

Withdrawing from the Sarkaria Inquiry

On 20 September, Sarkaria began his sittings at *Kanchi* on Greenways Road. The DMK engaged twenty-six lawyers, including senior counsels Shanthi Bhushan, G. Ramasamy, K.K. Venugopal and Govind Swaminathan.[61] The Commission received 168 affidavits from the public. All except Si.Pa. Adithanar withdrew from the proceedings, protesting the rejection of the request to examine the memorialists and the 760-plus witnesses. The AIADMK predictably ridiculed Karunanidhi 'for running away' from the Commission.

On 27 September, *Murasoli* published Karunanidhi's letter dated 26 September reiterating his requests to cross-examine the four memorialists and those who had submitted affidavits and not to treat the documents by the probe agencies as the main evidence.[62] In the event, Sarkaria would permit the examination of fourteen of the seventeen witnesses material to the aerial spraying and sugar scandal cases, but not all, citing the Supreme Court's decision in the Bakshi Gulam Mohammad case (1966) and other precedents.[63]

On 13 October, Karunanidhi said he was not running away and would participate if Sarkaria accepted their requests.[64] On 16 October, CBI brought criminal charges at the additional chief metropolitan magistrate's court in the wheat sale scandal, alleging that in 1974, two firms were favoured to sell wheat in the open market to make a huge profit.[65]

Having chosen to stay away from the proceedings, Karunanidhi now took his case to the public, openly criticizing the Commission for disallowing his requests and lambasting MGR and Kalyanasundaram as cowards for refusing to testify.[66] On 20 October, Sarkaria excoriated Karunanidhi's stand as 'motivated by extraneous considerations'. Six days later, V.P. Raman was blunt when he maintained that Karunanidhi and his associates were in 'strategic retreat' as they were in a 'morass' and 'irretrievably drowned' as the evidence was 'far too much to swallow'. Raman concluded that 'it was not a walkout in manly protest but a slinking away in morbid fear at the prospect of public exposure'. The same Raman would also advise MGR later that the findings were not substantive enough to allow for prosecution.[67]

On 9 November, *The Hindu* editorial scathingly said that Karunanidhi's approach violated fair play. But Karunanidhi was making 'fair play' an issue. On 11 November, *Murasoli* published a translation of the editorial. On 12 November, Karunanidhi said he wanted to make it available widely and that he had not discussed the criminal proceedings against him and knew how to treat a matter that was sub judice.[68]

Refer Constitutional Changes to People

On 21 October, Karunanidhi suggested that the proposed constitutional changes be placed before the people in the general elections as was done in the 1971 elections, fought on the key issues of bank nationalization and the abolition of privy purses. Pointing out that the parliamentary term was four years in the US and Japan, five years in the UK, Canada and West Germany, and three years in Australia, Karunanidhi took a jibe at the proposed idea of extending Parliament's term from five to six years, wondering what held the Congress (I) back from facing the public at the end of the five years.

He suggested elections be held within six months to seek the people's mandate.

Karunanidhi denounced the Sarkaria proceedings as partial, bitterly criticizing the Centre's attempt to vilify the DMK. Citing the treatment meted out to former Punjab chief minister Pratap Singh Kairon and former finance minister T.T. Krishnamachari in similar circumstances, Karunanidhi sarcastically remarked: 'But, that was all under the late Nehru'. Karunanidhi said that despite eighty MPs submitting charges against former Haryana chief minister Bansi Lal, he was not subjected to an inquiry and was promoted to defence minister. He would repeat this ad nauseam in later years. Karunanidhi scorned the three IAS officers called to testify in the aerial spraying and school textbook cases, pointing out that they were the subject of an investigation or had their houses raided by the CBI. He said the 168 affidavits were from industrialists who could not make the DMK administration bend to their wishes.[69]

On 25 October, Parliament began the debate on the Swaran Singh proposals. The Jan Sangh, Socialist Party, Bharatiya Lok Dal and Congress (O) said they would not participate. On 25 October, Era. Sezhian expressed the DMK's inability to participate, pointing out that neither the circumstances nor the moment was appropriate, with the possibility of a countrywide discussion being non-extant. He, however, said that the DMK welcomed any changes that envisaged socialist goals. On 29 October, Karunanidhi said that even those who supported the changes had expressed reservations about armed police being sent to states and shifting education to the concurrent list. CPI's Indrajit Gupta had argued against the extension of Parliament and other provisions, and the Congress (I)'s Hanumanthiah had warned that socialist ideals could not be forced down the throats of successive generations. IUML's Sulaiman Sait stated that the insertion to curb anti-nationalist forces was redundant. Karunanidhi said that it was for all the above reasons that the DMK and the Opposition had asked to restore basic freedoms and create conditions for a nationwide discussion. He said the new Parliament could consider these changes.[70]

Karunanidhi Convenes National Opposition Meeting

At the 20–22 November AICC (I) session at Guwahati, Indira Gandhi indicated that she would talk to the Opposition if they would cooperate and change their approach. Karunanidhi promptly welcomed the gesture.[71] On 15 December, on Karunanidhi's invite, leaders of the Opposition from the Congress (O), Bharatiya Lok Dal, Jan Sangh, Praja Socialist, Revolutionary Socialist and Akali Dal met at Sezhian's residence in Delhi. Among others, Asoka Mehta, A.B. Vajpayee and Biju Patnaik were present. Karunanidhi later recorded that 'no one can deny that this was the first and foremost reason for the birth of the Janata Party.'[72] Earlier, Rajaram and Sezhian had met Vajpayee when he was under house arrest and had urged him to work with Morarji Desai and Charan Singh, spurring the efforts towards the Janata Party.[73]

In his welcome address, Karunanidhi said that a way must be found to normalize the situation in the country. On some conditioning the talks to lifting the Emergency, Karunanidhi sagely said that conditionalities from either side would be unhelpful. The next day, leaders continued their meeting at H.M. Patel's house where a communiqué indicating their readiness for talks was finalized. Karunanidhi forwarded it with a letter to Indira Gandhi, expressing the Opposition's wish to engage in talks.[74] It is unclear if Indira Gandhi responded to this letter. However, events cascaded fast and Indira Gandhi felt emboldened to announce elections.

15

The Beginning of the Electoral Reverses

1977 Parliamentary Election

Parliamentary elections were called for 16 and 20 March 1977. The Emergency had welded the Congress (O), Charan Singh's Bharatiya Lok Dal, the Swatantra, the Socialist Party of India of Raj Narain and George Fernandes, Jagjivan Ram's Congress for Democracy and the Jan Sangh into the Janata Party, the first-ever merger of the Hindi heartland Opposition. On 15 February, DMK–Janata talks, or what remained of the Congress (O) in Tamil Nadu, were salvaged after Sanjiva Reddy intervened with Karunanidhi.[1] In the event, the Janata Party conceded the DMK's claim for an equal number of the forty parliamentary seats (nineteen each), including Puducherry. The DMK yielded Maran's Central Madras seat to P. Ramachandran, president of the state Janata Party. Maran shifted to South Madras. CPM was allocated two seats.[2] Arrayed against them was the AIADMK, Congress (I) and the CPI.

The following day, Sarkaria's interim report made it to the press before it was formally placed in the Rajya Sabha on 2 March. Finding against Karunanidhi, Anbil Dharmalingam and S. Madhavan, Sarkaria characterized the evidence as 'cogent, convincing and reliable'.[3] Karunanidhi rued that 'with the legal cases [Indira Gandhi wished to] finish the DMK without a trace.'[4]

The results saw an anti-Emergency wave sweep Indira Gandhi politically off her feet, ushering the motley Janata Party to power. The south had, however, stood by Indira Gandhi. A.V.P. Asaithambi was the sole DMK winner in Tamil Nadu (the DMK also won the Pondicherry seat), and Janata won three seats. Karunanidhi said the Emergency excesses were not felt down south, and in addition to the 'Indira wave', the 'film glamour wave' had affected the DMK alliance.[5] On 21 March, the Emergency was lifted.

1977 PARLIAMENTARY ELECTION

Party	Contested	Won	Votes	Percentage
AIADMK	20	18	53,65,076	30.04
INC	15	14	39,77,306	22.27
CPI	3	3	8,22,233	4.60
CPM	2	0	2,79,081	1.56
DMK	19	1	33,23,320	18.61
JANATA PARTY (JP)	18	3	31,56,116	17.67

Karunanidhi hoped that the Janata government would drop the Sarkaria-spawned cases. On 20 February, at the campaign's kick-off at the Marina, Desai, as Janata chairman, had said* that the Congress (I)'s friends in Haryana, under similar circumstances as Karunanidhi's, had not faced an inquiry and were also 'rewarded', adding that one should not be condemned before proven guilty.[6]

Yet, as there was no indication of relief, Karunanidhi set off to meet JP, who had a soft corner for him. JP was the architect of Opposition unity and played kingmaker, plumping for Morarji

---

* Karunanidhi says he could not attend this meeting owing to prior commitments.

Desai as the Janata prime minister. On 6 April, Karunanidhi and Maran called on JP at Mumbai's Jaslok Hospital. According to Karunanidhi, JP inquired and learnt that the cases were yet to be withdrawn and later sent a letter to Morarji Desai through him. Karunanidhi records that Desai grew momentarily 'silent' on seeing the contents, said he could not decide on his own, that it would require cabinet sanction and explained that JP had urged the cases against Karunanidhi be withdrawn.

Director General of Police V.R. Lakshminarayanan writes damningly: 'I know of the frantic attempts to sabotage these trials by approaching Shri Jaya Prakash Narain', but Desai turned down JP's 'fervent pleas' as 'he discovered that the cases were well-founded'.*[7] Desai's misgivings were not new. He had justified the electoral alliance with the DMK as 'a wrong inevitable [in the fight against] evil'.[8]

Karunanidhi repeatedly argued that the treatment meted out to him was patently unfair and cited the case of Parkash Singh Badal.[9] Desai felt that corruption cases differed from the political ones.[10] Ironically, the cases against Karunanidhi were withdrawn in 1980 under an Indira Gandhi administration following a DMK–Congress (I) rapprochement.

Third Split

Sarkaria's immediate fallout was within the party. On 10 April, after a petition calling for the abolition of his post as president, Karunanidhi wrote to Nedunchezhian to say that 'very close friends' were engaged in a signature campaign against him and 'though few', he feared the harm to the Kazhagam and had chosen to resign. This would be the first of Karunanidhi's many aborted resignations intended to shock and awe, succeeding all the time. Nonetheless,

---

* Karunanidhi, however, points to Royappa's affidavit claiming that Lakshminarayanan wanted him to perjure against Karunanidhi. *Nenjuku Needhi*, 3: 146–47.

Nedunchezhian followed suit. Taking the moral high ground, he said, 'The Kazhagam's leadership that had taken credit for the past election victories, should also shoulder the responsibility for the defeat in the recent elections.' This self-righteous candour would come to haunt him.[11]

Pulavar Govindan, P.U. Shanmugam, N. Veerasamy and K. Veeramani now arranged for the two leaders to meet. Anbazhagan rushed with a resolution from the executive asking them to reconsider, and Karunanidhi and Nedunchezhian complied. Their resignations lasted for twenty-eight hours. But the euphoria was short-lived.[12] On 15 April, Nedunchezhian, K. Rajaram, S. Madhavan, Era. Sezhian, T.K. Srinivasan, P.U. Shanmugam, Rama Arangannal, Si.Pa. Adithanar and others quit the DMK. Nedunchezhian said that he received 'harsh' letters faulting his stand of owning up to defeat and, when 'feelings of enmity and hate' prevailed, he did not wish to be in anyone's way. Karunanidhi expressed disbelief, said he would step down and invited Nedunchezhian to return and run the party. On 17 April, at a Marina meeting, Karunanidhi extended the invite again but to no avail.

On 20 April, in an open letter, Karunanidhi movingly recalled their thirty-five-year friendship, Nedunchezhian walking seven miles to his wedding and other instances to tease out the depth of their bonds and begged him for the honour of dying with his ties to him and Anbazhagan intact. Asking him to rush back, Karunanidhi said that he was 'waiting; until the eyes would not bear remaining open.'[13] But Nedunchezhian remained unmoved. Describing Karunanidhi as a 'dictator', Nedunchezhian and others came up with sixteen charges. Karunanidhi called them traitors and position seekers. Karunanidhi now penned an essay titled 'Et tu Brute'. He needn't have bothered. They were political ciphers with little mass support.

On 8 May, at the inaugural of his Makkal Dravida Munnetra Kazhagam (People's DMK), Nedunchezhian wondered why the

Kazhagam, which had had a streak of success under Anna, faced defeat under Karunanidhi.

> People had begun to be disappointed and disgusted with Kalaignar Karunanidhi's leadership. Consequently, the DMK suffered a crushing defeat in Dindigul, Coimbatore assembly, parliamentary by-elections and Puducherry election. He alone is responsible for the ministry's dismissal . . . on eight charges.
>
> As reasonable as it is to own and enjoy Kazhagam's honour, fame, and success, it would be equally fair to own responsibility when Kazhagam meets with decline, humiliation, and defeat.[14]

Nedunchezhian assured that there would be no 'worship of individuals' in his Makkal DMK. Nedunchezhian failed to say there would also be no Makkal DMK for very long and that it was just a bridgehead to the AIADMK.[15] Never a leader in his own right, Nedunchezhian merged his party with the AIADMK in four months—on 17 September. However, his arrival would also trigger Manoharan's exit as there was room for only one number two. Wasn't Nedunchezhian the permanent number two?

Ananda Vikatan now lampooned the DMK as a boat with holes. On 15 May, the Madurai general council, attended by 462 of the 577 members, chose Anbazhagan as general secretary and Sadiq Pasha as treasurer and amended its rules to create the post of a deputy general secretary.[16] The colourless Anbazhagan would play the loyal number two till Karunanidhi's death.

1977 Assembly Election

Karunanidhi's isolation continued with the Janata shutting the door on the DMK for the assembly elections. Karunanidhi positively spun the situation. With allies, they would have ended up fighting for only a hundred seats, leaving the other hundred to the Janata and the rest to others, he said. They could fight all seats now.[17] Karunanidhi, who had refused to part with a single assembly seat in 1971, was prepared to concede an equal number of seats now.

The DMK fielded candidates for 230 seats, allotting the rest (four) to smaller allies. Karunanidhi was proud that forty candidates were MISA internees. The AIADMK fought in alliance with the CPM and IUML. Congress (I) and CPI fought together. Popular weekly *Kumudam* placed Congress (I), Janata and the AIADMK for the first three places and the DMK last.[18]

The AIADMK won the four-cornered race, ushering in a long political winter for Karunanidhi. The DMK's forty-eight seats, and forty-two lakh votes, nonetheless, belied all earlier analyses. Karunanidhi pointed out that the DMK and Janata could have claimed 137 seats, which would have gone up to 150 seats with the CPM.[19] He pointed out that the difference between the DMK and the AIADMK was just ten lakhs, reminding his siblings of the DMK's long-standing demand for proportional representation.[20]

1977 ASSEMBLY ELECTION

Party	Contested	Won	Votes	Percentage
AIADMK	200	130	51,94,876	30.36%
INC	198	27	29,94,535	17.50%
CPI	32	5	4,96,955	2.90%
CPM	20	12	4,77,835	2.79%
DMK	230	48	42,58,771	24.89%
AIFB	6	1	50,831	0.30%
JP	233	10	28,51,884	16.67%

In Opposition

Karunanidhi proved a good shepherd to his DMK flock during this politically parched period. Internally, however, he was in a hurry to end his exile. Even as early as 1978, Karunanidhi reportedly tested the waters within for reconciliation with Indira Gandhi. Understandably, the party had little appetite for such an early about-turn. In 1980, Karunanidhi would finally reach an understanding with Congress (I), sharing equal seats. However, these efforts to defeat MGR proved Sisyphean.

The tables now turned against him, Karunanidhi was the Leader of the Opposition while his bête noire MGR was the chief minister. Each obsessed over the other, and their relationship was best known only to them. In August 1978, commenting on MGR, Karunanidhi said, 'Pure cine glamour has brought him success,' adding:

> He was a stunt actor, nothing more. He used the films to project himself. He painted himself as God. As in his films, he also plays a double role in his politics. He wants prohibition to show people his Gandhian ideals. What ideals? He is not even a true Tamilian. Although he gives his age as 61, people say he's at least 65 or 66.[21]

Only months later, MGR opined that Karunanidhi was a 'terrorist'.[22] Outside the House, they spewed spite on the other, yearning for the other's fall. Yet, in the legislative assembly, they showed a grudging respect with MGR vaunting the fact that they addressed the other as 'Andavane!', or 'God'. And thanks to the years of friendship, the early years of struggle and indignities, tireless pursuit, mutual help and success—moments of tenderness would sometimes come to the fore.

The rapport was such that in August, in a public meeting, DMK legislator Nellikuppam Krishnamurthy said their camaraderie caused doubts in the cadres, who deserved an explanation. Underplaying it as business, Karunanidhi said that it was not as 'suspected to look into the almanack for a date for the merger of the DMK and the ADMK'. It was a Freudian slip, and a merger would almost happen in two years. On MGR's request, DK's K. Veeramani became a gofer to an incredulous Karunanidhi, who told Veeramani he was the third emissary and was unsure of MGR's sincerity. This backchannel continued until Janata leader Biju Patnaik, on Charan Singh's behest, brought the idea of a merger into the open in September 1979.

Test of Wills

Indira Gandhi's 29–30 October visit became the first test of wills between the two leaders. At the last minute, on 27 October, the DMK executive decided on black flags for the former prime minister. Karunanidhi wrote a passionate appeal to cadres and led the protest at Saidapet. In Madurai, Indira Gandhi's car came under attack. Police used sixteen rounds of tear gas and baton-charged the crowd, even as Indira Gandhi sat in her car. DGP Mohandas said that but for the police intervention, it would have been another Sriperumbudur (where Rajiv Gandhi was assassinated). Pazha Nedumaran, who was in the car with her, had physically shielded Indira Gandhi from the assault. In its aftermath, *India Today* commented that the '48-hour tour ended in a grand fiasco, leaving behind two dead, 200 wounded and over 1000 in jail', while Congress (I) and MGR claimed Indira Gandhi would have been murdered.[23] Karunanidhi touted the day when Indira Gandhi and India understood the DMK as 'heirs of the Self-Respect movement'.[24] But on 29 October, in the public meeting at the Marina addressed by Indira Gandhi, Tamilarasu Kazhagam leader Ma.Po.Si. said his 'DMK friends had made Tamils cringe in shame before the world.' Director General of Police K. Mohandas said that the Janata Party had put the DMK up to the task. Karunanidhi denied this and called the protest a 'duty'.[25]

Karunanidhi and the cadres were arrested and interned for forty days.[26] Thousands now filled the jail, seeking their leader's release. On 9 December, Karunanidhi was released.[27] However, Karunanidhi and 134 others were later charged with, among other things, conspiracy to murder Indira Gandhi. On 4 August 1995, the Supreme Court upheld the High Court's earlier dismissal of these cases. Unlike the wheels of justice, in a little over two years, the exigencies of politics would see Karunanidhi and Indira Gandhi travel in the same vehicle as allies.

A peeved and spurned MGR declared then, 'If the Congress (I) can have an alliance with a man like Karunanidhi, there is no reason why it cannot have one with someone like me who had ordered police firing to protect Amma from Karunanidhi's goons when she visited Madras four years ago.'[28]

Sarkaria Findings

On 4 January 1978, Karunanidhi moved the first of the two DMK no-confidence motions against the MGR administration, charging that it acted contrary to Anna's policies and, perhaps taking a dig at MGR's purported desire for a merger and added that 'the two parties cannot unite as far as ideology is concerned'.* He charged that the 'AIADMK implemented mini-MISA on Indira Gandhi's advice to finish off the DMK' in the black-flag protest.

On Sarkaria's interim findings, Karunanidhi insinuated that most charges could not be substantiated. Instead of focusing on good governance and planning welfare schemes, the MGR administration was focused on the DMK and was tirelessly repeating the same charges.[29] MGR appeared prepared. He said that CPM's P. Ramamurti had told him that Sarkaria would never reach the courts and that the cases would be dropped if they did, and said the problem was that witnesses were recanting their testimonies.[30]

On 12 May, Sarkaria's final report was placed before Parliament.[31] Sarkaria found substance in fourteen of the twenty-eight charges inquired, of which two were against Karunanidhi. The following

---

* On 19 February 1979, Sadiq Pasha moved the second.

Source: https://en.wikipedia.org/wiki/P._Ramamurthi

CPM's P. Ramamurti was a fierce critic of the Dravidian
movement who had in 1967 entered into a poll pact with
the DMK and the Swatantra Party

day, Karunanidhi said that all charges would have been dismissed if
Sarkaria had permitted the examination of witnesses.[32] On 19 May,
Karunanidhi asked at a public meeting in Mumbai if there was one
justice for Janata's ally Parkash Singh Badal and another for him.[33]

Sarkaria found that Karunanidhi unduly favoured 'Sathyanaryana
Bros' in the contract for pipes for the Veeranam Project and said,
'The responsibility for this huge waste of public money [of Rs 6 crore]
must rest squarely on Shri. Karunanidhi and Shri. Sadiq Pasha.'
Karunanidhi attributed the waste to bureaucratic delays and cited
Hirakud and Bhakra Nangal projects as examples.[34] Sarkaria said
Sathyanarayana Bros' Purushotham 'exploiting his friendship [with
Maran] to influence Karunanidhi' was established. Purushotham
had given Rs 59,202 worth of construction material for the 'Murasoli

Building without accepting payment from Maran—a fact admitted by Maran himself'.

Sarkaria further said that in the aerial spraying case, on 17 November 1970 and 22 September 1971, Karunanidhi received illegal gratification of Rs 25,000 and Rs 1,17,273, respectively. He added that Karunanidhi and Anbil Dharmalingam had 'conceived in concert a plan to bring down the Aviation Operators to their heels and make them submit to their extortionate demands for gratification in the shape of commission . . .'[35]

Similarly, Sarkaria found that P.U. Shanmugam and Karunanidhi received 'illegal gratifications in cash aggregating Rs 13,21,296' from sugar mills for creating the conditions to manipulate prices.

Sarkaria concluded that the Nedunchezhian Trust had received a donation 'from a student's parent as consideration for securing his admission in a college' and committed other improprieties. In March 1979, Karunanidhi, commenting on Nedunchezhian being made the general secretary of the AIADMK, asked, 'Could there be anything more disgraceful . . .?'[36]

The Commission said that P.U. Shanmugam abused his office to 'extract or collect funds' for his trust; the DMK's Anna Trust could not explain 'an excess deposit of Rs 1,06,000' and AVM Charities denied a donation of Rs 10,000 that the trust claimed. The Muthuvelar Arakkattalai run by Karunanidhi's nephew Amirtham, it said, had illegally diverted temple funds.

Sarkaria found that Si.Pa. Adithanar abetted the founding of four shell lift irrigation societies to obtain loans from the State Land Development Bank to the tune of Rs 17,40,000 and, although the loan was repaid, Adithanar was behind the attempts to 'intimidate, suborn or tamper with witness', the Commission said. The irony was Nedunchezhian, S. Madhavan, P.U. Shanmugam, Sathyavanimuthu, Adithanar and Madurai Muthu, named by MGR, later joined him.

Karunanidhi, however, insisted that nothing was proven besides the aerial spraying case and the sugar deal.[37] In 1998, speaking about Sarkaria, Karunanidhi said the alleged corruption amounted to Rs 50 lakh. As the chief minister in 1989, he revealed that on 15 November 1977, Advocate General V.P. Raman had advised Chief Minister MGR that it was neither advisable nor possible to launch a prosecution successfully for mere impropriety or irregularity and, on 24 October 1979, noted that 'with the exception of the allegation which related to aerial spraying none of the other allegations inquired into by the Sarkaria Commission can be successfully pursued further in a criminal prosecution' as the charges were not substantive enough to institute cases.[38] In 1989, the Karunanidhi administration closed the file. However, senior counsel and Congress (I) leader P. Chidambaram noted that year: 'I tell you even today, in the sugar deal, Karunanidhi was charged that he took money on this date, and Supreme Court judge Sarkaria, listing [the dates], said, "Yes, he had taken this amount."'[39]

The Sarkaria Commission, in retrospect, and considering Jayalalithaa and Sasikala and the 2G controversy, now appears tame. Time had taken the sting out of the Commission, and Sarkaria is better known nationwide for his 1984 Centre-state Relations report. In 1998, Karunanidhi pointed out that he had written seventy-six movies and produced ten, of which three were with MGR, and the successful films were 'very profitable'. His family members were writers, directors, producers and businessmen, Maran's son Kalanidhi Maran runs Sun TV and everyone's source of income is regular and 'there is no room for a case against my family or me for having amassed disproportionate assets to income'.[40] Yet, the phrase 'scientific corruption' attributed incorrectly to the Commission has stuck to Karunanidhi.

Karunanidhi turned the tables on MGR when, on 31 January 1979, speaking at Nagercoil, he alleged that a deal for buying ships from Bulgaria had been hatched for $11 million for the chief minister to siphon off a crore and a half.[41] On 3 February, in an 85-minute speech, Karunanidhi called it the 'scandal of the century', alleging that a crore had already been swindled and shared. MGR said that if it was proven that he had taken a single paisa, he 'will not be alive'.[42] Nedunchezhian pointed out later that the decision would have to be made with the approval of the Centre and the Bulgarian government, and neither an agreement nor a purchase occurred.[43]

Warming up to Indira Gandhi

Earlier, on 24 January 1978, speaking in Yavatmal (Maharashtra), Indira Gandhi owned up to the excesses during the Emergency. Soon, she would speak in a similar language in Tiruchi in February.[44] On 2 April, speaking in Madurai, Karunanidhi referred to Indira Gandhi's recent speeches and that the DMK would no longer consider her a political untouchable.[45] Yet he had to wait till Thanjavur for MGR's mea culpa.

The following day, George Fernandes hoped that Karunanidhi would not do anything to support a 'fascist'. Karunanidhi said the change in Indira Gandhi should be welcomed and added, 'DMK will seek reconciliation but not surrender.'[46] On 11 April, in a missive titled 'For Fernandes's Attention', Karunanidhi said that while cases against Parkash Singh Badal were withdrawn, those against him continued and wanted those who preached to do some introspection themselves.[47] Despite his angst, Karunanidhi supported the Janata candidate, Veerendra Patil, against Indira Gandhi in the 5 November 1978 Chikmagalur by-election.[48] Supported by the regional satrap, Devaraj Urs, Indira Gandhi won the election, only to be expelled from Parliament on 19 December 1978 and jailed for a week for alleged obstruction of a 1975 parliamentary probe of Sanjay Gandhi's auto-manufacturing business.

Thanjavur—MGR's Volte Face

Indira Gandhi was widely believed to be planning a run from Thanjavur in the by-election on 17 June 1979 with AIADMK support. On 14 May, press reports said that Karunanidhi would run against her. Karunanidhi said that the district secretaries and others had proposed the idea, and a final decision would be taken on 21 or 22 May.[49] Anbazhagan indicated at a public meeting that 'Thanjavur was not Chikmagalur, the chief minister of Tamil Nadu was not Devaraj Urs and Karunanidhi was not Veerendra Patil'.[50] The portents of a rich drama were everywhere.

MGR appeared committed to supporting Indira Gandhi's candidacy until the evening of the 20th. However, later that night, after meeting Desai with Rajaram, MGR declared that if she contested, it could give rise to a 'serious law and order problem' and said he wanted to avert 'another Madurai'. Desai had asked MGR if he was 'a friend or foe of us (Janata)' and asked him to 'be decisive and frank.' He had no issue with MGR supporting another Congress (I) candidate. MGR had much respect for Desai, and Desai, a teetotaller, was fond of MGR.[51] Much earlier, on 6 May, Karunanidhi had foreseen such a possibility in Thanjavur. Karunanidhi termed MGR's reasons 'scare tactics', described him as an 'all India jester', and reasoned that MGR had dropped Indira Gandhi, fearing an inquiry commission.[52]

The Congress (I) fielded its district chief, and MGR canvassed for him against the DMK's Anbil Dharmalingam. Congress (I)'s S. Singaravadivel beat A. Dharmalingam. In the second by-election in Nagapattinam, the DMK-supported CPI candidate, K. Murugaiyan, defeated the AIADMK's M. Mahalingam. Citing the 1977 election results for Thanjavur's six assembly segments, Karunanidhi pointed out that the DMK would have come first if they had fought separately, adding that MGR had 'hid behind the Congress (I)'s strength' in Thanjavur.[53] Thanjavur led to a serious rethink in the Congress (I) camp, and in a year, Karunanidhi would be fighting in the comfort of Congress (I)'s company.

Reservations on Economic Criterion

On 2 July, the MGR administration's decision to introduce an economic criterion limiting reservations to backward classes with an annual income limit of Rs 9000 presented an unexpected gift to the DMK.* Anna had somewhat set a precedent when he announced free education up to the pre-university level for children of needy parents whose annual income was not above Rs 1500, irrespective of caste.

Despite the DMK's pushback, MGR refused to roll back the measure. Karunanidhi suggested that if MGR had to introduce the economic criterion, he could do so in the 50 per cent general category but not touch the 31 per cent earmarked for the backward. MGR said that he was willing to conduct a referendum on the issue. Karunanidhi said MGR should have considered it earlier, adding that reservations were needed until castes were eradicated.[54] By a majority decision, the Madras High Court, however, upheld the MGR Government order. Yet, this victory would prove pyrrhic. The DMK–DK protests would have to be controlled by force, and MGR himself would do an about-turn.

Karunanidhi revealed in 1995 that the issue of reservations for economically weaker sections had stood in the way of the merger of the Kazhagams in 1979, as MGR was initially averse to conceding this point.[55] Four decades later, on 9 January 2019, the Bharatiya Janata Party government passed the 103rd amendment, reserving 10 per cent for 'economically weaker sections'. The amendment has

---

* MGR had spoken about need-based reservations earlier. Kerala had such reservations and MGR had reportedly acted on Kerala's former chief minister Achutha Menon's advice. T.S. Subramanian, 'Milestones in a Long Journey,' *Frontline*, 31 August 2018, 48.

been legally challenged. Incidentally, the DMK and the AIADMK were one of the few parties that opposed the measure.[56]

Merger Talks Come out in the Open

In the autumn of 1979, Odisha leader and Steel Minister Biju Patnaik and Minister of State Karur Gopal, at Prime Minister Charan Singh's behest, stepped in to try their hand at reuniting the Kazhagams. Charan Singh felt that if the Dravidian parties joined, all forty seats could be won, and Indira Gandhi's southern bastion could be breached. On 12 September, Patnaik met Karunanidhi, who posited six conditions for the merger: 1. The reunited party to function as the DMK; 2. Party flag could be the AIADMK flag; 3. MGR to continue as chief minister; 4. DMK need not be part of the ministry; 5. Posts of the president, general secretary, treasurer, etc., could be decided later; and 6. Importantly, MGR rescinds the economic criterion. Patnaik would meet MGR soon thereafter.

On 13 September, at 11 a.m., MGR entered the State Guest House, fondly addressing Karunanidhi as 'Andavane!' Anbazhagan accompanied Karunanidhi, and MGR took Nedunchezhian, Manoharan and Panruti S. Ramachandran. For forty minutes, the two leaders met privately. MGR, confirming the conditions, assured Karunanidhi that the executives and the general councils of the two parties could meet separately on a fixed day to pass the merger resolution.

The two leaders later told the press they had discussed some 'basic issues'.[57] That evening at Vellore, MGR repudiated the agreement and claimed that Karunanidhi wanted the merged entity to be called DMK and the AIADMK's flag and election symbol changed. On 14 September, Karunanidhi revealed that Patnaik had proposed an alliance between the two parties, but he had sought reunification, for only as a merged entity could they rescind the order on economic criterion. MGR, who was reluctant to concede the sixth condition, came around later, but those opposed to reservations for the backward persuaded MGR against it.[58] On 21 September, Karunanidhi alleged that the talks were intended to derail the DMK-Congress (I) alliance and for MGR to forge an alliance instead.[59] The US consul general, on the other hand, recorded that Karunanidhi had used the meeting to 'set up MGR'[60] and said that the real issue was 'who should be seen to rejoin whom, with Karunanidhi insisting that MGR come back to the DMK he left in 1972'.[61]

On 1 April 2009, at a public event, Karunanidhi blamed the other Ramachandran for the failed merger: 'I know who had played spoilsport . . . I don't want to name him . . . But without his name, history would be incomplete . . . He was Panruti Ramachandran, who had travelled along with MGR to Vellore after our meeting . . .' After learning that MGR's fans' association head had come under attack, S. Ramachandran told MGR that while they could get together at the top, the cadres could not work together. The merger was, in any case, a mirage and would have never worked. The party had split purely because of the two men's egos, and the majority in both camps was deeply invested in the separation. Yet both leaders played along to Patnaik's idea even as they kept their options open. While MGR had hosted breakfast for Congress (I) leader Karuppiah Moopanar on 13 September, Karunanidhi was booked to fly to Delhi on the 14th to meet Indira Gandhi to stitch an electoral deal. Clearly, in the game of cravenness to woo Congress (I), Karunanidhi had beaten MGR—this time.

In June, Cho Ramaswamy had smelt a rat and asked him about a tie-up with the Congress (I). Karunanidhi's riposte was that the journalist's 'imagination was boundless'. 'Would we yield for lowly electoral successes?'[62] But that is exactly what he would do.* On 23 June 1980, Sanjay Gandhi died in an air crash. He was considered

---

* On 12 September, he wondered that if the DMK had won ten or twelve seats in Parliament and in the event the cases were withdrawn, then would it not be a sham to say that Morarji is a disciplinarian and honest. *Murasoli*, 13 September 1978, 1.

an extra-constitutional authority and the reason behind some of the Emergency excesses. Yet, Karunanidhi, in his tribute, described him as 'India's future hope'.[63]

On 15 September, Karunanidhi met Indira Gandhi after a hiatus of four years and then met her in the company of C.M. Stephen, R. Venkataraman and R.V. Swaminathan to reach an electoral understanding under which the DMK and the Muslim League would contest seventeen and the Congress (I) twenty-three seats, including Puducherry. Karunanidhi called the rapprochement a 'huge turning point in politics'.[64]

While MGR commented, 'Let the wicked go with the wicked; we shall align with the righteous', Devaraj Urs, Karnataka's chief minister who had fallen out with Indira Gandhi, called it an 'unholy alliance'.[65] From then on, Karunanidhi began to sing hosannas to the understanding. On 21 September, he said that there were some 'painful events' in between, 'but for the nation's sake, we must bind ourselves with the events of political change'.[66] On 28 September, he called it a 'noble alliance!'[67] On 25 September, reacting to Desai's comment that Karunanidhi had requested the withdrawal of the cases on him, Karunanidhi said that there was nothing wrong with it.[68]

Earlier, in July, Charan Singh had revived his Lok Dal, split the Janata Party and on 28 July 1979, took over as prime minister with Congress (I) and AIADMK support. On 19 August, Bala Pazhanoor and Sathyavanimuthu of the AIADMK became the first-ever central ministers from a regional party. However, as Indira Gandhi withdrew support within a month, Charan Singh quit to continue as caretaker prime minister. MGR chose to return to the Janata Party for the 1980 parliamentary polls (Lok Dal was a non-entity in the state), and the two ministers quit on 23 December. MGR cut a sorry figure, but he had set a precedent, and rightly bragged later that he had sent a Christian and an Adi Dravida to the Centre.[69]

1980 Parliamentary Poll

On 30 September, speaking at the Marina, Karunanidhi said they were renewing a long-standing relationship to eliminate poverty, end inequalities and steer an era of social justice, concluding, 'We do not want a *tamasha* at Delhi . . . We believe only Thirumathi Indira Gandhi can give us a stable government.'[70] Indira Gandhi claimed that they had come together with a 'purpose' and a 'principle'; they believed in the same socio-economic programmes, and astonishingly said that the DMK Government had 'made a genuine effort to implement our twenty-point programme'. She added, 'There had never been a moment when we thought we agreed, but behind the scenes there was something else'; and the disagreement 'was never on basic national issues'.

She said she had accepted responsibility for the mistakes and had lost the government, adding that she reciprocated Karunanidhi's desire for cooperation, for it was for 'a great cause—the cause of our country'. [71] Earlier, Indira Gandhi had indicated to party workers that after the 'drama' of Thanjavur, it had become clear that the AIADMK was not reliable and was not keen on a tie-up. She claimed the DMK government was removed because its term was nearly over.[72] At the 1 December election conference at Salem, Karunanidhi coined the famous slogan, '*Nehruvin magale varuga! Nilayana aatchi tharuga!*—Nehru's daughter welcome! Give us a stable government.'[73]

On 6 January, *Murasoli* published separate appeals to voters from Indira Gandhi and Karunanidhi. In her appeal, Indira Gandhi said that India had greatly lost its dignity under the Opposition, said she could do good with the DMK and asked for people's vote to build a 'strong and glory-filled India'.[74]

The Congress (I) won all but the Gobi and Sivakasi seats, where it lost to the AIADMK.

The DMK won all sixteen seats and was rewarded with G. Lakshmanan becoming the Deputy Speaker of Parliament. The

Congress (I) led in 119 and the DMK in 83 of the 234 assembly segments. In the Puducherry assembly elections, the DMK won fourteen seats, INC ten, the CPI one, Janata three and independents two. The AIADMK failed to win a single seat.

1980 PARLIAMENTARY ELECTION

Party	Contested	Won	Votes	Percentage
AIADMK	24	2	46,74,064	25.38%
INC	22	20	58,21,411	31.62%
CPI	3	0	6,60,940	3.59%
CPM	3	0	5,91,869	3.21%
DMK	16	48	42,36,537	23.01%
IUML	1	1	2,32,567	0.08%
JP	9	0	14,65,782	7.96%

MGR attributed the DMK–Congress (I) victory to sympathy for Indira Gandhi. Locally, the twenty-lakh-strong farmers association and a section of the police were disaffected, and the harsh prohibition statute had backfired among women. Karunanidhi said that while people wished for Indira Gandhi to return, it was a vote of no-confidence against MGR.[75] On 9 January 1980, *Murasoli* said, 'Glamour politics had been sent to the grave.'[76] 'The days of Ramachandran's political hegemony are numbered' was the epitaph that *India Today* wrote for MGR.[77] Was it?

16

Again in the Opposition

On 19 January 1980, the DMK executive announced a three-phase agitation from 29 January against the economic criterion.[1] Five days later, on 24 January, the chief minister revoked the order and, in a complete turnaround, increased reservations for the backwards from 31 to 50 per cent. The DMK patted itself on the back, but the truth was that MGR had taken the wind out of the DMK's sails.

That day, shaken by the rout in the parliamentary polls, MGR also diluted the stringent measures against drinking, allowing permit holders to rise to a staggering 9,00,000 from 8000. Karunanidhi commented: 'MGR has now virtually opened liquor shops and made the Prohibition Act a dead letter.'[2] On 9 February, the MGR government withdrew cases against farmers.

On 15 February, the DMK and allies handed over a memorandum containing forty charges against MGR to the visiting President and the governor and the following day to the prime minister in Delhi.[3] Two days later, on 17 February, the MGR government and eight other state governments were dismissed.

On 3 March, Manoharan joined the DMK, claiming later that he was a 'walking corpse' under MGR.[4] On 3 April, Karunanidhi disclaimed 'vote politics' in taking back the deserters, claiming that it was the 'sign of a compassionate heart'.[5] But none was politically consequential.

Faustian Bargain

On 4 April, Karunanidhi revealed that the DMK and Congress (I) would contest 109 seats each, and the chief ministerial candidate would be known 'with time'. Karunanidhi said he would have settled for 'even fewer seats' to redeem Tamil Nadu, which was 'engulfed in darkness'.[6] But it was a Faustian bargain. As he was kept guessing on the coalition's chief ministership, on 16 April, Karunanidhi spun the situation positively, phrasing the issue before the electorate as: 'It is not who should be; it is rather who should not be chief minister.'[7] Perhaps Karunanidhi had spoken *Aram*. He was not to be. On 13 April, *Murasoli* published a Press Trust of India story claiming sources in Delhi had revealed that Karunanidhi would be chief minister. Karunanidhi said this was agreed upon at the 1 March meeting with Indira Gandhi.[8]

However, M.P. Subramaniam, the new Congress (I) state president, would deny any knowledge of the accord. The Congress (I) dissension and its anxiety to win a larger number of seats than its ally to deny it the chief ministership would do the alliance in. On 20 April, Indira Gandhi finally confirmed the 1 March agreement, making a bad situation worse, torpedoing any Congress (I) hopes of leading the coalition and taking away the incentive to make the alliance work. Eight years later, on 20 December 1988, Congress (I)'s P. Chidambaram termed the chief ministership and the equal number of seats for the DMK as 'very wrong decisions . . . politically and morally.'[9]

The DMK promised: free university education, debt relief to farmers, a department for the welfare of government staff, concessional gold for weddings for the poor, free housing plots for the rural poor, a Rs 100 stipend for registered unemployed graduates and housing for Dalits and fisherfolk.[10] Although similar, the AIADMK's promise of a kilo of free rice for every five kilos, a job per family and a rupee a day for those below the poverty line caught the voters' imagination.[11]

Yet, on 29 May, Karunanidhi prophesied that MGR would not end up even as the Leader of the Opposition, projecting 180 seats or more for the alliance the following day.[12] Karunanidhi was wrong. As voters differentiated between parliamentary and assembly elections, the AIADMK won 129 seats and recaptured power. The DMK's vote share fell to 22 per cent, thanks to the fewer seats it contested (the fewest ever). Worse still, Karunanidhi could only win by 699 votes in Anna Nagar, the lowest margin in his political career. MGR described Karunanidhi as 'a spent force' and lost no time in mending relations with the Centre.[13]

1980 ASSEMBLY ELECTION

Party	Contested	Won	Votes	Percentage
AIADMK	177	129	73,03,010	38.75%
INC	114	31	39,41,900	20.92%
CPI	15	9	5,01,032	2.66%
CPM	16	11	5,96,406	3.16%
DMK + IUML 6	118	38	42,48,790	22.55%
AIFB	2	1	65,536	0.35%
GKNC	10	6	3,22,440	1.71%
JANATA PARTY	95	2	5,22,641	2.77%
TN KAMARAJ CONG 6 + INC (URS)	9	3		

GKNC or Gandhi Kamaraj National Congress is led by Kumari Anandan. TN Kamaraj Congress led by Pazha Nedumaran and INC (Urs) fight as part of AIADMK alliance. TNKC wins three of six seats. INC (Urs) loses all three seats.

Karunanidhi explained that he was 'never out of step' with Indira Gandhi, but local differences led to Adi Dravidas deserting the DMK, and the commitment on the chief ministership boomeranged.[14] Karunanidhi later lamented that to have trusted 'cats and foxes' was the DMK's mistake.[15]

On 3 June, at his fifty-sixth birthday meeting at the Marina, Karunanidhi pontificated that the difference between the two fronts was just nine lakh votes, that twenty-five lakh had changed course since the parliamentary elections, and, likewise, the nine would not take long to change. Attributing MGR's victory to his many promises, Karunanidhi impishly added that one could expect the venue for the rice pick-up the day after MGR's cabinet was in place! Yet, the speech is known more for Karunanidhi's hurt and angst at being spurned.

Comparing himself to the 'house dog' that refuses to quit its keeper despite being beaten and chased away, Karunanidhi said that despite the defeat, he remained theirs. Again, comparing himself to a mother who does not drop her child because it had peed on her and instead endearingly calls the child her eyes and jewel, Karunanidhi concluded his speech by saying, 'I will always serve you.'[16]

Enter M.K. Stalin

But he was not alone. A successor was emerging in M.K. Stalin. Karunanidhi's investment in his eldest son Muthu had proved a mirage. A MISA-minted Stalin was of a different mettle. As a teenager, Stalin had founded the DMK's Gopalapuram Youth Association and graduated to staging propaganda plays later. At the fortieth staging of his *Murase Muzhangu* (Oh! Drumbeat!), MGR as *Periya thanthai*, or uncle, echoed Karunanidhi's concern, openly counselling Stalin to concentrate on his studies.[17] But in 1976, with the Emergency internment, the die was cast.

Anna and Periyar

Photo credit: 'Stills' Gnanam

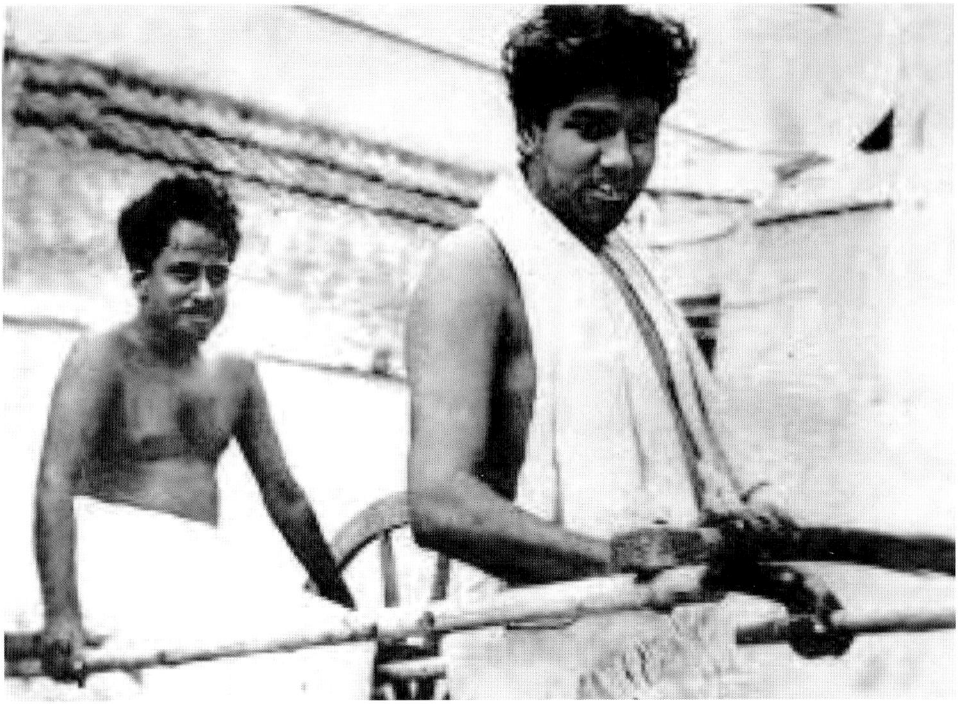

Photo credit: 'Stills' Gnanam

Formative years: Anna with E.V.K. Sampath

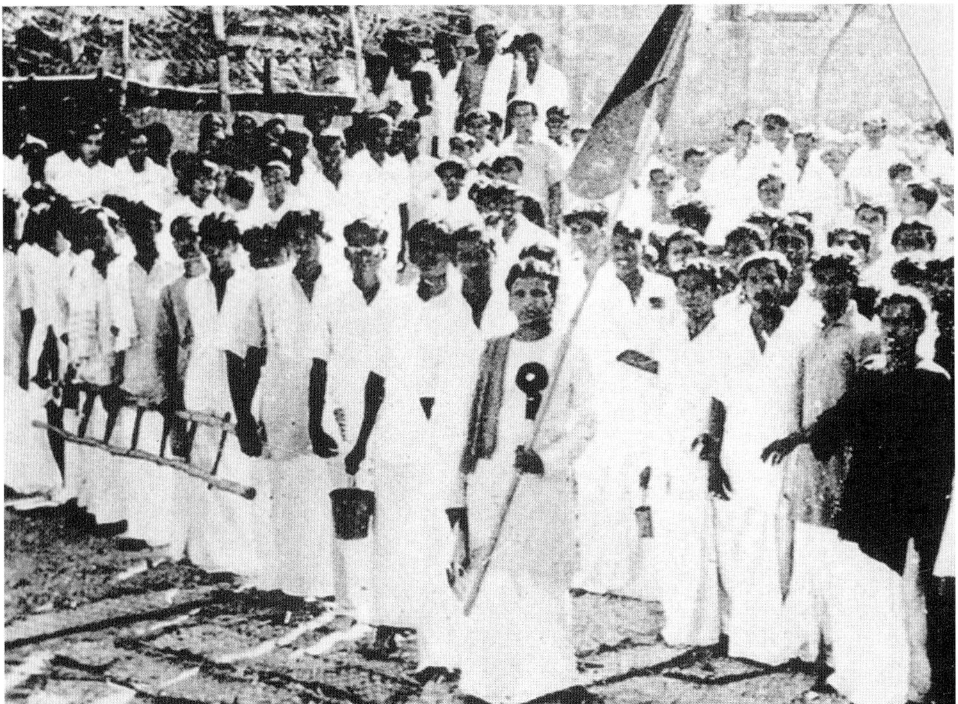

Photo credit: 'Stills' Gnanam

Karunanidhi leading a protest in the early years

Three chief ministers in the making: MGR, Anna and Karunanidhi with actress Bhanumathi and movie mogul S.S. Vasan

Anna and Rajaji

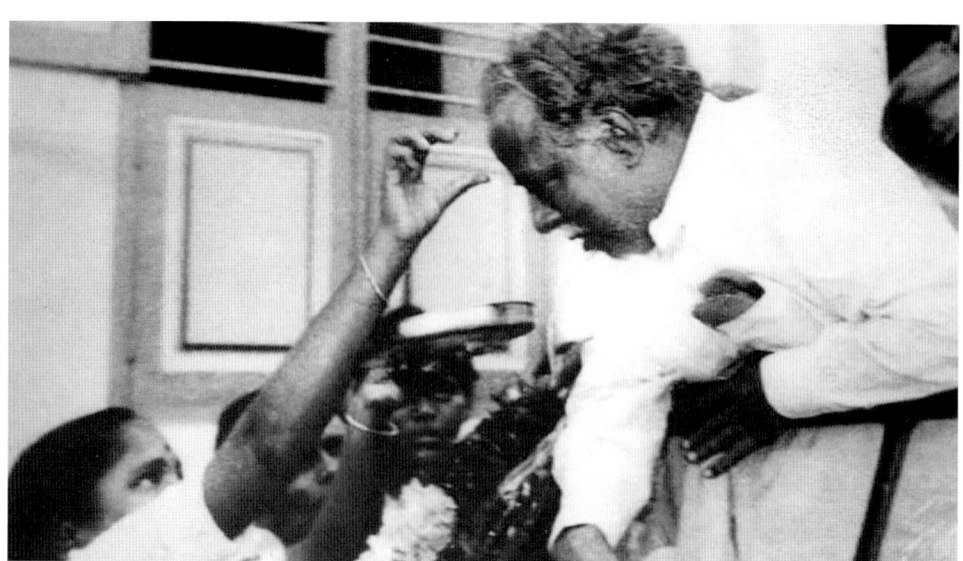

Leader of the traditional ally Indian Union Muslim League, Quaid-E-Millath Muhammad Ismail, with Anna

Photo credit: 'Stills' Gnanam

Anna on the campaign trail

Photo credit: 'Stills' Gnanam

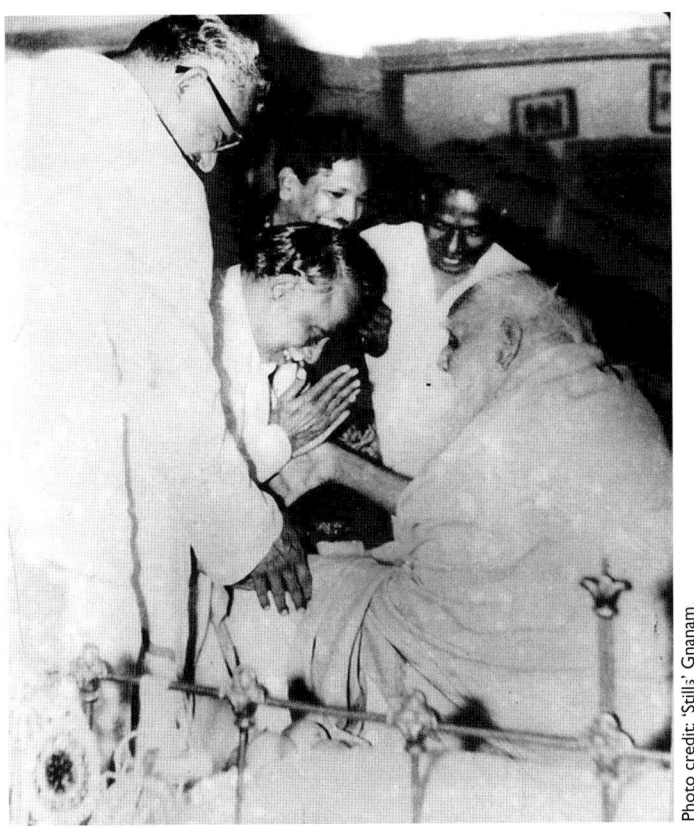

Nedunchezhian, Anna, Karunanidhi and Anbil Dharmalingam
seeking mentor Periyar's blessings after the 1967 victory

Chief Minister Anna, Public Works Minister Karunanidhi and Rama Arangannal (in the car)

Photo credit: 'Stills' Gnanam

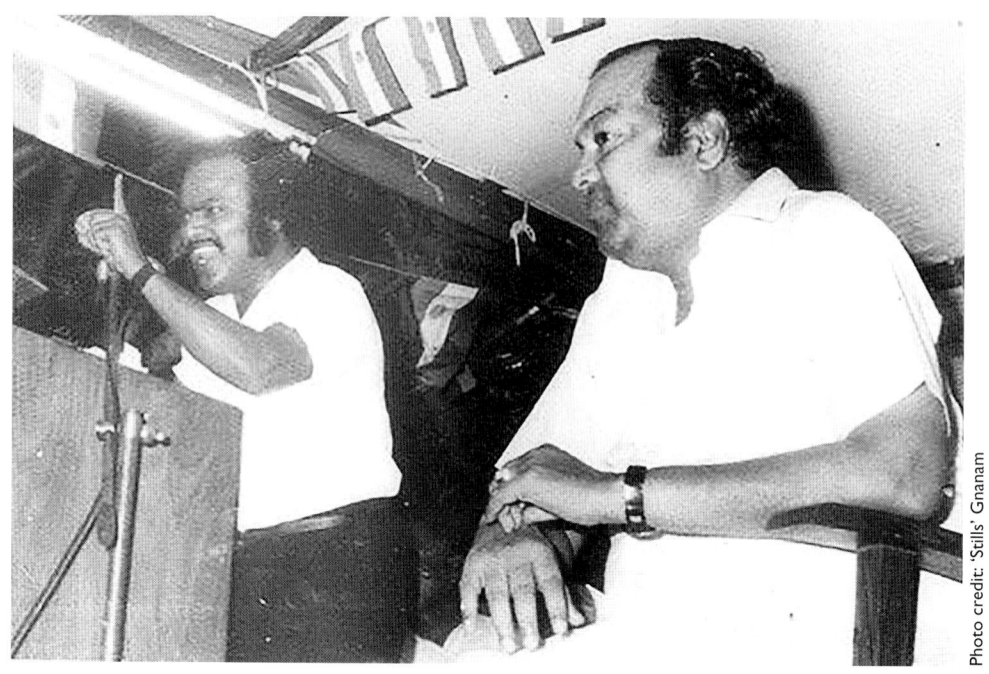

The author Jayakanthan (at the dais) and the poet Kannadasan—Kamaraj's feisty supporters

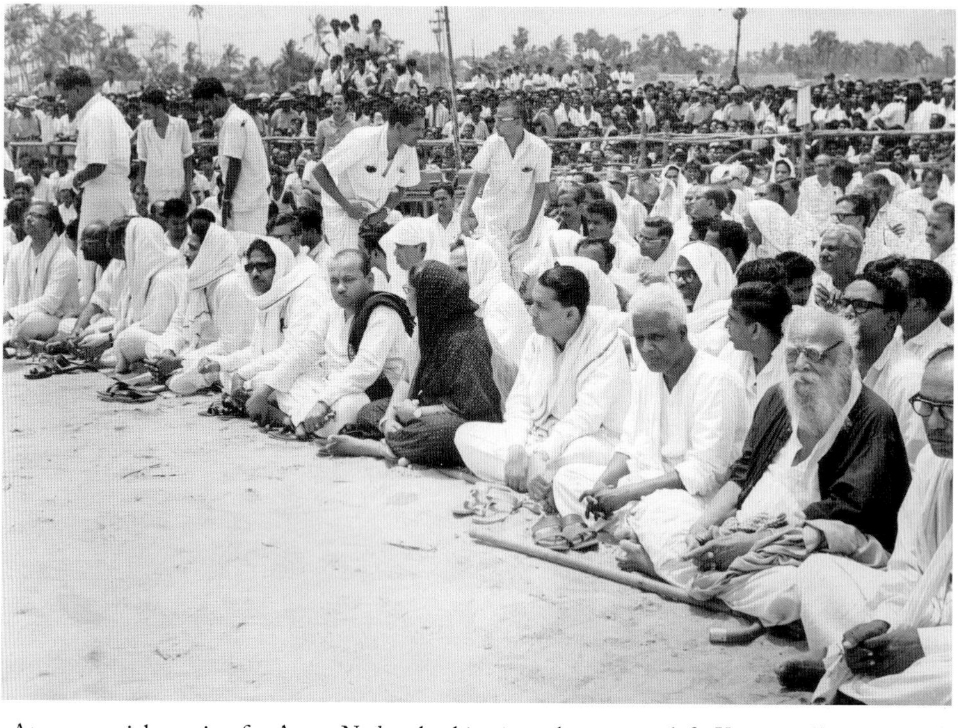

Photo credit: 'Stills' Gnanam

At a memorial meeting for Anna. Nedunchezhian is to the extreme left. Karunanidhi is wearing dark glasses, to his left is Mathiazhagan. From right to left are N.V. Natarajan, Periyar, Pulavar Govindan and Sadiq Pasha. Behind Govindan is S. Madhavan

Karunanidhi with his mother, Anjugam

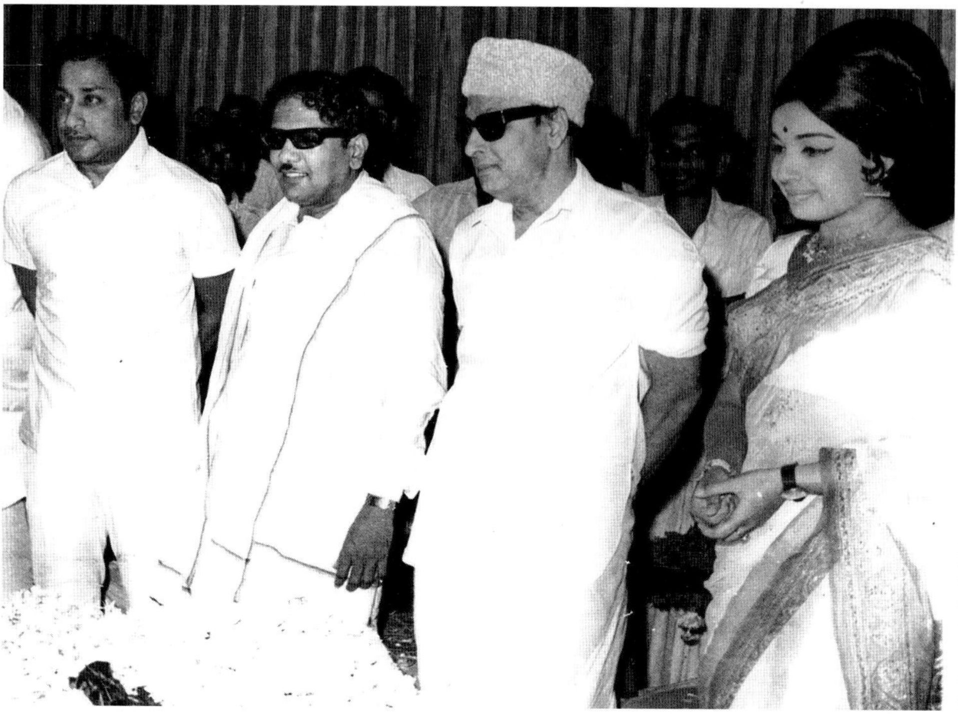

Photo credit: 'Stills' Gnanam

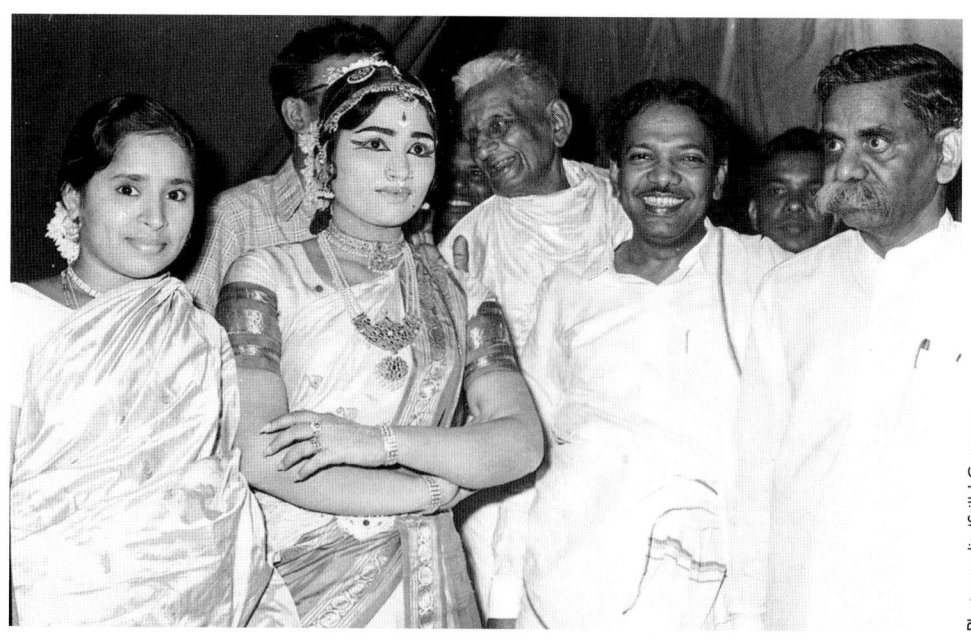

Sivaji Ganesan, Karunanidhi, MGR and Jayalalithaa at the *Savaale Samaali* (1971) movie felicitation

Photo credit: 'Stills' Gnanam

Karunanidhi with Tamilarasu Kazhagam's Ma.Po.Si., or Ma.Po. Sivagnanam (with a thick moustache). Ma.Po.Si. was behind the Tamil Nadu name change and was the architect of the state autonomy demand. The inclusion of Tiruttani into Tamil Nadu is also credited to him

On 21 July 1980, Karunanidhi inaugurated the party's youth wing at the Madurai Jhansi Stadium. Karunanidhi wrote that membership was open to those aged fifteen to thirty years and not 'a day more'.[18] The new wing soon eclipsed the others.[19] On 2 August 1982, a five-member coordination committee of M.K. Stalin, Tiruchi Siva, Parithi Ilamvazhuthi, Walajah Hassain and Tharai Manian was announced. Anbazhagan claimed that since Karunanidhi's entire family had 'given themselves to the Kazhagam', there was no need 'to separately entrust specific tasks' by making Stalin the secretary.[20] Karunanidhi appeared coy about his son's role but not for long. On 18 April 1983, Stalin became secretary and 5 June 2003 deputy general secretary and on 23 January 2009 treasurer. Soon, Stalin was anointed *Thalapathi*, or commander, a title once reserved for the Dravidar Kazhagam's Pattukottai Azhagiri and Anna. Whatever Stalin lacked, he made up for it with industry. For thirty-four years, he led the wing before stepping down at sixty-three and being elevated to working president on 4 January 2017.[21]

In 2016, Karunanidhi said that Stalin had elevated himself to be 'DMK's future leader' with his hard work. Therefore, he was his 'political heir'.[22] But in 1993, the party had split on this. Stalin later characterized 'dynastic politics' as a 'very complex issue', adding that Anna handpicked Murasoli Maran and citing him as Karunanidhi's doing was 'absurd'. Stalin said his public life had spanned fifty years, and he had risen 'gradually with industry and everyone's approval'. He concluded that dynastic politics was part of 'India's culture, an all-India phenomenon, and present in all fields'.[23] In 2016, Stalin assured that neither his son nor his son-in-law would join politics.[24] But we are getting ahead of ourselves.

Tit for Tat—The Ray Commission

Karunanidhi would embarrass and expose the MGR administration as inept, notoriously corrupt and in bed with the liquor lobby. On

18 January 1981, Karunanidhi alleged a scam of Rs 12 crore in the illicit diversion of rectified spirit to Kerala and sought an 'impartial central inquiry'. On 4 February, Karunanidhi blamed the chief minister for being on the take.[25] Three days later, Karunanidhi charged that MGR cared for Kerala's interests more than he did for Tamil Nadu and added that 'Keralites are doubly fortunate for they have two chief ministers fighting for Kerala's interests: one there and one here'.[26]

On 10 February, MGR appointed Justice Kailasam, a friend, to head an inquiry. From 22 February, the DMK began picketing to press for Kailasam's recusal. That day, Manoharan and M.K. Stalin, among others, were taken into custody and released after five weeks.[27] In all, some 7500 had courted arrest.[28] Meanwhile, Kerala's CPM Chief Minister E.K. Nayanar hinted that 'DMK men' were also involved and appointed an inquiry commission.[29]

The MGR administration inexorably moved to the other end of the prohibition spectrum. On 6 April, the amendment to the Prohibition Act led to the opening of 14,000 toddy and liquor shops.[30] On 10 May, Karunanidhi alleged a Rs 3-crore bribe in awarding bottling licenses and claimed a crore had already passed hands.[31]

Four days later, the CBI withdrew the aerial spraying case against Karunanidhi, reasoning that key witnesses had recanted.[32] MGR's political career had been built around the Sarkaria Commission, but, in the end, the way the Commission came into being and its discarded findings proved purely political.

On 29 May, as Justice Sadasivam replaced Kailasam, Karunanidhi termed it 'an eye wash commission'.[33] These manoeuvres of MGR were of no avail. On 18 June, history repeated itself when Indira Gandhi named the Justice S.K. Ray Commission on the rectified spirit scandal. Ray was given six months to submit his report.[34] The report never saw the light of day. Both Tamil Nadu and Kerala contended before the Supreme Court that the move was redundant as they had their own probes.

Meanwhile, as private entities made a killing in the liquor contracts, on 16 June, the DMK executive suggested that the state take over production, blending and bottling or entrust it to cooperatives.[35] On 4 August, Karunanidhi alleged MGR's liquor licensing improprieties came to Rs 5 crore.[36] In October, he upped this figure to Rs 20 crore.

Karunanidhi had been picking at the chinks in MGR's armour, one by one—from the aborted ship deal, rectified spirit and the scams in bottling, blending and liquor licensing. But there was no silver bullet yet. On 30 October, a frustrated Karunanidhi said that however much they 'shout at the top of their lungs', MGR believed he could not be shaken.[37] MGR made light of Karunanidhi's charges but felt compelled to appoint the K.S. Ramamurthi Commission that day. Ramaprasada Rao would take over from Ramamurthi and, in April 1984, clear MGR and his colleagues.[38]

Ethnic Issue—1981

Earlier, from 4 to 10 January 1981, the Fifth World Tamil Conference was held in Madurai. Karunanidhi stayed away, complaining that he was not properly invited, rendering it an exclusive MGR show as the latter wished. Nonetheless, the litmus test for Tamil affinity lay twenty miles south of Tamil Nadu in Sri Lanka, where Tamils faced an uneasy existence.

The week-long ethnic violence in Sri Lanka and the burning down of the Jaffna public library on 31 May–1 June saw passions inflamed in Tamil Nadu. On 7 June, Karunanidhi appealed to Indira Gandhi to treat it as a 'humanitarian issue' and followed up with a meeting with her on 25 June.[39] MGR met the prime minister separately, and on 21 August, the assembly adopted a unanimous resolution urging the prime minister to protect the Tamils. Further, in a first, it called for a shutdown on 12 September.

Before long, the issue became hostage to competitive politics. Karunanidhi complained that MGR was 'not serious' and announced the picketing of the Sri Lankan mission for 29 August. Denied permission, he turned the picketing into a recurring one and courted arrest on 15 September.[40] His arrest led to at least five, including a woman, burning themselves to death while eleven suffered burns for their leader.[41] On 25 September, Karunanidhi appealed against the 'sacrificial fire' that he said burnt his heart, and on the following day, pointed out that neither Anna nor he 'accepted' this course.[42] However, on his release on 29 September, Karunanidhi spoke differently: 'The Tamils have woken up because a leader backed by the masses and revered had been imprisoned. The self-immolations symbolize the awakening of the Tamil people.'[43]

In trying to paint MGR as supine, Karunanidhi had pushed the envelope. During the thick of the agitation, Indira Gandhi cryptically replied, 'Ask the local leaders' about the alliance with the DMK. The shift became apparent on 31 October when after meeting MGR, the prime minister welcomed support from all parties in the 29 November Tirupattur assembly by-election, prompted by the Congress (I) incumbent's death. The AIADMK had choreographed the sequence of events conveying its support offer through the Intelligence Bureau's M.K. Narayanan. The Congress (I) had to simply say it welcomed the support.

MGR justified the political trapeze act by saying that the incumbent's party should retain the seat caused by the member's death. On 8 November, Karunanidhi wondered who would succeed if the deceased were independent. Writing about this period later, he said that 'Indira Gandhi had developed some bitterness and malice' towards the DMK but did not elaborate.[44] The Congress (I) forbade the DMK and AIADMK to campaign from its platforms. Karunanidhi was in a pickle. He chose to stay away in a selective feint of self-respect, but his declaration that he would not end the alliance added insult to the self-inflicted injury.[45] In twenty months, the DMK would be pushed out.

Long March Seeking Justice

On 24 November, Karunanidhi made public the copy of the Justice Paul Commission report concerning the 26 November 1980 death of a temple verification officer—provided to him as Leader of the Opposition, inviting criminal charges against him, his two government aides and nephew Murasoli Selvam.* Paul had concluded that 'homicidal violence' had taken place and recommended the dismissal of the trustees before an inquiry.

On 13 February 1982, Karunanidhi, asking that the guilty be brought to book, led the DMK walkout in the assembly. On 15 February, he chose the 180 km *Needhi Kaetu Nediya Payanam* (Long March Seeking Justice) from Madurai to Tiruchendur to press his claim. En route to Madurai, an official met him in his train at Villupuram to relay the chief minister's appeal to give up the march. Karunanidhi declined, saying it would help the chief minister overcome his reluctance to punish the guilty.

On D-Day, 30,000 workers joined their leader. On the second day, as Karunanidhi's legs swelled, a music band stepped in to cheer their leader while MGR telephoned him to plead again that he discontinue the walk. A thoughtful chief minister had also sent an ambulance. Karunanidhi walked 200 km over eight days, met two lakh people and termed the march a 'new record!' On reaching Tiruchendur, he addressed a massive rally while sitting, owing to the swelling in his legs.[46]

Nutritious Noon Meal Scheme

On 1 July 1982, MGR joined the children of Paappakurichi village in Tiruchi district at lunch to inaugurate the now celebrated Chief

---

* The two aides were placed under suspension and Karunanidhi was arrested and later released. On 7 February 1989, the DMK government withdrew the case. *Murasoli*, 11 February 1989, 5.

Minister's Nutritious Noon Meal Programme (CMNMP) for school pupils.[47] On 11 October 1987, Finance Minister Nedunchezhian put the number of total beneficiaries since 1983 at 92 lakh. The nation had rarely seen a scheme of this magnitude. A job per family and free toothpowder for children were introduced on 2 September and 14 November 1982. In 1987, free veshtis and saris were handed out, and plans for free footwear were afoot. The age of freebies had arrived.[48] Freebies would expand to include gas stoves, colour TVs, laptops, bicycles and scooters over time.*

The meal scheme put the DMK on the back foot and on 17 September, Karunanidhi denied that he opposed the scheme and alleged that half the money was spent on AIADMK men and that the rice was bad.[49] However, MGR alluded that Karunanidhi had said that 'Rs 250 crore has been meaninglessly spent' and asked: 'Won't the people of Tamil Nadu figure him out after this?'[50] Unsurprisingly, the DMK was compelled to continue the programme, adding eggs twice a week and promising milk in the 2016 elections. On 15 September 2022, as chief minister, M.K. Stalin, in a throwback to the Justice Party's scheme, began a free breakfast scheme for primary school children in 1500 government-run schools.[51] The scheme was announced in 2016 by Jayalalithaa but was never put into place.

Enter Jayalalithaa

On 4 June 1982, MGR's longest reigning female lead, Jayalalithaa, joined the AIADMK and debuted two weeks later at the Cuddalore conference, making an impression. Cuddalore collector V.S. Chandralekha introduced her to Sasikala Natarajan, a video rental shop owner. Jayalalithaa met Sasikala's husband, M. Natarajan, two years later.[52] Sasikala's job was to video-shoot Jayalalithaa's meetings. Sasikala would later become a surrogate sister to her.[53]

---

* On 26 August 2022, the Supreme Court said a three-judge bench would take up pleas to review its 2013 judgment that tied freebies to the directive principles.

In January 1984, Jayalalithaa said, 'Today, MGR is everything to me' and when he was no more, reiterated, 'He was everything to me!'[54] The most-paired female lead with MGR, Jayalalithaa had staged a comeback after a decade in MGR's life, this time as his female lead in the political theatre.

On 18 August 1982, MGR named Jayalalithaa a member of the high-level committee overseeing the noon meal scheme. In January 1983, she was made propaganda secretary,[55] bringing gravitas to this otherwise low-key function. MGR entrusted her with the February 1983 Tiruchendur by-election and Jayalalithaa proved herself.[56] On 24 March 1984, MGR nominated her to the Rajya Sabha and she was elected on 29 March 1984.[57] She was allotted seat number 185, the very seat where Anna had sat from 1962 to 1967.

At public meetings, women came in large numbers to see this elegant woman, their heartthrob's favourite heroine. But Jayalalithaa's imperiousness and importance caused heartburn amongst senior leaders. She soon appeared both a blessing and a liability.

Jayalalithaa understood early on that her relevance depended on her opposition to Karunanidhi, and she took this as a personal mission.

Jayalalithaa and Karunanidhi viciously disliked each other. Jayalalithaa taunted Karunanidhi as a 'dark force' and the 'head of a family administration' while he described her as a 'witch', 'vampire' and 'corruption queen'. On 24 September 1991, Chief Minister Jayalalithaa claimed that the DMK's mean campaign that she was a *paapaathi* (an offensive term to indicate a Brahmin woman) had failed. People instead considered her to be from the 'caste that serves us (them)'.[58]

Tiruchendur was the first time Karunanidhi deigned to take note of her when he described her as a shooting star or a star with a tail in Tamil, implying that she was hanging on to MGR's coattails.[59] In January 1984, Jayalalithaa complained of Karunanidhi's 'cowardice' in letting his proxies respond to her, that he could not answer a single question of hers, and that DMK speakers spoke in 'filthy language' about her.[60]

Back to Tiruchendur: Karunanidhi attributed the AIADMK's razor-thin win to malpractice and termed Tiruchendur a 'turning point'. [61] Karunanidhi's sentiment was justified. After the September 1982 Periyakulam parliamentary by-election, this was the second by-election that the DMK had fought on its own. In Periyakulam, the DMK had polled nearly as many votes singly as it had in 1980, together with Congress (I).[62] The DMK-Congress (I) alliance was all but broken, and the Congress (I) had fielded its candidates in both Periyakulam and Tiruchendur.

Southern Chief Ministers Meet

The formal break-up with the Congress came about unexpectedly. On 20 March 1983, other than the Congress (I) chief minister of Kerala, four southern chief ministers met for ten hours in Bengaluru to discuss Centre-state relations under the aegis of Karnataka Chief Minister Ramakrishna Hegde. MGR's presence left Karunanidhi with no option but to instruct his Puducherry man to join. MGR's proposed Southern Council of Chief Ministers was announced but never met. Congress (I) General Secretary C.M. Stephen called the conclave 'highly dangerous, because it panders to the rising regionalist tendencies'.[63] In retrospect, there was much hype about the one-off meeting.

MGR attended the 28 May Vijayawada conclave but stayed away from the rest in Delhi, Srinagar, Kolkata and Delhi again, pointing out that after Bengaluru, the conclaves had moved away from Centre-state relations to opposition to Congress (I).[64] The DMK joined those meetings. Karunanidhi attended the Kolkata and the 21 August 1984 meeting in Delhi to discuss the N.T. Rama Rao government's dismissal in united Andhra Pradesh.[65]

Four days after Bengaluru, on 24 March, Indira Gandhi announced the Sarkaria Commission on Centre–state Relations.

Bengaluru had achieved what Karunanidhi's 1974 resolution could not. But then nearly a decade had passed, and Punjab was staring into Indira Gandhi's face. A Commission—the age-old trick in governance—was the answer.[66] On 29 March, welcoming the Bengaluru conference, Karunanidhi claimed there were 'twenty Quebecs in India' and urged the MGR administration to bring another resolution along the lines of his 1974 resolution.[67]

Despite the uneasiness between the two parties, the Puducherry DMK-Congress (I) coalition government experiment had lasted all this while. But with Bengaluru, the farce of the alliance had reached its end. The Congress (I) withdrew support, and the DMK's second Puducherry coalition experiment fell flat on its face on 24 June.[68] Karunanidhi claimed victimhood and pride in its wake. Three days later, DMK's G. Lakshmanan resigned as Deputy Speaker of Parliament. Karunanidhi was now free to don the principled Opposition leader's role. And the ethnic issue in Sri Lanka gave him all the excuses.

Karunanidhi Advocates Intervention in Sri Lanka

On 2 July 1983, addressing a rally on Sri Lankan Tamils, Karunanidhi said that they had been suffering for a long time, that Colombo had never permitted his visit, and that 'Indira Gandhi's compassion to Palestine Liberation Organization's Arafat or South Africa's Alfred Joe' (*sic*) should extend to Tamils as well. That day would come; if not, 'we will make it happen,' he said.[69]

As the Sri Lankan anti-Tamil riots peaked on 25 July, Karunanidhi called for a rally on 27 July and assembled a sea of humanity in seven hours to urge the Centre to act.[70] At the rally, Karunanidhi called for sending the Indian Army to Sri Lanka, as in Bangladesh.[71]

---

* He would rightly describe Sarkaria as a 'status quo' commission on its recommendations five years later.

On 30 July, Karunanidhi asked India to end its 'complacency' and emulate the 1974 Turkish intervention in Cyprus.[72] On 31 July, the DMK's executive called for a shutdown on 2 August, followed by picketing on 4 August and a stop-rail agitation on 5 August to press for military intervention. On 1 August, Karunanidhi called for India to create a separate Tamil state in Sri Lanka. He said:

> Suppose the interest in the Tamils is genuine, and the statement that Tamil Nadu is a part of India and Tamils are Indians is true. A part of that Tamil community is dying daily on the neighbouring island!
>
> Why cannot the Government of India come forward to enable a peaceful life permanently for them?
>
> Is this question unfair?
>
> Is this so difficult for the Centre to answer?
>
> I humbly ask this on behalf of the DMK to Indira Gandhi, madam.
>
> How do we resolve this issue?[73]

Indira Gandhi had meanwhile begun a covert assistance programme to train Tamil militants for strategic leverage even as India lent its good offices.

On 5 August, as the Centre cancelled trains, the DMK declared victory.[74] Indira Gandhi told Parliament that the events had caused 'anguish and anxiety to the entire nation', and although India did not wish to interfere, India was not 'just any country' to Sri Lanka.[75]

After a series of protests[76] the finale was reached on 10 August when Karunanidhi and Anbazhagan resigned their assembly seats, faulting the state and the Centre for their 'inability to protect Tamils', not dispatching the army and not seeking UN peacekeeping forces or inviting Sri Lankan Tamil leaders to hear them out. *Murasoli* headlined the resignations as a 'renunciation' and 'sacrifice'. Karunanidhi said that the Tamil race's future had become a question mark[77] and later encouraged DMK cadres to collect a million signatures from 15–20 August to urge UN involvement.*[78] On 11 August, Karunanidhi set fire to the Sri Lankan Constitution's Sixth Amendment banning secessionist advocacy and said that 'Tamil Eelam' was the only solution.[79]

That day, the DMK walked out in Parliament on the prime minister's 5 August statement calling for talks and a solution within Sri Lanka's unity and integrity. On 12 August, Karunanidhi said that Indira Gandhi put good relations with Sri Lanka before the Tamils.[80] On 16 August, MPs Maran and C.T. Dhandapani met the prime minister at her request to suggest that India condemn the incidents, raise it at the UN and seek international observers.[81] In the Rajya Sabha, Maran lamented that the Centre had not condemned the July incidents and then read out the 1971 parliamentary resolution on Bangladesh to contrast its approach.[82] Indira Gandhi replied: 'We have condemned and we do condemn genocide and where and we realize the harassment of and injustice to the Tamils of Sri Lanka.' Maran now called for recognition of the Tamil Eelam movement on the lines of the Front de Liberation Nationale (FLN) of Algeria that India had recognized.[83]

Karunanidhi later said it had taken 50,000 DMK cadres courting arrest, sixteen immolations of which ten were fatal, and his and Anbazhagan's resignations and the signatures to the UN to prompt Indira Gandhi to use the term 'genocide'.[84] Meanwhile, MGR and his ministers sported black shirts for a month from 16 August.

On 25 August, Indira Gandhi's special envoy, G. Parthasarathy (GP), called on Karunanidhi and MGR on his way to Colombo. Karunanidhi said that the DMK's position was well known. On 28 August, Karunanidhi said that if the Centre sent troops to Sri Lanka, the Congress (I) could rule Tamil Nadu for ten years, and

---

* The million signatures came to 1000 pounds and were handed over to the UN on 13 October 1983. *Murasoli*, 5 December 1983, 1–2.

the DMK would not make an attempt at power.[85] The next day, he unveiled the portraits of fallen Tamil militants in an event and advised them to unite.[86] On 27 October, speaking on a government resolution condemning Sri Lanka, MGR asked if the DMK demand for the army was for the militants or the Indian plantation Tamils who had been taken to the island from Tamil Nadu by the British to work in the tea plantations and lived amongst the majority Sinhalese. Roughly half the Tamil population in Sri Lanka, the Indian plantation Tamils' needs were not aligned to that of the Sri Lankan Tamils. Situated geographically amongst the Sinhalese, they sought better living conditions and a peaceful coexistence. In fact, they feared a backlash from the secessionist advocacy of their Sri Lankan Tamil brethren. He added that the militants he had met preferred arms and equipment and did not want army help.

Emphatic that Eelam Tamils should win Eelam and not Tamil Nadu, MGR pointed out the fate of the plantation Tamils amidst the larger Sinhala populace in case of such an eventuality. (On 8 August 1984, Indira Gandhi said in Parliament: 'The other Tamils who are in the plantations are completely spread out and defenceless. This is an extremely complex situation.'[87]) MGR wondered if his critics had 'a conscience' for saying he had no affinity for Tamils, adding that he and Karunanidhi had 'eaten from the same leaf* and Karunanidhi should bear this in mind.[88] He said he was a Tamil when he was in the DMK and had become a non-Tamil afterwards. On support to the Centre, MGR said that those who advocated confrontation all the time and no cooperation were being unfair.[89] The DMK could never respond to MGR.

MGR also sported and cultivated a personal relationship with the most promising of the militants—Liberation Tigers of Tamil Eelam's (LTTE) Velupillai Prabhakaran. The Tigers did not look

---

* A Tamil way of saying that they were bosom friends.

to Karunanidhi until MGR passed away, and Prabhakaran never officially met him.

In April 1984, MGR issued a public invitation to the militant leaders. Karunanidhi followed suit. The leaders of the Tamil Eelam Liberation Organization (TELO), Eelam Revolutionary Organization of Students (EROS) and Eelam People's Revolutionary Liberation Front (EPRLF) met Karunanidhi. But not the LTTE. MGR cancelled his meeting but wished to separately see LTTE's Prabhakaran and People's Liberation Organization of Tamil Eelam (PLOTE)'s Uma Maheswaran. To MGR's question as to why the LTTE chose not to meet Karunanidhi, LTTE's political adviser Anton Balasingham tactfully replied that Karunanidhi's invite was to score over him. MGR smilingly said: 'You have understood Tamil Nadu politics well.' MGR's support to the Tigers was under the table; he gave them a foothold in Tamil Nadu until 1986.[90]

AIADMK Woes

On 29 March 1984, Jayalalithaa was elected to the Rajya Sabha and later chosen as AIADMK parliamentary party deputy leader. Vaiko of the DMK too was re-elected that day.[91] The following day, Karunanidhi was elected to the legislative council.[92]

Jayalalithaa's arrival had led to upheaval within. The 20 May assembly by-elections where AIADMK and Congress (I) were allied and the rebellion of Excise Minister S.D. Somasundaram (SDS) were pointers to the party's drift. Jayalalithaa undertook a major campaign. Yet the DMK wrested the Mayiladuthurai seat from AIADMK and retained Anna Nagar, improving its earlier performance by an additional 9000 votes. Congress (I) took Thanjavur from the DMK. The AIADMK held on to Uppiliapuram. A jolted MGR vowed to cleanse the party of 'racketeers, liquor barons and capitalists'. Five days later, Jayalalithaa resigned as propaganda secretary. On 20 August, she reminded MGR to act on her 25 May resignation to preempt 'leaders like Somasundaram . . . leaving the party' because of her.[93] It was too late and too little.

On 30 August, S.D. Somasundaram said that people suspected the integrity of those at the very top of the administration. On 1 September, the general council expelled Somasundaram from the party. MGR asked that day whether it is 'deserved, just and moral' for SDS to accuse him, wondering in Tamil folklore style if Somasundaram, 'who makes this abominable accusation, will live well?' SDS reacted by saying that MGR's true face was showing, and he had proof of MGR's wrongs. Mohandas said MGR's health suffered a serious setback because of SDS.

On 2 September, MGR accepted Jayalalithaa's resignation. Jayalalithaa claimed later that MGR assured her that he would reinstate her in 'one or two months' but had taken ill. [94] On 3 September, Somasundaram was dismissed from the ministry. Somasundaram now claimed that Jayalalithaa was the 'de facto chief minister' and that MGR was 'the number one in the kingdom of the corrupt'.[95] Karunanidhi said that MGR, who had claimed to be a Buddha, 'has been unmasked'.[96]

MGR Takes Ill—Indira Gandhi Killed

On 5 October, with his kidneys failing him, MGR was admitted to the Apollo Hospital. He later suffered a stroke. As MGR fought for his life, humanity rose, offering prayers for his recovery. On 22 October, Karunanidhi joined the multitude, penning one of the most moving missives, saying that prayer meant appeal and that he, an atheist, would also pray, concluding: 'Like the fog that disperses with the rays of the sun, let your illness disperse!'

On 31 October, Indira Gandhi's assassination convulsed India. Karunanidhi rightly said that she was the last of the leaders known in India's nooks and crannies, that there was much she was to accomplish and that she should have lived long.[97] As Rajiv Gandhi, a pilot and her son, was sworn in as prime minister that day

Karunanidhi commented that the 'take off' had been good. Still, one would have to wait to see the 'landing'.[98]

On 5 November, MGR was airlifted to the US for medical treatment. On 11 November, Karunanidhi reminisced about their friendship and suggested holding elections on MGR's return, as he deemed it an honour to face MGR.[99] A week later, he recalled MGR kissing him on his forehead soon after his budget speech as chief minister in 1969. Yet, during the elections, the DMK wondered if MGR was alive.

1984 General Election

General elections for Parliament and the assembly were held on 24 December 1984 in Tamil Nadu. MGR was fielded from Andipatti. On 21 November, MGR affixed his thumb impression and subscribed to the oath of affirmation in the presence of the consul general in New York. That day, Karunanidhi proposed that he travel at DMK expense with two physicians to verify that MGR was well enough to do these things on his own.[100] Karunanidhi attributed this to the machinations of the Centre and said it was not good that Rajiv Gandhi would engage in such 'political chicanery' even at the outset of his long public career.[101]

The eight-party DMK-led alliance included an emaciated Janata, the two communist parties, the Farmers and Workers Party, Nedumaran's Kamaraj Congress, IUML and Tamil Nadu Forward Bloc. The DMK manifesto promised streamlining the meal scheme, yearly bonuses for government servants, free bus passes for students, free power for farm pump sets, free saris for women, the waiver of crop loans and an end to the 'liquor empire'. The manifesto promised an inquiry by a high court judge on MGR's illness and treatment. It said Tamil Eelam was the only solution.[102]

A member of the legislative council, Karunanidhi chose not to contest. His task was, however, cut out. He had to overturn the latent sympathy for MGR. He tried to do it, for the most part, deftly. Harping on his friendship with MGR, Karunanidhi addressed the

AIADMK cadres as 'siblings', claiming that MGR had once accepted him as leader and his government would pay for his medical bills—all the while questioning the state of MGR's health, insisting that MGR was not aware of what was being done in his name. [103]

Even the 'Moon Had Blemish'

Karunanidhi appeared desperate. On 3 December, Karunanidhi asked AIADMK cadres to entrust the chief minister's chair to him in trusteeship, only to hand it over to a healthy MGR on his return.[104] Manoharan later said that the speech backfired with the AIADMK cadres. But MGR's man Friday R.M. Veerappan was not taking any chances. On 7 December, he released three photos showing MGR reading a newspaper in his bed and walking with a stick to discredit Karunanidhi's 'lie'. Karunanidhi wondered if MGR would talk to him if he placed a call.[105] Karunanidhi also wondered if the Constitution would allow an 'invalid' to hold office.[106] On 8 December, he said at Srivilliputhur that people were ready for a 'major change' after seven years of misrule.[107] But Karunanidhi was not prepared for what followed.

On 9 December, a video of MGR holding and reading newspapers, eating and smiling was released. Shown along with Indira Gandhi's funeral footage, the video restored confidence in MGR's health and invoked sympathy. Further, the campaign saw Jayalalithaa suitably break down in meetings, assuring her audience that her leader was well and would return healthy.[108]

As a stiff contest loomed, on 15 December, Karunanidhi lamented in Tiruchi that he had been 'punished' for seven years, wondered what his crime was and admitted to shortcomings in his rule. He claimed that even the 'moon had blemish' and that the wrongdoings were unbeknownst to him, and that he had dealt with them whenever they were brought to his knowledge.[109] In utter humility, he said elsewhere, 'I will be the sandals to your feet.'[110]

Photo credit: Wideangle Ravi Shankaran

Jayalalithaa and MGR at the Madurai All World MGR Fans Association
Conference, 1986

The AIADMK–Congress (I) alliance won thirty-seven
parliamentary seats and 193 assembly seats. The North and Central
Madras seats had saved the DMK's total rout. Jayalalithaa later
claimed that she had won the election for the party.[111] Despite
the twin sympathy waves, the DMK won twenty-four of the 167
seats it contested. M.K. Stalin lost by a narrow 2292 votes to K.A.
Krishnaswamy. In a first, a Hindu nationalist won as an independent
in Padmanabhapuram.

1984 PARLIAMENTARY ELECTION

Party	Contested	Won	Votes	Percentage
AIADMK	12	12	39,68,967	18.36%
INC	26	25	87,55,871	40.51%
CPI	3	0	7,38,106	3.41%
CPM	3	0	6,14,893	2.84%
DMK	27	2	55,97,507	25.90%

TN Kamaraj Congress and GKNC contest one seat as DMK and AIADMK allies
respectively.

1984 ASSEMBLY ELECTION

Party	Contested	Won	Votes	Percentage
AIADMK	155	132	80,30,809	37.03%
INC	73	62	35,29,708	16.30%
CPI	17	2	5,67,527	2.62%
CPM	16	5	5,97,622	2.80%
DMK + IUML 8	175	24	63,62,770	29.34%
JP	16	3	4,93,374	2.28%

On 28 December, as the AIADMK legislature party elected MGR as their leader, Jayalalithaa walked out 'in a huff'. R.M. Veerappan said that she canvassed in Delhi for a coalition government to be led by her and he pushed back.

As Jayalalithaa fronted Nedunchezhian as chief minister, R.M. Veerappan said she would take over from Nedunchezhian after her Rajya Sabha term. 'That is the conspiracy', he insisted.[112] Jayalalithaa alleged MGR was kept hostage by the Janaki-R.M. Veerappan cabal.[113]

In his 30 December letter, Karunanidhi cheered the siblings, saying that some votes decided Socrates's fate by condemning him to death, but time had made the Greek philosopher immortal.[114] The difference between the two fronts was only 31 lakh, he said, adding that if 16 lakh had chosen to vote the other way, the results would have been different.[115] But this was a counterfactual.

17

Third Opposition Stint

Like King Vikramaditya and his repeated trips to capture the *Betaal,* Karunanidhi remained undeterred in his mission to unseat MGR. Consigned a third time to the Opposition, and this time not even the Leader of the Opposition, Karunanidhi fought hard to stay relevant—consummately employing the ethnic and language issues and keeping the party pulsating with life.

Jayalalithaa Marginalized

MGR's illness had split the AIADMK in two, and according to S. Ramachandran, MGR served as a 'bridge'.[1] R.M. Veerappan said he did a balancing act 'to retain control'.[2] It was a bit of both. A less-kindly Maran described MGR's third administration as 'a vegetable government'.[3]

On 20 January, the anti-Jayalalithaa camp reached for the jugular, removing her as the deputy leader in the Rajya Sabha. The following day, Jayalalithaa claimed MGR's wife Janaki was 'controlling the whole show against' her and a 'cabal of conspirators' held MGR 'prisoner'. Seeking an impartial inquiry, she wondered why they were afraid to let her meet MGR.[4] She explained her fighting spirit thus:

I do not have families to protect, business interests to protect . . . I have no husband, no children, no family, no relative, no ties, no bindings. If you ask me what I am living for, I am not living for myself, what do I have in life . . . I don't even have any friend . . . I am only living for the public cause which is why I have that courage.[5]

Journalist Solai records that 'Jaya was so ambitious that she wanted to become the chief minister when MGR was hospitalized', which was not lost on her opponents. On 3 February, Veerappan called her a 'fourth rate lady' and suggested that she was trying to 'capture' the party[6] and later claimed it was his 'moral duty to destroy her evil force'.[7]

On 5 February 1985, MGR returned to a hero's welcome and was sworn in on 10 February. On 14 February, 3 March and 18 March, in all, twenty-four ministers were sworn in, making MGR's third cabinet the largest in Tamil Nadu's history.[8]

On 19 February, Jayalalithaa met MGR at Fort St George for half an hour.[9] On 30 March, at the party's general council, Nedunchezhian indicated that MGR would drop ten to eleven corrupt ministers.[10] On 6 April, Karunanidhi, branding all of them corrupt, said that the chief minister was no exception and questioned the usefulness of MGR's proposed action.[11]

Karunanidhi Ups the Ante

Rajiv Gandhi had assured Jayewardene that his Sri Lanka policy would be an 'Indian policy', free from pressure from Tamil Nadu. Still, the pressure was unrelenting from the DMK.[12] From 15 March to 15 June, the implacable Karunanidhi penned sixteen letters advocating a robust Indian role. On 18 March, he claimed in the legislative council that 'India was afraid of Sri Lanka, a turkey berry country', adding there would be no Tamils left if this inertia continued. They would just get together the following year to pass a condolence motion.[13] On 24 March, he announced a month-long picketing of central government offices and a campaign for ten million signatures for Eelam.[14]

On 2 April, addressing India's security sensitivities, Karunanidhi asked that there be no fear that Eelam would lead to a separate Tamil Nadu. Such thought, he said, could arise only if the annihilation of Sri Lankan Tamils was not stopped.[15] On 26 April, he announced the creation of the Tamil Eelam Supporters Organization (TESO) to lobby for Eelam.*[16] The next day, he said that, unlike MGR, a DMK government would have passed a resolution for Tamil Eelam. Voted into power thrice later, Karunanidhi did no such thing. Ironically, it was Jayalalithaa who passed a resolution on 25 March 2015 that came close to calling for Eelam.†[17] On 16 May, Karunanidhi courted arrest and was released on 30 May. In all, some 30,000 people had courted prison in picketing. Finally, Karunanidhi chose to mark his sixty-second birthday as Eelam Tamils Rights Day and receive contributions for the Lankan Tamils.[18]

Meanwhile, the India-sponsored talks between the Sri Lankan government and Tamil groups in Thimpu in July and August collapsed. The ham-handed deportations on 24 August of LTTE's A.S. Balasingham, TELO adviser N. Satyendra and S. Chandrahasan prompted Karunanidhi to lead a large TESO rally the next day where he said that if the Centre could not bring forth a solution, Tamil Nadu could do it by running training camps for the state's youth.[19] On 27 August, giving the prime minister three days to reverse the deportations, Karunanidhi called for a stop-train agitation for 30 August. On 29 August, Chandrahasan returned. Satyendra chose not to return and Balasingham returned several

---

* On 13 May, he enlisted the Dravidar Kazhagam, Nedumaran's Kamaraj Congress and Ayyanan Ambalam's Forward Bloc as part of TESO.
† The assembly resolution urged the Centre to move a resolution in the United Nations Security Council, including a referendum on the creation of Eelam.

weeks later. On 30 August, 2500 DMK volunteers courted arrest in a stop-train protest.[20, 21]

MGR Plays His Last Card

On 5 September, Jayalalithaa was reinstated as propaganda secretary and R.M. Veerappan was divested of his information portfolio. Her profanest critic, Kalimuthu, remarked, 'MGR, like Lord Shiva, has swallowed poison to save the party.'[22] But like the poison lodged in Shiva's throat, Jayalalithaa's comeback was difficult to swallow for her opponents. As they rebelled, MGR shocked his cabinet colleagues on 28 October by announcing that he was quitting, only to reverse his decision after R.M. Veerappan's moving speech on his indebtedness to him and Nedunchezhian's and Rajaram's intercession.

MGR had played his last card. However, its effect wore off quickly. Kalimuthu termed Jayalalithaa's reinstatement an 'enigma' and indicated the limits to MGR's diktat: 'To say "yes" to everything that the leader does, temple cows can be appointed as ministers.' He added that eighty-five MLAs were opposed to any plan to make Jayalalithaa deputy chief minister.[23] On 1 November, the chief minister clarified that there would be no deputy. Asked if the storm had subsided, he said: 'Even a gentle breeze was not there.'[24] But the storm continued to rage and MGR, till his death, played arbiter. Meanwhile, the DMK and allies marked 8 December as a protest day against MGR's 'misrule'.[25] However, the AIADMK won by a comfortable margin against the DMK in the 17 December Cheyyar assembly by-election. MGR had campaigned for R.M. Veerappan's nominee.

Local Body Election—Council Abolition

On 24 January 1986, R.M. Veerappan was given back his information portfolio and three additional subjects. More disconcertingly for

Jayalalithaa, in a signed statement in *Anna*, the party organ, MGR asked that the party bodies in Jayalalithaa's name be dismantled, adding that he was only reiterating his warning of December 1983.[26]

Mohandas said MGR plotted the 23 February civic elections to help restore order. Instead, they exposed the party's decline. Neither MGR nor Jayalalithaa campaigned. For the first time, eighteen-year-olds voted for local bodies, an election held after fifteen years. The DMK won sixty-four and its allies eight of the ninety-seven townships. AIADMK won eleven of the fifty-eight townships in which it put up candidates.[27]

Karunanidhi asked those elected to carry out their duties with humility, responsibility, fairness and service-mindedness.[28] With a third of the seats in the legislative council to be filled from the local bodies, the possibility of Karunanidhi serving as the Leader of the Opposition in the council had emerged.*

In mid-April 1986, MGR nominated actress 'Vennira Aadai' Nirmala, his counsel N.C. Raghavachari and G. Swaminathan to the council. On 21 April, a writ petition challenged Nirmala's nomination as she was declared insolvent in 1984. Nirmala cleared the debt but withdrew her candidacy after the governor asked MGR to explain her nomination.[29]

Three weeks later, on 14 May, Nedunchezhian moved a one-sentence resolution in the chief minister's name to abolish the sixty-six-year-old legislative council. He said that the chief minister had decided after consulting ministers, such as himself, during the past seven-eight months and that the move would cut down expenditure. The previous day, Karunanidhi pointed out in the council that twenty

---

* In 1986, the term of the local body heads would be reduced to three years from four, and in 1987, it provided for the right to recall of elected officials on charges of corruption or abuse of position. *Tamil Nadu Legislative Assembly (Eighth Assembly) Review: 1985–88*, 53. (Chennai: Legislative Assembly Department, 1988). Accessed 1 May 2022, https://assembly.tn.gov.in/archive/8th_1985/8threview_85-88.pdf; On 14 May, Karunanidhi wondered why the MGR government did not bring a statute to recall ministers. *Murasoli*, 16 May 1987, 1.

to thirty boards, including one for poultry, had been formed, and the governor cost Rs 30 lakh annually. In contrast, the council cost only Rs 25 lakh. Karunanidhi offered to quit to save the council.[30]

Karunanidhi Grows Silent on the Ethnic Issue

Earlier, on 4 May, the TESO 'Save Sri Lanka Conference' in Madurai brought A.B. Vajpayee, N.T. Rama Rao, H.N. Bahuguna and other leaders together. MGR called for an all-party meeting on 3 May. P. Chidambaram and Romesh Bhandari, minister of state and foreign secretary, travelled to Colombo for talks from 29 April to 4 May. Karunanidhi remarked that every time the DMK or TESO voiced support for the Tamils, it was 'routine' for the state and the Centre to show that they were engaged.[31]

At the conference, Karunanidhi said that the Centre had no 'definite policy' on Sri Lanka and followed an 'indifferent' course.[32] Two of the conference's three resolutions called on India to give up its 'nonchalant' attitude, approach the issue not as a mediator but as the country with 'direct and close links' with the Tamils, explore all avenues to ensure that Tamils lived as equals and bring up Sri Lanka's 'genocide' in international forums. The third resolution appealed to international financial institutions and donors to withhold aid. In his welcome speech, Karunanidhi alleged that the Sri Lankan government was not sincere, and Rajiv's engagement provided an 'alibi' for Colombo to seek international aid. He announced that the second Save Ceylon Tamils Conference would be held in Andhra Pradesh.

In a consultative meeting with the militants, including the LTTE and the moderate Tamil United Liberation Front (TULF) earlier, Karunanidhi appealed for the militants' unity and to the LTTE to spare TELO leader Sri Sabaratnam's life, only to see his appeal fall on the LTTE's deaf ears, when two days later, Sabaratnam was killed.[33] On 8 May, Karunanidhi said he was 'very confounded'.[34] On

18 May, unveiling the slain militant's photograph, Karunanidhi said that until the militants united, he would remain 'silent'.[35]

However, on 24 May, with no let-up in the violence, the DMK called for a total stoppage on 31 May to spur the Centre to action. On 29 May, saying they could not be in a place where opposition was voiced to the Eelam idea, the DMK walked out of the all-party meeting. Earlier, the 3 May all-party meeting had endorsed a solution within a unified Sri Lanka.[36] Karunanidhi then asked cadres to mark his birthday by donating to the Eelam cause for the second year.[37] On 4 June, he announced he would distribute the Rs 2.75 lakh collected by the five militant groups at the birthday. The LTTE, however, chose not to take the money and, despite reminders, would not even contact the DMK.[38] But from then on, for the next nine months, Karunanidhi maintained a deafening silence on the issue.

Batting for Prabhakaran

Earlier, on 8 November 1986, police picked up Prabhakaran and other militants following a shootout at Choolaimedu. In its aftermath, Prabhakaran complained that they were 'arrested, interrogated and detained as common criminals'. Rs 40 crore worth of military equipment was also seized but returned to the LTTE on MGR's orders.[39] Karunanidhi maintained a stoic silence. The shootout had caused public aversion.

A week later, on 16 November, on the margins of the 16–17 November South Asian Association for Regional Cooperation (SAARC) summit in Bengaluru, Prabhakaran refused to accept Jayawardene's devolution offer despite the pleas of the Indian team and MGR's persuasion. Soon, the Chennai police confiscated LTTE's communication equipment and those of the other groups. Prabhakaran began an indefinite fast on 22 November, embarrassing the state and the Centre, leading MGR to order the return of the equipment. The vicissitudes of Tamil Nadu's hospitality now clear, Prabhakaran shifted to Sri Lanka.[40]

That day, breaking his silence briefly, Karunanidhi described the seizure as a 'betrayal' and lambasted the Centre and the state.[41] But Karunanidhi had chosen to make virtue out of necessity. The LTTE had hitherto shunned him. Karunanidhi was sore, but the Tigers had forged ahead of the other groups and held the cards to a solution. On 24 November, Karunanidhi injected a sense of high-mindedness into his predicament when he said that regardless of the LTTE's 'respect' for him and the DMK, the party 'cannot harbour old ill-feelings' and his 'little party' would speak for the 'haplessly murdered Tamils'.[42]

Disqualification of DMK Legislators

Earlier, on 27 September, the DMK executive announced a protest for 17 November, setting on fire copies of Part XVII of the Constitution on Hindi and demanding the incorporation of Nehru's assurance into the Constitution.[43] From 19 September to 13 February 1987, Karunanidhi dedicated thirty-three of his thirty-five letters to the issue, stirring the DMK cadres to action following the annual Hindi week circular of the Centre's Press Information Bureau calling staff to observe a 'Hindi week' from 16 September and identifying seven areas for Hindi usage.[44] To Home Minister Buta Singh's explanation that it was routine, Karunanidhi said that routine did not mean it was justified.

Meanwhile, on 21 October, MGR axed ten ministers, including R.M. Veerappan and Kalimuthu.

At the 8–9 November Anti-Hindi Conference in Coimbatore, Karunanidhi termed the protest a continuation of the fifty-year struggle against Hindi and said 15,000 had volunteered to participate on 17 November.[45] On 13 November, MGR stole a march on Karunanidhi when an assembly resolution in his name echoed the

DMK demand. Karunanidhi claimed the resolution was the result of the DMK's protest and made it clear that the protest would continue.[46] This was a mistake.

On 16 November, at the send-off for Anbazhagan, who was to engage in the protest the following day, Karunanidhi laboured the point that the protest meant no dishonour to the Constitution and that Anna had conceived the exact protest in 1963,[47] and that it was setting a piece of paper on fire and nothing more. A pre-emptive arrest foiled Anna, yet he was awarded a six-month prison term. Importantly, Karunanidhi underestimated MGR's resolve.

The next day in Chennai, Anbazhagan burnt a piece of paper with the constitutional provision on Hindi as part of the protest in seven of the constituencies in the city. Along with Anbazhagan, six legislators, twelve women and three children were among the 302 arrested that day.[48] On 20 November, Karunanidhi wrote to ten Opposition chief ministers urging them to pass resolutions on Nehru's assurance in their assemblies. No one seemed to oblige him. On 24 November, Speaker P.H. Pandian disqualified the seven legislators, prompting Maran to compare Pandian's action to Roman emperor Caligula's attempt to make his favourite horse, Incitatus, a Roman senator.[49]

Insisting only the Election Commission could decide,[50] Karunanidhi indicated that he was willing to give his life.[51] On 9 December, he got into the act and obtained a ten-week prison term. On 10 December, *Murasoli* said that 17,566 were in jail.[52] Charges were pressed under the Prevention to National Honour Act on several arrested. However, they were released on 2 February 1987, sixteen days before the term. Karunanidhi's internment saw six commit self-immolation, three poison themselves to death and nine others die in police firing.[53] On 22 December, following a bitter four-hour-long debate, a government resolution disqualifying ten DMK legislators was adopted by 131 votes to twenty-four, consequently bringing down the DMK strength to fourteen.[54] While Karunanidhi said that

MGR had taken 'revenge', Anbazhagan unsuccessfully mounted a legal challenge the next day.[55]

V.P. Singh Emerges

On 11 April 1987, Defence Minister Vishwanath Pratap Singh (VP), the Raja of Manda, resigned from Rajiv Gandhi's cabinet. As finance minister, VP's actions against tax fraud and foreign exchange violations had earned him a reputation as being cleaner than Mr Clean, his boss. But on 9 April, when VP announced that his ministry was probing Rs 30 crore in kickbacks on HDW submarine purchases—when the prime minister was also defence minister—he had overreached. Five days later, Swedish Radio claimed that arms manufacturer A.B. Bofors had paid commissions to the tune of Rs 64 crore in the sale of its howitzer guns to India.[56]

On 13 April, Karunanidhi said that Mr Clean had come under a cloud and, borrowing Kamaraj's famous idiom for the Kazhagams, said that Rajiv and VP were 'planks from the same [Congress] puddle'.[57] Ironically, VP ended up as the closest prime minister to Karunanidhi. On 2 October 1987, VP founded the Jan Morcha party, and it soon became the rallying point for the anti-Congress (I) political forces, which coalesced into the National Front on 6 August 1988. On 11 October 1988, the Jan Morcha merged with the Janata Party and the Lok Dals to become the Janata Dal. Riding a popular wave, VP became president of the Janata Dal. Janata Party president Chandra Shekhar conceded ground to VP, stating, 'There is a difference between a president and a leader.'[58]

Karunanidhi Breaks Silence

On 2 January 1987, Colombo imposed a fuel ban on Jaffna, triggering a humanitarian crisis. Karunanidhi broke his long silence on 10 February. That day, the administrative committee passed a comprehensive resolution covering Karunanidhi's recently cultivated and future affection for the LTTE. Mentioning Prabhakaran and the LTTE, the resolution blamed MGR and the intelligence agencies for sowing discord amongst militant groups and MGR's 'treachery' and the Centre's indifference for bringing the Tamils to the brink. It claimed that if the message of the May 1986 TESO resolution had been heeded, the dire situation in the Jaffna peninsula would not have happened.[59]

On 13 February, Karunanidhi said that the language struggle's first phase had concluded, and the struggle for the safety of the (Sri Lankan) Tamil nation would commence.[60] On 15 February, he called for rallies on 16 February and led a rally in Chennai.[61] On 7 March, Karunanidhi said that the Tamils' situation was worse than in 1983 and that the Sri Lankan and Indian governments were 'duping the Tamil people'. Claiming that MGR was not 'sincere' and that he side-tracked and 'maligned' the DMK's agitations, Karunanidhi said that the chief minister's opposition to Eelam had weakened the cause. He complained that MGR viewed the issue along partisan lines and that the LTTE 'avoided meeting [him] often'.[62] On 10 March, Karunanidhi sent a telegram to the prime minister urging action and, on 23 April, wondered if the Centre was waiting for the 'death of the last Tamil' so that it could once and for all pass a condolence resolution.[63] On 27 April, the MGR government, under pressure to be seen doing something to mitigate the situation, announced financial aid, amounting to Rs 4 crore, to two LTTE proxy organizations. On 29 April, Karunanidhi said that the money would 'tend to the wounds' of the Tamils.[64]

Karunanidhi now asked that his birthday be marked as a condemnation day against the Centre. On 3 June, his birthday, India dispatched a flotilla of fishing boats with thirty-eight tons of food, only to see the Sri Lankan navy turn them back. On 4 June, Operation Poomalai (Garland) saw India air-drop food. Former Sri Lankan High Commissioner Bernard Tilakaratna said later that

Rajiv had initially favoured the Sri Lankan military campaign to the finish. Still, MGR had persuaded him to change his mind.[65]

However, on 9 June, a strident Karunanidhi said that 'deceptive drama' would not save Tamils.[66] Keeping up the heat, on 17 June, he hit below the belt, claiming that the ships and air-drop were prearranged between Jayawardene and Rajiv to divert attention from the Bofors and other scandals.[67] On 28 June, he said it was time to send warships to Sri Lanka.[68]

Accord a Sacrificial Altar

India's actions forced Sri Lanka's hand, and on 29 July, Rajiv and Jayawardene inked the Indo–Sri Lanka Accord in Colombo. Opposed to the agreement, Prime Minister Ranasinghe Premadasa avoided the signing ceremony. The accord provided for the merger of the north and the east provinces and nominal devolution. The militants were required to give up arms, and India sent a peacekeeping force (IPKF). On 30 July, in a statement in Parliament, Rajiv claimed, 'The Agreement meets the basic aspirations which animated the Tamils struggle.'[69]

The prime minister had called Opposition leaders separately earlier to discuss the accord. On 28 July, Maran intuitively opined to Rajiv that the accord would not be complete without the LTTE as a signatory.[70] Karunanidhi termed the pact 'hasty', said it was doomed to fail and later foresaw great disappointment for the Tamils.[71] He said that India's signature 'is as clownish as the Registrar of Marriages signing in place of the bridegroom'. On 31 July, recalling the story of the bundle of twigs that could be broken when separated, he blamed Jayawardene, Rajiv and MGR for dividing the militants in the lead-up to the accord.[72] Karunanidhi said the fact that the IPKF would be under Jayawardene's command made its purpose clear.[73] On 4 August, Prabhakaran, in a rally in Jaffna, asked, 'What do we do when a superpower beyond our means has decided to determine our political destiny?'[74] On 26 August, the Tiger leader said that the accord could never be accepted.[75]

Arivalayam

The opening of 'Anna Arivalayam (Abode of knowledge)', the DMK's new office, was scheduled for 16 September 1987. Arivalayam resulted from the 15 May 1985 instruction for the party to vacate its government-assigned office for its legislature party.[76] Karunanidhi saw an opportunity in the setback. He chose to construct a modern office for the party on land bought on Anna Salai as early as 1971.[77] A bank loan of Rs 50 lakh was raised for the Rs 1-crore project, and on 10 June 1985, Karunanidhi appealed for contributions.[78] Three weeks later, with his appeal bringing in just Rs 1 lakh, Karunanidhi wrote anxiously about the project's completion, the interest and the money needed.[79] Karunanidhi undertook an intensive tour from the end of March through June, collecting Rs 63 lakh, of which Rs 46 lakh went towards the Arivalayam fund.[80]

The opening, however, coincided with the Vanniyar Sangam's call led by Dr Ramadoss for a roadblock protest for 17–23 September to press its demands for an exclusive 20 per cent reservation in the state and 2 per cent in central services. The Sangam's earlier blockade in May 1986 had halted traffic in the state, and thousands were arrested. A one-day blockade of trains had followed in December 1986.

Matters were made worse when the agitation was brought forward by six hours to midnight, pitting the returning DMK cadres and the protesters against each other. Violence between the Vanniyar Sangam and the protesters and the Vanniyar Sangam and Adi Dravidas led to twenty deaths.[81] Karunanidhi lamented that the 'untoward atmosphere' could have been averted if only the authorities had informed them about the roadblock being brought forward. [82] Ramadoss, however, apportioned blame to the DMK for the mix-up of the dates and the violence. He more damagingly added that 'Karunanidhi did not say a word to welcome the peace efforts, for peace between our two communities [Vanniyas and Adi Dravidas] does not serve his interests'.[83] The damage was done.

IPKF–LTTE Hostilities

On 3 October 1987, the Sri Lankan military intercepted seventeen LTTE militants on the high seas, who were later kept in the joint custody of the army and IPKF. On 5 October, the militants consumed cyanide on learning of the army's plans to transport them to Colombo. Twelve died. On 6 October, the LTTE held India responsible, saying it had forewarned the IPKF.[84] An LTTE rampage against Sinhalese and Muslims began. The IPKF's intervention to disarm the LTTE led to hostilities from 10 October, leading to 1200 soldiers and 660 LTTE cadres dying before the IPKF exited in 1990.[85] Some dubbed the fiasco as India's Vietnam.

On 11 October, MGR, who was in the United States, held the Sri Lankan government responsible and appealed for a ceasefire. That day, Karunanidhi called the accord the 'sacrificial altar built for Sri Lankan Tamils' and said that discussing the wrongs of the past would not lead to a solution to the present. He said that Jayawardene had succeeded with the help of the Indian Army, where the Sri Lankan Army failed.[86]

On 13 October, LTTE's Kittu, Subramaniam and Rahim met Karunanidhi and delivered Prabhakaran's letter seeking support to stop IPKF action. A similar letter had been sent to MGR. With MGR's help limited to mere appeals, Prabhakaran had turned to Karunanidhi, who did not let him down. That day, Karunanidhi called for rallies on 15 October for a ceasefire and talks with the Tigers and DMK protest meetings for 17–18 October.[87] At the 15 October rally, Karunanidhi wondered about the 'sad irony' of the IPKF liberating Jaffna from Tamils and suggested that Rajiv liberate Aksai Chin instead. He also sent telegrams to eight Opposition chief ministers urging them to use their good offices to stop the killings.[88] Karunanidhi claimed that Jayawardene had used the IPKF to thwart a coup.[89] A series of DMK-sponsored picketing and rallies followed.

On 29 October, Karunanidhi forwarded a letter from twenty-eight Sri Lankan Tamils to Rajiv, listing IPKF's excesses and appealing for the cessation of hostilities.[90] On 1 November, he asked IPKF to return to its 9 October positions and asked India to first cease-fire, which would 'ease the way' to a solution.[91] On 9 November, speaking at Salem, Karunanidhi warned of a repeat of 1965 if the army action did not stop.[92]

That day, Rajiv told the Rajya Sabha that the LTTE's attacks on the Sinhalese and Muslims would have spawned unprecedented violence, the victims would have mainly been Tamils in the south and the central highlands, and there was no alternative to disarming the LTTE.

On the LTTE's tactics, Rajiv pointed out that the LTTE 'need not keep on sending telegrams to Tamil Nadu and other places', that it could get in touch with the IPKF quicker and that this could be done in thirty minutes. He claimed no gaps between the LTTE and Tamil groups and India on the accord save Eelam.[93]

Karunanidhi and Maran chose to listen but not hear. On 22 November, Maran claimed 'Rajiv had Tamil blood on his hands'.[94] As the DMK processions, cycle rallies, human chains and meetings against 'Rajiv's killings' became the order of the day, Karunanidhi justified it by saying that there 'would be no Tamil in Sri Lanka tomorrow' otherwise.[95] On 19 December, Karunanidhi said that Rajiv and the Congress (I) had acquired 'indelible blemish'.[96] On 21 December, he questioned MGR's 'right to sanction' the killings and Rajiv's 'right to kill' and the following day said that the DMK would show black flags to Rajiv Gandhi.[97, 98]

A Gracious Goodbye to MGR

The DMK's unremitting agitational approach ended abruptly on 24 December 1987 when MGR breathed his last. An era had come to an end. Karunanidhi's condolence message was gracious and revealed the depth of their friendship amidst the political enmity:

> I am overcome with shock and melancholy hearing that my dear friend Dr MGR has passed away. Our friendship blossomed in 1945 with Jupiter Pictures' *Rajakumari*, directed by A.S.A. Samy, in which he starred as the hero, and I was the scriptwriter . . . We remained extremely friendly even after the changed political circumstances and through our differences.
>
> [MGR] reigned as the unparalleled hero of Thamizagam's film world. He created a new era in the film arena. Few had made the film world theirs as he did and conquered it the way he did. He has the honour of making his party, the ADMK he founded in 1972, rise to power quickly. None would not praise his resolute will to serve tirelessly—even through his two-three years of illness—during the ten years he served as chief minister. He shone through his ceaseless hard work and not giving up, winning people's affection.

The Kazhagam's activities were suspended and flags flew at half-mast for a week.[99]

As a boy used a crowbar to strike at his statue to tear it down hours after MGR's death on 24 December, Karunanidhi wrote on 27 December that 'the little brother' had not stabbed him in the back but in his heart and therefore he was at peace. Tamil valour considers being stabbed from behind a disgrace. Karunanidhi had invoked Sangam honour even in his statue's fall. A man of many firsts, Karunanidhi now earned the dubious distinction of seeing his statue being felled in his own lifetime while Lenin's and Stalin's statues were brought down long after their deaths.[100] Karunanidhi did not agree for the statue to be re-erected.[101]

18

Karunanidhi vs Jayalalithaa

Karunanidhi's public career was set to plumb new depths and scale new heights. The lady he had hitherto failed to acknowledge—Jayalalithaa—would emerge to take her mentor's place and continue the anti-Karunanidhi war. In February 1988, Karunanidhi rebuked the interviewer who asked what he thought of Jayalalithaa: 'Do not drag me into all this' and listed Nehru and Indira Gandhi as people whom he had been associated with or politicked with to buttress the notion that his new political nemesis was way beneath his dignity.

But Jayalalithaa brought her mojo and rose to become a cult in her own right. Karunanidhi could only ignore her at his own peril. Karunanidhi was an example of those who were either blessed or cursed with a long political career and its perils of dealing with those that one deems lesser than oneself.[1] And in 1989, he may have inadvertently aided her resolve to stay put in the all-male political arena. A lady of many firsts, Jayalalithaa reigned over Tamil Nadu as a czarina but also became the first chief minister to be convicted for disproportionate wealth in a lower court. The case against her in the Supreme Court abated owing to her death.

In the early years, Jayalalithaa proved highly volatile, often making intemperate and coarse remarks and allegations that defied logic or reason. She made herself inaccessible and went into long absences. She had at least twice quit public life—on 18 March and 18 December 1989. She attributed the first to reasons of both health and the indignities of public life. She claimed on that occasion, and later, that she was a reluctant politician 'forced' into politics by MGR.[2] Yet, she ushered in a certain pride and hope to womenfolk, becoming representative of their aspirations and serving as a vehicle for the anti-DMK political forces.[3]

AIADMK Splits

As her leader lay in state, Jayalalithaa stood her ground at MGR's head for two days, allegedly braving the physical harassment meted out to her by Janaki's supporters. R.M. Veerappan blasted her for conducting 'political commerce' with MGR's body. Jayalalithaa encountered more humiliation when she was pushed out of the funeral carriage. She did not join MGR's final journey.

On 1 January 1988, Jayalalithaa took over as general secretary, formally dividing the party. She said later that she was 'bulldozed' into the position and claimed on that occasion that MGR had told 'everyone' that either he had to go 'to counter Karunanidhi or any other big political leader' or send her.[4] Janaki led the other faction. She was only a front. R.M. Veerappan was the brain and the force behind her. On 2 January, Janaki and Nedunchezhian were elected leaders of the respective AIADMK legislature parties.

With ninety-seven of the 133 legislators, Janaki commanded a majority in the legislature party. But the cadres were with Jayalalithaa, and she claimed a repeat of 1972.[5]

On 7 January, Janaki Ramachandran was sworn in as the first woman chief minister of Tamil Nadu and was given three weeks to prove her majority.[6]

'Scar on Democracy'

On 20 January, Karunanidhi clarified that the DMK would vote against the Janaki ministry.[7] On 28 January, at the eleventh hour, the Congress (I) chose to renege its commitment to back Janaki, leading to the most despicable incidents in the assembly. That morning when the House met, Speaker P.H. Pandian said that five Congress (I) legislators had informed him that they had resigned. He adjourned the House to noon (the five were considered loyal to Sivaji Ganesan; one retracted the resignation).

When the House reconvened, the Speaker disqualified six former ministers: Nedunchezhian, S. Ramachandran, Thirunavukkarasar, Aranganayagam, Tiruchi Soundararajan and K.K.S.S.R. Ramachandran. He adjourned the House to 3 p.m. Immediately, a bout ensued between the two factions. In the melee, Congress (I)'s Sivaraman assumed the Speaker's chair, revoked the disqualifications, announced a motion of no confidence in Pandian and the ministry and, claiming the resolutions were passed, adjourned the House sine die.

At 3 p.m., when Pandian reconvened the House a third time, Sivaraman and Pandian jostled for the chair. According to *Murasoli*, Sivaraman sat on Pandian's lap, triggering another jousting, the arrival of the Jayalalithaa faction and Congress (I) musclemen and a free for all. On the Speaker's invite, helmeted policemen arrived and unleashed a baton charge, driving away the Opposition MLAs. Several Congress (I) legislators were injured, some seriously.

When the House resumed a fourth time at 3.30 p.m. in the absence of the Jayalalithaa faction and the Congress (I) members, the Speaker ironically disqualified the AIADMK members for defying the AIADMK whip from being present and voting for the motion. Pandian put the confidence motion to a vote and said that ninety-nine had voted in favour, eight DMK had voted against (four members could not return to the House as it was shut), and three from IUML and the lone Janata member were neutral. The Speaker declared the motion carried.[8] S. Ramachandran termed it a 'cruelly contrived majority'. *Frontline* later captioned it as Tamil Nadu's Day of Shame.[9] The prime minister termed it a 'scar on democracy' and, on 30 January, President's rule was imposed. Janaki had been chief minister for twenty-four days.[10] The Congress (I) offered various explanations for its volte-face. One was horse trading; the other was that Janaki sought the DMK's support.

On the 28th morning, after the Speaker adjourned the House to noon, the Janaki camp's Raghavanandam, Madhavan, Rajaram and others met Karunanidhi to seek the DMK's support.[11] But when R.M. Veerappan and Janaki telephoned Karunanidhi for support, they turned the raison d'être of the AIADMK and MGR's legacy on its head.[12] A moment of danger justified anything, R.M. Veerappan said later.[13] The House's effective strength was 222. With the resignation of five Congress (I) members and six Jayalalithaa faction legislators' disqualification, the Janaki government required 107 votes. The DMK's twelve votes could make or break the government.[14] Karunanidhi commented that within two days of conferring the Bharat Ratna on MGR, Congress (I) had stabbed his wife in the back. Betrayal is 'Congress culture', he concluded.[15] S. Ramachandran dubbed the Janaki–Veerappan faction and Karunanidhi 'natural allies'.[16]

Meanwhile, R.M. Veerappan reiterated that Jayalalithaa was 'no major political force'.[17] The politically savvy R.M. Veerappan was wrong this time. On 9–10 February, Jayalalithaa addressed massive meetings in Madurai and Thanjavur, respectively. At Madurai, she claimed her detractors conspired to kill her, she wished to commit sati but did not, as she had promised MGR to continue his work.[18]

Prabhakaran Saved by DMK Vigil

On 14 February, Karunanidhi, referring to *The Hindu* report that Prabhakaran was encircled, said that the LTTE leader could be removed, but the 'deluge' in its aftermath could not be contained.[19] On

19 February, Prabhakaran addressed a letter to Karunanidhi, calling him the 'hope of the Eelam Tamils'.[20] On 20 February, Karunanidhi kept a 'largely attended' fast in Chennai.[21] On 28 February, he warned Rajiv of an 'upsurge' if Prabhakaran's life were taken.[22] On 1 March, Jayalalithaa described the LTTE as 'young and idealistic'.[23]

On 4 March, Karunanidhi said the prime minister was 'butchering thousands of innocent Tamils in the name of disarming the Tigers' and called it Rajiv's 'impudence in the cause of saving his own prestige and his lack of maturity'.[24]

On 15 March, the DMK joined the Opposition's all-India shutdown call against Rajiv's governance.[25] On 29 March, Karunanidhi published a harrowing letter from a father in Sri Lanka, narrating how his son had been picked up by the IPKF, tortured and handed over dead. Karunanidhi wondered how many fathers, mothers and wives anguished thus.[26]

On 21 March, Jayalalithaa called for an immediate halt to IPKF operations and warned against any harm to Prabhakaran.

On 6 June, Karunanidhi declared that despite 20,000 IPKF surrounding him, Prabhakaran's life had been spared because of the DMK's 'vigil' and even the 'Ganges's waters would be unable to wipe away the Tamil blood on Rajiv's hands'.[27]

Rajiv's Election Pitch

Earlier, on 21 April, Rajiv arrived to participate in the 22–24 April AICC (I) session at Maraimalai Nagar, 45 km from Chennai, travelling to the session by train in second class to make contact with the public en route. On arrival, he had said at the Chennai airport that twenty years of Dravidian rule had led to the state losing its prominent place.[28] At the session, Rajiv announced a Rs 1500-crore development plan for Tamil Nadu. Although he decried government subsidies in food, clothes, chappals and electricity without the government having the money to pay salaries, Rajiv clarified that

MGR's noon meal scheme would continue. The AICC (I) political resolution called VP the 'prophet of untruth'.[29]

Rajiv's description of the Dravidian rule as a dark period turned into a refrain in his subsequent visits and election campaign. On 27 April, Karunanidhi argued that it was not that the Congress (I) alone cared for the nation and that the other parties cared only for votes.[30] On 12 May, Karunanidhi, speaking at Vridachalam, asked voters to compare his 'dark rule' with the earlier Congress rule and vote for him based on his work and achievements.[31] Three days later, speaking at Coimbatore, Karunanidhi said that if they commanded him to be their 'servant', he would serve them again and claimed that he need not become chief minister to acquire 'splendour' or 'status'.[32]

The four leaders resented Jayalalithaa's autocratic style; her inaccessibility; the power of her aide, M. Natarajan; the lack of transparency in handling party funds; and the absence of a senior position for Nedunchezhian. In response, Jayalalithaa used an unprintable simile for the four. Nedunchezhian, for his part, described her as 'Karunanidhi in a sari'.[33] The four leaders, in turn, 'expelled' her. Jayalalithaa had discarded their advice for a tie-up with the Congress (I). Wishing to 'form a government of our own', she said, 'People have accepted me as a leader in whom they have complete faith.'[34] Her hubris would consign her to the Opposition. On 2 July, Jayalalithaa issued a statement in which she said that Sasikala and Natarajan were 'family friends', had nothing to do with politics and had been of assistance to her from the days of MGR with his 'full support', and expelled Nedunchezhian, S. Ramachandran, Aranganayagam and Thirunavukkarasar.[35] The problems that would bedevil Jayalalithaa's political career would surface early on.

National Front

After seven months of exploratory talks, on 6 August, the Janata Dal, Lok Dal, Congress (S), Jan Morcha, Asom Gana Parishad (AGP),

Telugu Desam and the DMK came together to form the National Front (NF) with VP as convenor and N.T. Rama Rao as chairman. Karunanidhi was appointed to the eleven-member presidium and Murasoli Maran to the policy-drafting committee.[36] As early as 16 October 1987, Karunanidhi, writing in *Dinamani*, referred to Rajiv's government as the 'rule of the elites' and envisaged an alliance of regional parties at the Centre.[37] The Congress (I)'s sclerosis would begin in 1989, while the BJP and the regional parties would move into that space. A two-party system of the Congress (I) versus the Opposition was to lead to a tripartite system where the next twenty-five years would see coalition governments with a major say for the regional parties.

The NF was the first experiment in Opposition unity on the part of Left forces, Hindi heartland parties, the DMK and the AGP. The strangest of bedfellows, they had rallied behind VP, the knight in shining armour, to bring down Rajiv. Jayalalithaa would later describe their alliance as one between 'mice and frogs'.[38]

On 7 August, in an overture to the DMK, the NF resolution moved by Karunanidhi called for a ceasefire and a negotiated settlement in Sri Lanka.[39] On 8 August, again in a major concession to the DMK, the NF's 71-point programme gave up mentioning the three-language formula and instead promised to implement Nehru's assurance and re-examine Centre-state relations 'de novo' as well as implement the 1980 Mandal Commission recommendations calling for reservations for other backward classes (OBC) in central government institutions within a year. An exultant Karunanidhi penned six letters titled 'A Beginning', signifying the gains the DMK had made with the Front.[40]

The 17 September public launch of the National Front (NF) in Chennai proved to be a DMK show, with NF leaders heralding Karunanidhi as the next chief minister of Tamil Nadu. But the NF's inherent contradictions had to be contained. Devi Lal required persuasion from VP and others to drop his original plan of speaking in Hindi at the rally.[41]

Rajiv had initially termed Dravidian rule regressive, but from November 1988, he zeroed in on the seven years of Karunanidhi rule. Karunanidhi lamented that the prime minister's speeches were not prime ministerial but more akin to an 'uncouth fourth-rate speaker.'[42] On 20 December, P. Chidambaram characterized Karunanidhi's rule as 'seven years of social and economic ignominy' and the twenty years of Anna, Karunanidhi and MGR rule as the 'dark age' and the DMK as a 'poisonous movement'.[43]

When talks with Congress (I) broke down, Jayalalithaa said she was 'relieved', adding that an AIADMK government was one of the 'preconditions' for any alliance.[44] Turning it into a four-cornered contest, both parties had unwittingly handed over victory on a platter to the DMK. The DMK fought the election in the company of IUML and the Janata Dal.

1989 Assembly Election

As early as September, Karunanidhi had dispatched some trusted 'friends' in the Kazhagam to the districts to identify suitable candidates. Additionally, Karunanidhi said some journalists were sent independently as 'spies' on the same mission. The data and information were analysed to screen over 3000 applicants.[45] Of the 197 candidates, thirty-seven were lawyers, eleven doctors, twenty-six graduates and seven women.[46] The manifesto announced a 30 per cent reservation for women in government services and local bodies; a five-cent housing plot for the rural poor; a grant of Rs 5000 for girls below the poverty line who had passed Class VIII; free university education for the most backward, scheduled castes and tribes; compartmental reservation for the most backward and reservation on the economic criterion in the open quota; parity in state employees' salaries with their central counterparts; and an insurance scheme for the unorganized sector and agricultural workers.[47] Congress (I) promised total prohibition. Jayalalithaa promised to write off cooperative loans for farmers. Teaming up with Sivaji Ganesan's Tamizhaga Munnetra Munnani (TMM), Janaki promised a kg of rice for Re 1 for those below the poverty line.[48]

On 1 January 1989, Karunanidhi began a nineteen-day campaign tour.[49] Jayalalithaa had called the IPKF engagement 'one big mess', described the DMK as her 'enemy number one' and declared, 'It is going to be a fight between me and Karunanidhi.'[50] The prime minister's many visits and intense campaign against the DMK, however, turned the battle into Rajiv vs Karunanidhi.[51]

Rajiv promised Kamaraj rule, invoked Indira's memory and promised even to do away with Nehru's three-language formula. Then, the prime minister spilt bile claiming that 'The DMK leaders had made a vain bid to kill Indira Gandhi' and they had joined hands with the 'champions of Khalistan'.[52] Karunanidhi stoked Dravidian pride and asked voters if they wanted to be ruled from Delhi or Chennai.[53] Jayalalithaa, meanwhile, drew the largest crowds.[54] She made several promises. She termed 'rooting out corruption at all levels' as one of her 'major promises to the people'.[55]

With a 33.18 per cent vote share, the DMK won 146 seats. Karunanidhi was elected from the Harbour constituency, and Stalin from Thousand Lights, his first innings as a legislator. In 1984, its tally was twenty-four seats with 29.5 per cent of the votes. Now, it had won two-thirds of the seats. A 4 per cent swing had brought it a rich haul.

AIADMK secured 21.15 per cent of the votes and twenty-seven seats. Congress (I), hoping to capture power, came third with twenty-six seats and polled 19.83 per cent. Janaki's faction faced a humiliating defeat with 9.19 per cent of the votes, with the controversial former Speaker, Pandian, being the sole winner. Janaki finished third behind the DMK winner Asaiyan and Jayalalithaa's candidate. Karunanidhi revealed that he did not wish even someone named Ramar, the DMK's first choice whose name was the diminutive of the late leader MGR, to contest against his widow Janaki, and Asaiyan was chosen. Janaki's ally Sivaji Ganesan suffered a disgraceful defeat in Thiruvaiyaru. Janaki retired from politics, paving the way for the party's reunification. Elected to the assembly from Bodinayakkanur, Jayalalithaa quit the Rajya Sabha on 24 January 1989 and took over the party's reins to become the state's first woman Leader of the Opposition. On 10 February, the two AIADMK factions united and the next day, was granted the twin leaves symbol.[56] Yet, her hopes of coming to power had been dashed.[57] She would become reclusive.

1989 ASSEMBLY ELECTION[58]

Party	Contested	Won	Votes	Percentage
DMK + ABDUL LATHEEF MUSLIM LEAGUE 5	203	151	80,39,155	33.34%
AIADMK JAYA	203	29	52,81,454	21.90%
INC	217	26	48,67,125	20.19%
AIADMK JANAKI	177	1	22,02,497	9.13%
CPM	21	15	8,51,351	3.53%
CPI	13	3	2,95,170	1.22%
JANATA DAL (JD)	10	4	2,82,647	1.17%
IND	20	5		

Critics alleged that the Sasikala–Natarajan duo had put Jayalalithaa on a high horse, blighting a Congress (I) alliance. Together, they had polled more votes than the DMK in 146 constituencies. Karunanidhi, however, pointed to the 1980 DMK–Congress (I) defeat. He described the 1989 vote as a 'decisive one' against the Congress (I) and added that the days of glamour or sympathy were over, and people had voted on issues and parties. In two years, he would have to eat his words.[59]

19

Exile Ends—Briefly

1989

On 27 January 1989, Karunanidhi and his compact seventeen-member cabinet were sworn in at the Valluvar Kottam. Chief Minister Karunanidhi said the DMK's success heralded Opposition victory and described VP, chief ministers N.T. Rama Rao of united Andhra Pradesh, S.R. Bommai of Karnataka, E.K. Nayanar of Kerala and other National Front leaders on the dais as 'those who would take upon the responsibility of ruling India tomorrow'. Karunanidhi expressed hope for resolving the Cauvery issue to the southern chief ministers.[1]

Later that day, the chief minister alleged a 'scorched earth policy' during the governor's rule. He said he stared at an 'empty treasury' with a minus Rs 70-crore cash balance and an 'empty granary'. He added that commitments of even Rs 50,000 could not be passed without scrutiny and sought the Centre's assistance. Karunanidhi clarified there were no plans to open arrack shops as many families were inveigled by liquor (yet, in March 1991, he would introduce 'cheap liquor') and promised the price of rice would stay the same despite the Centre raising it. Karunanidhi said that for Sri Lanka an interim arrangement providing the 'fruits of Eelam' was also desirable in place of Eelam. He also promised a clean and accountable government.[2]

Rajiv's 'DMK Initiative'

Karunanidhi, the adept administrator, hit the road running. On 9 February, in a speech resembling vintage Karunanidhi, the chief minister told the Conference of Chief Ministers of States that the onus of keeping states within India rested on the Centre, observing that the situation is such that the 'lynchpin is trying to separate from the wheel'.[3]

Rajiv asked Karunanidhi to stay behind after the conference.[4] The following morning, Minister of State for External Affairs Natwar Singh briefed Karunanidhi on the ethnic issue. Later that evening, the prime minister told Karunanidhi and Maran that he would arrange for Maran and Vaiko to officially travel to Jaffna on an Indian Air Force flight to meet Prabhakaran and would get in touch with the chief minister on his return to Chennai. Rajiv outlined an arrangement similar to the Palestine Authority with Prabhakaran as chief minister.[5]

But three days earlier, on 6 February, spurred by ambition and adventure, the party's feisty MP, Vaiko, left clandestinely for Jaffna. It would mark the beginning of the end of his political career in the DMK. In his letter that reached Karunanidhi two days later, Vaiko said he would convey his leader's message for pragmatism to Prabhakaran and added his wish to see Karunanidhi as the 'one who changed the destinies of the Eelam Tamils'. As Vaiko's visit became public, Anbazhagan stated on 20 February that the MP had not taken permission from the leadership.[6] On 4 March, *Murasoli* published Vaiko's letter. That evening, Vaiko returned to India.

Vaiko brought pizazz to the DMK. His rousing speeches and proven organizational skills had won him a following. However, Vaiko's ambition and LTTE affinity had gotten the better of him.

Twenty years younger than Karunanidhi and ten years older than Stalin, Vaiko was the rising star and had to be reined in. Ko. Si. Mani and Arcot Veerasamy met Vaiko and sought his agreement for 'temporary suspension'. An easily excitable man, Vaiko wept and promised the letter the following day, only to change his mind.[7]

Vaiko as a follower—pre-1993

Photo courtesy: Yahoo News

Vaiko met an irate Karunanidhi on 5 March, after which he briefed the press at the party headquarters against Karunanidhi's advice. He said he had committed a wrong, claiming his leader had forgiven him like a mother.[8] The next day, the mother damned the ego trip 'highly irresponsible' and as 'adventurism', saying that it served his 'publicity' ends but would not 'problem solve' (*sic*).[9] Karunanidhi was right. Vaiko's act, perhaps a flourish of youth, was overreaching and foolhardy. But his daring, Karunanidhi knew, would capture the imagination of the younger cadres, and any action against Vaiko would confer a halo around his head.[10]

On 15 March, on his visit to the Planning Commission, Karunanidhi met Rajiv Gandhi at the latter's request that day and the following day. As Karunanidhi regretted Vaiko's clandestine visit, Rajiv said graciously that there was no need to discuss it and that he would send word through Maran on future contacts. Recalling the rendezvous, Karunanidhi said that Rajiv's graciousness surprised him even four years later.[11]

Maran later revealed in Parliament that under the prime minister's 'DMK Initiative', Vaiko, S. Kandappan and Maran were to meet Prabhakaran in Jaffna. It was not meant to be.[12] The 25 March assembly incidents (described below) greatly altered the political context. Karunanidhi openly lamented ten weeks later that those close to Rajiv were conspiring to 'throw mud' at the DMK.[13] Chandra Shekhar's principal secretary, S.K. Misra, stretches the point when he writes that Rajiv and Karunanidhi 'hated each other, and Rajiv Gandhi was keen to see [Karunanidhi] out of office.'[14]

As the 'DMK Initiative' floundered, on 2 May, Maran wrote tongue-in-cheek to Rajiv, wondering if there was a political reason for the lack of follow-up. In his 15 May reply, Rajiv listed the dates of contacts made by his office with Maran and pointed out that the ball was in the DMK's court, adding that there was a communication gap somewhere.[15]

But the discussion was moot. President Ranasinghe Premadasa's election in Sri Lanka deprived the Indians of any initiative. Despite their enmity for each other, Premadasa, the LTTE and the radical Sinhala Janata Vimukthi Peramuna (JVP) were united in wanting the IPKF to leave. On 4 May, Premadasa chose to open talks with the LTTE to undercut the JVP—cruelly mocking the IPKF's efforts to disarm his foe. If the President had calculated that he could take on an IPKF-battered LTTE after seeing out the Indians, it was a dangerous gambit. In doing so, he had thrown a lifeline to the LTTE, gasping for breath. On 1 June, Premadasa openly called for the IPKF's exit by 29 July, the second anniversary of the accord.[16]

Despite these ungainly developments, Karunanidhi and Maran met Rajiv on 15 June in Chennai on the latter's visit one last time. Rajiv asked that Maran meet him in Delhi.[17]

VP later revealed that Karunanidhi had not moved forward after this, as with the Congress (I) warming up to the AIADMK, he feared any such move could be used against him. According to VP, Rajiv sent for Maran in May or June. He told him to convey to Prabhakaran that if he distanced himself from Premadasa, he would ensure that matters were settled on 'favourable terms for him—which means he was virtually promising him Eelam.'[18] But Rajiv may have overestimated the DMK's links to the LTTE while underestimating the LTTE's ability to better their record of irrational behaviour. Karunanidhi would note later that even as the Centre cooled its heels after 25 March, the DMK could not get in touch with the LTTE.[19]

On 2 July, the DMK general council called for the prime minister to 'reconsider' his Sri Lanka policy and bizarrely asked him to obtain assurances from Premadasa to prevent 'fratricide'; and perhaps in tune with the emerging thinking in Delhi, recommended a phased withdrawal of the IPKF. On 12–13 July, in his meeting with Premadasa, Rajiv's special envoy Deshmukh agreed to IPKF withdrawal by 30 September.[20]

Fulfilling Election Promises

Earlier, on 17 February, the chief minister made waves when he detailed how rules were amended and bent for profiteering by distillery owners, costing the state a loss of Rs 100 crore annually. Describing it as 'Himalayan corruption; a recurring corruption', the chief minister claimed to have 'liquidated the liquor empire'.[21] Karunanidhi's broad brush had painted MGR as the patron saint of the 'liquor empire'. Jayalalithaa could only feebly protest that she knew nothing about the charges, adding that 'raking up charges against a dead person is sheer political vendetta . . . and we will not allow this vilification of a great leader like MGR to continue.'[22] She need not have bothered. Despite the damning evidence, MGR's image remained intact. Soon thereafter, Karunanidhi abolished forty-one of the seventy-seven sinecure political positions created by his predecessor.[23]

Fair-weather AIADMK politicians now made a beeline to the DMK and on 19 February, the executive asked the leadership to hasten slowly in admitting them.[24] Karunanidhi set into motion a process of admitting second-tier leaders seeking fresh pastures or disillusioned with Jayalalithaa. The irony was that many of these erstwhile MGR and Jayalalithaa men performed better and rose quickly. In 2021, M.K. Stalin took eight such men into his thirty-five-member cabinet.

His aborted term saw a slew of welfare measures and handouts even as the chief minister doubled down on his promises. On 20 February, Karunanidhi piloted an assembly resolution to revive the legislative council. Similarly, a bill that day increased the term of local bodies from three to five years, omitted the recall provisions of the heads and restored the powers curbed in 1986, i.e., inspection of midday meal centres, maintenance of schools, appointment of agriculture and sub-health-centre-related staff. On 1 March, in a major move at women's empowerment, a bill set aside 33 per cent representation for women in local bodies.[25]

On 13 March, the Karunanidhi cabinet accorded a 20 per cent sub-reservation for thirty-nine most backward (MBC) and sixty-eight de-notified communities from the 50 per cent reserved for 201 backward communities.[26] The 1982 Ambashankar Commission estimated that backward classes numbered 217.49 lakh, and 105 lakh were the most backward. Of the most backward—the Vanniyars, estimated at 65.05 lakh—were the largest while the others made up 39.95 lakh; with the 17.19 lakh de-notified, their total came to 122.19 lakh. These 122.19 lakh were to share the 20 per cent. Karunanidhi clarified that exclusive reservation in the name of caste as the Vanniyar Sangam demanded would not have stood judicial scrutiny. He offered to review the system in a year.

Ramadoss, however, said that Karunanidhi had 'stabbed his heart'. The Vanniyar Sangam now demanded a caste count by a judge from outside the state and a caste-wise quota in six months. Karunanidhi argued that the other castes would reject such an enumeration. Later, on 1 May, the Vanniyar Sangam blocked roads, and a youth died in police firing. Karunanidhi revealed that Ramadoss's original claim was only 18 per cent along with just ten other castes with the Vanniyas, and he suggested including the de-notified communities.[27]

25 March Assembly Incident

Ramadoss certainly got under Karunanidhi's skin. But, Jayalalithaa remained the centre of gravity of his political opposition. She had kept away from campaigning in the 11 March Madurai East and Marungapuri by-elections and yet the party had won.[28] Her presence was perhaps not as pivotal as she had imagined.

A concatenation of events in the next days revealed Jayalalithaa as a capricious, dejected and reluctant politician when she resigned from the assembly and quit public life. On 18 March, close to midnight, some newspapers received an envelope with a statement in Tamil where Jayalalithaa said she was quitting public life due to the indignities and her indifferent health, and in her one-line letter in English to the Assembly Speaker, she said that her resignation from the House would take effect from 15 March.[29]

Earlier on 18 March, police had raided her associate Natarajan's house on a cheating complaint by a party worker, alleging that the refundable fee of Rs 20,000 towards a party ticket had yet to be returned. It was here that the police had laid their hands on the ill-fated letter. Natarajan had intercepted the correspondence en route to newspaper offices. On 19 March, as newspapers broke the story,

Jayalalithaa said she had asked Natarajan to hold on to her letter as she had reversed her decision following pleas from party leaders and alleged that the chief minister was behind the leak. The 'leak' had seriously recoiled. Jayalalithaa chose to stay the course and proved she was at her best with her back against the wall.[30]

Karunanidhi denied the allegation. He said that on the evening of 18 March, Speaker Tamilkudimagan had informed him that he had received the letter from an unknown messenger and he advised him to write to Jayalalithaa for confirmation. Karunanidhi said that his government was not 'vindictive [or] narrow-minded' to act on the letter.[31] Jayalalithaa confirmed that she had written the letter but denied she had forwarded it to the Speaker. On 22 March, Tamilkudimagan announced that he had not accepted the letter. Jayalalithaa now railed against the police action, met the governor seeking Natarajan's release and, on 24 March, with the support of Congress (I), conducted an impressive rally against the DMK's 'vindictiveness'.

The assembly convened on 25 March against this backdrop. Congress (I) deputy floor leader Kumari Anandan, Jayalalithaa and her colleagues had given notice of privilege motions against the possession of the letter and publication.[32] Jayalalithaa alleged her phone was being tapped and said the chief minister and his cabinet should resign. The Speaker said he would rule on the motions on 27 March and asked the chief minister to present the budget.[33]

As the chief minister rose, Jayalalithaa said a person charged with 'criminal acts' should not be reading the budget. Karunanidhi claimed that DMK MLAs sat like 'dolls', for having learnt that a ruckus was planned, he had asked them to remain 'still [like] cowards'.[34] In response to Jayalalithaa's encore taunt—'criminal'—Karunanidhi covered the mike and said something that *The Hindu* later reported was inaudible and the *Indian Express* reported referred to an erstwhile Telugu actor with whom Jayalalithaa was once intimate, saying, 'Go tell him.'[35]

According to Karunanidhi, at this point Jayalalithaa directed her colleagues to 'punch him', and Sengottaiyan and others lunged forward and pandemonium broke out. An AIADMK member pushed the centre table dividing the treasury benches and the Opposition in the melee. In the resultant impact, the small podium hit the chief minister, who lost his balance, and his glasses were broken. Kannappan, Ko. Si. Mani, Duraimurugan and others formed a protective ring around Karunanidhi, who later blamed Sengottaiyan.[36] The chief minister was whisked to safety, and the Speaker adjourned the House. After politically breaking up with Jayalalithaa, Thirunavukkarasar said that no one punched Karunanidhi and that Jayalalithaa had desired a ruckus in the belief that the government would be dismissed like Janaki's.

Meanwhile, the DMK ministers went after Jayalalithaa throwing budget papers, paperweights and other missiles, even as Thirunavukkarasar, K.K.S.S.R. Ramachandran, Moopanar and others formed a protective ring around Jayalalithaa as she hid behind a table.

Karunanidhi later said that when their leader was 'attacked', the DMK men could not take it any further.[37] On 9 April, Maran, in a public meeting, wondered if they were 'eunuchs' to remain still when the 'leader of five crore Tamils' was assaulted.[38] As she was escorted out by her partymen, a minister allegedly pulled at Jayalalithaa's sari.[39]

Exiting the assembly tousled and teary-eyed, Jayalalithaa claimed that Duraimurugan had tugged at her sari and tore it, that she fell and hurt her knee badly, and that Karunanidhi had used a vulgar word to abuse her. In a statement later that day, she said she would not attend the assembly 'until a situation is created where a woman could feel safe' and called for the government's removal. Borrowing a phrase from her mentor, she declared the assembly 'dead' and said that if she were to return, she would only do so 'as chief minister'.[*40]

---

[*] On 30 December 1989, Jayalalithaa stepped down as Leader of the Opposition and chose S.R. Radha in her place.

Karunanidhi called Jayalalithaa a 'top-notch actress' trying to pre-empt the imminent revelation of some 'horrendous corrupt deals', but she would end up like King Canute, who attempted vainly to stop the tide.[41]

Three days later, on 28 March, a composed Karunanidhi denied Jayalalithaa's charge of phone tapping and said that the original complaint against Natarajan included Jayalalithaa. Still, he had advised the police commissioner to exclude her. The next day, a conciliatory Karunanidhi, referring to Jayalalithaa's charge, said that 'he was ashamed if something like that had happened' and claimed that she was 'like a sister to him' adding, however, that the charge against Duraimurugan was deliberate. Walking down memory lane, Karunanidhi said that no one had objected when his wife and family were body-searched during the Emergency and famously concluded that this was because he 'was a commoner, lowly and a Shudra. That's it.'[42] On 5 August 2018, Duraimurugan said that if he had pulled at her sari, she would have 'killed' him.[43] On 5 March 2003, Chief Minister Jayalalithaa insisted that she was attacked viciously and described the DMK defeat in 1991 as punishment 'for their wrongs'. Anbazhagan said that she was 'tense' that day and nothing like what she said had happened.[44]

The day's ugly incidents had grossly overshadowed the budget speech delivered after the exit of AIADMK and Congress (I) members. The speech had a few historic firsts in relation to women's empowerment. Karunanidhi announced equal rights in ancestral property for women, free education up to undergraduate degree for poor and middle-income women, a grant of Rs 50 for two months for women prior to and after birth, a monthly stipend of Rs 50 for widows and destitute women, Rs 5000 for marital expenses for women schooled up to the eighth grade, a scheme to provide jobs for 40,000 women, and exclusively reserving first- and second-grade teacher positions for women. Welfarist measures included 5 kg of free rice for the poor on three occasions (extended to five later), free sari and veshti for the poor, housing for weavers and pavement vendors, a primary health centre for every 20,000 people, debt relief for farmers, and a solatium of Rs 10,000 for lorry, auto, taxi and bus drivers and construction workers deceased in accidents*.[45]

The 25 March incident galvanized a dispirited Jayalalithaa and brought synergy to an AIADMK–Congress (I) alliance that failed to materialize earlier. On 30 April, Jayalalithaa said that although she wanted out, Karunanidhi had given her the 'resolve to continue' and declared ominously for Karunanidhi: 'I have no time for illnesses now.' She said that Congress (I) was never a foe, that she was 'capable of taking on Karunanidhi' herself, and that he should apologize and drop the ministers involved and she would return to the assembly.[46] However, Jayalalithaa would again go into political hibernation.

Politics of Rice

On 26 August, hosting a public meeting of the National Front leaders, Karunanidhi said that with his Nagarpalika and Panchayat Raj bills,† Rajiv was attempting to usher in a unitary form of government.[47] Karunanidhi said:

> They say the central government would contact the local bodies directly. I ask: Then why a state government? Why don't you do away with it? No states; no chief minister. Let there be one prime minister. Let that prime minister declare he is the dictator. Isn't this a challenge to a chief minister's self-respect?[48]

---

* On 7 March 1990, cheap liquor 'to poorer sections who are desirous of consuming liquor' was introduced. Karunanidhi said this was a way to combat spurious liquor. Accessed 1 May 2022, https://indiankanoon.org/doc/1890249/?type=print.
† The bills would pass in 1993 under Narasimha Rao. Accessed 1 May 2022, https://rsdebate.nic.in/bitstream/123456789/264715/1/PD_151_16081989_21_p180_p222_22.pdf, Cols, 180-194.

Relations between Tamil Nadu and the Centre were fraught. The rice, palm oil and sugar allocations to the state had considerably dwindled, and the shortage was making a difference to the smooth functioning of the PDS.

From 18 October, the DMK conducted 'surge meetings' for five days, demanding the adequate release of rice, oil and sugar.[49] But the party was simultaneously preparing itself for elections. That day, Karunanidhi announced free saris and veshtis for 50 lakh families with less than Rs 200 monthly income.[50] On 22 October, another 33 lakh families with Rs 300 monthly income were included.[51] Previously, on 17 October, power tariff for farmers was reduced from Rs 75 to Rs 50 benefiting an estimated nine lakh farmers.[52]

1989 Parliamentary Election

Parliamentary elections were to be held in Tamil Nadu on 24 November. As Jayalalithaa shed her hibernation, *India Today* explained it as her being shaken by a poll that showed less than a third of the people surveyed considered her to be serious about politics. Jayalalithaa was named the eternal general secretary in the August general council.[53] In its manifesto, the DMK sought IPKF's withdrawal, more railway lines, airports, a Cauvery tribunal and Cauvery delta oil and gas.[54] Karunanidhi asked Tamil Nadu voters to emulate their northern counterparts—where opinion polls showed an anti-Congress (I) trend—to vote against Rajiv.[55] Jayalalithaa, however, turned it into a Karunanidhi vs Jayalalithaa battle, the AIADMK manifesto describing the DMK in power as a 'political accident' and seeking a vote on who should govern the state.[56]

On 15 November, Karunanidhi said that he was not worried about the talk of dismissal. Rajiv Gandhi would not become prime minister and power did not matter to him. This would become his refrain during the campaign.[57] In her campaign speeches, Jayalalithaa harped on the 25 March incident and asked voters to drive 'these modern day Dushasanas and Duryodhanas out of power'.[58]

Two days before polling, Karunanidhi foresaw thirty seats for the alliance.[59] Nationally, the National Front won 143 seats and was the second-largest component after Congress (I) with 197 seats. The south, however, had voted for Congress (I). In Tamil Nadu, the DMK alliance suffered a rout. The CPI saved the day, winning Nagapattinam. For the first time since 1957, the DMK went without representation in Parliament. Jayalalithaa said that people had rejected the DMK.[60] On 29 November, Karunanidhi said in Delhi that the 'superstition that only the Congress (I) could form a government in the Centre was the reason for its success in the South.'[61]

At the National Front inaugural in Chennai (from left to right) N.T. Rama Rao, Karunanidhi, V.P. Singh, S.R. Bommai and Ram Vilas Paswan (bearded)

1989 PARLIAMENTARY ELECTION

Party	Contested	Won	Votes	Percentage
INC	28	27	1,05,24,027	39.86%
AIADMK	11	11	45,18,649	17.12%
DMK	31	0	70,38,849	26.66%
CPM	4	0	9,65,838	3.66%
CPI	2	1	5,39,316	2.04%
JD	2	0	3,74,902	1.42%

The BJP fought in three places and polled 0.29 per cent. Paatali Makkal Katchi (PMK), the politicized Vanniyar Sangam from July 1989, contesting in thirty-two of the forty seats, including Puducherry, won 5.82 per cent of the votes and finished third in 120 assembly segments.[62]

Karunanidhi and Prime Minister VP Singh

On 30 November, Karunanidhi said that regardless of who would be prime minister, the 'unity of the National Front' would be its gift for the people who voted it to power.[63]

From the outset, unity remained at a premium. On 2 December, VP was sworn in as prime minister. But before that, on 1 December, VP proposed Devi Lal, and Chandra Shekhar seconded him, only to see Devi Lal withdraw and propose VP instead.[64] Devi Lal, the compromise candidate in collusion with the neo-Opposition leader VP, who had delivered the National Front, had pulled a fast one on Chandra Shekhar, the vintage Opposition leader. With less than 16 per cent of the vote and a quarter of the seats, VP had performed a feat but had earned an implacable foe in Chandra Shekhar, who told journalists: 'This is the first chapter of value-based politics.'[65] The comeuppance would surprisingly take another eleven months.

Murasoli Maran, Karunanidhi and his favourite Prime Minister, VP Singh

VP promoted federalism and economic liberalization and, in the end, even became a social justice champion. Despite their dismal performance, he had included the DMK, TDP and AGP in his ministry. Maran was now a cabinet minister, a first in the annals of DMK history. Unsurprisingly, Karunanidhi celebrated VP. On 3 February 1990, VP agreed to Karunanidhi's request to name the Chennai international and domestic airports after Anna and Kamaraj, respectively. It is a different matter that no arrivals or departures mention these names.[66] On 2 June 1990, when VP constituted the Cauvery Water Disputes Tribunal, he gave Karunanidhi and Tamil Nadu a substantial gift. The May 1975 demand had finally come true.[67] Only four days earlier, on 28 May, the VP government had constituted the Inter-State Council. Karunanidhi would later note that VP 'could accomplish what could not be done in the last 40 years'.[68] VP had also reactivated the National Development Council, which met outside Delhi in Chennai on Karunanidhi's suggestion.

In later years, Karunanidhi would wangle several ministers at the Centre. But this period was the height of his power and authority. Karunanidhi's chemistry with VP was exemplary, as seen in the body language, hugs and embraces. He considered him a sibling.[69] To VP, Tamil Nadu proved an oasis from the parched political Hindi desert where his political foes gave him no respite. No surprise that Chandra Shekhar later claimed Chennai dictated to Delhi.[70] Karunanidhi was never more influential than he was in the eleven months of VP's rule.

Negotiating Fraternal Peace

The ground realities in Sri Lanka had radically changed, and India's Sri Lanka policy now took a 180-degree shift. VP called the IPKF 'a mistake' and set 31 March 1990 as the deadline for the withdrawal. India's High Commissioner J.N. Dixit wrote that VP and External Affairs Minister I.K. Gujral were motivated to prove Rajiv 'was not right'. [71] In a complete turnaround, the Indian establishment treated the issue as Sri Lanka's domestic issue, and Karunanidhi wanted matters left to the LTTE.[72]

On 11 December, Karunanidhi met VP, Gujral and High Commissioner L.L. Mehrotra to discuss modalities for a resolution in Sri Lanka.[73] Later, engaging four Tamil groups, the erstwhile votary of Eelam pointed out that they should settle for autonomy and unity.[74] On 15–16 December, Karunanidhi and Maran met LTTE's Balasingham and Yogi in Chennai.[75] Balasingham's wife Adele records that Karunanidhi and Maran visited them thrice.

Karunanidhi inquired whether the LTTE would share power with EPRLF, which controlled the North Eastern Provincial Council (NEPC) thanks to the LTTE boycotting the polls; the LTTE desired fresh elections and Balasingham 'convinced' Karunanidhi that they would sweep it. Karunanidhi finally endorsed the LTTE's position.[76]

After briefing the prime minister on 20 December, Karunanidhi said that the LTTE had announced its intention to return to the democratic process, the ball was in the Centre's court, and his task had concluded.[77] On 4 January 1990, in a first, Sri Lanka's Foreign Minister Ranjan Wijeratne, after meetings in Delhi, flew to Chennai for a 'courtesy call' with Karunanidhi.[78] On 7 January, EROS and on the following day, Mehrotra, and on 8 and 9 January, NEPC chief minister Varadaraja Perumal met Karunanidhi. On 24 January, Rajiv claimed Karunanidhi had forsaken Tamil interests in Sri Lanka.[79]

On 11 February, at the DMK's sixth state conference's plenary, Karunanidhi said that the LTTE was gaining 'public support in a major way' in places vacated by IPKF but asked the LTTE not to 'victimize the weak'.[80] Yet, it was apparent that Karunanidhi had chosen to brace the inevitable. A US consul general cable said that Karunanidhi had asked other militant groups to 'bury their differences with the LTTE and support their obvious power position and assist in developing a viable Tamil political environment'. In other words, Karunanidhi asked the other groups to take the path of least resistance or meet their fate. But the India-allied Tamil groups proved reluctant to face their changed fate.[81]

On 16–17 February, the LTTE representatives met Karunanidhi, and the other groups met him on 17 February in Chennai. On the 18th, he met with all the groups and again on 22 February with EPRLF, ENDLF, PLOTE and TELO. Dixit records that on 28 February, S. Jaishankar, who was the first secretary, conveyed to Varadaraja Perumal, in Trincomalee, New Delhi's recommendation that he dissolve his government. Karunanidhi refused permission for two chartered ships carrying 1355 pro-Indian group Tamils, including women and children, to dock at Chennai. Yet, he could only postpone the LTTE's viciousness.[82] VP said later that the concern was for India to avoid the war's spillover.[83]

Karunanidhi stayed away from the reception on 24 March, marking the last IPKF contingent's return. As his absence drew all-round flak, including from allies, on 30 March, Karunanidhi justified his stand as directed against Rajiv's decision that he said led to 1800 IPKF and 5000 innocent Tamil deaths. Emphasizing that the DMK had much respect for the armed forces, Karunanidhi said that this did not mean support when they erred and pointed to the Opposition that the US Army involvement in Vietnam faced from US law-makers.[84] The US cable indicated that the chief minister's absence may have been to please the LTTE. [85]

Seeking Cauvery Tribunal

On 19 April, Karunanidhi and his Karnataka counterpart Veerendra Patil held talks for nearly three hours in Chennai on sharing Cauvery waters.[*]

Later that day, following the failure of the talks, Karunanidhi read out a statement in the assembly that twenty-five rounds of talks over the twenty years had not led to a solution and Tamil Nadu would seek a tribunal.[86]

Congress (I) Claim of LTTE Camps

As the Congress (I) began to make claims of LTTE camps in Tamil Nadu on 8 May, Karunanidhi offered to join the legislators and journalists if they could identify the camps and added that the LTTE's de facto Eelam obviated any need for Tamil Nadu. Besides, the LTTE never availed Indian training, he said.[†] Emphatic that he was 'openly blaming RAW' for earlier dividing the militants and now seeking to create differences between the state and the Centre,

---

[*] Karnataka's position was that 670 tmc was available, its needs were 414 tmc and Tamil Nadu's were 444 tmc and the 188 tmc shortfall be equally divided. Tamil Nadu maintained that the 444 tmc was after the 100 tmc it would forgo and its needs could not be reduced any further.

[†] *Murasoli*, 9 May 1990, 1, 8. However, RAW founder R.N. Kao is quoted as describing as 'disaster' the policy of training and arming the LTTE. Rohan Gunaratna, *Indian Intervention in Sri Lanka: The Role of India's Intelligence Agencies* (Colombo: South Asian Network on Conflict Research, 1993), 26.

Karunanidhi hoped the prime minister would take appropriate action.[87] There appeared to be little coordination between the different organs of the government that often worked at cross purposes. RAW seemed to have a mind and agenda of its own. Yet, on 13 May, the prime minister said that he did not agree with the chief minister.[88]

On 19 June, the allegations of the existence of camps did not matter any more. That day, Karunanidhi organized and briefed nine chief ministers, several Union ministers and national leaders to explain 'the nuances of the Sri Lankan Tamil problem, and how to solve it', and obtained their support. As he stepped out, the news of LTTE viciously mowing down Padmanabhan, twelve of his colleagues and an Indian national in a shootout in Chennai, greatly embarrassed their new patron saint, who lamented that the militants had staged their fratricide in Tamil Nadu itself.[89]

On 6 September, Rajiv told Parliament that Tamil Nadu's law-and-order situation was 'very close' to that of Kashmir, Punjab and Assam, which were troubled.[90]

VP Announces Mandal

Relations between VP and Devi Lal began to flounder when VP asked Devi Lal's son, Om Prakash Chautala, to step down as Haryana's chief minister in the aftermath of violence and poll-rigging in the Meham by-election in February. Elected from a second constituency in May, in an election marred by the deaths of twelve, and reinstated as chief minister on 12 July, Chautala stepped down four days later owing to opposition within the National Front. Devi Lal hit back, calling VP 'spineless' and his opponents 'wimps'.[91]* On 1 August, VP dropped Devi Lal, who promptly called for a peasants' march on

---

* On 12 July, Jayalalithaa expelled Thirunavukkarasar, K.K.S.S.R. Ramachandran and others from the party. On 1 August, the Thirunavukkarasar faction expelled Jayalalithaa.

9 August. On 7 August, to undercut Devi Lal, VP announced his 'momentous decision of social justice' in Parliament to implement Mandal, turning into another backward classes (OBC) champion.[92]

The report excluded many dominant proprietary castes like Jats—to which Devi Lal belonged, and Devi Lal wanted included.[93] On 15 August, the prime minister played his second card, wooing Muslims when he declared Prophet Mohammed's birthday a national holiday.

On 20 August, Karunanidhi moved a government resolution to thank the Centre on Mandal that was passed unanimously. While Tamil Nadu patted itself for its pioneer role in social justice for the OBCs in the Hindi heartland, violent protests convulsed the north. Upper caste students self-immolated from 19 September. The BJP felt politically under siege.[94]

On 15 September, BJP president Lal Kishan Advani announced a rath yatra for a Ram temple at Ayodhya and was arrested on 23 October in Bihar, a Janata Dal state. As though on cue, BJP withdrew support for VP the following day.

On 27 October, Karunanidhi extended free power to all farmers adding another Rs 30 crore to the Rs 350-crore loss from subsidies to the Tamil Nadu Electricity Board.[95] The price of rice was lowered, and the 12 kg per month was increased to 20 kg, costing another Rs 58 crore in subsidies.

On 7 November, in a first, the V.P. Singh government was voted out of office. Earlier, on 5 November, Chandra Shekhar split from the Janata Dal to call his faction Janata Dal (Socialist or S), claiming the support of sixty-eight MPs. Karunanidhi said VP had been felled like Caesar in the Roman Senate for Mandal. With Congress (I) support, Chandra Shekhar was sworn in on 10 November as prime minister. But his days were numbered. And so were Karunanidhi's, with a truculent Chandra Shekhar beholden to Congress (I) and AIADMK.

20

Twice Bitten

Cho Ramaswamy writes that Jayalalithaa did not believe Chandra Shekhar's 'minority government' would dismiss the Karunanidhi government.[1] Yet, her demand for the dismissal only grew shriller. The Congress (I) played second fiddle. On 7 November, Rajiv Gandhi said in Parliament that the 'linkage between . . . DMK and the LTTE is very clear'. He claimed that the coastal waters were under Tiger control, said the government could not protect Sri Lankan political refugees and concluded that the gravity of the situation was not realized.[2] Karunanidhi rebutted Rajiv's 'absolute lie' as 'unbecoming of a former prime minister' and said that he had tarnished Nehru's fame.[3] Karunanidhi spoke of the nexus between MGR and the LTTE and Indira Gandhi's policy of covert training for the militants. He said the law-and-order situation in Tamil Nadu was comparatively healthier than in other states. Nonetheless, it was equally valid that the LTTE had found a sympathetic administration in Karunanidhi's and at the Centre with VP*.[4]

---

* LTTE's Kasi Anandan, in his deposition to the Jain Commission, said that the LTTE had 'very friendly relations with Karunanidhi', enjoyed better freedom of movement and were able to communicate from Jaffna to Tamil Nadu under the Karunanidhi and VP government. Accessed 2 April 2022, http://media1.intoday.in/indiatoday/images/JainCommissionReport.pdf.

But criticism of Karunanidhi turning a blind eye to the LTTE's activities was not limited to Rajiv Gandhi. On 15 November 1990, Vice Admiral L. Ramdas fired the first official salvo, claiming that a hundred Sri Lankan militants apprehended on the high seas and handed over to the state authorities were released without proper scrutiny. Karunanidhi said that Rajiv's 7 November speech, the renewal of the Congress (I) refrain of LTTE dominance, and the vice admiral's remarks—all possessed the 'ulterior motive' of getting rid of his government.[5] The next day, the prime minister told Parliament that Tamil Nadu and Assam were on 'the brink' and asked their chief ministers 'to restore peace and law and order'; otherwise, he said 'things would take their own course'.[6]

Karunanidhi dispatched Manoharan, who enjoyed a friendship with the prime minister, to troubleshoot for him. On 18 November, after meeting with the prime minister, Manoharan said that Chandra Shekhar had replied 'not at all' to his query about whether he intended to dismiss the DMK government. But this was only the beginning of the prime minister's prevarication. On 27 November, Chandra Shekhar reiterated that law and order should be 'brought under control' in the state.

Meanwhile, in June 1990, Jayalalithaa had asked Natarajan to leave Poes Garden as he 'overstepped his limits' and Jayalalithaa 'did not like his highhanded way and interference', and she and Sasikala ceased all contacts with him.[7] She issued a statement 'disowning' M. Natarajan. She said he was not a party man, a family friend or an aide.[8]

On 3 December 1990, the chief minister personally apprised the prime minister and heard him reiterate his assurances. However, ten days later, on 14 December, in Chennai, Chandra Shekhar sang a different tune when he asked the Tamil Nadu government not to 'take liberties with the Centre and pay heed to his advice on important national issues'. Later that day in Lucknow, addressing his Janata Dal workers, Chandra Shekhar famously remarked, 'Days are gone when the Union Government used to dictate from Madras.' (On 10 January 1991, he repeated the same in Parliament.) Karunanidhi rejected the charge.[9] On 25 December, the prime minister, on a visit to the Kanchi Mutt, said at Kanchipuram that 'some forces here are threatening the very existence of the State' and later claimed that no one wished to dismiss a government. Still, if there were apprehensions, then he would have to act. That evening, Jayalalithaa hosted a tea for the prime minister at her Poes Garden residence, where she reiterated her request for dismissal. On 29 December, she flew to Delhi to meet Rajiv. Later that evening, she submitted a 'confidential' memorandum against the DMK government to Chandra Shekhar and, the following day, to the President. Rajiv would later have dinner with Jayalalithaa in Chennai, and in January, the Congress (I) would follow up with its memorandum to Chandra Shekhar against the DMK government.

On 3 January 1991, Karunanidhi met Chandra Shekhar after attending the National Development Council in Delhi and said that Chandra Shekhar treated him like a prime minister should treat a chief minister.[10] But dismissal loomed large, and at the 6 January general council, Karunanidhi rued that the militants had created a conducive climate for the lies and the campaign against the DMK.[11] That day, Karunanidhi asked if it was Indira Gandhi or him who had sanctioned thirty-one camps for the militants and if there were no law-and-order issues between 1983 and 1986 in the state. Borrowing a line from Churchill's 14 July 1941 speech that 'London can take it again' in anticipation that it would be bombed as in the previous year, Karunanidhi said that 'The DMK will take it' about the dismissal.

On 7 January, Karunanidhi undertook a two-day tour of 272 villages in the northern districts to launch his free housing scheme for Dalits. Elsewhere, in Parliament that day, and for the next four days, except 9 January (when Parliament was not in session and the prime minister spoke on the issue to the consultative committee of

MPs of the home ministry), the DMK government's alleged nexus to the LTTE remained the focus in both Houses.

On 10 January, AIADMK's Thambi Durai said that the entire state 'expect[s]' dismissal and BJP's Jaswant Singh suggested Art. 256, under which the Centre could direct the state. CPI's Indrajit Gupta said the prime minister should think 'twenty times before using the powers in the Constitution'.[12] Chandra Shekhar denied that dismissal was a quid pro quo for AIADMK support. Even as an ordinary member, he had written to the home minister on LTTE activity and the chief minister's reaction, but the letter was not even acknowledged. The prime minister said he would 'think a hundred times before dismissing an elected government'.

Yet in the same breath, he claimed links between the LTTE and the United Liberation Front of Assam (ULFA), alleged six ULFA centres in Tamil Nadu and, in the most damaging revelation, claimed, 'for ears only' information to the chief minister was landing in the LTTE's headquarters in Jaffna. He was unsure if it was with the chief minister's 'knowledge and connivance'. He had not resorted to Art. 256 yet, and then the 'point of [no] return' would have been reached. Assuring that he 'has no intention to dismiss Shri. Karunanidhi's Government', he added that the chief minister 'should not go on giving statements challenging the Government of India. This morning he has come out with a statement that he will fight it back. I don't fight; I don't want confrontation. But the days are gone when the Government of India will be run from Madras. It will be run from this House and this Parliament.'[13] The prime minister had woven a whodunit for Congress (I) and the AIADMK. But a political analyst would later describe the charge of ULFA finding a haven in Tamil Nadu as 'idiotic'.[14]

On 11 January, Chandra Shekhar met Opposition leaders from the Rajya Sabha to allay their fears of an impending dismissal even as Maran, speaking that day in the Rajya Sabha, termed the prime minister's allegations as 'canards' and his assurances as 'double thinking and double talk'. Maran claimed the prime minister was 'under severe pressure from his masters, the Congress (I) Party.'[15] On 13 January, Karunanidhi formally wrote to the prime minister rebutting the charges. On 25 January, he took to the assembly to ask if he was a 'traitor' and to argue that such information had to be shared to operationalize the decision taken with the prime minister. He denied that any 'secret' was shared.[16]

Earlier, on 18 January, in his address to the House, Governor S.S. Barnala claimed that while there were communal clashes elsewhere, Tamil Nadu enjoyed calm and peace.[17]

Meanwhile, on 21 January, Moopanar was recognized as the Leader of the Opposition, with Thirunavukkarasar and two other legislators breaking off from the AIADMK.[18] On 28 January, the defence minister met Karunanidhi twice at Madurai on his way to Colombo to discuss the ethnic issue.[19] That day, Congress (I) and AIADMK carried out a roadblock protest to press dismissal. The following evening, Opposition leaders led by VP met President Venkataraman even as Karunanidhi reached out to him through an aide and was advised that he do something 'fantastic'—like arresting all the militants. That evening following the militants' arrest, the President assured the aide that 'everything will become right'.[20] However, it was not to be.

Dismissed—A Second Time

On 30 January, Law Minister Subramanian Swamy met Barnala in Delhi, followed by Minister of State for Home Subodh Kant Sahai and later RAW and IB officials. Karunanidhi later wondered if RAW and IB were running the government. That night at 9.30 p.m., an Opposition delegation led by VP met the President, who claimed he had no information on the dismissal. Yet, minutes later, Venkataraman had signed on the dotted line, Karunanidhi rued later.[21] His government had been dismissed.

On 1 February, Karunanidhi called for Venkataraman's resignation for acting as Chandra Shekhar's 'puppet' and called

Barnala a 'noble man' for demurring on the dismissal.[22*] Barnala had refused the customary governor's report that would have formed the basis for dismissal. The constitutional provision 'otherwise' under Art. 356 had therefore been invoked. From then on, Karunanidhi would advocate removing the 'otherwise' clause. Three years later, the Bommai case in 1994 set limits to the use of Art. 356 and brought it under judicial review.[23] On 25 February, Chandra Shekhar told Parliament that when dismissal was discussed, Barnala had told them that the chief minister kept him in the dark and that the Centre possessed the information and it was for it to act.[24]

On 26 April 1994, in his deposition to the Jain Commission, Chandra Shekhar said he chose to take action 'at that very point of time so that no mischief could be played by the DMK government'.[25] S.K. Misra, former principal secretary to the prime minister, said that the decision was based on merit and Chandra Shekhar was in 'deep anguish'.[26] However, *Frontline* titled the whole burlesque as 'Goebbelsian (sic) propaganda—Kafkaesque trial'.[27] Karunanidhi said that Chandra Sekhar had temporarily saved his government by dismissing the DMK government but presciently noted that 'They will pat [Chandra Shekhar] . . . Then they will stab him in the back'.[28] On 6 March, Congress (I)'s withdrawal of support on the pretext that Rajiv was being spied upon led to the fall of the Chandra Shekhar government.

On 25 February, Chidambaram outdid Chandra Shekhar when he charged the Karunanidhi and the National Front governments with 'coverup' of the LTTE's illegal activities. He alleged that in the aftermath of Padmanabha's murder, on 26 June 1990, Karunanidhi

---

[*] On 6 February, the National Front conducted a nationwide protest shut-down in which 25,000 people courted arrest. Prabhu Chawla, 'Parties gear up for polls in Tamil Nadu,' India Today, 28 February 1991. Accessed 1 May 2022, https://www.indiatoday.in/magazine/indiascope/story/19910228-parties-gear-up-for-polls-in-tamil-nadu-814083-1991-02-27; *Murasoli*, 6 February 1991, 8. On 13 February, Barnala resigned when he was asked to shift to Bihar. Karunanidhi, *Nenjuku Needhi*, 4: 337.

asked two LTTE emissaries to take him 'into confidence' before their operations so that he could 'warn' his police to back off. Chidambaram said that on 17 February 1990, Karunanidhi made a 'most pernicious change' in policy, shifting law and order from the chief secretary to the home secretary, a 'close relative' and considered 'the Deputy Chief Minister of Tamil Nadu', which was reversed on 2 February following his government's dismissal.[29] On 27 February, Karunanidhi retorted that Chidambaram had proven that he was not fit to have served as a minister of state and pointed out that in Congress (I)-ruled Karnataka and Maharashtra, law and order was in the home secretary's remit. He said the chief secretary had 'overall charge' despite the change he had effected. Karunanidhi did not respond to Chidambaram's more negative charge of his meeting with the LTTE emissaries.[30] He appeared to have chosen to fight another day.

That day was 18 March, when Karunanidhi chose to turn the bizarre charges against him to his advantage. Speaking in Patna at the National Front's election campaign kick-off, Karunanidhi introduced himself as an 'enemy' of the country and a 'dangerous person' who had provided confidential information. While he had been imprisoned twenty times for language and public issues, he said those who had never been to prison, except in films (read Jayalalithaa), had called him a traitor.[31] But Karunanidhi's reference to Jayalalithaa as 'Rajiv's political girlfriend' saw Jayalalithaa retort that, 'Irked at being challenged by a woman, Karunanidhi had been talking about womanhood in a derogatory manner' and condemned the silence of the other National Front leaders present and called upon women's groups to protest.

Rajiv's Death Crushes the DMK

Elections to Parliament and the assembly were held on 26 June in Tamil Nadu. The DMK fought in alliance with the two communists,

Janata Dal and Thirunavukkarasar's Anna Puratchi Thalaivar Thamizhaga Munnetra Kazhagam (APTTMK).[32]

Jayalalithaa launched her campaign on 18 April together with Rajiv. She attacked Karunanidhi and the DMK government as anti-women and tore into the cheap liquor scheme.[33] A DMK campaign song on Jayalalithaa's private life further pushed women's groups away from the DMK.[34] Additionally, for the DMK, a new political foe in the PMK and its leader Ramadoss had emerged who had characterized Karunanidhi as a 'betrayer of the LTTE and the Mandal causes' and promised to name a Dalit as chief minister.[35]

Paatali Makkal Katchi (PMK) founder Dr S. Ramadoss

On 1 May, Karunanidhi began his campaign and was buoyed by the crowds.[36] Karunanidhi highlighted the Cauvery Tribunal, Mandal and his government's schemes and said that he sought justice.[37] On 11 May, Karunanidhi said that the DMK alliance would win 180 seats.[38] VP and Barnala also campaigned for the DMK alliance.

On 21 May, Rajiv's life was cruelly cut short by an LTTE suicide bomber at Sriperumbudur, 40 km southwest of Chennai, blotting the LTTE for good and greatly damaging the Tamil cause. Had he lived, Rajiv would likely have blossomed into a more seasoned and effective leader.

On 22 May, Vazhapadi Ramamurthy said that the 'assassination was a handiwork of the LTTE with active support from the DMK'.[39] The resultant fury was taken out on *Murasoli* and the communist organ offices and establishments owned by DMK leaders.[40] On 25 May, in a rally to condole Rajiv's death, Karunanidhi said that his government had protected Rajiv during his many visits while the governor's administration had failed.[41]

Rajiv's assassination echoed deeply in the south, and the AIADMK–Congress (I) alliance won all forty parliamentary seats, including the lone Puducherry seat. Karunanidhi was the sole DMK winner in the assembly elections. However, even in its worst defeat, the DMK had polled 22.46 per cent of the votes, showing its committed cadre and support base. In addition to the sympathy factor, the PMK had eaten into the DMK's support in the northern districts.[42] The PMK debuted in the assembly with the election of Panruti S. Ramachandran. Jayalalithaa had won both the Bargur and Kangeyam seats.

The sympathy wave's depth and spread were complete, but the Congress (I) had also tipped the balance in the AIADMK's favour. However, on 29 June 1992, Jayalalithaa claimed that even without Rajiv's murder, the AIADMK would have netted the same victory, for voters wished 'to teach a lesson to those who tried to malign and harm her and to restore MGR's rule' and therefore 'no person, force or event could have stopped this result'.[43] Notably, the DMK would not win a single by-election since 1989; in 1993–94, the AIADMK would win by-elections on its own. Yet, Jayalalithaa could have been gracious. Vazhapadi Ramamurthy said that Jayalalithaa was trying to 'delude herself'.[44]

1991 PARLIAMENTARY ELECTION

Party	Contested	Won	Votes	Percentage
DMK	29	0	5,601,597	22.69%
JD	5	0	718,222	2.91%
CPM	3	0	611,358	2.48%
CPI	2	0	503,762	2.04%
AIADMK	11	11	4,470,542	18.1 %
INC	28	28	10,510,569	42.57%

1991 ASSEMBLY ELECTION

Party	Contested	Won	Votes	Percentage
DMK + IUML	176	2	55,36,668	22.46%
CPM	22	1	7,77,532	3.20%
CPI	10	1	3,05,143	1.20%
JD	15	1	4,15,947	1.70%
APTTMK	9	3	3,41,104	1.38%
AIADMK	168	164	1,09,40,966	44.39%
INC	65	60	37,43,859	15.19%
THAYAKA MARUMALARCHI KAZHAGAM (T. RAJENDAR)	11	2	3,71,645	1.50%
PMK	194	1	1,45,56,456	5.91%
IND	145			

The AIADMK-Congress (I) alliance won all the seats in the parliamentary polls. On 22 June, Karunanidhi blamed the sympathy wave, the 'wanton blame' and the 'Goebbelsian' (*sic*) propaganda on the DMK in relation to Rajiv's death for the rout and, personalizing the defeat, resigned his seat.[45] On 21 June, P.V. Narasimha Rao was sworn in as prime minister of a minority government.

Chief Minister Jayalalithaa

On 24 June, Jayalalithaa took over as the chief minister with an eighteen-member cabinet composed of MGR-era veterans and later entrants.[46]

Tamil Nadu saw a repressive administration led by a self-involved, thin-skinned, self-destructive, cavalier, vengeful and extravagant Jayalalithaa. 'He who has great power should use it lightly', said Seneca, but Jayalalithaa was neither politically mature nor ready to handle such power. From the outset, Jayalalithaa, along with Sasikala, was buffeted by asset-grabbing charges. Public life reached a new nadir.* However, a self-assured Jayalalithaa also proved decisive and combative in an all-male arena, reaching national heights like no other regional leader—making and unmaking a prime minister in 1998–99, fighting for the state's rights, crushing the LTTE and instituting schemes for women and children. Women stood by her, except in 1996. She extricated herself from much of the legal nightmare that followed her like her shadow, and when it appeared that she was at the end of her legal tether, death intervened to save her dignity.

To the DMK, five years of dystopia were made worse by Vaiko's absence from late 1993. On 25 June, the day after she took over, the Cauvery Tribunal's interim award of 205 thousand million cubic feet of water was announced. The Centre's decision to seek Supreme Court advice on gazetting the order saw Jayalalithaa confront the Centre. Minister of State Vazhapadi Ramamurthy quit his ministerial

---

* Her lieutenant turned political foe S. Thirunavukkarasar's speech in the assembly on 25 March 1999 lists several of her oddities and several violent incidents allegedly caused at her behest. Karunanidhi, *Nenjuku Needhi*, 5: 959–69.

position and won Jayalalithaa's appreciation. At the same time, ministers P. Chidambaram and M. Arunachalam faced a boycott from AIADMK MPs and MLAs. On 16 August, Chidambaram's car and convoy came under attack in Tiruchi, showing the sway she held over her supporters, not to mention her style of expressing dissatisfaction.[47] On 11 December, much to Jayalalithaa's credit, the tribunal's interim order was gazetted. However, as the later events showed, this was not the end of the road for Tamil Nadu.[48]

In her 15 August Independence Day speech earlier, Jayalalithaa vowed to retrieve Katchatheevu. In the 24 August by-elections to Kangeyam, Jayalalithaa fielded R.M. Veerappan, her fiercest critic, whom she had brought into the cabinet. R.M. Veerappan won but would enjoy an uneasy relationship. The AIADMK also won Musiri. The DMK won the Harbour and Egmore seats against Congress (I) candidates. AIADMK–Congress (I) relations began to sour as Congress (I) believed that the AIADMK had played dirty there.

TADA, LTTE Ban, Acid Attack

But the DMK was facing problems of its own. On 18 November, Vaiko's brother, V. Ravichandran, was arrested under the Terrorist and Disruptive Activities Prevention Act (TADA) and charged in the Padmanabha murder case. The following day, Anbazhagan said in a statement that Ravichandran's non-registration with the police of Sri Lankans who had sought refuge in his house was against 'DMK practice and . . . policy'.[49] Vaiko would later chafe that the party had one policy for his family and another for Subbulakshmi Jagadeesan and her husband, arrested on 9 January 1992 on charges of harbouring two Sri Lankans involved in the Padmanabha murder.[50] Earlier, the party marked the 75th anniversary of the Dravidian movement in Madurai on 21–22 December with much fanfare. Vaiko was lustily cheered at the conference, next only to Karunanidhi.

On 18 February 1992, the *mahamaham* festival at Kumbakonam ended in tragedy when the police baton-charged crowds to prevent them from getting too close to the bathing enclosure where Jayalalithaa and Sasikala offered prayers and ritually bathed each other, causing a stampede that killed over forty-eight people. Karunanidhi pointed an accusing finger at Jayalalithaa's pomp for the tragedy. He said that MGR's trips to the Mookambika Temple were without a fuss.[51]

On 14 May, Home Minister S.B. Chavan read out a statement banning the LTTE in India. Maran said that Jayalalithaa had pressurized the Centre.[52] On 14 May, Karunanidhi pointed out that it was unclear how, after banning the LTTE, the Centre would resolve the ethnic issue as the LTTE was integral to any solution.[53]

On 19 May, former Tamil Nadu Industrial Development Corporation (TIDCO) managing director V.S. Chandralekha was the victim of an acid attack that scarred her face. Gadfly Subramanian Swamy blamed Jayalalithaa for the attack, as Chandralekha had earlier stood in the way of the Tamil Nadu Small Industries Corporation Limited (TANSI) land sale to her and Sasikala. Jayalalithaa and Sasikala had together bought two properties belonging to TANSI. Jayalalithaa was accused of abusing her office to buy the properties below market prices and the properties would be returned on the Supreme Court's instructions.[54]

On 14 August, Jayalalithaa announced the Justice S. Sivasubramaniam Commission to inquire into nine corruption charges against Karunanidhi and his family. Karunanidhi quoted the adage, 'Those whom the Gods want to destroy, they first make them mad' and alleged that Jayalalithaa was not of 'sound mind and had decided to do anything' against him and his family. He described it as a 'captive commission' under a judge of Jayalalithaa's court.[55*]

---

* The Commission ended in a whimper five years later when Sivasubramaniam, without holding a single sitting or issuing any affidavits, pronounced the charges baseless. *Murasoli*, 15 April 1997, 1, 8; T.S.S. 'A Surprise Probe,' *Frontline*, 11 September 1992, 20.

DMK Memo against Jayalalithaa

On 16 September, Karunanidhi, Anbazhagan, Sadiq Pasha, Manoharan
and Maran presented a memorandum of '18 grave criminal offences'
totalling Rs 100 crore against Jayalalithaa, eight ministers and fifteen
civil servants and others to Governor Bhishma Narain Singh, seeking
his permission to file complaints against Jayalalithaa. The allegations
included a Rs 40-crore bribe in returning the Ramachandra Medical
College to its founder N.P.V. Ramaswamy Udayar (taken over by
the DMK government on 25 June 1989); a Rs 28-crore kickback in
the disinvestment of Southern Petrochemical Industries Corporation
(SPIC); the improper sale of Empee Distillery to its former owner; and
the TANSI land purchase below market prices by Jaya Publications, of
which Jayalalithaa and Sasikala were partners.[56]

On 2 October, in a similar memorandum, Subramanian
Swamy called for Jayalalithaa's disqualification for violating the
Representation of the People Act as a legislator since her Jaya
Publications had a subsisting contract with the State Text Book
Society to supply text books worth Rs 94 lakh.[57] (On 21 April
1993, Swamy presented a memorandum to the President listing
thirty-eight corruption charges against Jayalalithaa.)[58] Neither the
petitioners nor Jayalalithaa would have foreseen the apocalyptic
nature of these complaints. Why would Jayalalithaa, an intelligent
woman of an affluent background, get into such a morass? Who
could fathom her actions other than Sasikala now that Jayalalithaa is
no more? Karunanidhi, however, attributed her actions to the 'lack of
basic conviction to do good to the people' and wondered: 'How can
we expect something that is not in her?'[59] Jayalalithaa nonetheless
claimed that her 'conscience was clear' about the charges. [60]

On 21 November, Karunanidhi's former home secretary, R.
Nagarajan, suspected in the leak of Jayalalithaa's resignation letter on
18 March 1989, was arrested under TADA for aiding and abetting
the LTTE. Nine days later, on 30 November, Nagarajan blamed
Chief Minister Karunanidhi and his chief secretary for turning a

blind eye to the LTTE. Karunanidhi called it 'false and baseless' and said he was 'prepared to face the gallows'.[61]

Nagarajan later said he became the DMK administration's 'bureaucratic scapegoat' for the Jayalalithaa administration. At the same time, Ravichandran and Subbulakshmi Jagadeesan were the 'political face' to establish the earlier charge of the DMK–LTTE nexus.[62]

Ayodhya, By-Elections

Nationally, Hindu outfits like the Bajrang Dal and Vishwa Hindu Parishad were preparing for a *kar seva* or voluntary service at the Ayodhya Babri Masjid complex. On 23 November, at the National Integration Council, Jayalalithaa said that conditions for the proposed kar seva be created even while preserving the mosque.[63] Three days later, on 26 November, Karunanidhi said that the DMK would extend support to the Centre against the kar seva, as it did during the Chinese incursion and the 1965 Indo–Pak war.[64] However, on 6 December, the kar sevaks razed the mosque's towers. Karunanidhi wondered if the Indian Army, which could not protect the mosque, could defend India. Jayalalithaa called for a shutdown to protest the destruction.[65]

On 16 March, she wondered in the assembly what the army was doing when the Babri Masjid was torn down. And, on 28 March, Jayalalithaa claimed that 'Coming as I do in the Dravidian tradition of EVR and Anna', she would have no truck with the BJP, which had supported the kar seva.[66]

Earlier on 9 March 1993, Jayalalithaa formally ended the uneasy alliance with Congress (I). Earlier, TNCC (I) president Vazhapadi Ramamurthy, speaking at Erode, had said that she had turned into the 'BJP's mouthpiece' and that he would present a list of corruption charges before the people in two months.[67] 'Some people were abusing and ridiculing me, while others were waiting to stab me in the back', Jayalalithaa reasoned.[68]

On 1 June, Jayalalithaa made good on her electoral promise by shutting down the cheap liquor shops at a loss of Rs 390 crore to the exchequer.[69] On 18 July, she kept a dramatic fast that lasted for eighty hours, described as a 'Brahmastra' (the ultimate Hindu mythological weapon) by her to pressure the Centre to issue a directive under Art. 256 to Karnataka to implement the interim order on Cauvery. She ended her fast after Union Water Resources Minister V.C. Shukla promised in person to set up two committees to ensure the implementation of the award. Karnataka promptly said that it would boycott the committees.[70] On 21 July, Karunanidhi called the committees redundant and said that they would render the tribunal ineffective and ignore its interim award.[71]

As the AIADMK won the 19 September Palani Parliament and Ranipet assembly seats on its own by reduced margins, Jayalalithaa said, 'The Congress (I) as a party has vanished with this election and the DMK has been driven to the edge of despair.'[72] Jayalalithaa had campaigned for two weeks in Ranipet. The DMK had fielded Subbulakshmi Jagadeesan at Palani.[73] CPM suggested that there was a tacit understanding between the DMK and Congress (I) in Palani. Karunanidhi said that the 10 per cent increase in the votes in Palani for the DMK gave the lie to the CPM claim.[74] CPM would ditch the DMK in the next election for Vaiko.

In less than two months, the DMK would be convulsed by its most serious challenge since MGR—Vaiko.

21

Fourth Split

Seventh State Conference

On 26–28 March 1993, the seventh state conference was held in Coimbatore. On 25 March, at 3.30 p.m., a fire consumed 4 lakh sq. ft of the pandal. Karunanidhi suspected 'sabotage and conspiracy' and said that in its long journey, the DMK had experienced and overcome numerous trials and declared, 'The DMK will take it.' The conference, he made clear, would proceed as scheduled.[1]

On 26 March, the general council requested Karunanidhi for an action plan against Hindi spreading its tentacles like an 'octopus'. The council asked the Centre to abandon the new economic policy and recall the Jayalalithaa-sympathetic governor. Opposing the 72nd and 73rd constitutional amendments on local bodies, the council condemned BJP and AIADMK support for the Ayodhya kar seva and urged that the exclusion of the 'creamy layer' and the 50 per cent cap on reservations by the Supreme Court in the Indira Sawhney case be addressed.[*,2]

---

[*] On 16 November 1992, the Supreme Court in the Indira Sawhney case upheld the 27 per cent OBC reservation but struck down the 25 September 1991 10 per cent reservation on economic criterion by the Narasimha Rao government and capped reservations at 50 per cent.

337

The inevitable liberalization process that had begun with VP was out in the open like a bleeding wound in Chandra Shekhar's time and would gallop with Narasimha Rao at the helm and become an unstoppable juggernaut with the signing of GATT on 15 April 1994. In 1991, the DMK's protestations were marked to GATT Director-General Arthur Dunkel's Draft deemphasizing protectionist measures, with Karunanidhi and his ilk punning on Dunkel by adding the Tamil letter *tha* before it to make it sound like *Thadangal* or 'impediment' to India's growth. Ironically, liberalization had freed states to woo foreign investment more spiritedly. The DMK's opposition was feeble and, at best, could prevent some disinvestments later. But the party, like many others, was quietly falling in line. It would come out of the closet in 2001.

At the plenary on 28 March, Karunanidhi announced a stop-train agitation for 20 April and a 'continuous' programme to deface Hindi signboards. Listing instances where Hindi had made inroads, Karunanidhi said that telecast time in Tamil was reduced, and even the thirty-minute cooking programme on TV bore a Hindi name. All India Radio conducted a 15-minute Hindi class every afternoon; even peons in the central government offices were compelled to have a working knowledge of Hindi, and signboards of central government offices sported Hindi names transliterated into English and Tamil. Life Insurance Corporation's schemes bore Hindi names, invitations of central government offices in Tamil Nadu were in Hindi, and instructions for yarn packings to bear labels in Hindi were in Hindi. He said that day's directive of Hindi as a requirement from 15 August for All India Radio news editors signified that non-Hindi speakers were 'second class citizens'.

The Elephant in the Room

But the conference was better known for other things. Much to the leadership's unease, Vaiko had emerged as the most popular individual, next only to Karunanidhi. The long-standing ovation he received as he rose to speak was another testimony to this. His clandestine visit to Sri Lanka had already brought his ambition into the open. In the 20–21 May 1992 party elections, Vaiko supporters in North Arcot district had pledged to fight for Vaiko as an 'alternate leader' on the lines of the LTTE's Mahatiya, Prabhakaran's 'alternate'. Unsurprisingly, they were not elected.[3]

In early 1993, the Madurai district secretary, Pon. Muthuramalingam, who was at odds with Karunanidhi's elder son, M.K. Alagiri, had arranged meetings for Vaiko with a welcome poster describing Vaiko as the 'DMK's third chapter' after Anna and Karunanidhi. The issue of succession was now the elephant in the room, and both sides were queasy. At the conference, Vaiko felt compelled to vouch that he would never become a 'traitor'.[4] *Murasoli* did not publish this part of the speech.[5] Similarly, Anbazhagan suddenly gushed that he could not think of a 'leader other than Karunanidhi to preserve' and lead the DMK.[6] In a box message, *Murasoli* equally felt the urge to assert that the Stalin-led youth wing's rally lasted for two and a half hours and made the deduction that it was 'one more proof that all youth are on Kalaignar's side'.[7]

Karunanidhi chose to address the issue head-on. He revealed that he had recently told a US journalist that the DMK was 'not the Shankara Mutt'—to anoint an heir but a democratic organization where the party would choose his successor.[8] Like Louis XIV, who claimed he was the State, Karunanidhi had become the party long ago. But he had not expected the much younger and ambitious Vaiko to command an organic following and become a threat—not just for succession plans within the DMK, if any, but for Karunanidhi himself.

Symptomatic was the sudden popping up of fans' associations in Vaiko's, Pon. Muthuramalingam's and his rival M.K. Alagiri's names, frontally challenging the leadership's authority. In a similar situation, MGR had asked that the Jayalalithaa fans' associations be disbanded. Karunanidhi chose to emulate him. On 7 June, the former town secretary of Palayamkottai and the 21 Ward secretary, both Vaiko loyalists, were expelled.[9] That evening, Karunanidhi, at a public meeting, claimed that some magazines were 'mischievously' making a mountain out of a molehill, that there was 'no confusion in the DMK', and that the associations 'would not be allowed. And none need to worry about it.' He said that naming the *mandrams* after the living had given 'room for mischief and skirmishes' and concluded with a swagger that 'these rustles cannot rattle this seasoned fox'.[10]

On 9 June, Vaiko chipped in, damning the naming of *mandrams* after him as 'mischievous'.[11] But the elephant in the room would not go away. On 16 June, Karunanidhi tried to save face for himself and his opponents when he faulted the intelligence agencies for stirring confusion and asked the DMK faithful to overcome it.[12] Ironically, only five months later, Karunanidhi would rely on an unconfirmed intelligence report to precipitate matters. On 23 June, while solemnizing a wedding, Karunanidhi described the DMK as a 'fortress', said that he would not hesitate 'to remove the grass and the shrubs', and prophesied that those trying to break the Kazhagam would be 'finished without a trace'.[13] Meanwhile, Vaiko, in a public meeting at Thoothukudi, claimed that 'like the salt is inseparable from the sea and the red from the blood', he was 'inseparable from Kalaignar'.

Manoharan Becomes Collateral

Manoharan became an unexpected casualty in the shadow tussle. Articulating his own frustration, he had told an interviewer as early as January that he would oppose any action against Vaiko. Manoharan was sore that he was not part of the DMK Trust, whose by-laws required trustees to be from elected party positions. Karunanidhi let it go, then. A captivating speaker but an armchair politician and a self-styled intellectual, Manoharan owed his nominated deputy general secretaryship to Karunanidhi. Karunanidhi invariably referred to Manoharan as his 'younger brother', and Manoharan described Karunanidhi as 'my family's elder'; yet on 22 June, an impetuous Manoharan penned a poem of very poor taste punning on the word 'nomination' in the DMK-sympathetic *Dinakaran* daily.

Titled *Karuvin Kutram* (The Embryo's Crime) or Karunanidhi's Crime, with Karu being the diminutive of Karunanidhi, Manoharan took potshots at Karunanidhi, suggesting that he was the reason for all the bane in the party. As is typical in the Dravidian movement's political discourse, the next day, *Dinakaran* carried a riposte by Maduranthakam Arumugam, who had never penned anything, much less a poem, but by his election to the executive, had found a place in the DMK Trust.[14] Titled *Kaalathin Kutram*! (The Fault of Time) and outdoing Manoharan in poor taste and innuendo, it painted Manoharan as selfish and inebriated in the evenings and his station in life as a creation of the creator (read Karunanidhi).[15] Maran and Stalin asked that Manoharan be sacked, and twenty-seven of the thirty district secretaries offered support. A shocked Manoharan now claimed that his poem was on Jayalalithaa. However, this clever-by-half response failed to prevent his expulsion on 24 June, and N. Veerasamy was appointed in his place.[16] Manoharan now said that he would remove Karunanidhi and capture the leadership.[17]

On 26 June, at a public meeting in Madurai, Vaiko swore fealty to Karunanidhi even as he sought justice for Manoharan. Pon. Muthuramalingam did the same. They were out of line and were promptly pulled up.

On 28 June, Karunanidhi said that Manoharan had stooped to the level of a very vulgar Congress speaker of yesteryears, fallen prey to 'evil forces', and the poem was a 'gift' from him and he would also bear this ignominy.[18] He added that Manoharan had described Maduranthakam Arumugam and Kovai Ramanathan nominated to the DMK Trust as 'wastrels and coolies' and blamed him in his poem for their nominations. The next day, Manoharan met Karunanidhi and pitiably claimed that district secretaries Pon. Muthuramalingam, Senji Ramachandran and Lakshmanan had spurred him to take on Karunanidhi.

On 3 July, at the party executive, Anbazhagan showed letters of apology from Vaiko and Muthuramalingam for their 26 June speeches and disclaimers from the three district secretaries that they had prodded Manoharan. But Manoharan's surrender was of no avail, at least not yet. Karunanidhi claimed after the executive that the thirty district secretaries and state convenors had supported the action and that the decision stayed.[19] On 17 July, he reiterated that for the 'indignity committed' by Manoharan, there could be no other resolution but his expulsion.[20] However, Manoharan would be forgiven and rehabilitated on 1 December.

On 5 July, an olive branch was extended to the rebels when Alagiri, in a public meeting, apologized for calling them 'traitors.' On 8 July, *Murasoli* published a piece circuitously criticizing K.P. Kandasamy, *Dinakaran*'s managing director and a former DMK minister, for its pro-Vaiko stance.[*, 21] On 16 July, Karunanidhi cited the Nehru family, Dr Subbarayan, his son Mohan Kumaramangalam and grandson Rangarajan Kumaramangalam, Rajaji and his son Narasimhan and Narasimha Rao and his son who was a minister in Andhra Pradesh, asking how Stalin was different from them. Karunanidhi concluded: 'They can be! But, since I am not from a high caste, my son cannot be . . ., isn't that it?'[22]

---

* K.P. Kandasamy's *Dinakaran* group of publications did well. According to *Frontline*, Kandasamy's commercial success was not to the liking of the *Murasoli* group, which floated *Thamizhan* daily but had to shut it down as it failed. Karunanidhi was disappointed that Dinakaran had taken a pro-Vaiko stand despite him having elevated K.P. Kandasamy to ministership and helping sort out proprietary issues with *Dinakaran*. T.S. Subramanian, 'Tussles for Power,' *Frontline*, 30 July 1993, 29–30. Kalaippuli S. Thanu, 'Unmaigal Solven,' *Vikatan*, 24 December 2020. Accessed 1 May 2021, https://www.vikatan.com/news/general-news/series-by-kalaippuli-s-thanu-8.

Shadow Tussle

The leadership had won thus far. Then, out of the blue, on 3 October, Karunanidhi read to the media a previous day's communication from the chief secretary to him that the central government had 'come across unconfirmed information that the LTTE have plans of eliminating you [Karunanidhi] to promote the interests of V. Gopalsamy.'[23] Karunanidhi said later that, following consultations, he chose to accept the security cover. The letter's implication was dire: the LTTE allegedly preferred Vaiko for the DMK leadership. Was the threat credible? It did not matter, and Vaiko was caught off guard. That evening, a highly emotional Vaiko said the exposé had struck him like a 'thunderbolt', and he would sacrifice himself for his leader.

The following day, DK's Veeramani counselled Karunanidhi to assess the report's credibility, while PMK's Ramadoss saw it as an attempt to malign Vaiko and send him out. In a statement, the LTTE denied the allegation of its involvement and characterized the development as an 'intra-party issue'. Karunanidhi termed the reference to the intra-party issue as 'unnecessary'. Karunanidhi said he did not wish to comment on a question that Vaiko had not denied links to the LTTE.[24]

On 6 June, Manoharan blamed Subramanian Swamy and Maran for the report. That day, former director general of police V.R. Lakshminarayanan wrote in *Dinamani* that intelligence information was usually 'half-truths' and the insinuation 'knowingly or unknowingly conducted political mischief'. On 7 June, *Murasoli* questioned the writer's integrity.[25]

The intelligence letter had forced the succession issue into the open. On 5 October, in an emergency executive meeting, Karunanidhi told the district secretaries, 'There cannot be two swords in a scabbard. Of late, Gopalsamy has regarded himself as a leader and acting so.' Of the twenty-nine district secretaries who attended, twenty-one wished for immediate disciplinary action. The other district secretaries had approached Anbazhagan to convene the general council, but he had washed his hands off, saying, 'Time is past. I cannot do anything.' According to Vaiko, the district secretaries had told Anbazhagan that 'the party would be ruined'.

The leadership pushed on. On 7 October, in a lengthy statement, Karunanidhi attributed the crisis to the intelligence agencies and Vaiko's 26 June Madurai speech adding that Vaiko should have spoken to him privately on Manoharan. Vaiko and Pon. Muthuramalingam had tendered written apologies for the 26 June speeches. But the issue did not end there, said Karunanidhi. What was the issue then? Karunanidhi finally came out to charge that some projected Vaiko as the 'future', 'alternate' or 'equal leader', and Vaiko behaved appropriately of this.[26]

Like an old patriarch who had been ignored, Karunanidhi listed the younger brother's lack of respect towards him, adding that Vaiko made no effort to contact him even after the revelation of the 'shocking' news (the intelligence report) to explain himself. But what explanation did he expect, or what explanation could Vaiko have proffered? He added that as elections secretary, Vaiko had not worked in the October by-polls nor inquired about him when his van came under attack at Ranipet.[27] In his rejoinder, Vaiko indicated that Karunanidhi wished to expel him and, alluding to Stalin, said that Karunanidhi knew who was being portrayed as the 'next leader'. He said he did not receive an invite to campaign in the elections and lamented that Karunanidhi had not condemned Subramanian Swamy's description of him as 'cancer'. With speculation that Vaiko would be expelled any time, Dhandapani of Nochipatti became the first victim by self-immolation outside Vaiko's house. An emotional Vaiko carried his body to the cremation ground and gave an oration that the *Indian Express* equated to Mark Antony's speech. There would be five others.

That night, Karunanidhi, for the last time in his political career, announced that he was retiring as the leader on 10 October, seeking 'peace of mind' and release from his 'bottled-up emotions', adding that this had been on his mind for some months and that he would engage in literary and social pursuits.[28]

The next day, Vaiko matched his leader's histrionics when, in a statement, he poignantly lamented that 'the leader himself [was] calling me a murderer'. Earlier, to a question in his 3 October press conference as to why the LTTE was targeting him, Karunanidhi had reportedly responded, 'The reason is mentioned in the letter', and *Dinakaran* had published it. In one stroke, Vaiko had seized the high ground. Comparing himself to the fallen Ramayana antihero Kumbakarna, a melodramatic Vaiko said he would give his life for Karunanidhi. The DMK would, however, consider him as the other brother Vibhishana who chose to join his brother's enemy Rama and was, therefore, a traitor.

Karunanidhi quickly realized the implication of the charge. On 8 October, he flatly denied that such a question was ever posed or that he had answered it. He said that Vaiko had 'manufactured' it and compared Vaiko's allegation of an imminent expulsion to 'fighting with a shadow'.[29] On 9 October, Anbazhagan refuted Vaiko's allegation that a plot to remove him had been in the making for months, said that Vaiko did not come to meet him like the other secretaries, and a resolution depended on the acceptance of the 'truths' and that Vaiko was in a hurry to lead.[30] At noon that day, Karunanidhi said that he was taking back his resignation after seeing five people commit self-immolation.[31]

On 12 October, Maran refuted Vaiko's allegation that he was plotting to get Vaiko arrested under the National Security Act.[32] That day, Karunanidhi repeated that Vaiko was 'fighting with his shadow' and that he had been as patient as he could with him, but Vaiko 'could have killed [him] instead of his current speeches'. He said he could have removed him after his clandestine trip to Sri Lanka, but he did not.[33]

On 13 October, Anbazhagan, in response to the demand from Vaiko's side to convene the general council, said that the general council had met on 26 March and since it met only once a year, that would happen only six months later.[34] On 14 October, Veerapandi Arumugham indicated that the leadership would not act against Vaiko. Vaiko, however, pressed ahead. In the 16 October *Dinathanthi* interview, Vaiko claimed that Maran and Stalin used Subramanian Swamy as an 'instrument' to remove him from the party.[35] On 20 October, Anbazhagan asked that Vaiko not come up with 'newer charges' when the matter had been put to rest, as indicated by Veerapandi Arumugham.[36]

On 22 October, Karunanidhi issued another statement in which he wondered how Maran, Alagiri and Stalin could have conspired in a letter forwarded by the state government from the Centre. Karunanidhi said it was 'highly astonishing' that Vaiko was creating the illusion that action had been taken against him when Anbazhagan clarified that no action was contemplated.[37] Karunanidhi said it could not be ruled out that the LTTE might have plotted Vaiko's takeover of the DMK.[38] To this, Vaiko said that Karunanidhi was not Anna and he was not Sampath. That day, commenting on Vaiko's statement, Karunanidhi admitted that he was not Anna, implying that Vaiko could be Sampath.[39]

On 25 October, in response to a question as to whether there was a 'power struggle' within the DMK, Karunanidhi said that even when Anna's end was just a few hours away, the question of succession had not arisen. But in his case, although he had two to three more years in his term, aspirations for leadership had been underway for a year. In response to Vaiko's contention that Karunanidhi was afraid to convene the council, Karunanidhi said that the general council was a 1120-strong body and had to convene only five to six months later and that if a third of the members requested it in writing, the secretary general would consider convening it. To the question on Maran, Alagiri and Stalin's involvement in the Vaiko affair, a greatly annoyed Karunanidhi said, 'Let us burn the three at Anna Salai.'[40]

On 26 October, Vaiko alleged at a public meeting at Kudavasal that the intelligence letter was a conspiracy hatched by Karunanidhi, wondering how the leader could do this.[41] On 27 October, in a lengthy statement, Veerapandi Arumugham said that Vaiko had rejected the offer of talks.[42] In this game of cat and mouse, Vaiko seemed to enjoy some sympathy both within and outside the party. As both sides hardened their positions, on 30 October, in Madurai, Karunanidhi indicated that 'betrayal' would no longer last in the party.[43]

On 1 November, Anbazhagan served a show cause notice on Vaiko, accusing him of several lapses and indicating that he had designs on the leadership.[44] He characterized Vaiko's taunt that the leadership was afraid to convene the general council as 'insulting'. He wanted Vaiko to show cause in a week.[45]

But there still appeared to be hope. On 2 November, Veerapandi Arumugham issued his third statement, offering again to serve as a mediator.[46] But Vaiko proved implacable. He made personal remarks about Veerasamy and jeered at Karunanidhi's ad nauseam remark that he 'possessed a heart to bear anything'. 'Sitting in the security of a head constable and two gun-wielding constables, if Karunanidhi says: "I possess a heart to bear anything", won't people laugh at reading Karunanidhi's remark?' he pilloried Karunanidhi. In response, on 6 November, Veerasamy referred to Vaiko in the singular, making it clear that the leadership had made up its mind. And perhaps that was what Vaiko wished to achieve.[*,47] On 29 March 2009, Karunanidhi wrote that Vaiko had asked Duraimurugan who had told him that he would succeed Karunanidhi and counselled

---

[*] During this time, Vaiko had sought actor Rajinikanth's sympathy for him, albeit unsuccessfully. After a three-hour meeting arranged by filmmaker Kalaipuli S. Thanu, Vaiko lamented that Rajinikanth had asked him to stay put with Karunanidhi. 'It appeared that he was asking me to endure more humiliation,' Vaiko had lamented. Kalaippuli S. Thanu, 'Unmaigal Solven,' *Vikatan*, 31 December 2020. Accessed 2 December 2021, https://www.vikatan.com/government-and-politics/series-by-kalaippuli-s-thanu-9.

patience: 'What if our leader lives to a hundred like Periyar or Rajaji? When would I become the leader then?'[48]

Expulsion

In his 7 November response, Vaiko said that the seven-page show-cause notice was written to 'somehow achieve [his] exit from the DMK and public life', which was a 'planned conspiracy'. Vaiko said that following the arrest of his younger brother Ravichandran, Ko. Si. Mani and T.R. Baalu had met him armed with a prepared resignation letter for his signature, and he had told them to give him poison instead. On 2 July, he had poured his heart out about the leader's efforts to 'politically finish' him, only to hear Anbazhagan say, 'Stalin can sit on his lap, can you? You have to accept all this in politics.' When Vaiko wondered if this was democratic, Anbazhagan ended the discussion by saying, 'Nothing can be done against Kalaignar. You withdraw for a year by not addressing meetings.' Vaiko denied all the 'false charges' and said that only the general council could decide on the issue and that the general secretary was duty-bound to convene the council.[49]

In retrospect, Vaiko's and the leadership's actions were a clear tragicomedy and a farce. Vaiko would face the same accusations in 2021 when he installed his son into a critical position in his party. As three more supporters set fire to themselves, Vaiko said he was 'a wounded man', and Karunanidhi should have 'consoled' him.[50] Four days later, on 11 November, the long-deferred action came when Anbazhagan expelled Vaiko for anti-party activities.[51] Vaiko said that Karunanidhi wanted cadres to believe he was a 'murderer' and that he was about to be 'crucified' without a trial, and claimed a 'solid majority' in the general council and a revolt against the 'undemocratic attitude' of Karunanidhi and Anbazhagan. However, Vaiko had overestimated the dissent.

Unlike his predecessors, E.V.K. Sampath, MGR and Nedunchezhian, Vaiko now laid claim to the DMK. On 25

November, the executive meeting at Salem attended by 138 out of 178 members endorsed Vaiko's expulsion and the nine district secretaries and others who had sided with Vaiko. Six others had sent letters expressing support for the majority decision.

At the executive, Karunanidhi said that Vaiko had placed him in an awkward situation where, at his first meeting with the prime minister, he had to apologize to Rajiv Gandhi, who was 'yearning to keep the DMK from capturing power' for the clandestine visit. But Rajiv was gracious about the visit and had asked him to stay behind to discuss the ethnic issue, and Karunanidhi was pleased with the talks. But just then, *Junior Vikatan* published details of Vaiko's visit, forcing him to release Vaiko's letter to the media. Vaiko's misadventure had created a situation where a solution to the ethnic issue had slipped away then, leading to refugees reaching Tamil Nadu and 'begging', harming the DMK and leading to the dismissal of the ministry.

Karunanidhi claimed that Vaiko was a 'publicity seeker', which he said was the cause of the present crisis. He said he had fallen for Vaiko's 'emotive acting' and was not surprised that Veerapandi Arumugham, the go-between, had not suspected the act. He said that even as he sang his praise, Vaiko was, in parallel, preparing for the mantle but was disappointed that Karunanidhi 'was still there' and that he had 'woken up and had escaped'. Karunanidhi revealed that women's wing leader S. Sargunam had suggested that he or Stalin clarify that Stalin would not be president and, in response, he had said that such a statement could be issued if there was such a thought, and that the DMK was a democratic movement. There was 'no "dynastic" politics here'.[52]

On 1 December, Manoharan was readmitted. Had Karunanidhi invited him back, or had he returned on his own? Karunanidhi said that it was both. The leadership had moved fast against Vaiko's rival moves.[53] But it would grate Karunanidhi so much that, on 3 December, he pointed out that Anna, Sampath and MGR had founded their party and flag. He said the rebels believed in 'confrontational politics', perhaps believing that if they seeded such a violent culture, this soil would become ready for an arms culture.[54]

On 26 December, Vaiko convened a general council at Tiruchi, claiming that 447 of the 825 members attended, and relieved Karunanidhi and Anbazhagan of their positions. Vaiko was elected as general secretary.[55]

On 29 December, the DMK general council convened in Thanjavur and attendance was videotaped. Karunanidhi said that 908 of the 1151 members attended. Out of them, 758 were members directly elected, and 150 were ex-officio members. Karunanidhi said that 335 rebels were removed and 150 appointed in their stead. The general council passed resolutions asking LTTE-sympathetic journals to stop their interference in intra-party affairs immediately.[56] Ten non-attendees sent telegrams and letters agreeing to abide by the majority decisions of the council.[57]

Vaiko's pretensions as the real DMK forced the party to seek and obtain an interim injunction on 8 April 1994 at the munsif courts at Karur and Coimbatore, which was made absolute on 26 April by the Madras High Court. On 3 May, the Election Commission recognized the Karunanidhi-led DMK as the real DMK. In his autobiography, Karunanidhi wrote theatrically later that if the party were lost to traitors, he would have died.[58]

Vaiko formed his Marumalarchi (renaissance) DMK or MDMK on 6 May 1994.* Vaiko declared Jayalalithaa the MDMK's 'number One political enemy' and said his priority was to fight her corrupt government. He termed Karunanidhi 'a spent force.'[59] Was he?

---

* Vaiko remains the Dravidian leader who had spent more than four years in jail with the Emergency internment and later POTA. He is credited with having written thousands of letters from his prison cell to cadres. Ra. Aravindraj, 'Vaiko vazhkai varalaaru,' *Vikatan*, 3 April 2021. Accessed 22 May 2022, https://www.vikatan.com/government-and-politics/politics/biography-of-mdmk-leader-vaiko.

22

Veshti-Clad Tamils

'Samooga Neethi Kaatha Veeranganai'

1993 was a year of internal strife and contention with Jayalalithaa for the championship of social justice. Like in Greek myths, their competitive politics always entailed a binary outcome. Here, the surprise winner was Jayalalithaa. In a bizarre turn of events and much to Karunanidhi's chagrin, the Dravidar Kazhagam led by K. Veeramani, priding itself as the sole guardian of social justice, became Jayalalithaa's stormtrooper and adviser for the retention of 69 per cent reservations in the wake of Indira Sawhney.[*] So, in the end, when Veeramani certified Jayalalithaa, a Brahmin, the 'Samooga Neethi Kaatha Veeranganai' or 'Protector of social justice', the irony was not lost, and Karunanidhi was miffed.

---

[*] The Dravidar Kazhagam had been at the forefront of the struggle for affirmative action. It opposed economic criteria in reservations. In 1980, MGR reversed his decision on economic criteria in reservations and, in an about-turn, increased reservations for backwards from 31 to 50 per cent. With 18 per cent reserved for Scheduled Castes, reservations stood at 68 per cent, one of the highest in the country. In 1990, acting on a Madras High Court order, the DMK government reserved a percentage for Scheduled Tribes, taking total reservations to 69 per cent. K. Veeramani, the DK general secretary, took it upon himself to work with the government to retain the status quo.

On 15 March 1993, Jayalalithaa constituted a Backward Classes Commission headed by M.S. Janarthanam, a former judge, in pursuance of the Supreme Court's direction and on 22 March, her government filed a review petition in the Indira Sawhney case.[1] On 27 July, the Madras High Court, in response to writ petitions against admissions procedures in professional colleges, directed status quo for the 1993–94 academic year but compliance with the 50 per cent capping after that. However, on 25 August, the Supreme Court stayed the high court order on a writ petition from the non-governmental organization (NGO) Voice (Consumer Care) Council, and the NGO filed a contempt petition when Tamil Nadu breached the stay.

On 1 September, DK cadres set fire to copies of the Supreme Court's stay, and on 13 October, the DK approached the Madras High Court against Indira Sawhney. On 6 November, a DK conference suggested the state enact an Act under Article 31C to protect the status quo.

On 9 November, in a special session, the Tamil Nadu assembly passed a unanimous resolution calling upon the central government to amend the Constitution to override Indira Sawhney. Yet, two days later, on 11 November, Tamil Nadu tendered an unconditional apology in the Voice NGO's contempt petition to the Supreme Court and on 22 November, submitted 'affidavits of compliance' with Indira Sawhney. Caught between the Supreme Court and realpolitik, Jayalalithaa was walking both sides of the road. But this step put her on the back foot.[2] Karunanidhi embarrassed Jayalalithaa, as Janus, asserting that she had no 'genuine feeling for the issue'. He said, instead of an apology, she should have fought back. Karunanidhi pointed out that at the time of Mandal, Jayalalithaa demanded an economic criterion for reservations for the backward.[3]

On 26 November, at an all-party meeting, Veeramani handed over a draft bill to the chief minister. On 30 December, Jayalalithaa piloted the Tamil Nadu Backward Classes, Scheduled Castes and

Scheduled Tribes Bill 1993 under Article 31-C, passed unanimously the following day. Not to be outdone, on 23 January 1994, Karunanidhi led a DMK rally in Chennai to press for early presidential assent and to place the Act under Schedule IX of the Constitution to exclude it from judicial review. Yet, the rally was more to demonstrate that Vaiko's expulsion had not dented the party.[4]

On 7 February, DK urged people to send telegrams to the President for early assent to the statute. But presidential assent was nowhere on the horizon. On 14 June, the DMK convened an all-party meeting and called for picketing on 17 June.[5] But Jayalalithaa upstaged Karunanidhi, declaring a closure that day, and when the picketing was deferred to 20 June, Karunanidhi and others were arrested and released that evening.

On 25 June, Jayalalithaa led a delegation to the prime minister, even as some Opposition parties, including the DMK, chose not to join her. On 24 and 26 June, Karunanidhi called her trip 'useless' and an 'eyewash'. To argue that she was not sincere, Karunanidhi asked her to issue an advertisement to deny her government's affidavits of compliance to the Supreme Court. Jayalalithaa had taken two-page advertisements to counter the Opposition, pointing out that particular circumstances in Kashmir, Karnataka and Arunachal Pradesh allowed for more than 50 per cent reservations.

On 28 June, Karunanidhi wrote to party leaders across India for support. After the DMK convened an all-party meeting the following day, Karunanidhi asked DMK MPs to lobby political parties for a constitutional amendment. On 10 July, *Dinamani* published the leaders' responses to Karunanidhi. On 18 July, Jayalalithaa emulated Karunanidhi, writing to leaders across India. Meanwhile, the Jayalalithaa government increased the number of seats in professional courses to offset the loss of seats from implementing the Supreme Court verdict.

Despite Karunanidhi's protestations of Jayalalithaa's insincerity in social justice, she displayed vicious intolerance to any move thwarting her efforts. On 13 July, Anna University's vice chancellor was threatened with knives for his stand to implement the 50 per cent capping. On 21 July, Voice's senior counsel K.M. Vijayan was brutally attacked. The CBI later charged AIADMK's S.D. Somasundaram and thirteen others in connection with the assault. In August 2012, the Madras High Court acquitted the accused, as witnesses failed to corroborate the prosecution.[6]

On 19 July, the Tamil Nadu Act received presidential assent. On 23 August, the 67th amendment, including it in the Ninth Schedule, was passed, ending this phase of the battle.[*][7] Consequently, on 8 September, Veeramani conferred the title 'Samooga Neethi Kaatha Veeranganai' on Jayalalithaa at Vallam, Tiruchi. Earlier, on 2 September, at Kumbakonam, a greatly irked Karunanidhi said that he had been in public life for fifty-six years and was not 'yearning for this recognition' and did not have to 'beg' for it. Such recognition, he said, would happen in the future, even if some 'parsimonious minds' (read Veeramani) were holding back. He said that history would record his 27 June letter to VP and his letter to other leaders and their responses.[8] On 9 September, solemnizing a wedding, Karunanidhi used the Ramayana metaphor to paint Veeramani as Vibhishana and himself as the fallen king Ravana.[9]

Unity against Seshan

Karunanidhi, Jayalalithaa and Vaiko would unite against Chief Election Commissioner T.N. Seshan. In October 1994, Karunanidhi, Vaiko and Anna's widow Rani Annadurai filed suits for a permanent injunction against the book *Seshan: An Intimate Story*, penned by a scribe on T.N. Seshan's narration. In Chapter 9, titled 'Report on a "Bully"', Seshan, collector of Madurai during the 1965 anti-Hindi

---

[*] On 2 February 2021, the Supreme Court agreed to examine a petition seeking an immediate stay on the 69 per cent reservation arguing that it violated the principle of equality.

agitation, hinted at a CIA connection to Anna in fomenting the riots. On 16 October, the Madras High Court ordered a six-week ban.

Jayalalithaa first approached the court regarding the book's tenth chapter, 'An Affair, with MGR', which she contended contained defamatory material on her mentor. Soon after, she took exception to comments on Anna, contending that both leaders had been defamed. Karunanidhi, Vaiko and Rani adopted the arguments of Jayalalithaa's counsel.[10] On 18 October, Seshan expressed regret and undertook to exclude the offending portions.[11] Yet, on 27 November, AIADMK men blocked the exit road from the airport for Seshan, and later the hotel he stayed in came under attack.[12]

Permission to Prosecute Jayalalithaa

The unity against Seshan's book was a one-off. On 15 April 1995, Karunanidhi and Anbazhagan presented a 539-page document listing twenty-eight corruption charges against Jayalalithaa and others to Governor Channa Reddy, seeking sanction to prosecute her. The complaint that would seal Jayalalithaa's legal fate was listed as the twenty-fifth. But it stuck. Trouble had begun even earlier for Jayalalithaa on 25 March, with the governor permitting Subramanian Swamy to prosecute her in response to his 2 November 1993 request for sanction.[13] In one of her few comments on these attempts,* Jayalalithaa said, 'My conscience is clear,' adding that voters would judge her in 1996. In this, she was right.[14]

On 7 April, Channa Reddy faced the wrath of an AIADMK crowd, including a minister, that mobbed him at the Egmore railway station. AIADMK men threw stones, eggs and footwear at the governor's convoy in Tindivanam three days later.[15] On 8 April, acid

---

* On 16 March 1994, Vazhapadi Ramamurthy and six other party leaders handed over a memorandum to Governor Channa Reddy listing thirty-eight corruption charges against Jayalalithaa.

bulbs, soda bottles and stones were thrown at Subramanian Swamy in a public meeting. AIADMK women made obscene gestures and shouted expletives at Subramanian Swamy on his visits to the high court complex later. On 26 April, Nedunchezhian moved a motion for the governor's recall, with 169 voting in support and thirty-seven against and two abstaining.[16] Jayalalithaa startlingly claimed on the occasion that the governor had 'misbehaved' with her in August 1993 when she called on him.[17]

On 30 May, advocate R. Shanmugasundaram suffered a vicious attack resulting in multiple fractures and the loss of the little finger on his left hand. His criminal complaint against the purchase of TANSI land was to be filed in court the next day by the joint secretary of the DMK's legal wing, R. Sai Bharathi. In 1993, Bharathi filed a writ petition to cancel the sales.[18] The attack triggered a stand-off between the judiciary and the Jayalalithaa government, and on 20 June, the Madras High Court directed that the case be handed over to the CBI.[19]

Against this background, the 7 September wedding of her foster son came as the last straw. Dubbed 'the mother of marriages', its vulgar pomp attracted such attention that the *New York Times* wrote about it.[20]

'Even God Cannot Save Tamil Nadu'

Opposition to Jayalalithaa's excesses had brought together the DMK, CPI, PMK, Vazhapadi Ramamurthy's Thamizhaga Rajiv Congress, All India Forward Bloc and Bhartiya Republic Party. Actor Rajinikanth unexpectedly joined the fray when on 21 July, at his *Basha* movie felicitation, in the presence of the movie's producer, R.M. Veerappan, he spoke of the rising bomb culture in Tamil Nadu and urged the chief minister to bring urgent legislation to empower the police against the menace.[21] Eleven days earlier, on 10 July, two homemade bombs had been hurled at film director Mani

Ratnam's house following the release of his movie *Bombay*, exploring an inter-religious marriage, topping the several bomb incidents that had preceded Jayalalithaa's four years.[22]

Veerappan was summoned the following day by an indignant Jayalalithaa, who ticked him off for not rebutting Rajini and claimed that he welcomed praise only for MGR and enjoyed it when she was criticized. On 1 September, she dropped Veerappan from the cabinet and, on 17 September, expelled him from the party. (Veerappan was dropped on 20 May 1992 for the first time, but taken back on 17 May 1993.) Rajini Peravais (associations) sprang up and Karunanidhi assessed that the impact of a Rajini-Veerappan political entry would only be known over time.[23] Clearly, the DMK was unsure about Rajini's potential and, even more so, whether it was to its detriment or benefit. But soon, Rajini would put the DMK at ease.

Karunanidhi and Rajinikanth

Photo courtesy: Wordpress.com

On 18 September, in a statement, Rajinikanth, blaming himself, apologized to Veerappan, Veerappan loyalists and MGR fans for Veerappan's situation. At the Anna birth anniversary meeting at Karaikudi two days earlier, Veerappan had lauded Rajini.[24]

Earlier, on 27 September, Rajinikanth, in a statement, famously said: 'If . . . Jayalalithaa is voted back to power, even God cannot save the people of Tamil Nadu.' Even Rajinikanth would not have estimated the statement's rallying cry. It was no surprise that *Murasoli* published the statement on its third page. The actor said that he was disappointed, like the multitudes, that Jayalalithaa used her office not to serve but for her selfishness and pomp. He said 'time' would decide his entry into politics.[25] Again, in a significant relief to career political leaders, Rajinikanth, in a television interview on 12–13 December, ruled out his entry into politics, but spoke about extending support to parties striving for good governance.[26]

Rajinikanth's stand must have warmed the cockles of Karunanidhi's heart. In a Pongal interview on 14 January 1996 with *Dinamani*, in response to a question as to why the DMK was not critical of Rajinikanth who had no record of public service, Karunanidhi made it clear that, with Rajinikanth 'not entering politics, not confronting the DMK and minding his profession . . . What was the need for me to censure him?'[27]

Rajinikanth enjoyed a mass following that won him the superstar title. His fans' associations were a robust presence across the state. Although apolitical, the actor, Jayalalithaa's neighbour at Poes Garden, appeared to be biding his time for a political role. At least his scriptwriters and lyricists made him mouth words to that effect in movies. His cult status saw Rajinikanth deign to preach, and preach to Jayalalithaa in particular. At the 20 April Film Workers Housing event, Rajinikanth sang plaudits for Jayalalithaa for her gesture of providing free land for housing for film workers. Still, he also rendered a homily saying that Jayalalithaa owed her office not to the wealthy but to the poor, and she would be hailed as the 'leader of the poor' if she were to do good. [28] If Jayalalithaa was displeased at this patronizing, she did not show it.

Two days later, on 22 April, at the Chevalier award ceremony for Sivaji Ganesan, Rajinikanth was blunter. He said Jayalalithaa should have honoured Sivaji Ganesan by naming the Film City after him. (She had named it after herself.) To change was humane, and she had done it with this grand felicitation for the actor, he said. 'Whoever errs, I would point it out,' Rajinikanth declared.[29]

Congress (I) Alliance

Oblivious to the tide against Jayalalithaa and underestimating the enmity between her and Karunanidhi, National Front leaders sought her out. On 21 July, Karunanidhi called it an 'insult' that some National Front leaders had visited Jayalalithaa to invite her to the National Front and issue statements adding that it would be an 'additional insult' if they were to return to the DMK that the AIADMK had spurned them.[30] But then Karunanidhi had been quietly warming up to the Congress (I), and the National Front leaders had only given him an excuse to quit their Front.

There were other smaller irritants. In an interview with Sun TV in late December, Vazhapadi Ramamurthy, an ally, pitched for a coalition government in the state. On 24 December, Karunanidhi cited the 1980 election results as a vote against coalitions and added that Vazhapadi Ramamurthy's comments that the DMK should carry out an *Agni Pravesh* (a cleansing act to prove one's innocence by immersion in fire) on the Rajiv Gandhi murder and that the study of Hindi be facilitated in government schools made his presence in the seven-party alliance untenable.[31] Vazhapadi Ramamurthy, in turn, claimed that the 'DMK was afraid that it cannot swindle in a coalition', described Karunanidhi as a 'spectacled snake' and said that he would not retract his accusation about the DMK's links to the LTTE.[32]

But tailwinds were steering the DMK. On 26–28 January 1996, the eighth state conference in Tiruchi declared that the DMK aimed to defeat the corrupt governments at the state and the Centre. The media described the event as the DMK's 'second coming'.

Karunanidhi warned that unless a 'complete and genuine federal system is put in place', there would be many a Kashmir. He said that the DMK would contest all 234 seats.[33]

On 6 March, Rajinikanth prohibited using his name and image for political purposes.[34] Two weeks later, on 20 March, Karunanidhi reiterated that he was not opposed to an alliance with Congress (I). But there were no takers. On 27 March, the Narasimha Rao-led Congress (I) announced an alliance with the AIADMK 'in the larger national interest'. Karunanidhi rued later that President R. Venkataraman tried hard to keep the 'Brahmin Empire from falling because of the 'natural affinity between Brahmins'.[35]

Earlier, Jayalalithaa had met Narasimha Rao in Hyderabad at his family wedding and reportedly offered to sponsor the Congress (I) campaign. Even as Cho Ramaswamy described the Rao–Jayalalithaa alliance as a 'business transaction', Rajinikanth, on 29 March, said in a statement from the US that Jayalalithaa had 'bought Delhi' with her ill-amassed wealth but could not 'purchase' the Tamil people or the state.[36] 'Political Pact with Ex-Film Star May Bring Down India's Premier,' warned the *New York Times* later. Yet at the moment, Rajiv's killing was still fresh, and so were the DMK's sympathies, until then, for the LTTE. In his diary, Narasimha Rao attributed the decision to ally with Jayalalithaa to the Congress Working Committee.[37] That day, Moopanar floated the Tamil Maanila Congress (TMC) at Tirupparankundram, terming the alliance as being against the 'self-respect' of the Tamils.[38]

On 31 March, thanks to Rajinikanth and Cho Ramaswamy, Karunanidhi and Moopanar announced an electoral alliance.[39] The following day, Rajinikanth said that the accord was the 'handiwork of God' to save Tamil Nadu and asked people to overthrow Jayalalithaa's rule.[40]

Rajinikanth met Narasimha Rao thrice and had spoken on the phone to him about her 'misrule', asking him to do something about it. To the question of whether he would join them, he had said no and had expected the Congress (I) to align with the DMK or go alone after this. On Swami Dayanand Saraswathi's prodding, he called Narasimha Rao to ask him to ally with the DMK and, in lieu, promising to campaign, only to hear the prime minister say that it was not up to him but to the parliamentary board. He was shocked when the alliance was finalized later that evening. After this, he urged the 'giants' Karunanidhi and Moopanar to join hands.[41]

He asked people to use their vote as Brahmastra against Jayalalithaa and not to be content with Rs 50 rupees but demand Rs 500 or Rs 1000 for votes (if cash was offered) as it was their money.[42] Rajinikanth's support would play a critical role in sending Jayalalithaa home. Twenty-one years later, on 15 May 2017, Rajinikanth, however, termed his support 'a political accident'.[43] 'She was distressed because of my words. I was one of the main reasons why she lost in 1996,' Rajinikanth would say in her aftermath and added that she proved to be 'golden hearted'.[44]

DMK–TMC Focus on Corruption

Earlier, on 17 March, the DMK–PMK seat-sharing talks broke down. Karunanidhi revealed that the PMK had initially pitched for sixty assembly and ten parliamentary seats, and the DMK's final counteroffer was twenty-five assembly and two parliamentary seats. A day earlier, Ramadoss had alleged that Karunanidhi was vindictive towards the PMK. A confident Karunanidhi said they would 'part as friends'.[45] Both parties had chosen to gamble. But this time, Karunanidhi was sailing a tide. Switching sides without scruples, the PMK would prove crucial in two years to the AIADMK's success in the 1998 parliamentary elections.

The DMK manifesto said that only the DMK front could eliminate the 'corrupt central and state governments' and promised severe action against the corrupt, confiscating their corrupt properties, and an 'open government' that would be 'transparent'.[46]

The party undertook to work for a 'safety net' from the ills of the new economic policy, an ombudsperson-like structure, and lobby for Sethusamudram and Thoothukudi to be made a free port. Notably, it promised total prohibition.

The DMK–TMC's central focus yet remained Jayalalithaa's corruption. On 6 April, when the *Indian Express* pointed out that it was not as though corruption had begun with Jayalalithaa and asked if the DMK was not considered the 'fount of corruption', Karunanidhi, as is his wont, wondered if the Rajaji and the Kamaraj administrations were free of scandals. This was vintage Karunanidhi, equating himself with Rajaji and Kamaraj—paragons of virtue who were never accused of personal corruption. Or, for that matter, Karunanidhi's mentor, Anna. Karunanidhi was right when he said that, compared to the Jayalalithaa administration, the corruption in his DMK administration was as minor as 'mustard', and scandal those days meant taking money from industrialists and the rich.[47]

On 7 April, Karunanidhi asked voters to 'liberate Tamil Nadu' by electing the DMK alliance.[48] That week, Rajinikanth recorded a video famously repeating that 'If Jayalalithaa is voted back to power, even God cannot save Tamil Nadu'.[49] Sun TV repeatedly played the video on its channel.

The DMK–TMC alliance was turbocharged with Rajinikanth's support. If the TMC used Rajinikanth's image of him on a bicycle in his film *Annamalai* to popularize its bicycle symbol, Karunanidhi began many of his speeches thus: 'Our alliance has the blessings of my dear younger brother, superstar Rajinikanth.' Karunanidhi asked voters not to give even a single seat to the AIADMK as it would be 'akin to "letting a bandicoot into" a food store'. Karunanidhi said he would prosecute Jayalalithaa and confiscate her 'ill-gotten' wealth.[50]

Jayalalithaa tried to turn it into a personal battle between her and Karunanidhi. 'Do you want Karunanidhi—who was rejected four times by the people, tried to murder Indira Gandhi, helped the killers of Rajiv Gandhi and even tried to kill me through a road accident—to return to power?' She claimed that all these people (Karunanidhi and Moopanar) had come together to oppose her only because she was a woman. But it did not work this time. She charged Moopanar with 'having a hand in Rajiv Gandhi's assassination'. On 11 April, at Usilampatti, a voter flung a chappal at her and her van was pelted with stones. Aware of antipathy, she had denied tickets to 117 of the 158 sitting MLAs, including ten ministers. Ramadoss and Vaiko targeted both Karunanidhi and Jayalalithaa. Vaiko said: 'Jayalalithaa is the flood of corruption, but Karunanidhi is the fount. The flood will go away, but not the fount.'[51]

On 9 April, in response to Jayalalithaa's campaign that the DMK would do away with prohibition, Karunanidhi promised to strictly enforce prohibition and appoint a thousand women per district to carry out propaganda against drinking.[*] To her question on their prime ministerial candidate, Karunanidhi said the person identified by them 'will be prime minister'.[52] On 16 April, Karunanidhi characterized the contest as between 'the good and evil'.[53] In an op-ed in *Dinamani*, Karunanidhi asked voters to elect the DMK alliance for a 'Strong India and a prosperous Tamil Nadu'. He said that he was seventy-two years old, had been in public life for fifty-seven years, and would 'serve Tamil and Tamil people' until nature permitted him.[54]

The DMK won all but four of the 176 seats for which it put up candidates. The TMC won all but one of the forty seats, and the minor allies fared well. The MDMK came a cropper. Its ally CPM won one seat. The BJP began its assembly innings with a seat in Padmanabhapuram. Dr K. Krishnaswamy, a Pallar leader (Devendra Kula Vellalars since 22 March 2021) who had become prominent during the Kodiyankulam incident,[†] was elected as

---

[*] *Murasoli*, 9 April 1996, 1.
[†] On 26 July, following the disfiguring of the statue of Muthuramalinga Thevar, eighteen people were killed. On 31 August, the police, in the guise of apprehending the murderers from the earlier murder of Maravars, allegedly launched an attack on

independent from Ottapidaram, beginning the legislative debut of the Dalit leaders. Jailed during the Emergency for nine months, Krishnaswamy, once of a Marxist-Leninist persuasion, described the Dravidian movement as 'an utter failure now . . . suppressing the Dalit people'.[55] The PMK had won four seats and had performed creditably in the Vanniyar pockets.[56]

The AIADMK hurtled to a humiliating defeat, winning just four seats and taking down the Congress (I). Jayalalithaa lost to a little-known DMK candidate in Bargur by a margin of more than 8000 votes. All seventeen ministers who ran lost. Thirunavukkarasar and Thamaraikani had won their seats owing to their standing with their constituents.

Karunanidhi called it a 'great, silent revolution' and, using Lincoln's words, said the results proved that: 'You can fool some of the people all of the time, and all of the people some of the time, but you cannot fool all of the people all of the time.'[57]

Jayalalithaa said the AIADMK believed that 'vox populi, vox dei'. She said that she has 'faced vicissitudes both in her private and public life, and the AIADMK has grown by facing trials and tribulations from the days of MGR'. But the following day, she disputed the DMK's victory as 'genuine' and said she suspected 'massive conspiracy and wide-spread rigging'.[58] She also disclaimed that there was a 'Rajini wave'. Three days after the rout, she told an interviewer that Sasikala would remain her friend and sister forever. 'No one has the right to question this.'[59] Jayalalithaa's hubris, the vulgar display of pomp and pelf at her foster son's wedding, the violence and the widespread corruption had done her in. Vaiko rightly said it was a wave against the AIADMK, not a yes vote for the DMK–TMC alliance.[60] Chandralekha said that Karunanidhi

---

Kodiyankulam, a Dalit village 40 km from Thoothukudi. The Jayalalithaa-ordered Gomathinayagam Commission was boycotted by the Dalits and, in November 1999, the commission exonerated the police of excesses. S. Viswanathan, 'A village ruined,' *Frontline*, 20 October 1995, 40–41.

and Moopanar had harvested the fruits of Subramanian Swamy's and her campaign.[61]

On 19 May, when asked to what he owed his party's victory, Karunanidhi stated: 'Jayalalithaa and how she ruled the state.'[62] He suggested that Rajinikanth had nailed the zeitgeist, adding that if Rajini, Moopanar, or even he had spoken in favour of Jayalalithaa, it would not have garnered this kind of traction, for people were so bitter with her. Karunanidhi said that he would not be vindictive.[63]

1996 ASSEMBLY ELECTION

Party	Contested	Won	Votes	Percentage
DMK + INL 5*	182	173	1,14,23,380	42.07%
TMC	40	39	25,26,474	9.30%
CPI	11	8	5,75,570	2.12%
AIADMK	168	4	58,31,383	21.47%
INC	64	0	15,23,340	5.61%
BJP	143	1	4,90,453	1.81%
JP	50	1	1,50,134	0.55%
CPM	40	1	8,51,351	1.68%
MDMK	177	0	15,69,168	5.78%
JD	16	1	1,17,801	0.43%
PMK	116	4	10,42,333	3.84%
ALL INDIA INDIRA CONGRESS (Tiwari)**	46	0	2,09,942	0.77%

* Abdul Latheef broke away from the IUML in 1988 and in 1994 merged
his faction with Ibrahim Sulaiman Sait's Indian National League INL;
**AIIC Tiwari is led by Vazhapadi Ramamurthy in Tamil Nadu.

In Puducherry, the DMK won seven, the TMC six and CPI three, for a simple majority. On 27 May, a DMK–CPI coalition headed by R.V. Janakiraman was sworn in. TMC lent outside support. AIFB won a seat as part of the DMK alliance.

The DMK–TMC alliance won all parliamentary constituencies except the lone Puducherry seat won by Congress (I).

Two Veshti-Clad Tamils

Karunanidhi was sworn in as chief minister for a fourth time on 13 May, with twenty-four colleagues. To a question as to whether Stalin was excluded because he was his son, Karunanidhi said yes.[64] But there were other plans for this son. Karunanidhi discounted Jayalalithaa's fear that he would act vindictively, saying he was 'no sadist' but would not stand in the way of the law.[65]

Left to right: P. Chidambaram, Karunanidhi, Chandrababu Naidu, G.K. Moopanar and Deve Gowda

Photo courtesy: Indian Express

Nationally, the parliamentary elections had thrown up a hung Parliament. The BJP had won 161 seats and the Congress (I) 140. The Janata Dal had won seventy-nine, CPM fifty-two and CPI thirty-two seats. With thirty-nine seats between them, the DMK and TMC together would prove decisive in government formation. P. Chidambaram had, on the occasion of the TMC–DMK alliance, said that Karunanidhi and Moopanar would be the 'two veshti-clad Tamils' who would decide the next prime minister.[66] That prediction would come true.

23

1996–2001: Momentous Years

Jayalalithaa, Jain and the BJP

Karunanidhi considered this term his 'golden period' and lists the Thiruvalluvar statue, the Cauvery River Water Authority (CRWA), welfare boards for unorganized labour, Tidal Park, Samathuvapurams* and the farmer shandies as key accomplishments. He could have added his endeavours to turn Chennai into Asia's Detroit, roping in Hyundai to build its automobile plant in 1996.[1] But in that respect, he was only standing on Jayalalithaa's shoulders. In 1995, by signing an MoU with Ford to set up shop, she opened Chennai as a destination for automobile manufacturers. On 19 May 1996, Karunanidhi said Ford Mahindra had approached him to set up a plant and, with an impish smile, added that he had 'not expected anything from them in return'.[2]

1969, when he helped elect V.V. Giri as President and played an important part in helping Indira Gandhi retain power, was more of a political blip in Karunanidhi's political career. In twenty-five years, much had changed. Yogendra Yadav says that the three Ms of Indian politics—Mandal, Mandir and Market—had allowed 'latent

---

* Samathuvapurams were housing projects promoted by the state government that were meant for people of all castes, including Dalits, to live together.

367

forces to surface in electoral politics', bringing a third alternative to the Congress (I) and the BJP from 1989 to 2014, save for the 1991–96 period.

Thus, this was a heady period for Karunanidhi in Delhi. Along with the Left, Chandrababu Naidu and Moopanar, he played a central role in choosing the United Front prime ministers, Deve Gowda and Inder Kumar Gujral.

In 2011, Tamil Nadu would have the highest representation in the council of ministers. Many believed coalitions had come to stay. They had not anticipated Narendra Modi.

At the same time, in Tamil Nadu, from the late 1980s, the lower OBCs—read Vanniyars—and the Dalits (the Pallars and the Paraiyars) flexed their muscles in a more determined manner, a sad commentary on the failed Dravidian narrative of inclusiveness. Ramadoss, Krishnaswamy and Thirumavalavan made caste kosher in the electoral arena in the land of the birth of the Bhakti movement and Periyar.[3]

Taking Centre Stage

On 10 May 1996, Karunanidhi—politically in a good place—appealed to VP to take over the prime minister's mantle with support from the Left, DMK, Telugu Desam and AGP. Parrying a question on support for the BJP, Karunanidhi said that he did not consider the BJP politically 'untouchable'.[4] Still, the following day, he ruled out support for the BJP.

On 14 May, Tamil Nadu House in Delhi was a hive of activity, with chief ministers Chandrababu Naidu, Deve Gowda, Jyoti Basu and Lalu Prasad Yadav, CPM leader Harkishan Singh Surjeet, CPI's Indrajit Gupta, Samajwadi Party's Mulayam Singh Yadav, Tamil Maanila Congress's Moopanar, and AGP leaders holding consultations. Post the 1989 elections, the DMK and AGP had no parliamentary presence, and the TDP had just two seats. But now in 1996, Karunanidhi, with thirty-nine seats between him and Moopanar, had become the pivot of these efforts.

The Janata Dal, the communists, the DMK, TMC, TDP, AGP and six other parties had banded together as the Third Front. With Congress (I) extending support to this 'secular' constellation, Karunanidhi, Deve Gowda, Chandrababu Naidu and Lalu Prasad Yadav visited VP to urge him to assume the prime minister's position. When VP, who was suffering from terminal cancer, expressed inability, Karunanidhi cited Narasimha Rao, who, despite ill health, was prime minister, and VP appeared inclined. Nevertheless, he had decamped when Surjeet, Jyoti Basu, Mulayam Singh Yadav, Lalu Prasad Yadav and Moopanar visited him in the evening. Later that night, VP visited Karunanidhi to explain that he feared they might convince him.[5] Advani, however, records that VP had turned down the offer 'more out of compulsion than choice', for the Congress (I) would have never supported him.[6]

Jyoti Basu was now offered the mantle, only for the CPM politburo to shoot it down. Basu later described it as a 'historic blunder'. The Third Front settled on Deve Gowda, whom Gujral described as 'The Darkest of the Dark Horses'. But then, it was meant to be. As Advani put it, they wished to 'Stop-the-BJP-at-any-cost' and 'Stop-the-other-person-from-becoming-PM'. In the process, a man little known outside Karnataka and with no Hindi and some English had made it to the prime minister's post.[7]

Earlier, on media reports on Moopanar's candidacy, Karunanidhi said he would be 'the happiest if Moopanar became prime minister'.[8] Surjeet indicates that Moopanar did not want it and they settled on 'the person sitting next to him'. Moopanar operated outside Tamil Nadu in English. He was not a people's leader, although that became his sobriquet. Moopanar was seized by the doubts that would engulf any southern politician who was no one beyond his state. Narasimha Rao, the first prime minister from the south, was an exception. He was a Delhiite because of his long years in Delhi as MP and minister. He was also fluent in Hindi. It would require Deve Gowda with no Hindi and with little Delhi exposure prior to his prime ministerial stint to dispel the myth. By then, Moopanar's time would have passed.

The Third Front submitted a list of 170 members to the President. However, the delay in the Congress (I) letter of support saw Atal Bihari Vajpayee, with 187 seats with allies, sworn in on 16 May as prime minister. On 20 May, the Third Front was formally christened the United Front.[9] On 19 May, Karunanidhi revealed that Vajpayee had telephoned him seeking the DMK's support. Describing him as 'a very likeable person', Karunanidhi noted that he was in a party that he 'completely disliked' and even engaging in a discussion on Hindutva would be tantamount to compromise.[10] On 27 May, Maran, speaking against the motion of confidence, said: 'Not that I love Thiru Vajpayee less, but I love my people, my language, my culture and the brothers and sisters of the minority community more.'[11] In two years, Karunanidhi and Maran would eat their words. Vajpayee resigned that day, drawing the curtains down on his twelve-day stint as prime minister.

On 1 June, Deve Gowda was sworn in as prime minister, with Congress (I) support. Janata Dal President Lalu Prasad Yadav was under a cloud with the fodder scam of Rs 930 crore. While assailing Jayalalithaa as the 'Corruption Queen', Karunanidhi was in the splendid company of Lalu Prasad Yadav and a prime minister whose intolerance to corruption was debatable.

Lalu Prasad Yadav broke the Janata Dal on 5 July 1997 and installed his wife Rabri Devi on 25 July 1997 as chief minister of Bihar when he had to step down after an arrest warrant. On 23 September, Sitaram Kesri became Congress (I) provisional president and, the following June, its president. He had pending cases against him. The contradictions could not have been more glaring.

At any rate, Maran was named industries minister and T.G. Venkataraman, a Vanniyar, as Karunanidhi meticulously records, minister for surface transport. TMC's Chidambaram was named finance minister, and M. Arunachalam minister of urban planning. Tamil Nadu had unprecedently obtained four cabinet berths.[12]

Sasikala Arrested

On 20 June, Sasikala was arrested for Foreign Exchange Regulation Act (FERA) violations,* after which the demand for Jayalalithaa to end her ties with Sasikala grew corybantic. Fat lot Jayalalithaa cared.[13] On 25 June, Jayalalithaa expelled S.D. Somasundaram, S. Aranganayagam and S. Kannappan for demanding that she send Sasikala away and asked of them: 'Can I ask them to send their wife from their home?'[14] Jayalalithaa said Indira Gandhi did not send away Sanjay Gandhi despite the criticisms levelled against him and wondered if 'Mr Karunanidhi [would] expel Mr Maran or Mr Alagiri and his various other progeny from his household', as his family members had attracted much criticism.[15]

Photo courtesy: India Today

Jayalalithaa and Sasikala

---

* Sasikala spent eleven months in jail before she was granted bail.

However, on 27 August, she said that she was 'distancing' herself from Sasikala, 'who had in the minds of the people emerged as an alleged power-centre and an extra constitutional authority'. She said this was 'in deference to the wishes of my party men, the general public and my friends and well-wishers'. She also disowned Sudhakaran as 'a foster son' and said she would 'continue to be a mother or sister to all my partymen'. She disclaimed that her decisions were influenced by 'any single family or person and never will they be'.

But nobody, most of all Karunanidhi, believed that explanation for a second. Karunanidhi said that Jayalalithaa had 'rehearsed the script with Sasikala on her [24 August] prison visit' and was 'trying to pull the wool over people's eyes again'. In Jayalalithaa's aftermath, Sasikala would reveal that they had enacted the charade for 'the outside world'.[16]

Karunanidhi repeatedly argued that Sasikala was only a shield, her properties were in a thousand places, but it was Jayalalithaa's money behind it all.[17] Karunanidhi's attempts to drive a wedge between the two women, however, came unstuck. Sasikala would not swerve. The jail term only brought them closer.[18]

Mayor of Chennai

But there were other feats to savour. On 29 September, Krishna waters flowed into Tamil Nadu. Karunanidhi described the day as more joyous than his wedding day and said that Chennai would get 440 million litres instead of 240 million litres of water daily. In response to Maran's suggestion to clean the Cooum river, Karunanidhi said that 'politics has been cleansed of Cooum (Jayalalithaa)'.[19]

Stalin was fielded for the Chennai mayoral race in the 12 October local body polls. It was a well-thought-out apprenticeship plan. With Rs 200 crore for Chennai's improvement, a first, Stalin was given ample resources to excel.[20] Jayalalithaa withdrew her candidate to support Subramanian Swamy's candidate, V.S. Chandralekha, against

Stalin. Four cases that Subramanian Swamy had launched against Jayalalithaa were pending. But nobler principles were at play—or so she said—to fight 'dynastic politics and to save democracy'. She had found Karunanidhi's soft underbelly. There would be no respite henceforth for him. On 14 September, walking into her snare, Karunanidhi wondered if Jayalalithaa–Sasikala politics, the foster son's wedding and the distancing drama were not 'family politics'.[21] Stalin, for his part, claimed that his dad had entrusted him to the people.[22]

Jayalalithaa retorted:

> All powers are with one family in Tamil Nadu. No one has done what Karunanidhi has done. His son-in-law is a minister in the Centre. Stalin is contesting as the Chennai Mayor. Alagiri is the undeclared mayor of Madurai. Another son is in Coimbatore (*sic*). It is not healthy that all authority resides in one family.[23]

Stalin, however, won by 3.2 lakh votes, becoming the first popularly elected mayor of the city.[24]

Jayalalithaa Arrested

On 5 December, the cabinet decided to arrest Jayalalithaa and set up special courts.[25] A junior minister's comment that people wondered why action was delayed helped clinch the issue. Karunanidhi had trod carefully lest he was accused of a witch hunt.

On 7 December, Jayalalithaa was arrested for allegedly receiving Rs 8.53 crore in kickbacks for purchasing 45,302 colour TV sets for village community centres. The administration appeared keen to take full advantage of the spectacle. *Frontline* reported that 'as if on cue, the driver took his time . . . and a police officer was seen urging photographers to take pictures' of Jayalalithaa in a police van. 'Naalai Namadhe' (Tomorrow is ours),' she said to her followers as she stepped into the police van. 'The days of extinction of this (DMK) regime are approaching,' she added. [26] While in prison and at her political weakest, she would yet tell *The Hindu* that 'The wheel will come a full cycle.' She kept her word.[27]

Jayalalithaa spent twenty-eight days in prison before she obtained bail. She revealed later that the period before her arrest was more agonizing and depressing than prison. She had considered bidding goodbye to politics to free herself from the web of cases, and towards this end, she had probed through Thirunavukkarasar and Moopanar if the cases would be dropped, but in vain.[28]

TMC, PMK, MDMK and CPM welcomed the arrest, while BJP and DK called the action vindictive. The DMK tried hard to appear more than gracious in dealing with Jayalalithaa. The following day, Law Minister Aladi Aruna said that despite the judge ordering ordinary class, she was given 'special class' and issued a room with an attached bathroom and toilet, a fan, a bed and two pillows (from home), a table, a chair, a standing fan, a comforter, mineral water and mosquito mats.[29] On 9 December, Chandra Shekhar, however, said in Parliament, 'the way Sushri [Ms] Jayalalithaa has been treated is just a shame.' He said, 'As an accused, she is not a culprit. It is yet to be proved that she has done some wrong.'[30]

A five-day Department of Vigilance and Corruption (DVAC) search of Jayalalithaa's properties in Chennai and Hyderabad from 7–12 December yielded 28 kg of gold, 500 kg of silver, 10,500 saris and property documents.[31]

Jayalalithaa faced seven other cases in the special courts. In addition, CBI probed money-laundering charges about a $3,00,000 'gift' from Bankers Trust in 1992; and income tax proceedings for her non-disclosure of income of Rs 1.04 crore for the financial year 1993–94.[32] Additionally, Sasikala, former ministers and civil servants faced thirty-nine cases.[33]

Jayalalithaa would extricate herself from this legal morass in almost all but the disproportionate wealth case. She set up a team to handle her finances, legal issues, political strategy and public relations. The team was in place for ten months and she permitted candid advice on the next steps and the consequences. On 14 and 17 December, S. Kannappan and S. Muthusamy were arrested on corruption charges.[34]

Pudukkottai By-Election

In the 9 February 1997 Pudukkottai by-election, the DMK candidate P. Mari Ayya won by 12,024 votes, less than a third of his deceased predecessor. Jayalalithaa had stayed away on health grounds. The AIADMK candidate had carefully avoided Jayalalithaa and relied on MGR's image. Yet the DMK's high-gear campaign on corruption had failed to gain much traction.[35]

Jayalalithaa claimed that the DMK had slandered her freely, foisted false charges and cases, jailed her and harassed her, and suggested that people had disapproved of these measures. Karunanidhi nonetheless claimed that the verdict was an endorsement of his eight-month rule's 'amazing achievements'.

Moopanar Let Down

On 30 March 1997, the Congress (I) withdrew support for Deve Gowda. Gujral records that Sitaram Kesri, who had a few cases against him, suspected that Gowda was engaged in 'blackmail'.[36] Outwardly, Kesri complained that the prime minister failed to give 'due respect or recognition to the Congress'.[37] On 11 April, the Gowda government lost the confidence vote. The search for a new prime minister began. This time, it would place Karunanidhi's role under a cloud.

On 16 April, asked if Moopanar would become prime minister, Karunanidhi said that no one had expressed interest and he, Moopanar and Chandrababu Naidu were working towards a 'good end'.[38] The next day, Karunanidhi told presspersons that if Tamil Nadu had a shot at the prime ministership, they should expect the DMK to put forward Moopanar and no one else. That day, Chidambaram visited Gujral to explore if he would accept the prime ministership, to which Gujral gave a tepid yes. When Gujral wondered if Moopanar was in the running, Chidambaram 'was not so candid'. However, Chidambaram had probed if Gujral would take Moopanar into his cabinet and, conversely, if Gujral would serve under Moopanar.[39]

On 19 April, Gujral met Karunanidhi at the latter's request. Gujral was lobbying for himself. Karunanidhi says Gujral was getting ready to go to Bihar Bhavan to persuade Lalu Prasad Yadav to back him.[40] That evening's steering committee meeting chose I.K. Gujral as its prime ministerial candidate. While welcoming the choice, Chidambaram said that the TMC was pained that some camps in the United Front had questioned the integrity of the TMC and, therefore, would not be part of the government. Jyoti Basu denied that the Left had such suspicions.

On 20 April, Karunanidhi revealed that before the steering committee unanimously settled on Gujral, he had personally canvassed for Moopanar. Despite Biju Patnaik's death on 17 April, he had gone to Surjeet's house and the next day to Lalu Prasad Yadav and Sharad Yadav's house to lobby for Moopanar. As Lalu Prasad Yadav plumped for Karnataka's S.R. Bommai, Karunanidhi had wondered why Tamil Nadu could not be considered this time, as Karnataka had already had a prime minister. But both Surjeet and Lalu Prasad Yadav were firm that the next prime minister should also be from the Janata Dal. 'When the Left and the Janata Dal—the two large fronts—have other views, what can I do?' Karunanidhi asked. He said that AGP's Mahanta also supported the Left's position. Meanwhile, Mulayam Singh Yadav visited Karunanidhi to seek support for his candidacy. CPM batted for Mulayam Singh Yadav, but Lalu Prasad Yadav's opposition to a fellow Yadav's rise ended it. Gujral, an 'impartial candidate', had emerged as the consensus candidate in Chandrababu Naidu's consultations through the process of elimination. On repercussions in Tamil Nadu's politics, Karunanidhi said that it is not that he and Moopanar had fought a contest.[41]

TMC's N.S.V. Sithan said that if Karunanidhi and Chandrababu Naidu had decided to make Moopanar prime minister, they could have done so. A police official alludes to hearing Karunanidhi saying that he could not imagine himself (as chief minister) repairing to the airport to receive or see off Prime Minister G.K. Moopanar.[42] There were limits to a fellow Tamil's rise, and certainly not at one's political expense. On 21 April, Karunanidhi blamed a few newspapers for the 'rumours' and said that CPM did not extend support to Moopanar, which was not personal. Karunanidhi expected the TMC to be part of the ministry.[43]

On 21 April, close to midnight, Karunanidhi, Chandrababu Naidu, CPM's Sitaram Yechury and Maran met Moopanar at his residence for an hour, asking him to ignore the press reports, after which Gujral finalized the cabinet list at 3 a.m. the following day. In addition to Maran and Venkataraman, T.R. Baalu was taken into the council of ministers.[44]

On 22 April, in an interview with *Kumudam*, Karunanidhi denied that he had not seriously worked for Moopanar's candidacy, adding that he had to struggle even to parse out if Moopanar was in the running. He had tasked Maran to ask Moopanar if he was interested, as he feared Moopanar would be 'shy' if he confronted him directly. Moopanar told Maran that his friends were saying so about him and that he did not wish to hurt their sentiments, so had kept mum. Karunanidhi said that on 14 April, on their return flight from Delhi, he had directly asked Moopanar if he 'had such a thought', and Moopanar had responded dismissively, 'Forget it; it is only a three-month job.'[45]

On 23 April, as discussion raged on his role on Moopanar, Karunanidhi said, 'The truth will come out.'[46] Moopanar did not do much to squelch the speculation about Karunanidhi's half-hearted advocacy for him. This must have irked Karunanidhi. On 27 April, when asked why he had not sought the prime ministership heading a party larger than the TMC, Karunanidhi famously said: 'I know my height.'[47] Deve Gowda, from the south with no Hindi, had proven that anything was possible. So, did Moopanar not know his place?

Frontline said that Moopanar's candidacy was a media imagination.[48] However, Surjeet indicated that Moopanar's candidacy would have been accepted if the mid-term election prospects did not loom large. In such a scenario, the north would be the major battlefield and, therefore, there was a need to select a leader from there. Surjeet said that Chidambaram had suggested Moopanar's name. Still, before his trip to Moscow, he had explained why this was impossible, and Chidambaram 'saw the reason behind it and left', said Surjeet.[49] On 6 May, when the press lingered on the issue, Moopanar said: 'Go to the next question.'[50] Janardhan Thakur, however, writes, 'Moopanar was boiling with impotent rage.'[51]

AIADMK Division

The AIADMK was wrestling with difficulties, too. On 19 May, Jayalalithaa expelled Thirunavukkarasar, deputy general secretary, for 'groupism' and fraternizing 'with the permanent foes and traitors of the party'. Jayalalithaa said: 'If insects attack a big banyan tree, the branches should be lopped off to prevent the entire tree from being blighted.' Thirunavukkarasaar said at public meetings that the AIADMK should own up to its 'mistakes' and work to 'revive MGR's memory'.[52]

Salem Special Conference

At the 27–29 June special conference in Salem, in a throwback to the early years of the DMK, Karunanidhi called cadres to build 'a Tamil society of the Sangam age, which had no caste distinction' in the twenty-first century, remove Article 356 and 'redefine and recast the federal equation'. An exclusive youth wing session on 28 June saw speakers hail Stalin as the 'future hope'. V.P. Rajan, who opened the session, said to Stalin, 'Tamil Nadu is in your hands.'[53]

As *The Hindu* commented that 'short of the anointing ceremony' of Stalin, everything happened at the conference, Karunanidhi launched a broadside at the daily saying:

This (the DMK) is not a king's palace. I am not a king. Nor is Stalin a prince . . . I will not be bothered if a yellow paper writes— because I don't have a sacred thread and I have not performed *upanayanam* for Stalin—that only the anointing ceremony of Stalin remains to be done. But this (*The Hindu*) is a newspaper of tradition. Son and grandson have succeeded grandfather as Editor there. Should dynastic succession be only there?

Karunanidhi revealed that many of his cabinet colleagues had wanted him to give Stalin a ministerial berth in May 1996, but he did not. Pointing out that Stalin was later elected as mayor of Chennai, Karunanidhi said, 'I did not offer that post to him on a silver platter.' *The Hindu* editorial counselled patience and tolerance to the chief minister the following day.[54]

Jain's Interim Report

More worrisome developments awaited Karunanidhi. On 9 November, *India Today* published excerpts of Justice Milap Chand Jain's 5280-page interim report on Rajiv Gandhi's assassination.[55]

On page 925 of volume vii, Jain said: 'The assassination of Shri Rajiv Gandhi would not have been possible the way it was materialized without the deep nexus of LTTE operatives with the Tamils in Tamil Nadu and tacit support from the State authorities and the law enforcement agencies.'[56] He added that 'there was tacit support to LTTE by Karunanidhi and his Government and law enforcement agencies.' Jain blamed VP for removing the special cover and Chandra Shekhar for not properly assessing the threat to Rajiv Gandhi.

Jain had prejudged the issue and, in one sweep of the pen, had damned all Tamils. *Frontline* called it a 'witch hunt' of the DMK, and VP.[57] VP claimed, 'Jain has just paraphrased the Congress (I) affidavit' and described it as 'justice retired'.[58] In his 28 February 1998 final report, Jain would redial his findings.[59]

But for now, the damage was done. On 14 November, senior leader Arjun Singh attacked Kesri, who was suspected of reaching a deal with the prime minister on the report. Others like K. Karunakaran, Pranab Mukherjee and K. Vijayabhaskara Reddy wanted the DMK expelled. On 16 November, Kesri called on Sonia Gandhi and, on 18 November, demanded the expulsion of the DMK, dismissal of the DMK government, action against VP, punitive measures against Narasimha Rao and proceedings against P. Chidambaram (who was monitoring Rajiv Gandhi's security and thus was responsible for the lowered security cover).[60] The previous day, Karunanidhi clarified that the DMK ministers would not resign and would provide a 'point-by-point rebuttal with documentary proof' in a parliamentary debate.[61] Gujral had underestimated Congress (I)'s resolve to smoke out the DMK in proving its loyalty to the Gandhi dynasty.[62]

On 20 November, pandemonium ensued when the Action Taken Report (ATR) dismissing Jain's allegations was tabled in Parliament. That day, Karunanidhi termed the blame on the DMK as 'baseless and motivated' and added that Jain had damned all the people of Tamil Nadu and that none of the accused was from the DMK. The trial court's verdict would be out on 28 January 1998, and, in the meantime, no rational person would fault the DMK, as it was 'unthinkable, dangerous and inhuman' to do so.[63] Karunanidhi rejected the Congress (I) suggestion of withdrawing from the ministry until investigations concluded and there was clarity. He said later that the Congress (I) was looking for an excuse and would have still withdrawn support to Gujral, for it felt that it would do well if elections were called.[64]

That day, Kesri formally wrote to Gujral asking him to 'Drop the DMK ministers', failing which his party would withdraw support. On 21 November, the United Front core committee formally rejected the demand. Maran suggested they 'counterattack' Congress (I) with the Thakkar Commission that accused Indira Gandhi's aide R.K. Dhawan of involvement in her assassination. Gujral records that 'Karunanidhi had his own apprehensions' on his suggestion of referring the entire Jain Commission report to a three-judge committee of the Supreme Court.[65] Karunanidhi said that the issue had 'boomeranged' and that there was 'no redemption for the Congress (I)'.[66]

On 23 November, the DMK shot down Gujral's suggestion through VP of a Joint Parliamentary Committee (JPC) inquiry. On 24 November, Gujral formally responded to Kesri's 20 November letter expressing his inability to concede the demand. Gujral says that some Congress (I) leaders tried to lure Moopanar and Mulayam Singh Yadav, but Moopanar refused to ditch the DMK.[67] Karunanidhi refers to CBI director Raja Vijay's account that when he met Jayalalithaa in the presence of the Special Investigation Team's D.R. Karthikeyan, she eagerly wondered when they would arrest Karunanidhi.[68]

On 28 November, the Congress (I) withdrew its support, and Gujral resigned. He remained in a caretaker capacity until 19 March 1998.

Coimbatore Tragedy

On 14 February 1998, tragedy struck Coimbatore when bomb attacks in thirteen places killed fifty-nine persons (forty-six Hindus and thirteen Muslims), including ten women and a child, and injured over 200. L.K. Advani was to have addressed an election meeting at

3 p.m. By 3.30 p.m., a big crowd had gathered to hear Advani, who was delayed. Ten were killed, and Karunanidhi said hundreds may have died if the meeting had begun as scheduled.[69]

This attack was attributed to Islamic radicals. Karunanidhi would later point out that the attacks were 'to avenge the death of eighteen Muslims' in November–December 1997 in police action with Hindu militants. Eight Hindus also died on that occasion. The army was called in. Karunanidhi later traced the cycle of violence to a constable's killing by Al Umma radicals on 29 November 1997.[70] In the secular Dravidian discourse, minorities were above reproach, but who could explain the action of the extremists? The inhuman attacks changed Coimbatore, the industrial hub of Tamil Nadu, from a Leftist bastion to a BJP stronghold, giving the lie to the all-encompassing Dravidian identity of the Dravidian parties. The DMK, a staunch advocate of minority interests, was unprepared for this radicalism in its backyard. That evening, Al Umma and Jihad Committee were banned. Three weeks later, on 7 March, Karunanidhi ruled out any 'political context' and said that it was 'out and out the handiwork of Islamic radicals'.[71]

Earlier, on the morning of 15 February, accompanied by Moopanar, Karunanidhi left on a special flight to Coimbatore. In a carefully worded statement, Karunanidhi said that his government would not tolerate 'majoritarian or minoritarian violence' and clumsily added that it was not wrong to assume that the violence was an 'instigation by foreign forces'.[72] Karunanidhi later explained that after the 28 January 1997 killing of Palani Baba, a Muslim activist, by the RSS, 'Muslim radicals were angry with Hindu radicals'. Therefore, he had to speak about majoritarian radicalism, and he had dealt with Islamic radicals 'severely'. By 24 April, 158 people would be accused and 102 arrested.[73]

The AIADMK, BJP, PMK, MDMK, Janata Party and Vazhapadi Ramamurthy's Thamizhaga Rajiv Congress demanded Karunanidhi's resignation.[74]

1998 Parliamentary Election

Parliamentary elections were held in Tamil Nadu on 16, 22 and 28 February.

Jayalalithaa sensed that the BJP would form the next government and daringly struck an alliance with the hitherto-shunned BJP, giving it much-needed credibility in Tamil Nadu. Ramakrishna Hegde and Mamata Banerjee would follow suit.[75] Equally daringly, she stitched an alliance with her bitterest critics: the PMK, the MDMK and Vazhapadi Ramamurthy's Thamizhaga Rajiv Congress. Subramanian Swamy was already an ally. Except for the MDMK and the PMK, the others were non-entities. Vanniyar and voluble, Vazhapadi Ramamurthy was, however, a valuable catch. 'Tell me, who is not corrupt in this country? Is Karunanidhi above corruption? Is Maran above corruption? Is Moopanar above corruption? Is Chidambaram above corruption?' he said in justification of his alliance with Jayalalithaa.[76]

The DMK fought in alliance with the TMC and the CPI. But, after two years, the TMC's utility to milk any remaining antipathy against Jayalalithaa was to be tested. The DMK and TMC kept the CPM out—the DMK for its sin of dalliance with the MDMK and the TMC for blocking Moopanar's premiership.[77] Leaving out the PMK, Thirunavukkarasar's MGRADMK, and Puthiya Thamizhagam was a mistake. Karunanidhi must have been aware of this, at least about the PMK. Unable to concede the PMK's demand, and more so to criticize it lest it alienated the Vanniyars, he could only rue that 'foxiness' had crept in, separating the 'Doctor' [Ramadoss] from the DMK and making him enter into an 'unholy friendship'. However, Ramadoss had made it public that the PMK would align with the party that gave it the highest number of seats. Karunanidhi would be more imaginative in 1999, giving the PMK nine seats.[78] Congress (I) headed a third front with Thirunavukkarasar. CPM fought in two seats on its own.

The DMK took credit for the ban on radical outfits, the post-Coimbatore arrests of hundreds, and the Rs 2-lakh compensation to the deceased's family. The party noted 333 bomb explosions and 135 deaths in 'Amma's five-year rule' and wondered about the action and compensation.

Karunanidhi described the BJP as an 'octopus' whose arms the RSS, Hindu Munnani and Vishwa Hindu Parishad 'spread terrorism, religious hate and people-to-people conflict,' and his firm policy was not to allow it in the state. 'This is the soil prepared by the likes of Periyar, Anna, Perunthalaivar Kamaraj, Quaid E Millath [Muhammad Ismail], Jeevanadam—there is no room for religious forces. We declare that there should be no place.'[79]

'I will tear off his mask,' Jayalalithaa said of Karunanidhi and referred to the 'dynastic rule of the Karunanidhi family that has ruined the state in the last two years'. She blamed Karunanidhi for the mid-term poll and projected Vajpayee and a stable government.[80]

The results took many by surprise. AIADMK won eighteen and its allies twelve seats. The DMK and TMC tally had dropped to five and three. CPI won one. In Tenkasi and Sivakasi, Dr Krishnaswamy's Puthiya Thamizhagam candidate polled more than 1,00,000 votes.[81]

1998 PARLIAMENTARY ELECTION

Party	Contested	Won	Votes	Percentage
AIADMK	22	18	67,31,550	26.30%
PMK	5	4	15,48,976	6.00%
BJP	5	3	17,57,645	6.90%
MDMK	5	3	16,02,504	6.30%
THAMIZHAGA RAJIV CONGRESS (TRC)	1	1	3,65,557	1.40%
JP	1	1	2,66,202	1.00%
DMK	17	5	51,40,266	20.10%
TMC	20	3	51,69,183	20.20%

Party	Contested	Won	Votes	Percentage
CPI	2	1	6,28,360	2.50%
INC	35	0	12,23,102	4.78%
MGRADMK	3	0	2,78,324	1.09%
CPM	2	0	1,61,452	0.63%

DMK won the lone Puducherry seat.[82]

Rajinikanth's support of the DMK–TMC front did not matter this time. The absence of the CPM, PMK, the Janata Dal, Thirunavukkarasar's party and Puthiya Thamizhagam saw the DMK lose ten seats.[83]

In less than two years, stability had pushed the issue of corruption to the background.

Besides, the DMK administration was perceived as '"soft" on minority fundamentalism'.[84] Karunanidhi said, 'People were mesmerized by the slogan of stability . . . [and] the shock administered by the bomb explosions.' The BJP candidate C.P. Radhakrishnan from Coimbatore won by the highest margin in the state.

On 6 March, at the United Front steering committee, Surjeet suggested that constituents rally behind Congress (I) to ward off Hindutva. The DMK was willing to forgive Congress (I)'s charges against it. But Chandrababu Naidu, whose principal opponent was the Congress (I) in his state, hedged. The beginning of the end of the United Front was in sight.

Equally, with 181 seats, the BJP's chances of a government were in striking distance. With thirty seats, Jayalalithaa and her allies was the largest bloc in the National Democratic Alliance (NDA) and the BJP needed them achingly. Jayalalithaa had bounced back. She would make parties with just one seat in Parliament, such as Vazhapadi Ramamurthy, sit at the cabinet table.

24

Tail Wagging the Dog
An Inauspicious Beginning

No one had held the Centre hostage as Jayalalithaa did, regularly pushing it off a cliff, exhausting it and leaving it with little time or room for governance as in the thirteen months of Vajpayee's second stint.

Invoked by mad priest Subramanian Swamy, Jayalalithaa became a malevolent goddess. The goddess's whims and fancies lay underneath the palimpsest of her demands. The BJP tried to propitiate her but could not concede her central demand—the dismissal of the DMK government made openly but denied with impunity.

Jayalalithaa's blunderbuss to the Scandinavian-style egalitarianism of Delhi's politics showed her as politically callow. Seeing an 'uncharacteristically glum' Vajpayee, journalist Vinod Mehta wondered if something was wrong, and Vajpayee said: 'After you, Jayalalithaa is coming.' Vinod Mehta added: 'And then he laughed for the first time.'[1] Such was her power.

At the 9 March NDA meeting on the National Agenda for Governance, Jayalalithaa placed six high-minded demands: acceptance of the Cauvery Tribunal's interim award; nationalization of inter-state rivers; constitutional safeguards for 69 per cent reservation; a third of the jobs reserved for women in central establishments; all scheduled languages to become official and lastly, Tamil Nadu to store 152 feet water in Periyar.[2]

The next day, Jayalalithaa told the media that the Karunanidhi government encouraged 'anti-national forces', namely Pakistan's spy agency, the Inter-Services Intelligence, provided sanctuary 'to religious fundamentalists' and ought to be dismissed. This would become her refrain.

Promising 'unconditional support' for the Vajpayee government, Jayalalithaa went hammer and tongs at Sonia Gandhi. She said it would be a 'national tragedy' if she were to become prime minister and a 'disgrace' to the nation. Four days later, on 14 March, Sonia Gandhi was named Congress (I) president.[*3] In addition to ingratiating herself to the BJP, Jayalalithaa shared its contempt for Rajiv Gandhi's widow. She felt that, unlike her, Sonia Gandhi had not earned her place.

Sonia Gandhi ignored Jayalalithaa. A prickly Karunanidhi said he had a record of service to the nation and suggested that Jayalalithaa had committed all kinds of betrayals (he listed five kinds), including betraying her mentor. 'Vajpayee is not a madman to listen to those like Jayalalithaa', he said, concerning her call for his government's dismissal.[4]

On 12 March, Jayalalithaa said she was holding back on her letter of support to the Vajpayee government, expecting a 'favourable reply' to her demands. However, Cho Ramaswamy writes that Sharad Pawar had called Jayalalithaa, and she believed in the possibility of a Congress (I) government led by him. The next day, highly placed but unnamed BJP sources were cited as saying that Jayalalithaa had

---

[*] On 16 May 1999, Sharad Pawar, P.A. Sangma, and Tariq Anwar wrote to Sonia Gandhi to suggest that she propose an amendment to the Indian Constitution that the offices of President, vice president and prime minister be held by 'natural-born citizens'. The three were expelled.

cloaked her demands in high principle, demanding finance and home portfolios for Subramanian Swamy and Vazhapadi Ramamurthy, the DMK government's dismissal and hinting obliquely that cases against her be withdrawn.[5]

Jayalalithaa hit back, saying she was not treated with respect in Delhi and the 'unfounded reports' pained her. She asked Vajpayee and Advani to 'touch their conscience' to say she had sought their assistance on her cases. Most cases were in the state's domain, and in the only case where the CBI was involved, the finance ministry had no role, she pointed out. She reiterated that she would offer outside support.[6]

On 12 March, Jayalalithaa was taken aback when Vajpayee met the President at 7.30 p.m. and furnished a list of 240 MPs from whom he had letters of support. Realizing that she was earning a bad name in holding back government formation, she returned to the BJP option but not before she fulminated against Ramakrishna Hegde and the BJP and declared support from the outside. She said Hegde would not allow her to speak about Cauvery and mocked her at the 9 March meeting even as the BJP leaders simply watched.

The BJP wanted her to be part of the government for stability, and Jaswant Singh was dispatched.[7] Jaswant Singh was the first of the BJP envoys whose predicament *Rediff* portrayed when it described him as the 'minister for Jayalalithaa affairs' with cabinet rank.[8] On 14 March, after the President reportedly sent her a fax about her support, she sent in her letter of support.[9] On 15 March, Jayalalithaa indicated she and her allies would join the government.[10] MDMK opted out.

Vajpayee won the 28 March vote of confidence with TDP support. On 23 April, Chandrababu Naidu quit as the convenor of United Front. But more body blows were in the making for the Front.

Thanks to Jayalalithaa, Vazhapadi Ramamurthy, the sole MP of his party, sat in the cabinet. AIADMK's M. Thambidurai was the law minister, and Sedapatti Muthiah was the surface transport minister. There were other firsts. The finance ministry was bifurcated to accommodate Jayalalithaa's nominee with independent charge of revenue, banking and insurance. 'Jayalalitha virtually annexes finance ministry', read the *Rediff* headline.[11]

Sasikala faced four charges of FERA violations with the Enforcement Directorate (ED). Her nephews V. Bhaskaran, T.T.V. Dhinakaran and V. Sudhakaran faced seven.[12] R.K. Laxman's cartoon showed a nervous Vajpayee on a chair, with the rug under the chair held aloft by Jayalalithaa.[13]

On 2 April, Vajpayee poured cold water on her demand for the DMK government's dismissal. Replying to Pranab Mukherjee, Vajpayee said his government had no such intention and would not misuse Article 356. Jayalalithaa expressed surprise at the statement and said it must have been in context. Yet this did not prevent her from claiming that the 'DMK government's days are numbered'.[14]

But it was Muthiah who, on 7 April put in his papers after a special court framed corruption charges against him. Jayalalithaa, in a deeper mess than her minion, now chose to grandstand. On 15 April, she wanted all charge-sheeted ministers dropped, and the AIADMK executive called on the Centre to take steps to 'immediately remove the DMK government'.[15]

Upping her ante, on 18 April, she wrote the prime minister to remove Communications Minister Buta Singh, Ram Jethmalani and Ramakrishna Hegde, who too faced charges, or re-induct Muthiah. On 19 April, Jethmalani suggested that Vajpayee 'call her bluff'. Hegde advised Vajpayee to seek a fresh mandate instead of constantly giving in to Jayalalithaa's 'blackmail'. On 20 April, Buta Singh was dropped.[16] Vajpayee said he had sought clarifications from the others.

On 23 April, the AIADMK ministers asked Vajpayee to 'advise Mr Hegde to either shut up or get out'. On 25 April, Jaswant Singh met Jayalalithaa in Chennai to restore peace. The DMK executive meeting that day condemned the dismissal demand from an 'enemy party' as 'blatant blackmail' and 'devoid of any merit at all'. Karunanidhi termed the resolution 'only a reply to the threats from some terrorists in Poes Garden'.[17]

On 23 April, tabling a white paper on the culprits of the Coimbatore blasts, Karunanidhi attributed 'the spread of religious fundamentalism' to the Ayodhya mosque's destruction.[18] Jayalalithaa described the white paper as 'black paper', alleging that Karunanidhi had given room for Islamic radicals against the BJP.[19] Three days later, speaking to Cho Ramaswamy, Karunanidhi denied he was 'mainly opposed to Hinduism' and said he was only against 'religious fanaticism'. Explaining his presence at Iftar events, he said Muslims did not invite him to a mosque, and if Hindus were to invite him outside a temple premises, he would accept the invite.[20]

On 26 May, Karunanidhi introduced the Tamil Nadu Prevention of Terrorist Activities Act (POTA), 1998.[21] Jayalalithaa said POTA would be used against political opponents.

On 7–8 and 11 June, AIADMK members in both Houses of Parliament walked out, demanding the dismissal of the DMK government. On 13 June, P. Chidambaram pointed out the BJP's dilemma as a lack of a two-thirds majority in the Rajya Sabha and its inability to make Jayalalithaa understand this.[22]

Yet Jayalalithaa appeared to desire a fait accompli and any obstacle overcome later. Vazhapadi Ramamurthy said so in so many words. On 18 June, Jayalalithaa reiterated her call for dismissal. The following day, she charged the BJP of two-timing Karunanidhi and issued a 'friendly warning' claiming an 'explicit understanding' of the dismissal of the DMK government and terming it 'non-negotiable'. She asked that the President not assent to POTA.[23]

On 21 June, Advani disclaimed any discussion on dismissal, adding there would be no dismissal under 'pressure'. On 23 June, Jayalalithaa, in a fifteen-page statement, accused the BJP leadership of 'selective amnesia', adding that Advani was 'not bothered about national security'. She then stayed away from the 27 June coordination meeting citing ill health. Ramadoss faxed a statement reiterating the allies' call for dismissal.[24]

On 4 July, Nedunchezhian, AIADMK presidium chairman, announced that the AIADMK's 'continued support is for the present'. Later that day, the minister of state for coal, Biju Janata Dal's Dilip Ray and George Fernandes met Jayalalithaa.[25]

On 16 July, in a twelve-page letter, she and her allies asked the prime minister to notify the 30 May 1997 Cauvery draft scheme in the gazette. Karunanidhi for his part asked Vajpayee to finalize and notify the scheme before 21 July.[26] On 19 July, Jayalalithaa again administered a 'friendly warning' to the BJP and asked them not to take her support for granted.[27]

Jain's Final Report

On 31 July, Advani tabled Jain's final report in Parliament, which said that the LTTE had turned Tamil Nadu into a 'rear base' between 1989–91. The Action Taken Report or ATR referred to the Commission's 'serious observations in its Interim Report' and entrusted the inquiry on Karunanidhi to the Multi-Disciplinary Monitoring Agency (MDMA).[28] Jayalalithaa promptly demanded Karunanidhi's resignation to enable an 'impartial investigation' and called for filing a first information report.[29] Karunanidhi dismissed the ATR as a 'major fraud' under 'mindless pressure' from Jayalalithaa.[30] On 2 August, Jayalalithaa called for Karunanidhi to be charge-sheeted.[31]

But it was not that Jayalalithaa alone was baying for Karunanidhi's head. On 19 August, Manmohan Singh, Arjun Singh, Pranab Mukherjee and others met Advani to submit a seven-page letter where: 'The Congress insists that the government direct the agency to investigate all matters relating to Mr M. Karunanidhi as adverted

by the Commission and proceed against him in a court of law, if
warranted by the evidence which will be uncovered.'[32]

Threat of Withdrawal of Support

On 7 August, under the prime minister's aegis, an agreement was
reached for implementing the Cauvery interim award and forming
a Cauvery River Authority (CRA) and a monitoring committee on
the sharing of waters.[33] But without Karnataka's goodwill, none of
this could be put to work, as later events would reveal.[34] Jayalalithaa
called it 'a sell-out' and said, 'Possibly there was a quid pro quo',
suggesting that Karunanidhi's nod was in return for exclusion from
the ATR.[35] She and her allies demanded the original 1997 draft
scheme failing which she warned of 'disastrous consequences'.*[36]
This time, Jayalalithaa was deadly serious, as Vajpayee would reveal
later.[37]

On 12 August, George Fernandes and Pramod Mahajan flew
down to meet her and were spoken to through the intercom when
Jayalalithaa called the agreement a fait accompli presented to her.
When they finally saw her in the afternoon, she complained that the
prime minister had deserted her and let Karunanidhi steal the show
on Cauvery.[38] That night, Ramadoss and Vazhapadi Ramamurthy
met the prime minister in Delhi, and Vazhapadi Ramamurthy
denied a crisis later. He was being economical with the truth.

But Jayalalithaa's brinkmanship had led the allies away from
her. On 13 August, they told Jayalalithaa that they would not follow
her lead if she withdrew support. Yet, to save face for her, they
authorized her to take 'appropriate decisions at the appropriate time'
on continuing support.[39]

---

* On 10 November 1997, Tamil Nadu approached the Supreme Court to direct the
Centre to gazette the 30 May 1997 draft plan. On 12 August 1998, the Supreme
Court was to take it up for consideration.

That day, Bezbaruah, the director of the Enforcement Directorate, was 'repatriated' to the Delhi government, and the media pegged it on to the 12 August Fernandes-Pramod Mahajan and Jayalalithaa meeting.[40] The following day, Fernandes again met Jayalalithaa. The same day, N.K. Singh, Montek Singh Ahluwalia and others were transferred. Jayalalithaa denied her hand in the transfers.

Why would Jayalalithaa fuss about media reports on her this time? It is hard to know. On 16 August, Jayalalithaa wrote to the prime minister to reverse Bezberuah's transfer. She alleged that some 'very close to the Prime Minister's office' were on the take from a 'well-known group of publications' and condemned the 'cunning attempt' to make her a 'scapegoat' for the transfer. She said she discussed the Cauvery issue with Fernandes and Mahajan and no other subject.[41] That day, Fernandes chimed in, supporting her.[42]

Vajpayee, Badal, Karunanidhi and Advani

Photo courtesy: News 18.com

Karunanidhi said Jayalalithaa was in the habit of making grave charges and had now levelled them against the prime minister himself.[43] Vajpayee told *Star News* there would be no inquiry unless Jayalalithaa provided proof of bribery.[44]

On 24 August, Maran released Advani's 19 August response to him, describing the inclusion of Karunanidhi's name in the ATR as an 'inadvertent error'.[45] That day, Jayalalithaa asked Karunanidhi to seek an open pardon for 'ruining Tamil Nadu's stand that the Cauvery dispute could be resolved only by the water dispute tribunal and the Supreme Court'.[46]

Allies Are Ingrates

In his 14–15 September interview with the *Indian Express,* Karunanidhi indicated he would support the BJP if it proved secular. He said no prime minister, much less Vajpayee, can achieve anything when 'it was a daily battle to stay alive'.[47]

But Jayalalithaa was at war with all the allies. On 15 September, marking Anna's 90th birth anniversary at Tiruchi, she warned: 'Those who kick the ladder after climbing on it will break their legs.' She ominously reiterated her promise to 'lodge Karunanidhi in the same jail cell' where she was kept.[48]

That day, in an impressive MDMK show at the Marina, showcasing the prime minister, Advani and others, Era. Sezhian remarked that 'Tamil Nadu and the Dravidian parties have come to terms with Vajpayee' and the other way around. Sezhian had carefully chosen his words. He said Vajpayee, not BJP.[49]

On 16 September, answering a journalist's question, Vajpayee said that he had raised the question of support with Karunanidhi and told him that the BJP was indeed 'secular' and did not need a certificate on secularism from the others. Asked whether his government would complete its term, the prime minister quipped, 'I can't say.' Vajpayee said he had already asked the attorney general to investigate the Bezbaruah transfer.[50]

That day, George Fernandes met with Jayalalithaa.[51] Jayalalithaa termed the DMK's support hypothetical the next day and said she would comment, 'If that happened.' She had underestimated Karunanidhi.[52]

Rabri Devi Government's Dismissal

On 22 September, following a spate of violence against Dalits, the Union cabinet recommended dismissing the Rabri Devi government while keeping the assembly suspended.[53] Yet, the cabinet rejected the demand for the DMK government's dismissal.[54] On 26 September, the President returned the cabinet resolution on Bihar.[55]

On 9 October, Jayalalithaa met Vajpayee and later Advani to discuss the law and order situation in Ramanathapuram and elsewhere and the reported threat from Osama bin Laden. She later described the ties with the BJP as 'purely a seat adjustment' and said AIADMK 'would stick to the Dravidian identity', and asked the BJP to keep the Ayodhya issue frozen for at least twenty-five years and focus on service delivery, infrastructure and jobs.[56]

Photo courtesy: Tamil Samayam.com

Jayalalithaa and Vajpayee

On 7 December, Jayalalithaa said the AIADMK should not be held responsible for a mid-term poll. She supported the Opposition closure call for 11 December and disbanded the AIADMK front.[57]

Two days later, Jayalalithaa admitted that the relationship with the Centre and the BJP was 'uneasy'.[58] The relationship was erratic, defying rationale or analysis. Thus, on 17 December, the Centre told the Supreme Court that the state government could not transfer cases to special courts.[59] On 19 December, Karunanidhi alleged that the Vajpayee government 'has come out in the open to rescue the Jayalalithaa group' and his hopes that 'Mr Vajpayee would ensure honesty and probity in public life have been belied'.[60]

Pitying the Centre's plight, Thirunavukkarasar said, 'One wonders who the Prime Minister is, Vajpayee or Jayalalithaa.' A *Dinamani* cartoon pithily portrayed the BJP government's pickle showing the prime minister with a shovel having erected a tombstone after burying the cases and telling a puzzled spectator: 'Did we not say that we will wipe out corruption?'[61] Finance Minister Yashwant Sinha records that Jayalalithaa handed over a 'note about her income tax cases' after hosting lunch. 'The prime minister innocently asked me about the envelope . . . and its contents,' Sinha wrote. He said he did not act on her request.[62]

The Centre's genuflections, nonetheless, fell short of Jayalalithaa's needs. On 30 December, Admiral Vishnu Bhagwat, the chief of the Indian Navy, was sacked on account of 'security considerations'.[63] A perceptive Jayalalithaa soon spotted the political potential for her from the clumsy affair. On 2 January 1999, she suggested that a commission of retired service chiefs probe the circumstances.[64] It was her way of bringing focus to her requests.[65]

However, on 9 January, after a call from Vajpayee on 7 January on cabinet expansion, she termed her demand for an inquiry as 'only a constructive criticism of an ally'.[66] On 10 January, she said for the first time that she has a 'very good working relationship' with the Centre but noted that in case of a mid-term poll, her 'AIADMK will not be a cause for it'.[67]

On 3 February, Jayalalithaa said she had difficulties with the joint statement from the 2 February coordination meeting. On her continued support, she indicated she would take 'an appropriate decision . . . at the appropriate time. Wait and see.'[68]

That day, Fernandes met Jayalalithaa and later claimed the meeting had no 'special significance'.[69] However, on 8 February, media reported that on 5 February, the Centre had issued a notification transferring forty-six corruption cases, including the eight against Jayalalithaa, to four regular courts.[70] However, on 14 May, the Supreme Court quashed the notification as 'bad'.[71]

On 12 February, following two massacres, the Rabri Devi government was dismissed. Karunanidhi termed the Dalit deaths 'reprehensible' but said it could not justify the dismissal. Jayalalithaa reiterated that 'Tamil Nadu is a better case for President's rule'.[72] Yet, on 19 February, Vajpayee said, 'Dismissing the DMK government is like dismissing my own government.'[73] On 20 February, Jayalalithaa reiterated her demand and made it clear that her support was only for Vajpayee and was not transferable.[74] On 9 March, the Vajpayee government restored the Rabri Devi government. What Chidambaram had foreseen for Tamil Nadu had played out in Bihar. But Jayalalithaa failed to take note.

Jayalalithaa's Delhi Visit

On 26 March, Jayalalithaa began her five-day Delhi visit. The 27 March coordination meeting decided against a Joint Parliamentary Committee inquiry. The prime minister hosted an exclusive lunch the next day, preceded by his son-in-law's visit to Jayalalithaa's suite. Despite her posturing, she did not raise the Bhagwat issue. Instead, she demanded nine AIADMK ministers, including Subramanian

Swamy, to replace Vazhapadi Ramamurthy with her nominee and to appoint twenty-five officials in specific posts.[75]

Fernandes met her on 29 March to explain his position.[76] However, that day's main event was the 'tea' hosted by Subramanian Swamy, where Jayalalithaa met Sonia Gandhi, claimed they were 'old friends' and described the meeting 'a political earthquake'.[77] Sonia Gandhi's aide R.D. Pradhan writes that she was 'wary' of Jayalalithaa.[78] However, she had her compulsions. Cho Ramaswamy writes that the BJP government was moving forward on Bofors and waiting for the President's sanction to prosecute Rajiv Gandhi's former External Affairs Minister Madhav Singh Solanki.

The next day, BJP's Rangarajan Kumaramangalam predicted Jayalalithaa would probably pull the plug on the government and asked her to 'conform or quit'.[79] On 31 March, Jayalalithaa said she did not see herself as prime minister 'but anything is possible in politics'.[80] According to Cho Ramaswamy, her astrologers had predicted that she would become prime minister in April while political pundits banked on MPs not wishing re-election, Mulayam Singh Yadav not countenancing a Congress (I) government, Jyoti Basu declining and, in the event, Jayalalithaa becoming a serious contender.[81]

On 1 April, Nedunchezhian and six others, in a joint statement, asked that the prime minister clarify if he agreed with Kumaramangalam and if so, he needed to only tell them and 'in one hour' they would inform the President that they were 'no longer supporting a Government that does not want us to stay in it'.[82] That day, Jayalalithaa ruled out the possibility of a Congress (I)-led government with AIADMK support for the moment.[83]

On 3 April, Vajpayee said it was Kumaramangalam's opinion.[84] That day, the AIADMK general council demanded Bhagwat's reinstatement or Fernandes be shifted and a JPC inquiry. 'If you try our patience for too long, we will throw out the driver [BJP] and run the train ourselves,' Jayalalithaa warned. 'This warning is different. The situation is entirely different,' she said, promising 'exciting developments'. Jayalalithaa had upped the ante. There was no turning back now.[85]

On 5 April, the cabinet met without the AIADMK ministers and rejected the demands.[86] Jayalalithaa asked her two ministers to quit and, in a lengthy statement, claimed that 'never has a cabinet met with the single-point agenda of slighting an ally that is responsible for the majority'. She blamed Fernandes and Advani as slipshod on national security, claimed that the LTTE had access to ministers and an LTTE representative met a senior minister in Delhi.[87]

On 9 April, AIADMK withdrew from the coordination committee. Advani and Vajpayee telephoned Karunanidhi on 9 and 10 April, respectively for support.[88]

Karunanidhi's About Turn

On 11 April, Karunanidhi said that the DMK could not be in the same front as Jayalalithaa. On 12 April, Maran met Moopanar to explain the DMK shift towards the BJP. That day, Jayalalithaa said the doors had been shut as the BJP had made calls to the DMK.[89] On 13 April, Moopanar met Karunanidhi and claimed they opposed both the BJP and the AIADMK.

But later that day, the DMK executive, in a resolution, described Jayalalithaa as the 'greatest enemy' and 'the biggest threat to the state and the nation'. Karunanidhi had stiffed his allies. And famously justified it: 'Jayalalithaa's corruption is more dangerous than communalism.'[90] But Karunanidhi was candid: 'We are running a political party. At this juncture, we need to save our party—as well as our government . . .'[91] Jayalalithaa had only herself to blame.

On 14 April, Jayalalithaa formally withdrew support to the BJP government. Before emplaning to Delhi, she said she would form a third front and indicated she could become prime minister.[92] That evening, she met Sonia Gandhi for seventy-five minutes. However, the next day, Sonia Gandhi pitched for a Congress (I) government supported by others.[93]

On 15 April, Karunanidhi said he felt 'insulted' that Surjeet and Bardhan had met Jayalalithaa the day before, claimed the Left's moves had 'certainly fragmented' the Third Front and that they would get to see Jayalalithaa's true colours.[94] CPM's Sitaram Yechury said if the DMK had chosen to change its stand, the Left should 'not be used as an excuse'.[95]

That day, moving the motion of confidence, Vajpayee foreseeing the mess to follow, wondered what would follow the BJP's aftermath. On 16 April, Maran speaking on the motion, said, 'We have no other choice . . . We support Atalji and never can we support the mother of corruption . . .'[96] Janata Dal president Sharad Yadav exclaimed: 'We sacrificed the United Front Government for the DMK, which has now ditched us.'[97]

On 17 April, Vajpayee lost by one vote and Sonia Gandhi telephoned Jayalalithaa for support.

No Coalition

On 19 April, Jayalalithaa and Mulayam Singh Yadav met Sonia Gandhi.[98] Their efforts however, had come to naught. On 21 April, Sonia Gandhi and Manmohan Singh met the President and proposed a Congress (I) minority government headed by Manmohan Singh.[99] But Mulayam Singh openly ruled out support. He had also scotched Jayalalithaa's ambition, telling her that even he had been told that he should become prime minister and that these things should not be taken seriously.[100] The following day, he floated Jyoti Basu's name. Jayalalithaa toed his line, and Surjeet supported Basu. Gujral writes that Surjeet was two-timing Sonia Gandhi while promoting Basu.[101] The Left and TMC met that day and asked Karunanidhi to reconsider his support for the BJP. Karunanidhi said they should have convened the meeting before the confidence vote.[102]

Later that night, Lalu Prasad Yadav and Jayalalithaa told Sonia Gandhi that her choices were limited to a Third Front-led coalition government led by Basu or a leader of the Congress (I)'s choice. As Sonia Gandhi baulked, Jayalalithaa lost her temper and Lalu Prasad Yadav had to calm both ladies.[103] Jayalalithaa later claimed she proposed Basu to stave off a Sonia Gandhi prime ministership, but 'Sonia scuttled the move as she did not want an Indian to be prime minister.' On 24 April, Jayalalithaa met the President even as the impasse continued. On 25 April, the CPM politburo agreed to Basu as prime minister, provided the Congress (I) extended outside support.[104] This, however, was a no-go for Congress (I). That day, Sonia Gandhi admitted to the President that she did not have the requisite numbers.[105] The Opposition had imploded. Vajpayee continued in a caretaker capacity and excelled. Jayalalithaa's action led to another general election, but she never regretted her action.[106]

Manjolai and Samathuvapurams

Back home, Moopanar moved closer to a third alternative. On 23 July, a brutal police attack on a rally led by Dr Krishnaswamy and the TMC in solidarity with workers at a tea estate in Manjolai in Tirunelveli district saw seventeen victims (eleven Dalits) drown in the Thamiraparani river.[107] Karunanidhi appealed to Moopanar not to make common cause with Krishnaswamy.[108] On 13 November, the Justice Mohan Commission controversially exonerated the police.[109]

Frequent caste clashes saw Karunanidhi launch, on 17 August, the first Samathuvapurams at Melakottai close to Madurai. The 103 townships accommodated 100 people of eighteen castes, with forty being Dalits.[110] Karunanidhi called it the 'acme of [his] achievements' although critics have dismissed them as tropes of 'spatial equality'.[111] Two decades later, the virility of caste has rendered the symbolism almost dead.[112]

Alliances

On the one hand, Karunanidhi embarked on creating Samathuvapurams. On the other hand, he was in a hurry to embrace the PMK. On 3 May, he met Ramadoss and, on 2 August, allotted nine seats for the PMK–TRC combine. Ramadoss's bazaar-style bargaining had again paid rich dividends.[113]

Similarly, political expediency helped paper over differences with 'betrayers'. As early as 19 May, Vaiko called on Karunanidhi and said it was like a 'son who had left to set up his family visiting his father'. A gracious Karunanidhi wondered, 'What is there to forgive?' in Vaiko. Whether Stalin approved the rapprochement, he characteristically responded: 'He is in the DMK!' Karunanidhi also refused to be drawn into Sonia Gandhi's foreign nationality controversy.[114]

In a lengthy resolution on 2 June, the general council opting for an alliance with the NDA avoided any mention of the BJP. On fielding candidates against the TMC, Karunanidhi asked the reporter to read the Gita, which said that even kin did not matter when it came to battle.[115]

Moopanar crossed the political Rubicon tying up with Krishnaswamy and Thol. Thirumavalavan's Dalit Panthers (later Viduthalai Chiruthaigal Katchi or VCK) and Janata Dal (S).[116]

Puthiya Thamizhagam's Dr S. Krishnaswamy, pioneer in founding a Dalit political outfit

Viduthalai Chiruthaigal Katchi's Thol. Thirumavalavan who has had more political success than his southern counterpart Dr S. Krishnaswamy

Karunanidhi indicated that his campaign would focus on India's need for a 'good, bold and efficient Prime Minister. Vajpayee fits the bill on all these counts.'[117] The DMK manifesto assured there would be no harm to minorities, and it would rise in their defence and sacrifice itself if any harm befell it.[118]

On 21 August, at the Marina, Vajpayee cited the proverb—a friend in need is a friend indeed—to describe the DMK's support at the vote of confidence and mentioned Jayalalithaa playing truant from the beginning. He said that on the eve of Independence Day in 1998, she threatened to withdraw support, demanding cases be withdrawn, probes halted and the DMK government dismissed. He said dealing with the AIADMK was 'one of the most painful periods' of his political career.[119]

Jayalalithaa termed the BJP 'a poisonous tree' and vowed to end the 'family politics' pursued by Karunanidhi, a 'dark force'.[120] She said she was not projecting Sonia Gandhi as prime minister because the Congress (I) was not doing so.[121] In Villupuram, the only place they were to appear together, Jayalalithaa, claiming she was caught up in a 'sea of humanity', stood up Sonia Gandhi.[122]

1999 Parliamentary Election

Parliamentary elections in Tamil Nadu were held on 4 and 11 September. The DMK–BJP alliance won twenty-six seats. Nationally, the BJP won a total of 182 seats. The AIADMK and allies won fourteen seats. Jayalalithaa said, 'It was neither a setback nor a defeat for us.'

Vazhapadi Ramamurthy lost in Salem, where Jayalalithaa had campaigned for three days. Ramamurthy later blamed Ramadoss for his defeat, and the two Vanniyar leaders drifted apart. Sasikala's nephew T.T.V. Dhinakaran won in Periyakulam. Karunanidhi claimed the results 'proved that the minorities remain with the DMK'. On the AIADMK's ten seats, Karunanidhi, in an allusion to Dhinakaran and T.M. Selvaganapathy, who faced corruption charges, said some voters preferred certain corrupt acts.[123]

1999 PARLIAMENTARY ELECTION

Party	Contested	Won	Votes	Percentage
DMK	19	12	62,98,832	23.13%
PMK	7	5	22,36,821	8.21%
BJP	6	4	19,45,286	7.14%
MDMK	5	4	16,20,527	5.95%
JP	1	1	2,66,202	1.04%
MGRADMK	1	1	3,96,216	1.46%
TRC	1	0	3,38,278	1.24%
AIADMK	24	10	69,92,003	25.68%
INC	11	2	30,22,107	11.10%
CPI	2	0	6,95,762	2.56%
CPM	2	1	6,39,516	2.35%
TMC + VCK	27	0	19,46,899	7.15%
PT	10	0	5,68,196	2.09%

Jayalalithaa admitted that with the TMC, more seats could have been won but mocked its claim that it would re-establish Kamaraj rule. 'Kamaraj himself could not bring that back,' she said.[124]

Tamil Nadu later got twelve members in the Council of Ministers, the highest for any state.[125]

On 14 November, Karunanidhi inaugurated the first 109 *Uzhavar Santhais* or farmers' shandies, where farmers sold their produce directly to the consumer.[126] On 1 January 2000, Karunanidhi unveiled the 133-ft Thiruvalluvar statue in Kanniyakumari and said he was in a 'trance' as he pressed the button.[127]

The DMK's alliance with the BJP would not be such a transfixing event. Karunanidhi frequently turned an apologist for the BJP government and soft-pedalled on controversial issues. He banked on Vajpayee as the moderate face of the BJP. But Vajpayee had his limitations. On 6 February, the prime minister termed the RSS a 'cultural and social organization' in response to the Gujarat government permitting government staff to participate in RSS activities. On 8 February, Karunanidhi compared the RSS to the Dravidar Kazhagam; although they were different, he said that he came from the Dravidar Kazhagam. Moopanar said the 'compulsions of power' had made Karunanidhi term the RSS a social organization and pointed out Karunanidhi's 7 March 1999 write-up, where he had said that the RSS 'does not respect humanitarianism . . . does not subscribe to communal harmony or the belief that all religions are one. Such persons are in power today. In support of such a regime, there are some *parivars* and retinue. Their atrocities and high-handed acts have made India bow its head in international forums.' Moopanar described Karunanidhi's change as a 'travesty of the times' and said Anna, if alive, 'would have shed tears of blood'.[128]

Jayalalithaa Convicted

But Moopanar was not in a better place himself. On 28 January 2000, in a desperate gamble to stay relevant, the TMC announced support for the AIADMK in the 17 February by-elections walking back on the raison d'être for its emergence.[129] DMK and its allies won two of the three seats. Jayalalithaa had taken the first step towards Moopanar's TMC on 24 October 1999 when she met a convalescing Moopanar with a bouquet.

On 2 February, Jayalalithaa was convicted and sentenced to one-year rigorous imprisonment in the Pleasant Stay Hotel case.[130] That day, AIADMK men burnt a college bus in Dharmapuri, burning three female students alive. On reviewing ties, Moopanar quoted a Kural couplet that said one should apply one's mind before a decision and then stick to it.[131]

But Karunanidhi read more into Moopanar's decision to stay the course with Jayalalithaa. On 6 April, he said in the assembly that the TMC believed that Jayalalithaa was 'finished' and would go 'to jail', the cadres would move to the TMC, and it could come to power. He added that AIADMK cadres were not so naïve and would not accept any other leadership. On this, the TMC staged a walkout.[132]

Cine Star Rajkumar's Release

On 30 July, forest brigand Veerappan abducted Kannada actor Rajkumar and three others. His demands included amnesty and the release of fifty-eight detainees. Jayalalithaa charged the Karunanidhi government with complacency, if not connivance, called for a CBI probe and asked that his demands be rejected. Karunanidhi and his Karnataka counterpart S.M. Krishna were understandably opaque about their dealings with Veerappan. Journalist Nakkheeran Gopal played emissary, but it was Tamil nationalist Pazha Nedumaran's sixth visit as emissary that would see Rajkumar freed after a 108-day ordeal.

Karunanidhi said that he and Krishna had pursued an 'extraordinarily cautious and careful approach' to ensure that there was 'not even a small strain' between the Tamils and Kannadigas.

Pazha Nedumaran who symbolized principled politics,
but had become a hardcore Tamil nationalist

Jayalalithaa, however, called for a white paper and said Rajkumar alone was in a position to 'reveal the whole truth behind the entire sordid drama'. On 2 September 2002, as chief minister, she alleged that a Rs 30-crore ransom was paid for the release. S.M. Krishna denied it.[133]

Alagiri's Rebellion

On 20 August, Alagiri, Karunanidhi's eldest son from Dayalu Ammal, worried that his safe outpost was being raided by his younger sibling's Trojans and termed the new entrants from the AIADMK as 'political businessmen'.[134] Sent away to Madurai in 1989 ostensibly to look after *Murasoli*, the enfant terrible had turned into a DMK puissant. On 19 September, Anbazhagan asked cadres to stay away from Alagiri.[135] On 22 September, Karunanidhi called it an intra-party affair.[136] On 25 September, Karunanidhi said Alagiri was not removed as he had not renewed his five-year membership.[137]

On 9 October, a special court sentenced Jayalalithaa and five others to three years and two years rigorous imprisonment in the

TANSI cases. On 31 October, the Madras High Court suspended prison terms but not the conviction.[138] The 28 August 1997 Election Commission order stipulated disqualification from the trial court's judgment except for legislators or parliamentarians who had appealed.[139] Jayalalithaa became ineligible to contest elections from the date of conviction and for a further period of six years from the date of release.

25

Jayalalithaa Back in Power

PMK Bolts DMK Alliance

On 17 January 2001, a confident Jayalalithaa said that independent agencies and police surveys had found that 60 per cent favoured her in the upcoming elections, and she would contest independently and form a government.[1] Jayalalithaa's confidence was somewhat understandable. The DMK's ties with the BJP had politically isolated it, and anti-incumbency was latent despite good governance. The PMK—the political weathercock—was the first to detect the changing winds. Such calculations would inform the PMK's decisions till 2009.

On 6 February, Ramadoss said: 'Big brother M. Karunanidhi tried to destroy us at every step. Sister (Jayalalithaa) extended a friendly hand of support. That is why we left the DMK and joined the AIADMK.' Karunanidhi later revealed that Ramadoss wanted Vazhapadi Ramamurthy out, and he first took it up with NDA convenor George Fernandes, indicating that Ramadoss would leave the NDA otherwise and then approached the prime minister, who asked him to 'wait at least one week,' by which time Ramadoss had exited. Vazhapadi Ramamurthy too left, 'angry' that Vajpayee had not taken him into his cabinet, explained Karunanidhi.[2]

On 7 February, Karunanidhi denied the allegations and said the doctor had already made up his mind.[3] In a new low, Karunanidhi now turned to caste parties. It was equally poor political judgement. Engaging in sophistry, he argued that the PMK (Vanniyar), the New Justice Party (Mudaliar) and Kannappan's Makkal Tamil Desam (Yadava) bore no caste names and there were 'no exclusive caste parties'. To a question why the PMK changed its stance every election, Karunanidhi light-heartedly quipped: 'Only because there are elections every time.'[4]

Courting Castes

But Karunanidhi was unnerved. He publicly called on Moopanar to return to the DMK alliance. On 16 February, Puthiya Thamizhagam became the first of the numerous caste parties to join the DMK front.[5]

Meanwhile, the DMK's southern flank saw revolt, with Alagiri declaring he would contest as an independent. On 6 March, Karunanidhi described himself as a scion of Manu Needhi Chola who, at the call of a cow whose calf was killed under his son's chariot, rode his chariot over his son.[6] Karunanidhi was no Manu Needhi Chola. He was just a preening blowhard. Alagiri was not Veedhividangan, the Chola's pliant son.

Additionally, the 18 March alliance with the MDMK came unstuck with Vaiko, particularly on three seats. On 9 April, Karunanidhi said he had offered alternate seats, yet Vaiko had left and Karunanidhi blamed it on his 'zodiac'.[7] The elephant in the room was Stalin, and both parties avoided admitting it. The MDMK feared it would aid Stalin's ascension. The DMK worried that Vaiko would stand in his way if the party failed to get a majority.[8]

The DMK contested 167 seats and the BJP twenty-one. Most caste outfits that mattered had been accommodated. But Karunanidhi was in for a rude surprise.[9]

Maran Retires

On the evening of 14 April, Karunanidhi was to announce the list of DMK candidates. Hours earlier, at Maran's behest, calls were made to news agencies to announce his retirement from active politics for health reasons. The truth was that the party list emphasized loyalty to the emerging leader, and the naked display of caste outfits parading as DMK's allies was not to Maran's liking. Maran had lost out to Stalin in guiding party affairs.[10] Karunanidhi never discussed the issue.

Between 25 November 2000 and 26 February 2001, Karunanidhi penned twenty-four letters on his government's achievements.[11] He touted the lifting of seven million out of poverty and a million women benefiting from women's self-help groups as the highest of his achievements, adding that per capita income rose from Rs 11,894 in 1995–96 to Rs 18,786 in 1999–2000.

Equally, he was no more apologetic about the DMK's support for economic reforms. He said newer economic reforms, globalization and liberalization had impacted all countries, and the differences between capitalist, socialist and communist states was blunted. China's astonishing growth and Russia's shocking changes would impact one's ideas. Information technology was changing the world into a global village, and change alone was permanent.[12]

Jayalalithaa's Papers Rejected

The AIADMK had its share of woes. The PMK's insistence on the Puducherry chief ministership led to a separate Congress (I)–TMC alliance after Jayalalithaa decoupled the states. On 5 March, she agreed to share the Puducherry chief ministership for the first half term with the PMK and allotted ten of the thirty elected seats. But there was more trouble ahead.

Jayalalithaa filed her nominations from Krishnagiri, Andipatti, Bhuvanagiri and Pudukkottai. Her papers were rejected on 24 April as the Representation of the People Act (RPA) allowed for a maximum of two nominations; additionally, her convictions disqualified her. But Jayalalithaa blamed Karunanidhi for the rejections and said, ultimately, 'Dharma will win.'[13] Karunanidhi said Jayalalithaa had 'willingly trapped' herself and that the law had merely caught up with her.[14]

On 30 April, an undaunted Jayalalithaa said she was her party's chief ministerial candidate because 'the people will not accept anyone else'. She said she was now contesting in all 234 seats. Yet, on 7 May, in an NDA election rally at the Marina, Prime Minister Vajpayee claimed no one knew who would be chief minister if the AIADMK front was returned to power.[15]

Comeback

The AIADMK alliance polled 49.89 per cent of the vote against the DMK-led alliance's 38.03 per cent. With over a 10 per cent lead, the AIADMK won 132 seats and allies sixty-five. The DMK won twenty-eight seats and its allies nine. Fifteen ministers lost. Jayalalithaa said her victory was 'expected' and claimed that the law and order, the inefficient public distribution system and the closure of a hundred factories led to the DMK's defeat.[16]

A sullen Karunanidhi said he considered the 'verdict a reward . . . for the successive achievements of our rule in the past five years'.[17] Karunanidhi blamed the sympathy stoked by the 'false propaganda' that he was responsible for rejecting nominations for the defeat. On 6 June, he pointed out that the AIADMK had stitched a strong alliance, and MDMK had dispersed votes.[18] Karunanidhi did not mention the damage caused by Alagiri, to whom at least ten DMK candidates owed their defeat by small margins. On 13 May, Karunanidhi said he would restructure the organization, rev up party work and ask Anbazhagan to lead the DMK legislature group.[19]

2001 ASSEMBLY ELECTION

Party	Contested	Won	Votes	Percentage
AIADMK	141	132	88,15,387	31.44%
TMC	32	23	18,85,726	6.73%
PMK	27	20	15,57,500	5.56%
INC	14	7	6,96,205	2.48%
CPM	8	6	4,70,736	1.68%
CPI	8	5	4,44,710	1.59%
AIFB	1	1	39,248	0.14%
IND + INL	2	2	1,03,971	0.40%
IUML	1	0	30,497	0.11%
TMMK	1	0		
DMK + IND 18	185	31	86,69,864	30.92%
BJP	21	4	8,95,352	3.19%
PT	10	0	3,55,171	1.27%
MAKKAL TAMIL DESAM KATCHI	6	0	2,57,126	0.92%
PUDHIYA NEEDHI KATCHI	5	0	1,96,740	0.70%
MGRADMK	3	2	1,29,474	0.46%
MGR KAZHAGAM	2	0	1,36,916	0.49%
KONGUNADU MAKKAL KATCHI	1	0	40,421	0.14%
THAMIZHAR BHOOMI	1	0	45,002	0.16%
MDMK	211	0	13,04,469	4.65%

In Puducherry, the Congress (I)–TMC alliance won.

Karunanidhi Arrest

On 14 May, Jayalalithaa and five ministers were sworn in. Karunanidhi said, 'If this is right, then Lalu Prasad Yadav should also be allowed to become chief minister.'[20] Chief Minister Jayalalithaa said she would not 'take revenge' or act 'in a vindictive manner'.[21] She did not mean it.

On 17 May, DMK MLA Parithi Ilamvazhuthi was arrested for attacking a polling agent. Karunanidhi prophesied such events as a 'continuum'. But no one, much less Karunanidhi, was prepared for what happened on 30 June.[22]

That day, Karunanidhi was arrested in a predawn swoop in a Rs 12-crore scam in constructing nine flyovers in Chennai.[23] Overnight, the women's ward was converted to a common ward, and Karunanidhi spent five nights in the same cell where he had once lodged Jayalalithaa. Stalin surrendered later that day.

Maran and T.R. Baalu were arrested for preventing police from performing their duty. A Sun TV crew promptly appeared at Karunanidhi's residence and recorded the happenings. Thanks to advocate K.S. Radhakrishnan, the video was smuggled out from under the police's nose and the edited clip where Karunanidhi screamed, 'They are killing me' even as police officers elbowed and bodily lifted him was played ad nauseam by Sun TV.[24] Jaya TV, on the other hand, showed footage where things were calm and took a turn for the worse after the arrival of Maran.

Karunanidhi was produced before a judge at 4.30 a.m. and broke down recounting his ordeal. On his way to the jail, he told the press: 'They dragged me. They tore my shirt. When we arrested her, we treated her with respect.' He wrote *Aram Vellum* (Truth will triumph), for a journalist as comment.[25] Karunanidhi was released on 4 July on 'humanitarian grounds' and in consideration of 'his old age'.[26] But Jayalalithaa had greatly diminished the man and herself.

The nature of the arrest raised revulsion and condemnation.[27] Karunanidhi later claimed that forty people had died, unable to bear the unjustness of it all.[28] Union Law Minister Arun Jaitley described the action as a 'personal agenda' overriding 'the rule of law'.[29] The prime minister condemned the arrest and spoke to the chief secretary about Karunanidhi's and Maran's well-being. That day, an alarmed Union cabinet called for the governor's report and dispatched a home ministry team. Earlier, the NDA coordination committee meeting sent a team led by George Fernandes to Chennai.[30]

Jayalalithaa defended the police action, saying that the Sun TV footage was a 'deliberate and stage-managed stunt' and the voice in the tape was not Karunanidhi's. 'His lips did not move,' she said. She claimed Maran had pushed Karunanidhi, and a policeman prevented him from falling. She said Maran and Baalu behaved 'like street rowdies and goondas', and wanted them dropped from the cabinet.[31]

On 1 July, after visiting Karunanidhi and Maran, Fernandes opined there was no other option but President's rule.[32] That day, an unfazed Jayalalithaa offered an elephant in Guruvayur to the temple's deity.[33]

On 3 July, Maran and Baalu were released.[34] Maran claimed that the police hit him in the chest, where he has a pacemaker and carried him out like a 'parcel'.[35] On 4 July, Karunanidhi was released, but the charges remained. Karunanidhi broke down twice that day while briefing the press on his release.[36] Maran suspected the operation was aimed to 'eliminate . . . Karunanidhi.' He asked for the 'extraordinary remedy' of President's rule.[37] But the NDA government did not have the political strength to impose Article 356. So despite all the hubbub, its hands were tied. No wonder later, on 5 November 2002, asked if he was satisfied, Karunanidhi said: 'What action have they taken that I should be satisfied?'[38]

On 7 July, Stalin was granted bail. Jayalalithaa set up an inquiry commission led by Justice A. Raman, a retired high court judge, which the DMK boycotted.[39] 'Do you need a mirror to look at the wound on your palm?' Karunanidhi asked. Jayalalithaa said that while Karunanidhi claimed he would face justice, 'he always ran away from it'.[40]

On 10 July, Jayalalithaa issued a ten-page statement in a question-and-answer format. She said the police manual rules were clear: a political leader with a mass following must be arrested only after midnight. Then, why was she arrested during the day? Because

Karunanidhi had no choice. Under the rules, no woman should be arrested and kept in police custody between 6 p.m. and 6 a.m.[41] In 2004, she denied it was vengeance and said she never regretted her action.[42]

On 21 September, a five-judge constitution bench struck down Jayalalithaa's appointment as illegal and unconstitutional. That day, a T.T.V. Dhinakaran protégé and a nominee of the Sasikala family, O. Panneerselvam was named chief minister. Hadn't Lalu Prasad Yadav set a precedent of rule by proxy? However, there was good news for Jayalalithaa. On 4 December, the Madras High Court acquitted her of the TANSI and the Pleasant Stay Hotel cases. Describing it as 'God's mercy', Jayalalithaa quoted Subramanya Bharati that 'conspiracy will encircle dharmic life, but dharma will triumph'.[43] On 26 December, she was acquitted in the coal import scam case.[44] When questioned if justice would be done on appeal to the Supreme Court, Karunanidhi commented: 'How can I say this beforehand? Only some can say which court would render justice. I cannot.'[45]

On 24 February 2002, Jayalalithaa sprinted to victory from Andipatti, defeating her DMK rival.[46] Alagiri and Stalin had closed ranks to campaign for the DMK candidate. On 2 March, Jayalalithaa and a twenty-six-member cabinet were sworn in.

On 24 November 2003, the Supreme Court upheld the Madras High Court verdict in the TANSI case but not before observing that Jayalalithaa 'must atone her conscience' and the properties must be returned. Subramanian Swamy, who had originally obtained sanction to prosecute Jayalalithaa, blamed the DMK for mishandling the case. Jayalalithaa said it was 'God's will'.[47]

In mid-December, the Kannagi statue at the Marina was removed as a lorry had damaged its pedestal on 6 December. Karunanidhi claimed Jayalalithaa's astrologers had advised her to remove it and termed the removal 'a challenge to Tamil pride'.[48] Political commentator Gnani Sankaran compared DMK's 'passion' for Kannagi to 'some children who never outgrow a teddy bear'.[49]

Godhra

But the strains in the DMK–BJP alliance following Karunanidhi's arrest were set to grow. On 27 February 2002, a Sabarmati Express coach was set on fire by a Muslim mob, killing sixty Hindus and sparking widespread sectarian violence in Gujarat that killed more than 1000 people, mostly Muslims. Chief Minister Narendra Modi was accused of complicity, although a Supreme Court-appointed Special Investigation Team cleared him. But his detractors continue to link him to the sordid incidents.[50]

On 28 February, Karunanidhi condemned the incident. Jayalalithaa's query that day, 'Why are those who vociferously deplore the attacks on minorities silent on the Godhra killings?' was enthusiastically welcomed by the state BJP, greatly annoying Karunanidhi.[51] On 3 March, Karunanidhi reiterated his trite observation that the majority should 'embrace' the minority while the latter should 'respect' the majority. He blamed the deaths on the insistence of some to build a temple at the disputed site in Ayodhya and added that the DMK would quit if the BJP showed 'religious affinity . . . and parochialism'.[52] Justifying the decision to stick with the BJP, Karunanidhi later said, 'One cannot leave an alliance on every issue that crops up.'[53]

On 23 March, Jayalalithaa, in the presence of BJP leaders, launched the free meal scheme at sixty-three shrines at the Kapaleeswarar temple.[54] On 24 March, the DMK general council asked the NDA not to 'deviate an inch' from the common agenda while claiming that Vajpayee had put a 'full stop' to the Godhra carnage. But Karunanidhi declared the DMK's ties to the state BJP dead.[55]

Vaiko, Nedumaran Arrests

In an unexpected overture to India, on 10 April, LTTE supremo Prabhakaran described Rajiv Gandhi's assassination as 'tragic' and called for lifting the ban on the LTTE in India.[56] The ban had deprived the LTTE of a rear base. Prabhakaran was naïve to believe that words of contrition or remorse would set the clock back to the pre-Rajiv assassination era for the LTTE. On 16 April, the Tamil Nadu assembly, in a resolution, said Tamils were 'shocked' at the statement and called for the Indian Army to go to Sri Lanka and capture Prabhakaran for him to face trial if the Sri Lankans could not apprehend him. While the PMK and communists walked out, the DMK stayed neutral, although its members shouted slogans like 'Do not victimize Tamils'. The PMK voted against the motion. The previous day, the Puducherry assembly had passed a similar resolution.[57]

On 11 July, Vaiko was arrested under POTA and the Unlawful Activities Prevention Act 1967 for his 29 June speech supporting the LTTE.[58] Karunanidhi condemned the arrest.[59] The BJP was, as in Karunanidhi's arrest, in a fix. On 19 July, George Fernandes called on Vaiko after declaring he should not be in prison. Fernandes, however, injected grandness into the Centre's inability to intervene when he supinely said that Vaiko did not 'need our support'.[60]

On 1 August, Pazha Nedumaran was arrested for a speech on 13 April for his LTTE affinity.[61] Slamming it as yet another misuse of POTA, this time it was Karunanidhi's turn to quote Subramanya Bharathi: 'Those who utter truth had to undergo imprisonment, and those who became the slaves of lies would prosper.'[62] On 5 November, Karunanidhi visited Vaiko in jail and said they had brotherly ties.[63]

Jayalalithaa Spews Bile

On 14 August, the TMC merged with Congress (I) in Madurai. Sonia Gandhi said the state was among the first three when Kamaraj ruled, but today 'people from every other walk of life are undergoing untold miseries in the state'.[64] On 28 August, Jayalalithaa said she opposed the idea of Sonia Gandhi, a 'foreigner' becoming prime minister and claimed she had not supported Sonia Gandhi's candidature in 1999.[65]

Congress (I) spokesperson S. Jaipal Reddy reminded Jayalalithaa of her support 'to a government to be formed by the Congress (I) led by Mrs Sonia Gandhi'. He attributed her criticism to the need to free herself from criminal cases.[66] On 31 August, Jayalalithaa claimed the reference to Sonia Gandhi was to identify the party and nothing more and termed it 'a crying shame' and the 'moral bankruptcy' of Congress (I) that it would project Sonia Gandhi as prime minister.[67] On 2 September, she referred to Sonia Gandhi as Antonia Maino Gandhi and a 'political businesswoman', adding that her only qualification for the prime ministership was a 'marriage certificate' to Rajiv Gandhi.[68] On 7 September, hedging his bets, Karunanidhi said, 'When Sonia Gandhi herself does not want to react, why should the DMK?'[69]

Cauvery—Emotions Overflow

With the monsoons delayed, Cauvery became a serious flashpoint. While Karnataka pleaded inability to abide by the distress-sharing formula, Tamil Nadu claimed that Karnataka had increased the storage capacity of its dams. In a strong gambit, Jayalalithaa chose to rely squarely on the Supreme Court and herself. On 2 April, posturing, she described the CRA as a 'toothless wonder' and said she would ignore it.[70] But Karunanidhi deemed it as 'arrogance' and destructive.[71] On 10 July, Tamil Nadu filed a comprehensive suit at the Supreme Court to ensure the interim award.[72]

Jayalalithaa did attend the 27 August CRA meeting chaired by the prime minister, only to walk out when her Karnataka counterpart S.M. Krishna expressed his inability to release water.[73]

On 3 September, the Supreme Court ordered Karnataka to release 1.25 tmc ft of water daily until the CRA's final decision.[74] On 8 September, the CRA asked Karnataka to release 0.8 tmc ft of water. Tamil Nadu approached the Supreme Court for a minimum of 1.25 tmc ft.[75] From this point, the issue turned hugely emotional. Karnataka held a closure on 12 September, protesting the CRA decision.[76] On 16 September, police opened fire on farmers attempting to lay siege to the Kabini dam, and two days later, after a farmer killed himself by jumping into the dam, Karnataka suspended the release of water. Jayalalithaa asked Krishna to quit if he could not control the law and order situation.[77]

On 20 September, she called for an all-party meeting finally. Karunanidhi, who had complained that she ignored the Opposition, now said they 'are not slaves to attend meetings at such short notice'.[78] After the all-party meeting, Jayalalithaa called for the Centre to take over dams and to dismiss the Karnataka government. Tamil Nadu filed a contempt petition.[79] On 22 September, Karunanidhi blamed the impasse on Jayalalithaa's 'twin-track approach', saying: 'On the one hand, the chief minister has approached the courts, and on the other, she wants talks with Karnataka'.[80] But this criticism was unfair and ignored the essential bottleneck: political will. Jayalalithaa was knocking on all doors.[81] On 24 September, Kannada film star Rajkumar led a protest march.[82] On 29 September, Karnataka farmers held a rail blockade.[83]

In Tamil Nadu, the Tamil film fraternity led by director Bharathiraja announced a protest at Neyveli Lignite Corporation on 12 October to press for the stoppage of electricity to Karnataka. On 5 October, farmers laid siege to Kabini and Krishnarajasagar (KRS) reservoirs, and Krishna announced an eight-day march in solidarity.[84] On 6 October, Jayalalithaa called to sack the Karnataka government.[85] That day, Karnataka banned Tamil TV channels and movies.[86] On 7 October, Krishna commenced his walk.[87]

Karunanidhi boycotted the all-party meeting that day but suggested a day's closure.[88] On 9 October, Tamil Nadu observed a closure. That day, Rajinikanth said he was not consulted on Neyveli.[89] Bharathiraja retorted, 'A guest cannot become head of the household.'[90] This was a reference to the fact that notwithstanding his success in the Tamil film industry and his huge fan following in Tamil Nadu, Rajinikanth was a Bengaluru native who had moved to Chennai for his film career. On 12 October, the film fraternity and Rajinikanth held separate fasts at Neyveli and Chennai.[91]

On 17 October, the Supreme Court asked Karnataka to release 'some water' immediately.[92] On 28 October, Karnataka began to release water.[93] The issue continued to be fraught for some time. On 7 November 2003, an irate Jayalalithaa said that she would openly blame the prime minister and the Centre and said if the BJP, Congress (I) and Janata Dal were to go to Thanjavur Delta for votes, voters would 'chase them away' for their betrayal.[94]

Animal Sacrifice, Conversions, Karunanidhi 'No Chanakya'

Meanwhile, on 28 August, Jayalalithaa wrote to district authorities to enforce the Tamil Nadu Animals and Birds Prevention of Sacrifice Act banning animal sacrifices in temples.[95] On 5 October, the Tamil Nadu Prohibition of Forcible Conversion of Religion Ordinance, 2002, banned religious conversions by 'force or fraud'.[96] On 24 October, referring to the 'twin tumbler' system where Dalits were served in a separate tumbler at tea stalls, Karunanidhi said that Hindus and the government should try and erase untouchability. Karunanidhi also claimed that the word 'Hindu' meant a 'thief' and cited a 1970 Hindi publication which said that Islamized Persians considered the word Hindu 'kafir', 'black', 'looter' and 'slave'.[97] As the Kanchi Shankaracharya, among others, criticized him, Karunanidhi dithered: 'Maybe it means someone who steals the heart.'[98]

On 18 December, in an in-camera two-day AIADMK general council meeting, Jayalalithaa admitted that Karunanidhi was a literary figure but said he was no 'Chanakya'. She thought of calling it quits, but Karunanidhi, filing case after case against her, made her reconsider her decision.[99]

Savarkar Portrait

On 26 February 2003, President Abdul Kalam unveiled a portrait of Hindu Mahasabha leader Vinayak Damodar Savarkar, popularly Veer Savarkar, in Parliament. The entire Opposition barring former prime minister Chandra Shekhar boycotted the event.[100] Karunanidhi sidestepped the issue. Instead, on 27 February, he waxed eloquent on the sales of his *Tholkaapiya Poonga* book in an event organized by Alagiri in Madurai.[101]

'Krishnas Sacrificed in the New Mahabharata'

However, the pleasure from Madurai did not last long. Party elections were announced for 19 May. On 20 May, former minister Tha. Kiruttinan was murdered in Madurai, and two days later, Alagiri was arrested. Kiruttinan's widow said her husband had stood against Alagiri's wish to stack the posts in the south with his men. She wailed to Stalin who came to pay respects to the deceased: 'Look at the fate of my husband, who was loyal to the party and you.'

Karunanidhi said Alagiri's arrest aimed to smear the DMK. On 24 May, he wrote to the prime minister and home minister alleging that the state government was trying to implicate a senior party functionary for the murder falsely.[102] Anbazhagan described the siblings as 'trees that have naturally grown in the garden of the DMK' adding that Karunanidhi's four children had served the party and that Stalin was in prison and concluded: 'If Stalin cannot be in politics, nobody else deserves to be in politics.'[103] On 2 June, Stalin was named one of the three deputy general secretaries and S. Duraimurugan the principal secretary, a newly-created post signifying his upward mobility.[104]

But the murder had become political fodder for Jayalalithaa. 'There is a Dhritarashtra even today. In his palace, there is more than one Duryodhana. Even Krishnas (Kiruttinan is Krishna's Tamilized version) are sacrificed in their battle for power. This is a new kind of Mahabharatha,' she said of the sibling rivalry. An incensed Karunanidhi suggested that Jayalalithaa was Putana, the demoness who tried to suckle infant Krishna to death.[105]

1.76 Lakh Government Staff Dismissed

On 1 July, 13 lakh government employees struck work, protesting the rollback of dearness allowance and certain pension benefits. But Jayalalithaa was not any other chief minister. Invoking the Essential Services Maintenance Act (ESMA), she dismissed 1.76 lakh staff, bringing the strikers to their knees and winning praise from a public sick and tired of the babus.[106] But not Karunanidhi and the Left. Government staff formed a solid vote bank and also served as election officials. Karunanidhi flayed Jayalalithaa's approach as 'destructive' and claimed 'womenfolk [of the staff's family] were cursing her'.[107]

Ending BJP Ties

But Jayalalithaa was a headstrong leader. She had gotten away with jailing Karunanidhi, Maran and Baalu. What was the use of being a coalition partner if the DMK could not count on the BJP for help? In a calibrated move, Karunanidhi began the withdrawal from the alliance. Thus, on 21 September, at the Villupuram district conference, former Law Minister Aladi Aruna, in a choreographed speech, wondered whether 'an alliance, friendship or relationship' existed between the DMK and the BJP, adding that whenever the DMK's 'self-respect was at stake', the Centre had abandoned them.[108]

On 15 October, Sonia Gandhi phoned Karunanidhi to thank him for condemning the previous day's attack on its Thanjavur MP

Mani Shankar Aiyar, following a spat between him and Jayalalithaa at a meeting in Nagapattinam.[109]

On 15 December, 1.5 lakh DMK workers courted arrest, demanding repeal of POTA and protesting the Centre's and the state's 'anti-people policies' and on 20 December, the DMK quit the NDA. Karunanidhi listed the Vajpayee government's 'fluctuating' stand on Ayodhya and the state BJP 'ridiculing and deriding the DMK' among the reasons for the exit.[110] The alliance's shelf life had expired, minorities had to be wooed and Karunanidhi had already identified new pastures. MDMK quit on 30 December and the PMK on 12 January 2004.

Karunanidhi, who had hedged on Sonia's foreign origins, now said it would be 'uncivilized to call her a foreigner when she has become a daughter-in-law of India'. He would later coin the phrase 'Indira's daughter-in-law welcome! India's Lakshmi, victory to you!!'[111] Karunanidhi stitched a formidable seven-party alliance called the Democratic Progressive Alliance (DPA). The AIADMK had only the BJP as an ally. The results were easy to discern.

Rajinikanth Takes on Ramadoss

On 11 April 2004, in an eight-page statement, Rajinikanth, with an elephantine memory, described PMK founder Ramadoss as the 'king of violence' who had called him a 'dirty swine wallowing in mud' and asked his fans to oppose the PMK.[112] Twenty months earlier, on 16 August 2002, PMK cadres had vandalized cinemas where *Baba*, a flop, was released. Ramadoss took exception to the actor glamorizing smoking in *Baba*. Rajinikanth vowed to teach Ramadoss a lesson. But the feud had begun after Ramadoss wondered at Poompuhar what Rajinikanth, who 'made crores and crores in Tamil cinema', had given in return. Earlier, Rajinikanth had called for forest brigand Veerappan's death at a 100th-day celebration of a Puneeth Rajkumar (son of actor Rajkumar) film. Veerappan was a Vanniyar.[113]

Karunanidhi carefully avoided any comment. However, on 14 April, a reporter pushed the envelope, wondering if Karunanidhi's silence on Rajinikanth was because of the 'political blow from MGR'. Incensed, Karunanidhi said: 'No one can beat me. If I beat, no one can bear it.' Karunanidhi ended the meeting abruptly when another reporter wondered if he was referring to Rajinikanth.[114]

'Sun—Son—Grandson'

On 23 November 2003, Maran passed away. Karunanidhi was greatly distressed. Only ten years younger to his maternal uncle Karunanidhi, Maran was his conscience. Shy and reserved Maran spoke his mind fearlessly to the DMK functionaries, often playing the bad cop. A screenwriter like his uncle, Maran soon became the DMK's face in Delhi. Fluent in English, he articulated the DMK's ideals with passion. Maran helped Karunanidhi navigate the maze of Delhi's politics and was credited for Karunanidhi's decision to ally with Indira Gandhi in 1980 and the BJP in 1999. As commerce minister, Maran was credited for passionately protecting India's interests in the Doha round of talks on the WTO. As industries minister, he was instrumental in bringing investments to the state. From 2001, Maran's stars were on the decline. A younger Stalin, eager to fill his father's boots, had begun to assert himself. Yet, till he lived, Maran stood by his uncle.

As Karunanidhi fielded the thirty-eight-year-old Dayanidhi Maran in place of his late father, on 4 March, a *Dinamani* cartoon showed Karunanidhi, Stalin and Dayanidhi as 'Sun—Son—Grandson'.[115] Jayalalithaa brought in as many as twenty-nine new faces, mostly district secretaries. One of them was 'Edappadi' Palaniswami, a former MP.[116]

On 6 May, at an NDA rally in Chennai, Vajpayee addressed Jayalalithaa as '*Anbu sagodhari*' (beloved sister) and said: '*Naam inaivom, nathigalai inaippom,*' (we will unite, and join the rivers as well). Jayalalithaa called Karunanidhi a 'betrayer' of Tamil Nadu's interests, Ramadoss a 'caste fanatic', Vaiko a 'braggart' and the communists 'philosophical chameleons'.[117]

Karunanidhi highlighted the past unease between Vajpayee and Jayalalithaa, while Jayalalithaa asked the electorate to choose Vajpayee instead of a 'half-baked novice', Sonia Gandhi.[118]

Vaiko was released on bail on 7 February 2004 after 577 days. His fifty-five-day campaign drew large crowds; many thought he was chief minister material. However, Sun TV ignored Vaiko.[119]

In the 2004 parliamentary elections, the DPA won all forty seats, including Puducherry. Karunanidhi conceded that it was 'the alliance's strength'.[120] Advani diplomatically alluded that the AIADMK had taken the BJP down.[121]

2004 PARLIAMENTARY ELECTION

Party	Contested	Won	Votes	Percentage
AIADMK	33	0	85,47,014	29.80%
BJP	6	0	14,55,899	5.10%
DMK + IUML 1	16	16	70,64,393	24.60%
INC	9	9	41,34,255	14.40%
PMK	5	5	19,27,367	6.70%
MDMK	4	4	16,79,870	5.90%
CPI	2	2	8,52,981	3.00%
CPM	2	2	8,24,524	2.90%

Jayalalithaa had stopped free power to farmers and hut dwellers, introduced Honour ration cards for those earning Rs 5000 per month who were then delisted, hiked rice prices, power and bus charges, regulated conversions, enforced a ban on animal sacrifices in temples and in September 2002, fired 10,000 road workers.[122] Jayalalithaa said the polls were meant to decide who would rule at the Centre.[123] But she soon reversed her decisions.

'ATM Ministries'

The Congress (I) had won 145 seats. The BJP came a close second with 138 seats. The centre-left United Progressive Alliance (UPA) was formed post elections. The UPA did not command a majority but received support from other left-leaning parties united in wanting to prevent the incumbent NDA a second term. On 22 May 2004, Manmohan Singh was sworn in as prime minister.

Karunanidhi camped for eight days in Delhi. On 23 May, Karunanidhi said the promised portfolios were not allotted, and his ministers would not assume office until 'the mistakes are rectified'.[124] Karunanidhi blamed the coterie around Sonia Gandhi and Prime Minister Manmohan Singh but said he did not know who meddled with the promise. 'That seems to be the secret,' he said. When asked if it was a 'P. Chidambaram secret', Karunanidhi retorted: 'I don't know. It could be Chidambaram (finance minister) secret or Mayavaram (Mayiladuthurai) secret.' (Petroleum Minister Mani Shankar Aiyar had been elected from Mayiladuthurai.)[125]

Although Manmohan Singh sought ten days, all of the DMK's demands were met the next day following Sonia Gandhi's intervention.[126] The *Indian Express* commented, 'Without giving an inch, [the DMK] got more than a mile'.[127] When questioned why the DMK did not seek the irrigation portfolio, Karunanidhi said that with the Cauvery dispute, it would not be appropriate for Karnataka or Tamil Nadu to hold it.[128] On 31 May, Karunanidhi said they demanded shipping for implementing Sethusamudram and Colachel harbour projects.[129] However, the impression was that the DMK was after the cash cow portfolios—described as 'ATM ministries'. Dayanidhi Maran was made the minister of information technology. Over the moon on Dayanidhi Maran's performance, Karunanidhi said in December, 'If he were a Brahmin, he would be praised as Thirugnana Sambandan, but he is only the grandson of a Shudra.'[130]

Tamil Nadu had twelve ministers, of which seven were of cabinet rank, the highest ever.[131] PMK's Anbumani Ramadoss, at thirty-five, was health minister. He was not a member of Parliament. But he had a higher qualification. He was Ramadoss's son. In the initial years, Ramadoss would declare that people should whip him if anyone from his family ever took to politics. A horsewhip sat on a chair next to him. The theatrics left a deep impression on the Vanniyars, who saw the physician as the cure for their social ills.

It took only a decade before Ramadoss's son, Anbumani replaced the whip. The Vanniyars did not mind. After all, they were used to politicians making grand promises and not keeping them. They acknowledged him as *Chinna Ayya* (junior *ayya*).[132]

On 13 June, actor Vijayakanth, speaking at Kallakurichi, commented on politicians becoming ministers without being elected. Claiming that farmers were reduced to eating rats in Thanjavur, Vijayakanth wondered if anyone asked for the agriculture or water resources portfolios. 'They were after portfolios that would fetch income,' he concluded. PMK cadres burnt Vijayakanth's effigy and the fans' association offices and threatened to stop screening his films, but on 22 June, the PMK called for a unilateral ceasefire.[133] Vijayakanth considered himself a modern-day MGR and entertained notions of greatness. But little would he or the PMK know that his political entry would come about this way.

On 12 October, Tamil was declared a classical language. Karunanidhi considered it a great achievement and expected this to encourage the study of Tamil in universities worldwide. This has yet to happen, and some other languages have been declared classical, watering down the privilege. Ironically, as early as 5 May 1984, Jayalalithaa had advocated classical language status for Tamil along the lines of Sanskrit.[134] On 2 July 2005, the Sethusamudram project was inaugurated. Jayalalithaa now opposed the scheme on environmental concerns.[135]

Veerappan and Jayendra Saraswathi

On 18 October, the Special Task Force (STF) ended a twenty-year hunt in twenty minutes, killing Veerappan and three of his associates. Jayalalithaa said that the STF's activities 'bottled up' during Karunanidhi's tenure, and she had motivated the STF after she returned to power in 2001.[136]

On 11 November, Deepavali day, Jayendra Saraswathi was arrested for the 3 September murder of A. Sankararaman, the manager of the Varadharajaswamy Temple at Kanchipuram. Karunanidhi initially called it 'an honest action' and 'commendable'. Karunanidhi had wondered how long the police would let the culprits off the hook and on 13 November, Stalin was to lead a fast in Kanchipuram. Months earlier, on 6 June, Jayendra Saraswathi had told the *Times News Network* that Jayalalithaa's *ahankara* (arrogance) did her party in'. On 14 November, Karunanidhi advised that 'a new captain' be found and added that the 'institution should not be allowed to die'.[137] On 22 November, Karunanidhi said, 'There is a streak of political background and vengeance in Jayalalithaa's action. Answers to a number of doubts in both the cases (Veerappan and the Shankaracharya) have not come.'[138] Jayalalithaa dismissed political or personal motives and said the arrest was one of the 'most painful decisions' of her political career.[139]

2006 Assembly Election

On 14 September 2005, *Puratchi Kalaignar* or revolutionary artist Vijayakanth (44) founded his Desiya Murpokku Dravida Kazhagam (National Progressive Dravidian Party or DMDK) at Thoppur near his home town Madurai. Symbolizing a blend of nationalism and Dravidian ethos, the actor would enjoy a respectable welcome until his style of politics and health subdued him. Vijayakanth said his family would not hold any position.

On 26 January 2006, Vaiko met Karunanidhi for an electoral tie-up. But the camaraderie between the two leaders while Vaiko was interned had long ceased.[140] In mid-February, fishing in troubled waters AIADMK presidium chair K. Kalimuthu wondered, 'Is Karunanidhi willing to announce Vaiko will be made deputy chief minister?'[141] On 19 February, Vaiko said he 'will not kneel before anybody'.[142] On 27 February, the VCK signed up for an alliance with the AIADMK. DMK had refused it seats.[143]

On 4 March, unhappy with the DMK's offer of twenty-three seats, Vaiko met Jayalalithaa and was given thirty-five seats. Both leaders said they put the past behind them, and Vaiko said: 'The DMK tried to ditch me, crush me and destroy my party.'[144]

On 28 March, the AIADMK manifesto promised 'an able administration'.[145] On 29 March, the DMK manifesto promised quality rice at Rs 2 per kg, free gas stoves to poor households, waiver of property loans of farmers, free power for weavers and revival of the marriage assistance scheme.[146] Importantly, the manifesto promised the landless two acres of land and free colour television sets for households without TVs. [147] P. Chidambaram called the manifesto the 'hero of 2006'.[148] On 4 April, Jayalalithaa challenged the feasibility of the TVs, saying it would cost Rs 15,000 crore and wondered about the money for it.[149] On 5 April, Karunanidhi said only Rs 540 crore were required a year, and if the 'loot [of the distilleries] is stopped', TVs can be distributed. Jayalalithaa capitulated and tried to outdo the DMK when on 17 April, she promised 10 kg of free rice and 4 gm of gold free later for thalis for poor girls and waiver of farmers' cooperative loans.[150] But it was too late. Vijayakanth pointed out that he had offered freebies such as Rs 10,000 per girl child in the bank for her wedding and free cows. [151]

Jayalalithaa described the polls as 'probably, the last battle with our traditional rivals'. Karunanidhi said that it showed 'her culture', adding, 'Yes, it is the final war between two schools of thought, dictatorship and democracy.' On Jayalalithaa's declaration that there was no scope for a coalition government, Karunanidhi said, 'That is her view.'[152]

Karunanidhi said that freebies, minorities and alliance strength would favour the DMK alliance. Karunanidhi predicted 118 seats for the DMK, but the party fell twenty-two seats short of a simple majority.

2006 ASSEMBLY ELECTION

Party	Contested	Won	Votes	Percentage
DMK + IND 4	132	96	87,28,716	26.50%
INC	48	34	27,65,768	8.40%
PMK	31	18	18,63,749	5.70%
CPM	13	9	8,72,674	2.70%
CPI	10	6	5,31,740	1.60%
AIADMK + IND 5	189	61	1,07,68,559	32.60%
MDMK	35	6	19,71,565	6%
VCK	9	2	4,26,321	1.30%
JD(S)	1	0	23,628	0.07%
DMDK	232	1	27,64,223	8.40%

DMDK polled 8.40 per cent and Vijayakanth was elected from Vriddachalam, a Vanniyar stronghold. DMDK candidates polled more votes than the losing margins of the AIADMK candidates in eighty seats and DMK candidates in forty-eight seats. Vijayakanth said, 'People were ready to welcome a big change.' Were they?

26

'Thamizhinath Thalaivar'?

Karunanidhi's last term as chief minister between 2006 and 2011 signified the apogee of his influence in Delhi till 2009, though he stayed as part of the UPA-II government till 2013. DMK ministers made both national policy and headlines with the 2G scandal. Karunanidhi soon got bogged down in family disputes, having created many centres of power within. Worse still, the fierce champion of the Sri Lankan Tamil cause watched the misery of the loss of the lives of tens of thousands of innocent civilians there as the civil war came to a bloody end in 2009. We will never know if his resignation as chief minister over the issue would have brought a ceasefire and saved the deaths of thousands. But Karunanidhi would have lived up to his self-declared title as *Thamizhinath Thalaivar*. He threw away a historic opportunity.

Karunanidhi was reluctant to use his power for positive gain on his avowed goals of regional autonomy or official status to all languages, and except for the questionable usefulness of designating Tamil as a classical language, nothing much was achieved during these years. In the end, this was an opportunity that the octogenarian squandered away.

On 13 May 2006, Karunanidhi and his thirty-one-member cabinet were sworn in. Karunanidhi, a man of many firsts, now had the dubious honour of heading the first-ever DMK government without a majority. Jayalalithaa harassed Karunanidhi, terming his government a 'minority government'.[1]

Every time Jayalalithaa dubbed it a 'minority government', extra cash flowed to the Congress (I) legislators' kitty from the DMK administration. Three years later, in August 2009, an exasperated Karunanidhi chose to hit below the belt when he crassly retorted, 'I would henceforth address her only as Mrs Jayalalithaa,' as opposed to Ms.[2]

On 3 June 2006, Karunanidhi launched the Rs 2 per kg rice scheme.[3] The DMK won five of the six corporation councils in the 13 and 15 October elections to local bodies. In Chennai, the DMK 'outdid' the AIADMK's record of 2001 in violence, booth capturing and rigging. *Frontline* described it as 'Farce in Chennai'.[4]

Cauvery Final Award

On 5 February 2007, the Cauvery Water Disputes Tribunal awarded Tamil Nadu 192 tmc ft of water annually and the states to 'proportionately reduce' their shares at times of distress. Karunanidhi said the award gave 'consolation', but the AIADMK, MDMK, DMDK and PMK opposed it. Jayalalithaa wanted the Karunanidhi government to resign even as she pitched for the Centre to notify the award.[5]

Family Matters

On 7 May, the Kalanidhi Maran-owned *Dinakaran* published the results of a poll on the most efficient central minister from Tamil Nadu. Predictably, Dayanidhi, with 64 per cent, topped the list, followed by Chidambaram with 27 per cent and T.R. Baalu with 7 per cent. Anbumani Ramadoss polled 1 per cent, prompting PMK cadres to burn copies of the daily. On 8 May, Karunanidhi said he did not trust such polls, that *Dinakaran*'s poll had become 'an instrument to create bitterness between allies', and that the ranking was not in the right order.[6]

On 9 May, *Dinakaran* published the results of a second poll to the question: 'Who should be Kalaignar's political heir?' Seventy per cent had plumped for Stalin. Two per cent each favoured Alagiri and Kanimozhi. Others received 20 per cent. Even in Madurai, Alagiri was less preferred to Stalin. Alagiri said that the Maran brothers were up to mischief.[7] The poll also ranked the police as the most corrupt of the departments.

Within hours, arsonists owing allegiance to Alagiri threw petrol bombs into the *Dinakaran* office in Madurai. Two young engineers and a security guard were burnt to death in the resultant fire. *Dinakaran* staff blamed Alagiri supporters, and Kalanidhi Maran said he stood by the claim that Alagiri was behind the dastardly incidents.[8] That day, Karunanidhi condemned the act, promised action and termed the poll 'an undesirable act'. He also reminded that he had often repeated that the DMK was a democratic organization where the successor would not be chosen in a hereditary manner.

On 10 May, *Dinakaran* carried pictures of the police standing by while the arson and violence occurred. Its headlines said: 'Unable to digest the opinion polls, M.K. Alagiri runs amok—attacks through rowdies'. That day, Karunanidhi told the assembly that *Dinakaran* had published the 7 May poll against his wishes, and he was 'puzzled' by its timing and was shocked by the poll's publication and the ministers' ranking. He said Chidambaram was 'an economist', Anbumani Ramadoss was a 'dynamic' minister, and they 'shone', and the poll was 'hurtful' to them and their parties. He pointed out that Dayanidhi Maran had excluded himself from the poll. He said Kanimozhi was a poet and had expressly said she had no interest in a political career, and Alagiri had no interest in party posts. Karunanidhi announced a CBI investigation since his family was involved.[9]

The following day *Dinakaran*'s headlines read: 'Put an end to Alagiri's atrocities' and quoted Kalanidhi Maran as saying that he would not quit until the authorities took action. On 11 May evening, Karunanidhi celebrated fifty years of his legislative career. Sonia Gandhi and the prime minister took part. Dayanidhi Maran was absent but Alagiri was present.

Jayalalithaa and Vaiko demanded the government's dismissal and Vijayakanth, Karunanidhi's resignation.

The brothers, it appeared, had staged a quiet coup. On 13 May, the DMK's administrative committee empowered Karunanidhi and Anbazhagan to 'remove' Dayanidhi Maran from the cabinet and to seek his explanation.[10] Electricity Minister Arcot N. Veerasamy revealed that Dayanidhi Maran had threatened the home secretary in the aftermath of the violence, warning that if she did not maintain law and order, he would meet the President and take it up with him.

Dayanidhi Maran resigned the following day. On 15 May, Dayanidhi Maran said Karunanidhi had been 'misled' by someone who 'tried to capitalize on the opportunity'. On the issue of destabilizing Stalin, he said, 'Such a situation never occurred nor will occur.' Maran added that he had planned to abolish mobile roaming charges from 3 June—the birthday of Karunanidhi.[11]

Karunanidhi moved quickly. He chose to send Kanimozhi to Delhi, and on 6 June, she was elected to the Rajya Sabha. Kalaignar TV took shape in September, and Dayalu Ammal and Kanimozhi acquired shares. Kanimozhi's stakes in Kalaignar TV would later land her in trouble. But for now, things were bright.

Tata's Letter

Environment Minister A. Raja was named in Dayanidhi Maran's place. The prime minister took over Raja's environment portfolio.[12] But Karunanidhi had expelled the ghost to embrace the vampire. Raja's term would prove controversial and hugely damaging to the

DMK, although a CBI court cleared him of any wrongdoing in 2017.

On 13 November, Ratan Tata handwrote, as Vinod Mehta put it, a 'cringing, absurd and potentially explosive note' to Karunanidhi. On the issue of spectrum, 'his [Raja's] stated policies for most part have been legally sound, rational and well-reasoned', Tata said in his letter. Tata Teleservices had jumped the queue, and Raja had granted it a licence. Tata continued: 'It is essential that history praises the vision, creativity and high growth achieved by you and your minister.' . . . 'DMK can possibly claim telecom to be its greatest achievement and most significant contribution to the nation's growth,' said Tata. The Niira Radia tapes would later put the letter into context, suggesting Tata lobbied to get Raja into the IT ministry again in 2009 and keep Dayanidhi Maran, who had asked him for a 'hefty bribe', out of IT.[13]

Ironically, Dayanidhi Maran had, in February 2008, told the US consul general that 'When people get into power, they lose concentration and start focusing on making money' and that the DMK would lose half the seats if they continued 'as they are'.[14]

On 21 November 2008, Karunanidhi again charged the brothers with attempts to 'create a feeling of intense dislike' among his children. Karunanidhi said that after the senior Maran's death, shares held by his family in the Sun TV group were 'taken in a hurry' by the brothers for Rs 100 crore. 'Where was the need for such a hurried partition? What was the profit of Sun TV then?' he asked, implying that they had been short-changed.[15]

Dayanidhi Maran hurriedly convened a press conference to deny the charges. He released Kalanidhi's point-by-point reply in a detailed twelve-page letter to Karunanidhi. Kalanidhi claimed that Karunanidhi had congratulated him after the Nielsen poll was published by the English press and said the Tamil translation be published in *Murasoli*. He said that 'someone called from Chennai and suggested that instead of attacking the buses, they could target the *Dinakaran* office'. Kalanidhi claimed attempts were made to crush the Sun TV network when Kalaignar TV took about 250 employees of Sun TV. 'Even if they had come on their own as claimed by Kalaignar TV, how could it be justifiable?' he asked.[16]

But blood proved thicker. On 1 December, the family reconciled. 'Eyes grew moist, and heart sensed sweetness,' said Karunanidhi. Although his eldest daughter Selvi and Stalin were believed to have helped the patch-up, Karunanidhi credited Alagiri for the reconciliation and Stalin, who had joined him in his efforts.[17] Sun TV's stock gained 12.25 per cent the next day.[18] *Caravan* said no one knew what brought the change of heart but pointed to lobbyist Niira Radia's conversation with journalist Vir Sanghvi, where she said that Dayanidhi Maran gave Dayalu Ammal Rs 600 crore.[19]

Eelam IV War

The family war had ended well. The Eelam IV war proved more dangerous to Karunanidhi's self-declared moniker *Thamizhinath Thalaivar*. On 2 January 2008, the Sri Lankan Army captured Kilinochchi. The Tigers were in retreat. As the civilian population suffered, on 23 April, Karunanidhi moved the first of the four assembly resolutions in 2008–09, urging India to bring the two warring parties to the negotiating table.[20] But these resolutions failed to get traction in Delhi.

Worse still, the Indians were actively abetting the war effort against the LTTE.

Karunanidhi Blinks First

On 14 October, an all-party resolution boycotted by the AIADMK asked the Centre to stop the civil war 'in Eelam' within two weeks. Acknowledging 'Indian military aid is resulting in the genocide of Tamils', it called for India to immediately end such assistance, failing which all MPs from Tamil Nadu may resign by 29 October.[21] The term 'Eelam' had been used for the first time in an official statement. Jayalalithaa, however, wondered if Karunanidhi '[has] the guts to dissolve the state government' instead.[22] Even Dayanidhi Maran dubbed the resignation of the DMK MPs a 'drama' to the US consul general and said that Karunanidhi's 'blackmail' had alienated Sonia Gandhi.[23]

On 15 October, Jayalalithaa said the calls for a ceasefire were 'a farce . . . as India cannot stop a civil war in another country'.[24] However, on 18 October, the prime minister spoke to Sri Lankan President Rajapaksa to ensure the safety of Tamil civilians. On 22 October, External Affairs Minister Pranab Mukherjee told both Houses of Parliament that India had reiterated its 'conviction that there is no military solution to the ethnic conflict'.[25] On 19 October, the film fraternity held a rally at Rameswaram. Film director Senthamizhan Seeman said that Delhi feared an independent Sri Lankan Tamil state would lead to repercussions in India. He wondered how Gandhian India could aid the Sri Lankan government in finishing off the Tamils.[26]

On 26 October, Basil Rajapaksa, brother and senior adviser to President Rajapaksa, visited India to assure that the 'safety and well-being of the Tamil community in Sri Lanka is being taken care of'. Significantly, 'both sides agreed that terrorism should be countered with resolve', meaning the campaign against the LTTE and India's military would continue unimpeded.[27]

That day, Sonia Gandhi telephoned Karunanidhi, and Pranab Mukherjee flew down to request that Karunanidhi not precipitate matters. Karunanidhi readily pirouetted for Mukherjee, who made it clear that if Karunanidhi carried out his threat, Congress (I) would withdraw support to the DMK ministry. Standing outside Karunanidhi's Gopalapuram residence, Mukherjee said, 'We were never part of the ceasefire (initiated by Norway) nor did we break it. So we cannot restore it.' Karunanidhi stomached the slap. Turning into an apologist for the Centre and even the Sri Lankan government, he claimed that the Sri Lankan government had promised not to attack civilians. The next day, he floated a relief fund.[28]

On 2 November, Karunanidhi pontificated: 'Should we not be conscious of India's limitations?' and added that the purpose of the resolution would have been defeated if only the DMK MPs had resigned, and that there would be no one to exert pressure on the Sri Lankan government if the government at the Centre had fallen.[29]

On 4 November, Jayalalithaa claimed that Karunanidhi 'performed an inexplicable somersault', suddenly woke up to the issue and said his resolutions were 'totally overlooked'. She said Karunanidhi had failed to answer her questions if India's military help was not a fact and if Karunanidhi was not abetting the murder of the Tamil people.[30] On 17 April 2017, Mahinda Rajapaksa gushed: 'We didn't have to ask! . . . India helped us in every possible way. We didn't want to publicize it, tell the press too much.'[31] On 22 September 2020, he admitted that without India's help, Sri Lanka would not have won the war.[32]

On 5 November, Karunanidhi lamented the cacophony of the Opposition and said instead, if there was harmony, it would aid the Centre's efforts.[33] Two days later, Karunanidhi lamented that the militants (read LTTE) had not shown the same enthusiasm in unity as they showed in 'building graves for the fallen in the fratricidal war'. He said he alone could not help end the tragedy, and his opponents were engaged in 'trickery' to 'embarrass' and end his government's life.[34] On 12 November, Karunanidhi moved another resolution demanding a ceasefire, and on 4 December, led an all-party delegation to meet the prime minister. On 27 December, he said he was appealing for a ceasefire 'with teary eyes'. Who was Karunanidhi appealing to? The Sri Lankan Army or the UPA Government of which his DMK was a constituent, which was abetting the war against the Tigers? The DMK general council, in a resolution, asked for the external affairs minister to visit Sri Lanka to press for a ceasefire.[35]

Meanwhile, the 9 January 2009 Thirumangalam assembly elections saw an unprecedented 90 per cent turnout. Cash was distributed through morning newspapers and slipped through the door. Alagiri had pulled out all the stops, making it popular as the Thirumangalam formula. But Thirumangalam could only provide a brief respite from the ethnic issue.

On 12 January, Ramadoss, Veeramani and Thirumavalavan met Karunanidhi to urge Pranab Mukherjee to visit Sri Lanka and agreed on a common action plan. However, on 15 January, Thirumavalavan unilaterally chose to go on a fast for a ceasefire but gave up the fast on 18 January. Ramadoss suggested that the next phase of the agitation, lasting ten days, should bring Tamil Nadu to a 'standstill' and asked Karunanidhi to say yes and leave the rest to them to bring the Indian government 'to its knees'.[36]

Sacrificing Tamils

On 18 January, Jayalalithaa, thinking she was taking on Karunanidhi, said innocent civilians would die in any war, and Sri Lanka was no exception.[37] She predicted the DMK being shown the door before the year-end and the AIADMK taking its place. On 20 January, Karunanidhi said that some parties had turned the ethnic issue into 'opposition to Congress (I) . . . and change of government [in the state]' and read the pressure on him to conduct an 'unruly revolution' as a conspiracy aimed at his dismissal.[38]

On 23 January, Karunanidhi moved a resolution titled 'Alas, the Tamil race in Sri Lanka is being destroyed—a final appeal to the government' and imploring it 'to save the Tamils'. He said repeated requests had been fruitless; this was the 'last appeal'. In his speech, Karunanidhi said he would lose power if Eelam could be attained. However, he would later say he would have lost his government if he had gone against the Centre on Sri Lanka.[39] Resolutions had been moved on 7 December 2006, 23 April and 12 November 2008 earlier. Karunanidhi would tout this as a major improvement over the AIADMK's approach.[40]

On 29 January, Muthukumar, 26, set himself on fire, accusing the Centre of being blind to the ethnic issue and criticizing Karunanidhi as a political opportunist. Muthukumar succumbed to his burns.[41] That day, Anbazhagan told the assembly President Rajapaksa had agreed not to bomb the safety zones [where Tamils would take refuge]. He claimed the DMK was neutral vis-à-vis the LTTE.[42] The DMK leadership's faith in the Sri Lankan government's words was embarrassingly disingenuous. But the sweetness of power made everything acceptable.

On 3 February, the executive resolved to hold rallies on 7, 8 and 9 February. As Ramadoss said he was disappointed, Karunanidhi retorted that Ramadoss and others would not have been disappointed if the resolution had said he was quitting.[43]

On 5 March, Jayalalithaa charged that the 'self-declared Thamizhinath Thalaivar' and the Centre he supported were watching the genocide. She went on a solidarity fast with the suffering Tamils on 9 March.[44] That day, Karunanidhi told a DMK rally that there was no option but to plead, 'Oh, mother! Save the Tamils', and if the war ended in defeat, Prabhakaran be treated with 'respect' like Alexander treated King Porus. Ramadoss said Karunanidhi's comparison of Mahinda Rajapaksa to Alexander made 'Tamils hang their heads [in shame]'. After endless pleas to the Centre for a ceasefire, the DMK called for closure on 23 April in Tamil Nadu and Puducherry.

On 16 April, the AIADMK manifesto promised to press for a separate Eelam.[45]

On 17 April, in telegrams to Sonia Gandhi, the prime minister and the foreign minister, Karunanidhi asked that India end diplomatic relations if it did not heed the foreign minister's call for a ceasefire. On 18 April, Jayalalithaa charged Karunanidhi with enacting 'drama after drama', pretending he was concerned for the Tamils there.[46]

On 21 April, Karunanidhi said he would 'deeply regret' if
Prabhakaran was killed. A day prior, Karunanidhi had created a stir
by saying that he did not consider Prabhakaran a terrorist. He said
later that he was misquoted.[47]

Jayalalithaa, however, charged that history would not forgive
Karunanidhi for betraying the Sri Lankan Tamils. Karunanidhi said
on 22 April that she was the 'one who certified that the ongoing war
is not against Tamils, but only against the LTTE' and asked: 'Will
history forgive you?' He also recalled that Jayalalithaa had remarked
in January that it was normal for some civilians to be killed in war.

In his missive that day, Karunanidhi said if he quit as some urged
him to, even the little support the Tamils have now would disappear.
He concluded:

Let those blame throw blame.

Those who are wise would know the truth

But the hearts of the world's Tamils are in deep distress—

Wiping that grief—Is it not in the hands of the Centre?

What can we do?

Except to cry, weep and lament![48]

Jayalalithaa wondered: 'If Karunanidhi can't apply adequate pressure
on the Union government now, when will there be a ceasefire?' 'And
if India, a big power in the region, did not intervene and take strong
measures, which other country would do so?' she asked.[49]

On 23 April, Karunanidhi said the Tamil cause should not be
lost because of 'some betrayers'. Jayalalithaa termed the day's closure
call 'a farce and a drama' and refused to join it.[50] Gandhian People's
Movement leader Tamilaruvi Manian had urged Karunanidhi to use
his influence to stop the air raids against civilians. Karunanidhi said
the Centre would not heed him. At Manian's suggestion that he
lead an all-party delegation, Karunanidhi wondered if Jayalalithaa,
Vaiko or Ramadoss would join him. Manian then suggested that the

DMK's ministers at the Centre resign and heard Karunanidhi say: 'They would say goodbye.' Manian said they could not easily dismiss those gestures and finally suggested that Karunanidhi resign and take to the streets. He argued that Tamil Nadu would be behind him, leading to a resolution, and the DMK would romp home with 200 seats in the mid-term election. But Karunanidhi was not moved.[51]

On 24 April, Foreign Secretary Shivshankar Menon and National Security Adviser (NSA) M.K. Narayanan met President Rajapaksa in Colombo. On 25 April, speaking at a public meeting in Salem, Jayalalithaa said that if she had a role in the next government at the Centre, she would 'take the required steps for Eelam'.[52]

Karunanidhi had said that even an ordinary worker of the DMK would not do the lowly act of betraying the Tamil race for the sake of positions, frills, status or authority. But this time, the Karunanidhi of *Purananuru* times gave a thousand explanations to justify his holding tight to power. On 26 April, Karunanidhi, without any sense of irony, listed the 'two important tasks before the DMK' : to save the Lankan Tamils and to win the 2009 elections.[53]

But the pressure on him was such that on 27 April, Karunanidhi announced an indefinite fast to 'sacrifice' himself to bring about a ceasefire. Karunanidhi had played the last but one card. But it was pure optics. The prime minister and home minister phoned him, and a few hours later, in a choreographed action, Sri Lanka announced the end of combat operations with 'heavy calibre weapons, combat aircraft and aerial weapons, which could cause civilian casualties'. Karunanidhi called off his fast at 1 p.m. The fast had lasted a few hours. On 3 May, he wrote that if he had not succeeded in his fast, he would have been next to the graves of Sankaralingam and LTTE's Dileepan. This, he insisted, was the absolute truth.[*54]

---

[*] Sankaralingam died on 13 October 1956 after 76 days of fasting on several demands including to rename Madras State Tamil Nadu and LTTE's Dileepan died on 26 September 1987 after a twelve-day fast on a number of Sri Lankan Tamil-related demands.

Jayalalithaa, Vaiko, Ramadoss and Vijayakanth called the fast 'a deceitful drama'. Jayalalithaa rightly wondered, 'How can we call the mere stoppage of dropping bombs a ceasefire?' Karunanidhi had forsaken his Sri Lankan brethren. Ten days after leaving the UPA on the differences on the issue of the Sri Lankan Tamils, on 29 March 2013, Karunanidhi said that the exit had achieved nothing except to fulfil the desire of those like Jayalalithaa. Similarly, it would have achieved nothing if he had pulled out his ministers then. He termed as 'conjecture' the thesis that the mass killings would have been halted if the DMK had taken such a stand. 'Has the Eelam Tamil issue been resolved? Did India bring amendments to the US resolution? Did it adopt a resolution with the amendments in Parliament? All that has happened is the exit of the DMK. But the DMK is not the least sorry,' he wrote.[55]

Karunanidhi would also later charge Pranab Mukherjee of 'misleading' him on 27 April 2009 that the use of heavy weapons had ceased. But Karunanidhi surely was not so naïve to swallow Pranab Mukherjee's claim hook, line and sinker.[56] On 7 March 2013, he improvised when he said he did not know that the Sri Lankan ceasefire announcement was 'false' and that he had been truthful to his conscience.[57]

Foreign Secretary Shivshankar Menon damagingly records that 'despite differences in public posture on the issue in Tamil Nadu and Delhi, there was cross-party understanding on the basis of policy towards Sri Lanka with both the Dravida Munnetra Kazhagam (DMK) and the All India Anna Dravida Munnetra Kazhagam (AIADMK) party, as a result of considerable hard work by Pranab Mukherjee and Narayanan, as I found when I met alone with very senior Tamil Nadu politicians in Chennai'. Menon writes that the Rajiv Gandhi murder 'had caused a shift in broader Indian attitude, which came to be more in line with those of the Sri Lankan government'. Clearly, both the Kazhagams wanted the LTTE vanquished. What they had not bargained for was the unjustifiable civilian casualties as the Sri Lankan Army pursued the LTTE with impunity, and the LTTE used civilians as human shields.[58]

No Election Issue

Tamil filmmakers Bharathiraja and Seeman, vocal in their support for Sri Lankan Tamils, chose to work against Congress (I) candidates, now singling out Chidambaram. Harsh words were reserved for Sonia Gandhi. Bharathiraja said, 'As revenge for being widowed, she has widowed 2.5 lakh Tamil women. But what else can you expect from a lady from the land of Mussolini?'[59]

Seeman called the conflict 'a direct war between Sonia and Prabhakaran' and alleged that India had given Sri Lanka Rs 2000 crore worth of assistance to finish the Tamil resistance and said Chidambaram must answer for it. He said India's complicity was evident in its silence to every expression of Sri Lanka's thanks to India for its support.[60] On 18 May 2009, Seeman formed the Naam Thamizhar Iyakkam. This social outfit subsequently turned into a political party named Naam Thamizhar Katchi (NTK), which sees LTTE's Prabhakaran as a guiding force and advocates ultra Tamil nationalism.

Elections to Parliament were held in Tamil Nadu on 13 May 2009. But the ethnic issue would not gain traction as an electoral issue. The 20 kg of rice at Re 1 a kg and the National Rural Employment Guarantee Scheme of employment for 100 days a year at Rs 80 a day were plusses.

The DMK fielded Thirumangalam hero and 'by-election specialist' Alagiri from Madurai. It was a Dhritarashtra-like decision but meant to move Alagiri away to Delhi and establish Stalin's fiefdom in the state. Yet, on 18 October 2010, Jayalalithaa alleged in Madurai that 'In Tamil Nadu there are two governments—one in Chennai headed by Karunanidhi and his son M.K. Stalin, the deputy chief minister—and the other in Madurai under Alagiri and his associates'.[61] Responding to criticism from the communists on Alagiri's candidacy, Karunanidhi said, 'Oh my gosh! What a fuss! Why do they fear this child so much? Their fear hops on to me that even I fear Alagiri.'[62] Alagiri promised an international airport, a jasmine oil factory, a unit of the All India Institute of Medical Sciences (AIIMS) and making Madurai a 'clean city, green city and E-city'.

Karunanidhi highlighted the benefits of being part of the coalition at the Centre, turning the original DMK slogan on its head 'Vadukku vazhangugirathu, therku therukirathu' (north gives, south progresses) about central funds, the infrastructure projects and investments in IT, telecom and industrial sectors in the state.[63]

On 6 May, Karunanidhi was forced to emulate Jayalalithaa, promising to take 'all efforts to ensure that 'Eelam' is created'. Jayalalithaa said that if a 'favourable' government was returned, she would ensure that the Indian Army was sent to help create 'Eelam'.[64] On 9 May, Prime Minister Manmohan Singh cited international law and said that it was not 'easy to march armies' into a sovereign country, and those advocating it knew that these were 'tall promises'.[65] Jayalalithaa shot back: 'Indira Gandhi sent troops to East Pakistan. Is the Congress telling me that she didn't understand international law?'[66]

The DMK and allies won twenty-seven of the thirty-nine seats while the AIADMK front won twelve. Alagiri's margin was more than 1.4 lakh votes. All PMK candidates lost. The DMDK scored 10.1 per cent of the votes, and in fourteen seats, the party had polled more than the margins of victory of the DMK-Congress (I) candidates.

The ethnic issue felled a few of Congress (I)'s top candidates, former ministers E.V.K.S. Elangovan, Mani Shankar Aiyar, R. Prabhu and TNCC (I) president K.V. Thangabalu. P. Chidambaram scraped through with a mere 3000-plus votes after two recounts. Two years later, Jayalalithaa accused Karunanidhi of overturning the result in Chidambaram's favour and Chidambaram of 'fraud'.[67]

As the results defied electoral arithmetic, the US consul general said, 'Among others, the DMK's unparalleled ability to deliver cash handouts to voters, and possible vote-tampering as factors contributing to the Congress–DMK alliance's victory.'[68]

2009 PARLIAMENTARY ELECTION

Party	Contested	Won	Votes	Percentage
AIADMK	23	9	69,53,591	22.20%
PMK	6	0	19,44,619	6.40%
MDMK	4	1	11,12,908	3.70%
CPI	3	1	8,64,572	2.80%
CPM	3	1	6,68,729	2.20%
DMK	21	18	76,25,397	25.10%
INC	15	8	45,67,799	15.00%
VCK	2	1	7,35,847	2.40%
IUML	1	1	3,60,474	1.19%

A disappointed Jayalalithaa said, 'Money power has won over democracy' and remained indoors.[69]

On 18 May, Karunanidhi said that 'prevention of destruction and ensuring a lasting peace was the immediate responsibility of India'.

The following day, in Delhi, he said that Sonia Gandhi and the prime minister should take a 'more firm interest in the Sri Lankan Tamils' issue'. The DMK and other parties wanted UN intervention, Mahinda Rajapaksa and Sarath Fonseka to be tried for war crimes, the internally displaced to return, and UN and INGOs to take part in the reconstruction and rehabilitation of Tamils.

Eelam War IV Ends—Blame Game Begins

Eelam War IV, which had begun in August 2006, ended on 18–19 May in a twenty-two-hour battle which ended Prabhakaran's life.

The ethnic issue had been brutally put to bed. A UN panel found that both sides committed serious human rights violations and that up to 40,000 people might have been killed in the final five months alone.[70] On 27 March 2014, the United Nations Human Rights Council (UNHRC) would finally vote to open an international inquiry into alleged war crimes by both sides.[71]

On 22 May, in a statement that avoided any reference to Prabhakaran or his death, Jayalalithaa said, 'The decimation of the LTTE or the killing of its leaders cannot wipe away the injustice meted out to this large community that has as much roots in Sri Lanka as the Sinhala majority.'[72] Karunanidhi said he did not wish to comment on Prabhakaran's death.[73]

On 27 May, the UNHRC passed what Human Rights Watch called 'a deeply flawed resolution on Sri Lanka', reaffirming the principle of non-interference and largely commending the Sri Lankan government for its post-war policies.[74] Amnesty International described the vote as a 'low point for the human rights council'. European countries, Canada, Chile and Mexico had supported an inquiry into allegations of human rights excesses by the Sri Lankan Army and the Tigers using civilians as human shields.[75] In April 2010, Sri Lanka created the Lessons Learnt and Reconciliation Commission (LLRC), whose report, published in December 2011, largely exonerated the government forces.[76]

On 29 May, President Mahinda Rajapaksa said he had fought India's war.[77] On 23 June, Shivshankar Menon said Rajapaksa was 'in a way right'.[78] In 2019, Sri Lanka's Defence Secretary Gotabaya Rajapaksa said that along with Presidential Adviser Basil Rajapaksa and President's Secretary Lalith Weeratunga, they were in regular contact from day one with an Indian team comprising Shivshankar Menon, National Security Adviser M.K. Narayanan and Defence Secretary Vijay Singh outside normal channels and said they 'solved' 'very sensitive' issues and they 'had a very close relationship'. Gotabaya Rajapaksa said that the Sri Lankan team visited India many times and that 'Tamil Nadu was putting pressure. We understood that and did certain things that helped them (India)'.[79] But, the Sri Lankans need not have feared Karunanidhi's pressure, for he admitted to an interviewer this time that he was not planning to confront the Centre. 'In the Sri Lankan issue, if I had gone against the Centre, I would have lost my government,' he said.[80]

On 1 July, in the debate on the Sri Lankan Tamils, Karunanidhi even went a step further:

> There should be diplomacy in anything. If we wish to help the Tamils there, we can't say things in anger and hate on the Sinhalese, which becomes counterproductive . . . We could speak valiantly. A feisty speech, a stormy speech, a speech with the force of the sea waves and a volcanic speech—so we can praise speeches. But we must make sure that we do not upset the Sinhalese more. This is what I call diplomacy.[81]

In August 2009, UK's Channel 4 News broadcast video footage apparently showing government troops summarily executing Tamils during the final push of the war. The Sri Lankan government denied abuses.

27

Second UPA

Nationally, in the 2009 parliamentary elections, the Congress (I) improved its performance to 206 from 145 in 2004. On 4 May, Karunanidhi described Sonia Gandhi as 'pure gold' and the 'epitome of sacrifice' and asked her to take over as prime minister.[1] The Congress (I) decided to enforce its 2004 strength-to-post formula of a cabinet berth for every six MPs and a minister of state for every three MPs that it could not enforce then.[2] On 21 May, the DMK said the Congress (I) formula was unacceptable.

Sonia Gandhi and Manmohan Singh called Karunanidhi on 21 May late at night.[3] *Rediff* reported that Rahul Gandhi had reservations about T.R. Baalu and Raja.[4] However, on 22 May, Prime Minister Manmohan Singh clarified there was no reservation. Karunanidhi said the two 'had been the target of some Delhi-based satellite television channels'.[5]

On 28 May, the DMK ministers were inducted. Alagiri got chemicals and fertilizers, Raja was back in IT and Dayanidhi Maran got textiles. S.S. Palanimanickam, S. Jagathrakshakan, S. Gandhiselvan and actor Napoleon became ministers of state. Karunanidhi had sacrificed Baalu for Alagiri. Alagiri's choice for Parliament was already a bad decision. Karunanidhi had compounded his mistake. Having elevated Alagiri, he named Stalin deputy chief minister the following day. It was a clumsy political trapeze. It did not work.[6]

Alagiri was uncomfortable with English and Hindi and, under the rules, was not allowed to speak Tamil.[7] On 14 September, Jayalalithaa said it was an insult to Tamil and asked the DMK to pull out of the UPA government.[8] After fifteen months, when Alagiri finally spoke in Parliament, the BBC reported it.

However, Karunanidhi's major problems would be centred elsewhere with Raja and Dayanidhi.

On 5 December, Karunanidhi said he had achieved many of his goals except a new assembly complex, the Anna library and the World Classical Tamil Conference in June 2010. After that, he would retire.[9] On 15 January 2010, Karunanidhi again hinted that he wished to follow in the footsteps of Jyoti Basu, Periyar and Nelson Mandela and that the deputy chief minister should continue the good work.[10] However, despite these periodic pronouncements, Karunanidhi was averse to becoming a figurehead and never stepped down.

Stalin's biography was released on 9 March. Speakers hailed the deputy chief minister's 'accessibility'. On 24 March, Karunanidhi asked the media to be patient until the June World Tamil conference, saying he would consider both views on whether to continue as chief minister or to pass the mantle to Stalin.[11] But there was opposition within.

The DMK retained the Pennagaram assembly seat in the 27 March by-elections. The PMK finished second, while the AIADMK and DMDK candidates forfeited their deposits.[*12] Alagiri was absent from the by-election campaign. He left for Australia on 24 March and told *Junior Vikatan* that day that in his father's aftermath, he

---

[*] Pennagaram was the eleventh by-election since October 2006. The DMK won eight seats, and its ally, Congress (I), the rest. Ten voters exercised the Rule 49-O (from the Conduct of Election Rules, 1961), NOTA or None of the above option of not voting for any candidate.

refused to accept anyone other than Karunanidhi as his leader. He concluded that no one could measure up to Karunanidhi.[13]

2G

Earlier, on 29 November 2008, Subramanian Swamy had written to the prime minister seeking sanction to prosecute Raja under the Prevention of Corruption Act. The following year, an NGO Telecom Watchdog complained to the Central Vigilance Commission (CVC) about irregularities in spectrum allocation.[14] From July 2009 onwards, the Opposition parties raised the spectrum allocations issue in Parliament, demanding a probe.[15] On 21 October 2009, CBI filed a first information report (FIR) against unknown officers of the Department of Telecommunications, unknown private persons/ companies and others.

On 31 March 2010, the Comptroller and Auditor General (CAG) reported large-scale irregularities in auctioning 2G spectrum licenses. On 3 May 2010, as demands for A. Raja's resignation rocked Parliament, Karunanidhi stood by Raja, saying that the Opposition was levelling 'malicious charges' [because] 'Raja is a Dalit'.[16]

On 6 May, the Raja and Radia telecon was made public. That day in a statement, Jayalalithaa charged Karunanidhi of 'shamelessly playing the Dalit card'.[17]

On 25 May, the Delhi High Court dismissed the NGO, Centre for Public Interest Litigation's (CPIL) petition seeking a probe into the scam by a Special Investigation Team or the CBI and in August moved the Supreme Court. On 13 September, the Supreme Court asked the Centre and Raja to reply in ten days to CPIL and others on the allegation that there was a Rs 70,000-crore scam. On 24 September, Subramanian Swamy moved the Supreme Court seeking direction to the prime minister to sanction Raja's prosecution. On 8 October, the Supreme Court asked the government to respond to the 31 March CAG report.

On 29 October, the Supreme Court pulled up the additional solicitor general for Raja's continuation in the cabinet and the delay in the investigative work. On 10 November, when the CAG estimated the presumptive loss at a whopping Rs 1.76 lakh crore, all hell broke loose.[18] That day, Jayalalithaa urged 'the people of India' to send a one-line telegram to the President urging Raja's dismissal. The following day she said that if the Congress (I) could 'summon up the political will to act against Raja', she would save it from collapse unconditionally, offering to make the loss of the eighteen MPs through her nine and with other parties. She asked Sonia Gandhi to forget the past misunderstanding, noting that her party was thirty-eight years old, she had a political career of twenty-eight years, and when one spends so much time in politics, 'there are bound to be ups and downs, and there is bound to be a past. But in politics, if you keep harping on the past and looking back you cannot move forward,' she suggested to Sonia Gandhi. On 12 November, Karunanidhi claimed that 'the doors are closed to Jayalalithaa', revealing his anxiety about continuing the ties with the Congress (I). His daughter Kanimozhi's explanation the previous day to Pranab Mukherjee of Raja's innocence had however, failed.[19]

Karunanidhi pronounced Raja 'not guilty' and said he had followed procedures in place and adopted by his predecessors Pramod Mahajan and Arun Shourie. On 14 November, the Congress (I) core committee chose to drop Raja, and Manmohan Singh rang Karunanidhi to suggest that Raja quit. Pranab Mukherjee spoke to Karunanidhi thrice on the phone to outline the seriousness of the issue. Raja met Karunanidhi twice and on 14 November told reporters in Delhi and Chennai he had done 'nothing wrong' and would not resign. He later drove to the prime minister's residence in Delhi to tender his resignation. Two days later, Kapil Sibal was named in Raja's place. Jayalalithaa said it would be just 'symbolic tokenism' if it were not followed up with an inquiry.[20] She said Raja had left 'after a virtual avalanche of public opinion was mobilized' after her interview and the 'millions of telegrams' to the President. Karunanidhi said Raja was asked to resign to allow the functioning of Parliament and said the stalling of parliamentary proceedings during the previous year was part of a pre-planned effort to achieve the ouster of Raja, a Dalit.[21] While Karunanidhi claimed the loss was 'presumptive', Jayalalithaa said the loss was not presumptive, only the amount was.[22] On 8 December, Karunanidhi said he would proceed against Raja without compunction if proven guilty.[23]

On 15 December, Subramanian Swamy filed a criminal complaint before the Special Judge, CBI to set in motion the provisions of the Prevention of Corruption Act against A. Raja and later included P. Chidambaram.[24] That day, the Supreme Court granted senior counsel Prashant Bhushan's plea on behalf of CPIL, Telecom Watchdog (both activist groups) and journalist Paranjoy Guha Thakurta for the CBI to probe the spectrum scam thoroughly. Bhushan had attached a CD with 140 of the recordings of the lobbyist Niira Radia's conversations. On 19 November, *Outlook* published the conversations and a second tranche on 11 December. The tapes showed A. Raja and Kanimozhi, and others talking to Radia about securing the telecom portfolio for Raja while keeping Dayanidhi out of it, Kanimozhi aspiring for a minister of state with independent charge and Dayanidhi Maran's poor opinion of Alagiri and an alleged payment of Rs 600 crore to his grandaunt Dayalu Ammal.[25]

On 17 December, Karunanidhi wondered if anyone would believe that Dayanidhi Maran had paid Rs 600 crore to his grandmother and if this could be proved, and if those who alleged it came out in their name to make such an allegation, he would face them in the court.[26] On 21 December 2010, Karunanidhi called the allegation that Raja got his IT ministry after lobbying as 'mischief'. Just because there was a tape, it would not become true, he said and cited the conversation of Rs 600 crore to Dayalu from Dayanidhi as proof of the unsubstantiated claims. He said his meeting with Ratan Tata did not mean 'corruption' and added that Raja had followed his predecessors in spectrum allocation and cited Arun Shourie's contention that the scam could be some Rs 30,000 crore, not Rs 1.67 lakh crore.[27]

On 21 December 2017, a special CBI court acquitted Raja, Kanimozhi and fifteen others in the 2G spectrum scam.[28] Judge O.P. Saini said, 'Some people created a scam by artfully arranging a few facts. A huge scam was seen by everyone where there was none.'[29]

Manmohan Singh said the 'massive propaganda' against the UPA was 'without any foundation'.[30] Subramanian Swamy said the government 'must prove its bonafides by filing an immediate appeal in High Court'. He prophesied that the 2G verdict would be overturned like the case of Jayalalithaa's high court acquittal.[31] On 19 March 2018, the Enforcement Directorate and CBI filed appeals at the Delhi High Court. The appeals are pending.

2011 Assembly Election

On 1 February 2011, after finalizing the alliance with the Congress (I) for the assembly elections, Karunanidhi said, 'The sky is clear and there are no hurdles in our way.' However the following day, the CBI named Raja the first accused and arrested him. On 3 February, the DMK general council argued that 'just because a person is arrested, he does not become guilty', and its resolution said that the DMK had been an 'open book'. Karunanidhi said he stood by Raja, who was 'languishing in jail and paying the price for making mobile phones affordable to the people'.[32]

On 8 February, the CBI arrested DB Group's Shahid Balwa.[33] On 17 February, judge Saini remanded Raja for fourteen days. The following day, CBI raided Kalaignar TV and questioned Sharad Kumar, managing director of the channel, in connection with an alleged transfer of Rs 214 crore arranged by Cineyug Films from Shahid Balwa's DB Group, a main beneficiary of the 2G allotment. Kalaignar TV claimed the money was returned with interest.

The DMK was in a straightjacket and the Congress (I) could strong arm Karunanidhi into giving it sixty-three seats of its choosing, fifteen more than in 2006. On 4 March, Karunanidhi revealed that he had offered his ally fifty-one, fifty-three and fifty-eight and finally sixty seats. Yet, that day, the Congress (I) had intimated from Delhi its demand for sixty-three seats—that it would choose.[34] The following day, Karunanidhi threatened to withdraw his six ministers. But when the Congress (I) failed to blink, Karunanidhi capitulated. The DMK ended up contesting 119 seats, the lowest since 1980.[35]

Earlier, on 4 March, Vijayakanth met Jayalalithaa, and the DMDK was later allotted forty-one seats. Jayalalithaa had once accused Vijayakanth of trying to usurp MGR's legacy, and on 23 October 2006, she alleged the actor came drunk to the assembly and the actor, in turn, wondered whether she had ever filled his cup.[36] The bad blood would never be overcome. Jayalalithaa revealed later that she 'did not wish the least' to ally with Vijayakanth but bowed to the wish of her party men. Vijayakanth, however, maintained that the AIADMK was desperate for a tie-up, and he 'blindly' agreed to deliver the people from the 'atrocities of the DMK regime'.[37] Circumstances had forced them into an alliance but the two actors would never put up a joint presence in the campaign.

On 16 March, Jayalalithaa unilaterally announced the AIADMK slate of 160 candidates, including some seats sought by allies but climbed down after she realized they would go their separate ways.[38] On 19 March, the MDMK blamed Jayalalithaa's 'arrogance' for offering thirteen seats and quit the alliance.

On 17 March, Karunanidhi promised women 35 kg of rice, free laptops to college students from below-poverty-line families and free mixers and grinders. On 22 March, Stalin added that

Photo credit: Wideangle Ravi Shankaran

Jayalalithaa and Vijayakanth as allies, 2011. Seated to the left is CPI's A.B. Bardhan

they might also give refrigerators and washing machines. But this time, Jayalalithaa outdid them when a week later, on 24 March, she promised 20 kg free rice for all, twenty litres of drinking water daily to those below-poverty-line and 4 gm of gold for underprivileged women. She matched the mixers and grinders promise while adding a fan, extended laptops to high school children, free 'modern, green' homes of 300 sq. ft to 3 lakh families, 60,000 cows for 6000 families and sheep for poor families. She had certainly learnt her lessons from 2006.[39]

Karunanidhi bandied his medical insurance scheme, the 108 ambulance service and the scheme to convert twenty-one lakh huts to concrete houses. On 27 March, Karunanidhi listing his achievements, said he expected 'the expression of gratitude from people who enjoy these benefits every day'.

Jayalalithaa launched a vicious attack on Karunanidhi's family, alleging that they 'must be the richest in the world' and adding that with ministers in the state and the Centre, 'they have earned more than any other family in the world'. CPM's Prakash Karat called the DMK and the Congress (I) 'brothers in corruption'.[40]

The AIADMK won 147 of the 160 seats by margins ranging from 10,000 to 73,000 votes. The DMDK won twenty-nine seats, the CPM ten, CPI nine, actor Sarath Kumar's All India Samathuva Makkal Katchi and the Manithaneya Makkal Katchi (MNMK) two each and PT, RPI, AIFB and the Kongunadu Ilaignar Peravai one each. The DMK won only twenty-three seats. Eighteen ministers, including Anbazhagan, were defeated. Congress (I) won just five seats, PMK three, the VCK none and the Kongu Nadu Munnetra Kazhagam (KMK) one.

2011 ASSEMBLY ELECTION

Party	Contested	Won	Votes	Percentage
AIADMK (IND 5)	165	150	1,41,50,289	38.40%
DMDK	41	29	29,03,828	7.90%
CPI(M)	12	10	8,88,364	2.40%
CPI	10	9	7,27,394	2%
MNMK	3	2	1,81,180	0.50%
PT	2	2	1,46,454	0.40%
AIFB	1	1	88,253	0.20%
DMK (IND 5)	124	23	82,49,991	22.40%
INC	63	5	34,36,432	9.30%
PMK	30	3	19,27,783	5.20%
VCK	10	0	5,55,965	1.50%
KMK	7	0	3,70,044	1.00%

Jayalalithaa said her priority was to restore 'the rule of law', which had 'totally deteriorated'. 'First the debris has to be cleared, and then the house has to be rebuilt. It is not an easy task,' she said. She claimed she restored the state's fiscal health twice in 1991 and 2001 and said 'the havoc that has been wrought in Tamil Nadu is beyond description'. Karunanidhi said people had given him rest and sarcastically said he congratulated them. The three-year-long power crisis, soaring prices, the grassroots corruption and the 2G scam had all done the DMK in.[41] Anbumani Ramadoss later alleged that the AIADMK gave Rs 200 each to all voters, a little more than the DMK. He said Rs 1000 per vote could result in a victory margin of 40–50,000 votes, Rs 500 in 20,000–30,000 votes and Rs 250 to 300 in 10,000 votes.[42]

There was more trouble ahead for the DMK's first family. On 25 April, in its 53-page supplementary chargesheet, the CBI accused Kanimozhi of entering into a criminal conspiracy with Raja for allegedly accepting illegal gratification to route money related to the 2G scam through Kalaignar TV in which she held 20 per cent shares.[43] Earlier, responding to questions on the DMK's possible exit from the UPA in the event of his family members' figuring in the chargesheet, Karunanidhi had shot back, 'Is that your desire?' 'Being a woman, you should not talk as if you are heartless,' he told the woman reporter.[44]

However, another woman—Jayalalithaa—in a statement called for Kalaignar TV founded with 'graft money' to be taken off the air and Kanimozhi and all the other members of the Karunanidhi family who had directly or indirectly benefited to be arrested. She was surprised that Dayalu Ammal was left out in the chargesheet. Vijayakanth also wondered why Dayalu Ammal was excluded and suggested that Karunanidhi resign on moral grounds or that his government be dismissed.[45]

On 27 April, the DMK's high-level implementation committee expressed surprise at the inclusion of Kanimozhi's and Kalaignar TV head Sharad Kumar's names and said it would face the issue legally. The resolution attacked the press and some political leaders whose 'culture and way of life is to indulge in corruption' (read Jayalalithaa) but saw the 2G issue as a rare opportunity to tear the UPA apart, shake the DMK and remove Karunanidhi from political leadership. An emotional Karunanidhi said he had personally brought a reluctant Kanimozhi to attend the meeting, and it was not to save his daughter 'but to save the party's image' and added that he would not make an issue of his difficulties and 'pawn' the party.[46]

On 16 May, Jayalalithaa was sworn in as chief minister. Vijayakanth became the Leader of the Opposition. But relations between the two leaders soon frayed and reached a new low. On 1 February 2012, Vijayakanth lost his cool and made uncouth gestures towards the treasury benches. Jayalalithaa described his actions as 'most disgusting' and said it showed what would happen when those undeserving reached new heights. The AIADMK would have won the elections without the DMDK and the seats allotted to the DMDK as people had decided to end the DMK rule. She 'regretted' and was 'ashamed' that she had joined hands with the DMDK. The DMDK was 'fortunate enough' to strike a deal with the AIADMK and said its MLAs, its principal Opposition status and ascent were made possible by her AIADMK. She ominously added that the DMDK had peaked, and henceforth would only see descent. Karunanidhi commented that the AIADMK had its own 'unique' way of handling Opposition parties.[47] However, Jayalalithaa's words would ring true. This was the apogee of Vijayakanth's political career and the efforts in 2014 and 2016 to position him in the lead by a non DMK–AIADMK front would prove disastrous for him and his sponsors.[*]

Kanimozhi Arrest

On 20 May, Kanimozhi was arrested pending trial. Kanimozhi later said that it did not add up for her that the DMK was in power at the Centre, she was the chief minister's daughter and yet she ended up in jail. She hoped to 'unravel the facts' one day.[48] 'If you have a daughter who faces arrest for an offence not committed by her, how sad will you be? I'm saddened the same way,' Karunanidhi said.[49] On his birthday, a reflective Karunanidhi mentioned the Tamil

---

[*] Vijayakanth passed away on 28 December 2023.

adage, 'Friendship with the bad will result in trouble.'[50] Two days later, Karunanidhi, the father, told a public meeting at Tiruvarur: 'Kanimozhi is in Tihar jail, either it could be due to the Centre's order or complacence' adding that 'a flower kept there (Tihar) will wither away quickly due to the temperature'.[51]

On 22 May, Karunanidhi wrote, 'The arrest is a vendetta against DMK and my family from Kanniyakumari to the Himalayas', and he was confident of winning the 'final war'. Karunanidhi said Kanimozhi's 'only crime' was to heed his advice and become a shareholder in Kalaignar TV.[52] Five months after the arrest, in an interview with *Ananda Vikatan*, Kanimozhi's mother said that until Sita immersed herself into the fire, she was considered a suspect and so was her daughter.[53]

On 10 June, Karunanidhi snapped at mediapersons after the high-level action committee meeting asking him about DMK–Congress (I) ties and Kanimozhi. 'Why do you keep asking about Kanimozhi and High Court bail? Even today, the Madras High Court has ruled against the state government's stand on a uniform syllabus. Why don't you ask me about that? You have come here with an agenda,' he raged. On 14 June, in a long letter, Karunanidhi lamented that twenty-two of the thirty-one questions from the media were on the two issues. He said that the questions were intended to end the DMK–Congress (I) alliance hoping for criticism from him that could be blown up later to create confusion.[54]

But there was more trouble ahead. On 6 July, the CBI's declaration that it had evidence against Dayanidhi Maran saw him resign the following day. On 10 October, Kalanidhi and Dayanidhi Maran's residences were raided.[55]

On 28 November, Kanimozhi made bail.

Resolution on Economic Sanction on Sri Lanka

On 3 June, UK's Channel 4 premièred a special hour-long investigation titled *Sri Lanka's Killing Fields* at the 17th session of the Human Rights Council (30 May–17 June 2011) in Geneva.[56] Sri Lanka denounced it as the work of the LTTE supporters. India had said the events of the war needed to be examined but said its concern was the welfare of the Tamils.[57]

On 8 June, the Tamil Nadu assembly adopted a unanimous resolution seeking economic sanctions on Sri Lanka by India to 'rein in' Colombo on the Tamil issue and pressing for speedy rehabilitation of displaced Tamils. Launching a scathing attack on Karunanidhi, Jayalalithaa said the DMK's 'selfish nature and helplessness' did not yield any tangible benefits for the suffering Tamils. Vijayakanth sarcastically added, 'The credit for eliminating the Tamil race in Sri Lanka went to the DMK.'[58] Karunanidhi said, 'Jayalalithaa, who had said the Sri Lankan Army was not deliberately killing the Sri Lankan Tamils, and it was common for innocent people getting killed in a war, was now behaving as if she is concerned about the Sri Lankan Tamils.'

Meanwhile, on 19 December, Jayalalithaa expelled Sasikala a second time and thirteen others, including T.T.V. Dhinakaran. She told the 30 December general council that Sasikala and her kin had been sent home for good but cited no reasons for her action. But on 31 March 2012, Sasikala was readmitted after she claimed in a two-page letter to Jayalalithaa that she was in the dark about her kin's alleged 'conspiracy to usurp the party and power'.[59]

India Votes against Sri Lanka

Sri Lanka opposed a US resolution in the UNHRC that year for 'promoting reconciliation and accountability' recommended by Sri Lanka's domestic inquiry, LLRC. On 29 February 2012, Karunanidhi stressed that India should not 'at any cost' back Sri Lanka on the vote.[60] On 6 March, Jayalalithaa penned a second letter to Prime Minister Manmohan Singh reiterating her demand that India support the US-backed resolution, condemn Colombo and initiate action for an economic embargo on the country.[61] On 9 March, Karunanidhi wrote to the prime minister along similar lines. On 12 March, the prime minister proffered a diplomatic response to Karunanidhi without committing anything. On 13 March, the AIADMK and DMK forced an adjournment of the Rajya Sabha and disrupted the House on the issue.

On 14 March, Jayalalithaa said she had written twice to the prime minister, and his response to her letters was 'not satisfying'. That day, Channel 4 released the second video, 'Sri Lanka's Killing Fields. War Crimes Unpunished released'. On 19 March, as the prime minister told Parliament that India was 'inclined to' back the US resolution, Karunanidhi called off a DMK fast but said he had also considered pulling out his ministers from the UPA.[62] On 22 March, in a first, India voted against Sri Lanka. The US-backed resolution called for implementing Sri Lanka's reconciliation commission recommendations and for the UN High Commissioner of Human Rights to provide technical assistance.[63] Jayalalithaa and Karunanidhi both claimed credit for India's vote.[64]

28

Jayalalithaa Returns

TESO's Second Avatar

On 19 April 2012, Karunanidhi said, 'The song of freedom is ringing in the ears of Tamils across the world. The blood and tears shed by Sri Lankan Tamils will not go in vain. If not tomorrow, it will come into existence one day.'[1] On 25 April, he said that five years earlier, he had remarked that Tamil Eelam was his 'unrealized dream' and now he wished to revive TESO towards it. Karunanidhi, however, clarified that he was no longer calling for a Bangladesh-style Indian intervention but for India to take steps towards a UN resolution for a referendum for Sri Lankan Tamils on Eelam.[2] Five days later, the defunct TESO was revived. Justifying his decision and in an obvious dig at Jayalalithaa's 2009 comment during the Eelam IV war, Karunanidhi said he could not take a stand such as 'people dying in war is normal'.[3] Yet, on 16 July, following a visit by P. Chidambaram the previous day, Karunanidhi said the proposed TESO conference in August would not have Eelam on its agenda and claimed the 'priority is to ensure safety and a good living to the Sri Lankan Tamils'.[4] But, the 12 August conference was named the Eelam Tamil Rights Protection Conference.

On 8 August, the Ministry of External Affairs said it objected to using the term 'Eelam' in the title. That day, quoting the line *Eelathu unavum Kaazhaga thakkamum* from *Pattinapalai*, a Sangam work about boats at the ancient Poompuhar port laden with food from Eelam and other items from Myanmar, Karunanidhi pointed out that the term was two millennia old.[5] On 11 August, the ministry withdrew its objection but advised against 'any declaration or outcome' challenging Sri Lanka's unity.[6]

A chary Karunanidhi studiously avoided using the word 'Eelam' at the preliminary meeting before the conference, and justified his ambivalence by reiterating that the priority was to heal the Tamils. He nevertheless assured that within his lifetime, he would struggle to realize his dream with his followers.

The conference adopted fourteen resolutions, the most salient of which urged India to pilot a UN resolution for Eelam while scrupulously eschewing the term. Karunanidhi's compulsions as a coalition partner were painfully evident.

Karunanidhi also told the delegates that, like the rest of the world and India, he was 'misled' by Colombo's announcement of ending the hostilities in 2009.[7] If Karunanidhi expected the Opposition to believe his disingenousness, he was sorely mistaken. In a resolution on 27 August, the AIADMK executive interpreted Karunanidhi's admission as confessing to his responsibility for the 'mass killing of Lankan Tamils in 2009'.[8]

On 1 and 5 November, Stalin and Baalu handed copies of the resolutions to UN Deputy Secretary-General Jan Eliasson in New York and Navnethem Pillai, UN High Commissioner for Human Rights in Geneva. Karunanidhi also sent the resolution to the President, prime minister and Sonia Gandhi.

US Resolution for Accountability

On 29 January 2013, Karunanidhi said he desired that India back the US co-sponsored resolution in the UNHRC on *'Promoting reconciliation and accountability in Sri Lanka*, calling Sri Lanka to conduct an 'independent and credible' probe into allegations of human rights violations.[9] On 5 February, TESO passed resolutions asking India to facilitate a resolution in the UNHRC towards a UN referendum for Sri Lankan Tamils to live in dignity and with rights—longhand for Eelam. Asked whether TESO was still in favour of a Tamil Eelam, Karunanidhi said, 'Yes, yes, yes.'[10] On 8 February, Karunanidhi and Stalin participated in a black flag demonstration against Sri Lankan President Mahinda Rajapaksa's visit to Delhi.

On 19 February, *The Hindu* published new photographs of Prabhakaran's twelve-year-old son Balachandran, believed to have been shot dead in cold blood—from Callum Macrae's documentary *No War Zone: The Killing Fields of Sri Lanka*. In an op-ed, Macrae hoped for the 'new evidence' to spur India to support the US co-sponsored resolution.[11]* On 21 February, Jayalalithaa said the boy's death brought memories of 'genocidal killings of Jews under Hitler's rule in Germany' and Karunanidhi posed, 'The Tamils of Tamil Nadu wondered if the Indian government should still support the barbaric Sinhala regime.'[12] On 5 March, after a TESO picketing was foiled, Karunanidhi called for a shutdown on 12 March to press the Centre to back the US co-sponsored resolution. On 7 March, at a TESO conference in Delhi, Stalin called for 'a credible, independent, international inquiry' and added, 'A lasting political solution lies in a referendum.'[13] On 9 March, Karunanidhi asked India to pilot a resolution for a referendum for the Lankan Tamils' 'protection'.[14]

Against an uptick in emotions in the state, on 15 March, Karunanidhi indicated that it would be 'meaningless' for the DMK to continue in the ministry if India failed to move the DMK amendments, declaring that 'genocide and war crimes' were committed, and rooting for a time-bound independent,

---

* Between 2012 and 2014, the US-backed resolutions in the UNHRC were aimed at some accountability. Thereafter, the resolutions were intended to maintain US influence.

international investigation to ensure perpetrators were punished at the International Court of Justice.

That day, External Affairs Minister Salman Khursheed told the Rajya Sabha that India was 'absolutely committed to . . . ensure that there must be accountability' and do what it did the previous year and likely support the procedural resolution, a follow-up of the previous year's resolution. Khursheed concurred with an AIADMK member that the investigation must be 'impartial, transparent and independent'. Yet, it was clear that India would not push for an 'independent' inquiry, which meant an international inquiry. The following day, in his letter to the prime minister and Sonia Gandhi, Karunanidhi said he was writing 'with immense mental agony and a feeling of having been let down by the Government of India', indicating it would become 'meaningless' for the DMK to continue in the ministry if India failed to move the DMK-suggested amendments. On 17 March, Karunanidhi reiterated his demand.

DMK Quits UPA

On 18 March at 5.30 p.m., Defence Minister A.K. Antony, Finance Minister Chidambaram and Health Minister Ghulam Nabi Azad flew down to meet Karunanidhi, who held fast to his demands and added a fresh one that Parliament adopt a resolution incorporating the two amendments and the parliamentary resolution be fused with the US co-sponsored resolution. As Azad objected to the additional demand, 'sparks flew' as Karunanidhi, in a long-delayed reaction, vented out to the trio that on 27 April 2009, Pranab Mukherjee and Chidambaram misled him by saying that hostilities had ceased, urging that he give up his fast.

Still, Karunanidhi told the press that the trio had assured him his requests would be met. This was not to be. On 19 March, at the end of his tether, Karunanidhi announced the DMK's withdrawal from the cabinet, charging the Centre with 'watering down' the

US co-sponsored resolution and disregarding the DMK-suggested amendments. 'When a situation has been created that will not benefit Eelam Tamils, it will be a big harm to the Tamil nation for DMK to continue in government,' he reasoned. Karunanidhi said he felt that the UN and India had both 'betrayed' the Sri Lankan Tamils, and the Centre had let him down badly, but rejected the suggestion that the party should have quit in 2009 as 'perverse'. When asked about talks of India's military assistance to Sri Lanka even before 2009, Karunanidhi said 'if this were true', it would be among the issues to be investigated in the future. Chidambaram said he did not know what happened 'between last night and this morning' and described it as a 'canard' that India was behind the watered-down US resolution.[15] Even as DMK members celebrated in the open, Jayalalithaa called Karunanidhi's decision a 'deceitful drama'.

That day, in a rare show of unity with her arch-rival Karunanidhi, Jayalalithaa, in a letter to the prime minister, demanded that the government take 'historic' and 'courageous' steps to move amendments to the US-backed resolution as well as an independent resolution to strengthen it.

Prior to the vote on 21 March, India had pushed for seven written amendments in six paragraphs, calling for an independent and credible investigation but falling short of calls for an international inquiry as Karunanidhi and Jayalalithaa had demanded and failing to term the violations 'genocide'. But even this was too late, and the sponsors pleaded that the resolution would be 'broadest-possible' and a consensus had already been reached. In the end, India read out a statement.[16] Karunanidhi called the resolution adopted 'misshapen' and 'useless'.[17] Tamil Nadu's demands for an impartial inquiry would not matter in the following years. The international pressure on Sri Lanka would ease even as the US and other Western nations would settle for a domestic inquiry.

But there were small symbolic concessions that the Centre accorded Tamil Nadu. On 25 March, the DMK executive called

India to boycott the Commonwealth Heads of Government Meeting (CHOGM) scheduled for 15–17 November in Colombo and to table a resolution against Sri Lanka before the UNHRC. The next day, Jayalalithaa wrote to the prime minister along similar lines and said she would not permit Sri Lankan cricketers to play in the Indian Premier League (IPL) matches in Tamil Nadu.[18] The next day, she moved a resolution in the assembly that asked India to stop calling Sri Lanka a 'friendly nation', call for an independent international inquiry, impose an economic embargo and move a UN resolution for a referendum on Eelam.[19]

On 16 July, in a resolution, TESO insisted that India boycott the CHOGM.[20] On 24 October, Jayalalithaa moved an assembly resolution asking India to 'completely' boycott the November CHOGM meet and take steps to 'suspend' Sri Lanka until it took steps to ensure equality for Tamils and, in a follow-up resolution on 12 November, expressed 'deep anguish' at India's decision to send its external affairs minister to the meeting. It said India's support for Sri Lanka's President to head CHOGM for the next two years would bring it 'perpetual infamy'.[21] Manmohan Singh skipped CHOGM, but Salman Khursheed was present. Canadian Prime Minister Stephen Harper also stayed away, citing 'the absence of accountability' for human rights violations.[22]

'I Would Propose Only Stalin'

Earlier, on 3 January 2014, Karunanidhi, while welcoming Dalit youth from the PMK into the DMK, said to them that after him, 'the answer is Stalin, who is seated here'.[23] Still, there was pushback from an expected quarter. On 4 January, in response to posters by Alagiri supporters announcing a parallel general council, the DMK high command disbanded the Madurai urban district unit and appointed new office-bearers temporarily. They were all Stalin's supporters. The following day, in an interview with *Puthia Thalaimurai TV*,

Alagiri made it clear that he would not accept anyone except his father as his leader, even if his father were to ask him to do so. He claimed decisions were taken without his knowledge and that he only learnt about the DMK's decision to quit the UPA through the media. Pouring cold water on the party's anxiety to ally with Vijayakanth, Alagiri said the actor lacked political etiquette, and he never considered him a political leader.[24] Elsewhere, Vijayakanth told the DMDK general council that day that he joined the AIADMK alliance in 2011 because of Alagiri's disparaging remarks against him.[25]

The next day, Stalin snubbed his elder brother at Tiruchi, retorting that he doesn't read such 'unnecessary news items'.[26] On 6 January, Karunanidhi chided the 'mischief makers' for misreporting that he had identified Stalin as his political heir and pointed out that he did not mention that in his aftermath, Stalin would succeed him as the DMK president. The general council chose the leader, but if he were allowed to propose, he would 'propose only Stalin's name. The general secretary had already proposed Stalin's name, and I am just seconding his proposal,' he said, adding that the 'general council does not meet on one's whims and fancies'.[27] Alagiri shot back, citing Karunanidhi's refrain, 'The DMK is not a mutt where it picks its successor.'[28]

On 7 January, Karunanidhi called Alagiri's 5 January interview remarks 'not only regrettable but also condemnable' and said it was up to the 'authorized high command' to decide on alliances. He warned of disciplinary action and even expulsion for those who spoke out of turn.[29] But Vijayakanth was only symptomatic of the siblings' rivalry.

On 23 January, the leadership took the first step against Alagiri when it suspended five more of his supporters in response to the opening of a police case on a complaint from an Alagiri supporter against the party's Madurai rural district secretary, a Stalin supporter, under the Scheduled Castes and Scheduled Tribes (Prevention of Atrocities) Act.

The following day, Alagiri charged into Karunanidhi's bedroom with his elder daughter Kayalvizhi and her husband and reportedly took him to task.[30] That day, Anbazhagan issued a brief statement suspending Alagiri for criticizing the party's plans for an electoral alliance with 'certain parties' and for foisting cases against party cadres (read Stalin's men).[31] Karunanidhi amplified that the suspension would not affect the party as the south zone secretary post 'was created for Alagiri.' Desperate for a tie-up with the DMDK, the leadership had straightened Alagiri for being out of line. But the actor was not going to oblige the DMK.

'Will anyone beat his or her father?' Alagiri retorted about rumours that he had behaved rudely with his father on 24 January, alleged his suspension was planned and that he had taken up the suspension of five more of his supporters and the irregularities in the party polls with Karunanidhi that day. 'But I did not get a proper reply. I have now been suspended. Democracy is dead in the DMK,' he said.[32]

But that proved the last straw, as Karunanidhi would reveal four days later when he said that Alagiri's words that day 'broke his heart'. 'You may have listened to his interview on a news channel. He has nurtured an inexplicable hatred for Mr Stalin. On 24 January, he entered my bedroom . . . and told me that Stalin would die in three or four months,' Karunanidhi added.[33] But this was not the last of Alagiri. Ironically, he would support a Vijayakanth-led third front in the 2014 parliamentary TV polls.

Vijayakanth Charts His Course

On 6 March, Vijayakanth revealed that he had begun talks with the BJP. Earlier, on the BJP's request, Gandhiya Makkal Iyakkam's Tamilaruvi Manian had gone back and forth with the DMDK, MDMK and PMK to stitch the National Democratic Alliance. His efforts had paid off, and Vijayakanth chose to head the third front.

On 14 March, Alagiri met BJP president Rajnath Singh in Delhi and offered to support the NDA. On 23 March, Vaiko met Alagiri in Madurai and claimed he had sought Alagiri's support for their front. Later, Alagiri, commenting on Karunanidhi's upcoming visit to Madurai on 13 April, said his dad might see him then and if he did, he said 'he [Karunanidhi] may even be sidelined from the party.'[34]

This proved the last straw. On 25 March, Anbazhagan expelled Alagiri. An undaunted Alagiri said he would not be intimidated by 'such threats by some self-appointed leaders in the party', accused Karunanidhi of being 'partial' to Stalin and said he would always be part of the DMK as 'Anna Arivalayam was built with my hard work, too.'[35]

'Lady or Modi?'

On 24 February, her birthday, Jayalalithaa announced candidates for all forty parliamentary seats, including Puducherry, indicating that the AIADMK would withdraw in places to be allocated to the communists. The AIADMK had participated in the two meetings of the Left-mooted eleven-member 'Third Front' at the national level earlier.[36] However, closer to the polls, Jayalalithaa, banking on a hung Parliament and wishing to maximize her chances of playing kingmaker, chose to go it alone. So, on 4 March, she dispatched a few ministers to the CPM to tell them they would part as friends.[37]

On 25 February, Jayalalithaa appealed for votes for the AIADMK to 'take India forward'. The AIADMK manifesto promised to scale up her popular welfare schemes nationally, eradicate poverty, create ten crore jobs in five years and reiterated its resolve to move the UN to hold a referendum on Eelam. Among other promises were the increase of the income tax ceiling up to Rs 5 lakh, including Scheduled Caste converts to other faiths in the list of Scheduled

Castes and 33 per cent reservation for women in legislative assemblies and Parliament.[38]

In contrast, the DMK's manifesto said the party would urge the Centre to take steps for conducting a UN-supervised 'referendum' for the Sri Lankan Tamils for a permanent political solution but without naming Eelam. In a first in a decade, the manifesto did not promise any freebies.

Instead, it promised a waiver of education loans, opposed foreign direct investment in retail, raising income tax exemption to Rs 6 lakh for men and Rs 7.20 lakh for women and appointing a million women as people's welfare workers and a million youth as road workers for maintaining the 13,000 km Golden Quadrilateral roads.[39]

Stalin, who led the DMK campaign, undertook a punishing thirty-nine-day campaign tour. Lacing his speech with facts and humour, Stalin made fun of Jayalalithaa hopscotching in and out of a helicopter, mimicked the police security radio chat about Jayalalithaa's arrival and take-off: 'Over. She has gone up. Over. The helicopter has started flying. Over,' and then asked his audience to 'say "over" to Jayalalithaa's rule', leaving the crowd in splits. He said hers was 'a government of mere announcements' and 'empty promises'.[40]

On 18 April 2016, speaking in Karur, Stalin took on Senthilbalaji, whose 'influence' he said kept him undisturbed through fifteen reshuffles in the Jayalalithaa cabinet. He claimed Senthilbalaji was even considered for the chief ministership when Jayalalithaa was in jail. 'Senthilbalaji and his brother control Karur district through corruption, land-grabbing and looting. Everyone knows about him.'[41] Stalin could have hardly guessed that in seven years' time, Senthilbalaji would be part of his cabinet and he would be his biggest defender even after the Enforcement Directorate arrested him.

Jayalalithaa undertook a gruelling fifty-one-day campaign. She said the Congress (I)'s 'taraka mantra is corruption everywhere and in everything', citing the 2G, Coalgate, Westland Helicopter, Rolls Royce Hawk Aircraft and Commonwealth Games scams and adding that when a government at the Centre was formed with AIADMK's help, then 'India will dazzle and Tamil Nadu twinkle'. Jayalalithaa did not take on the BJP or its prime ministerial candidate, Modi until the end when she laid out data to show Tamil Nadu was ahead of Gujarat and posed who was better, *'Gujarat's Modiyaa or Tamil Nadu's intha ladyaa?'* (Gujarat's Modi or this lady?) to lusty cheers.[42]

Jayalalithaa and Narendra Modi

Photo courtesy: AP file photo

The AIADMK polled 44.92 per cent of the votes and won thirty-seven of the forty seats in its best-ever parliamentary performance. The DMK polled 23.60 per cent. The third front won an impressive 19 per cent votes, 75 lakh votes and the BJP and the PMK a seat each. However, caste and faith helped those two wins. The Puducherry seat was won by the BJP-allied All India N. Rangasamy Congress (AINRC), which had broken away from the Congress (I) in 2011.

Tamil Nadu had decisively chosen Jayalalithaa over Modi. But Modi had arrived nationally, winning a thumping majority for the BJP.

2014 PARLIAMENTARY ELECTION

Party	Contested	Won	Votes	Percentage
DMK	34	0	95,75,850	23.60%
VCK	2	0	6,06,110	1.50%
MANIDHANEYA MAKKAL KATCHI (MNMK)	1	0	2,36,679	0.60%
IUML	1	0	2,05,896	0.50%
PT	1	0	2,62,812	0.60%
AIADMK	39	37	1,79,83,168	44.92%
INC	39	0	17,51,123	4.30%
BJP	7	1	22,22,090	5.50%
PMK	8	1	18,04,812	4.40%
MDMK	7	0	14,17,535	3.50%
DMDK	14	0	20,79,392	5.10%

Rajiv Gandhi Convicts' Release

On 18 February 2014, the Supreme Court commuted the death sentences of three of the seven convicts in the Rajiv Gandhi assassination to life, citing inordinate delays in deciding their mercy pleas and adding that the state could exercise its remission power to release the convicts. The following day, Jayalalithaa declared that her government would seek the Centre to give its views 'within three days', after which she said she would set them free. Under the Criminal Procedure Code, the state had to 'consult' the Centre. Jayalalithaa's decision was seen as a political 'masterstroke' pleasing Tamil nationalist sentiments.[43] However, the next day, acting on the Centre's petition, the Supreme Court stayed the decision.[44]

On 2 December 2015, the Supreme Court clarified that the term 'consultation' with the Centre implied 'concurrence', making it clear that the release was in the Centre's gift. The Dravidian parties, the PMK and the Tamil nationalist Naam Thamizhar Katchi were for the release on humanitarian grounds even as the Congress (I) vehemently opposed it. Ironically, although Jayalalithaa had set the ball rolling, the seven would walk free under a DMK government in 2022 after the Supreme Court decisively intervened again on humanitarian grounds. On 11 November 2022, thanks to the apex court, Perarivalan walked free after thirty-one years in prison. The chief minister hugging Perarivalan that day evoked mixed reactions, however. That day, the Supreme Court directed the release of the six remaining convicts. On 28 November 2022, they all walked free.[45]

Against a New Dam on Mullaiperiyar

Jayalalithaa fiercely opposed Kerala's efforts to build a new dam on the Mullaiperiyar. Kerala, the upper riparian state, contended the existing dam was unsafe, and water storage beyond 138 feet would lead to the dam bursting at its seams. On 8 May 2014, the Supreme Court reaffirmed its 27 February 2006 decision, finding for Tamil Nadu and allowing the state to raise the water level to 142 feet.[46] On 17 February 2022, Kerala asked for a review of the 2014 verdict, renewing its plea to build a new dam. Tamil Nadu contends that the dam would hurt farmers heavily dependent on the Mullaiperiyar waters.[47]

Jayalalithaa Convicted and Jailed

If Jayalalithaa was disappointed that her hopes of a central role in Delhi were dashed, there was more bad news in the offing. On 27 September 2014, Special Judge John Michael D'Cunha, in his 1136-page order in Bengaluru, found Jayalalithaa guilty in the 'disproportionate wealth' case, sentencing her to four years' simple imprisonment under the Prevention of Corruption Act and a fine of Rs 100 crore. Jayalalithaa stood disqualified as an MLA and, under the law, was barred from contesting elections for another ten years.

Sasikala, Ilavarasi and Sudhakaran got a sentence of four years and a fine of Rs 10 crore each under the Indian Penal Code. 'Heady mix of power and wealth is the bottom line of this case,' the judge observed. Jayalalithaa had claimed it was a 'witch-hunt' by her opponents and sought a lenient sentence due to her diabetes and hypertension. Jayalalithaa and the three others appealed the verdict.

The case had taken eighteen years to reach a conclusion. Anbazhagan, who had impleaded himself in the case and requested that it be tried outside Tamil Nadu, expressed happiness, and Stalin said that 'truth has triumphed'. The original complainant, Subramanian Swamy, said: 'She was corrupt' and added that it gave him great pride that a 'sessions court judge stood up to all this and gave a correct judgement'.[48]

On 27 September, Jayalalithaa stepped down, and two days later, O. Panneerselvam was sworn in as chief minister. Jayalalithaa, Sasikala, Ilavarasi and Sudhakaran were lodged in the Parappana Agrahara prison, about 20 km from Bengaluru. Newspaper reports suggested that 150 had died of shock unable to bear the development; forty of those had taken their lives.[49] On 17 October, the Supreme Court granted bail to the four accused. Jayalalithaa's counsel had pleaded on health grounds, and Subramanian Swamy did not object.[50] Jayalalithaa largely stayed indoors for seven months until she won the appeal.

Jayalalithaa Acquitted

On 11 May 2015, Justice Kumaraswamy, in his 919-page order, said that his calculations showed that the disproportionate assets were only 8.12 per cent and citing the Supreme Court's ruling in the Krishnanand Agnihotri case said that when the difference was less than 10 per cent, the accused could be acquitted.[51] On 23 June, the state of Karnataka appealed.

Jayalalithaa was sworn in on 23 May as chief minister and was elected from the R.K. Nagar constituency in a by-poll on 27 June.

The DMK did not field a candidate. Karunanidhi reasoned that the election would have been a mockery of democracy and as the assembly elections were within a year.[52]

The stage was thus set for the elections. On 20 July, Karunanidhi, in a volte-face on his liquor policy, held out the promise of total prohibition if the DMK was voted to power. 'Drinking has affected even women and children,' Karunanidhi rued.[53] The senior Ramadoss said the announcement 'sounded like an appeal for clemency to me', asking Karunanidhi to shut down the distilleries of the DMK men instead if he was sincere about his promise.[54]

On 17 October, in a first, Stalin refuted the charge that the DMK was anti-Hindu, alleged that it was a well-planned campaign to project the party as anti-Hindu, that 90 per cent of the family members of party leaders and cadres were Hindu and that the DMK did not 'stand in the way of those who have faith'.[55]

Namakku Naame

While Karunanidhi relied on prohibition to deliver the DMK, his son's son-in-law, V. Sabareesan, was turning to political consultants to deliver his father-in-law. *The Hindu,* as early as 8 September 2014 identified the son-in-law thus: 'Sabareesan has Mr Stalin's ears and holds sway over his decision-making. A typical backroom boy, he follows Mr Stalin like a shadow, pulls the strings and is in touch with bigwigs, much to the consternation of partymen.'[56] Thanks to Sabareesan and the consultants, Stalin launched a mass contact programme where he undertook an 1100-km tour for five months, covering the 234 assembly constituencies of the state. Karunanidhi came up with the name *Namakku Naame* (We for us) for the tour that began in Kanniyakumari on 20 September.

The 63-year-old Stalin tried to buck his white shirt-veshti image and sport a younger look. There were 1.38 crore young voters in the 18–29 age group, constituting 23 per cent of the 5.82 crore electorate. With coloured shirts and sleeves rolled up, trousers and Puma sports shoes, Stalin's mass contact programme saw him walk, smile, press the flesh, pose for selfies, drink tea at roadside shops, ride a scooter, drive an autorickshaw and plough fields. A social media connect campaign was also launched.[57] Karunanidhi took to Twitter to greet his son as *Thalapathi* at the conclusion of the tour on 12 February 2016 at T. Nagar.[58]

Two days earlier, speaking at a wedding, Jayalalithaa, as is her wont, narrated a short story of a father-son duo where the father, at his son's request, teaches the son that politics is a dangerous art where there is no room for sentiments. One should strive to learn on one's own, the father said. Yet, as the son was insistent, the father asked him to climb up a ladder to the loft, where the papers of his 'political shenanigans' were kept and from which the son could take his lessons. However, as the son neared the loft, the father took his hands off the ladder causing the son's fall. The father told the son: 'If you were to learn everything, then would anyone respect me any more?' The son concluded that it was his first lesson and that he would have to fend for himself and could not count on his dad. Jayalalithaa alluded to Stalin's *Namakku Naame* as his theatrics to climb the political ladder on his own, as his father would not help him.[59]

Vijayakanth Wishes to Be 'King'

On 5 October, the Makkal Nala Koottiyakkam (People's Welfare Front or PWF), floated jointly by the MDMK, CPI, CPM and VCK, came into being with Vaiko as its convenor.[60] On 23 December, even as Karunanidhi publicly invited Vijayakanth to ally with the DMK, the PWF met Vijayakanth and offered to project him as their chief ministerial face.

On 25 February 2016, eight of the twenty-nine DMDK legislators formally joined the AIADMK and Vijayakanth lost his position as the Leader of the Opposition.

Karunanidhi, meanwhile, reiterated his calls to Vijayakanth. But the actor kept hedging his bets. Vijayakanth's grand illusion of himself was given vent when, on 20 February, at Kanchipuram, the actor asked his audience if he should be king or kingmaker and received the response 'king'.

On 9 March, a hopeful Karunanidhi said, 'The fruit is ripening. It is yet to be decided when it will fall into the milk,' on Vijayakanth tying up with the DMK. However, the following day, Vijayakanth said he would go it alone. On 21 March, an unyielding Karunanidhi said he had still not lost hope.

On 23 March, Vijayakanth threw in his lot with the PWF. The actor reasoned that the PWF had said that he would be king and they the kingmakers, and he 'immediately signed the seat-sharing agreement' and agreed to a coalition government. Vijayakanth was unhappy with how the DMK 'spun' the negotiations, painting him as ambitious and demanding the deputy chief ministership and a high share of seats later in the local body elections. Once AIADMK-bitten Vijayakanth was now twice shy of the DMK, unsure that it would be any different. [61]

Vijayakanth's decision had made it easier for Jayalalithaa who was aiming to spread her wings and soar high. On 4 April, Jayalalithaa announced candidates for 227 of the 234 seats, leaving six to seven minor allies and named candidates for all the thirty Puducherry seats and seven Kerala assembly seats. The DMK gave forty-one seats to Congress (I), five to IUML, four to the MNMK, four to PT, and three to the breakaway DMDK.

The DMK manifesto promised prohibition, waiver of education loans, tablets or laptops with an Internet connection, a 10 GB per month download option for 16 lakh students and smartphones for poor families.[62] The AIADMK manifesto promised 100 units of power every two months free (to 78 lakh households); farm and education loan waivers; free laptops for Standard X and XII students; Amma banking cards to avail government services; 50 per cent subsidy on scooters for women and free mobile phones for all ration card holders. Jayalalithaa more credibly promised phased prohibition and sought votes on her performance. The 2011–16 term was a quieter one, with many of the welfare schemes reaching the rural women and the lower rungs of society.

On 8 May, in an interview with *Sun News*, Stalin said: 'Neither will my son nor will my son-in-law join politics. For that matter, I can assure that no one from my family will join politics.'[63] On 12 May, Karunanidhi told NDTV he would be the chief minister if his party won the 16 May assembly election, and Stalin had to wait 'till nature does something to me' and incredibly claimed: 'Stalin himself doesn't want to become Chief Minister. He wants DMK President (Karunanidhi) to become Chief Minister.'[64] If Stalin was disappointed, he did not show it. The DMK now tried to argue that it would get experience and youth by choosing the father-son duo to govern. Non-committed voters probably saw only Karunanidhi's infirmity.

Social media and technology were aggressively used to connect with voters, and full-page advertisements were taken out on the day before the elections by the DMK and others. But, the Kazhagams were taking no chances. Money poured into the constituencies from both sides, and ingenious ways were crafted to get money to voters without attracting the notice of the Election Commission or the opponent. As D. Ravikumar of the VCK said: 'I was confident. Just a day before the election date, everything changed. Money was raining. Money defeated us.' His leader Thirumavalavan lamented that it was 'near-total bribery' later. *Frontline* said that except for the six seats in Kanniyakumari district, all the 228 constituencies saw organized cash distribution. The cash-for-vote formula was imported from Karnataka's 2007 experience, according to the magazine and then in 2009, Tirumangalam saw its crude power.[65]

2016 ASSEMBLY ELECTION

Party	Contested	Won	Votes	Percentage
AIADMK + IND 7	234	136	1,78,06,490	40.88%
DMK + IND 3	180	89	1,36,70,511	31.39%
INC	41	8	27,74,075	6.42%
IUML	5	1	3,13,808	0.73%
MNMK	4	0	1,97,150	0.46%
PT	4	0	2,19,830	0.51%
DMDK	104	0	10,34,384	2.39%
MDMK	29	0	3,73,606	0.86%
CPI	25	0	3,40,290	0.79%
CPM	25	0	3,07,303	0.71%
TMC	26	0	2,30,711	0.53%
VCK	25	0	3,31,849	0.77%
PMK	232	0	23,00,558	5.32%
NAAM THAMIZHAR KATCHI (NTK)	231	0	4,58,007	1.06%

In the six-corner contest, the AIADMK won 131 of the 227 seats it contested and three of its minor allies won a seat each. In 2011, the AIADMK fought in the company of the DMDK, the communists and the Puthiya Thamizhagam. Its calculated risk in the security of Vijayakanth not joining forces with the DMK had paid off. Jayalalithaa's return broke the trend of the Kazhagam's alternating in office since 1989.

The arithmetically stronger DMK–Congress (I) alliance won ninety-eight seats and the DMK eighty-nine, the largest in its Opposition history. The Congress (I) won eight and the IUML one. The smaller allies came a cropper. The PMK spoiled the DMK's chances in at least thirty constituencies, and the party lost twenty-one seats by a margin of 3000 votes.

But the elections dealt a crushing blow to Vijayakanth's ambition to be king. The actor himself faced a disastrous rout in Ulundurpet, losing to the AIADMK and his deposit. Voters seemed aghast at Vijayakanth's lack of poise as he spat at reporters and often raised his hand at his own cadres. Vaiko, for his part, was no man of equanimity either. His caste-laced remarks on Karunanidhi showed his frustration and the levels to which he could stoop.[66]

On 23 May, Jayalalithaa was sworn in as chief minister for a sixth time. Within the first thirty minutes, she had signed off on shutting down 500 Tamil Nadu State Marketing Corporation (TASMAC) shops, moved up the opening hours of TASMAC stores to noon from 10 a.m., 100 units of free power, waiver of crop loans, one sovereign gold for nuptial chains or thali, free power to looms and free breakfast for students in government schools. However, the free breakfast awaited implementation until 15 September 2022 by her DMK successor, Stalin.[67]

50th Year as DMK President

On 27 July 2018, Karunanidhi became the first leader to enter the fiftieth year as party president. In ten days, the DMK patriarch would breathe his last.

29

The Titans Are Gone

Karunanidhi Fades Away

Earlier, on 25 October 2016, Karunanidhi fell ill due to a drug-related allergy. On 16 December, the nonagenarian underwent a tracheostomy to improve his breathing. From then on, the DMK leader, who had mesmerized Tamil audiences for eight decades, could not speak or write like before. As Karunanidhi had said more than once, only nature could have forced his hand, and finally, it had. Like an old general, Karunanidhi was beginning to fade away, and for once, the five-decade president of the DMK had truly become a figurehead.

Power and authority had been slipping from Karunanidhi's hands since the 2001 elections, even as the ageing leader fought to stay relevant. He could have graciously left on a high note while he was still chief minister in 2011. Karunanidhi reportedly told Duraimurugan that if he retired, he would fade into oblivion, and even Duraimurugan would not care to visit him. Tamil politics has yet to see a Lee Kwan Yew.

On 4 January 2017, Stalin was elected working president at the general council, which witnessed some tender moments. An emotional Duraimurugan invoked Anna's 1956 invitation to Nedunchezhian as he beckoned Stalin to lead them: 'Anna said *Thambi vaa. Thalaimai thaanga vaa.* [Younger brother come forward to lead].' I borrow his words.' A visibly moved Stalin said he considered the position as a 'responsibility'.[1]

Jayalalithaa No More

Earlier on 4 December 2016, Jayalalithaa suffered a cardiac arrest, and her end appeared near. She was brought in an unconscious state to Apollo Hospital for 'fever and dehydration' on 22 September and on 30 September, Dr Richard Beale, an intensivist from the United Kingdom, was flown in. Karunanidhi urged that a photograph of the chief minister at the hospital be released, but the AIADMK shot it down.[2]

On 5 December 2016, Jayalalithaa was announced dead, and two hours later, around 11.30 p.m., Panneerselvam was sworn in as chief minister in a stopgap arrangement. The BJP was believed to have weighed in on the status quo. This time, however, Panneerselvam did not see himself as an interim arrangement. Ironically, Panneerselvam belonged to the same Kallar community as his finders Sasikala and Dhinakaran. But fifteen years is a long time, and Panneerselvam had gotten bold enough to challenge his handlers.

Panneerselvam could not be faulted for thinking that he could be chief minister. The bell had tolled on the era of mass leadership with Jayalalithaa's departure and an unwell Karunanidhi. A late entrant into public life, Jayalalithaa struck it alone in her mentor's absence and eventually succeeded in her quest to walk out of MGR's shadow.

Overwhelmed by MGR's widow, her cohorts and Karunanidhi in MGR's aftermath, Jayalalithaa surprised many with her stomach for politics. The penny had dropped instantly for her. Her principal foe was Karunanidhi, and she outdid her mentor in opposing him. Karunanidhi simply ignored her, letting the DMK's second-rung leadership engage her. But after the 1989 elections, he did not have

Edappadi K. Palaniswami and O. Panneerselvam

this luxury. She was indeed the legatee to the MGR mantle. Not bound by friendship or shared experiences, it became a no-holds-barred game between the two—each outdoing the other in coarse language and obscene comparisons in the mutual denigration game.

Imperious, impetuous and impertinent, Jayalalithaa became a cult for her party men and women. To many others, she remained an enigma with a streak of self-destructiveness and her inexplicable sibling affection for Sasikala. Yet, the desire for self-preservation saw her repair and rebound.

She was unlike any other leader. Leaders, including prime ministers, visited her at her residence. Except for her campaigning during elections, she was almost an armchair politician. Even her mentor did not have this luxury. She had such goodwill with the cadres that she could hibernate. Her aura and stature were such that she could conduct politics by sitting in her Poes Garden residence and issuing statements almost daily. These were aimed at Karunanidhi, his administration, his family and politics.

In contrast, Karunanidhi had to engage party men on a constant basis. Not a day passed without the DMK leader tending to party affairs at the party office, writing at the *Murasoli* office, touring the state, addressing a public event or meeting press persons. Karunanidhi was ever active till his illness made it impossible.

Karunanidhi responded to almost every one of Jayalalithaa's statements. If he was reinforcing her political standing, he also did it for himself. Ironically, the two depended on the other to be relevant.

Jayalalithaa did not have to engage in outreach constantly or meet party men daily as Karunanidhi did. Consequently, when Jayalalithaa visited her party office, she made news.

It was during the elections that she met the masses and turned on her charm. Unlike Karunanidhi, she had no Stalin or even Anbazhagan to give her a hand. She carried the burden of the AIADMK campaign singly but on her terms. She offered no seat on the dais for even alliance candidates who stood with folded hands until she finished reading from her political hymn sheet. She was the centre of gravity of the anti-DMK-Karunanidhi forces.

Women adored her with her warts and all. Flocking in droves to get a glimpse of her, they soon began to lend their ears to her. She was initially their leader's sweetheart. But she quickly came to embody women's power and mojo in an all-male political space. Seeing powerful men prostrate before Jayalalithaa may have sent a shiver of delight in these women, even as non-Tamils were nonplussed and even Tamils wondered about the decorum of it all. Jayalalithaa

famously dismissed it as 'Indian tradition and culture' and argued
that MLAs and MPs prostrated before Karunanidhi, but the media
chose not to notice it. She claimed that anything to do with her was
blown up, and the prostration had stopped after she issued public
statements.[3] It never stopped.

The abject subservience of her ministers and party men showed
she was the queen bee. Even MGR had not commanded such
authority. But 'Amma' was a czarina. She could have used this
unprecedented authority to bulldoze change and better people's lives.
Instead, her first term was notorious for the graft and ostentation
and the Sasikala family's power. She fell precipitously in 1996. Many
wrote her off politically. The next years proved excruciating for her
with the barrage of legal cases and the relentless prosecution. She
had wanted out, but amnesty was not the strong suit of her political
foe. To be fair to Karunanidhi, public opinion limited his options
and amnesty for criminal cases for a politician in India would have
been unprecedented.

Despite Jayalalithaa's excesses and the inexplicable bonds to
the Sasikala family, the Tamil populace proved indulgent towards
her. Was it because she was a woman or because she was the only
alternative to Karunanidhi? Or was it because her prosecutor had
once been accused of corruption himself, or is public memory short-
lived? Or is it that the expectations of probity in public life have
greatly diminished over the years?

Chastened somewhat, she stitched a formidable alliance with
her erstwhile critics and the politically untouchable BJP to stage
a remarkable comeback in 1998. With the largest number of MPs
after the BJP, she held the reins of the NDA, but again, her decisions
bordered on the irrational to the bizarre.

Her vicious attacks on Sonia Gandhi fall into this genre. How
does one explain them? Although she claimed she had nothing
personal against Sonia Gandhi, it is likely that she felt that Sonia
Gandhi had everything given to her on a platter while hers was

a path of humiliation and indignities. After the failed alliance in 1999 with the Congress (I), her repeated diatribes on Sonia Gandhi upended any cooperation with the party, even indirectly after 2001. On 11 November 2010, as the DMK found itself in the thick of the 2G issue, she asked Sonia Gandhi to consider the fact that her political career spanned twenty-eight years and there were bound to be 'ups and downs', asking her to treat bygones as bygones and move forward.

Back to 1999: like in a snake-and-ladders game she had returned to where she had started after a thirteen-month roller-coaster ride with the BJP. Worse still, her enemy, the DMK, was ensconced at the Centre. Although the AIADMK never made it to the Centre after this, she aimed for a national role from this time on.

But isn't all politics local? That year, she reached out to one of her fiercest critics—Moopanar. Having to choose between a BJP-allied DMK and Jayalalithaa, the raison d'être for his Tamil Maanila Congress, Moopanar chose Jayalalithaa, helping her stage a remarkable comeback in 2001.

The second term showed her as politically savvier and a strong leader. Her drive against the LTTE and its patrons, her handling of the government staff strike, Cauvery, Mullaiperiyar, forest brigand Veerappan, the Kanchi pontiff and the tsunami showed her firm hand.

She enjoyed more aura and authority than all her predecessors. Yet, she had to bow out in 2006 to a stronger DMK alliance. But Karunanidhi had paid a high price—he had to give away seats liberally to rope in allies. Consequently, he earned the dubious distinction of heading the only DMK minority government. She harassed him on this score. By 2009, Karunanidhi was beset by other problems, such as the 2G scandal, a more assertive Congress (I) at the Centre, the Eelam IV war, load-shedding, a worsening law and order problem, not to mention his balancing act with his sons.

The DMK's bungling in the law and order and power fronts saw Jayalalithaa return to power a third time in 2011. However, she had to stoop to conquer—reluctantly tying up with Vijayakanth. It was a comedown for both. In months, they were the bitterest of rivals again.

But this was also the term her many welfare schemes were hatched. Freebies such as mixers and grinders, goats and 20 kg of rice monthly rained on the poor. Government and aided school children and colleges received free laptops, while free bicycles were distributed to Plus Two students.

Her welfare schemes were eponymously touted 'Amma'—Amma Canteens to Amma Salt. She was 'Amma' for her party men. 'Amma' was ubiquitous now.

In 2014, her national ambitions were out in the open, and she created history, winning thirty-seven parliamentary seats. Politically, she would come into her own in 2016. No more was she in her mentor's debt. However, she was fighting the Disproportionate Assets case and failing health. Death saved her the indignity of having her fate decided by the Supreme Court. She left on a high note.

Chief Secretary raided

Only two weeks after Jayalalithaa's death, on 21 December, income tax (I-T) officials raided the house of Chief Secretary P. Rama Mohana Rao following the arrest of sand mining baron Shekhar Reddy and two associates after seizing cash worth Rs 133 crore and 135 kg gold from the 8 December raids held in Shekhar Reddy's residence and offices. The chief secretary's office at Fort St George was also part of the raids, with central reserve police personnel posted for security, even as Chief Minister Panneerselvam was at the secretariat. Stalin called the raids a 'disgrace to the state'.[4]

On 27 December 2016, Rama Mohana Rao wondered, 'Where is [the] state government?' and caustically added, 'If madam had been alive, would this happen to Tamil Nadu?'[5] Media reports later indicated a diary seized during the raids allegedly mentioned Panneerselvam and others on the take from Shekhar Reddy.[6]

Panneerselvam, however, denied any links. In March 2017, ED arrested Shekhar Reddy and his two associates for money laundering. Shekhar Reddy would make bail later.[7]

If the raids were inexplicable, so was the 28 September 2020 CBI decision to drop charges for lack of evidence against Shekhar Reddy and five others after dragging them to court for illegal conversion of demonetized currencies, causing a Rs 247.13 crore loss to the government.[8] Stalin termed it as the 'BJP's gift' to the AIADMK and wondered how, after 'perusing 800 documents and investigating 170 witnesses, the CBI was not able to find which bank converted the notes'.[9]

Jallikattu

The Jallikattu protests again tested Panneerselvam's mettle. Jallikattu, or the bull-taming sport, was traditionally held at Alanganallur next to Madurai during the Pongal harvest season in mid-January. In 2011, the Centre included bulls in the list of animals prohibited for training and exhibition. The Animal Welfare Board of India (AWBI) cited the notification to seek a ban on violent sports involving animals, and in May 2014, the Supreme Court banned the sport. In 2016, as the Union Environment Ministry sought to undo the ban by revoking its 2011 order, the Supreme Court clamped again.[10] Thus, with the prospect of another year without Jallikattu, thousands began congregating on 17 January 2017 at the Marina Beach, urging the state and the Centre to repeal the ban. The sport signified Tamil valour and culture, but none had foreseen it to touch the Tamil collective consciousness as it would. The crowds, who were a few thousand, soon swelled to lakhs, making the rest of the country sit up and take notice. The spontaneous protests spread to Alanganallur and other parts of the state.

None had foreseen the organic protest—a watershed moment for Tamil identity and unprecedented in the state's history. Pushed around on the Sri Lankan Tamil issue, Cauvery, Mullaiperiyar and the hydrocarbon issues, Tamils appeared to have had enough, and the pent-up frustrations had broken into a deluge; the feeling of being let down by a political system where Supreme Court decisions were fair to their state on water-sharing were mere trophies and would be hard put to translate into reality—had built up a welter of feelings and anger. The Jallikattu ban was the last straw. The moral force of the protests was such that it could keep out politicians and enlist broad public support.

Panneerselvam was under immense pressure to overturn the ban. On 20 January, the fourth day of the protest, Panneerselvam, after meeting the prime minister the previous day, promulgated an ordinance that received the governor's assent. The protesters had tasted victory. However, some saw the ordinance as a palliative, and the more vocal elements began to move the goalposts to more fundamental issues. Police broke the gathering with excessive force matching the protestors in lawlessness.[11]

Sasikala Comes out of the Closet

In any case, Panneerselvam had managed to tame the bull. But Sasikala, moving surely towards the chief minister's chair, was a different matter. She was chosen as general secretary of the AIADMK on 29 December 2016. Five weeks later, on 5 February 2017, Panneerselvam stepped down after duly proposing Sasikala's name as the AIADMK legislature party leader. However, on the 7th evening, Panneerselvam sat with his eyes closed at the Jayalalithaa memorial for forty minutes, after which he claimed that Sasikala and senior party leaders forced him to resign and that he would withdraw his resignation if party cadres so wished. Panneerselvam also claimed that Jayalalithaa told him to take over as chief minister and that her spirit later told him that he should come out and tell the truth to the people of Tamil Nadu. On 25 November 2019, *Thuglak* editor S. Gurumurthy claimed that he was the one who was behind Panneerselvam's revolt.

Sasikala moved quickly to quell the rebellion. She dismissed Panneerselvam from the post of party treasurer and appointed Dindigul Srinivasan in his place. On 8 February, MLAs owing allegiance to Sasikala were taken to a resort close to Mahabalipuram. That day, Stalin, in a Facebook post, said people had not voted for Sasikala to become chief minister and urged Governor Vidyasagar Rao 'to take a good decision liked by people' and 'considering factors like the imminent Supreme Court verdict in the [disproportionate] assets case and the question of a stable regime'.[12] The next day, Sasikala met the governor to stake her claim to be sworn in as chief minister. The governor, however, would not move.

On 14 February, the Supreme Court convicted Sasikala, Ilavarasi and Sudhakaran in the 21-year-old Disproportionate Assets case for four years each. Sasikala was barred from holding public office or contesting elections for ten years. The case against Jayalalithaa had abated.[13] Should Panneerselvam have waited?

Hours later, Sasikala chose Edappadi K. Palaniswami as the legislature party leader. The revolt within the AIADMK's Mukkulathor leaders would ironically see the Gounders rise within the party, ending the Mukkulathor sway that had begun with Sasikala's ascent. On 15 June 2021, Sasikala accused Palaniswami of turning the AIADMK into a 'one-caste party'.[14]

A four-time legislator from his native Edappadi constituency and a one-time MP, Palaniswami was a propaganda and organization secretary who had called upon Sasikala to become the chief minister and crawled to touch her feet, leading to ad nauseam taunts from Stalin later.[15] Hours before she left for Bengaluru on 15 February to turn herself in, Sasikala revoked the suspension of her nephew T.T.V. Dhinakaran, appointing him as the deputy general secretary. Dhinakaran was to officiate as the general secretary in her absence. The AIADMK was now divided.

On 17 February, the Panneerselvam faction (Puratchithalaivi Amma) expelled Sasikala as general secretary while Sasikala and her nephew Dhinakaran headed the faction known as Amma with Palaniswami as the head of the government. But Sasikala and Dhinakaran had grossly underestimated Palaniswami. Palaniswami soon proved he was his own man, showing an uncanny ability to use his perch to consolidate his position, politically defang Sasikala and Dhinakaran, neutralize Panneerselvam and become the first non-mass-based leader of the AIADMK. Palaniswami stayed the full term and would be known for both the Thoothukudi police killings and his decision to grant horizontal reservation to rural children in medical colleges and for declaring the Cauvery delta as a green zone free of hydrocarbon activity.

Keen on stability, Palaniswami quickly built bridges to the BJP. He supported the BJP's move to revoke Article 370, pass the Citizenship (Amendment) Act (CAA) and batted for the three abortive farm bills and simultaneous elections. In turn, it appeared that the AIADMK's former ministers under the DVAC and CBI radar had the BJP's protective arm around them. In the process, he earned the DMK's snark—that he was a stooge of the BJP. Yet, he was no pushover. He stood his ground in 2021, refusing the BJP's exhortations to take back Dhinakaran and Sasikala. Electorally, however, the BJP would prove a liability with the minorities deserting the AIADMK.

On 19 February 2017, Palaniswami won the confidence vote with 122 votes for and eleven against. Speaker P. Dhanapal had rejected the Panneerselvam faction's demand for a secret ballot and the DMK's demand for a postponement of the vote. Before the vote, the DMK plunged the House into chaos, with its MLAs seen breaking mikes and furniture, throwing papers, standing on tables and heckling the Speaker. Two MLAs separately occupied the Speaker's chair. The marshals forcefully evicted the eighty-eight DMK MLAs and the lone IUML MLA before the vote. Stalin claimed that his shirt was torn. Dhanapal for his part claimed his shirt was torn and he was insulted because he was a Dalit. Congress (I) members had walked out. Stalin called the Palaniswami government Sasikala's 'proxy'.

But Palaniswami was all but that. If the DMK had aimed at the chaos to call for President's rule, the ruse badly failed. Palaniswami slowly but surely began chipping at Sasikala's hold over the party.

On 28 February, the Panneerselvam camp petitioned the President for a probe into the circumstances surrounding Jayalalithaa's death.[16] On 22 March, the Election Commission froze the AIADMK election symbol and barred the use of 'AIADMK' till the final order. The two factions now chose to explore a merger. On 19 April, Panneerselvam made the merger conditional on the ouster of Sasikala and Dhinakaran from the party. That day, the Palaniswami faction held a consultative meeting and decided to 'delink' the party and the government from Sasikala's family.[17] On 25 April, Dhinakaran was arrested by the Delhi Police for allegedly attempting to bribe Election Commission officials for the two leaves symbol for the Amma faction. Dhinakaran made bail on 1 June.[18]

On 10 August, Palaniswami made up for the crawling episode when his faction invalidated Sasikala's appointment of Dhinakaran as deputy general secretary and added that the office bearers appointed by Jayalalithaa would lead the party. On 17 August, the Palaniswami government announced an inquiry commission by retired high court judge Arumugasamy to probe Jayalalithaa's death.* With these moves, on 21 August, the two factions merged. Panneerselvam was named convener and Palaniswami, the co-convener. An eleven-member steering committee was also named. On 16 February 2018,

---

* On 18 October 2022, the commission's report was submitted in the assembly. Oblivious of the AIIMS medical experts' committee's findings, which did not find any wrongdoing, Arumugasamy found fault with V.K. Sasikala and others and suggested further investigation against them.

Panneerselvam said that the prime minister had encouraged him to merge and join the ministry.[19]

The next day, nineteen MLAs owing allegiance to Dhinakaran withdrew support to the Palaniswami government, reducing it to a minority. One of them retracted later. On 18 September, the Speaker disqualified the eighteen MLAs under the anti-defection law.

R.K. Nagar By-Election

On 21 December 2017, Dhinakaran won the R.K. Nagar by-poll as an independent by a margin of more than 40,000 votes, surpassing Jayalalithaa's winning margin by 1162 votes. The AIADMK candidate finished a distant second while the DMK candidate forfeited his deposit. The DMK had engaged in tactical voting to shore up Dhinakaran's chances whom it saw as a Trojan horse that would bring down the Palaniswami government but, in the process, lost its security deposit. On 15 March 2018, Dhinakaran launched the Amma Makkal Munnetra Kazhagam (AMMK) in Melur next to Madurai. On 25 October 2018, the Madras High Court upheld the disqualification of his eighteen MLAs.

Rajinikanth Says 'System Is Corrupt'

There were other false messiahs. On 17 May 2017, Rajinikanth praised Stalin as 'a great administrator', Anbumani Ramadoss as 'a very intelligent person', Thirumavalavan as working 'tirelessly for Dalits' and Seeman as 'a warrior' and observed that 'the system is corrupt. People are fed up. We need to change the system together'.

In a duet in his 1995 film *Muthu*, Rajinikanth had sung that he would decide at the right time if he should enter public life, and in response, his female lead chimed that it sounded like a plan. As we saw earlier, 1995 was a turbulent year for Rajinikanth, leading to his stand against Jayalalithaa, the apogee of his political sway. Yet, he had spurned the suggestions of Moopanar and others to take the lead. Rajinikanth was content simply aiding Moopanar and the DMK's efforts to unseat Jayalalithaa. In 1998, when he instructed his fans to work against PMK's MP candidates, his magic was already gone. Yet unmistakably, the actor remained the most popular after MGR with a cult status, and speculation continued on his political entry.

On 31 December 2017, Rajinikanth ended all speculation when he declared that 'It is now or never' and indicated that his party would be launched in January 2018. Rajinikanth asserted that his party would capture power and 'give honest, transparent, corruption-free, spiritual, secular politics without caste, creed or religion'. He made it clear that he would not be chief minister.[20] Describing his politics as one 'based on spirituality, not on religion or caste', Rajinikanth said, 'The system has to change. Democracy has been corrupted. It needs to be cleansed.'[21]

Rajinikanth with Tamilaruvi Manian: An aborted stab at clean politics

Photo courtesy: R. Senthil Kumar/PTI

On Rajinikanth's invitation, Gandhiya Makkal Iyakkam founder Tamilaruvi Manian became his adviser. For three years, the two met regularly, discussing ways to provide good governance. They had decided to choose a competent candidate in his/her forties to lead their government. However, on 29 December 2020, Rajinikanth backed out, citing his health condition. The announcement came as a huge disappointment to his fans and those who believed in alternative politics.

Makkal Needhi Maiam

Three weeks earlier, on 21 February 2018, unlike Rajinikanth, Kamal Haasan chose to take the plunge, floating his Makkal Needhi Maiam (MNM) in Madurai. The actor said that his fans 'are rising now as they could not tolerate the injustice being done to the people by the past and present governments'.[22] Delhi chief minister and Aam Aadmi Party leader Arvind Kejriwal said, 'Now you can vote for an honest party, for Kamal Haasan,' adding that the DMK and AIADMK were 'corrupt parties'.[23]

Makkal Needhi Maiam founder Kamal Haasan

Photo courtesy: *The New Indian Express*

NEET

Palaniswami had skilfully staved off the internal threat. However, the National Eligibility Entrance Test (NEET) or a single window entrance examination across India for medical courses prescribed by the Medical Council of India (MCI) would become a hot potato.[24] Both the Kazhagams contended that NEET disadvantaged rural and economically underprivileged children and favoured those from the central board (CBSE). In the initial years, other states had sought time to standardize the syllabus. Those who favoured NEET said it promoted meritocracy and curtailed the commercialization of medical education.

Meanwhile, minority institutions like the Christian Medical College of Vellore legally challenged the MCI's authority to control admissions. On 18 July 2013, in a 2-1 split verdict, the Supreme Court said that the MCI and the Dental Council of India had no authority to prescribe all-India medical entrance tests. The court's decision came on 115 petitions challenging the MCI notification on NEET for admission. [25]

On 29 July 2013, Chief Minister Jayalalithaa urged Prime Minister Manmohan Singh to drop the Centre's move to reintroduce NEET.[26] When NEET was finally to be implemented, Jayalalithaa secured exemption in 2016–17 and wanted Tamil Nadu 'not to be forced to implement the NEET even in the future.'

However, on 11 April 2016, the Supreme Court reversed its earlier stand, saying the 2013 verdict was without any discussion within the bench.[27] In February 2017, the Tamil Nadu assembly passed two bills seeking exemption from NEET. However, on 22 August 2017, the Supreme Court ordered Tamil Nadu to introduce NEET.

Anita, a school-topper Dalit girl who could not pass NEET and had waged a campaign against the exam, brought focus to the issue when she committed suicide on 1 September 2017.[28] On 18 September 2017, the President withheld assent to the bills. NEET would not go away, and the issue would fester with more student deaths related to the exam.

Cauvery Management Body

On 16 February 2018, the Supreme Court passed the 465-page Judgment on the Cauvery Water Dispute, modifying the Cauvery Water Disputes Tribunal (CWDT) award of 2007 and reducing Tamil Nadu's share by 14.75 thousand million cubic feet. The verdict was good for another fifteen years. The CWDT had ordered that a Cauvery Management Board (CMB) be set up to implement its 2007 order. On 1 April, Tamil Nadu filed a contempt petition against the Centre for 'wilfully disobeying' the court's order. On 5 April, the DMK and allies called for a state-wide closure. On 6 April, a group of farmers in Tiruchi partially buried themselves in the sand in an effort to draw the Centre's attention. On 7 April, Stalin launched a rally to 'retrieve Cauvery rights' at Mukkombu near Tiruchi, blaming the Palaniswami government for failing to exert enough pressure on the Centre to form the CMB.[29] On 8 April, Rajinikanth warned that the Centre would earn Tamil Nadu's wrath if the CMB were not formed immediately. The AIADMK held a hunger strike on 10 April.[30]

On 1 June, the Centre announced the Cauvery Water Management Authority (CWMA) and the Cauvery Water Regulation Committee (CWRC). But this was not the end of the road for Tamil Nadu, as we saw in August 2023 when Tamil Nadu approached the Supreme Court again for its agreed share of waters. A permanent consensual distress-sharing formula alone can end this endemic dispute.

Sterlite Deaths

On 22 May 2018, thirteen people died in police firing when protestors went on a rampage demanding the closure of Vedanta's Sterlite copper smelting plant in Thoothukudi as it polluted groundwater. Congress (I) president Rahul Gandhi described the police action 'state sponsored terrorism', and Stalin called for the plant's shutdown and Palaniswami to quit. Actors Kamal Haasan and Rajinikanth also faulted the government. On 28 May, the Palaniswami government shut down the plant. The following day, speaking in the assembly, Palaniswami blamed the DMK for the violence and said that the UPA government gave clearances for Sterlite's expansion four times and the DMK government had also given several clearances as well as land for Sterlite's expansion.[31]

DMK President Stalin

On 7 August 2018, Karunanidhi passed away, ending an epoch. A few hours earlier, Stalin had met Palaniswami against the advice of his DMK colleagues, seeking the state government's permission to bury his dad alongside the DMK founder leader Anna in the Madras Marina. He had set aside his honour and met the chief minister, held his hands and pleaded. Palaniswami said the law was against it but agreed to consider the issue only to turn it down ten minutes later.[32] However, the Madras High Court later cleared the legal impediment. Stalin said he would have died if it was not to be.

On 14 August 2018, the DMK executive committee elevated Stalin as president and Duraimurugan as party treasurer. On 28 August, the general council endorsed Stalin as president. Stalin began his acceptance speech with a slightly altered version of his father's customary salutation: *En uyirilum melaana Kalaignarin anbu udanpirappukale* (Beloved brethren of Kalaignar who are dearer to me than my own life). 'I am not Kalaignar, I can't speak like him; no one can; I can't match his mastery over the language. But, I can dare to try,' a humble Stalin admitted. He said Anbazhagan, his 'elder father' had long seen the portents of leadership in him. He said the DMK's four pillars were rationalism, self-respect, social justice and

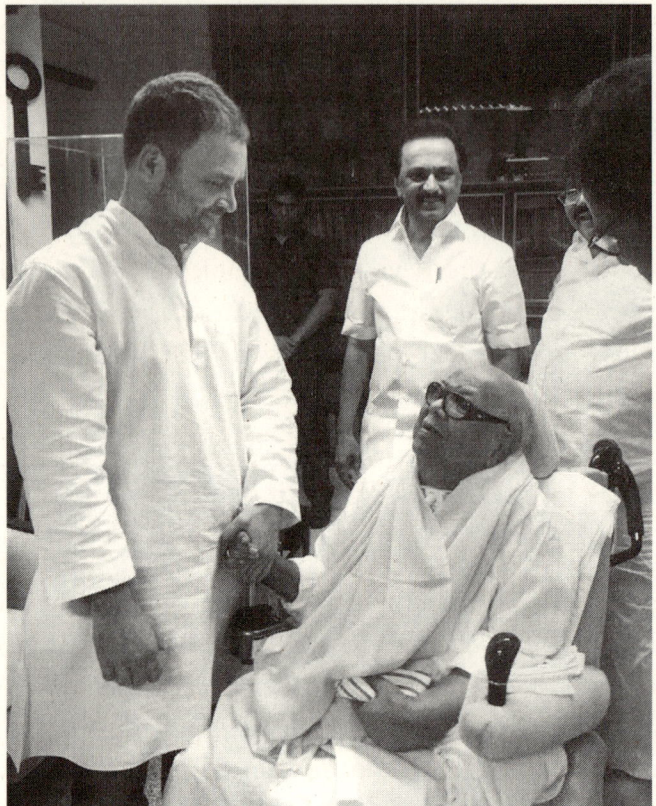

Photo courtesy: PTI

Rahul Gandhi calling on an ailing Karunanidhi

equality. He alleged that the Centre, with its 'religious fanaticism' was striking at the roots of education, arts, literature and religion and the state government had mortgaged people's welfare, and the DMK's first duty would be to 'throw out the thieves' of the state.

Stalin said he pondered the challenges before them and dreamt of a 'beautiful future'; the dream was where he, the Kazhagam, the Tamils, the country and the world would be 'anew beautifully [and] live happily'. He said the Kazhagam's cadres did not believe in caste supremacy and considered every living being their sibling and lent a helping hand to the needy. 'We don't believe in God. But, we respect those who believe.' Stalin beckoned cadres: 'Come with me

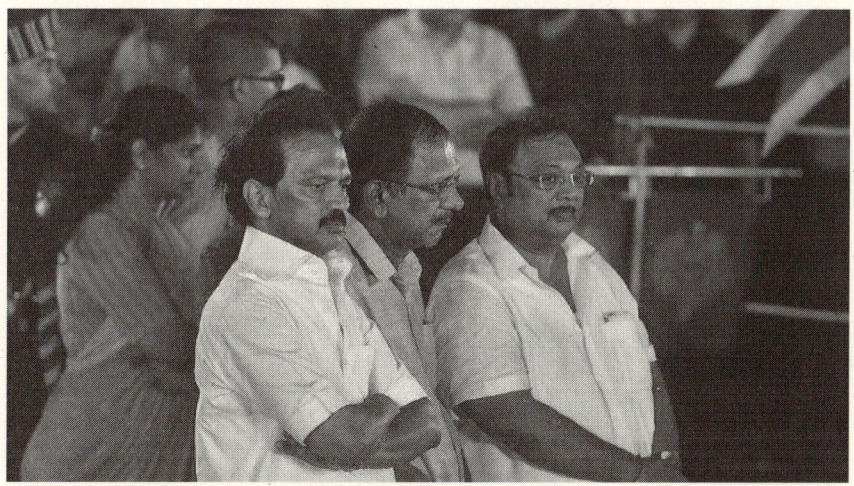

Photo courtesy: PTI

From left to right: Kanimozhi, Stalin, Tamilarasu and Alagiri at Karunanidhi's
funeral. Eldest son M.K. Muthu and elder daughter Selvi are missing in the picture

and join hands. I am not asking you to follow me. We can walk
together . . . to prevent saffronization of this country and throw out
the spineless ruling party in the state.' Borrowing a line from his
father's script in *Parasakthi*, he said his call was not to 'feel the breeze
but to jump the fire'.[33]

30

M.K. Stalin in Power
Kodanad Whodunit

The year 2019 had not begun well for Chief Minister Palaniswami. On 11 January, Samuel Mathew, a journalist, released a sixteen-minute video linking him to the heist-cum-murder at the Kodanad tea estate belonging to Jayalalithaa. On 23 April 2017, a security guard at the estate was murdered, and some valuables and three cases of documents went missing. Police blamed an eleven-member gang. Five days later, the first two accused met with separate road accidents, killing the first and seriously injuring the second, although his wife and daughter died. On 3 July, the estate's computer operator was found dead.

On 14 January 2019, Stalin met Governor Banwarilal Purohit and urged him to remove Palaniswami and set up a Special Investigation Team.[1] On 18 January 2019, Palaniswami called it a 'drama scripted by the DMK to defame . . . and discredit' him, and later obtained a court order against the DMK linking him to the crimes.[2] However, on 7 September 2023, Udhayanidhi Stalin, in a tweet, said Palaniswami 'cannot hide for long . . . hoping to escape the Kodanad murder-robbery and corruption cases'.[3]

2019 Parliamentary Election

Despite the court gag, Stalin concluded his 2019 parliamentary campaign by saying people knew what happened in Kodanad and that he had a right to ask questions.[4]

Parliamentary elections were conducted on 18 April in Tamil Nadu. Earlier, on 16 December 2018, Stalin proposed Rahul Gandhi as prime minister, whom he said could defeat the 'fascist' Narendra Modi.[5] When his proposal failed to gain traction, Stalin, without any sense of irony, said, 'If we do not propose [Rahul Gandhi], then who will?'[6]

Among others, the DMK made promises on Centre-state relations, a separate budget for agriculture, abolition of NEET, waiver of educational loans, free train travel for students and return to the more favourable old pension scheme for government staff. The party promised to push for the appointment of one crore youth with Standard X schooling as road workers and for the Centre to employ fifty lakh women as people's welfare workers on the lines of the state's *Makkal Nala Paniyalargal* or people's welfare staff appointed in 1990 to employ educated youth in 12,617 village panchayats and later discontinued by the AIADMK government. The party made constituency-wise promises for the twenty-two assembly seats that faced by-polls.[7]

The AIADMK proposed an Amma National Poverty Eradication Initiative (ANPEI) named after Jayalalithaa, envisaging a direct transfer of Rs 1500 monthly to the poor, promised to work for the release of the Rajiv Gandhi assassination convicts, scrap NEET and for the Centre to give up foreign direct investment in retail.[8]

Dr Ramadoss, who had on 8 April 2018 said that 'until rain, sea water, the world and Tamil existed [he] would never ally with the DMK or the AIADMK', was part of the AIADMK alliance as it had earmarked 10.5 per cent within the 20 per cent compartmental reservations.[9]

The DMK alliance won all but one of the thirty-nine seats by large margins. With twenty-three MPs, the DMK was the third-largest party in Parliament after the BJP and the Congress (I). An anti-Modi wave defined the vote in Tamil Nadu, making it the most anti-Modi state after Kashmir and Punjab. It was a sweet and sour victory for the DMK as nationally, the Modi-led BJP had been returned with a massive mandate.

2019 PARLIAMENTARY ELECTION

Party	Contested	Won	Votes	Percentage
DMK + IND 4	24	24	1,43,63,332	33.52%
INC	9	8	54,05,674	12.61%
VCK	1	1	5,00,229	1.16%
CPI	2	2	10,31,617	2.40%
CPM	2	2	10,18,225	2.37%
IUML	1	1	4,69,943	1.09%
AIADMK + IND 2	22	1	83,07,345	19.39%
PMK	7	0	22,97,431	5.36%
BJP	5	0	15,51,924	3.66%
DMDK	4	0	9,29,590	2.16%
TMC	1	0	2,20,849	0.50%

In the by-polls to the assembly, the DMK's strength rose to 101 with its haul of thirteen seats, but its dream of unseating the AIADMK had come to naught. With nine seats from the by-polls, the AIADMK had 123 MLAs, six more than the halfway mark. Tamil Nadu stayed close to the truism that its voters differentiated between assembly and parliamentary elections.

Anbazhagan Passes Away

On 7 March 2020, Anbazhagan, the nominal number two and general secretary since 1977, passed away. Respected as *Perasiriyar* (professor) in the party, he was known for his mild manners and remained a quiet force behind Karunanidhi. He officiated at Karunanidhi's family events. DMK flags flew at half-mast for a week. On 9 September, Duraimurugan was elevated to general secretary and T.R. Baalu was made treasurer.

Agriculture Zone and Horizontal Reservations

Palaniswami primed himself for the assembly elections in 2021. In the environment versus development debate, his government was pressured to prioritize agriculture and the environment. Nammalvar, an organic farming scientist, campaigned against the Cauvery Bed Methane project following the Union Ministry of Environment and Forests' nod in 2012. Following an expert study, on 8 October 2015, Jayalalithaa had banned the project.

On 15 February 2017, the Centre announced Neduvasal as one of the forty-four areas earmarked for hydrocarbon contracts nationwide, setting off protests.[10] Three months later, Kathiramangalam witnessed protests following a 'leak' in an Oil and Natural Gas Commission's (ONGC) pipeline on a private farm.[11]

The DMK lent its voice to the protests, including the one against the Rs 10,000 crore 277.3 km long expressway connecting Salem and Chennai, reducing travel time by half. Stalin claimed 'nearly 8000 acres of agricultural land will be lost.'[12] In a series of protests against the land acquisition for the project, at least five people committed suicide.[13] However, in power, the DMK would be confronted with the dilemma of development versus the environment. In August 2022, it indicated that it was likely to back the expressway project.[14] The DMK also faced stiff opposition from local villagers on its plans to build a second airport for Chennai at Parandur. In power in 2006–11, it faced opposition to its plans to acquire lands for special economic zones and satellite towns.

On 20 February 2020, Palaniswami took the wind out of the DMK's sails when the assembly passed the Tamil Nadu Protected

Agricultural Zone Development Bill, cancelling the 19 July 2017 notification declaring forty-five villages of Nagapattinam and Cuddalore districts as a Petroleum, Chemicals and Petrochemicals Investment Region (PCPIR).[15] The announcement was widely hailed.

On 15 September, the assembly passed the bill to provide a 7.5 per cent horizontal reservation in undergraduate courses in medicine for government school students.[*][16] On 26 February 2021, acceding to the PMK demand, a bill granting 10.5 per cent reservation to Vanniyars within the existing reservation of 20 per cent for most backward classes was passed.[†]

Run-up to the Election

On 22 December, the DMK submitted a ninety-seven-page complaint accusing Palaniswami, Panneerselvam and ministers S.P. Velumani, P. Thangamani, R. Kamaraj, C. Vijayabaskar, R.B. Udhayakumar and D. Jayakumar as corrupt.

Stalin and Palaniswami were the chief ministerial faces of their parties. The DMK allied with the Congress (I) and others while the AIADMK fought in alliance with the BJP and the PMK. Palaniswami had pushed back on the BJP's suggestion to accommodate Dhinakaran. (Dhinakaran's AMMK and DMDK fought the elections together.)

Palaniswami also made an about-turn on the 11 December 2019 CAA, expediting citizenship for minorities from Pakistan, Afghanistan and Bangladesh, fearing persecution. Protests erupted all over India, and the DMK spearheaded it in Tamil Nadu. On 14 March 2021, the AIADMK's 163-point manifesto promised to make the Centre reconsider the CAA.[17] Earlier, on 17 February

---

[*] On 26 August 2021, the Stalin-led DMK government extended this to all professional courses.
[†] On 31 March 2022, the Supreme Court declared the quota unconstitutional.

2020, Palaniswami had accused the DMK of misleading the people on CAA and asked that the party point out who from Tamil Nadu had been affected.[18] But elections had forced the compromise. Waiver of education loans, free housing, an annual subsidy of Rs 7500 to farmers, a government job per family, a washing machine, Arasu Cable TV connection, solar stoves to poor families and six LPG cylinders per family were the other promises.

The DMK made 500 election promises, including setting up a separate ministry to oversee their implementation. It promised to reduce the price of LPG cylinders by Rs 100 each, waive education loans, open 500 Kalaignar canteens, reduce milk price by Rs 3 per litre and make a one-time payment of Rs 4000 to ration card holders and Rs 10,000 to farmers for a new motor.

The key electoral promise of the Kazhagams remained the DMK's promise of Rs 1000 and the AIADMK's Rs 1500 monthly for one crore women household heads. Yet, both appeared to have been inspired by the MNM founder Kamal Haasan's 21 December 2022 vision envisaging 'payment' to homemakers for their work at home.[19] Both parties promised one-year maternity leave up from six months. The DMK also promised to provide Rs 24,000 as maternity assistance.

But the party was not taking any chances—political strategist Prashant Kishor had been hired to deliver it.

2021 ASSEMBLY ELECTION

Party	Contested	Won	Votes	Percentage
DMK + MDMK 6 + IND 9	188	133	1,74,27,615	37.70%
INC	25	18	19,76,527	4.27%
VCK	6	4	4,57,763	0.99%
CPI	6	2	5,04,537	1.09%
CPM	6	2	3,90,819	0.85%

Party	Contested	Won	Votes	Percentage
IUML	3	0	2,22,263	0.48%
AIADMK + TMC 6 + IND 6	191	66	1,53,89,569	33.29%
PMK	23	5	17,58,774	3.80%
BJP	20	4	12,13,510	2.62%
AMMK	165	0	10,85,985	2.35%
DMDK	60	0	2,00,157	0.43%
SOCIAL DEMOCRATIC PARTY OF INDIA (SDPI)	6	0	28,060	0.06%
AIMIM	3	0	3,134	0.01%
MNM	154	0		2.35%
NTK	234	0	30,42,307	6.58%

The DMK polled 37.70 per cent of the votes and won 133 seats, including those who fought on its symbol. With sixty-six seats and a 33.29 per cent vote share, the AIADMK had held itself independently, although ten of its ministers had been routed. The party had fought a close race in some seats, with Duraimurugan winning by a margin of less than 1000 votes. In a historic first, two VCK candidates won in non-reserved seats The BJP won four seats, but its vote share fell to 2.62 per cent. In Coimbatore South, Kamal Haasan lost to the BJP candidate in a closely fought race. The MNM polled 2.52 per cent and the AMMK 2.35 per cent. The AMMK played spoilsport to the parent AIADMK in twenty constituencies. Naam Thamizhar Katchi improved its vote share to 6.58 per cent from 1 per cent in the 2016 polls and 4 per cent in the 2019 parliamentary elections.

Chief Minister Stalin

The long wait for Stalin had come to an end. On 7 May 2021, Stalin was sworn in as chief minister with a thirty-five-strong cabinet.

Tamil ultra nationalist Naam Thamizhar Katchi founder Senthamizhan Seeman—a magnet for Tamil youth

P.T.R. Palanivel Thiaga Rajan, with a political legacy and finance background, was appointed finance minister. Duraimurugan, ranked number two, was given the portfolio of water resources and made the Leader of the House. Stalin's picks for the chief secretary, the director general of police and the head of the Directorate of Vigilance and Anti-Corruption (DVAC) were known for their professionalism. The day after taking over as chief minister, the scheme to allow women to ride free in government city buses was launched.[20] On 21 June, a five-member economic advisory council headed by the former Reserve Bank of India (RBI) Governor Raghuram Rajan was announced. Stalin said his goal was to make Tamil Nadu a one trillion-dollar economy.

The chief minister began with a fund of goodwill. During his campaign, Stalin had promised to order a detailed probe into Jayalalithaa's death and to bring corrupt AIADMK ministers to justice.[21] His government began to act on the second promise. On

22 July, M.R. Vijayabhaskar became the first of the former ministers raided by the DVAC for disproportionate wealth.[22] On 11 August, S.P. Velumani, on 16 September, K.C. Veeramani, on 18 October, C. Vijayabaskar, on 15 December, P. Thangamani and on 19 January 2022, K.P. Anbalagan and R. Kamaraj on 8 July 2022 were raided by the DVAC.[23] Palaniswami and Panneerselvam condemned the raids as 'political vendetta'. They should know that, as Amma's government and theirs did the same.[24] If the DMK shouted foul when the ED and IT acted against the DMK, the DVAC appeared to be the Kazhagam's own version of the central agencies. Independent institutions were no longer apolitical.

However, after being thrown out of the AIADMK on 11 July 2022, Panneerselvam sang a different tune, arguing that the government was 'doing its duty'. Another former minister, K.T. Rajendra Bhalaji, was arrested on 5 January 2022 for misappropriation of Aavin funds and later made bail. Velumani and C. Vijayabaskar were raided more than once, with the last raids on 13 September.[25] But the DMK, Palaniswami said, was throwing stones from a glass house and described the raids as an attempt to divert the attention from the Supreme Court's directive against the Minister for Electricity, Prohibition and Excise, Senthilbalaji and its anti-people actions.[26] Earlier, on 8 September, the apex court had restored the cash-for-jobs criminal case against Senthilbalaji.

Annamalai and Governor Act as Opposition

On 8 July 2021, Annamalai was appointed the president of the BJP's state unit. The thirty-six-year-old former Indian Police Service officer, with his flamboyant style, began to convert the BJP into the most vocal Opposition party even as the AIADMK was in a power struggle. Young, dynamic and brash Annamalai's guerrilla style politics of revelations calling the DMK corrupt kept the BJP alive in the public consciousness.

Photo courtesy: K. Annamalai

BJP's state leader K. Annamalai energizing the cadres

Two months later, on 9 September, R.N. Ravi was appointed governor of the state. Also, a former Indian police official, Governor Ravi, seemed to be in competition with Annamalai to get under the DMK's skin. To the two former police officials, the DMK administration could do nothing right.

Ravi proved unusual in many respects. He sat on bills, refused to follow the script in the customary address to the assembly, staged walk-outs, dismissed a tainted minister and reversed it equally swiftly, refused to swear in a minister, inviting the Supreme Court's intervention and did not hold back on criticizing the DMK administration and needling the Dravidian movement.

Together with some social media critics, Annamalai and the governor hogged the Opposition space rendering Palaniswami a milquetoast Leader of the Opposition.

Bills against NEET

Ravi could not shed the impression of gubernatorial filibustering of bills and delaying sanction for prosecution of the AIADMK's former ministers for corruption. He vehemently opposed the DMK's efforts to do away with NEET. Tamil Nadu continues to plough a lonely furrow on NEET while the other states have not uttered so much as a squeak.

In its 14 July 2021 report, the Justice A.K. Rajan Committee on NEET listed twenty reasons for eliminating the exam.[27] It said that the percentage of rural students dropped from 65.17 per cent in 2016–17 in the pre-NEET year to 49.91 per cent in 2020–21, and that of Tamil medium students fell from 14.88 per cent in 2016–17 to a mere 1.99 per cent in 2020–21.[28] The panel suggested that the state assert its constitutional rights or pass legislation to override NEET and base admissions on Standard XII results.

On 13 September, the Tamil Nadu Admission to Undergraduate Medical Degree Courses Act 2021, seeking to exempt students from NEET, was passed. On 4 October, the chief minister wrote to twelve Opposition chief ministers 'to put up a united effort to restore the primacy of states' in education and seek their support against NEET.[29]

The NEET bill was passed again on 8 February and sent to the President after Ravi returned it. On 26 April, the chief minister said the governor's job was only that of a 'postman' forwarding bills to the President. On 12 August 2023, Governor Ravi said he would 'never ever!' give his assent to the NEET bill as he did 'not want my children to feel intellectually disabled'.[30] The next day, a nineteen-year-old student who failed to clear NEET twice committed suicide, and the following day, his father killed himself, bringing acuity to the issue. On 14 August 2023, Stalin wrote to President Droupadi Murmu, requesting her assent to the bill to save lives.

Earlier, on 26 January 2022, the chief minister announced an All India Federation of Social Justice and, on 3 February, wrote to leaders of thirty-seven political parties calling on them to 'come together as a true Union of States with conviction', to ensure 'Everything for Everyone' and underscored the 'threat posed by religious hegemony'.[31]

'Dravidian Model'

On 7 May 2022, marking the first anniversary of the DMK in power, Stalin said, 'The name of my goal is the Dravidian model', defining it as inclusive growth and social justice.[32] The strongest objection to the term came from Ravi, who derided it as a 'political slogan' and a 'desperate bid to sustain an expired ideology, an ideology that does not relish the idea of *Oru Bharatham*, one India'.[33]

Sleepless Nights

On 9 October, after being elected as the president of the DMK for a second term, Stalin told the party general council that the actions of some of his cabinet colleagues and party leaders gave him 'sleepless nights' as he woke up 'with the worrying thought of whether our party seniors, cadres or ministers have said or done something wrong' and compared himself to a 'drum beaten on both sides'. To point out that the buck stopped with him, Stalin said, 'If it rains too much or doesn't rain, I will be blamed.'[34]

The thirty-five-strong cabinet could only count a handful of ministers as involved, dynamic and performing. Worse still, some were even a source of embarrassment. One minister had manhandled a party councillor in public, and another threw a stone at a party worker for not bringing a chair.

DMK Files

But there were more serious systemic problems, claimed Annamalai. On 14 April 2023, Annamalai released a fifteen-minute video clip termed the 'DMK Files', alleging the chief minister's family members and colleagues of amassing ill-gotten wealth amounting to Rs. 1.34 lakh crore. He charged the chief minister and his son-in-law with money laundering and accepting 'corrupt money' from foreign shell companies and demanded to know the details of the investors in Udhayanidhi Stalin's Red Giant Movies. Annamalai contended that as deputy chief minister, Stalin was paid a bribe of Rs 200 crore for the 'tweaking of tender regulations' to favour a multinational company in the Chennai Metro Rail project, adding that he would file a complaint with the CBI. The DMK called Annamalai's allegations 'a joke' and challenged him to proceed, wondering what the CBI had been doing since 2014.[35]

Ominously for the AIADMK, Annamalai also indicated that before the 2024 parliamentary polls, he would expose the 'corruption of all the parties' adding, 'If you do not want me to continue this, go talk to Delhi [leaders] and get me changed [as the president]'.[36] An annoyed Palaniswami told mediapersons the following day to ask him about 'seasoned political leaders' and not about Annamalai, who he said was 'trying to become a big man' through his 'sensational interviews'.[37] Annamalai rubbed salt in Palaniswami's wounds the next day when he made it clear: 'We have no friends here. Everyone here is our enemy . . . whoever has indulged in corruption will be viewed as an enemy. The plank of the 2024 parliamentary elections is corruption.'[38] But Annamalai's principal political adversary remained the DMK.

Four days later, on 20 April, Annamalai tagged a sensational twenty-six-second audio clip claiming the voice in the clip belonged to Palanivel Thiaga Rajan, who, in a conversation with a journalist, alleged that Udhayanidhi Stalin and Sabareesan have made '30,000 crores' in a year.[39] Annamalai said, 'With every passing day, these substantiate the claims made by us in #DMKFiles.'[40]

Finance Minister Thiaga Rajan dismissed the clip as the work of a 'blackmail gang'. Annamalai challenged him to produce a tape with similar content but with his voice.[41] On 25 April, Annamalai released a second clip of fifty-seven seconds with the same voice praising the BJP's 'one man, one post' rule and criticizing the DMK for 'lack of system'. Annamalai tweeted, 'Listen to the DMK ecosystem crumbling from within.'[42]

On 10 May, in the first cabinet change, the minister for dairy development, who was in the news for all the wrong reasons, was dropped. The next day, Thiaga Rajan was moved to information technology and Udhayanidhi Stalin and T.R.B. Rajaa, son of treasurer T.R. Baalu, were sworn in as ministers. Ranked tenth, Udhayanidhi Stalin was allotted the portfolio of youth welfare and sports development and special programme implementation. Palaniswami promptly called to put an end to family rule.[43]

Photo courtesy: Udhayanidhi Stalin

Heir apparent Udhayanidhi Stalin with his father, M.K. Stalin

On 26 July, Annamalai submitted a 'trunk' full of DMK files-II documents to Ravi detailing corruption charges against nine DMK ministers. In a sixteen-minute video, Annamalai alleged Rs 5600 crore corruption in the IT, transport and health departments and demanded a reply.[44]

Palaniswami Ends Dual Leadership

The AIADMK was in stasis. Mocked as 'Mr Humble' by his detractors, Panneerselvam, the AIADMK's coordinator, was not the most dynamic man to lead the party. Palaniswami had already asserted himself as the chief ministerial face of the party over him. Now, with no government to keep, he had turned inwards and was on an overdrive to end the dual leadership. As Panneerselvam resisted the putsch, on 11 July 2022, Palaniswami alleged that Panneerselvam had a 'relationship' with the DMK and expelled him. After a see-saw legal battle between the two factions, Palaniswami was named the sixth general secretary of the AIADMK on 28 March 2023.[45] On 20 April 2023, the Election Commission recognized Palaniswami as the general secretary of the AIADMK.

On 8 May 2023, Panneerselvam and Dhinakaran said they would work together against the 'evil force' DMK and 'betrayers' in the AIADMK.[46] Palaniswami called Panneerselvam and Dhinakaran 'traitors' and 'the "B" team of DMK'.[47]

Governor Refuses to Follow Script

Earlier, on 9 January 2023, Governor Ravi, sensing that passages he had omitted were being read out, walked out of the assembly without waiting for the national anthem to be played after the chief minister moved a resolution to record the text provided by his state government and not the speech delivered. In his address,

Ravi had skipped references to secularism, the state as a haven of peace and omitted mention of Periyar, Ambedkar, Kamaraj, Anna, Karunanidhi and the 'Dravidian model'. In his resolution, the chief minister said the governor's action was 'against assembly traditions'.

Earlier, 'Quit Tamil Nadu' slogans were raised against Ravi and DMK MLAs shouted, 'Don't impose BJP, RSS ideology.' Also earlier, Congress (I) and VCK members hailed 'Tamil Nadu'. On 4 January, Ravi had suggested Thamizhagam as a more appropriate name for the state.

The DMK's allies boycotted the governor's address and raised slogans against the delay in clearing bills. Twenty-one bills, including the one on the ban on online gambling, were pending. The governor returned the 19 October 2022 bill on 8 March 2023 with queries. It was readopted on 23 March 2023.[*, 48]

On 6 April, the governor said withholding assent meant the bill was dead. Stalin responded saying that Ravi 'should not think of himself as The Great Dictator' and the party tweeted Ravi's face with a Hitler moustache.[49] On 10 April, the assembly adopted a resolution urging the Centre and the President to instruct Ravi to give his assent to bills in a timely manner. Piloting the bill, Stalin faulted Ravi's 'whims and fancies' for the delays, converting the Raj Bhavan into a 'political Bhavan' and said that by keeping the bills pending, the governor was acting against the welfare of the people.[50] The governor finally cleared the anti-gambling bill that day.

But this was not the end.

On 4 May, speaking to the *Times of India*, Ravi came out strongly against the DMK government and its ethos. He dubbed the government text of his assembly speech as 'neither policies nor programmes, but propaganda. They were inaccurate, they were lies.'

---

[*] In December 2022, the Justice K. Chandru panel said seventeen committed suicide owing to online gaming in the three years in the state.

The governor cited a number of incidents, from the Popular Front of India (PFI) banned as a terrorist organization in September 2022, the sand mafia (on 25 April 2023, a village administrative officer was killed in his office in Thoothukudi allegedly by the sand mafia) to the Kallakurichi school violence where a girl committed suicide and protestors set fire to vehicles and fought the police to depict the law and order situation as far from satisfactory. He said he was duty-bound to speak the truth and could not describe Tamil Nadu as a 'haven of peace' as the text specified.

The governor said the 'Dravidian model' played down the national freedom movement and tried to erase the sacrifice of the state's freedom fighters and, in an indirect reference to the Justice Party and Periyar's dalliance with the British, glorified the collaborators of the British.

Claiming that no bills were pending, the governor lamented that the youth in Tamil Nadu were 'completely insulated' from the happenings in the rest of the country and 'education standards have gone down terribly', which is reflected in the poor performance of its students in the civil services. The governor echoed the concerns of many when he said that 90 per cent of the state's engineering graduates 'are unemployable' and wondered how, barring a few associate professors with twelve, fifteen years' experience 'the rest got the job'.[51]

On 7 May, speaking at an event to mark the second anniversary of his government, Stalin hit back: 'BJP-ruled state Manipur is burning. Is Tamil Nadu burning like Manipur?' On PFI, Stalin said the governor was raking up incidents before 2021 and 'trying to demean DMK's rule'. 'Why should the governor, who is supposed to be a part of the government, act like an Opposition leader?' Stalin wondered. Stalin claimed that Dravidian had vanquished 'Sanatana Dharma, Varnashrama, Manu Needhi, and caste discrimination' and has the power to defeat the Aryan ideology.'[52]

Senthilbalaji Epitomizes the Fall in Public Life

Ravi struck back in an unexpected manner. At 7 p.m. on 29 June, he sent a five-page letter informing the chief minister of his decision to remove Senthilbalaji from the council of ministers as his continuation would be detrimental to the course of justice. The governor's action was unprecedented. Five hours later, in a second letter that was brief, Ravi said he was keeping his decision in abeyance on the advice of the Union Home Minister that it would be prudent to seek the opinion of the attorney general.

Earlier, on 14 June, Senthilbalaji was arrested in a cash-for-jobs scam while he was the transport minister from 2011 to 2015 in the Jayalalithaa government. In a show of solidarity, Stalin and his colleagues visited Senthilbalaji at the hospital, who had complained of chest pain during the arrest. Palaniswami however, claimed Stalin was 'scared' that Senthilbalaji would 'spill the beans' and went to see him after his arrest. Senthilbalaji later underwent a heart bypass surgery.[53]

Senthilbalaji had begun with the MDMK and had moved to the AIADMK in 2016 and later to AMMK but switched to the DMK in 2018. In 2019, he won as a DMK candidate and was given the weighty portfolios of electricity and excise.[54] In 2021, the ED had filed a case against Senthilbalaji and others under the Prevention of Money Laundering Act (PMLA). On 30 July 2021, the Madras High Court quashed the proceedings as the minister said he had returned the money and that he had reached a compromise with the aspirants. In other words, Balaji had admitted to taking money. But now that he had returned it, he contended that there was no cause of action. On 16 May 2023, the Supreme Court took a dim view of the high court's order and ordered a fresh investigation against the minister and others. Following this, on 23 May and 13 June, the ED raided forty locations connected with Senthilbalaji and his brother.

Yet, on 15 June, Senthilbalaji was retained as minister without portfolio, overriding the governor's objection to his continuance owing to 'moral turpitude'.[55] Rajaji, Krishna Menon, Lal Bahadur Shastri and Murasoli Maran were ministers without portfolio under different circumstances. But, this was the first time that a minister in custody for corruption had been retained. On 2 July, the chief minister claimed his ministers were targeted as he was helping forge a national alliance, pointed out that Jayalalithaa continued in office until she was convicted, that the former AIADMK ministers raided by I-T and ED were at large and said the governor was 'unable to stomach' the DMK's good governance.[56]

On 5 July, Law Minister S. Regupathy wrote to Ravi urging him to accord early sanction to prosecute four former ministers in relation to the 'gutkha scam' and corruption charges.[57]

Three days later, on 8 July, Stalin wrote to President Droupadi Murmu complaining that the governor's pending nod exhibited his partiality and concluded that Ravi was 'unfit' to hold such a 'high post'. He said Ravi was conducting an 'ideological and political conflict with the democratically elected Dravida Munnetra Kazhagam,' and alleged that he was involved in attempts 'to topple the state government.'[58] Ravi, however, proved to be full of surprises, as we will see below.

On 18 July, the Indian National Developmental Inclusive Alliance (INDIA), comprising twenty-eight Opposition parties, including the DMK, was formed.

DMK Government 'Most Corrupt'

On 28 July, flagging off Annamalai's six-month-long En Mann En Makkal march (My land, my people) at Rameswaram, Home Minister Amit Shah said that Stalin should be 'ashamed' for retaining Senthilbalaji as a minister and damned the DMK government as the 'most corrupt' in the country.[59] Stalin in return, termed the pada yatra a *pava yatra* (a march of sin) 'to wash away sins and apologise for the 2002 Gujarat riots and the [current] happenings in Manipur'. He said central ministers were also facing cases and wondered if Shah had the guts to ask Modi about it. Regarding dynasty politics, Stalin said, 'Is there no dynasty politics in the BJP? I can list it.'[60]

In a tweet, Annamalai said that it was the DMK and the party's 'first family' that had committed many sins, including the ceding of Katchatheevu, the killing of Tamil fishermen by the Sri Lankan Navy during the UPA's rule and the killing of Tamils during the final Eelam war.[61]

Rs 1000 Monthly Grant to Women

On 15 September, Stalin inaugurated the 'Kalaignar Magalir Urimai Thittam' scheme in Kancheepuram, providing a monthly rights grant of Rs 1000 to 1,06,50,000 woman family heads. Earlier, on 5 September, the scheme providing girls from Standard VI to XII in government schools Rs 1000 till their undergraduate degree, diploma and ITI courses was launched. Six lakh students were to be beneficiaries.

Sanatana Dharma

On 3 September, Udhyanidhi Stalin shot to national attention when he compared Sanatana Dharma to 'mosquitoes, dengue, malaria, fever and corona,' and said it should be eradicated like them.[62] On 14 September, Modi joined issue with Udhayanidhi Stalin when he said at a rally in Madhya Pradesh that the INDIA alliance wished to erase 'Sanatana Dharma', which gave inspiration to Swami Vivekananda and Lokmanya Tilak, and that the INDIA alliance were to 'divide the country and society' and should be stopped. He called the INDIA alliance the '*Ghamandia* [arrogant] Alliance'.[63] On 19 November, while addressing two election rallies in Rajasthan, the prime minister said, 'The entire country has witnessed what they said about Sanatana [Dharma]. Getting rid of Sanatana will mean annihilating the culture of Rajasthan. Will you allow this to happen?'[64] On 21 November, Udhayanidhi Stalin said that the prime minister was taking his five-minute speech on Sanatana Dharma across the country.[65]

Unlike in the north, where Sanatana Dharma was a synonym for Hindu Dharma, the Tamil Saivite and Bhakti traditions identified it with Brahminism.[66] However, Tamilaruvi Manian, distinguishing between Varnashrama and Sanatana Dharma, points out that it is the former that speaks to caste.[67,*]

AIADMK Quits NDA

On 25 September, the AIADMK ended ties with the BJP-led National Democratic Alliance (NDA). In a resolution, the party said Annamalai's comments on Jayalalithaa have hurt the AIADMK cadre. Earlier, on 12 June, Annamalai obliquely said that Jayalalithaa was convicted of corruption and the state was the leader in corruption. The AIADMK called him 'inexperienced, irresponsible, and motivated'. Annamalai backtracked the following day, saying the AIADMK had misinterpreted his remarks.[68] But that was only a strategic retreat.

On 18 September, Annamalai's true intentions of how he saw the Kazhagams were out in the open when he observed that in 1956

---

* On 4 March 2024, the Supreme Court had pulled up Udhayanidhi Stalin saying he 'abused his rights', and that he is 'not a layman but a minister'. Krishnadas Rajagopal, 'SC to hear plea of T.N. Minister to club FIRs,' *The Hindu*, 5 March 2024, 1, 8; on 6 March 2024, Justice Anita Sumanth of the Madras High Court, disposing of writ petitions seeking the removal of the two DMK lawmakers and the HR and CE minister, held Udhayanidhi Stalin's and A. Raja's comments as 'perverse' and 'divisive' and factually and historically inaccurate and 'revealed an alarming lack of understanding of Hinduism'. Mohamed Imranullah S., 'Sanatana Dharma row | Udhayanidhi Stalin, A. Raja statements "perverse, divisive", says Madras High Court,' *The Hindu*, 6 March 2024, 2.

in Madurai, Anna had mocked the notion of divinely ordained gifts such as oratory, as the Hindus believe, that Muthuramalinga Thevar took strong exception to the speech the following day and Anna subsequently hid himself in Madurai and could only travel after apologizing. Although Anna addressed a meeting soon thereafter in Madurai, he refused to engage Thevar as his supporters had desired and there is certainly no record of Anna's expression of regret.[69]

Relations between the two parties had been stormy, with Annamalai eclipsing the AIADMK as the principal Opposition and unsparing in his criticism of the Kazhagam's corruption. At a personal level, the two-generation-younger Annamalai from the same Vellalar Gounder community posed an additional threat to Palaniswami. Palaniswami had successfully outmanoeuvred his AIADMK benefactor Sasikala, handler T.T.V. Dhinakaran and rival Panneerselvam. But Annamalai, the political upstart, was energizing the state BJP, hogging the media limelight and was genuinely popular for a novice. He appeared an uncanny adversary, perplexing Palaniswami and others.

The AIADMK leadership was miffed that the BJP leadership had failed to rein in Annamalai, a loose cannon. In any case, the BJP had proven a liability and, focused on the 2026 assembly elections, the party had chosen to dump the BJP.

In the long term, going it alone suits Annamalai's ambition to build the party as well.

Governor to 'Engage' with Chief Minister

On 1 November, Tamil Nadu approached the Supreme Court alleging that Governor Ravi was causing a 'constitutional deadlock' by his 'politically motivated conduct' and asked that the court fix an 'outer time limit' for the governor to act on the bills and government orders.[70] On 6 November, the Supreme Court exhorted the governors to do some 'soul searching', noted that they were not 'elected by the people' and wondered, 'Why should parties be made to approach the SC for the Governors to act?'[71] Four days later, it expressed 'serious concern' over the delay by the Punjab and Tamil Nadu governors in giving assent to bills.[72]

On 13 November, Ravi returned ten pending bills, including the two passed by the previous AIADMK government, simply saying that he 'withheld assent'. Most of the bills related to shifting the authority to appoint vice chancellors from the governor to the state government. On 18 November, the assembly readopted the ten bills, throwing the ball back into the governor's court. Stalin, moving the resolution to readopt the bills, claimed that the governor was 'not able to digest the development of Tamil Nadu', and was against Tamil culture, literature and social justice.[73]

On 20 November, the Supreme Court noted that the bills had been with the governor since January 2020 and he had returned them after the matter had reached the court and wondered 'What was the governor doing for three years?'[74] On 22 November, in his affidavit to the Supreme Court, Ravi said he had accorded sanction on 13 November to prosecute former AIADMK ministers C. Vijayabaskar and B.V. Ramanna in the gutka scam.[75]

On 28 November, the governor forwarded the readopted bills to the President and informed the assembly on 30 November, a day before the hearing in the Supreme Court. On 1 December 2023, a three-judge bench headed by Chief Justice D.Y. Chandrachud said the governor, having withheld his assent to the bills on 13 November, cannot now refer the repassed bills to the President, adding that the governor had no option but to grant his assent to the bills in the re-enacted form. In the end, the chief justice urged the governor to engage with the chief minister.[76] On 31 December, Stalin met the governor at his invite to ask that he get the bills back and grant consent for the prosecution of former ministers K.C. Veeramani and M.R. Vijayabhaskar.[77]

'Something Is Rotten in the State of Denmark'

The DMK would also face difficulties from a completely unexpected front. Justice Anand Venkatesh of the Madras High Court appeared to believe in judicial activism and had become a thorn in the administration's flesh. On 10 August, in a surprising move, he suo motu ordered the revision of the acquittal of Higher Education Minister K. Ponmudy, his wife and friend, in a disproportionate assets case from 2002. The judge described the 30 June 226-page acquittal by the Vellore principal district judge after only four days of hearing and just before the judge's retirement as 'a shocking and calculated attempt to manipulate and subvert the criminal justice system'.

On 22 August, the judge took up the discharge of Revenue Minister K.K.S.S.R. Ramachandran and Finance Minister Thangam Thennarasu. Quoting Shakespeare's 'Something is rotten in the State of Denmark,' the judge opined that something was amiss with the Srivilliputhur Special Court for MP/MLA Cases and noted that 'upon change of power in the state in 2021, the identities of the accused and the prosecution were obliterated' and the courts chose to play wise. He said if the special court's approach were emulated elsewhere, the special courts trying MPs and MLAs would be 'writing a collective obituary to the cases under the Prevention of Corruption Act'.[78]

On 30 August, the judge took up the withdrawal of a disproportionate assets case against former chief minister O. Panneerselvam in 2012, terming it a 'cruel joke' and saying that 'DVAC has unfortunately become a 'chameleon and has begun to take its colours depending upon who is in power. Unfortunately, courts have also acted in tandem'.[79] The DMK had earlier accused the judge of following a 'pick and choose' policy in suo motu revisions. On 8 September, the judge took up Minister for Rural Development I. Periyasamy and former AIADMK minister B. Valarmathi's graft cases.[80]

On 13 February 2024, Senthilbalaji resigned from the cabinet a day before the hearing of his bail petition. Two weeks later, on 28 February, Justice Venkatesh denied bail, agreeing with the ED's contention that Senthilbalaji remained influential even as he ordered the completion of the trial within three months.[81]

On 26 February, Justice Venkatesh reinstated the corruption case against Rural Development Minister I. Periyasamy, ordering the completion of the trial by July 2024.* The judge termed the minister's 17 March 2023 trial court discharge from an alleged irregular government plot allotment case as 'completely specious and perverse'. The judge has initiated six *suo motu* criminal revisions against the acquittal or discharge of politicians from corruption cases.[82]

In addition to Periyaswamy, Senthilbalaji, Thennarasu, ministers Duraimurugan, K.K.S.S.R. Ramachandran, Anitha Radhakrishnan, P. Geetha Jeevan and E.V. Velu face legal issues.

Earlier, on 21 December 2023, Justice G. Jayachandran of the Madras High Court sentenced Higher Education Minister K. Ponmudy and his wife to three years in prison and a Rs 50 lakh fine each for a corruption offence. Ponmudy stood disqualified as a legislator and minister. On 11 March 2024, the Supreme Court suspended Ponmudy's conviction and jail sentence. (The bench also suspended his wife's sentence but not her conviction.) That day, the DMK government approached the governor to re-induct Ponmudy into the cabinet only to hear on 17 March Ravi cite 'constitutional morality' from taking Ponmudy back. On 21 March, the Supreme Court asked the governor to keep aside his 'subjective perceptions' and stop 'defying' the court. Consequently, Ponmudy was sworn in on 22 March.

---

* On 8 April, the Supreme Court stayed the trial.

2024 Parliamentary Election

Tamil Nadu went to the polls on 19 April.

Elections in Tamil Nadu have witnessed the liberal distribution of cash and gifts for decades now. Still, the 27 February 2023 Erode assembly by-poll created a new record when the ruling DMK created 'pens' where potential voters were required to be present the whole day as a demonstration of their loyalty and away from poaching by rivals. In return, they were provided meals and a daily allowance of Rs 500. On weekends, the DMK provided households poultry, meat and fish. Additionally, gifts poured in, in the form of pressure cookers, silverware, laptop cases, silver anklet strings and even washing machines for households with more than ten votes. The DMK-supported Congress (I) candidate won by a huge margin against the AIADMK candidate. But neither the DMK nor its opponents covered themselves with glory. Tamil Nadu's politics had touched a new low.[*]

Unlike in 2019, the state saw a four-cornered contest led by the DMK, the AIADMK, the BJP and the NTK. The DMK front added MNM to its allies. The BJP-led NDA had roped in the PMK, TMC, the AIADMK's expelled leader O. Panneerselvam, and T.T.V. Dhinakaran's AMMK and other smaller parties. Edappadi Palaniswami had promised a 'mega alliance' on 6 November 2022. But his AIADMK was left with just the DMDK, PT, and SDPI.

Till 16 April, Prime Minister Modi visited the state eight times in 2024 and launched scathing attacks on the DMK and the INDI alliance. On 4 March, he said the DMK had a problem with the Centre directly sending money to the beneficiary accounts and that he wished to tell the DMK 'that Modi will not let you loot the money of the people of Tamil Nadu, and the money you

---

[*] Tamil Nadu held the record for the second-highest seizure of cash to voters at Rs 460 crore. Gujarat was first. ECI, 15 April 2024. Accessed 21 April 2024, https://pib.gov.in/PressReleaseIframePage.aspx?PRID=2017913.

looted will be recovered and spent for the people of the state. This is Modi's guarantee.'[83] The DMK ran campaign ads later that said the cooking gas price was Rs 440 in 2014 and Rs 818 today. 'When will we recover from the price hike! Can we still trust warranty [and] guarantees?' it posed. DMK online ads where Stalin called voters to 'save the nation' were ubiquitous all the way up to the *New York Times*. Modi had also claimed that the country's '140 crore people' were his family, whereas the DMK and Congress (I) believed in the 'family first' motto. Stalin retorted that the ED, I-T and the CBI were the prime minister's families.[84]

On 15 March, Modi said the INDIA bloc's 'history is of scams and their policies are focussed on coming to power to loot the public'.[85] And on 19 March, with T.T.V. Dhinakaran and Dr Ramadoss by his side Modi said, 'DMK-Congress means big corruption, DMK-Congress means one-family rule', described the two parties as two sides of the same coin and said the INDI alliance was deliberately insulting Hinduism and wondered how this could be allowed. Modi's roadshow in Coimbatore the previous day received an unprecedented show of support.*

On 22 March, Stalin hit the stump in Tiruchi with a scathing attack on Modi over the electoral bonds, saying the prime minister had no right to speak about corruption. He promised that the 'Centre's misdeeds would be exposed once the INDIA bloc is voted to power'. Charging the BJP for failing to do anything for Tamil Nadu, he said the Centre returned just 29 paise for every rupee of tax from Tamil Nadu. He claimed the AIADMK was now in a 'secret alliance' with the BJP.[86]

Palaniswami interpreted Stalin's and Udhayanidhi's refrain of a 'secret alliance' as the result of 'the election fear' as they were disappointed that the AIADMK sans the BJP would now attract minority support.[87] Taking a jibe at Modi's roadshows Palaniswami wondered: 'Has he given anything to the state?', adding that the

---

* On 9 April, Modi held a roadshow in Chennai.

people of Tamil Nadu were educated and knew 'who has toiled for them'. On 10 April, the prime minister claimed that the 'DMK has first copyright on corruption [and the] entire family [was] looting Tamil Nadu'. Stalin said Modi was the right choice for the 'chancellor of the university of corruption'.[88]

Manifestos

The DMK manifesto promised a reduction in the prices of LPG, petrol and diesel to Rs 500, Rs 75 and Rs 65, respectively, a monthly sum of Rs 1000 for women nationwide, a caste census every five years, exemption for Tamil Nadu from NEET, repeal of the CAA, prevention of the implementation of the Uniform Civil Code and the National Education Policy, statehood for Puducherry, the appointment of governors in consultation with chief ministers, removal of Articles 356 on President's rule and Article 361 providing immunity for governors, a branch of the Supreme Court in Chennai, removal of toll booths on national highways, *Tirukural* as 'National Book', end government's divestment, completion of the Sethusamudram project, waiving off farm loans, government to cover premium for crop insurance, waiver of educational loans, a free SIM card with one GB data per month for college students, formation of State Development Council including chief ministers, replacing the current NITI Aayog with the Planning Commission, reclamation of Katchatheevu, recommendation to share cess revenues with states and the Finance Commission to increase the horizontal devolution of tax revenue from 42 per cent to 50 per cent, a cleaning programme for the Cauvery, Tamirabarani and Vaigai rivers, a Metro Rail line from Koyambedu to Ambattur, a separate Railway budget, Metro rail for Tiruchi, Tirunelveli, Salem, Thoothukudi and Thanjavur, Madurai and Thoothukudi upgraded to international airports, all major Union and state government offices to operate entirely on solar power by 2030 and increased subsidy for Electric Vehicles.[89]

The AIADMK also proposed to ensure that revenue from cess and surcharge is shared with states, removal of toll charges, Rs 3000 monthly assistance and six gas cylinders a year for women below poverty line, a monthly pension of Rs 5000 and a minimum support price for agricultural produce, to exert pressure on the Centre to stop Mekedatu dam at Cauvery, push for the Cauvery-Gundar-Vaigai interlinking project and also the Godavari-Cauvery, Parambikulam-Aliyar and Pandiyar-Punnapuzha linkage schemes, appointment of governors in consultation with chief ministers; a branch of the Supreme Court in Chennai, statehood for Puducherry, 33 per cent quota for women in legislature, daily wages in the case of the Mahatma Gandhi National Rural Employment Guarantee Scheme increased to Rs 450, dual citizenship for Sri Lankan Tamils, Sri Lankan Tamils and Muslims under the CAA, medical admission on plus two marks, separate lanes on national and state highways for two-wheelers, a Chennai-Nagapattinam waterway via Cuddalore, an international cricket stadium and an AIIMS in Coimbatore and IIT and IIM in Madurai.[90]

The AIADMK chose fresh faces for thirty-two of the thirty-three seats it contested. The DMK chose fresh candidates for eleven of its twenty-one seats. Six were from DMK families where a parent or sibling was related to the candidate. The AIADMK and Congress fielded three such candidates each. The MDMK chose Vaiko's son, Durai Vaiko, for its only seat, while the PMK fielded Anbumani Ramadoss's wife and the DMDK Vijayakanth's son, Vijay Prabhakaran. The BJP fielded Radhika Sarathkumar whose husband Sarathkumar had merged his party with the BJP.

Ravi Does It Again

On 12 February, for a second time in a row, Governor Ravi refused to read out the customary inaugural address of the legislative assembly and later walked out of the House.

After extending wishes and quoting a Kural couplet, Ravi expressed his inability to read the remainder of the prepared text, which was critical of the Centre and declared that the Citizenship (Amendment) Act would be not implemented in the state. Ravi said he disagreed with the text on 'factual and moral grounds', and reading it would amount to 'constitutional travesty'. Speaker M. Appavu then read the prepared address in Tamil and in the end, described the governor as 'a follower of Nathuram Godse and more' adding that the people of Tamil Nadu and the assembly were prepared for them, at which Ravi walked out of the House. Later, the assembly unanimously adopted a resolution to take the prepared text of the speech on record.

The Raj Bhavan later charged that the Speaker 'lowered the dignity of his chair and grace of the House', adding that Ravi left the House to preserve the dignity of his office.

It said the government ignored the governor's advice on playing the national anthem at the beginning and end of the address. Appavu said the national anthem was played at the end of the address as per convention. He said Ravi had written a letter to him on the same last year, and the issue was resolved.[91]

DMK and Electoral Bonds

On 15 February 2024, a five-judge Supreme Court Constitution Bench struck down as unconstitutional the 2018 electoral bonds scheme facilitating the anonymous funding of political parties. Highlighting the 'deep association' between money and politics, the Bench rejected the Centre's contention that citizens do not have a 'right to know' and ordered the State Bank of India, the bond seller, to disclose all details on the bonds to the Election Commission of India for public viewing. Details showed that the BJP was the largest beneficiary nationwide and the DMK in the state. On 17 March, addressing a public meeting in Mumbai at the culmination of Rahul

Gandhi's Bharat Jodo Nyay Yatra, Stalin termed the bonds the BJP's 'white-collar corruption' and asked, 'Can such a prime minister talk about corruption?'[92] On 4 April 2024, *The Hindu*'s cartoonscape showed Modi telling the people, 'I have strong bonds with you . . .'[93]

'Drug Kingpin'

On 25 February, *Murasoli* carried the party general secretary Duraimurugan's short note announcing the 'permanent removal' of Jaffer Sadiq, the deputy organizer of the DMK's NRI wing for Chennai-West, for bringing 'disrepute' to the party and advising cadres to desist from any contact. The following day, Narcotics Control Bureau (NCB) officials said that they had busted an international drug cartel which, over three years, exported approximately 3500 kg of pseudoephedrine, valued at over Rs 2000 crore, and that the kingpin was absconding. On 27 February, Annamalai identified the kingpin as Sadiq. Soon, videos and photos of Sadiq with Stalin, Udhayanidhi Stalin and the director general of police emerged. On 29 February, Annamalai posted an 11:34-minute video alleging Sadiq's links to the DMK's first family. The video clocked several lakh views and thousands of comments.

On 4 March, the prime minister, on a visit to the state, expressed 'deep concern' and alleged that 'With the blessings of the ruling party here, Tamil Nadu is witnessing uncontrolled drug smuggling and selling, everywhere'. That day, Edappadi Palaniswami charged in a video message that M.K. Stalin was 'taking Tamil Nadu to the abyss'.

On 9 March, the NCB took Sadiq into custody in Delhi. The following day, Palaniswami led an AIADMK delegation to Governor Ravi, seeking an independent inquiry into the Sadiq affair, considering the accused's 'closeness' with Stalin and the police chief. Later that day, Ravi noted that the recent developments, including drug seizures, 'confirmed the worst fears about prevalence of drugs in the state'.

Law Minister S. Regupathy said the BJP had deployed the NCB to 'besmirch and intimidate' the DMK and 'provide political mileage for the BJP during the elections.' The DMK's top leadership, however, maintained a deafening silence. On 10 March, the BJP alleged that Sadiq produced a film directed by Udhayanidhi Stalin's wife Kiruthiga Stalin. That day, it said the DMK had become 'Drug Marketing Kazhagam'.[94]

Actor Vijay Takes the Plunge

On 2 February, actor Vijay ended all speculation about his interest in politics and took the plunge, converting his Vijay Makkal Iyakkam, a fan body engaged in service activities, to a political party, the Tamilaga Vettri Kazhagam (TVK). Vijay described his political entry as 'paying a debt to Tamil Nadu's people.' In a three-page statement, Vijay said he does not consider politics as 'yet another profession' but a 'sacred service of people'. 'I have learnt not just the heights of politics but its depths from seniors in politics. Politics is not my hobby; it is my quest,' he said. Pronouncing himself against 'corruption' and 'divisiveness', Vijay said his TVK would not contest or support any party in the upcoming parliamentary elections. On 8 March, Vijay launched a membership drive to enrol two crore members before the 2026 state assembly elections.

Delimitation and Simultaneous Elections

On 14 February, the assembly 'unanimously' adopted two resolutions against the Centre's 'One Nation, One Election' proposal and the proposed delimitation after 2026.

While moving the resolutions, Stalin termed the 'One Nation, One Election' policy 'a dangerous, autocratic thought, and needs to be opposed'. He described delimitation as 'a sword hanging over the head of Tamil Nadu' and alleged a 'conspiracy to reduce the representation of Tamil Nadu (in Parliament). We need to oppose both in one voice,' he said. 'Even with 39 seats, we are begging the central government. If the number of seats further reduces, Tamil Nadu will lose its rights and fall behind,' he said.[95]

Stalin said simultaneous elections would necessitate dissolving democratically elected legislative assemblies before their term. He wondered if the state assemblies would be dissolved if the Union government lost its majority and also if elections would be called in the case of a state government's fall. 'Is there anything more comical than this?' he asked. Ironically, Karunanidhi had justified advancing the assembly elections in 1971, a year before its term and clubbing it with the parliamentary elections as a savings measure. On 14 March, the High-Level Committee led by former President Ram Nath Kovind recommended fresh elections to constitute the new Lok Sabha or state assembly for the unexpired term of the House in the event of a hung House, a no-confidence motion, or any such event.

Katchatheevu Again

On 31 March, Prime Minister Modi posting on X said: 'Eye-opening and startling! New facts reveal how Congress callously gave away Katchatheevu . . .'[96,*] The post was based on a Right to Information Act (RTI) response that Annamalai had obtained that made public Karunanidhi's dual stand of going along with Indira Gandhi's stance to give away the island while opposing it fiercely in public and how Prime Minister Nehru had termed the island as 'inconsequential' and Indira Gandhi was eager to gift the islet to Colombo. It was not clear when the RTI was filed or when the reply was received.

---

[*] T. Ramakrishnan, 'Lok Sabha elections | Katchatheevu issue unlikely to have electoral impact in Tamil Nadu,' *The Hindu*, 1 April 2021. Accessed 2 April 2024, https://www.thehindu.com/elections/lok-sabha/lok-sabha-elections-katchatheevu-issue-unlikely-to-have-electoral-impact-in-tamil-nadu/article68016513.ece.

Clearly, the BJP wished to paint the DMK and the Congress (I) as duplicitous and mistakenly saw it as an election issue.

Katchatheevu was an issue as Indian fishermen venturing close to the island had been regularly harassed, arrested and shot at by the Sri Lankan Navy. Jayalalithaa had vowed to reclaim the island in her Independence Day address as chief minister on 15 August 1991. On 31 October 1991, the assembly adopted a resolution to claim the island back. A decade later in 2001, Jayalalithaa realistically suggested that India negotiate a lease in perpetuity for fishing. However, in 2008, the Jayalalithaa government decided to take a legalistic approach and moved the Supreme Court to annul the 1974 and 1976 agreements. On 8 June 2011, her government adopted a fresh assembly resolution to implead the revenue department in the case and on 3 May 2013, adopted another resolution demanding the island's retrieval. On 10 May 2013, Karunanidhi filed a separate petition in the Supreme Court to annul the accords.[97] More recently, on 31 March 2024 when Annamalai said that the state BJP was determined to retrieve the island, it was the first time a national ruling party had spoken about reclaiming the island.

But, the BJP's intentions were short-term and in the context of elections. Annamalai was a politician playing to the gallery. However, the prime minister proved no different when on 1 April, taking to X a second time and citing a *Times of India* story, Modi alleged that the 'DMK has done NOTHING to safeguard Tamil Nadu's interests. New details emerging on #Katchatheevu have UNMASKED the DMK's double standards totally. Congress and DMK are family units. They only care that their own sons and daughters rise. They don't care for anyone else. Their callousness on Katchatheevu has harmed the interests of our poor fishermen and fisherwomen in particular.'[98]

That day, Foreign Minister Jaishankar chimed in saying that the two Congress prime ministers 'gave no importance to Katchatheevu', disregarded the advice to negotiate fishing rights and 'the DMK was complicit . . .'[99] P. Chidambaram in a tweet referred Jaishankar to the RTI reply dated 27 January 2015 when Jaishankar was the foreign secretary justifying the circumstances under which India acknowledged the island belonged to Sri Lanka. He said Jaishankar had been reduced to 'a mouthpiece of the RSS-BJP'.[100]

On 2 April, Stalin posed in Vellore if the prime minister had ever taken up the issue of the Indian fishermen in relation to Katchatheevu with Sri Lanka during his many visits there, had ever condemned the arrest of Indian fishermen and had the guts to speak about China having renamed thirty villages in Mandarin in Arunachal Pradesh.[101]

Annamalai-Palaniswami Spat

On 13 April, Annamalai, campaigning for AMMK's Dhinakaran, said that the AIADMK 'was run for contractors' (some AIADMK candidates are contractors) and that the AIADMK will cease to exist and its cadres would rally behind T.T.V. Dhinakaran after 4 June (vote counting day). Palaniswami said it was rich coming from Annamalai—an 'appointed leader' who could not become 'even a councillor' and asked him to watch his words. He reminded him that in 1998, the AIADMK had to carry the BJP to the people as it was such an unknown entity.[102]

31

The Near Future

The DMK is in its seventy-fifth year. It had swum 'rivers of fire' as Karunanidhi had picturesquely described the trials and tribulations of the party. Its initial years were fraught and dangerous, and the party's militant course reflected its immature yet idealistic phase. But the pursuit of power would greatly soften the party's course.

Periyar had described the impending independence on 15 August 1947 as 'British-Bania-Brahmin Contractual Day'. His Dravidar Kazhagam had, since 1939, considered the British, Brahmin and Bania as enemies and characterized independence as a 'day of mourning'. Periyar could speak his mind freely. He did not seek political power and had years of service in the Congress behind him. His disciple Anna was politically inclined. He publicly demurred with his mentor, saying it was a day when one of the two enemies, the British, was leaving, and only the Bania remained. There was no mention of the Brahmin.

The guru and the disciple had begun to differ, and their relationship had been strained for a while. This penultimate difference, as Anna admitted, was his attempt to be on the right side of history. A brief rapprochement between the duo followed, and Periyar indicated he would step down and hand over the reins of the movement to Anna. But fearing that Anna would convert the social movement into a political one, Periyar settled on his aide, Maniammai.

Together, the guru and the lead disciple had preached identity and self-respect to the Tamils. Now, they would travel separately. The DMK was born.

At the DMK's public launch on 18 September 1949, Anna accused their 'political father', the seventy-year-old Periyar, of being authoritarian and, by marrying Maniammai, less than half his age, bringing infamy to them. Yet, in deference to his leader, he named Periyar the titular head and said their aims were the same—a socialist garden where 'Dravidam' would bloom.

DMK demagogues thundered *Dravida Nadu* or *sudukadu*! (Dravida Nadu or death) during the party's militant phase. But in 1957, the party openly took to elections. This had been the plan all along. The charms of democracy and power—of ministerships and its trappings—were irresistible. The erstwhile 'freedom fighters' had walked into its snare.

In 1962, the party gave up Dravida Nadu as an impending ban stared in the party's face. Anna reasoned that he could not take advantage of the Chinese menace. The truth was that Anna had chosen discretion over valour. The Chinese had saved Anna's face.

In 1967, Anna joined hands with Rajaji, now co-opting the 'wily Brahmin'. In 1971, when Karunanidhi joined hands with Indira Gandhi, the Bania had become an ally. On both occasions, the dalliance with the 'enemy' was to defeat the 'Pure Tamil' Kamaraj.

Earlier, in 1965, Anna denied the DMK was a party of 'expediency' and no principles: 'Federalism, full autonomy for the states and egalitarianism—are these not principles?' he posed to his interviewer.

That year, power appeared within striking distance.

Anna made the audacious promise of three measures of rice for a rupee, thus beginning the party's slippery slope. It was an impossible promise to keep, but it caught the voters' imagination and unseated the Congress.

Anna's death in 1969 propelled Karunanidhi to the forefront. Karunanidhi had long been front and centre of the party. In 1961, Anna had chosen Karunanidhi over Sampath. His faith in Karunanidhi was not misplaced. Karunanidhi had delivered in 1967. Of course, MGR's charisma played a vital role.

With its paternal populism, the Karunanidhi-led DMK laid the foundations of the welfare state. Kamaraj had made school education free and incentivized education for most backward castes. His accent on education, industry and agriculture laid the foundations for Tamil Nadu's strides. Karunanidhi launched the slum clearance programme, built houses for Dalits, streamlined the public distribution system and began a conscious programme to draw talent from the backwards and Dalits, bringing his administration closer to the people. MGR and Jayalalithaa built on this edifice.

Anna had envisaged a Tamil Nadu free of want, and while describing the DMK as the party of the modest, said the modest do not have to remain so. But he hadn't envisaged the modest being accused of seeking wealth by dubious means.

Periyar had long foreseen this. A fortnight after the DMK's founding, Periyar conceded to Jalagandapuram Kannan that he was nagged by worry. He said he had concluded that his principles could not be achieved politically. To fight elections, money would be needed, and once the DMK sought money, principles would take a backseat. Periyar continued:

If, by chance, DMK becomes the ruling party, then from that moment, the dilution of my principles would begin . . . for many would indulge in seeking wealth through authority. I know those who have cast their lot with Anna. They come from simple families. For many, the desire to live well would be there. Because of this, their activities will bring much ill name to the party.

Periyar ended presciently that those opposed to his principles would point to the corruption. He also foresaw the division of the party once in power. Anna was 'shaken' when he heard of his mentor's prognosis.[1]

The DMK's leaders have come a long way from travelling in borrowed cars and living in rental and modest houses. The party's top echelons are well-heeled, and even third-tier functionaries are visibly well-off. Quite a few of these success stories, however, remain mired in mystery. The vast majority of the party's cadres, nonetheless, remain modest.

To be fair to the DMK, the values of public life did not begin to drop after the DMK's rise to power. They have been on a steady downhill path from the time of independence. Anna, whose personal integrity was beyond reproach, had himself begun to make political compromises for the sake of power, as we saw.

The DMK is also not a service organization, although it has often bandied itself as one. It is a political party. It has to fight and win elections every five years. Anna had lived true to the dictum that politics is the art of the possible. Karunanidhi stretched it.

The party has been in power in the state for twenty-two years and has been part of a coalition for seventeen years at the Centre. For a 'Shudra' that Karunanidhi ad nauseam reminded others he was, the key infrastructure ministries the DMK held at the Centre saw one of the nation's best-known industrialists, Ratan Tata, write to Karunanidhi singing paeans. The DMK had long arrived.

Egalitarianism

The DMK can yet look back with some satisfaction on the distance covered with respect to egalitarianism or social justice—its core ethos. Karunanidhi slightly enlarged the reservations pie, and MGR expanded it to the maximum. Today, the state is known for both its paternal populism and reservations. Also, Karunanidhi was the most vocal advocate of Mandal, which again was realized during V.P. Singh's time, who, of course, had his own compulsions.

Thanks to affirmative action, many have found opportunities and challenges that they would not have otherwise found. Seven decades of reservations have brought changes on the ground. The party stands for the status quo and opposes economic criterion and 'creamy layer'. But how long should children be assisted to walk, especially when many have come of age? Is a prop in perpetuity for the backward classes the answer to social mobility? Generations have moved up, and it is time that no limits are placed to their fullest expression.

Ironically, affirmative action had also accentuated caste and made the DMK's objective of a casteless society problematic. Candidates are fielded on the basis of caste. MGR was the only one who could transcend this to some extent. His cult-like status enabled him to ignore caste and experiment with social engineering. He fielded a Christian from the fisherman community in the predominantly upper-caste Hindu constituency of Tirunelveli.

Winning Back the Disaffected

In recent decades, the DMK's narrative of inclusiveness has come under severe strain. In its preoccupation with the Brahmin-Non-Brahmin narrative, the Dravidian movement had rarely dealt with the tensions between the intermediaries and the Dalits. The 'Dravidian model' should touch the lives of the last of the marginalized. Samathuvapurams remain a Band-Aid. Thanks to reserved seats, Dalit representation is ensured, but these representatives remain tokenisms.

The Congress empowered the Dalits. This explains the absence of a Kakkan in the Dravidian movement on par with his colleagues in the Kamaraj cabinet of the upper castes. Kakkan served as home minister with Kamaraj and was not tokenized. Kamaraj made no fuss about Kakkan's Dalit moorings. He was simply the best man for the job.

Even as incidents against Dalits have been more frequently reported, the latest genre of Tamil films of marginalized assertion and their success at the box office lends to some optimism. *Mamannan* (Emperor, 2023) by Udhayanidhi Stalin joins this genre of films where the marginalized are pitted against intermediate communities but reach an accommodation. Cinema had once portrayed caste pride in movies such as *Thevar Magan* (Thevar's Son, 1992), *Chinna Gounder* (The Younger Gounder, 1992), *Yejamaan* (Boss, 1993) and *Naatamai* (Village Head, 1994).

It is heartening that film directors from marginalized communities have come of age and are creators of good cinema. But what we see is still cinema. The extant two-tumbler system—a tumbler for non-Dalits and another for Dalits, the 2022 Vengaivayal incident of faecal matter in the water tank in a Dalit hamlet (separate water tanks exist for Dalits in some hamlets) all display the chinks in the Dravidian narrative of inclusiveness.

How does the DMK disabuse the notion that it is a party of the intermediaries? The party has been receptive to the changes happening around it. One of its four deputy general secretaries must be a woman, and the other an Adi Dravida. Yet, real power vests with the district secretaries and only one of its seventy-two district secretaries is an Adi Dravida, and one a woman. Intra-party elections decide the outcome of the fiercely fought district contests, but success also depends on the leadership's blessings.

Elsewhere, the Dalit-predominant VCK has seventeen non-Dalit district secretaries in its 144 districts and sports three women, five Muslims, and a Christian. The party has two MLAs who are non-Dalits.[2] The Kazhagams would require much courage to emulate this feat.

On 28 August 2018, in his acceptance speech as president of the DMK, Stalin said, 'A race that does not change itself to suit

Jayalalithaa with Periyar

Photo credit: 'Stills' Gnanam

Jayaprakash Narayan and Karunanidhi

Photo courtesy: Subha News Photo Service

MGR's emergence brought about a brief rapprochement between Kamaraj (left) and
Indira Gandhi in 1974

Photo credit: 'Stills' Gnanam

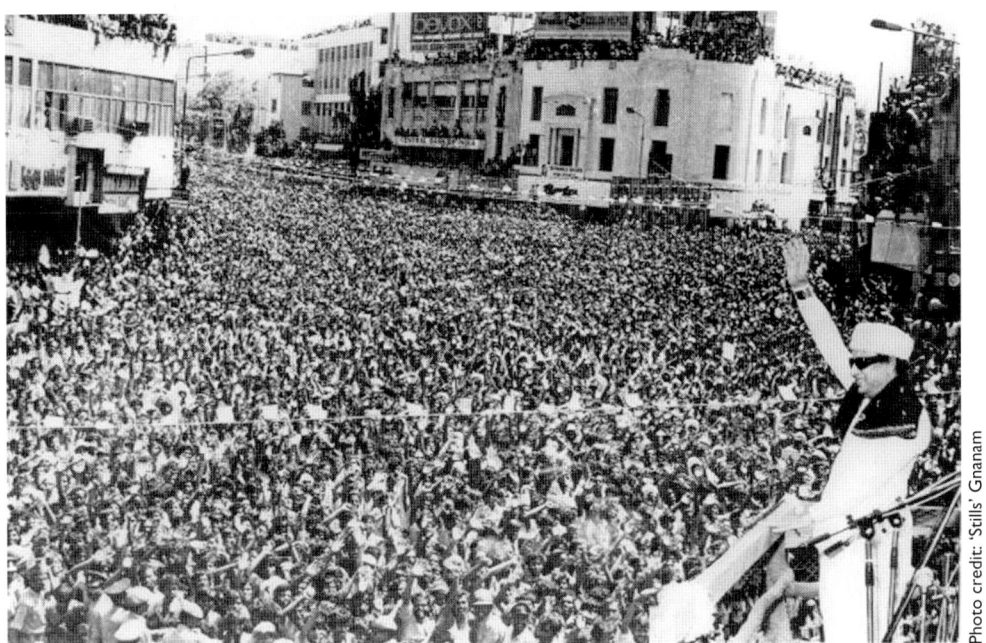

MGR at the public oath-taking ceremony when he became CM for the first time in 1977

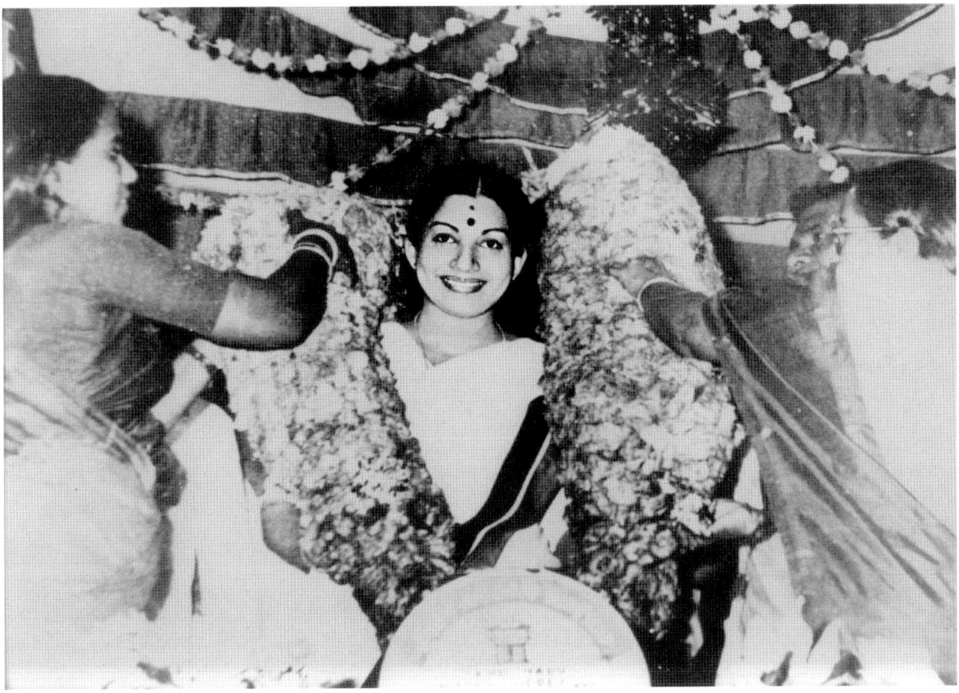

Photo credit: 'Stills' Gnanam

Jayalalithaa being felicitated. She is wearing a sari with the AIADMK colours as the border

MGR and Prabhakaran of the LTTE

Jayalalithaa, MGR and Janaki Ramachandran

Jayalalithaa as MGR's body lay in state after his death in December 1987

Photo credit: 'Stills' Gnanam

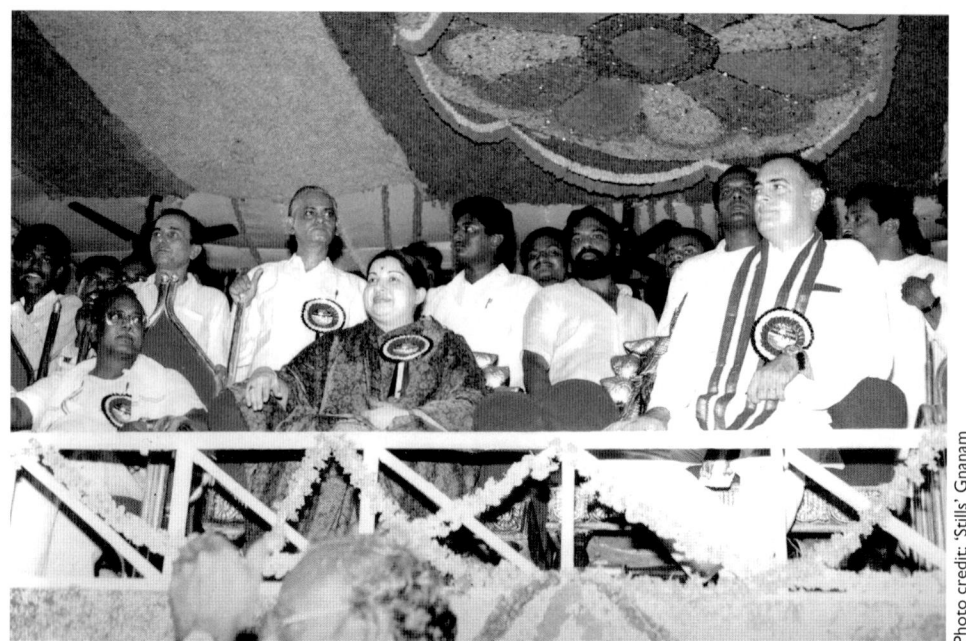

Vazhapadi Ramamurthy, Jayalalithaa and Rajiv Gandhi at a 1991 election rally

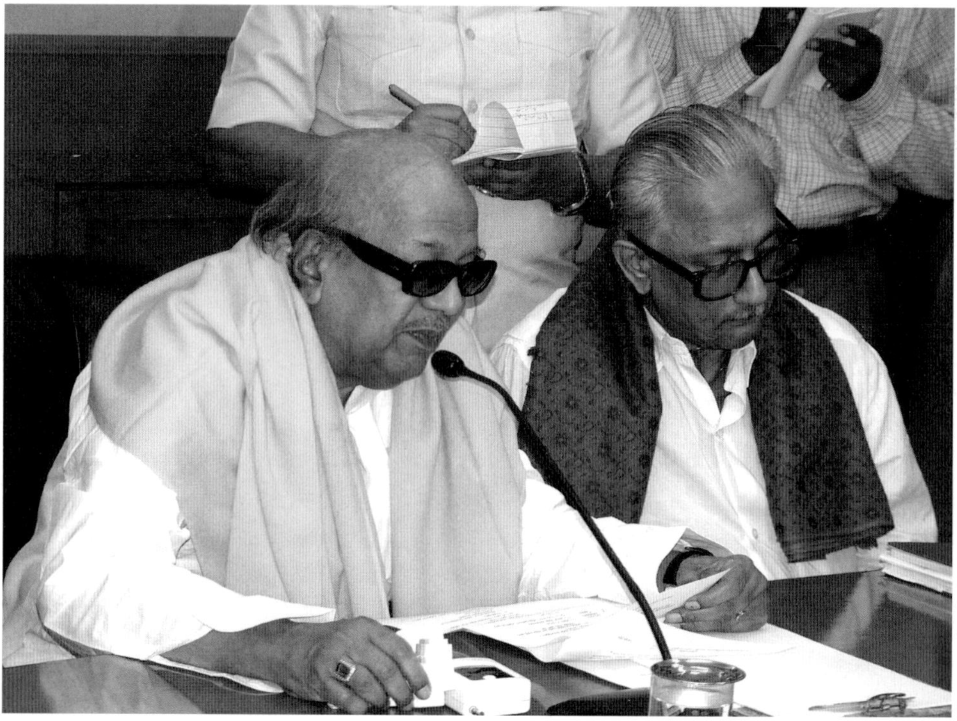
Photo credit: 'Stills' Gnanam

Karunanidhi and Anbazhagan

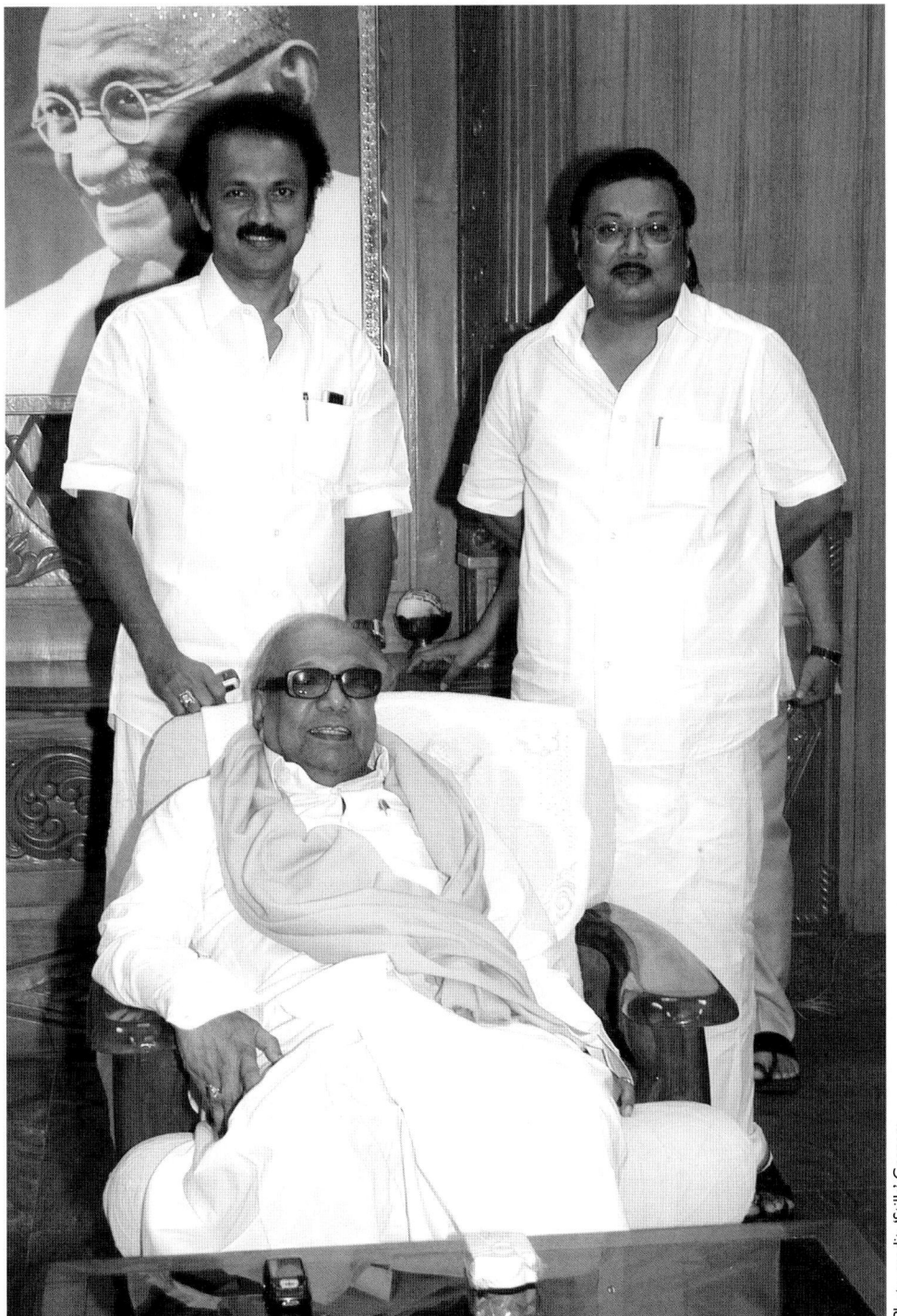

Karunanidhi with his sons M.K. Stalin and M.K. Alagiri in better times

The 2017 Jallikattu protests that rocked Chennai like never before

the changing times will not last,' indicating his willingness to accept change. Seven decades later, the DMK's challenges cannot be the same.

What are its challenges in the next twenty-five years? The challenges are substantial, and they remain jobs, sustainable development, graft, eradication of caste, weaning people away from freebies and subsidies and a calibrated liquor policy to end drunkenness.

This would require a leader who is a statesman willing to take electoral risks. With elections every five years, few, if any, politicians could be expected to transform into statesmen. But by learning from the past, we can be sure that with more awareness, the bar for leaders is likely to go up. Social media would play an increased role in spreading this awareness.

Jobs

Jobs remain the crying need of the hour. In June 2022, 2.21 lakh applicants competed for 444 sub-inspector posts in the state, showing the continued attraction for government jobs and especially the police.[3] Tamil Nadu has the second largest number of jobseekers (67.7 lakh) on the live register as of 2021 after West Bengal (77.6 lakh), as per the National Career Service data and the maximum number of scheduled caste and other backward caste jobseekers at around 17.3 lakh and 46.0 lakh. These aspirants most probably work in less ideal jobs even as they continue to populate the register. Tamil Nadu also had the highest number of women jobseekers (36.1 lakh) followed by West Bengal (24.6 lakh) and Maharashtra (18.9 lakh). Tamil Nadu has the maximum number of SC, ST and OBC jobseekers around.[4]

Subsidies

In 1967, the party gave up on its promise of a measure of rice per rupee for want of Rs 5 crore in a Rs 220-crore budget. Since

2011, the state has provided 5 kg of free rice per person. It looks like the party and the voters have come a long way. But have they? When an estimated thirty-five lakh immigrant workers have chosen the state to better their lives, the free rice to the needy does not add up.

Tamil Nadu spends close to a third of its Rs 3,65,321-crore budget, or Rs 1,13,643 crore, on subsidies, according to the Reserve Bank of India. These include subsidized power to farmers to support prices to cushioning the loss-making public sector undertakings like the Tamil Nadu Generation and Distribution Corporation Limited (TANGEDCO) and public transport corporations.

Close to a third of TANGEDCO's revenue in 2023 had to be made up by the state. They were subsidies and losses. Agricultural consumer subsidy was half of the overall subsidy in 2022 and 2023.[5] Similarly, the eight public transport corporations continue to incur a loss and are shored up by government funding. Of the seventy-seven state-run enterprises, a third were loss-incurring.[6] Increasing the efficiency of public sector undertakings and tapering off the subsidies, in the long run, would be good governance indicators.

Prohibition

Some 40 per cent, or Rs 45,000 crore, of the subsidies are from selling alcohol. This model of taking with the left hand and returning subsidies with the right hand and the handout culture requires serious introspection. Should not the scions of self-respect enable people to catch fish instead of handing out fish? This brings us to the bane of alcoholism.

Total prohibition has proved impossible even in Iran. The state owes, especially its women voters, the launch of a sustained campaign against drunkenness on the models of the anti-smoking campaign. This could be a fitting start for a party that promised total prohibition in 2016.

The Environment

Also, despite the DMK government's Meendum Manjappai and green initiatives and the party's environmental wing, the state's performance in the environmental rankings since 2016 has been slipping, according to the Centre for Science and Environment. Tamil Nadu scored just 4.4 out of 10, while Telangana topped with a score of 7.2, followed by Goa at 6.3, Maharashtra at 5.7 and Haryana at 5.5.[7] It would require all its imagination and the help of civil society and experts to keep Tamil Nadu green and environmentally friendly.

Water

Tamil Nadu is a lower riparian state. It is precariously dependent on water from its neighbours for its farming and drinking water needs. Water conservation should be foremost in the minds of Tamil Nadu's rulers. Changing to less water-intensive crops in a phased manner would be a good start. Despite the long years of struggle and an almost conclusive Supreme Court decision in 2018, the sharing of Cauvery waters remains problematic in the rain-scarce years. The two states would require all their imagination and political will to reach a regular distress-sharing formula. The state's legalistic approach to its water disputes with its neighbours has resulted in trophies but is still dependent on goodwill from the upper riparian state, as we have seen. A more enduring solution would require accommodation and courage between the upper riparian states and Tamil Nadu.

Secularism

In the battle between jobs, development, and the environment, the DMK has a worthy enemy.

The DMK's energies could be usefully channelled instead of wading into controversies like Sanatana Dharma. If Sanatana Dharma, as the DMK understands it, is the hegemony of a particular community, today, the DMK-aligned elites dominate the media to education to distilleries. Except in the temples, central appointments, music and art *sabhas* or academies and certain professions, the Brahmin's might has been largely subdued.

The BJP has already accused the DMK of Hindu phobia. Gone are the days of Karunanidhi's controversial pronouncements on the Hindu and Ram. Stalin had to concede that the DMK comprised 90 per cent Hindus, and in his acceptance speech as DMK president, said that though they were nonbelievers, they would respect believers. On 24 January 2021, Stalin even posed for photographs with a *vel* (spear of Murugan) given to him by a functionary. The ultra-Tamil nationalist Seeman, too, peddles a serious Tamil religious narrative.

Delimitation

As Chief Minister Stalin has identified, delimitation, which would rewrite the parliamentary seats in proportion to population, is a Damocles sword that hangs on Tamil Nadu's political power in relation to the rest of the country. Article 82 of the Constitution calls for the revision of seats after every census. The 84th amendment extended the 1976 freeze of the status quo until the next decennial census in 2021, which was postponed to 2026 because of the pandemic.

Tamil Nadu and the south could be victims of their own successes in slowing down population growth. Based on projections, in 2026, Tamil Nadu would gain ten more seats, but Uttar Pradesh's numbers would go from eighty to 143 while Kerala would remain the same.[8] A balance should be found to heed the need for better representation for the more populous states without diminishing the political power of those who have succeeded in slowing down the population growth.

Leadership

Leadership is not genetic. Tamil Nadu has been lucky to have a set of high-minded, stellar rulers and exceptional leaders such as Rajaji, Omandur Ramaswamy Reddiar, Kamaraj, Anna and his iconic successors. But the era of mass leadership might have come to an end. Chief ministers and leaders who are not charismatic but caring, accessible and intelligent, who walk the earth like normal mortals and attend to work like any government servant, would be a welcome change. Colossuses no longer walk Tamil Nadu. But is it too much of Tamils to ask that the high-minded and those seeking the public good again walk amidst them? For doesn't the Bible say in Proverbs 29:18: 'Where there is no vision, the people perish'?

Postscript

The INDI alliance led by the DMK in Tamil Nadu won all thirty-nine seats in Tamil Nadu and the lone Puducherry seat in the 2024 parliamentary election. The alliance's strength, the backing of the minorities, the DMK government's social programmes and a divided Opposition helped M.K. Stalin repeat his father's 2004 performance. However, the DMK's vote share fell from 32.76 per cent in 2019 when it contested twenty-four seats to 26.93 per cent with twenty-two seats. The DMK's work is cut out: jobs, development, environment and stanching the pervasive corruption.

The vote share of the AIADMK, which contested thirty-four seats with three smaller allies, fell to 20.46 per cent as opposed to 30.27 per cent in 2019 when it fought twenty seats in the company of the BJP, PMK, DMDK and others. The results are a wake-up call for the party and Edappadi K. Palaniswami. The BJP has performed creditably under its feisty state leader, K. Annamalai, in 'Periyar's soil'. It could well be the third player after the two Dravidian majors. Equally, NTK's Seeman's flamboyant leadership and ultra-Tamil nationalism seem to sway a sizeable section. With the BJP, NTK and actor Vijay crowding the political space, Tamil Nadu will likely move from a bipolar (led by the Dravidian majors) to a multipolar contest. A coalition era could be on the anvil. More choices bode well for the voters.

Appendices

PARLIAMENTARY ELECTIONS - DMK, AIADMK & INC

Year	Parties	Contested	Won	Votes	Percentage	Parties	Contested	Won	Votes	Percentage	Parties	Contested	Won	Votes	Percentage
		DMK+					AIADMK+					INC+			
1952	TAMILNADU TOILERS PARTY (TNTP)	7	4	8,89,292	4.46%	--	--	--	--	--	INC	74	35	72,53,452	36.39%
	COMMONWEAL PARTY (CP)	3	3	3,25,298	1.63%	--	--	--	--	--	--	--	--	--	--

Highlights:
*Of the 62, 13 are two-member constituencies providing for the election of scheduled castes/tribes, bringing the total number of representatives to 75.
*TNTP and CP are led by Vanniyar leaders S.S. Ramaswamy Padayachi and M.A. Manickavelu Naicker, respectively. In return for DMK support, they sign a pledge to advocate for Dravida Nadu.
*Other winners: Independents - 15, Socialist Party - 2, The Madras State Muslim League Party (MSMLP) - 1, and All India Forward Bloc (AIFB) - 1.
*Dravida Nadu party organ lists eight as winners as opposed to the seven as winners.

Year	Parties	Contested	Won	Votes	Percentage	Parties	Contested	Won	Votes	Percentage	Parties	Contested	Won	Votes	Percentage
1957	DMK	11	2	NA	NA	--	--	--	--	--	INC	41	31	50,94,552	46.52%

Highlights:
*The total number of constituencies is 34, out of which 7 are two-member constituencies, bringing the total number of representatives to 41.
*DMK fields 11 and lends support to 5 others.
*E.V.K. Sampath wins Namakkal and R. Dharmalingam, Tiruvannamalai. They become the first DMK MPs to win as independents as the party was yet to be recognized.
*Six other independents win.
*CPI contests 13 and wins 2 and Praja Socialist Party (PSP) contests 7 but wins no seats.

Year	Parties	Contested	Won	Votes	Percentage	Parties	Contested	Won	Votes	Percentage	Parties	Contested	Won	Votes	Percentage
1962	DMK	18	7	23,15,610	18.64%	--	--	--	--	--	INC	41	31	56,23,013	45.26%

Highlights:
*CPI contests 14, wins 2, polls 12,72,313 votes and 10.24%. AIFB fights and wins one seat, 19,853 votes and 1.41%. Swatantra contests 16 but wins none although it polls 13,00,526 votes and 10.47%.

Year	Parties	Contested	Won	Votes	Percentage	Parties	Contested	Won	Votes	Percentage	Parties	Contested	Won	Votes	Percentage
1967	DMK	25	25	55,24,514	35.78%	--	--	--	--	--	INC	39	3	64,36,710	41.69%
	SWATANTRA	7	6	14,14,208	9.16%	--	--	--	--	--	--	--	--	--	--
	CPM	6	4	10,57,542	6.85%	--	--	--	--	--	--	--	--	--	--
	IUML	1	1	1,80,392	1.17%	--	--	--	--	--	--	--	--	--	--

Highlights:
*Total number of seats are 39 following delimitation.
*On 14 January 1969, Madras State is renamed Tamil Nadu.

Year	DMK+					AIADMK+					INC+				
	Parties	Contested	Won	Votes	Percentage	Parties	Contested	Won	Votes	Percentage	Parties	Contested	Won	Votes	Percentage
1971	DMK	24	23	56,22,758	35.25%	--	--	--	--	--	INC (O)	29	1	48,53,534	30.43%
	INC (I)	9	9	29,99,567	12.51%	--	--	--	--	--	SWATANTRA	9	0	14,79,693	9.28%
	CPI	4	4	8,66,399	5.43%	--	--	--	--	--	SSP	1	0	1,41,605	0.89%
	AIFB	1	1	2,08,431	1.31%	--	--	--	--	--	--	--	--	--	--
	IUML	1	1	1,75,940	1.10%	--	--	--	--	--	--	--	--	--	--

Highlights:
*INC splits into INC (O) or Organization and INC (R) or Requisition led by Indira Gandhi in 1969. She splits Congress (R) in 1978 to form the current Congress, known after her as Congress (I).
*INC (O) allies with Rajaji's Swatantra in a 'grand alliance', but faces defeat.
*Kamaraj dies in 1975; the two Congress factions come together under Indira Gandhi's leadership; G.K. Moopanar heads the united Congress in the state. Remnants of the Congress (O) join others to form the Janata Party in 1977.
*First elections contested by DMK under the leadership of M. Karunanidhi. Karunanidhi aligns with Indira Gandhi against Rajaji-Kamaraj but offers her only parliamentary seats. In the event, INC (R) does not field candidates for the assembly.
*In a first, Periyar E.V. Ramasamy briefly canvasses for the DMK.
*M.G.R. breaks the DMK and founds his Anna DMK in 1972; later, All India Anna DMK.

Year	DMK+					AIADMK+					INC+				
1977	DMK	19	1	33,23,320	18.61%	AIADMK	20	18	53,65,076	30.04%	--	--	--	--	--
	JANATA PARTY (JP)	18	3	31,56,116	17.67	INC	15	14	39,77,306	22.27%	--	--	--	--	--
	--	--	--	--	--	CPI	3	3	8,22,233	4.60%	--	--	--	--	--

Highlights:
*DMK allies with the Janata Party (JP). DMK and JP win 1 and 3 seats, respectively.
*Two AIADMK MPs became union cabinet ministers in 1979 when Charan Singh broke the Janata Party to become prime minister with AIADMK support.

Year	DMK+					AIADMK+					INC+				
1980	DMK	16	16	42,36,537	23.01%	AIADMK	24	2	42,36,537	25.38%	--	--	--	--	--
	INC	22	20	58,21,411	31.62%	CPI	3	0	6,60,940	3.59%	--	--	--	--	--
	IUML	1	1	2,32,567	1.26%	CPM	3	0	5,91,869	3.21%	--	--	--	--	--
	--	--	--	--	--	JP	9	0	14,65,782	7.96%	--	--	--	--	--

Highlights:
*AIADMK wins Gobi and Sivakasi by thin margins.
*DMK's G. Lakshmanan becomes Deputy Speaker of the Lok Sabha.

Year	DMK+					AIADMK+					INC+				
	Parties	Contested	Won	Votes	Percentage	Parties	Contested	Won	Votes	Percentage	Parties	Contested	Won	Votes	Percentage
1984	DMK	27	2	55,97,507	25.90%	AIADMK	12	12	39,68,967	18.36%	--	--	--	--	--
	CPI	3	0	7,38,106	3.41%	INC	26	25	87,55,871	40.51%	--	--	--	--	--
	CPM	3	0	6,14,893	2.84%	GKNC	1	0	2,17,104	1.00%	--	--	--	--	--
	JP	5	0	9,11,931	4.22%	--	--	--	--	--	--	--	--	--	--
	TN KAMARAJ CONGRESS	1	0	1,44,076	0.67%	--	--	--	--	--					

Highlights:
*Sympathy wave trounces the DMK, which wins only North and Central Madras seats.
*AIADMK's M. Thambidurai becomes Deputy Speaker of the Lower House.
*TN Kamaraj Congress is led by Pazha Nedumaran. GKNC or Gandhi Kamaraj National Congress is led by Kumari Anandan.

Year	DMK+					AIADMK+					INC+				
1989	DMK	31	0	70,38,849	26.66%	AIADMK	11	11	45,18,649	17.12%	--	--	--	--	--
	CPM	4	0	9,65,838	3.66%	INC	28	27	1,05,24,027	39.86%	--	--	--	--	--
	CPI	2	1	5,39,316	2.04%	--	--	--	--	--	--	--	--	--	--
	JANATA DAL (JD)	2	0	3,74,902	1.42%	--	--	--	--	--	--	--	--	--	--

Highlights:
The DMK could not match the united AIADMK fighting with the Congress (I) as an ally.

Year	DMK+					AIADMK+					INC+				
1991	DMK	29	0	56,01,597	22.69%	AIADMK	11	11	45,18,649	18.10%	--	--	--	--	--
	JD	5	0	7,18,222	2.91%	INC	28	28	1,05,10,569	42.57%	--	--	--	--	--
	CPM	3	0	6,11,358	2.48%	--	--	--	--	--	--	--	--	--	--
	CPI	2	0	5,03,762	2.04%	--	--	--	--	--	--	--	--	--	--

Highlights:
*Rajiv Gandhi's assassination leads to a washout of the DMK alliance.

Year	DMK+					AIADMK+					INC+				
1996	DMK	17	17	69,67,679	25.63%	AIADMK	10	0	21,30,286	7.84%	--	--	--	--	--
	TMC	20	20	73,39,982	27.00%	INC	29	0	49,65,364	18.26%	--	--	--	--	--
	CPI	2	2	6,32,813	2.33%	--	--	---	---	--	--	--	--	--	--

Highlights:
*TMC is Tamil Maanila Congress, founded by G.K. Moopanar, protesting the Congress (I) alliance with Jayalalithaa.

Year	DMK+					AIADMK+					INC+				
	Parties	Contested	Won	Votes	Percentage	Parties	Contested	Won	Votes	Percentage	Parties	Contested	Won	Votes	Percentage
1998	DMK	17	5	51,40,266	20.08%	AIADMK	22	18	67,31,550	25.89%	INC	35	0	12,23,102	4.78%
	TMC	20	3	51,69,183	20.19%	BJP	5	3	17,57,645	6.86%	MGRADMK	3	0	2,78,324	1.09%
	CPI	2	1	6,28,360	2.45%	PMK	5	4	15,48,976	6.05%	UCPI	1	0	10,018	0.04%
	MGRADMK	3	0	2,78,324	1.09%	MDMK	5	3	16,02,504	6.26%	--	--	--	--	--
	CPM	2	0	1,61,452	0.63%	TRC - THAMIZHAGA RAJIV CONGRESS	1	1	3,65,557	1.40%	--				--
	--	--	--	--	--	JP	1	1	2,66,202	1.04%	--	--	--	--	--

Highlights:

*Vazhapadi K. Ramamurthy leads the Thamizhaga Rajiv Congress (TRC) contesting as an independent with the AIADMK-BJP alliance.

*Subramanian Swamy wins on a Janata Party ticket. Swamy operated as the rump Janata Party opposing the 1998 merger of the party with V.P. Singh's Jan Morcha and others to form the Janata Dal.

*Su. Thirunavukkarasar heads the MGRADMK. UCPI is the United Communist Party of India, a breakaway group of the CPI led by Tha. Pandian.

Year	DMK+					AIADMK+					INC+				
	Parties	Contested	Won	Votes	Percentage	Parties	Contested	Won	Votes	Percentage	Parties	Contested	Won	Votes	Percentage
1999	DMK	19	12	62,98,832	23.13%	AIADMK + INL	24	10	69,92,003	25.68%	--	--	--	--	--
	PMK	7	5	22,36,821	8.21%	INC	11	2	30,22,107	11.10%	--	--	--	--	--
	BJP	6	4	10,45,286	7.14%	CPI	2	1	6,95,762	2.56%	--	--	--	--	--
	MDMK	5	4	16,20,527	5.95%	CPM	2	0	6,39,516	2.35%	--	--	--	--	--
	MGRADMK	1	1	3,96,216	1.46%	--	--	--	--	--	--	--	--	--	--
	TRC	1	0	3,38,278	1.24%	--	--	--	--	--	--	--	--	--	--

Highlights:

*In a first, DMK allies with the MDMK.

*TMC forms a third front with VCK and IUML contesting as independents. Puthiya Thamizhagam (PT) and JP also join the front, losing in all the 38 constituencies contested in with a combined vote share of 9.32%.

Year	DMK+					AIADMK+					INC+				
	Parties	Contested	Won	Votes	Percentage	Parties	Contested	Won	Votes	Percentage	Parties	Contested	Won	Votes	Percentage
2004	DMK	16	16	70,64,393	24.60%	AIADMK	33	0	85,47,014	29.80%	--	--	--	--	--
	INC	10	10	41,34,255	14.40%	BJP	6	0	14,55,899	5.10%	--	--	--	--	--
	PMK	5	5	19,27,367	6.70%	--	--	--	--	--	--	--	--	--	--
	MDMK	4	4	16,79,870	5.90%	--	--	--	--	--	--	--	--	--	--
	CPI	2	2	8,52,981	3.00%	--	--	--	--	--	--	--	--	--	--
	CPM	2	2	8,24,524	2.90%	--	--	--	--	--	--	--	--	--	--

Highlights:
*IUML contested in one constituency with DMK symbol.
*A third front with VCK, Makkal Tamil Desam, Puthiya Thamizhagam, Janata Dal United led by George Fernandes, INL and others contested in 25 constituencies losing all.
*A fourth front with JP led by Subramanian Swamy and Puthiya Needhi Katchi contested in 31 constituencies losing all.

Year	DMK+					AIADMK+					INC+				
	Parties	Contested	Won	Votes	Percentage	Parties	Contested	Won	Votes	Percentage	Parties	Contested	Won	Votes	Percentage
2009	DMK	21	18	76,25,397	25.10%	AIADMK	23	9	69,53,591	22.88%	--	--	--	--	--
	INC	15	8	45,67,799	15.00%	PMK	6	0	17,36,000	5.71%	--	--	--	--	--
	VCK	2	1	7,35,847	2.40%	MDMK	4	1	11,12,908	3.66%	--	--	--	--	--
	IUML	1	0	3,60,474	1.19%	CPI	3	1	8,64,572	2.85%	--	--	--	--	--
	--	--	--	--	--	CPM	3	1	6,68,729	2.20%	--	--	--	--	--

Highlights:
*Actor politician Vijayakanth's DMDK enters fray; loses all 39 seats. Polls an impressive 10.3%.
*BJP contests alone and loses with a vote share of 2.3%.

Year	DMK+					AIADMK+					INC+				
	Parties	Contested	Won	Votes	Percentage	Parties	Contested	Won	Votes	Percentage	Parties	Contested	Won	Votes	Percentage
2014	DMK	34	0	95,75,850	23.60%	AIADMK	39	37	1,79,83,168	44.92%	INC	39	0	17,51,123	4.30%
	VCK	2	0	6,06,110	1.50%	--	--	--	--	--	--	--	--	--	--
	MANIDHANEYA MAKKAL KATCHI (MNMK)	1	0	2,36,679	0.60%	--	--	--	--	--	--	--	--	--	--
	IUML	1	0	2,05,896	0.50%	--	--	--	--	--	--	--	--	--	--
	PT	1	0	2,62,812	0.60%	--	--	--	--	--	--	--	--	--	--

Highlights:
*AIADMK's highest number of seats contested, won and votes polled.
*BJP ends up contesting 9 seats as papers of its candidate for Nilgiris is rejected as irregular; wins 1, polls 22,22,090, 5.50%.
*PMK contests 8, wins 1, polls 18,04,812 votes, 4.40%.
*MDMK contests 7, wins 0, polls 14,17,535 votes, 3.50%.
*DMDK contests 14, wins 0, polls 20,79,392 votes, 5.10%.
*MNMK is a Muslim party which was founded in 2009.

Year	DMK+					AIADMK+					INC+				
	Parties	Contested	Won	Votes	Percentage	Parties	Contested	Won	Votes	Percentage	Parties	Contested	Won	Votes	Percentage
2019	DMK	24	24	1,43,63,332	33.52%	AIADMK	22	1	83,07,345	19.39%	--	--	--	--	--
	INC	9	8	54,05,674	12.61%	PMK	7	0	22,97,431	5.36%	--	--	--	--	--
	CPI	2	2	10,31,617	2.40%	BJP	5	0	15,51,924	3.66%	--	--	--	--	--
	CPM	2	2	10,18,225	2.37%	DMDK	4	0	9,29,590	2.16%	--	--	--	--	--
	VCK	1	1	5,00,229	1.16%	TMC	1	0	2,20,849	0.50%	--	--	--	--	--
	IUML	1	1	4,69,943	1.09%	--	--	--	--	--	--	--	--	--	--

Highlights:
*First election in the absence of M. Karunanidhi and J. Jayalalithaa since 1989.
*VCK contests 1 seat on DMK symbol and one on a symbol allotted to it for that election.
*Other unrecognized parties contesting on DMK symbol include MDMK, Indhiya Jananayaga Katchi (IJK), Kongunadu Makkal Desiya Katchi (KMDK) with 1 seat each.
*Parties contesting on AIADMK symbol include PT and Puthiya Needhi Katchi (PNK), each contesting 1 seat. AIADMK's sole winner is O. Panneerselvam's son in Theni.

The data here relies on the Election Commission, party organs and open sources. This effort is not comprehensive or complete as not all seats or parties or independents could be accounted for. It tends to focus on the main formations and make sense of the data available.

LEGISLATIVE ASSEMBLY ELECTIONS - DMK, AIADMK & INC

Year	Parties	DMK+ Contested	Won	Votes	Percentage	Parties	AIADMK+ Contested	Won	Votes	Percentage	Parties	INC+ Contested	Won	Votes	Percentage
1952	TAMILNADU TOILERS PARTY (TNTP)	34	19	8,52,330	4.25%	--	--	--	--	--	INC	367	152	69,88,701	34.88%
	COMMONWEAL PARTY (CP)	13	6	2,18,288	1.09%	--	--	--	--	--	--	--	--	--	--

Highlights:
*Out of the total 309 constituencies in the undivided Madras State, 66 were two-member constituencies, 62 of which had one seat reserved for Scheduled Caste candidates and 4 for Scheduled Tribe candidates.
*A total of 667 independents contested, of which 62 won; votes - 47,58,768; percentage - 23.75%.
*TNTP and CP were led by Vanniyar leaders S.S. Ramaswamy Padayachi and M.A. Manickavelu Naicker, respectively. In return for DMK support, both Vanniyar leaders sign a pledge to advocate for Dravida Nadu. "
*More than 150 candidates, including the TNTP and CP sign the DMK pledge. Forty-three of these win.
*INC suffers heavy losses, which include the chief minister and much of the cabinet. Rajaji cobbles up a majority and becomes, for a second time, the first Tamil-speaking Brahmin premier of Madras State. (J. Jayalalithaa will be the third after Janaki Ramachandran.) Manickavelu Naicker joins his ministry while Ramaswamy Padayachi lends support from the outside.
*Ramaswamy Padayachi joins Kamaraj's ministry in 1954.

Year	Parties	DMK+ Contested	Won	Votes	Percentage	Parties	AIADMK+ Contested	Won	Votes	Percentage	Parties	INC+ Contested	Won	Votes	Percentage
1957	DMK	116	15	16,53,435	14.85%	--	--	--	--	--	INC	204	151	50,46,576	45.34%

Highlights:
*The total number of constituencies are 167, out of which 38 are two-member constituencies, making the House strength 205.
*In 1959, as a result of The Andhra Pradesh and Madras (Alteration of Boundaries) Act 1959, one member of the Andhra Pradesh Legislative Assembly was allotted to Madras, taking the total to 206.
*DMK's debut election. DMK fields 117 and supports another seven. Candidates run as independents on different symbols, including the rising sun.
*C.N. Annadurai, M. Karunanidhi and K. Anbazhagan are elected while Era. Nedunchezhian, poet Kannadasan, actor S.S. Rajendran lose.
*Of the 15 seats won, three were two-member constituencies. The party had lost by a few hundred votes to the Congress in 20 seats.

Year	Parties	DMK+ Contested	Won	Votes	Percentage	Parties	AIADMK+ Contested	Won	Votes	Percentage	Parties	INC+ Contested	Won	Votes	Percentage
1962	DMK	143	50	34,35,633	27.10%	--	--	--	--	--	INC	206	139	58,48,974	46.14%

Highlights:
*The total number of constituencies was 206 after two-member constituencies were abolished in 1961 by the Two-Member Constituencies (Abolition) Act, 1961.
*Anna faces defeat in his native Kanchipuram, but the DMK's showing ushers in the 1963 Sixteenth Amendment, requiring candidates to pledge to uphold India's unity. The DMK drops Dravida Nadu demand.
*Swatantra contests 94, wins 6, polls 9,91,773 votes and 7.82%; AIFB contests 6, wins 3, polls 1,73,261 votes and 1.37%, CPI contests 68, wins 2, polls 9,78,806 votes and 7.72% and Socialist Party contests 7, wins one, polls 48,753 votes and 0.38%.

Year	DMK+					AIADMK+					INC+				
	Parties	Contested	Won	Votes	Percentage	Parties	Contested	Won	Votes	Percentage	Parties	Contested	Won	Votes	Percentage
1967	DMK	174	137	62,30,552	40.69%		--	--	--	--	INC	232	51	62,93,378	41.10%
	SWATANTRA	27	20	8,11,232	5.30%		--	--	--	--	--	--	--	--	--
	CPM	22	11	6,23,114	4.07%		--	--	--	--	--	--	--	--	--
	PRAJA SOCIALIST PARTY (PSP)	4	4	1,36,188	0.89%		--	--	--	--	--	--	--	--	--
	IUML	3	3	95,494	0.62%		--	--	--	--	--	--	--	--	--
	SAMYUKTA SOCIALIST PARTY (SSP)	3	2	84,188	0.55%		--	--	--	--	--	--	--	--	--
	DMK-BACKED IND	2	2	70,665	0.46%		--	--	--	--	--	--	--	--	--

Highlights:

- The total number of constituencies was 234 and would remain the same in all future State Assembly elections.
- Anna promises three measures of rice for a rupee on his stump; Kamaraj defeated in his hometown, Virudhunagar, at the hands of a DMK student leader.
- MGR wins his first Assembly election from a hospital bed. He would perform a repeat in 1984.
- Si.Pa. Adithanar's Naam Thamizhar Katchi's four and Tamilarasu Kazhagam's two candidates fight under the DMK symbol.

Year	DMK+					AIADMK+					INC+				
	Parties	Contested	Won	Votes	Percentage	Parties	Contested	Won	Votes	Percentage	Parties	Contested	Won	Votes	Percentage
1971	DMK	203	184	76,54,935	48.58%		--	--	--	--	INC(O)	201	15	55,13,894	34.99%
	CPI	10	8	3,64,803	2.32%		--	--	--	--	SWATANTRA	19	6	4,65,145	2.95%
	AIFB	9	7	2,68,721	1.71%		--	--	--	--	TNTP	6	--	83,187	0.50%
	PSP	4	4	1,47,985	0.94%		--	--	--	--	SSP	2	--	17,491	0.02%
	IUML	7	6	1,91,730	0.44%		--	--	--	--	REPUBLICAN PARTY	1	--	25,667	0.15%
	TAMILARASU KAZHAGAM	2	1	43,436	0.2%		--	--	--	--					

Highlights:

- With a nominated member, the House's strength is 235. Three independents win, of which two defeat DMK candidates; CPM runs in 37 and Jan Sangh in five but fail to win a single seat.
- INC splits into INC (O) or Organization and INC (R) or Requisition led by Indira Gandhi in 1969. She splits Congress (R) in 1978 to form the current Congress known after her as Congress (I).
- INC (O) allies with Rajaji's Swatantra Party in a 'grand alliance,' but faces defeat.
- Kamaraj dies in 1975; the two Congress factions come together under Indira Gandhi's leadership; G.K. Moopanar heads the united Congress in the state.
- Remnants of the Congress (O) join others to form the Janata Party in 1977 in Tamil Nadu.
- First elections contested by DMK under the leadership of M. Karunanidhi.
- M. Karunanidhi aligns with Indira Gandhi-led INC (R); denies assembly seats to ally.
- Periyar E.V. Ramasamy canvasses for the DMK in a first.
- MGR breaks the DMK and founds his Anna DMK in 1972; later, All India Anna DMK.

Year	DMK+					AIADMK+					INC+				
	Parties	Contested	Won	Votes	Percentage	Parties	Contested	Won	Votes	Percentage	Parties	Contested	Won	Votes	Percentage
1977	DMK	230	48	42,58,771	24.89%	AIADMK	200	130	51,94,876	30.36%	INC	198	27	29,94,535	17.50%
	--	--	--	--	--	CPM	20	12	4,77,835	2.79%	CPI	32	5	4,96,955	2.90%
	--	--	--	--	--	--	--	--	--	--	--	--	--	--	--
	--	--	--	--	--	--	--	--	--	--	--	--	--	--	--

Highlights:
*Spurned by the Janata Party, DMK fights all but four seats where its ally, the Tamil Nadu Communist Party, led by C. Manali Kandasamy, fields candidates in three and the DMK extends support to the son of the iconic Ponnappa Nadar, in Killiyur.
*The DMK, AIADMK, Congress (I) and Janata Party (JP) enter into a four-way race. JP contests in 233 constituencies and wins 10 with a vote share of 16.67%.
*AIADMK supports 10 IUML candidates, Ponnappa Nadar's son in Killiyur, AIFB in Usilampatti and an independent in Thiruthuraipoondi, bringing the total to 234.

Year	DMK+					AIADMK+					INC+				
1980	DMK (IUML 6)	118	38	42,48,790	22.10%	AIADMK	177	129	73,03,010	38.75%	--	--	--	--	--
	INC	114	31	39,41,900	20.90%	CPM	16	11	5,96,406	3.16%	--	--	--	--	--
	IND	2	1	65,536		CPI	15	9	5,01,032	2.66%	--	--	--	--	--
	--	--	--	--	--	GKNC	10	6	3,22,440	1.71%	--	--	--	--	--
	--	--	--	--	--	AIFB	2	1	65,536	0.35%	--	--	--	--	--

Highlights:
*Karunanidhi agrees on sharing power with Congress (I) and on 17 June 1980, a common minimum programme promises free education up to the degree level for all, waiver of farm loans, making tillers owners and adoption of bright backward class students for higher studies.
*Karunanidhi wins by 699 votes in Anna Nagar, his lowest margin.
*AIADMK independents include Pazha Nedumaran-led TN Kamaraj Congress which contests six and wins three. INC (Urs) contests three seats but wins none.
*Janata Party contests 94 seats and wins 2 and 2.78%.
*GKNC or Gandhi Kamaraj National Congress is led by Kumari Anandan.

Year	DMK+					AIADMK+					INC+				
	Parties	Contested	Won	Votes	Percentage	Parties	Contested	Won	Votes	Percentage	Parties	Contested	Won	Votes	Percentage
1984	DMK + IUML 8	175	24	63,62,770	29.34%	AIADMK + RPI	157	133	80,30,809	37.03%	--	--	--	--	--
	CPM	16	5	5,97,622	2.76%	INC	73	62	35,29,708	16.28%	--	--	--	--	--
	JP	16	3	4,93,374	2.28%	GKNC	4	2	1,20,704	0.60%	--	--	--	--	--
	CPI	17	2	5,67,527	2.62%	--	--	--	--	--	--	--	--	--	--
1989	DMK + ABDUL LATHEEF MUSLIM LEAGUE 5 + TN FORWARD BLOC	203	151	80,39,155	33.34%	AIADMK (JL)	203	29	58,31,383	21.90%	INC	217	26	48,67,125	20.19%
	CPM	21	15	8,51,351	3.53%	CPI	13	3	2,95,170	1.22%	--	--	--	--	--
	JP	10	4	2,82,647	1.17%	AIADMK (JR)	177	1	22,02,249	9.13%	--	--	--	--	--
	--	--	--	--	--	TMM	49	0	--	--	--	--	--	--	--

Highlights:

*As MGR recuperates in a US hospital, the AIADMK decides to club the assembly elections with the parliamentary elections – a year before completing its full term.

*A member of the state Legislative Council, Karunanidhi chooses not to run.

*A Hindu Munnani-supported independent debuts from Padmanabhapuram. Two other independents also win.

Highlights:

*AIADMK divides into Janaki (JR) and J. Jayalaithaa (JL) factions and contest the elections separately. The AIADMK tally of two seats after unity is added to the JL's tally of 27.

*Thamizhaga Munnetra Munnani (TMM) led by actor Sivaji Ganesan allies with Janaki. Sivaji Ganesan loses to a DMK candidate in Thiruvaiyaru.

*BJP fields 36 candidates. None succeed. A total of 175 independent candidates contested and won 5 seats with 21,64,484 votes and 9% share.

*Abdul Latheef leaves IUML in 1988 over differences with the state head Abdul Samad, who breaks off ties with the DMK for its silence on fellow alliance partner CPM, describing the IUML as 'communal'. Latheef allies with the DMK. In 1994, he merges with the Ibrahim Sulaiman Sait-floated Indian National League (INL).

Year	DMK+					AIADMK+					INC+				
	Parties	Contested	Won	Votes	Percentage	Parties	Contested	Won	Votes	Percentage	Parties	Contested	Won	Votes	Percentage
1991	DMK	176	2	55,35,668	22.46%	AIADMK	168	163	1,09,40,966	44.39%	--	--	--	--	--
	TMK	11	2	3,71,645	1.51%	INC + INC (S) 1	66	61	37,97,076	15.19%	--	--	--	--	--
	CPM	22	1	7,77,532	3.15%	--	--	--	--	--	--	--	--	--	--
	JD	15	1	4,15,947	1.69%	--	--	--	--	--	--	--	--	--	--
	CPI	10	1	3,05,143	1.24%	--	--	--	--	--	--	--	--	--	--
1996	DMK + INL 5	182	173	1,24,23,380	42.07%	AIADMK	168	4	58,31,383	21.47%	--	--	--	--	--
	TMC	40	39	25,26,474	9.30%	INC	64	0	15,23,340	5.61%	--	--	--	--	--
	CPI	11	8	5,75,570	2.12%	--	--	--	--	--	--	--	--	--	--
	AIFB	1	1	75,324	0.28%	--	--	--	--	--	--	--	--	--	--

Highlights: (1991)

*AIADMK reunited under Jayalalithaa.

*Su. Thirunavukkarasar leads Anna Puratchi Thalaivar Thamizhaga Munnetra Kazhagam (APTTMK), contests 9 seats, wins 2 and 1.38%. Rechristens party later as MGRADMK.

*Rajiv Gandhi's assassination leads to a washout of the DMK. M. Karunanidhi becomes the sole winner. The DMK wins a by-election later, taking its tally to 2.

*S. Ramachandran becomes the first Paatali Makkal Katchi (PMK) legislator. PMK fields 199 candidates, polls 14,56,456 votes and an impressive 5.91%.

*Thayaka Marumalachi Kazhagam (TMK) is led by actor T. Rajendar.

*Indian Congress (Socialist) is led by Sarat Chandra Sinha.

Highlights: (1996)

*TMC is Tamil Maanila Congress headed by G.K. Moopanar, who broke away from Congress (I) protesting the alliance with Jayalalithaa.

*Jayalithaa suffers a humiliating defeat at the hands of a little-known DMK functionary.

*INL – Abdul Latheef heads Ibrahim Sulaiman Sait's INL or Indian National League in Tamil Nadu.

*PMK wins four seats, BJP, CPM, Janata Dal and Janata Party and independents win one each. BJP makes its debut in the assembly.

*MDMK fights in alliance with CPM; polls 5.78% but fails to win a seat.

Year		DMK+				AIADMK+					INC+				
	Parties	Contested	Won	Votes	Percentage	Parties	Contested	Won	Votes	Percentage	Parties	Contested	Won	Votes	Percentage
2001	DMK + IND 18	185	31	86,69,864	30.92%	AIADMK	141	132	88,15,387	31.44%	--	--	--	--	--
	BJP	21	4	8,95,352	3.19%	TMC	32	23	18,85,726	6.73%	--	--	--	--	--
	PT	10	0	3,55,171	1.27%	PMK	27	20	15,57,500	5.56%	--	--	--	--	--
	MAKKAL TAMIL DESAM - RAJA KANNAPPAN	6	0	2,57,126	0.92%	INC	14	7	6,96,205	2.48%	--	--	--	--	--
	PUDHIYA NEEDHI KATCHI - A.C. SHANMUGAM	5	0	1,96,740	0.70%	CPM	8	6	4,70,736	1.68%	--	--	--	--	--
	MGRADMK	3	2	1,29,474	0.46%	CPI	8	5	4,44,710	1.59%	--	--	--	--	--
	MGR KAZHAGAM - R.M. VEERAPPAN	2	0	1,36,916	0.49%	AIFB	1	1	39,248	0.14%	--	--	--	--	--
	KONGUNADU MAKKAL KATCHI (KMK)	1	0	40,421	0.14%	TMMK + INL	2	2	1,03,971	0.40%	--	--	--	--	--
	THAMIZHAR BHOOMI - KU.PA. KRISHNAN	1	0	45,002	0.16%	IUML	1	0	30,497	0.11%	--	--	--	--	--

Highlights:

*DMK independents include the northern Dalit dominant Dalit Panthers, later Viduthalai Chiruthaigal Katchi's (VCK) eight seats, Kongunadu Makkal Katchi (KMK), Thamizhaga Muslim Iykkya Jamaat (TMIJ), Congress Jananayaka Peravai (CJP) led by P. Chidambaram, Tamil Pattali Makkal Katchi (TPMK) - a PMK rebel, Tamil Nadu Mutharaiyar Sangam (TNMS), Kumari Anandan's Thondar Congress and Indian Uzhavar Uzhaippalar Katchi. Most of these were caste outfits.

*M. Appavu, originally of the Congress (I) and Speaker of the 2021 assembly, wins as an independent from Radhapuram constituency, bringing the total elected to 234.

*Dr. K. Krishnasamy of Puthiya Thamizhagam contests on a Janata Party ticket; becomes the first Dalit party leader to enter the assembly.

*Deserted by the TMC for its ties with the BJP, the DMK accommodates a host of caste-based parties and a one-man Muslim outfit - the TMIJ.

*P. Chidambaram founds Congress Jananayaka Peravai after breaking away from the TMC, protesting the alliance with the AIADMK.

*IUML, INL and the Tamil Nadu Muslim Munnetra Kazhagam (TMMK), founded in 1995 for the advancement of Muslims, all ally with the AIADMK.

*Vaiko's MDMK goes it alone; fails to win a single seat but polls 4.65%.

*Kongunadu Makkal Katchi of the Kongu Vellala Gounder Forum was founded ahead of the 2001 elections.

Year	DMK+					AIADMK+					INC+				
	Parties	Contested	Won	Votes	Percentage	Parties	Contested	Won	Votes	Percentage	Parties	Contested	Won	Votes	Percentage
2006	DMK + IND 4	132	96	87,28,716	26.50%	AIADMK + IND 7	189	61	1,07,68,559	32.60%	--	--	--	--	--
	INC	48	34	27,65,768	8.40%	MDMK	35	6	19,71,565	6%	--	--	--	--	--
	PMK	31	18	18,63,749	5.70%	VCK	9	2	4,26,321	1.30%	--	--	--	--	--
	CPM	13	9	8,72,674	2.70%	JD (S)	1	0	23,628	0.07%	--	--	--	--	--
	CPI	10	6	5,31,740	1.60%	--	--	--	--	--	--	--	--	--	--

Highlights:
*DMK promise of free television catches the voters' imagination. It also promises two acres of land to the landless. The second lowest number of seats since 1980 contested. J. Jayalalithaa mocks the DMK government with support of allies as 'minority ministry'.

*DMK independents include IUML, Dalit outfit Puratchi Bharatham and Forward Bloc (Vallarasu).

*AIADMK independents include INL, Indian National Trade Union Congress, Tamil Maanila Muslim League, Moovendar Munnetra Kazhagam and Forward Bloc (Santhanam).

*VCK and actor-politician Vijayakanth (Desiya Murpoku Dravida Kazhagam - DMDK) enter assembly. DMDK polls an impressive 3.4%. An independent wins in Thalli to complete the House strength of 234.

*Janata Dal Secular or JD (S) is the party founded by former prime minister Deve Gowda in 1999 when he broke off from Janata Dal.

Year	DMK+					AIADMK+					INC+				
2011	DMK + IND 5	124	23	82,49,991	22.40%	AIADMK + IND 5	165	150	1,41,50,289	38.40%	--	--	--	--	--
	INC	63	5	34,36,432	9.30%	DMDK	41	29	29,03,828	7.90%	--	--	--	--	--
	PMK	30	3	19,27,783	5.20%	CPM	12	10	8,88,364	2.40%	--	--	--	--	--
	VCK	10	0	5,55,965	1.50%	CPI	10	9	7,27,394	2%	--	--	--	--	--
	KMK	7	0	3,70,044	1.00%	MANITHANEYA MAKKAL KATCHI (MNMK)	3	2	1,81,180	0.50%	--	--	--	--	--
	--	--	--	--	--	PT	2	2	1,46,454	0.40%	--	--	--	--	--
	--	--	--	--	--	AIFB	1	1	88,253	0.20%	--	--	--	--	--

Highlights:
*DMK independents include IUML, Moovendar Munnetra Kazhagam and Perunthalaivar Makkal Katchi.

*AIADMK independents include All India Samathuva Makkal Katchi of actor Sarathkumar, Republican Party of India, All India Mcovendar Munnani Kazhagam and Tamil Nadu Kongu Ilaignar Peravai. MNMK, founded in 2009, is the political wing of the TN Muslim Munnetra Kazhagam.

*Courted by the DMK till the end, actor Vijayakanth decides to ally with J. Jayalalithaa, helping her return to power.

*Manithaneya Makkal Katchi (MMK), a Muslim party founded in 2009, contests three seats as part of the AIADMK alliance.

Year	DMK+					AIADMK+					INC+				
	Parties	Contested	Won	Votes	Percentage	Parties	Contested	Won	Votes	Percentage	Parties	Contested	Won	Votes	Percentage
2016	DMK + IND 3	180	89	1,36,70,511	31.39%	AIADMK + IND 7	234	136	1,78,06,490	40.88%	--	--	--	--	--
	INC	41	8	27,74,075	6.47%	--	--	--	--	--	--	--	--	--	--
	IUML	5	1	3,13,808	0.73%	--	--	--	--	--	--	--	--	--	--
	MNMK	4	0	1,97,150	0.46%	--	--	--	--	--	--	--	--	--	--
	PT	4	0	2,19,830	0.51%	--	--	--	--	--	--	--	--	--	--

Highlights:
*J. Jayalalithaa breaks the cycle of alternate rule by the Kazhagams from 1989. The maximum seats contested by the AIADMK ever. Independents include actor R. Sarathkumar, Thamimum Ansari's Manithaneya Jananayaga Katchi split from MNMK in 2016, RPI's C.K. Thamizharasan and others.
*Perunthalaivar Makkal Katchi, Tamil Nadu Peasants and Workers Party and Samuga Samathuva Padai contested a seat each on the DMK symbol.
*The DMDK led Third Front of MDMK, CPI, CPM, TMC and VCK projects Vijayakanth as chief ministerial candidate; fails to win a single seat. Vijayakanth himself is defeated in Ulundurpet. Loses deposit.
*The BJP formed the Fourth Front along with IJK losing in all the 234 constituencies.

Year	DMK+					AIADMK+					INC+				
	Parties	Contested	Won	Votes	Percentage	Parties	Contested	Won	Votes	Percentage	Parties	Contested	Won	Votes	Percentage
2021	DMK + MDMK 5 + IND 9	188	133	1,74,27,615	37.70%	AIADMK + TMC 6 + IND 6	191	66	1,53,89,569	33.29%	--	--	--	--	--
	INC	25	18	19,76,527	4.27%	PMK	23	5	17,58,774	3.80%	--	--	--	--	--
	VCK	6	4	4,57,763	0.99%	BJP	20	4	12,13,510	2.62%	--	--	--	--	--
	CPI	6	2	5,04,537	1.09%	--	--	--	--	--	--	--	--	--	--
	CPM	6	2	3,90,819	0.85%	--	--	--	--	--	--	--	--	--	--
	IUML	3	0	2,22,263	0.48%	--	--	--	--	--	--	--	--	--	--

Highlights:
*First election in the absence of M. Karunanidhi and J. Jayalalithaa.
*AIADMK announces 10.5 per cent of the 20 per cent compartmental reservations for Vanniyars.
*M.K. Stalin and Edappadi K. Palaniswami are the chief ministerial faces of the DMK and AIADMK respectively.
*DMK independents include E.R. Eswaran-led Kongunadu Makkal Desiya Katchi's 3 seats, M.H. Jawahirullah-led MNMK's 2 seats, AIFB's 1, T. Velmurugan-led Thamizhaga Vazhvurimai Katchi's (formed after leaving PMK) 1, Era. Adhiyaman's Aadhi Thamizhar Peravai's (a Dalit Arundhadiyinar outfit) 1 and the Marxist–Leninist Makkal Viduthalai Katchi led by S.K. Murugavel Rajan's 1.
*AMMK, DMDK, Muslim outfits Social Democratic Party of India (SDPI) and All India Majlis-e-Ittehadul Muslimeen (AIMIM) fight as allies but win no seats. AMMK polls 2.35%; DMDK 0.43%.
*Kamal Haasan heads a front with actor Sarath Kumar's All India Samathuva Makkal Katchi, IJK, JD (S) and other smaller parties. He loses to a BJP candidate in Coimbatore.
*NTK fields candidates in all 234 constituencies and polls an impressive 6.58%.

The data here relies on the Election Commission, the Tamil Nadu Legislative Assembly Reviews and open sources. This effort is not comprehensive or complete as not all seats or parties or independents could be accounted for. It tends to focus on the main formations and make sense of the data available.

Manifesto Highlights

YEAR	DMK	CONGRESS-O	AIADMK
1952	The DMK chooses to boycott the first general election, protesting that the Constitution was drafted without consulting the 'Dravidians' and is detrimental to their basic rights. Extends support to communists and 'non-Congress, honest, talented and forward-looking' candidates in return for their pledge to support and work for the cause of Dravida Nadu.	No collectivization of land. Establishment of Village Production Councils to direct, assist and market production and ensuring a better return, security of tenure and some interest in the land for the tiller. No wholesale nationalization but concerned with investment in the public sector. A mixture of industrial and decentralized cottage economy. Promise to safeguard foreign investment. Policy of non-alignment. Accent on democracy and socialism. Fight poverty, ignorance and inequality of opportunity through modern methods of production in line with the development of science and technology.	
1957	Seeks the right to self-determination to secede from the Union; political parity for big and small states by equal electoral representation and a ceiling for the Centre's authority and taxation powers. Proposes that all means of production be nationalized; a balanced five-year plan that would invest equally in the south and the implementation of schemes is left with the states. Plans to create a society where the minimum monthly salary would be Rs 100 and the maximum not more than twelve times that amount, industrialization and industries all over India and bold implementation of land reforms, expansion of agricultural cooperative farms and cattle farms, dairy, poultry and sales cooperatives in the cooperative sphere, free education up to tenth grade and education in the mother tongue, a rightful place for English, a Dravidian Research University and equal pay for central and state government staff. Tamils as ambassadors to countries with a significant Tamil populace, reduced defence expenditure and the money saved diverted into developmental schemes, a role for labour in capital and management, a single point sales tax, Devikulam, Peermedu and Tiruttani to be part of Tamil Nadu and Madras state is renamed Tamil Nadu. Promises to strive for a casteless and egalitarian society and the independence of Dravida Nadu. Says Kazhagam is capable of being a forceful Opposition in the legislature.	Goes to the people on the strength of its ten-year work in government and 'among the people', proclaims democracy and socialism as basic objectives and emphasizes self-reliance. Lists abolition of the Zamindari and Jagirdari systems, increased production of food, vast river valley schemes—Bhakra-Nangal, Damodar Valley, Hirakud, Tungabhadra and others, fertilizer factory at Sindri and the Chittaranjan Locomotive Factory, three large iron and steel plants in construction, the Integral Coach Factory in Madras, the reform of Hindu Law and the beginning of community development. Mentions atomic power for industrial development; states its vision of no exploitation and no monopolies and a socialist pattern of society, progressive participation of workers in industry and cooperative management of villages. Heavy industry balanced by small-scale and cottage industries and no nationalization of existing private industries, except where necessary or where they occupy a strategic position. All intermediaries to be progressively removed, so the cultivator owns the land and land ceilings to bring about a better distribution of land and intensified methods of cultivation on a cooperative basis. Establishment of industrial estates. Progressive steps to introduce prohibition in other parts of India. Peaceful integration of Goa, peaceful ties with Pakistan, opposition to South Africa's racial policy and declares Panch Shila as the basis of India's relations with the world. Reiterates India's efforts to get China's admission into the UN.	

YEAR	DMK	CONGRESS-O	AIADMK
1962	Proposes that the four southern states win independence and unite as a federal, socialist republic. Advocates proportional representation. Points out that it contested 116 seats in 1957 and polled seventeen lakh votes, while the Congress contested all 205 seats and won fifty lakh votes. Lists under thirty-six heads its work as a legislative opposition against price rise of food and essential items to its advocacy for earmarking Rs 1000 crore of the Rs 11,000 crore Third Five-Year Plan to Madras State and its suggestion of the Tamil words 'Thiru', 'Thirumathi' and 'Tamil Nadu' in lieu of the Sanskrit 'Sri', 'Srimathi' and 'Madras State'. Points out its opposition to Chinese aggression. Records its opposition to the institution of the governor, pledges to work for a socialist society with essential industries in the public sector, a free port, Salem Steel Plant, a nuclear plant, a desalination plant, Buckingham and Vedaranyam Canals linked for waterways, an automobile plant, a bone meal fertilizer and chemical fertilizer plant, rubber from coir, governmental crop insurance, removal of sales tax for food items and a single-point sales tax, three acres wet and five acres land for Adi Dravidas and landless, land ceiling at fifteen standard acres, 25 per cent seats each for Adi Dravidas and backward castes in cooperatives, delegation of powers and doubling of funds to panchayats, underground sewage in all townships, a university, amendment of the XVIIth part of the Constitution on language, legalization of Self-Respect marriages, a master plan for Madras and houses for Adi Dravidas next to their factories.	The manifesto resembles an abridged version of the Third Five-Year Plan. Lists schooling, the rise in life expectancy from 32 to 47.5 years and the extension of community development projects to nearly three-quarters of the nation's villages. Claims success in promoting economic development and social equality and decentralization of political power by Panchayati Raj. No hint of any specific plans for nationalization. Cooperative farming to be voluntary. Expresses concern over the possible growth of monopolies and concentration of economic power in the private sector. In a first, reference is made to the fixing of a ceiling on urban incomes to 'lessen the great disparities that exist today'. Envisages that at the end of the Third Plan, no village is without adequate provision of drinking water, a primary school and a proper approach road. Approves the three-language formula. Deplores revival of nuclear tests and calls for the ending of colonial domination in Africa. Resolves to continue to try and bring about the vacation of the illegal occupation of Indian territory under Pakistan and China. Points out that from 24 million boys and girls in schools in 1950–51, the figure has gone up to 46 million, and by the end of the Third Plan, is likely to reach 65 million. Emphasis on Community Development Programme leading to Panchayati Raj covering 72 per cent of the villages in agriculture, animal husbandry, village industries, social education, health and rural sanitation. Development of basic and heavy industries and small industry. Public sector to increasingly expand and play a dominant role, spread of service cooperatives through the rural areas and cooperative farming where possible. Universal free education to children in the age group five to eleven and provision of noon meals and uniforms for children with the cooperation of the people wherever possible. Land and certain essential amenities provided preferably on a cooperative basis to those with below average per capita income. Stands for a united non-sectarian and secular India.	

YEAR	DMK	CONGRESS-O	AIADMK
1967	Lists its legislative and parliamentary work under forty-nine heads. Dubs Congress party as that of the landed gentry while Kazhagam would implement land to the tiller. Pledges smaller fertilizer units, a 'land army' to make wasteland cultivable, temporary relief from debt for farmers, proportional representation, a referendum on major issues, culturally a more united south, and advocates more rights and residuary powers for states.	Mentions the compelling need for bringing banking institutions under social control and imposing limitations on urban income and property and a growing role for the public sector to achieve a 'socialist transformation of our society'. The commanding heights of the economy not to be in private hands and the State to play an active and dynamic role in planning, guiding and directing economic development. Import substitution to be pushed to the utmost. Plans for investment in the Fourth and Fifth Plans contemplate an increasing role for the public sector. Consumer cooperative stores to check price rise. Lower middle and working class people enabled to secure housing sites at a reasonable rate. Dispersal of industries to the utmost extent. Remunerative prices to the producer and the provision of adequate inputs of fertilizers, improved seeds, pesticides and credit. Centre and states to increase the tempo of social control over processing and marketing and to link these with credit. Free house sites or at concessional rates for all qualifying families by land acquisition. To strive to strengthen secular forces so that even the smallest minority in India enjoys an honoured place.	
1971	Seeks support highlighting the record of the four-year DMK administration. Cites the Salem Steel Plant, East Coast Road, Kalpakkam, Madras Water scheme, Thoothukudi deep sea harbour, nationalization of banks and buses, tax exemption for lands, land ceiling from thirty to fifteen standard acres, removal of food controls, a separate ministry for backward classes, a Slum Clearance Board, direct election of local bodies, more than ten new dams, a Backward Classes Commission, a Police Commission, free education up to pre-university (PUC), pension for teachers, Manu Needhi Scheme, name change of Akashvani to All India Radio, Dalmiapuram to Kallakudi, its 'No' to Hindi, advocacy of only powers necessary to be retained by the Centre and the rest to the states, state autonomy, socialist society without prejudice to property rights, a state planning commission, an Agricultural Productivity Council, an Industrial Marketing Society, Small Industries Development Corporation (SIDCO), trade welfare board and opposition to Hemawati dam on the Cauvery and concludes that the 'DMK is nation's servant and the lamp for the house.'	Promises a clean and honest administration, provision of minimum needs to all by 1975, a million residential units a year for middle and low-income groups, simplifying the tax structure and licensing system, farmer-oriented agricultural price policy and creation of a Rs 1000-crore fund to provide employment to every citizen towards establishing a 'democratic, socialist secular society'. Abolition of privy purses and princely privileges in an 'appropriate manner'. A mixed economy with 'public, private and cooperative sectors subject to regulations and control' and promise to simplify the licensing system, entrusting it to a 'semi-independent board'. Promise of a massive rural works programme, steps to promote the expansion of cottage and small industries and active association of labour with the management. All India Radio and Television to be independent corporations. Foreign policy to be 'truly and dynamically non-aligned'. Safeguards to fundamental right to property.	

YEAR	DMK	CONGRESS-O	AIADMK
1977	Promises a third 'Pay Commission'; terms the elections as the 'second independence struggle' and that the Kazhagam has paid a 'huge price' to fight 'Delhi dictatorship'. Alleges psychological torture of the families of the Kazhagam akin to that of Nazi Gestapo; says members of the Kazhagam 'suffered like Rome's Christians and South Africa's Blacks'. Lists achievements such as free education up to PUC; Slum Clearance Board, houses for Dalits and fisherfolk, legislation enabling Dalits as priests and pension for transport employees. Promises the revival of bonus for farmers and prices commensurate to production costs for farmers; two lakh houses for Dalits and fisherfolk, drinking water for all towns and villages, mini public health clinics and balwadis, Tamil script reform, a Thiruvalluvar statue in Kanyakumari, a committee to streamline farm tax, urban land tax, property tax and entertainment tax; study to see Vanniyar, Mukkulathor, Nadar, fisherfolk and Yadavas obtain more educational and job opportunities; to continue to urge the Centre that sugar mills are nationalized. An ombudsperson.		Promises to strive for the nationalization of inter-state rivers and linking the Ganga and the Cauvery. To uphold the wishes and dreams of C.N. Annadurai, and for this purpose, the chief minister and his cabinet to have direct contact with the masses. Promises a government independent of political motivations, simple living by ministers, enhancement of power generation, starting of two more nuclear stations in Tamil Nadu, review of the existing tariff on power for heavy industries, agriculture and domestic consumers and irrigation projects. Strive for minimum wages, bonus and labour participation in management. Free textbooks and fee exemption to poor students. Favours 'effective federal government' and more powers for states. To press for inclusion of Nehru's assurance on the continuation of English. Prices of foodstuff in consultation with farmers and inputs at concessional rates through cooperatives, minimum wages for labourers and priority to minor irrigation projects.
1980	Promises to strive to pull Tamil Nadu from 'state of stagnation' and 'dark age' during the AIADMK rule and put it back on the road to development. Says the task calls for the right perspective, Himalayan effort and wartime urgency. Proposes a farmer's development board with district committees to monitor implementation of agricultural schemes, sort out farmers' problems and periodically draw up fresh programmes, expert panels to suggest remunerative prices for farm produce and prices fixed every year at the commencement of the cultivating season. Promises to dispense with distraint proceedings and auction for recovery of loan arrears and find ways to implement the nine-point demands by the agriculturists' association headed by C. Narayanaswami. Pointing out that the AIADMK commitment of a Rs 50 monthly dole to the estimated twenty lakh jobless will come to Rs 120 crore per annum, suggests rapid industrialization to address unemployment and new industrial units. Promises licences in three months and provision of power and water to private sector units employing more than fifty persons. Proposes reservation for backward classes in the central government services and public sector undertakings, financial support up to university for brilliant but indigent students from the Backward and Scheduled Castes and efforts to find suitable placements for them; expert panel to suggest measures to improve State Power Board performance and urges Centre to take up the Hogenekal project. Promises to rationalize licence procedures and to bring twenty-seven more commodities under single-point tax, a personnel welfare department for government employees; and medical facility within five years for all villages and efforts to give a subsidy either in cash or as gold to poor families for 'thali' (nuptial chain).		A 10-point action programme for the uplift of the weaker sections of society, including women, Re 1 a day to every man and woman of employable age in families below the poverty line during unemployment; house sites for the homeless; preference to poor youth registered in employment exchanges, with employment to at least one in every family; and a monthly allowance of Rs 50 to unemployed graduates, including those with secondary grade training. Special nutrition allowance for three months at Rs 50 per month for poor lactating mothers; cash incentives to poor families in villages, Rs 100 to those on the verge of death due to starvation; 1 kg free rice to families below the poverty line for every purchase of 5 kg of rice; and free text and notebooks up to the tenth standard. A planning and development commission for agriculture with the chief minister as chairperson and agriculturists' representatives and steps to fix the support price for farm produce in consultation with farmers' associations. A welfare fund for farmers and supply of essential commodities at a fair price; promises to urge Centre to write off farmers' loans and in the event of the Centre's refusal, the state to discharge the debt within five years. Indigent agricultural labourers above sixty years to get pension and electricity to all hutments within five years. Thalis made of gold at subsidized rates for poor families. A 'permanent negotiating machinery' for government employees and representation for them in the legislative council. Policemen to have a single association from constable to inspector. Elementary schoolteachers to become government employees. Will urge Centre to declare inter-state river waters as national asset.

YEAR	DMK	CONGRESS-O	AIADMK
1984	Promises to work for 'wholesale federalism with autonomy for the states' and demands scrapping of Article 356 on President's rule in states. Promises noon meal scheme in the 'real and complete' way, weeding out 'corruption', immediate elections to local bodies, reintroduction of the bill to annul benami land transactions, free power supply for all agricultural pump sets, bus pass for village students, write off of tenancy lease arrears and the setting up of an expert Administrative Reforms Committee to streamline the state administration. Promises a 'Single Window Scheme' for granting licences to entrepreneurs in fifteen days and at least one industry in every panchayat union, a District Development Authority to pay special attention to industrialization, a separate government employees welfare department, interim relief and bonus to government servants and streamlining of the functioning of the land development and cooperative banks and a suitable debt relief policy. Promises an inquiry commission to go into the history of the illness and treatment given to the ailing Chief Minister M.G. Ramachandran. Asserts Tamil Eelam as the only solution while criticizing the Centre for not creating international opinion against the 'genocide' of the Sri Lankan Tamils. Comes up with the concept of creating a new model of modern villages along the highways to check the problem of migration to urban centres and to put an end to capitation fees in professional colleges, a Traders Welfare Board, implementation of the Mandal Commission recommendations and Rural Reconstruction and Development Bank branches in all taluks. Promises to bring in legislation to curb defection and end the 'reign by the liquor barons'.		As a follow-up of the self-sufficiency scheme, a rural reconstruction scheme to fulfil every village's basic needs. A family welfare scheme to meet the minimum needs of all families, a model rural economic development project in a village in each block offering employment opportunities to all adults and a five-year scheme to improve the lot of backward and depressed classes, including Adi Dravidas, washermen and barbers. An industrial policy that would permit automation where essential. Priority to construction of buildings for high schools. Free uniforms to all poor girls up to the 8th standard and free textbooks to poor boys and girls up to the 10th standard. 'Interim relief for state government staff and relief to the families of staff who died in harness raised from Rs 10,000 to Rs 20,000; bonus, two-way leave travel concession, exemption from professional tax and a separate department for the welfare of government servants. Assurance to teachers in government and aided schools to improve service conditions and a housing board. A time-bound programme for the development of Madras to make 'city beautiful'; appropriate land reform measures for recovery of income due to temples from their lands; provision of agricultural credit at 4 per cent interest and supply of farm inputs at concessional rates; and steps to solve the Cauvery water issue. Fight for state's rights and devolution of more powers towards a real federal set-up, equal rights for all languages and the continuance of English as an official language. Lists the noon-meal scheme benefiting 75 lakh children, supply of power to small farmers at concessional rates; extension of the crop insurance scheme to dry crops; grant of a special incentive of Rs 35 for a quintal of paddy; free veshtis and sarees to landless agricultural labour; free books and notebooks to children of widows, and insurance scheme for fishermen. Claims that during the seven years of the AIADMK rule, small-scale industries went up to 35,843 from 18,484 in 1977, 598 big and medium-scale industries of an outlay of Rs 1000 crores set up and 2432 new bus routes for 5234 villages and employing 29,540 persons were commissioned.

YEAR	DMK	CONGRESS-O	AIADMK
1989	Declares that it would oppose any move by the Centre to take away the powers of the states. The Constitution should be amended to provide for 'wholesome federalism with autonomy for the states'. Promises to fight for the continuance of English until all the national languages become official. Highlights a long list of achievements during the nine DMK years. Promises to restore the five-year term from the three and the powers taken away by the AIADMK government to the local bodies, grant them greater autonomy and financial assistance, and hold elections immediately for the corporations. Promises to urge the Centre to find a negotiated settlement for the Sri Lankan Tamils by bringing to the table all those concerned, including the LTTE. Streamline state administration and write off longstanding cooperative loan arrears of small farmers and abolish sales tax for agricultural pump sets and farm equipment. Mid-day meal scheme workers to be made permanent, industrial estates in the backward areas of each district, a 'reconstruction corporation for small scale industries', a Rs 100 crore soda ash plant at Vedaranyam, an institution for salt production, settlement of the Cauvery issue through negotiations, failing which to urge for a tribunal. Promises to revive the legislative council. Thirty per cent reservation in jobs for women in government, state corporations and local bodies, granting of Rs 10,000 for construction workers, lorry, taxi and autorickshaw drivers dying in harness, old age pension of Rs 50 for all agricultural labourers, retired workers and destitute above 60, hospitals for every 20,000 population, a rural housing agency, one lakh jobs every year for the educated unemployed, concrete houses for Adi Dravidas and free college education for Adi Dravidas, tribals and the most backward and increasing the minimum age for government jobs to 30.		AIADMK (Jayalalithaa) promises a corruption-free, 'clean, and efficient administration', total prohibition, law for equal rights to women in ancestral property, supply of rice at Rs 1.70 a kilo to the poor, increase of employment allowance to unemployed graduates, free bus passes to school and college students, pay parity to the state government employees with the central government staff, maternity and childcare centre in each panchayat, solatium of up to Rs 5000 to the family of fisherman dying out at sea and free education for women up to graduation. An autonomous body to advise and administer the temples under the religious and endowment department, priority to poverty alleviation schemes, an independent corporation for rural development, write-off of agricultural loans, free electricity to small farmers and agricultural inputs at subsidized prices and the abolition of land tax. Promises to strive to put an end to the 'bossy attitude of the Centre', acceptance in principle of exclusive reservation for the most backward and a special officer to conduct a caste census. Establish industrial states in all taluks, encourage private ventures and create conditions for entrepreneurs from outside to start new units in Tamil Nadu and urge for a tribunal on the Cauvery water dispute, early implementation of the Telugu Ganga scheme bringing Krishna waters to Madras, payment of life insurance premium for those below poverty line, speeding up of the Mass Rapid Transit System for Chennai and a master plan for development of the metropolitan area, and resolves to find a solution to the nearly thirty lakh unemployed on live register of the employment exchanges. A housing corporation for employees of transport corporations and the welfare of Harijans and a study into the working of government-owned corporations to close down the superfluous ones. The Congress offered a 26 per cent reservation in government jobs for women, the DMK 30 per cent, AIADMK (JR) 'a specified' reservation, while Jayalalithaa sought to enlarge the scope and functions of the Corporation for Women's Development and introduction of special job-oriented courses for women in rural areas.

YEAR	DMK	CONGRESS-O	AIADMK
1991	Promises four lakh free concrete houses for Adi Dravidas, free professional education for poor students, most backward classes and denotified communities, Adi Dravida and Scheduled Tribes and girls belonging to poor and middle-income families and free power supply to three lakh pump sets, enhancement of the family benefit to Rs one lakh for government employees, appointment of 10,000 additional teachers in the next five years and providing 10,000 houses for them during the same period, increase bus pass concession from 50 to 75 per cent for secondary, Plus Two and college students, a scheme to guarantee 150 days of employment per annum in forty-five drought-prone panchayat unions, the appointment of 25,000 Makkal Mala Paniyalargal every year in rural areas and training of educated unemployed youth, men and women to absorb them as teachers, adult education instructors and paramedical and health workers, distribution of rice at concessional prices, 10,000 free concrete houses for fishermen every year, writing-off of arrears of fishermen and also Taccavi loans and extension of the accident relief scheme for students with a compensation of Rs 10,000 to the family in the event of death and appropriate amount in the case of disability. A nutrition plan for children the age of six months and above at an outlay of Rs 350 crore, increase of the marriage assistance grant for girls of poor families from Rs 5000 to Rs 6000, maternity assistance for women belonging to poor households from Rs 200 to Rs 500 and assistance to poor families on the death of the breadwinner from Rs 3000 to Rs 5000. Promises to reopen all closed factories and establishments, implement minimum wages and social security measures for industrial workers, accord priority for resolving problems of women workers and provide 10,000 houses with looms for handloom weavers, drinking water for all villages in the coming year and expediting the Telugu Ganga project by 1993. Promises a high-level Administrative Reforms Commission to streamline the administration, grant benefits on recommendations made by the Police Commission and immediately elect corporations, municipalities, panchayat unions and panchayats. Urges the setting up of a Bench of the High Court in Madurai and presses for increased financial assistance to Tamil Nadu from the Centre and through the Finance Commission.		Reunited AIADMK promises to restore 'MGR rule' and provide a corruption-free, just, stable and responsive government and streamline the administration and a new and 'honourable' agreement between the Governments of India and Sri Lanka to end the sufferings and problems of the Sri Lankan Tamils; while disallowing the militants to use Tamil Nadu as a base for their 'anti-national or anti-social activities'. Total prohibition with the closure of the 'cheap liquor shops', measures to eradicate drug addiction and keep off adulteration in drugs. Special attention to agriculture, irrigation, power and industrial development. Advocates a judicious surface and sub-soil water use for irrigation and calls for an interim award from the Cauvery Waters Tribunal. Opts for a differential tax structure for dryland, garden, tank-fed and river-fed irrigation, proposes a special organization for fallow and wasteland management; and promises renovation and maintenance of tanks, ponds and all irrigation canals.

Private sector encouraged to participate in thermal projects; and maximum use of solar energy, including for desalination and Centre pressed to extend the gas grid to the south. Invite non-resident Indians (NRIs) and industries from other states to invest in Tamil Nadu with export-oriented units getting special priority; proposes a standing committee of experts on education and the promotion of technical and vocational education. Promises a Temple Administration Board, a special programme making available at least Rs 1 crore to each panchayat, immediate elections to all local bodies, protected water supply scheme to all villages and projects to recycle sewage water for industrial and other purposes. A New Pay Commission for government employees to study the anomalies and problems in the DMK government's decision to offer pay parity to the state employees with those of the Centre and solatium for the family of an employee dying in harness raised to Rs 60,000. Reiterates demand for 50 per cent reservation for the backward classes instead of the 27 per cent provided for in the Mandal Commission's recommendations; separate reservation for the poor among the backward classes, revamping of the nutritious meal programme and integrating it with education to make the centres into nursery schools, special education for women and handicapped, land reforms, teachers and labour welfare, special programmes for weavers and fishermen and highways maintenance. |

YEAR	DMK	CONGRESS-O	AIADMK
1996	Promises to root out the twin evils of criminalization of politics and politicization of criminals 'prevalent in Tamil Nadu in the last five years', an ombudsperson to inquire into the corruption charges against the chief minister, ministers and chairpersons of the state-owned corporations and announcement of the dates for local body elections and priority in bringing back communal harmony. Pledges to restructure the new economic policy and ensure a safety net for labour and weaker sections, to press for amending the Constitution to provide for wholesome and genuine federalism, make Tamil an official language at the Centre and empower the states to fix the percentage of reservations, implementation of 69 per cent reservation in letter and spirit to undo the 'injustice being perpetrated' by the AIADMK government 'feigning' to go by the 69 per cent but implementing only the 50 per cent reservation. Consumers to draw essential commodities in fair price shops on any date convenient instead of stipulated dates; introduce a 100-day employment guarantee scheme every year with priority to women in panchayat union areas, annually appoint 25,000 educated and jobless community welfare workers in rural areas, introduce self-employment for the urban poor and provide financial assistance for the educated unemployed under self-employment for educated unemployed youth. Provision of loans at low rates of interest to educated unemployed women and destitute to set up ventures, special loans for backward class and tribals for farming activities, creation of rural reconstruction and development bank in every taluk and Anna Village Renaissance Scheme under which a select village will be made a model village in every assembly constituency with all facilities. Urge the Centre to support a political solution acceptable to the Sri Lankan Tamils. Urges the people to throw out the 'most corrupt and fascist Government'.		Lists achievements and outlines plans for further development under thirty-six headings. Promises to campaign for more state autonomy and all efforts to weed out forces inimical to unity and religious harmony. On revenue administration reform, promises computerization of all land records and prioritizing reorganization of districts and blocks for simplified administration. Laboratories to meet the needs of agriculture, vocational education and industry. A high-level committee to study prospects of revamping secondary and higher education and efforts made towards students acquiring maximum skills. Provision to bring experts from abroad to lend their expertise to students of professional branches and priority for education in Tamil. Promises to press the Centre to extend to scheduled castes (SC) all benefits available to the backward classes (BC). Loans at low-interest rates for the BCs engaged in agriculture and industry through the Backward Classes credit bank and interest-free loans for BC students for overseas study. To press for all assistance through the Centre for the BCs—a delegation headed by the chief minister to take up the issue with the Centre. To strive for a 50 per cent reservation for women in all fields. Legislation to give priority to the local unemployed youth in non-technical jobs. Family welfare fund for government employees dying in harness to be increased from Rs 60,000 to Rs 75,000. Total prohibition in a phased manner. Highlights the approvals for various mega projects in the petrochemical, electronics and automobile sectors issued during the past five years and promises to maintain the tempo during the next five years. Other plans include mega projects for developing irrigation and roads, alternative power, health for all, revamping of the PDS, campaign for the implementation of the Sethusamudram project, besides welfare projects for women, children, fishermen, weavers and the aged.

YEAR	DMK	CONGRESS-O	AIADMK
2001	Vows to grow, produce and export more and claims it has fulfilled its promise in 1996 that it will usher in a second Green Revolution. Says focus would be on information technology, biotechnology and other cutting-edge sciences of the twenty-first century. To promote dry farming and wasteland development besides raising the groundwater table through micro-watershed management and other modern techniques, introduce 'contract farming' in cultivating fruits, vegetables and flowers while providing a market and remunerative price to horticulture farmers and encourage exports. Special incentives to boost farmers' export potential of medicinal plants and herbs. Promises to promote the intake of tender coconut water and promote multistoreyed cropping and other modern techniques in cultivation. Except for the very large ones, all irrigation sources entrusted to the respective water-user associations for maintenance. Points out the DMK government legislation for this purpose, and to the fact that forty-four irrigation tanks have been entrusted thus far. Claims to have come out with a transparent and investor-friendly industrial policy, pledges to pursue the same aggressively. Recognizing the crisis facing the textile industry, promises a comprehensive scheme to cover all aspects of the sector—from cotton cultivation to garment manufacturing and a task force to suggest social security measures to protect the interests of industry personnel. In view of the overwhelming response to the scheme, pledges to provide liquefied petroleum gas (LPG) connections to thirty lakh women over the next five years. Says environmental protection would receive special attention under the centrally-sponsored Rs 1700-crore National River Water Protection Scheme. Lists 'achievements' of the DMK governments—claiming first place in the country in rice productivity, oilseeds, investments in industry, containing AIDS and Infant Mortality Rate and the number of software professionals turned out from the state.		Promises corruption-free government and progressive developmental schemes to enable Tamil Nadu to become the country's 'most advanced state'. Assails the DMK administration for 'political interference, nepotism, corruption, malpractice, maladministration and heinous crimes' and commits to taking stringent measures to eradicate extremist, secessionist and separatist movements. Severely criticizes the DMK government's handling of last year's kidnap episode of actor Rajkumar and promises to 'reveal . . . all the sordid machinations of the outrageous drama' after putting down forest brigand Veerappan. Promises to urge the Centre to ban the Tamil Nadu Liberation Front, the TNLA, TNRT and other 'militant anti-national groups which are in league with Veerappan's gang'. To urge the Centre for legal action against M. Karunanidhi and other political leaders, 'lending support to the separatist, extremist and criminal forces'. Claims corruption in the present government had led to a 'money flow scarcity' and accuses the DMK of misusing a satellite television channel to suppress rival operators. Lists a series of 'scandals' in the public distribution system to the Tamil Nadu Electricity Board promising speedy remedial action and legal action. Criticizes the DMK and the BJP-led Centre for their handling of the Cauvery dispute; describes the forming of the Cauvery River Water Authority (CWRA) comprising four chief ministers and the prime minister as a 'betrayal' of the state; promises swift action for urging the government to enable Tamil Nadu to get its due legal rights in the Cauvery dispute and resolve the Mullaiperiyar dam issue, and urge the Centre to link the Pamba Achankovil and Vaigai rivers. Promises to urge the Centre to take steps to enable Sri Lankan Tamils to acquire their legitimate rights and a peaceful and dignified life; assures terrorism will 'never be allowed nor militants be ever permitted to use the state as their base'. An expert committee to undertake an industrial survey to locate new industrial areas and introduce state-of-the-art techniques to increase employment opportunities and modernize industrial units. A modern industrial development scheme to give special focus to drugs and pharmaceuticals, processed agro and food products, software industries and information technology and a Tamil NRI consortium to mobilize foreign investment. A pension scheme for the unorganized working class and fair wages for agricultural workers, free cooking gas connections for indigent women. Promises to urge the Centre to replace the three-tier administration system with a two-tier system by statute change. Assurance of two new reservoirs and desalination plants for Chennai.

YEAR	DMK	CONGRESS-O	AIADMK
2006	Promises a world of concessions and goodies especially to farmers and women: quality rice at Rs 2 a kg on ration cards, free colour television for every family 'for women's recreation and general knowledge', maternity assistance of Rs 1000 a month for six months, waiver of all cooperative farm loans and free electricity to weavers in addition to farmers, free gas stove to all poor women, a monthly financial assistance up to Rs 300 to unemployed youth, assignment of two acres to landless poor families, restoration of all concessions withdrawn to government employees and teachers and reservation for Muslim and Christians and implementation of the recommendations of the Sixth Pay Commission when announced, reinstallation of the Kannagi statue removed by the AIADMK government, re-establishing the MGR Film City and implementation of all DMK schemes discontinued by the AIADMK administration. Opposes disinvestment in public sector units; foreign direct investment in the retail sector; pledges to strive for 40 per cent share for states in gross tax revenue and to urge for doubling the royalty to the states. Says efforts would be made to secure 'Eelam Tamils' and prevent recurrence of arrests, abductions and killings of Tamil Nadu fishermen by the Sri Lankan Navy. Promises a probe into 'non-distribution' of financial assistance to the genuine victims in the tsunami-hit areas. To urge the Centre for constitutional amendments for the removal of the 'creamy layer' concept from reservation for the backward classes. Assures immediate elections to cooperatives dissolved in 2001 and to ask the Centre to bring in suitable amendments to remove the hurdles in the smooth functioning of the present three-tier local bodies. Promises to repeal the Tamil Nadu Essential Services Maintenance Act and revive the legislative council.		Promises to implement the Value-added Tax (VAT) after the Centre brings forward the necessary amendments acceptable to traders and producers. Assures a new 'Samadhan' scheme acceptable to all on tax arrears, flays the United Progressive Alliance (UPA) Government for permitting foreign direct investment in retail trade and faults the decision to reduce the interest rate for Employees Provident Fund from 9.5 per cent to 8.5 per cent while promising to continue to seek restoration of the original rate of interest. Opposes the Centre's decision to privatize the Neyveli Lignite Corporation, dubs Congress president Sonia Gandhi an 'extra-Constitutional power centre', demands probe against her in the wake of the Volcker Committee findings and calls for the constitution of an inquiry commission to investigate the 'Rs 700 crore submarine scam'. Accuses central ministers from Tamil Nadu of indulging in 'anti-Tamil Nadu activities', says the Sethusamudram Ship Channel Project was 'hastily implemented' without regard for the danger to the livelihood of thousands of fishermen and with scant regard for the environmental impact on the marine ecology of the region. Promises to urge the Centre to get Katchatheevu on 'lease in perpetuity'; points out the salient features of the draft scheme put forth by the state to the Cauvery Water Disputes Tribunal and promises continued constructive legal measures in this regard. Highlights various achievements and promises a 'fishermen protection scheme'; promises to urge the Centre to restore the subsidized rice scheme for the benefit of 50,730 Sri Lankan Tamil refugees, reiterates opposition to price rise and reduction in the quantity of rice in the public distribution system and promises to continue to supply rice at the 'present lowest rate'. Promises to provide employment in the next five years in the information technology sector to five lakh youths. Jayalalithaa rules out the possibility of a coalition government, confident party would return to power with absolute majority.

YEAR	DMK	CONGRESS-O	AIADMK
2011	Promises 35 kg free rice a month to the poorest of the poor (35 kg rice was supplied every month at Re 1 a kg to 18.64 lakh families—the poorest of the poor under the Centre's Antyodaya Annayojana [AAY] scheme). Promises distribution of free wet grinder or mixie to women and extension of a free power supply scheme for horticulture and coconut farming and 200 units of free power bi-monthly to handloom weavers from 100 units. Free bus passes for travel in local buses for senior citizens aged sixty and above, old age pension of Rs 500 per month hiked to Rs 750 per month. Metro Rail projects for Coimbatore and Madurai, extending the Chennai Metro Rail Project up to Mamallapuram and also up to Irungattukottai through the Sriperumbudur industrial area. Pledges to increase the financial assistance under the Kalaignar Housing Scheme from Rs 75,000 to Rs 1 lakh, free laptops to first-year students of the Backward Classes, Most Backward Classes, Scheduled Castes and Scheduled Tribes pursuing professional degree courses in government and government-aided colleges and to examine the demand for absorbing the interest of educational loans issued to students during 2004–09.		Promises a fan, a mixie and a grinder as freebies to all women, four grams of gold, in addition to Rs 25,000 as marriage assistance (Rs 50,000 and four grams of gold for beneficiaries holding a diploma or degree), six months of maternity leave along with Rs 12,000 assistance and bank loan to a maximum of Rs 10 lakh linked with 25 per cent subsidy for self-help groups. A 'Green Houses' scheme with houses powered by solar energy for families below the poverty line. For the landless poor, three cents of land free for house construction. Four sets of uniform and a pair of shoes for school students, scholarships for higher secondary-level students ranging from Rs 1000 to Rs 5000, laptops for all students in arts and science colleges, engineering colleges and polytechnics. Introduction of hospitals on wheels in rural areas and 24-hour telemedicine centres in 1500 villages, 5000 MW of additional power by 2013 and three-phase connection for all households; 20 kg free rice to all family card-holders and 20 litres of purified drinking water a month to all below poverty line (BPL) families. Separate manifestos announced for Tamil Nadu and Puducherry.

YEAR	DMK	CONGRESS-O	AIADMK
2016	Promises uninterrupted electricity, to enhance electricity production, monthly electricity billing, 20 kg free rice per month, total prohibition and to formulate schemes to offset the loss of revenue from prohibition, smartphones for poor families, tablets or laptops bundled with 3G/4G Internet connection and 10 GB per month download option for 16 lakh students, waiver of education loans, one lakh new jobs every year, new industries in south Tamil Nadu, to fill all vacant posts in government schools, Lok Ayukta, the Right to Service Act, a separate budget for agriculture, a ministry for irrigation, waiver of crop loans for small and micro farmers, reduction in price of Aavin milk by up to Rs 7 per litre, steps to include fishermen in the scheduled tribes list as 'marine tribes' and introduction of milk in the Nutritious Meal Scheme. Promises an Integrated Regulated Marketing Corporation in the place of TASMAC to ensure its workers do not lose their service seniority, a new organization under the Health Department and de-addiction centres in all districts for alcoholics. Promises to extend metro rail project to Mamallapuram and another line up to Sriperumbudur through Irunkattukottai and Oragadam industrial towns, teach English, French, German, Spanish, Arabic, Mandarin, Japanese and Russian in colleges and universities to enhance employment opportunities abroad for students and to review and upgrade 'Samacheer Kalvi' scheme every year. Training in organic farming in the name of Nammazhvar; revival of Sethusamudram Canal Project; increase of minimum support price for paddy; Tamil as official language in central government offices; maternity leave increase to nine months; Rs one lakh funding for entrepreneurs; all lakes/ water bodies desilted at Rs 10,000 crore; employment camps in districts; 750 units of free power for powerlooms; leather parks in Chennai, Dindigul and Vellore, Anna Unavagams, 200 check dams to prevent flooding at a cost of Rs 2000 crore; first-generation graduates to get preference for government jobs; scrapping of new pension scheme for government employees and teachers (that had done away with pension); withdrawal of cases against Kudankulam Nuclear Reactor protestors, medical colleges in all districts, 4th Police Commission, schemes to convert sea water to drinking water in coastal areas, efforts to revive Jallikattu, Rs three lakh subsidy for construction of concrete houses for low income groups and permission within sixty days for construction of houses, factories, offices, multistoreyed residential buildings and commercial buildings, and rationalization of fee for approval and reduction of stamp charges for transfer of property between blood relatives.		Promises 100 free units of power every two months; free cell phones for all ration cardholders, one sovereign gold for women ahead of marriages, 50 per cent subsidy for women for two-wheelers, maternity assistance of Rs 18,000, laptops with Internet for 10th and 12th Std students, free power to farmers, waiver of all farm loans, Rs 40,000 crore loans for farmers in 2016–21, continuation of old pension scheme for government employees, salary revision as per 7th Pay Commission and housing loan raised to Rs 40 lakh; Aavin milk at Rs 25 per litre, reimbursement of education loan of unemployed, training women to drive vehicles and subsidy to buy autorickshaws, Amma banking cards to avail interest-free loans and government schemes; free Wi-Fi at public spaces and breakfast under nutritious meal scheme. Rs 1 lakh for temples of local deities, phase-out of liquor, fisherfolk assistance hike to Rs 5000, separate housing for fisherfolk, no FDI in retail, 20 per cent land on Small and Mid-size Enterprises (SME) industrial parks reserved for SC/ST entrepreneurs, new granite policy, Lok Ayukta, Co-Optex coupons worth Rs 500 for Pongal festival for ration-card holders and 10 lakh houses through various housing schemes.

YEAR	DMK	CONGRESS-O	AIADMK
2021	Promise to create 5.50 lakh jobs in the government sector, a law to reserve 75 per cent of jobs for Tamils in industries in Tamil Nadu and private sector convinced to offer communal reservation in employment, waiver of education loan by students up to thirty years of age, who pursued school and higher education in Tamil Nadu, restoration and consecration of temples at Rs 1000 crore and Rs 25,000 grant for one lakh people to undertake Hindu spiritual tour, Rs 200 crore for restoring churches and mosques, monetary aid of Rs 4000 to ration cardholders impacted by COVID-19 and freeze on property tax revision till the economy revived from the pandemic. There was no mention of prohibition. Promises a separate ministry to implement the promises. Unveils the future DMK government's plan to increase the state's revenue through extraction of mines and minerals and prevent looting, proposes to create a separate ministry for mines and minerals and strengthen the 'technological capacity of TAMIN' for the purpose. Promises a special court to try the corruption charges against the AIADMK ministers; live telecast of assembly proceedings; law abolishing the NEET in the first assembly session; restoration of old pension scheme for government employees; monthly electricity billing cycle; and free milk for school students in the morning, Rs 100 subsidy per cooking gas cylinder, price of petrol and diesel reduced by Rs 5 and Rs 4 per litre and the price of Aavin milk reduced by Rs 3 per litre. Promises a proper inquiry into the death of former Chief Minister Jayalalithaa and prosecution of the guilty, to persuade the Centre to increase to Rs 25 lakh the annual income to determine creamy layer for central government institutions, press for reservation of BCs, ST/STs in private sector jobs and offer priority would be given for first-generation graduates in government jobs. Urge the Centre to make Tirukkural a 'national book'. Promises to give 40 per cent reservation for women in government jobs, increase in maternity leave to twelve months and Rs 24,000 as maternity assistance, 500 Kalaignar Unavagams on the lines of Amma Unavagam, night staying places for workers, piped drinking water in Chennai; smart cards for differently-abled people, free travel passes and motorized three-wheelers for travel, free sanitary napkins for government school/college girls; grievance redressal mechanism in every assembly constituency; resolution for petitions received by M.K. Stalin during the campaign; housing pattas in urban areas where there are no objections, enhanced old age pension of Rs 1500, enhanced assistance for destitute, widows and unmarried women above fifty years; Tamil Nadu River Protection Project; and steps for Indian citizenship for Sri Lankan Tamil refugees.		Over 163 promises: free houses, Rs 1500 per month credited to bank accounts of woman family heads to all ration cardholders, women to get a 50 per cent fare cut in town buses, distribution of solar-powered cooking stoves, washing machines and six LPG cylinders a year—to rice category ration cardholders, expansion of the rural employment guarantee scheme to 150 days from 100, Rs 7500 annual subsidy to farmers, educational loan waiver, government jobs to families without anyone in state service, ration items door-delivered (as in neighbouring Andhra Pradesh); laptops to students of self-financing classes of government schools, milk (200 ml milk or milk powder) to school students and children attached to anganwadis and Rs 2 cut in Aavin milk price, 'Amma banking card' scheme to provide interest-free loans (in association with banks) to help poor people repay loans in instalments and Rs 25,000 subsidy to purchase e-Autos, an Islamic university, increase in assistance to Hindu pilgrims to visit important centres of pilgrimage, hike of Haj subsidy from Rs 6 crore to Rs 10 crore and promise to bear the full fare for Jerusalem pilgrims, increase in the quota for women in government jobs to 40 per cent (from the current 30 per cent) and appropriate reservation for all castes. Promise to urge Centre to scrap the contentious Citizenship Amendment Act (CAA') and strive to bring education to the state list, increase in maternity leave for women government employees from nine months to one year and construction of new buildings with modern medical facilities for about 2000 Amma Mini Clinics. Build and provide houses free of cost in rural and urban areas under the 'Amma Illam Thittam' (Amma Housing Scheme) and interest on housing loans availed from cooperative housing societies waived on loan repayment. Steps to get fuel prices reduced, increase in subsidy under the Amma Green Housing Scheme from Rs 2.43 lakh to Rs 3.40 lakh, college students who have been getting 2 GB data to get it throughout the year, increase in social security pensions for beneficiaries, including senior citizens, from Rs 1000 to Rs 2000, 'Amma's gift (Amma Seervarisai)' of household items for newlywed couples under the state's marriage financial support scheme, free cable TV connections to rice ration cardholders and two free mosquito nets to poor and financial assistance to the differently-abled increased to Rs 2500 from Rs 1500. Promises continued support for the release of seven Rajiv Gandhi assassination case convicts, steps to ensure the welfare of Tamils in Sri Lanka and to press for dual citizenship for Sri Lankan Tamil refugees.

Notes

Preface

1   Gross State Domestic Product (Constant Prices), Reserve Bank of India, 19 November 2022. Accessed 21 September 2023, https://rbi.org.in/Scripts/PublicationsView.aspx?id=21415.
2   'Explained: What Is The Migrant Workers' Row That Has Gripped Tamil Nadu?,' *Outlook,* 7 March 2023. Accessed 21 June 2023, https://www.outlookindia.com/national/explained-what-is-the-migrant-workers-row-that-has-gripped-tamil-nadu--news-267966.

Chapter 1: Muthuvel Karunanidhi aka Kalaignar

1   *Murasoli*, 8 August 2018, 1.
2   Kalaignar (M. Karunanidhi), *Kalaignarin Kadithangal* (Chennai: Seethai Pathippagam, 2023), 1: 10.
3   C.N. Annadurai, 'Thambiudaiyaan Padaikanjaan,' (Anna's letter to thambis or younger brothers). Accessed 6 April 2020, http://www.annavinpadaippugal.info/sorpozhivugal/thambiyudayan.htm.
4   'M. Karunanidhi, 94: the end of an era,' *The Hindu,* 8 August 2018. Accessed 10 August 2018, https://www.thehindu.com/opinion/editorial/m-karunanidhi-94-the-end-of-an-era/article24626668.ece.
5   Karunanidhi, *Kadithangal*, 3: 236-40. Kavitha Muralidharan translated this piece.

6   'Karunanidhi responds to prime minister's charges,' 20 September 1976, US consul general cable. Accessed 1 December 2023, https://www. wikileaks.org/plusd/cables/1976NEWDE13883_b.html.
7   *Murasoli*, 4 June 1980, 1.
8   Karunanidhi, *Kadithangal*, 42: 45.

Chapter 2: DMK aka 'Teardrops'

1   Tiruchi Selvendran, *Thanthai Periyarudanum Thalaivar Kalaigarudanum Car Payanangalil*, (Chennai: Seethai Pathippagam, 2018), 21–23.
2   Rama Arangannal, 'Kaalathaal Maatra Mudiyatha Kanneer!', in *Anna Souvenir*, ed. C.N.A. Babu, (Chennai: Babu Pirasuram, 1972), 33–34.
3   Navalar Nedunchezhian, *Vaazhvil Naan Kandathum Ketathum*, (Chennai: Navalar Nedunchezhian Pathippagam, 2000), 177–82; T.M. Parthasarathy, *Thi.Mu.Ka. Varalaaru*, (Chennai: Bharati Pathippagam, 7th ed., 1998), 97–106.
4   R. Kannan, *Anna: The Life and Times of C.N. Annadurai*, (Gurgaon: Penguin Random House India, 2nd ed., 2017), 155–56.
5   Kannan, *Anna*, 159–63.
6   Nedunchezhian, *Vaazhvil*, 182–84; Parthasarathy, *Thi.Mu.Ka.*, 97–106.
7   Parthasarathy, 108–11.
8   Bishwanath Ghosh, 'In Search of Coral Merchant Street,' *The Hindu*, 4 May 2011. Accessed 1 May 2021, https://www.thehindu.com/features/ friday-review/history-and-culture/In-Search-of-7-Coral-Merchant-Street/article12058785.ece.
9   Ma.Po.Si., *Enadhu Porattam*, 2: 226–27, (Chennai: Poongodi Pathippagam, 2018).
10 Kalaignar M. Karunanidhi, *Nenjuku Needhi*, (Chennai: Thamizhkani Pathippagam, 2020), 1: 132; Kavignar Kannadasan, *Vanavaasam*, (Chennai: Vanathi Pathippagam, 2000), 117-19; Kannadasan, *Suyasaridham*, (Chennai: Vanathi Pathipipagam, 2000), 31.
11 K. Thirunavukkarasu, *Thi.Mu.Ka.: Prachanaygalum Pilavugalum Marumalarchiyai Noaki . . .*, (Chennai: Nakkeeran Pathippagam, 2022), 174.
12 Nedunchezhian, *Vaazhvil*, 185.
13 Kannan, *Anna*, 304
14 Ibid.
15 Ibid.
16 Ibid.

17   Nedunchezhian, *Vaazhvil*, 420.

18   Ajayan Bala, *Periyar*, (Chennai: Vikatan Pirasuram, 2009), 86.

19   K.P. Neelamani, *Thanthai Periyar*, (Chennai: Createspace Independent Publishing Platform, 2017), 97.

20   *'Periyar' Maraindhar: Periyar Vazhga*, ed., K. Veeramani, (Chennai: Dravidar Kazhagam, 2016), 22.

21   *Kudiarasu*, 11 September 1927.

22   *Selected Works of Jawaharlal Nehru, Second series*, ed., Mridula Mukherjee, (New Delhi: Jawaharlal Nehru Memorial Fund, 2009), 40: 87.

23   *Viduthalai*, 27 January 1950.

24   Kannan, *Anna*, 22.

25   *Dravida Nadu*, 13 November 1955, 2.

26   C.N. Annadurai, 'Kanchipuram Therthal Prachara Kootam', (Anna's speech at a Kanchipuram election rally). Accessed 6 April 2020, http://www.annavinpadaippugal.info/sorpozhivugal/1962_thaerthal.html.

27   Kalyani Ramasamy, *Nadipisaipular K.R. Ramasamy Ninaivugal*, (Chennai: Vasantha Publication, 2014), 99–100.

28   Kannadasan, *Vanavaasam*, 266.

29   Interview with M.S. Venkatachalam, 4 March 2012.

30   M.S. Venkatachalam, *My Days With Anna*, (Tiruchi, Tamil Kudil Pathippagam, 2010), 112–14.

31   Malarmannan, *Thi Mu Ka Uruvanadhu Yaen*, (Chennai: Kizhakku Pathippagam, 2009), 70–71.

32   *Maperum Tamil Kanavu*, (Chennai, Tamilthisai, 2022), 242–47; '"Padhavikkaga katchikku vandhavan alla; poraaliaaga!" – Duraimurugan gaatam'. Accessed 7 October 2020, https://www.vikatan.com/news/politics/dmk-treasurer-durai-murugan-explains-rumors-over-gs-post.

33   Kannadasan, *Manavaasam*, 75.

34   *Maperum Tamil Kanavu*, 303.

35   Ma.Po. Sivagnanam, *MGRudan Enakirundha Thodarbu*, (Chennai: Poongodi Pathippagam, 1995), 40, 226–27.

36   *Selected Works of Jawaharlal Nehru*, ed., Mukherjee, 41: 346.

37   S. Arulselvan, *Annavin Arasiyal Guru: 'Sunday Observer' P. Balasubramaniam*, (Chennai: Vikatan Pirasuram, 2017), 188.

38   Periyar's interview, *Ananda Vikatan*, 11 April 1965 cited in Arulselvan, *Annavin*, 195.

39   *Dravida Nadu*, 9 March 1952, 3–5, 8.

40   *Dravida Nadu*, 28 January 1951, 5.

41   *Dravida Nadu*, 19 November 1950, 8–10.

42   *Dravida Nadu*, 25 August 1957, 8–9.

43   *Dravida Nadu*, 22 September 1957, 10–11.

44   Kavignar Kannadasan, *Naan Paartha Arasiyal*, (Chennai: Kannadasan Pathippagam, 2007), 35–37.

45   Jayakanthan, *Oru Ilyakivadhiyin Arasial Anubhavangal*, (Madurai, Meenakshi Puthaga Nilayam, 1974), 148, 151.

46   *Periyar E.V.R. Sindhanaigal*, ed., V. Anaimuthu, (Chennai: Sithanaiyaalar Kazhagam, 1974), 3: 1826–827.

47   K. Velnambi, *Thamizhanai Uyarthiya Thalaimagan Uraigal*, (Chennai: Seethai Pathippagam, 2017), 379.

Chapter 3: Building the DMK

1   *Dravida Nadu*, 20 November 1949, 8, 11.

2   Karunanidhi, *Kadithangal*, 7: 321.

3   Kannadasan, *Naan*, 38–39.

4   Veerapandi Arumugham, *Dravida Iyakka Varalaatril En Payanam*, (Chennai: Gowra Publications, 2019). 18–19, 63.

5   *DMK Silver Jubilee Souvenir*, (Chennai: DMK, 1975), 63.

6   Kovai Ayyamuthu, *Enadhu Ninaivugal*, (Coimbatore: Vidiyal Pathippagam, 2010), 259.

7   Nedunchezhian, *Vaazhvil*, 169–71.

8   *Dravida Nadu*, 28 January 1951, 3.

9   Parthasarathy, *Thi.Mu.Ka.*, 142.

10   *Dravida Nadu*, 7 June 1953, 2.

11   *Dravida Nadu*, 15 October 1950, 1; Nedunchezhian, *Vaazhvil*, 223–24; Parthasarathy, *Thi.Mu.Ka.*, 154–55; Kavikondal M. Senguttuvan, *Nenjam Maravaa Nigazhchigal*, publication, (Chennai: Thamaraiselvi Pathippagam, 2002), 98–99.

12   *Dravida Nadu*, 21 July 1957, 5.

13   *Dravida Nadu*, 20 November 1949, 8, 11.

14   Nedunchezhian, *Vaazhvil*, 199–200.

15   *Dravida Nadu*, 30 July 1950, 1, 3.

16   *Dravida Nadu*, 30 July 1950, 4.

17   *Dravida Nadu*, 24 September 1950, 1, 3.

18   *Dravida Nadu*, 8 October 1950, 1,

19   *Dravida Nadu*, 1 October 1950, 1, 3.

20   *Dravida Nadu*, 8 October 1950, 3, 11.

21   *Dravida Nadu*, 15 October 1950, 7.

22 *Dravida Nadu*, 18 March 1951, 1, 3–4.
23 *Dravida Nadu*, 3 September 1950, 2, 8.
24 Kannan, *Anna*, 183.
25 *Dravida Nadu*, 17 September 1950, 1–8.
26 *Dravida Nadu*, 15 October 1950, 8.
27 *Dravida Nadu*, 12 November 1950, 1; *Dravida Nadu*, 19 November 1950, 8.
28 *Dravida Nadu*, 5 November 1950, 1; *Dravida Nadu*, 3 December 1950, 1.
29 *Dravida Nadu*, 24 July 1955, 15.
30 *Dravida Nadu*, 29 October 1950, 1.
31 *Dravida Nadu*, 5 November 1950, 6–7.
32 Parthasarathy, 141–45; *DMK Silver Jubilee Souvenir*, 75–76.
33 *Dravida Nadu*, 25 November 1951, 5.
34 Ibid., 1, 5.
35 *Viduthalai*, 5 November 1951.
36 *Dravida Nadu*, 13 April 1952, 8.
37 *Dravida Nadu*, 25 November 1951, 6.
38 For an interesting study on the communist idea of national self-determination, see Boris Meissner, 'The Soviet Concept of Nation and the Right of National Self-Determination,' in *International Journal* 32, (1976) 1: 56–81. Accessed 2 June 20202, http://www.jstor.org/stable/40542146.
39 *Dravida Nadu*, 5 December 1951, 1–4.
40 *Dravida Nadu*, 26 October 1958, 5-9; 11.
41 K. Velnambi, *Payanam*, (Chennai: Gowra Pathippagam, 2017), 3: 2761.
42 C.N. Annadurai, 'Muthal Maanila Maanadu,' (Anna's letter to thambis). Accessed 9 July 2021, http://www.annavinpadaippugal.info/sorpozhivugal/muthal_manila.htm.
43 Velnambi, *Thamizhanai*, 370.
44 *Dravida Nadu*, First Anniversary Issue, 24 September 1950, 2.

Chapter 4: Election, Kallakudi, Kamaraj

1 *Dravida Nadu*, 16 September 1951, 12.
2 The first day began with the procession from the party's office at Royapuram at 9 a.m. to the conference venue. At the grounds 'Dravida Nadu for Dravidians' rent the air as Anna hoisted the DMK flag.

Earlier, the Dravida Nadu national anthem was played. Maestro C.S. Jayaraman and Nagoor Hanifa performed the first day. In the evening, NSK spoke on his visit to Russia and at 10.30 p.m., a Telugu play and *Porattam* (Struggle) an all-women's play was staged. The second day saw Nedunchezhian, Sampath, Karunanidhi, Mathiazhagan and K. Manoharan make speeches. At 10 p.m., *Ilainjan Kural* (Youth's Voice) starring Karunanidhi and M.G. Chakrapani was staged. *Jameen Maaligai* (Zameen Mansion) and *Chandrodayam* (Moonrise) starring K.R. Ramasamy were staged on the third and the fourth day, respectively. *Dravida Nadu*, 9 December 1951, 6.

3   *Dravida Nadu*, 23 December 1951, 1–8.

4   *Dravida Nadu*, 2 March 1952, 5.

5   *Dravida Nadu*, 17 February 1952, 12.

6   Uttara Natarajan, *Plain Speaking: A Sudra's Story*, (New Delhi: Permanent Black, 2007), 179–80.

7   Ibid., 178.

8   Ibid., 179–83.

9   J.B. Kripalani, *My Times: An Autobiography*, (New Delhi: Rupa Publications, 2004), 747–48.

10   *Madras Legislative Assembly 1952–1957: A Review*, (Chennai: Legislative Assembly Secretariat, 1957). Accessed 21 January 2018, http://www.assembly.tn.gov.in/archive/1st_1952/Review_1-52-57.pdf.

11   A. Govindasamy Oru Sagaptham Centenary Souvenir, (Villupuram: AGS Pathippagam, 2017), 118–20.

12   *Enadhu Arasiyal Payanam*, ed., Thuglak Ramesh, (Chennai, The Alliance Publication Company, 2021), 233.

13   *Dravida Nadu*, 4 May 1952, 5, 7, 8.

14   *Dravida Nadu*, 11 May 1952, 1, 4–5, 9–10.

15   *Dravida Nadu*, 27 July 1952, 1–2.

16   *Dravida Nadu*, 27 July 1952, 8.

17   *Dravida Nadu*, 3 August 1952, 1–2.

18   *Dravida Nadu*, 21 December 1952, 1, 6.

19   *Dravida Nadu*, 28 December 1952, 1; *Dravida Nadu*, 4 January 1953, 1.

20   *Dravida Nadu*, 26 April 1953, 1.

21   *Dravida Nadu*, 28 December 1952, 1–5.

22   *Dravida Nadu*, 11 January 1953, 2.

23   *Dravida Nadu*, 11 January 1953, 1, 3.

24   *Dravida Nadu*, 22 February 1953, 1; *Murasoli*, 28 February 1988, 1.

25   *Dravida Nadu*, 9 January 1955, 16.

26   *Dravida Nadu*, 26 April 1953, 6.

27   *Dravida Nadu*, 26 April 1953, 6–7.

28   *Dravida Nadu*, 17 May 1953, 3.

29   *Dravida Nadu*, 17 May 1953, 3.

30   Parthasarathy, *Thi.Mu.Ka.*, 161; *Dravida Nadu*, 19 July 1953, 13.

31   Robert Trumbull, 'India Rioting Laid to Resentment of Dravidians at Language Reform; Proposal for a New Educational System as well as Opposition to Dominant Brahmins Are Also Factors,' *New York Times*, 17 July 1953, 4.

32   *Selected Works of Jawaharlal Nehru*, ed., Mukherjee, 19: 67.

33   *Dravida Nadu*, 7 June 1953, 5.

34   *Dravida Nadu*, 12 July 1953, 8.

35   *Dravida Nadu*, 26 July 1953, 1–5.

36   *Dravida Nadu*, 26 July 1953, 1.

37   *Dravida Nadu*, 17 July 1953, 13.

38   Robert Trumbull, supra 31.

39   *Dravida Nadu*, 31 July 1955, 15; Trumbull.

40   Kannadasan, *Vanavaasam*, 196–236.

41   *Dravida Nadu*, 15 November 1953, 7; *Dravida Nadu*, 2 August 1953, 15; *Dravida Nadu*, 27 September 1953, 9; *Dravida Nadu*, 27 September 1953, 8.

42   *Dravida Nadu*, 16 August 1953, 7; A.S. Venu, *Verdict on Verdict*, (Chennai: Kalai Mandram, 1953), 98.

43   *Dravida Nadu*, 4 October 1953, 6.

44   *Dravida Nadu*, 26 July 1953, 16; *Dravida Nadu*, 27 September 1953, 8.

45   *Dravida Nadu*, 29 November 1953, 1.

46   *Dravida Nadu*, 22 November 1953, 8; R. Kannan, *MGR: A Life*, (Gurgaon: Penguin Random House India, 2017), 82.

47   *Selected Works of Jawaharlal Nehru*, ed., Mukherjee, 24: 7.

48   Ibid., 8.

49   Venu, *Verdict*, 81–82.

50   *Govindasamy Centenary Souvenir*, 122.

51   A. Gopanna, ed., *Periyarum Perundhalaivarum*, (Chennai: Nava India Pathippagam, 2007), 8–35.

52   Kannan, *Anna*, 209, Jayakanthan, 35.

53   Cho Ramaswamy, *Ivargalai Sandhithen*, 2 vols (Chennai: The Alliance Publication Company, 2016), 1: 167.

54   Kannan, *Anna*, 220.

55   *Dravida Nadu*, 11 December 1955, 14.

56 *Dravida Nadu*, 11 December 1955, 16.

57 'Kalai ulaga kaanikai,' Anna's 18 December 1955 missive on fundraising for cyclone relief by actors. Accessed 1 March 2021, http://www. annavinpadaippugal.info/kadithangal/kalai_ulaga_kaanickai.htm.

58 P. Dheenadayalan, *MGR*, (Chennai: Sixth Sense Publications, 2014), 63.

59 Ibid., 57.

60 Kavignar Kannadasan, *Cinema Sandhayil Muppadhu Aandugal*, (Chennai: Kannadasan Pathippagam, 2013), 13.

61 Kannan, *Anna*, 222.

62 Ma.Po.Si. *Enadhu*, 2: 485–86; 497–506; 'Periyarai Puriyadha Periyaristugalum . . . Thamizh Desiyavadhigalum.' Accessed 22 November 2020, https://www.vikatan.com/government-and-politics/71321-does-periyarists-and-tamil-nationalists-understand-periyar; Kannan, *Anna*, 210.

63 Gopanna, *Periyarum*, 61.

64 *Dravida Nadu*, 29 January 1956, 3–6; *Dravida Nadu*, 4 March 1956, 18.

65 *Dravida Nadu*, 11 March 1956, 8.

66 Ma.Po.Si. *Enadhu*, 853.

67 On 29 January 1956, Karunanidhi moved a resolution at the Chidambaram general council to safeguard the rights of the Sri Lankan Tamils. On 22 June 1958, the party marked the 'Lankan Tamils Rights Protection Day'. Karunanidhi, *Kadithangal*, 44: 180–81.

Chapter 5: In Pursuit of Power

1 *Dravida Nadu*, 8 May 1955, 7–9.

2 *Dravida Nadu*, 8 May 1955, 7–9; C.N. Annadurai, 'Nedunchezhiyan Andrum! Indrum!!' Accessed 7 May 2020, http://www. annavinpadaippugal.info/kadithangal/nedunchezhiyan_andrum_ indrum.htm.

3 N. Vivekanandan, Iniyan Sampath and Kalpanadasan, eds., *E.V.K. Sampathum Dravida Iyakkamum*, Chennai, (2013), 273.

4 Ibid., 300.

5 'Irandaavadhu Maanila Maanaadu', Anna's speech on 20 May 1956 at the DMK's second state conference. Accessed 21 March 2024, https://www. annavinpadaippugal.info/sorpozhivugal/irandavathu_manila2_1.htm.

6 Malarmannan, *Thi Mu Ka*, 166.

7 Chokkan, *Annaandhu Paar*, (Chennai: Vikatan Pirasuram, 2009), 98.

8   Vivekanandan and others, *E.V.K. Sampathum*, 274.

9   *Dravida Nadu*, 27 May 1956, 4–6; *Dravida Nadu*, 3 June 1956, 11–17.

10   'Irandaavadhu Maanila Maanaadu', supra note 5.

11   *Dravida Nadu*, 12 August 1956, 3.

12   *Dravida Nadu*, 22 July 1956, 6.

13   *Dravida Nadu*, 5 August 1956, 15.

14   Gopannaa, *Periyarum*, 86.

15   *Dravida Nadu*, 16 November 1956, 3–5, 16.

16   *Dravida Nadu*, 29 September 1957, 13.

17   Parthasarathy, *Thi.Mu.Ka.*, 211, 213.

18   *Dravida Nadu*, 28 October 1956, 3.

19   Joyce Philomena Vernem, 'Nightmare in Ariyalur, a brave tale from 1956,' *The Hindu*, 2 March 2014. Accessed 17 April 2020, https://www.thehindu.com/opinion/open-page/nightmare-in-ariyalur-a-brave-tale-from-1956/article5740973.ece.

20   Veerapandi Arumugham, *Dravida*, 21–24.

21   Ibid., 24–28.

22   R. Muthukumar, *Indhia Therdhal Varalaaru*, (Chennai: Sixth Sense Publications, 2015), 54.

23   Ibid.

24   C.S. Poonjolai, 'Vazhga Vasavaalar'. Accessed 20 April 2020, http://www.arignaranna.net/arasiyal_main.asp.

25   Kavya Shanmugasundharam, ed., *Pasumpon Kalanjiyam: Thevarin Sorpozhivugal*, (Chennai: Kavya, 2nd ed., 2023), 376–78.

26   Muthukumar, *Indhia*, 52.

27   Venkatachalam, *My Days*, 28–34.

28   Gokul Rajendran, 'M Karunanidhi's victory march began from Kulithalai', *Times of India*, 9 August 2018. Accessed 2 January 2022, https://timesofindia.indiatimes.com/city/trichy/mks-victory-march-began-from-kulithalai/articleshow/65329424.cms.

29   *Dravida Nadu*, 1 September 1957, 3.

30   C.N. Annadurai, 'Municipal Elections and Party Politics,' *Homeland*, 25 January 1959. Accessed 20 April 2020, http://www.annavinpadaippugal.info/katturaigal/municipal_elections_and.htm.

31   Parthasarathy, *Thi.Mu.Ka.*, 214.

32   Ibid., 216–17.

33   'Alunarukku Annavin Paaraatu,' Anna's praise for the governor. Accessed 10 July 2019, http://www.annavinpadaippugal.info/sorpozhivugal/alunarukku_anna.htm.

34 'Sattamandrathil Annavin Mudhal Muzhakkam,' Anna's maiden assembly speech. Accessed 10 July 2019, http://www.annavinpadaippugal.info/sorpozhivugal/sattamandram_first.htm.

35 '4.7.57 Varavu Selavu Thitta Vivadthathil Anna,' Anna's participation in the discussion on the budget. Accessed 10 July 2019, http://www.annavinpadaippugal.info/sorpozhivugal/satta_04_07_1957_1.htm.

36 *Dravida Nadu*, 18 August 1957, 10–13.

37 *Kalaignarin Sattamandra Uraigal*, (Chennai: Poompuhar Pirasuram, 2008), 1: 19–22; *Kalaignarin Sattamandra Uraigal*, 9: 323–27.

38 *Dravida Nadu*, 29 September 1957, 15.

39 *Dravida Nadu*, 16 February 1958, 3; 'Aalunar urayin meedhaana vivaadha,' Discussion on governor's address. Accessed 22 May 2022, http://www.annavinpadaippugal.info/sorpozhivugal/300367_1.htm.

40 '"Governor's post like goat's beard", says Stalin,' *Times of India*, 16 November 2017. Accessed 20 June 2018, https://timesofindia.indiatimes.com/city/chennai/governors-post-like-goats-beard-says-stalin/articleshow/61665193.cms.

41 'Aluvalaga mozhi patriya vivadham,' Discussion on administrative language. Accessed 1 May 2022, http://www.annavinpadaippugal.info/sorpozhivugal/aluvalaga050960.htm.

42 Ibid.

43 *Dravida Nadu*, 16 March 1958, 11–12.

44 C.N. Annadurai, '16.3.60 Andru nadaipetra nidthinilai arikkai meedhaana vivadhathin podhu,' Anna's speech on the budget discussion. Accessed 2 January 2020, http://www.annavinpadaippugal.info/sorpozhivugal/satta_16_03_1960_1.htm.

45 C.N. Annadurai, 'Nyayangalai alatchiyapaduthuvathu aramalla,' Anna's speech in the assembly. Accessed 2 January 2020, http://www.annavinpadaippugal.info/sorpozhivugal/niyayangalai_alatchiyappaduthuvathu.htm.

46 '10.12.59 Andru nadaipetra governor uraviyin meedhaana vivadhathin podhu,' On 10 December 1959, discussion on the motion of thanks to the governor's address. Accessed 20 March 2020, http://www.annavinpadaippugal.info/sorpozhivugal/satta_10_12_1959_1.htm.

47 *Viduthalai*, 27 July 1957.

48 *Viduthalai*, 7 October 1957.

49 *Dravida Nadu*, 18 August 1957, 5.

50 Ibid., 12–13.

51 C.N. Annadurai, 'Nambikkainmaiyin meedhaana vivadham,' Anna's speech in the 31 October 1957 discussion on the motion of no confidence. Accessed 1 March 2020, http://www.annavinpadaippugal. info/sorpozhivugal/nambikkai301057_2.htm; http://www.annavin padaippugal.info/sorpozhivugal/nambikkai311057.htm.

52 *Dravida Nadu*, 24 November 1957, 16.

53 *Selected Works of Jawaharlal Nehru*, ed., Mukherjee, 40: 129.

54 Ibid., 388.

55 Ibid.

56 '17 July 1957 Kalvi maaniyathirkaana vettup preraraniyinpodhu', On the cut motion on the grants for education. Accessed 22 May 2022, ow.annavinpadaippugal.info/sorpozhivugal/satta_17_07_1957_2. htm; Bhaktavatsalam, *Enadhu Ninaivugal*, (Chennai, Jananayaga Seva Sangam, 1971), 47–48.

57 *Dravida Nadu*, 7 September 1958, 3; *Selected Works of Jawaharlal Nehru*, ed., Mukherjee, 40: 387.

58 *Dravida Nadu*, 7 September 1958, 3.

59 *Dravida Nadu*, 5 January 1958, 3–4.

60 C.N. Annadurai, 'The Twenty Days Itch,' *Homeland*, 2 February 1958. Accessed 20 April 2018, http://www.annavinpadaippugal.info/ katturaigal/the_twenty_days_itch.htm; C.N. Annadurai, 'Bull - Boxers Bellow,' *Homeland*, 9 February 1958. Accessed 20 April 2018, http:// www.annavinpadaippugal.info/katturaigal/bull_boxers_bellow.htm.

61 'Aalunar Urai Meedhaana Vivadham,' Discussion on the motion of thanks to the governor's address. Accessed 20 April 2018, http://www. annavinpadaippugal.info/sorpozhivugal/aalunar130258_2.htm.

62 *Selected Works of Jawaharlal Nehru, Second series*, ed., Mukherjee, 41: 346.

63 Ibid.

64 Gopanna, *Periyarum*, 95.

65 Ibid., 125.

66 *Dravida Nadu*, 19 April 1959, 3, 5.

67 *Dravida Nadu*, 26 April 1959, 4.

68 C.N. Annadurai, 'Chennai Maanagaraatchi: Thi Mu Ka Vetri - Paaraatu,' Anna's essay on the DMK's victory in the Chennai Corporation elections and the praise. Accessed 20 January 2020, http:// www.annavinpadaippugal.info/sorpozhivugal/chennai_maanagar.htm.

69 M. Karunanidhi, 'My Memories of Anna,' the *Illustrated Weekly of India*, 13 April 1969. Accessed 12 January 2019, https://archive.org/stream/

in.ernet.dli.2015.100844/2015.100844.The-Illustrated-Weekly-Of-India-Vol90-No14-26april-june1969_djvu.txt.

70   *Therkilirundhu Oru Suryian*, (Chennai: Tamilthisai, 2015), 117.

71   *Murasoli Pudhaiyal*, 17 March 1980, 3.

72   C.N. Annadurai, 'Significance of Six Months,' *Homeland*, 27 August 1967. Accessed 20 March 2021, http://www.annavinpadaippugal.info/katturaigal/significance_of_six_monts.htm.

73   *Kalki*, 20 April 1975, 31–32.

74   *MGRin Sattamandra Uraigal*, (Chennai: Government of Tamil Nadu, 2017), 181.

Chapter 6: First Split

1   Vivekanandan and others, *E.V.K. Sampathum*, 447–48.

2   Ibid., 392–401.

3   President's Order, 1960, Copy of Notification No. 2/8/60-O.L. (Ministry of Home Affairs), dated 27 April 1960. Accessed 20 March 2020, https://rajbhasha.gov.in/en/presidents-order-1960.

4   Vivekanandan and others, *E.V.K. Sampathum*, 402–04.

5   Ibid., 445.

6   India, *Parliamentary Debates*, House of Representatives, 7 August 1959, cols. 1398–99. Accessed 21 June 2020, https://eparlib.nic.in/bitstream/123456789/808945/1/pms_02_08_07-08-1959.pdf.

7   Vivekanandan and others, *E.V.K. Sampathum*, 437.

8   K.M. Selvaraj, *Maamanidhar Mathiazhagan*, (Chennai: Kaniyur Pathippagam, 2004), 166.

9   Vivekanandan and others, *E.V.K. Sampathum*, 460.

10   *Namnadu*, 13 February 1961.

11   *Dravida Nadu*, 26 February 1961, 5.

12   *Namnadu*, 27 February 1961.

13   *Namnadu*, 28 February 1961.

14   *Dravida Nadu*, 4 March 1961.

15   'Nidhinilai arikkai meedhaan vivadham,' Discussion on the budget, 8 March 1961. Accessed 20 March 20http://www.annavinpadaippugal.info/sorpozhivugal/nithi080361_1.html.

16   *Dravida Nadu*, 19 March 1961, 7.

17   Chokkan, *Annaandhu Paar*, 89.

18   Dheenadayalan, *MGR*, 104.

19   *Dravida Nadu*, 23 April 1961, 5–12.

Chapter 7: Soldiering On

1   Nedunchezhian, *Vaazhvil*, 340.
2   Ibid., 341–43.
3   K.S. Ramanujam, *The Big Change*, (Chennai: Higginbothams, 1967), 89, 129.
4   Ibid., 128.
5   *Mandram*, 15 February 1956.
6   C.N. Annadurai, 'Mozhiprachanai meedhaana vivadham,' Anna's 23 January 1968 assembly speech on the language problem. Accessed 2 February 2022, http://www.annavinpadaippugal.info/sorpozhivugal/230168_1.htm.
7   Ramanujam, *The Big Change*, 89–90.
8   Gopanna, *Periyarum*, 160–78.
9   *Murasoli Pongal issue*, January 1962.
10 P. Thangapandian, *Dravida Munnetra Kazhaga Therthal Arikkaigal*, (Chennai: Nalanda Pathippagam, 2008), 26 71.
11 Veerapandi Arumugham, *Dravida*, 36–39.
12 Malarmannan, *Thi Mu Ka*, 67–68.
13 Statistical Report on General Election, 1962 to the Legislative Assembly of Madras, (Election Commission of India, New Delhi, 1962). Accessed 20 May 2020, https://web.archive.org/web/20130127201143/https://eci.gov.in/eci_main/StatisticalReports/SE_1962/StatRep_Madras_1962.pdf.
14 Natarajan, *Plain Speaking*, 173–74.
15 Ara. Thiruvidam, *Thiruvallikeni Mudhal Thiruvarur Varai*, (Chennai: Gowra Pathippagam, 2018), 454.
16 *Selected Works of Jawaharlal Nehru*, ed., Mukherjee, 74: 447–62.
17 Chokkan, *Annaandhu Paar*, 123.
18 Ramanujam, *The Big Change*, 136.
19 Gopannaa, *Periyarum*, 195, 202; Karunanidhi, *Nenjuku Needhi*, (Chennai: Thirumagal Nilayam, 2018), 4:269.
20 J.B. Kripalani, *My Life*, 830–31.
21 A. Gopanna, *Kamaraj Oru Sagaptham*, (Chennai, Nava India publication, 2001), 204.
22 *Madras Legislative Assembly 1957–1962: A Review, March 1962*, (Chennai: Government of Tamil Nadu, 1962). Accessed 2 February 2019, http://www.assembly.tn.gov.in/archive/2nd_1957/Review_2-1957-62.pdf.
23 *Madras Legislative Assembly 1962–1967: A Review, (Chennai: Government of Tamil Nadu, 1967)*. Accessed 2 February 2019, http://www.assembly.

tn.gov.in/archive/3rd_1962/Review%203_62-67.pdf; Dheenadayalan, *MGR*, 121.

24   K. Rajaram, *Oru Saamaniyanin Ninaivugal*, (Chennai: Nakkheeran Pathippagam, 2014), 54; C.N. Annadurai, 'Soodum, Suvayum,' Anna's letter to thambis. Accessed 1 December 2018, http://www. annavinpadaippugal.info/kadithangal/soodum_suvayum_1_1.htm; ed., Thuglak Ramesh, *Enadhu*, 188-89.

25   *Madras Legislative Assembly 1957–1962*, supra note 22; *Daily Thanthi Varalaatru Suvadugal*, (Chennai: Daily Thanthi Publications, 2019), 435.

26   *Madras Legislative Assembly 1962–1967*, supra note 23.

27   Karunanidhi, *Nenjuku Needhi*, 1: 98–113.

28   C.N. Annadurai, 'Call My State "Tamil Nadu",' Anna's speech at the Council of States. Accessed 3 March 2019, http://www. annavinpadaippugal.info/sorpozhivugal/rajya_call_my_state.htm.

29   Gopanna, *Periyarum*, 198.

30   Ibid., 19.

31   Nedunchezhian, *Vaazhvil*, 352–54.

32   Venkatachalam, *My Time*, 140–41.

33   Ibid., 145–47.

34   Nedunchezhian, *Vaazhvil*, 354–55.

35   Abhinav Chandrachud, 'The House is in cession,' *Business Line*, 8 January 2018. Accessed 15 April 2019, https://www.thehindubusinessline.com/ blink/know/the-house-is-in-cession/article9926186.ece.

36   *Madras Legislative Assembly 1957–1962: A Review, March 1962*, supra note 23; http://www.annavinpadaippugal.info/sorpozhivugal/ desiya131159.htm.

37   India, *Parliamentary Debates*, Council of States, 25 January 1963, C.N. Annadurai's speech on the Sixteenth Amendment Bill, cols. 4890-891. Accessed 1 January 2018, https://rsdebate.nic.in/ bitstream/123456789/549556/1/PD_41_25011963_31_p4848_ p4952_29.pdf.

38   Ibid.

39   India, *Parliamentary Debates*, Council of States, 9 May 1963, Vote on the Sixteenth Amendment Bill, cols. 2831–896. Accessed 17 May 2019, https://rsdebate.nic.in/handle/123456789/544589?viewItem= searchfile:///Users/admin/Desktop/PD_43_09051963_15_p2831_ p2896_12.pdf.

40   Ramanujam, *The Big Change*, 228.

41   Velnambi, *Thamizhanai*, 368.

42 Nedunchezhian, *Vaazhvil*, 372.

43 Ma.Po.Si., *Enadhu*, 942–45.

44 Ibid., 362–64.

45 Kannan, *Anna*, 78–79.

46 Kannan, *Anna*, 280; *Madras Legislative Assembly 1957–1962*, supra note 23.

47 Periyar E.V. Ramasamy, 1, *Naan Sonnaal Unakku Yaen Kobam Vara Vendum?* ed., Pasu. Gowthaman, (Chennai: New Century Book House, 2017), 1: 599.

48 S.S. Thennarasu, *Pennilaatha Oorinile*, (Chennai: Thirumaran Nilayam, 1990), 51.

49 *Daily Thanthi, Varalaatrru Suvudugal*, 450–73; *Kalaignarin Sattamandra Uraigal*, 4: 174.

50 Thomas F. Brady, 'Shastri Reiterates Assurances Use of Hindi Won't Be Imposed,' *New York Times*, 4 February 1965, 6.

51 India, *Parliamentary Debates*, Council of States, 4 March 1965, Anna's speech on the motion of thanks on the President's Address, cols. 2001–002. Accessed 1 June 2019, https://rsdebate.nic.in/bitstream/123456789/533367/1/PD_51_04031965_12_p1975_p2104_4.pdf.

52 Ibid., col. 1992.

53 Periyar, Gowthaman, ed., 1: 675.

54 Ibid., 601–03.

55 Ibid., 622–23.

56 Ibid., 647.

57 India, *Parliamentary Debates*, Council of States, 9 May 1963, Anna's speech on the debate on the Sixteenth Amendment Bill, cols. 2831–896. Accessed 17 May 2019, https://rsdebate.nic.in/handle/123456789/544589?viewItem=searchfile:///Users/admin/Desktop/PD_43_09051963_15_p2831_p2896_12.pdf.

58 *Illustrated Weekly of India*, 26 September 1965.

59 Report of the Official Language Commission, 1956, Bombay, 1956, 401.

60 Tamilaruvi Manian, *Thi.Mu. Kazhagam: Sila Unmaigal, Sila Sandthegangal* . . . (Namakkal: Jeeva Puthagalayam, 2024), 62–64.

61 Gopanna, Kamaraj, 316.

62 Tamilvanan, *Thalaisirandha Kelvi Bathilgal*, (Chennai: Manimekalai Pirasuram, 1988), 43.

63 *Daily Thanthi, Varalaatru* 567.

64   *The Mail*, 16 June 1966, cited in Ramanujam, *The Big Change*, 142–44.

65   Ramanujam, *The Big Change*, 254.

66   Ma.Po.Si., *Enadhu*, 974–75.

67   Adiyar, 'Amarar Anna,' Anna memorial issue, *Ananda Vikatan*, 30 March 1969, 85.

68   C.N. Annadurai, 'Thambiyudayaan Padaikanjaan,' Anna's speech on 3 June 1968 felicitating M. Karunanidhi on his 44th birthday. Accessed 7 June 2018, http://www.annavinpadaippugal.info/sorpozhivugal/thambiyudayan.htm.

69   Ma.Po.Si., *Enadhu*, 949.

Chapter 8: In Power

1   *Kalki*, 8 January 1967, 3.

2   *Daily Thanthi, Varalaatru Suvadugal*, 482–83.

3   Thangapandian, *Dravida*, 72–83.

4   *Kalki*, 15 January 1967, 5.

5   Muthukumar, *Indhia*, 119.

6   Thiruvidam, *Thiruvallikeni*, 572.

7   Muthukumar, *Indhia*, 119.

8   Gopanna, *Kamaraj*, 250.

9   Thiruvidam, *Thiruvallikeni*, 469.

10   Velnambi, *Thamizhanai*, 376.

11   *Murasoli*, 22 March 1990, 2.

12   Ramanujam, *The Big Change*, 261.

13   *Daily Thanthi*, 14 February 1967.

14   Chokkan, *Annaandhu Paar*, 132.

15   Gopanna, *Kamaraj*, 250.

16   Cited in Ramanujam, *The Big Change*, 178.

17   Ramanujam, *The Big Change*, 12.

18   *Daily Thanthi, Varalaatru Suvadugal*, 489.

19   Tiruchi Satyendran, *Ini Oru Periyariyai Paarpoma?* (Chennai: Naam Thamizhar Pathippagam, 2009), 90–93.

20   Kannan, *Anna*, 303.

21   I owe this thought to Tamilaruvi Manian.

22   H.V. Hande, 'Kamaraj: A Stalwart Who Was Let Down By His Own People,' *Swarajya*, 19 July 2018. Accessed 30 August 2019, https://swarajyamag.com/politics/kamaraj-a-stalwart-who-was-let-down-by-his-own-people.

23 Senguttuvan, *Nenjam*, 109.

24 Natarajan, *Plain Speaking*, 174.

25 *Enadhu*, ed., Thuglak Ramesh, 189.

26 'Thavaru Seidha Podhu Thiruthungul,' Anna's radio interview on 7 March 1967. Accessed 2 June 2020, http://www.annavinpadaippugal. info/paettigal/thavaru_seithapothu.htm.

27 *The Hindu*, 16 February 1976, 1.

28 *Daily Thanthi, Varalaatru*, 486–87.

29 Nedunchezhian, *Vaazhvil*, 421.

30 Selvendran, *Ini?* 90–93.

31 Kavignar Karunanandam, *Anna Sila Ninaivugal*, (Chennai: Poovazhagi Pathippagam, 1986), 186–89.

32 C.N. Annadurai, 'Mozhiprachanai meedhaana vivadham,' Anna's 23 January 1968 assembly speech on the language problem. Accessed 5 June 2018, http://www.annavinpadaippugal.info/sorpozhivugal/230168_1.htm

33 https://viduthalai.in/2011-07-25-07-58-59/184276--q-q------.html.

34 C.N. Annadurai, 'Aalunar urai meedhaana vivadham,' Anna's 30 March 1967 reply to the motion of thanks to the governor's address. Accessed 5 June 2020, http://www.annavinpadaippugal.info/ sorpozhivugal/300367_1.htm.

35 Ma.Po.Si., *Enadhu Porattam*, 982–88; Karunanidhi *Kadithangal*, 7: 23.

36 Thiruvidam, *Thiruvallikeni*, 595.

37 'Prachanaygal pala,' Anna's 6 April 1967 press meet in Delhi, http:// www.annavinpadaippugal.info/paettigal/prachinaigal_pala.htm.

38 Muthukumar, *Madhuvilaku: Arasiyalum, Varalaarum*, (Chennai: Sixth Sense Publications, 2015), 73–75.

39 Adiyar, 'Amarar Anna,' Anna memorial issue, *Ananda Vikatan*, 30 March 1969, 88.

40 M. Bhaktavatsalam, 'Arignar Annavum naanum,' M. Bhaktavatsalam's 16 September 1984 recollection of his association with Anna, 21 July 2020, http://www.arignaranna.net/bakthavatsalam.htm.

41 C.N. Annadurai, 'Amaicharavaiyin meedhu nambikkailillath theermanam – vivadham thodarchi,' Fourth day of debate on the no-confidence motion. Accessed 21 July 2020, http://www.annavinpadaippugal.info/ sorpozhivugal/280868.htm.

42 T.R. Ramanujam, 'Anna – a gentleman CM'. Accessed 13 June 2020, http://www.arignaranna.net/trramanujam.htm.

43 C.N. Annadurai, 'Tamil Nadu 1967 satta peravai (thagudhinmaigal thaduppu) mun vadivu,' Anna's reply to the debate on the Tamil Nadu

Legislature (Prevention of Disqualification) Bill, 1967 (L.A. Bill No. 3 of 1967) (Act No. 3 of 1967)). Accessed 25 January 2020, http://www. annavinpadaippugal.info/sorpozhivugal/250367.htm; C.N. Annadurai, '1967–68 aam aandirkaana thiruttha varavu thittam arimugapatuthal,' Anna's 17 June 1967 speech introducing the revised budget for 1967–68. Accessed 25 January 2020, http://www.annavinpadaippugal.info/sorpozhivugal/110667_2.htm.

44　*Viduthalai*, 1 April 1967, 3.

45　C.N. Annadurai, 'Aalunar urai meeghaana vivadham (30 March 1967),' Anna's reply to the motion of thanks to the governor's address. Accessed 12 January 2010, http://www.annavinpadaippugal.info/sorpozhivugal/300367_2.htm.

46　*Dinamani Anna Centenary Souvenir*, (Chennai: *Dinamani*, 2009), 160.

47　'Kavana eerpu theermanam – kachatheevin meedhu ilangai arasu urimai kondaadal,' Anna's reply to the calling attention motion on the question of ownership of the island 'Kacha Theevu'. Accessed 14 June 2020, http://www.annavinpadaippugal.info/sorpozhivugal/250368.htm.

48　*Maperum Tamil Kanavu*, 214.

49　Kannadasan, *Vanavaasam*, 206.

50　*Maperum Tamil Kanavu*, 312–13.

51　*1974: Maanila Suyaatchi*, ed., Aazhi Senthilnathan, (Chennai: Aazhi Publishers, 2022), 571.

52　Nedunchezhian, *Vaazhvil*, 439–40; K. Velnambi, *Payanam*, 3: 2173; Thiruvidam, *Thiruvallikeni*, 587.

53　Thiruvidam, *Thiruvallikeni*, 588.

54　*Kalki*, 1 October 1967, 10.

55　*Kalki*, 21 May 1967, 8.

56　'1967–68 aandirkaana irudhi thunai arikkai peravai mun vaithal,' Anna tabling the grants for the 1967–68 supplementary budget estimates on 25 March 1968. Accessed 22 May 2023, http://www.annavinpadaippugal.info/sorpozhivugal/250368_2.htm.

57　*Dinamani Anna Centenary Souvenir*, 160.

58　C.N. Annadurai, '1967–68 aam aandirkaana thiruttha varavu thittam arimugapatuthal,' Anna's 17 June 1967 speech introducing the revised budget for 1967–68. Accessed 22 May 2023 http://www.annavinpadaippugal.info/sorpozhivugal/110667_1.htm; '1967–68 aandirkaana nidhinilai arikkai meedhaana podhu vivadham,' Anna's speech on the budget debate. Accessed 14 March 2020, http://www.annavinpadaippugal.info/sorpozhivugal/270667_2.htm.

59   *Kalki*, 9 July 1967, 7.

60   '1967–68 aandirkaana nidhinilai arikkai meedhaana podhu vivadham,' supra note 57.

61   C.N. Annadurai, '82 avadhu vidhiyin keezh thee vibathugal patriya arikkai,' Anna's statement on 8 July 1967 on the slum fires. Accessed 14 February 2020, http://www.annavinpadaippugal.info/sorpozhivugal/080767.htm.

62   Ibid.

63   *Kalki*, 10 March 1968, 7.

64   *Kalki*, 24 March 1968, 7.

65   *Maperum Tamil Kanavu*, 312–13.

66   '1967–68 aandirkaana nidhinilai arikkai meedhaana podhu vivadham,' supra note 57.

67   Thuglak Ramesh, ed., *Enadhu*, 168.

68   I owe this to Professor Naganathan, Chennai, 15 September 2021.

69   *Maperum Tamil Kanavu*, 311; *Therkilirundhu Oru Suryian*, 61–62; Tamil Nadu Civil Supplies Corporation. Accessed 21 June 2022, http://www. tncsc.tn.gov.in/.

70   '1967–68 aandirkaana nidhinilai arikkai meedhaana podhu vivadham,' supra note 57.

71   C.N. Annadurai, 'Othivaipu theermaanam-bathilurai,' Anna's reply to the adjournment motion on the slum fires. Accessed 6 January 2020, http://www.annavinpadaippugal.info/sorpozhivugal/070767.htm; '1967-68 aandirkaana nidhinilai arikkai meedhaana podhu vivadham,' supra note 57.

72   Ibid.

73   Ibid.

74   C.N. Annadurai, 'Chennai manila peyar Tamil Nadu . . .,' Anna's 17 August 1968 statement moving the resolution unanimously adopted on 18 July 1967 recommending that steps be taken by the State Government to secure necessary amendment to the Constitution of India to change the name of Madras State as 'TAMIL NADU'). Accessed 29 May 2020, http://www.annavinpadaippugal.info/ sorpozhivugal/170868_2.htm.

75   Velnambi, *Payanam*, 3: 2374–377.

76   'HT THIS DAY: Dec 14, 1967—Lok Sabha approves Language Bill,' *Hindustan Times*, 13 December 2021. Accessed 21 May 2022, https://www.hindustantimes.com/india-news/htthisdaydec-14-1967-lok-sabha-approves-language-bill-101639406770439.html; India, *Parliamentary Debates*, House of the People, 13 December 1967, cols.

6630–37;   https://eparlib.nic.in/bitstream/123456789/850957/1/04_
III_13-12-1967_p95_p151_PII.pdf, cols. 6630-637.

77   K. Velnambi, *Payanam*, 3: 2388.

78   The Official Language Resolution, 1968. Accessed 1 March 2022,
      https://rajbhasha.gov.in/en/official-language-resolution-1968.

79   *Tamil Nadu Legislative Assembly Quadrennial Review 1967–70, (Madras:
      Legislative Assembly Department, 1971)*. Accessed 2 May 2022, http://www.
      assembly.tn.gov.in/archive/4th_1967/Review%204_67-70.pdf.

80   M. Natarajan, 'Ullathaal Oruvare,' in *L.G. 70th Birthday Souvenir*,
      (Thanjavur, Thanjaivaazh Kannanthangudi Makkal Munnetra Sangam,
      2012).

81   C.N. Annadurai, 'Mozhiprachanai meedhaana vivadham,' Anna's
      23 January 1968 assembly speech on the language problem). 21,
      Accessed 1 January 2021, http://www.annavinpadaippugal.info/
      sorpozhivugal/230168_1.htm.

82   Ibid.

83   Ibid.

84   *Daily Thanthi, Varalaatru*, 506–07.

85   M. Natarajan, 'Ullathaal Oruvare,' supra note 81.

86   *Kalki*, 18 August 1968,7.

87   Jayakanthan, *Oru*, 354–56.

88   M. Natarajan, 'Ullathaal Oruvare,' supra note 81.

89   T.R. Ramanujam, 'Anna – a gentleman CM'. Accessed 13 June 2020,
      http://www.arignaranna.net/trramanujam.htm.

90   'Aria America payanam,' Anna's 15 April 1968 interview prior to his
      US visit. Accessed 13 June 2020, http://www.annavinpadaippugal.info/
      paettigal/ariya_america_payanam.htm.

91   Chockalaingam, 'Kandaar: Vetri Kondaar,' Anna's private secretary
      Chockalingam's interview on 16 February 1968 to *Kalki*. Accessed 22
      June 2020, http://www.arignaranna.net/chockalingam_interview.htm;
      Sidharth Bhardwaj, 'Bittersweet memories of battling the enemies
      of Goa,' *Times of India*, 23 August 2017. Accessed 17 August 2019,
      https://timesofindia.indiatimes.com/city/goa/bittersweet-memories-of-
      battling-the-enemies-of-goa/articleshow/58320913.cms.

92   M.S. Udayamurthi, *Americavil Anna-MGR*, (Chennai: Vidwan
      Pathippagam, 1975), 29.

93   Ibid., 30.

94   C.N. Annadurai, 'Maanila suyattchi muzhakkam,' Anna's speech at the 28
      July 1968 Tamilarasu Kazhagam's state autonomy conference. Accessed

1 April 2021, http://www.annavinpadaippugal.info/sorpozhivugal/maanila_suya.htm.

95 'Amaicharaviyinmeedhu Nambikkailillaath Theermaanan,' P.G. Karuthiruman's no-confidence motion on Anna's DMK ministry. Accessed 1 June 2020, http://www.annavinpadaippugal.info/sorpozhivugal/230868_1.htm.

96 Ibid.

97 Adiyar, 'Amarar Anna,' *Anna memorial issue, Ananda Vikatan*, 30 March 1969, 87.

98 'Amaicharaviyinmeedhu Nambikkailillaath Theermaanan.' supra note 96.

99 *Murasoli*, 28 March 1968, cited in *Kalki*, 7 April 1968, 8.

100 *Dinamani Anna Centenary Souvenir*, 29.

101 *Daily Thanthi, Varalaatru*, 536.

102 *Dinamani*, 5 February 1967, 1.

103 Jayakanthan, *Oru*, 364.

104 Ibid., 384.

105 *Kalaignarin Sattamandra Uraigal*, 1: 67–68.

106 *Kalki*, 9 February 1969, 4.

Chapter 9: Chief Minister Karunanidhi

1 S. Ramadoss, *Kazhagathin Kathai*, (Chennai: Puthiya Arasiyal Pathippagam, 2017), 11.

2 Karunanidhi, *Nenjuku Needhi*, 2: 25–26.

3 Interview with K. Manoharan July 1996.

4 Tiruchi Satyendran, *Ini?* 37–38.

5 Karunanidhi, *Kadithangal*, 9: 51.

6 Karunanidhi, *Nenjuku Needhi*, 2: 147.

7 Ibid., 6: 61–62.

8 Karunanidhi, *Kadithangal*, 43: 248.

9 Thiruvidam, *Thiruvallikeni*, 656–58; Karunanidhi, *Nenjuku Needhi*, 2: 148–51.

10 Karunanidhi, *Kadithangal*, 43: 248.

11 Nedunchezhian, *Vaazhvil*, 480–83; *Kadithangal*, 8: 193–94.

12 *Kalaignarin Sattamandra Uraigal*, 1: 63.

13 Karunanidhi, *Nenjuku Needhi* 2: 72–73.

14 *Summary Record of Discussions of the National Development (NDC) Meetings: Five Decades of National Building (Fifty NDC Meetings)*, 16–17.

15   *Murasoli*, 2 August 1994, 6.

16   Pupul Jayakar, *Indira Gandhi*, (Gurgaon, Penguin Random House, 2017), 210.

17   *Murasoli*, 5 August 1976, 4.

18   Zaheer Masood Quraishi, 'The Indian Presidential Election (1969),' *The Indian Journal of Political Science* 31: 1 (January–March 1970), 32–59.

19   Karunanidhi, *Nenjuku Needhi*, 6: 176-77.

20   Karunanidhi, *Kadithangal*, 5: 98–99; *Kalaignarin Sattamandra Uraigal*, 10: 151.

21   *Murasoli*, 20 October 1974, 1.

22   *Kalki*, 2 January 1976, 5.

23   P. Sabanayagam, *Service To The Nation*, (Chennai: Notion Press, 2019), 120.

24   *Kalaignarin Sattamandra Uraigal*, 1: 88.

25   Ibid.

26   K. A. Manikumar, 'Backward caste movement,' *The Routledge Handbook of the Other Backward Classes in India, Thought, Movements and Development*, (Gurgaon, Routledge India, 2022). Accessed 10 Nov 2023, https://www.taylorfrancis.com/chapters/edit/10.4324/9781003152873-16/backward-caste-movement-manikumar.

27   *Murasoli*, 17 August 1971, 1; *Navamani*, 4 April 1975, 1.

28   *Murasoli*, 8 July 1971, 4.

29   *Murasoli*, 14 November 1975, 1.

30   B. Sivakumar, 'Did M Karunanidhi change Tamil poet Thiruvalluvar's date of birth?', *Times of India*, 9 January 2017. Accessed 20 March 2019, https://timesofindia.indiatimes.com/city/chennai/did-karunanidhi-change-thiruvalluvars-date-of-birth/articleshow/59059750.cms.

31   Karunanidhi, *Nenjuku Needhi*, 5: 346.

32   Sabanayagam, *Service*, 123.

33   'DMK Government declares Tamil Thai Vaazhthu the State song,' *The Hindu*, 17 December 2021. Accessed 25 December 2021, https://www.thehindu.com/news/national/tamil-nadu/dmk-government-declares-tamil-thai-vaazhthu-the-state-song/article37981387.ece.

34   Ibid.

35   *Kalki*, 13 September 1970, 9.

36   *Murasoli*, 9 July 1971, 1.

37   Karunanidhi, *Kadithangal*, 5: 98–99; *Kalaignarin Sattamandra Uraigal*, 10: 151.

38 *Kalki*, 5 May 1974, 10; *Kalki*, 12 May 1974, 10; *Kalki*, 9 June 1974, 10.

39 *Murasoli*, 1 May 1981, 3.

40 R.R. Dalavai vs State Of Tamil Nadu on 7 May, 1976, 1976 AIR 1559, 1976 SCR 601; *Murasoli*, 5 November 1975, 3.

41 M. Natarajan, 'Ullathaal Oruvare,' in *L.G. 70th Birthday Souvenir*, (Thanjavur, Thanjaivaazh Kannanthangudi Makkal Munnetra Sangam, 2012).

42 *Murasoli*, 10 January 1974, 1.

43 *Murasoli*, 9 October 1971, 1.

44 Karunanidhi *Kadithangal*, 2: 12–13.

45 Ibid., 6: 119, 163.

46 *Murasoli*, 7 April 1976, 1.

47 *Kalaignarin Sattamandra Uraigal*, 10: 167–70; Karunanidhi, *Nenjuku Needhi*, 2, 139.

48 Thiruvidam, *Thiruvallikeni*, 691; Sangeetha Kandavel and Sanjay Vijayakumar, *Hindustan Times*, 2 November 2013, 'BHEL has made about 700 wheels for temple chariots in Tamil Nadu in over 45 years,' https://economictimes.indiatimes.com/bhel-has-made-about-700-wheels-for-temple-chariots-in-tamil-nadu-in-over-45-years/articleshow/25079898.cms?from=mdr.

49 *The Tamil Nadu Legislative Assembly, Fifth Assembly, Tenth Session, Second Meeting, Resume*, (Legislative Assembly Secretariat, 1974). Accessed 14 January 2019, https://assembly.tn.gov.in/archive/5th_1971/05_10_02.pdf.

50 *Murasoli*, 30 May 1989, 1; *Murasoli*, 3 June 1989, 3.

51 *Murasoli*, 27 June 1971, 5.

52 *Navamani*, 2 June 1975, 1; *Murasoli*, 8 May 1975, 1.

53 *Kalaignarin Sattamandra Uraigal*, 10:167–70; Karunanidhi, *Nenjuku Needhi*, 2: 139.

54 *Kalki*, 29 March 1970, 7; *Kalki*, 4 April 1970, 5; *Kalki*, 1 November 1970, 9.

55 Karunanidhi, *Kadithangal*, 6: 151; *Murasoli*, 8 August 1975, 4–5.

56 *Murasoli*, 11 February 1984, 1.

57 *Kalaignarin Sattamandra Uraigal*, 10: 215–22.

58 Ibid., 151–54.

59 *Murasoli*, 9 July 1971, 1.

60 *Kalki*, 25 July 1971, 10; *Kalki*, 13 December 1970, 10; *Kalki*, 20 December 1970, 9; *Kalki*, 10 January 1971, 10.

61 J.B. Kripalani, *My Life*, 854.

Chapter 10: 'Autonomy in the State and Federalism at the Centre'

1   *Kalki*, 27 June 1971, 9.
2   'From the Archives (September 14, 1970): Karunanidhi's reply,' *The Hindu*, 14 September 2020. Accessed 16 September 2020, https://www.thehindu.com/archives/from-the-archives-september-14-1970-karunanidhis-reply/article32593551.ece?homepage=true.
3   *Murasoli*, 7 May 1971, 1.
4   *Murasoli*, 2 July 1985, 2.
5   *Murasoli*, 13 March 1975, 1.
6   *Therkilirundhu Oru Suryian*, 113.
7   H. Maharajadhirajaaja Madhav Rao . . . vs Union Of India on 15 December, 1970, 1971 AIR 530, 1971 SCR (3) 9; Thiruvidam, *Thiruvallikeni*, 679.
8   *Kalki*, 20 September 1970, 7.
9   *Kalki*, 8 November 1970, 9.
10 *Murasoli*, 21 February 1990, 4.
11 *Murasoli*, 25 January 1971, 1.
12 'There was a sense of relief at elimination of DMK: Chidambaram Subramaniam,' *India Today*, 29 February 1976. Accessed 20 February 2020, https://www.indiatoday.in/magazine/cover-story/story/19760229-there-was-a-sense-of-relief-at-elimination-of-dmk-chidambaram-subramaniam-819063-2015-03-13.
13 *Kalki*, 14 February 1971, 5, 7.
14 H.V. Hande, 'Kamaraj: A Stalwart Who Was Let Down By His Own People,' *Swarajya*, 19 July 2018. Accessed 30 August 2019, https://swarajyamag.com/politics/kamaraj-a-stalwart-who-was-let-down-by-his-own-people.
15 *Daily Thanthi, Varalaatru*, 560–61; *Kalki*, 28 February 1971, 6.
16 *Kalki*, 14 February 1971, 5, 7.
17 Ilangovan Rajasekaran, 'Flawed script: Rajinikanth's comments on Periyar's 1971 rally,' *Frontline*, 1 February 2020. Accessed 3 June 2020, https://frontline.thehindu.com/the-nation/article30682576.ece.
18 Thiruvidam, *Thiruvallikeni*, 685; Srinivasan Ramani, D. Suresh Kumar, 'Ram, Ramasamy and Rajini: What happened in Salem in 1971?,' *The Hindu*, 22 January 2020. Accessed 30 January 2020, https://www.thehindu.com/opinion/op-ed/lord-ram-ev-ramasamy-periyar-and-rajinikanth-what-happened-in-salem-in-1971/article30618177.ece.
19 *Kalki*, 7 March 1971, 9.

20   'Fall-out from Salem,' *The Hindu*, 17 February 1971.

21   *Murasoli*, 17 February 1971, 6.

22   Muthukumar, *Indhia*, 141.

23   *Murasoli*, 22 February 1971, 6.

24   *Kalki*, 24 January 1971, 5.

25   *Therkilirundhu*, 114.

26   *Kalki*, 7 March 1971, 8.

27   *Kalki*, 21 March 1971, 7.

28   Aravindan Neelakandan, 'Remembering Kamaraj, The Kingmaker,' *Swarajya*, 16 July 2018. Accessed 20 July 2022, https://swarajyamag. com/culture/remembering-kamaraj-the-king-maker.

29   Nambi Marthandam, 'President Fakhruddin Ali Ahmed dismisses DMK ministry, places Tamil Nadu under President's Rule,' *India Today*, 29 February 1976. Accessed 1 February 2021.

30   *Murasoli*, 28 April 1974, 4.

31   *Murasoli*,

32   *Murasoli*, 21 September 1974, 1.

33   *Murasoli*, 21 June 1985, 2.

34   *Kalki*, 19 September 1971, 7.

35   *Kalki*, 6 February 1972, 7.

36   *Murasoli*, 18 September 1971, 1, 6.

37   *Murasoli*, 22 September 1971, 1, 4.

38   Kannan, *MGR*, 160-61.

Chapter 11: Second Split

1   *Kalki*, 23 July 1972, 6.

2   *Kalki*, 13 August 1972, 11.

3   Kannan, *MGR*, 161.

4   S. Swaminathan, *Karunanidhi: Man of Destiny*, (New Delhi: Affiliated East West Press, 2014), 61.

5   Karunanidhi, *Kadithangal*, 9: 5.

6   Kannan, *MGR* 169.

7   *Murasoli*, 9 May 1971, 1.

8   *Murasoli*, 17 October 1971, p. 2; *Murasoli*, 18 October 1971, p. 3.

9   Tamil Nadu take over of a strike,' *EPW*, 7, No. 4, (22 January 1972).

10   *Kalki*, 7 March 1971, 8.

11   Kannan, *MGR*, 163.

12   *MGRin Sattamandra Uragigal*, 511.

13   Durga Stalin, *Avaraum Naanum*, (Chennai: Uyirmai Pathippagam, 2018), 52–53.

14   Interview with Dr H.V. Hande, June 2018.

15   *Murasoli*, 14 August 1971, 1.

16   *Murasoli*, 14 December 1989, 1.

17   *Kalki*, 22 August 1971, 7.

18   *Murasoli*, 19 August 1971, 2.

19   *Murasoli*, 15 September 1971, 3.

20   *Murasoli*, 15 August 1971, 3.

21   *Murasoli*, 31 March 1971, 5.

22   *Kalki*, 21 May 1972, 5.

23   *Kalki*, 23 April 1972, 6; *Kalki*, 30 April 1972, 7.

24   *The Hindu*, 22 May 1972, 1.

25   *Kalki*, 4 June 1972, 9.

26   *India Today*, 15 August 1978.

27   *Namnadu*, 18 October 1972, 1.

28   Kannan, *MGR*, 58.

29   *Murasoli*, 21 September 1971, 3.

30   *Murasoli*, 25 October 1971, 4.

31   Bernard Weinraub: 'Movie idol leads sharp attack on Government of India State,' *New York Times*, 26 March 1973, 10.

32   *Murasoli*, 9 March 1976, 3.

33   *Murasoli*, 9 August 1972, 1.

34   Saidai Duraisamy, *Vergaluku Velicham*, (Chennai: Manidha Neyam Ilavasa I.A.S. Academy, 2018), 18.

35   *Murasoli*, 9 August 1972, 1; *Murasoli*, 29 August 1972, 1; *Murasoli*, 21 October 1972, 1; *Murasoli* 10 October 1978, 1.

36   *Kalki*, 20 August 1972, 10.

37   Ma.Po.Si., *MGRudan*, 44–45.

38   Kannan, *MGR*, 168.

39   T. Ramakrishnan, 'A look at the events leading up to the birth of AIADMK,' *The Hindu*, 18 October 2021, https://www.thehindu.com/news/national/tamil-nadu/a-look-at-the-events-leading-up-to-the-birth-of-aiadmk/article37046741.ece

40   Kannan, *MGR*, 172.

41   Kannadasan, *Naan*, 93–95.

42   Karunanidhi, *Kadithangal*, 5: 192–200.

43   Nedunchezhian, *Vaazhvil*, 494–500.

44   *Murasoli*, 13 August 1975, 2.

45   Kannadasan, *Naan*, 96–97.

46   Vellore Narayanan, *Oru Mayorin Ninaivugal*, (Chennai, Santha Pathippagam, 2006), 111–13.

47   Gopanna, *Kamaraj*, 350.

48   Saidai, *Vergaluku*, 28–29.

49   Ibid., 34.

50   *Enadhu*, ed., Thuglak Ramesh, 145–48, 52.

51   *Namnadu*, 17 October 1972, 1, 4.

52   Rule 20: 2, AIADMK Rules and Regulations.

53   Karunanidhi, *Kadithangal*, 2: 82.

54   Kannan, *MGR*, 178–79.

55   *MGRin Sattamandra Uraigal*, 500–03.

Chapter 12: Anna DMK

1   *Kalki*, 5 November 1972, 7; Cho Ramaswamy, *Ivargalai*, 1: 53.

2   T. Ramakrishnan, 'A look at the events leading up to the birth of AIADMK,' *The Hindu*, 18 October 2021. Accessed 1 December 2021, https://www.thehindu.com/news/national/tamil-nadu/a-look-at-the-events-leading-up-to-the-birth-of-aiadmk/article37046741.ece.

3   Cho Ramaswamy, *Adirshtam Thantha Anubhavangal*, (The Alliance Publication Company, 2016), 209–10.

4   Vellore Narayanan, *Oru*, 114–15.

5   Karunanidhi, *Kadithangal*, 19: 332.

6   *Kalki*, 19 November 1972, 9–10.

7   *Kalki*, 5 November 1972, 6.

8   *Daily Thanthi, Varalaatru* 578.

9   K. Kalimuthu to author, July 1996; Karunanidhi, *Kadithangal*, 7: 216.

10   *Enadhu*, ed., Thuglak Ramesh, 14–20.

11   *Kalki*, 26 November 1972, 3; *Thennagam*, 3 May 1975, cited in *Thuglak*, 1 June 1975.

12   *Murasoli*, 2 November 1976, p. 1; 1 September 1984, 1.

13   *Kalki*, 3 December 1972, 8.

14   Thiruvidam, *Thiruvallikeni*, 724–25.

15   Kannan, *MGR*, 190.

16   Selvendran, *Ini?* 20.

17   *Daily Thanthi, Varalaatru*, 576–78.

18   Tamilvanan, *Thalaisirandha*, 75.

19   *Kalaignarin Sattamandra Uraigal*, 10: 207.

20 Sunita Sekar, 'Rising star: The suspension that gave birth to the AIADMK,' *The Hindu*, 18 October 2016, https://www.thehindu.com/news/national/tamil-nadu/Rising-star-The-suspension-that-gave-birth-to-the-AIADMK/article15614155.ece.

21 *Kalki*, 4 March 1973, 8.

22 *Kalki*, 5 November 1972, 9.

23 *Daily Thanthi, Varalaatru*, 578.

24 Ibid., 578–81; *Sarkaria Commission of Inquiry, First Report*, 2, (New Delhi, Ministry of Home Affairs, 1977).

25 *Daily Thanthi, Varalaatru*, 579-80.

26 *Sarkaria Commission of Inquiry, First Report*, 1: 1; Nambi Marthandam, 'President Fakhruddin Ali Ahmed dismisses DMK ministry, places Tamil Nadu under President's Rule,' *India Today*, 29 February 1976. https://www.indiatoday.in/magazine/cover-story/story/19760229-president-fakhruddin-ali-ahmed-dismisses-dmk-ministry-places-tamil-nadu-under-presidents-rule-819615-2015-04-29.

27 Cho Ramaswamy, *Ivargalai*, 1:144; *Sarkaria Commission of Inquiry, First Report*, supra note 24.

28 Gopanna. *Kamaraj*, 351.

29 *Kalki*, 26 November 1972, 3.

30 K. Ramaswamy Sastry, 'A Chronicle of the DMK Split.' *EPW* 9, No. 13 (1974), 527–31. Accessed April 28, 2021. http://www.jstor.org/stable/4363540.

31 Kannan, *MGR*, 188.

32 Karunanidhi, *Nenjuku Needhi*, 2: 393–94; K. Ramaswamy Sastry, 'A Chronicle of the DMK Split,' supra note 30.

33 K. Ramaswamy Sastry, 'A Chronicle of the DMK Split', supra note 30.

34 'TAMIL NADU-The Politics of Repression,' *EPW*, 8, No. 31/33, Special Number (Aug., 1973), 1392–1393–395.

35 K.A._Mathiazhagan_vs_P._Srinivasan_And_Ors._on_27_February,_AIR 1973 Mad 371.

36 *The Hindu*, 3 December 1972, 1.

37 *Kalki*, 17 December 1972, 10.

38 Karunanidhi, *Nenjuku Needhi*, 2: 403; *Kalki*, 31 December 1972, 8.

39 *Kalki*, 11 March 1973, 6.

40 *Kalki*, 3 December 1972, 10.

41 Swaminathan, *Karunanidhi*, 66–67; *Daily Thanthi, Varalaatru Suvadugal*, 578–81.

42 *Kalki*, 24 December 1972, 7.

43 *Kalki*, 14 January 1973, 7.

44 *Kalki*, 11 March 1973, 7. On 24 February, Law Minister Madhavan responded saying Maharashtra's 1971 Lok Ayuktha act provided punishment for false charges. *Navamani*, 24 February 1973, 1, 3.

45 *Navamani*, 24 February 1973, 1, 3.

46 Karunanidhi, *Kadithangal*, 3: 207.

47 Kannan, *MGR*, 196.

48 Dheenadayalan, *MGR*, 308–11.

49 Kannan, *MGR*, 199.

50 *Kalki*, 1 July 1973, 6, 8.

51 Muthukumar, *Madhuvilaku*, 110–14.

52 *Murasoli*, 7 January 1991, 5.

53 *Kalki*, 25 November 1973, 10.

54 Sabanayagam, *Service*, 127–29.

55 *Kalki*, 2 December 1973, 2; *Kalki*, 23 December 1973, 14, *Murasoli*, 15 December 1973, 1.

56 *Murasoli*, 30 January 1974, 1–2.

57 *Murasoli*, 3 February 1974, 1.

58 T. Ramakrishnan, 'By-elections generally no shockers for ruling party,' *The Hindu*, 24 February 2012. Accessed 20 May 2019, https://www.thehindu.com/news/national/tamil-nadu/byelections-generally-no-shockers-for-ruling-party/article2925159.ece.

59 *Murasoli*, 13 March 1975, 1.

60 *Kalaignarin Sattamandra Uraigal*, 4: 61.

61 *1974: Maanila Suyaatchi*, 197.

62 *Murasoli*, 21 April 1974, 1, 4; *1974: Maanila Suyaatchi*, 569–73; *Murasoli*, 24 April 1974, 1.

63 *1974: Maanila Suyaatchi*, ed., Senthilnathan, 574–87.

64 Ibid.. xiv, 215–38.

65 Ibid., 244–47.

66 Ibid., 401-07.

67 Ibid.

68 Ibid., 436–39.

69 *Murasoli*, 21 April 1974, 1.

70 *1974: Maanila Suyaatchi*, 541; 565.

71 *Murasoli*, 27 October 1976, 1; *Murasoli*, 9 January 1974, 1; *Murasoli*, 18 February 1978, 1.

72 *1974: Maanila Suyaatchi*, 432–36.

73 Lakshmana Venkat Kuchi, 'M. Karunanidhi (1924–2018): A Legacy of National Relevance.' Accessed 31 March 2021, https://www.thehinducentre.com/the-arena/current-issues/article24623448.ece.

74 *1974: Maanila Suyaatchi*, 460.

75 *Murasoli*, 28 April 1974, 1; 1974: *Maanila Suyaatchi*, 467.

76 *Tamil Nadu Legislative Assembly Quinquennial Review 1971–76, 81*, (Chennai: Legislative Assembly Department, 1977). Accessed 22 January 2018, https://assembly.tn.gov.in/archive/5th_1971/5th-review-71-76.pdf.

77 Kalaignar, *Nenjuku Needhi* 2: 445.

78 *Murasoli*, 5 May 1974, 1, 4.

79 *Murasoli*, 10 January 1975, 4.

80 *Navamani*, 12 May 1974, 1.

81 Cho Ramaswamy, *Ivargalai Sandhithaen*, 1: 96.

82 *Murasoli*, 12 May 1974, 1.

83 *Navamani*, 1 July 1974, 3.

84 *Navamani*, 1 July 1974, 1; 'ADMK Leader Wants CM to Quit,' *The Hindu*, 30 June 1974, 7.

85 Diwakar and Akhlesh Singh, 'Karunanidhi, taken into confidence by Indira Gandhi on Katchatheevu deal, agreed to give Sri Lanka island', *Times of India*, 1 April 2024. Accessed 1 April 2024, https://timesofindia.indiatimes.com/india/karunanidhi-taken-into-confidence-by-indira-on-katchatheevu-deal-agreed-to-give-sri-lanka-island/articleshow/108924845.cms.

86 India, *Parliamentary Debates*, House of the People, 23 July 1974, cols. 187–201. Accessed 4 April 2024, https://eparlib.nic.in/bitstream/123456789/844070/1/05_XI_23-07-1974_p96_p104_PII.pdf.

87 *Murasoli*, 8 July 1974, 1–2.

88 Karunanidhi, *Kadithangal*, 42: 302–03.

89 Karunanidhi, *Nenjuku Needhi*, 2: 453–54.

90 Chief Minister M. Karunanidhi's speech on 15 August 1974 at Fort St. George, Chennai.

91 *Murasoli*, 24 August 1974, 1.

92 *Murasoli*, 25 September 1975, 1; *Murasoli*, 28 September 1975, 1; *Tamil Nadu Legislative Assembly Quinquennial Review 1971-76*, supra note 76.

Chapter 13: EMERGENCY

1 *Murasoli*, 16 March 1975, 1–2; 'Deteriorating situation at Vellore Medical College and Hospital,' 13 March 1975, US consul general

cable. Accessed 21 November 2018, https://wikileaks.org/plusd/cables/1975NEWDE03494_b.html; 'End of Vellore Hospital Strike, 19 March 1975, US consul general cable. Accessed 21 November 2018, https://wikileaks.org/plusd/cables/1975NEWDE03786_b.html.

2   *Kalki*, 30 March 1975, 7.

3   *Murasoli*, 13 March 1975, 1–2, *Murasoli*, 20 January 1975, 1.

4   *Murasoli*, 21 March 1975, 1; *Murasoli*, 25 March 1975, 1, 5; *Murasoli*, 23 April 1975, 1.

5   *Murasoli*, 6 November 1975, 1.

6   *Kalki*, 11 May 1975, 27–28.

7   *Kalki*, 25 May 1975, 50–54.

8   *Murasoli*, 8 May July 1975, 1.

9   *Murasoli*, 7 May 1975, 1; *Murasoli*, 8 May 1975, 1.

10 M.G. Devasahayam, 'Kalaignar Karunanidhi: Defending Democracy during Emergency,' The Hindu Centre, 9 August 2018. Accessed 10 September 2018, https://www.thehinducentre.com/the-arena/current-issues/article24640699.ece?homepage=trueOne.

11 'Shah Commission's Final Report,' *EPW*, 13, No. 39 (30 September 1978), 1660–662.

12 *Murasoli*, 28 June 1975, 1–4.

13 *Murasoli*, 2 January 1991, 4; *Murasoli*, 2 August 1994, 6.

14 'The Rediff Special,' Cho Ramaswamy's interview, 4 July 2005. Accessed 20 March 2018, https://www.rediff.com/news/2005/jul/04spec.htm.

15 Sabanayagam, *Service*, 141–42.

16 *Kalaignarin Sattamandra Uraigal*, 10:348.

17 'Views of DMK leader on current situation,' 7 July 1975, US consul general cable. Accessed 27 February 2018, https://wikileaks.org/plusd/cables/1975NEWDE09016_b.html.

18 'Political Situation in South India,' 8 July 1975, US consul general cable. Accessed 17 February 2018, https://www.wikileaks.org/plusd/cables/1975NEWDE09034_b.html.

19 *Murasoli*, 7 July 1975, 1.

20 *Murasoli*, 5 August 1976, 3; *Murasoli*, 25 August 1976, 3.

21 'Beach Speech,' 6 July 1975, (Chennai, DMK, 1975); 'Political Situation in South India.'

22 Karunanidhi, *Nenjuku Needhi*, 2: 481.

23 'Views of DMK leader on current situation.'

24 Ibid.

25 Karunanidhi, *Kadithangal*, 2: 119–23.

26 Ibid., 124–27.

27 *MGRin Sattamandra Uragial,* 9–10, 16, 50.

28 Ibid., 11.

29 *Murasoli*, 11 August 1975, 1.

30 'The Emergency in the South, 75 Days After,' 13 September 1975, US consul general cable. Accessed 14 January 2018, https://www.wikileaks. org/plusd/cables/1975NEWDE12389_b.html.

31 Kuldip Nayar, *Beyond the Lines*, (New Delhi: Roli Books, 2012), 230.

32 *Murasoli*, 28 September 1975, 1.

33 *Enadhu,* ed., Thuglak Ramesh, 171; *Murasoli*, 5 October 1975, 1; 7 October 1975, 1, 2.

34 *Murasoli*, 29 October 1975, 1.

35 'Karunanidhi calls for elections in Tamil Nadu,' 24 December 1975, US consul general cable. Accessed 2 February 2018, https://wikileaks.org/ plusd/cables/1975NEWDE17136_b.html.

36 *Murasoli*, 29 December 1975, 1–4; Karunanidhi, *Nenjuku Needhi,* 2,501–02.

37 William Borders, 'India to postpone elections a year,' *New York Times*, 30 December 1975, 1.

38 *Murasoli*, 28 December 1975, 1–2; *Murasoli*, 29 December 1976, 2; *Murasoli*, 11 September 1976, 1; 'Karunanidhi calls for elections in Tamil Nadu.'

39 India, *Parliamentary Debates*, Council of States, (Motion of thanks on President's address), 8 January 1976, col. 227, Accessed 1 February 2018, https://rsdebate.nic.in/bitstream/123456789/438540/1/ PD_94_08011976_4_p135_p242_18.pdf.

40 'Mrs. Gandhi Dismisses Opposition Government of a State and Takes Over Rule,' *New York Times*, 1 February 1976, 2; *Murasoli*, 10 January 1976, 1; Karunanidhi, *Nenjuku*, 2:505–06.

41 Karunanidhi, *Kadithangal*, 2: 204–06.

42 *Murasoli*, 26 January 1991, 2; Karunanidhi, *Nenjuku Needhi*, 2: 522.

43 Kannadasan, *Naan*, 108–111.

44 Sabanayagam, *Service*, 136–37.

45 https://www.wikileaks.org/plusd/cables/1976NEWDE01915_b.html.

46 India, *Parliamentary Debates*, Council of States, 8 January 1976, col. 95, (Proclamation on President's rule in Tamil Nadu). Accessed 3 March 2017, https://eparlib.nic.in/bitstream/123456789/856082/1/05_ XVI_09-03-1976_p101_p128_PII.pdf.

47 'Mrs. Gandhi says she imposed president's rule to head off planned violence by DMK.' 18 January 1976, US consul general cable. Accessed 20 January

2017, https://wikileaks.org/plusd/cables/1976NEWDE02457_b.html; Nambi Marthandam, 'President Fakhruddin Ali Ahmed dismisses DMK ministry, places Tamil Nadu under President's Rule,' *India Today*, 29 February 1976. Accessed 2 February 2018, https://www.indiatoday.in/magazine/cover-story/story/19760229-president-fakhruddin-ali-ahmed-dismisses-dmk-ministry-places-tamil-nadu-under-presidents-rule-819615-2015-04-29.

48 *Kalki*, 7 March 1971, 8.

49 'Situation in Tamil Nadu,' 2 February 1976, US consul general cable. Accessed 2 February 2018, https://www.wikileaks.org/plusd/cables/1976MADRAS00190_b.html; 'Tamil Nadu situation,' 6 February 1976, US consul general cable. Accessed 2 February 2018, https://www.wikileaks.org/plusd/cables/1976NEWDE01871_b.html.

50 Karunanidhi, *Nenjuku Needhi*, 2: 534.

51 Ibid.

52 Karunanidhi, *Nenjuku Needhi*, 2: 533.

Chapter 14: Suffering and Pain

1   'Tamil Nadu situation,' 6 February 1976, US consul general cable. Accessed 2 February 2018, https://www.wikileaks.org/plusd/cables/1976NEWDE01871_b.html; Coomi Kapoor, *The Emergency*, (Gurgaon: Penguin, Viking, 2015), 252.

2   Karunanidhi, *Nenjuku Needhi*, 2: 525–26.

3   Thiruvidam, *Thiruvallikeni*, 805.

4   *Murasoli*, 4 June 1978, 4.

5   Tha.Pa. Dillidurai, 'Deivathai Neril Kanden,' in *Arcot Veerasamy 80th Birthday Souvenir*, (Chennai: Muthu Vizha Committee, 2017), 213.

6   *Shah Commission Report: Lost and Regained*, ed., Era. Sezhian, (Chennai: Aazhi Publishers, 2011), cols. 19.288 to 19.299.

7   Tamilvanan, *Thalaisirandha*, 81.

8   *Murasoli*, 63 February 1976, 1.

9   *Murasoli*, 4 February 1976, 1.

10 Karunanidhi, *Nenjuku Needhi*, 2: 534–35; India, *Parliamentary Debates*, House of the People, cols. 14–18, 3 February 1976 statement on the constitution of the Sarkaria Commission of Inquiry. Accessed 1 January 2018, https://eparlib.nic.in/bitstream/123456789/854303/1/05_XV_03-02-1976_p11_p13_PII.pdf.

11 *Kalaignarin Sattamandra Uraigal*, 10: 437; 439.

12   *Murasoli*, 5 February 1976, 1.

13   *Murasoli*, 6 February 1976, 1.

14   *Murasoli*, 7 February 1976, 1.

15   *Murasoli*, 6 February 1976, 1.

16   *Murasoli*, 9 February 1976, 1.

17   'The old order changeth yielding place to the new,' 26 February 1976, US consul general cable. Accessed 17 February 2018, https://wikileaks. org/plusd/cables/1976NEWDE02897_b.html.

18   Ibid.

19   Kalaignar Karunanidhi, *Nenjuku Needhi*, 2: 544.

20   Karunanidhi, *Kadithangal*, 5: 50–51.

21   'Situation with the DMK,' 4 March 1976, US consul general cable. Accessed 31 March 2018, https://wikileaks.org/plusd/ cables/1976NEWDE03310_b.html; 'Views of Tamil Nadu chief secretary and of GOI adviser Dave on situation,' 18 February 1976, US consul general cable. Accessed 21 March 2018. Accessed 14 February 2018, https://www.wikileaks.org/plusd/cables/1976NEWDE02455_b. html.

22   *Murasoli*, 16 February 1976, 1.

23   Karunanidhi, *Nenjuku Needhi*, 2: 544–45.

24   D. Suresh Kumar, 'Indira's ban threat scared Karunanidhi: Cables,' *New Indian Express*, 10 April 2013. Accessed 20 April 2014, https://www. newindianexpress.com/states/tamil-nadu/2013/apr/10/indiras-ban-threat-scared-karunanidhi-cables-466663.html.

25   *Murasoli*, 9 September 1976, 3.

26   'G.K. Reddy's version of Tamil Nadu's takeover,' 6 February 1976, US consul general cable. Accessed 22 February 2018, https://www.wikileaks. org/plusd/cables/1976NEWDE01915_b.html.

27   *Kalaignarin Sattamandra Uraigal*, 10: 439.

28   Karunanidhi, *Kadithangal*, 1: 590–91.

29   *Murasoli*, 10 May 1979, 2.

30   *Murasoli*, 24 February 1976, 1.

31   Karunanidhi, *Nenjuku Needhi*, 2: 545.

32   *Murasoli*, 2 March 1976, 1; *Murasoli*, 3 March 1976, 1; Karunanidhi, *Nenjuku Needhi*, 2: 547.

33   Karunanidhi, *Nenjuku Needhi*, 2: 547–48.

34   *Murasoli*, 16 March 1976, pg.

35   Karunanidhi, *Nenjuku Needhi*, 2: 544.

36   Ibid., 548–49.

37 Karunanidhi, *Kadithangal*, 1: 618–19.

38 *Murasoli*, 5 April 1976, 1.

39 Ibid.

40 Karunanidhi, *Kadithangal*, 7: 784–85.

41 Karunanidhi, *Kadithangal*, 1: 731–32; *Murasoli*, 15 April 1976, 1–3; Karunanidhi, *Nenjuku Needhi*, 2: 510-15.

42 'DMK president Karunanidhi's assurances to GOI while attempting to revive DMK activities,' 30 April, US consul general cable. Accessed 14 February 2018, https://wikileaks.org/plusd/cables/1976NEWDE06326_b.html.

43 Karunanidhi, *Kadithangal*, 2: 29–31.

44 Ibid., 2: 43–44.

45 Karunanidhi, *Nenjuku Needhi*, 2: 553–54.

46 *Murasoli*, 15 February 1977, 1.

47 Karunanidhi, *Nenjuku Needhi*, 2: 558–62; Karunanidhi, *Kadithangal*, 18: 223.

48 *Murasoli*, 4 July 1976, 1.

49 Karunanidhi, *Nenjuku Needhi*, 2: 564–65.

50 *Murasoli*, 7 July 1976, 3; *Murasoli*, 2 October 1976, 1.

51 Karunanidhi, *Kadithangal*, 2: 252–53.

52 *Murasoli*, 10 July 1976, 1.

53 'More on Karunanidhi,' 3 September 1976, US consul general cable. Accessed 17 February 2018, https://wikileaks.org/plusd/cables/1976NEWDE13028_b.html.

54 *Murasoli*, 5 August 1976, 4.

55 *Murasoli*, 29 August 1976, 3.

56 *Murasoli*, 29 August 1976, 4.

57 'Mrs Gandhi's southern tour,' 17 September 1976, US consul general cable. Accessed 13 February 2018, https://wikileaks.org/plusd/cables/1976NEWDE13845_b.html.

58 *Murasoli*, 15 September 1976, 2.

59 *Murasoli*, 17 September 1976, 2.

60 'Karunanidhi responds to prime minister's charge,' 20 September 1976, US consul general cable. Accessed 2 July 2020, https://www.wikileaks.org/plusd/cables/1976NEWDE13883_b.html.

61 *Murasoli*, 20 September 1976, 1.

62 *Murasoli*, 27 September 1976, 4.

63 *Sarkaria Commission of Inquiry, First Report*, 19–21.

64 *Murasoli*, 3 October 1976, 1.

65   *Murasoli*, 17 October 1976, 1; M. Karunanidhi vs Union Of India on 20 February, 1979, 1979 AIR 898, 1979 SCR (3) 254.

66   Karunanidhi, *Kadithangal*, 11: 38.

67   'Karunanidhi on eve of appearance in court,' 2 November 1976, US consul general cable. Accessed 20 May 2023, https://wikileaks.org/plusd/cables/1976NEWDE15988_b.html.

68   *Murasoli*, 12 November 1976, 1.

69   'Karunanidhi on eve of appearance in court,' supra note 67.

70   *Murasoli*, 29 October 1976, 1. 3.

71   *Murasoli*, 10 December 1976, 1.

72   Karunandihi, *Nenjuku Needhi*, 2: 577.

73   *Enadhu*, ed., Thuglak Ramesh, 191–92.

74   Karunanidhi, *Nenjuku Needhi*, 2: 573–79; *Murasoli*, 16 December 1976, 1; *Murasoli*, 2 August 1994, 6.

Chapter 15: The Beginning of the Electoral Reverses

1   Karunandihi, *Nenjuku Needhi*, 3:50.

2   *Murasoli*, 13 February 1977, 1; *Murasoli*, 4 June 1989, 1.

3   'Sarkaria Commission: Karunanidhi partially guilty,' *India Today*, 15 April 1977. Accessed 21 May 2022, https://www.indiatoday.in/magazine/indiascope/story/19770415-sarkaria-commission-karunanidhi-partially-guilty-823648-2014-08-04.

4   Kannan, *MGR*, 223.

5   *Murasoli*, 22 March 1977, 1; *Murasoli*, 25 March 1977, 1.

6   *The Hindu*, 21 February 1977, 1.

7   V.R. Lakshminarayanan, *Appointments and Disappointments*, (New Delhi: Vikas Publishing House, 1988), 210.

8   Cho Ramaswamy, *Adhirshtam*, 273.

9   Interview with K. Rajaram, 20 June 2004; Karunanidhi, *Kadithangal*, 3: 131–32.

10   Cho Ramaswamy, *Adhirshtam*, 281–82.

11   Karunanidhi, *Nenjuku Needhi*, 3: 94–96.

12   *Murasoli*, 13 April 1977, 1.

13   Karunanidhi, *Kadithangal*, 3:1 3–21.

14   Nedunchezhian, *Vaazhvil*, 528–30.

15   Ibid., 528–30.

16   Karunanidhi, *Nenjuku Needhi*, 3: 121; *Murasoli*, 30 April 1977, 1.

17   *Murasoli*, 11 May 1977, 1; *Murasoli*, 26 May 1977, 1.

18   Karunanidhi, *Nenjuku Needhi*, 3: 123; Karunanidhi, *Kadithangal*, 9, 77.

19   Karunanidhi, *Nenjuku Needhi*, 3: 125.

20   *Murasoli*, 18 June 1977, 1.

21   Sunil Sethi, 'From the India Today archives (1978) | MGR: The celluloid politician,' *India Today*, 15 August 1978. Accessed 2 May 2021, https:// www.indiatoday.in/india-today-insight/story/from-the-india-today-archives-1978-mgr-the-celluloid-politician-2508277-2024-02-28.

22   *Murasoli*, 15 February 1979, 1.

23   'Indira Gandhi's two-day tour of Tamil Nadu ends in a grand fiasco,' *India Today*, 30 November 1977. Accessed 20 November 2018, https://www.indiatoday.in/magazine/indiascope/story/19771130-indira-gandhis-two-day-tour-of-tamil-nadu-ends-in-a-grand-fiasco-823484-2014-09-09.

24   Karunanidhi, *Nenjuku Needhi*, 3: 99.

25   *Murasoli*, 9 January 1978, 2.

26   Karunanidhi, *Kadithangal*, 3: 474.

27   'M.G. Ramachandran no match for DMK chief M.K. Karunanidhi,' *India Today*, 9 October 2014. Accessed 21 May 2022, https://www.indiatoday. in/magazine/indiascope/story/19780115-m.g.ramachandran-no-match-for-dmk-chief-m.k.-karunanidhi-822767-2014-10-09.

28   Kannan, *MGR*, 243–45.

29   *Murasoli*, 8 January 1978, 2.

30   *MGRin Sattamandra Uraigal*, 264–65.

31   *Murasoli*, 13 May 1978, 1.

32   *Murasoli*, 14 May 1978, 3.

33   *Murasoli*, 20 May 1978, 1.

34   *Murasoli*, 14 May 1978, 3.

35   *Sarkaria Commission of Inquiry, First Report*, 188.

36   *Kalaignarin Sattamandra Uraigal*, 4: 418.

37   Karunanidhi, *Kadithangal*, 3: 639–40.

38   Cho Ramaswamy, *Ivargalai*, 3: 384–85; Karunanidhi, *Nenjuku Needhi*, 5: 358; Ibid., 6: 324.

39   Cho Ramaswamy, *Ivargalai*, 3: 62.

40   Ibid., 385–86.

41   *Murasoli*, 1 February 1979, 2–3.

42   'DMK leader Karunanidhi charges M.G. Ramachandran govt with shipping deal scam,' *India Today*, 15 December 1979. Accessed 20 May 2020, https://www.indiatoday.in/magazine/indiascope/story/19791215-dmk-leader-karunanidhi-charges-m.g.-ramachandran-government-

with-shipping-deal-scam-822260-2014-02-18; *MGRin Sattamandra Uraigal*, 197.

43 R. Rangaraj, 'Tamil Nadu: Scams, pressure from Centre, MG Ramachandran steered the AIADMK through it all,' *Times of India*, 13 October 2021. Accessed 20 May 2022, https://timesofindia. indiatimes.com/city/chennai/tamil-nadu-scams-pressure-from-centre-m-g-ramachandran-steered-the-aiadmk-through-it-all/articleshow/86986376.cms.

44 'January 24, 1978, Forty Years Ago: Indira's Apology,' *Indian Express*, 24 January 2018. Accessed 1 May 2020, https://indianexpress.com/article/opinion/editorials/january-24-1978-forty-years-ago-indiras-apology-5036651/; Karunanidhi, *Nenjuku Needhi*, 3: 277.

45 Karunanidhi, *Nenjuku Needhi*, 3: 313.

46 *Murasoli*, 4 April 1978, 1–2.

47 *Murasoli*, 11 April 1978, 1.

48 Karunanidhi, *Nenjuku Needhi*, 3: 313.

49 *Murasoli*, 15 May 1979, 1.

50 'If Mrs. Gandhi runs, will Karunanidhi oppose her in Thanjavur?' 16 May 1979, US consul general cable. Accessed 22 May 2021, https://wikileaks.org/plusd/cables/1979NEWDE08498_e.html.

51 Cho Ramaswamy, *Adhirshtam*, 273.

52 *Murasoli*, 21 May 1979, 1.

53 *Murasoli*, 23 June 1979, 1; *Murasoli*, 15 June 1979, 6; Karunanidhi, *Kadithangal*, 4: 283–86.

54 *Murasoli*, 13 August 1979, 1-2.

55 S. Viswanathan, 'Jayalalithaa Playing a double role,' *Frontline*, 2 June 1995, 31.

56 'Parliament passes Bill to provide 10% quota for poor,' *The Hindu*, 9 January 2019. Accessed 10 March 2019, https://www.thehindu.com/news/national/parliament-approves-10-reservation-for-poor-in-general-category/article61553904.ece; Karunanidhi, *Kadithangal*, 4: 365–67.

57 *Murasoli*, 14 September 1979, 1; 'Tamil Nadu: Dramatic Meeting between Tamil Rivals.' 15 September 1979 US consul general cable. Accessed 29 March 2019, https://wikileaks.org/plusd/cables/1979NEWDE16796_e. html.

58 *Murasoli*, 15 September 1979, 4; *Murasoli*, 18 September 1979, 4; Karunanidhi, *Kadithangal*, 19: 326–27.

59 *Murasoli*, 21 September, 1.

60 'DMK Congress (I) Alliance jolts Tamil Nadu,' 19 September 1979, US consul general cable. Accessed 24 March 2018, https://wikileaks.org/plusd/cables/1979NEWDE17086_e.html.

61 'Dramatic Meeting between Tamil Rivals,' supra note 57.

62 Cho Ramaswamy, *Ivargalai*, 1: 396.

63 *Murasoli*, 24 June 1980, 1.

64 *Murasoli*, 16 September 1979, 1. The Congress (I) expelled Pazha Nedumaran for opposing the alliance. So much for gratitude in politics.

65 *Murasoli*, 18 September 1979, 1.

66 *Murasoli*, 21 September 1979, 1.

67 Karunanidhi, *Kadithangal*, 4: 434.

68 *Murasoli*, 26 September 1979, 1.

69 *MGRin Sattamandra Uraigal*, 507.

70 *Murasoli*, 2 October 1979, 1–2.

71 *The Hindu*, 2 October 1979, 11.

72 Ibid.

73 *Murasoli*, 3 December 1979, 4.

74 *Murasoli*, 6 January 1980, 1.

75 *Murasoli*, 9 January 1980, 1.

76 *Murasoli*, 9 January 1980, 3.

77 'Coming together of DMK and Congress(I) threatens stability of AIADMK administration,' *India Today*, 15 October 1979. Accessed 1 March 2019, https://www.indiatoday.in/magazine/indiascope/story/19791015-coming-together-of-dmk-and-congressi-threatens-stability-of-aiadmk-administration-822446-2014-02-20.

Chapter 16: Again in the Opposition

1 *Murasoli*, 20 January 1989, 1.

2 'Tamil Nadu Chief Minister M.G. Ramachandran waters down his prohibition law,' *India Today*, 29 February 1980. Accessed 2 February 2018, https://www.indiatoday.in/magazine/indiascope/story/19800229-tamil-nadu-chief-minister-m.g.-ramachandran-waters-down-his-prohibition-law-806463-2014-02-06.

3 *Murasoli*, 16 February 1980, 1–3.

4 *Murasoli*, 11 March 1980, 3.

5 Karunanidhi, *Kadithangal*, 4: 551–52.

6 *Murasoli*, 5 April 1980, 1; *Murasoli*, 6 April 1980, 3.

7 *Murasoli*, 17 April 1980, 1; *Murasoli*, 21 April 1980, 1.

8   *Murasoli*, 13 April 1980, 1.

9   Cho Ramaswamy, *Ivargalai*, 3: 55–56.

10   *Murasoli*, 21 April 1980, 1; *Murasoli*, 25 April 1980, 1.

11   Karunanidhi, *Kadithangal*, 4:5 89–90.

12   *Murasoli*, 30 May 1980, 3; *Murasoli*, 31 May 1980, 1.

13   'Karunanidhi does not exist without Congress (I) support: M.G. Ramachandran,' *India Today*, 31 October 1981. Accessed 1 February 2018, https://www.indiatoday.in/magazine/interview/story/19811031-karunanidhi-does-not-exist-without-congressi-support-m.g.-ramachandran-773402-2013-10-29.

14   'Dravida Kazhagam movement is as strong as ever: Karunanidhi,' *India Today*, 30 June 1980. Accessed 1 February 2018, https://www.indiatoday.in/magazine/cover-story/story/19800630-dravida-kazhagam-movement-is-as-strong-as-ever-karunanidhi-821221-2014-01-25.

15   Karunanidhi, *Kadithangal*, 8: 274.

16   *Murasoli*, 4 June 1980, 1–2.

17   M.K. Stalin, *Ungalil Oruvan*, (Chennai: Poompuhar Pathippagam, 2022), 186.

18   *Murasoli*, 22 July 1980, 2.

19   Karunanidhi, *Kadithangal*, 4: 668–69; *Murasoli*, 3 August 1980, 1–2.

20   *Murasoli*, 3 August 1982, 4.

21   'Thi.Mu.Ka virutcham endraal, ilainjarani adhan aaniver: Thi.Mu.Ka ilainjar ani uruvaana kadhai,' Kalaignar Seithigal, 7 April 2019. Accessed 2 May 2020, https://www.kalaignarseithigal.com/dmk/2019/07/04/dmk-youth-wing-journey-mk-stalin-to-udhayanidhi-a-recap.

22   'Aatipadaikum Anbil . . . alarum Arivalayam,' *Junior Vikatan*, 18 August 2020. Accessed 19 November 2020, https://www.vikatan.com/government-and-politics/politics/anbil-mahesh-dominating-in-dmk.

23   *Therkilirundhu*, 104–05.

24   'Udhayanidhi will not get into politics: Stalin,' *The News Minute*, 10 May 2016. Accessed 20 May 2018, https://www.thenewsminute.com/article/udhayanidhi-will-not-get-politics-stalin-42996.

25   *Murasoli*, 17 January 1981, 1; *Murasoli*, 18 January 1981, 1; *Murasoli*, 19 January 1981, 1; *Murasoli*, 5 February 1981, 1–2.

26   *Murasoli*, 8 February 1981, 2.

27   *Murasoli*, 29 March 1981, 1; *Murasoli*, 1 April 1981, 1.

28   *Murasoli*, 5 August 1981, 2.

29   'Liquor barons in Kerala determined to drown ruling LDF Government in rivers of spirit,' *India Today*, 28 February 1981. Accessed 19 February

2020, https://www.indiatoday.in/magazine/indiascope/story/19810228-liquor-barons-in-kerala-determined-to-drown-ruling-ldf-government-in-rivers-of-spirit-772715-2013-11-26.

30   *Murasoli*, 7 April 1981, 1.

31   *Murasoli*, 12 May 1981, 1.

32   *Murasoli*, 15 May 1981, 1.

33   *Murasoli*, 2 June 1981, 1.

34   'June 19, 1981, Forty Years Ago: Spirit scandal probe,' *Indian Express*, 19 June 2021. Accessed 21 January 2022, https://indianexpress.com/article/opinion/editorials/june-19-1981-forty-years-ago-spirit-scandal-probe-7365470/.

35   *Murasoli*, 17 June 1981, 1.

36   *Murasoli*, 5 August 1981, 3.

37   *Murasoli*, 31 October 1981, 1.

38   'Former HC judge to head one-man commission to probe Tamil Nadu's liquor problem,' *India Today*, 15 October 1982. Accessed 20 January 2019, https://www.indiatoday.in/magazine/investigation/story/19821015-former-hc-judge-to-head-one-man-commission-to-probe-tamil-nadus-liquor-problem-772287-2013-08-27;   'Liquor licences corruption case: MGR and other cabinet ministers get clean chit,' *India Today*, 15 April 1984. Accessed 19 January 2019, https://www.indiatoday.in/magazine/indiascope/story/19840415-liquor-licences-corruption-case-mgr-and-other-cabinet-ministers-get-clean-chit-802942-1984-04-15.

39   *Murasoli*, 8 June 1981, 1.

40   *Murasoli*, 31 October 1981, 1; *Murasoli*, 2 September 1981, 1; *Murasoli*, 7 September 1981, 1.

41   'Wave of violence envelops Tamil Nadu after Karunanidhi's arrest,' *India Today*, 31 October 1981. Accessed 25 January 2019, https://www.indiatoday.in/magazine/indiascope/story/19811031-wave-of-violence-envelops-tamil-nadu-after-karunanidhis-arrest-773399-2013-10-29; *Murasoli*, 11 October, 1.

42   *Murasoli*, 26 September 1981, 1; *Murasoli*, 26 September 1981, 1.

43   *Murasoli*, 31 October 1981, 1.

44   *Murasoli*, 9 November 1980, 1.

45   *Murasoli*, 17 May 1988, 3; *Murasoli*, 25 October 1981, 1; 'Congress (I) terminates alliance with DMK, indirectly welcomes support of AIADMK,' *India Today*, 30 November 1981. Accessed 29 March 2019, https://www.indiatoday.in/magazine/indiascope/story/19811130-

congressi-terminates-alliance-with-dmk-indirectly-welcomes-support-of-aiadmk-773454-2013-10-25.

46   Karunanidhi, *Kadithangal*, 5: 775.

47   C. Raghavan, 'Projects for the people,' *Frontline*, 9–22 January 1988, 15.

48   Krishnadas Rajagopal, 'All political parties on one side, everybody wants freebies: Supreme Court,' *The Hindu*, 23 August 2022. Accessed 28 August 2022, https://www.thehindu.com/news/national/all-political-parties-on-one-side-everybody-wants-freebies-supreme-court/article65801453.ece.

49   *Murasoli*, 19 September 1982, 1.

50   *MGRin Sattamandra Uraigal*, 509.

51   Divya Chandrababu, 'TN rolls out free breakfast scheme for primary school students,' *Hindustan Times*, 27 July 2022. Accessed 29 August 2022, https://www.hindustantimes.com/india-news/tn-rolls-out-free-breakfast-scheme-for-primary-school-students-101658946149832.html.

52   'I am prepared to face any probe, says Jayalalitha,' *The Hindu*, 3 July 1996, 15.

53   D. Suresh Kumar, 'From video rental shop to Fort St. George,' *The Hindu*, 6 February 2017. Accessed 7 February 2028, https://www.thehindu.com/news/national/tamil-nadu/From-video-rental-shop-to-Fort-St.-George/article17198966.ece.

54   Bhagwan R. Singh, 'Today MGR is everything to me,' the *Week*, 22 January 1984. Accessed 1 May 2019, https://www.theweek.in/webworld/features/society/mgr-jayalalithaa.html; 'Women in love,' the *Illustrated Weekly of India*, 1–7 May 1988, 12.

55   Ibid.

56   'Jayalalithaa: a political career with sharp rises and steep falls,' *The Hindu*, 6 December 2016. Accessed 20 August 2018, https://www.thehindu.com/news/national/tamil-nadu/Jayalalithaa-a-political-career-with-sharp-rises-and-steep-falls/article60644102.ece; Lakshmi Subramanian, 'My life with Jayalalithaa: V.K. Sasikala,' the *Week*, 18 July 2021, https://www.theweek.in/theweek/cover/2021/07/08/my-life-with-jayalalithaa-v-k-sasikala.html.

57   *Review of the work transacted by the seventh Tamil Nadu Legislative Assembly*, (Chennai: Legislative Assembly Department, 1980–1984), 181. Accessed 21 June 2020, https://assembly.tn.gov.in/archive/7th_1980/7threview_80-84.pdf.

58   *Tamil Nadu Legislative Assembly Debates, Official Report,* (Madras: Legislative Assembly Secretariat, 1991) 24 September 1991, Vol. 10, No. 1, 19–20.

59   *Murasoli,* 27 March 1983, 1–2.

60   '"Tholvi vandhaal odi pogamaaten!" Jayalalithaa sirapu paeti,' *Junior Vikatan,* 25 January 1984. Accessed 20 January 2018, https://www.vikatan.com/best-of-vikatan/vikatan-vintage/jayalalithaas-evergreen-interview-about-her-struggles-and-success.

61   *Murasoli,* 5 March 1983, 1–4.

62   *Murasoli,* 29 September 1982, 1.

63   'Conclave of four southern non-Congress(I) chief ministers surprisingly low-key,' *India Today,* 15 April 1983. Accessed 20 June 2018, https://www.indiatoday.in/magazine/special-report/story/19830415-conclave-of-four-southern-non-congressi-chief-ministers-surprisingly-low-key-770599-2013-07-22.

64   *MGRin Sattamandra Uraigal,* 517–20; 555–56.

65   Karunanidhi, *Kadithangal,* 7: 283–85.

66   *Murasoli,* 22 March 1983, 1.

67   *Murasoli,* 30 March 1983, 1–2.

68   Karunanidhi, *Kadithangal,* 7: 605; 'Coalition government in Pondicherry collapses as Congress (I) pulls out,' *India Today,* 15 July 1983. Accessed 20 July 2019, https://www.indiatoday.in/magazine/indiascope/story/19830715-coalition-government-in-pondicherry-collapses-as-congressi-pulls-out-770826-2013-07-19.

69   *Murasoli,* 4 July 1983, 1–4.

70   *Murasoli,* 27 July 1983, 1.

71   *Murasoli,* 29 July 1983, 1, 4.

72   *Murasoli,* 31 July 1983, 1.

73   *Murasoli,* 2 August 1983, 2.

74   *Murasoli,* 5 August 1983, 1.

75   India, *Parliamentary Debates,* House of the People, 5 August 1983, cols. 517–18. Accessed 20 November 2018, https://eparlib.nic.in/bitstream/123456789/809239/1/pms_07_12_05_08_1983.pdf.

76   *Murasoli,* 7 August 1983, 1.

77   *Murasoli,* 10 August 1983, 1; *Murasoli,* 11 August 1983, 1.

78   *Murasoli,* 11 August 1983, 4; See *Murasoli,* 23 December 1987, 1 where Karunanidhi claims twenty million signatures.

79   *Murasoli,* 14 August 1983, 1.

80   Ibid., 3.

81 *Murasoli*, 17 August 1983.

82 India, *Parliamentary Debates*, Council of States, 16 August 1983, cols. 359–60. Accessed 21 June 2018, https://rsdebate.nic.in/ bitstream/123456789/363058/1/PD_127_16081983_16_p254_ p422_11.pdf.

83 Ibid.

84 Karunanidhi, *Kadithangal*, 18: 33; *Murasoli*, 7 March 1987, 4.

85 *Murasoli*, 30 August 1983, 1.

86 *Murasoli*, 31 August 1983, 1.

87 India, *Parliamentary Debates*, Council of States, Statement on Sri Lanka, 8 August 1984, col. 310. Accessed 17 June 2018, https://rsdebate.nic. in/bitstream/123456789/337677/1/PD_131_08081984_13_p287_ p313_13.pdf.

88 *MGRin Sattamandra Uraigal*, 454–79.

89 Ibid., 499–507.

90 'Prabhakaran Speaks out about MGR,' YouTube video, 10:08, 3 February 2019, https://eelam.tv/watch/prabaharan-speaks-about- mgr_YVFp9jaHgA356Wm.html. Accessed 20 August 2023; Anton Balasingham, *Liberation*, (Mitcham, Fairmax Publishing Ltd. 2003), 2–17; T. Sabaratnam, 'MGR's Role in the Tamil Struggle.' Accessed 29 November 2018, https://sangam.org/pirapaharan-vol-2-chap-27-mgrs- role-in-the-tamil-struggle/.

91 *Review of the work transacted by the seventh Tamil Nadu Legislative Assembly*, supra note 57, 184.

92 *Murasoli*, 31 March 1984, 1.

93 'Riven by internal dissension, AIADMK Government virtually splits,' *India Today*, 15 September 1984. Accessed 21 June 2019, https://www.indiatoday.in/magazine/indiascope/story/19840915- riven-by-internal-dissension-ruling-aiadmk-government-virtually- splits-803272-1984-09-15.

94 K.P. Sunil, 'MGR is being kept a prisoner,' the *Illustrated Weekly of India*, 10 February 1985. Accessed 21 January 2020,https://archive.org/stream/ in.ernet.dli.2015.110086/2015.110086.The-Illustrated-Weekly-Of- India-Vol105-106-No368jan-june1985_djvu.txt.

95 Bhagwan R. Singh, 'Its wholesale corruption,' the *Week*, 16 September 1984. Accessed 21 June 2020, https://www.theweek.in/webworld/ features/society/sd-somasundaram-interview.html.

96 *Murasoli*, 4 September 1984, 3.

97 Karunandihi, *Kadithangal*, 7: 371–78.

98   *Murasoli*, 16 April 1987, 2.

99   Karunanidhi, *Kadithangal*, 7: 385–86.

100   Ibid., 7: 398–401.

101   Ibid., 7: 403–04.

102   *Murasoli*, 3 December 1984, 1, 3; *Murasoli*, 9 December 1984, 1.

103   *Murasoli*, 7 December 1984, 1–2.

104   *Murasoli*, 4 December 1984, 3.

105   'MGR banks on surge of sympathy for him to translate itself into votes,' *India Today*, 31 December 1984. Accessed 21 June 2019, https://www.indiatoday.in/magazine/nation/story/19841231-mgr-banks-on-surge-of-sympathy-for-him-to-translate-itself-into-votes-803521-1984-12-31.

106   *Murasoli*, 8 December 1984, 1; *Murasoli*, 9 December 1984, 1–2.

107   *Murasoli*, 10 December 1984, 1.

108   'MGR banks on surge of sympathy for him to translate itself into votes,' supra note 105.

109   *Murasoli*, 16 December 1984, 2.

110   Kannan, *MGR*, 346.

111   *Review of the work transacted by the seventh Tamil Nadu Legislative Assembly*, supra note 57.

112   K.P. Sunil, 'Grise,' the *Illustrated Weekly of India*, 7 February 1988. Accessed 1 May 2020, https://archive.org/stream/in.ernet.dli.2015.110083/2015.110083.The-Illustrated--Weekly-Of-Indiajanuary-july1988_djvu.txt.

113   *Review of the work transacted by the seventh Tamil Nadu Legislative Assembly*, supra note 57.

114   *Murasoli*, 30 December 1984, 1.

115   *Murasoli*, 31 December 1984, 1.

Chapter 17: Third Opposition Stint

1   K. Raghunathan and V. Jayanth, 'AIADMK split in 1984'—Interview with S. Ramachandran, *Frontline*, 6–19 February 1988, 14–15.

2   K.P. Sunil, 'Grise,' the *Illustrated Weekly of India*, 7 February 1988. Accessed 1 May 2020, https://archive.org/stream/in.ernet.dli.2015.110083/2015.110083.The-Illustrated--Weekly-Of-Indiajanuary-july1988_djvu.txt.

3   Anand Viswanathan, Prabhu Chawla, 'While Congress(I) keeps its guns trained on him, Karunanidhi shows he can hit back,' *India Today*, 15

February 1991. Accessed 22 January 2019, https://www.indiatoday. in/magazine/special-report/story/19910215-while-congressi-keeps-its-guns-trained-on-him-karunanidhi-shows-he-can-hit-back-814011-1991-02-15.

4   *Review of the work transacted by the seventh Tamil Nadu Legislative Assembly*, (Chennai: Legislative Assembly Department, 1980– 1984), 181. Accessed 21 June 2020, https://assembly.tn.gov.in/ archive/7th_1980/7threview_80-84.pdf.

5   R. Krishnaswamy, K. Raghunathan, K. Venugopal, 'Jayalalitha on the warpath,' *Frontline*, 26 January–8 February 1985, 19.

6   *Murasoli*, 4 May 1987, 2.

7   Kannan, *MGR*, 349–52; Sunil Sethi, 'Tamil Nadu CM M.G. Ramachandran returns home, health speculations laid to rest,' *India Today*, 28 February 1985. Accessed 1 May 2020, https://www. indiatoday.in/magazine/special-report/story/19850228-tamil-nadu-cm-m.g.-ramachandran-returns-home-health-speculations-laid-to-rest-769833-2013-11-27; 'AIADMK strongman responds to doubts,' *Frontline*, 26 January–8 February 1985, 17.

8   *Tamil Nadu Legislative Assembly (Eighth Assembly) Review: 1985–88*, (Madras: Legislative Assembly Secretariat, 1991), 13–17. Accessed 1 July 2019, https://assembly.tn.gov.in/archive/8th_1985/8threview_85-88. pdf; *Murasoli*, 15–16 February 1985, 1; 5 March 1985, 5.

9   S.H. Venkataramani, 'AIADMK chief MGR and Jayalalitha Jayaram were to all appearances happily reunited,' *India Today*, 15 March 1985. Accessed 1 June 2019, https://www.indiatoday.in/magazine/indiascope/ story/19850315-aiadmk-chief-mgr-and-jayalalitha-jayaram-were-to-all-appearances-happily-reunited-769880-2013-12-02.

10   *Dinamani*, 31 March 1985, 1.

11   *Murasoli*, 9 April 1985, 1.

12   J.N. Dixit, *Assignment Colombo*, (New Delhi, Konark Publishers, 1998), 29, 78.

13   *Murasoli*, 19 March 1985, 4–5.

14   *Murasoli*, 25 March 1985, 1.

15   *Murasoli*, 3–4 April 1985, 1.

16   *Murasoli*, 27 April 1985, 1.

17   *Murasoli*, 28 April 1985.

18   Karunanidhi, *Kadithangal*, 14: 305–07.

19   *Murasoli*, 26 August 1986, 4.

20   Karunanidhi, *Kadithangal*, 7: 621–22.

21   Ibid., 708.

22 S.H. Venkataramani, 'AIADMK MP Jayalalitha makes her comeback as propaganda secretary to thundering applause,' *India Today*, 30 September 1985. Accessed 1 May 200, https://www.indiatoday. in/magazine/indiascope/story/19850930-aiadmk-mp-jayalalitha-makes-her-come-back-as-propaganda-secretary-to-thundering-applause-802270-2014-01-07.

23 'Succession battle erupts between Veerappan and Jayalalitha as MGR falls ill,' *India Today*, 30 November 1985, https://www. indiatoday.in/magazine/indiascope/story/19851130-succession-battle-erupts-between-veerappan-and-jayalalitha-as-mgr-falls-ill-802209-2014-01-21.

24 Kannan, *MGR*, 361–62.

25 Karunanidhi, *Kadithangal*, 15: 210–14.

26 S.H. Venkataramani, 'R.M. Veerappan steals a march over his political foe Jayalalitha,' *India Today*, 15 February 1986. Accessed 1 March 2019, https://www.indiatoday.in/magazine/indiascope/story/19860215-r.m.-veerappan-steals-a-march-over-his-political-foe-jayalalitha-800591-1986-02-15.

27 S.H. Venkataramani, 'AIADMK suffers unprecedented defeat in municipal polls, DMK romps home a clear winner,' *India Today*, 15 March 1986, https://www.indiatoday.in/magazine/indiascope/story/19860315-aiadmk-suffers-unprecedented-defeat-in-municipal-polls-dmk-romps-home-a-clear-winner-800678-1986-03-15'; Karunanidhi, *Kadithangal*, 8:57; 67–68, 81, 86.

28 *Murasoli*, 1 March 1986, 1.

29 S.H. Venkataramani, 'Objections raised to nomination of actress to legislative council, MGR abolishes council,' *India Today*, 15 June 1986. Accessed 13 January 2019, https://www.indiatoday.in/magazine/indiascope/story/19860615-objections-raised-to-nomination-of-actress-to-legislative-council-mgr-abolishes-council-800945-1986-06-15.

30 *Murasoli*, 14 May 1986, 1, 4.

31 *Murasoli*, 3 May 1986, 1.

32 *Murasoli*, 5 May 1986, 1–2.

33 K. Venkataraman, 'M. Karunanidhi: A lifelong warrior for Sri Lankan Tamil cause, but misunderstood in the end,' *The Hindu*, 7 August 2018. Accessed 2 February 2019, https://www.thehindu.com/news/national/tamil-nadu/m-karunanidhi-a-lifelong-warrior-for-sri-lankan-tamil-cause-but-misunderstood-in-the-end/article61506000.ece.

34 Karunanidhi, *Kadithangal*, 8: 139–40.

35 *Murasoli*, 19 May 1986, 1, 3.

36   Karunanidhi, *Kadithangal*, 15: 396–400.

37   Ibid., 384–386.

38   'Eelath Thamizharum Kalaignarum.' Accessed 21 February 2022, https://kalaignar.dmk.in/2019/07/29/kalaignar-and-eezham/.

39   S.H. Venkataramani, 'Disarming of Sri Lankan Tamil militants in Tamil Nadu a blow to their battle for Eelam,' *India Today*, 30 November 1986. Accessed 25 February 2019, https://www.indiatoday.in/magazine/indiascope/story/19861130-disarming-of-sri-lankan-tamil-militants-in-tamil-nadu-a-blow-to-their-battle-for-eelam-801500-1986-11-30.

40   S.H. Venkataramani, Prabhu Chawla, 'India finds brokering of a settlement in Sri Lanka's crisis increasingly intricate,' *India Today*, 15 December 1986. Accessed 27 February 2019, https://www.indiatoday.in/magazine/special-report/story/19861215-india-finds-brokering-of-a-settlement-in-sri-lanka-crisis-increasingly-intricate-801547-1986-12-15; 'Anatomy of a witch-hunt,' *Frontline*, 29 November 1997. Accessed 21 January 2019, https://frontline.thehindu.com/cover-story/article30160454.ece.

41   *Murasoli*, 23 November 1986.

42   *Murasoli*, 25 November 1986, 4; *Frontline*, 5–18 March 1988, 99.

43   *Murasoli*, 28 September 1986, 1.

44   T.S. Subramaniam, 'Fire and thunder,' *Frontline*, 23 April 1993, 121.

45   *Murasoli*, 10 October 1986, 1.

46   Karunanidhi, *Kadithangal*, 16: 299–300, 305.

47   Ibid., 6: 202.

48   *Murasoli*, 18 November 1986.

49   *Murasoli*, 25 November 1986, 1, 3.

50   *Murasoli*, 3 December 1986, 1.

51   *Murasoli*, 29 November 1986, 1.

52   *Murasoli*, 10 December 1986, 1.

53   Karunanidhi, *Kadithangal*, 16: 349–52.

54   Ibid., 342.

55   *Murasoli*, 3 December 1986, 1; *Murasoli*, 24 December 1986, 3.

56   Debashish Mukerji, *The Disruptor: How Vishwanath Pratap Singh Shook India*, (Gurgaon, HarperCollins, 2021), 274.

57   *Murasoli*, 16 April 1987, 2.

58   Mukerji, *Disruptor*, 296.

59   *Murasoli*, 11 February 1987, 1.

60   Karunanidhi, *Kadithangal*, 16: 357.

61   *Murasoli*, 15 February 1987, 1; *Murasoli*, 17 February 1987, 1, 4.

62   *Murasoli*, 7 March 1987, 4.

63   *Murasoli*, 24 April 1987, 1.

64   Karunanidhi, *Kadithangal*, 17: 78–81.

65   'MGR Made Rajiv Change His Mind On Anti-LTTE Operation,' *Business Standard*, 17 December 1997. Accessed 21 January 2020, https://www.business-standard.com/article/specials/mgr-made-rajiv-change-his-mind-on-anti-ltte-operation-197121701068_1.html; https://www.indiatoday.in/magazine/cover-story/story/19870630-india-air-drops-relief-supplies-over-jaffna-despite-resistance-from-sri-lanka-799005-1987-06-30.

66   *Murasoli*, 10 June 1987, 1.

67   *Murasoli*, 18 June 1987, 1.

68   *Murasoli*, 30 June 1987, 1.

69   India, *Parliamentary Debates*, Council of States, Prime Minister's statement on the Indo-Sri Lanka Agreement, 31 July 1987, col. 302. Accessed 20 May 2019, https://rsdebate.nic.in/bitstream/123456789/305679/1/PD_143_31071987_5_p301_p311_10.pdf.

70   *Murasoli*, 29 July 1987, 1.

71   *Murasoli*, 30 July 1987, 1; *Murasoli*, 30 July 1987, 1.

72   *Murasoli*, 2 August 1987, 1.

73   Ibid.

74   'Velupillai Prabhakaran on the Indo Sri Lanka Accord,' Accessed 21 May 2020, https://tamilnation.org/ltte/vp/messages_speeches/870804suthumalai.htm.

75   *Murasoli*, 27 August 1987, 1.

76   Karunanidhi, *Kadithangal*, 9: 104.

77   Ibid., 9: 202.

78   Ibid., 14: 16–19.

79   Ibid., 7: 513.

80   Ibid., 17: 120–25.

81   Ibid., 7: 151.

82   S.H. Venkataramani, 'Agitation by backward Vanniyar community rocks Tamil Nadu,' *India Today*, 15 October 1987. Accessed 21 August 2020, https://www.indiatoday.in/magazine/indiascope/story/19871015-agitation-by-backward-vanniyar-community-rocks-tamil-nadu-799377-1987-10-15.

83   *Aside*, 16–30 November 1988, 23.

84   *Murasoli*, 7 October 1987, 1.

85 '30 years of the Indo-Sri Lanka Accord,' *The Hindu*, 18 August 2017. Accessed 1 May 2020, https://www.thehindu.com/news/international/30-years-of-the-indo-sri-lanka-accord/article 19517964.ece.

86 *Murasoli*, 12 October 1987, 1.

87 *Murasoli*, 14 October 1987, 1.

88 *Murasoli*, 16 October 1987, 1; *Murasoli*, 17 October 1987, 2.

89 Karunanidhi, *Kadithangal*, 17: 166–171.

90 *Murasoli*, 30 October 1987, 1.

91 *Murasoli*, 2 November 1987, 1.

92 *Murasoli*, 11 November 1987, 2.

93 India, *Parliamentary Debates*, Council of States, Prime Minister's statement on Sri Lanka, 9 November 1987, col. 333. Accessed 1 May 2020, https://rsdebate.nic.in/bitstream/123456789/296005/1/PD_144_09111987_2_p297_p336_17.pdf.

94 *Murasoli*, 22 November 1987, 3.

95 *Murasoli*, 11 December 1987, 1.

96 *Murasoli*, 22 December 1987, 1.

97 Ibid.

98 *Murasoli*, 24 December 1987, 1.

99 *Murasoli*, 25 December 1987, 1.

100 *Murasoli*, 27 December 1987, 1.

101 Karunanidhi, *Nenjuku*, 4: 239–40; *Murasoli*, 28 December 1987, 1.

Chapter 18: Karunanidhi vs Jayalalithaa

1 T.S. Subramanian, 'No opportunistic decisions', *Murasoli*, 27 December 1987, 1.

2 B. Kolappan, 'The reluctant actor and politician,' *The Hindu*, 2 October 2016. Accessed 1 July 2019.

3 Prabhu Chawla, 'I was bulldozed into joining politics,' says Jayalalitha,' *India Today*, 30 April 1989, https://www.indiatoday.in/magazine/interview/story/19890430-i-was-bulldozed-into-joining-politics-says-jayalalitha-816028-1989-04-30.

4 K. Raghunathan and V. Jayanth, 'I don't have a double edged tongue'—Interview with Jayalalithaa, *Frontline*, 23 January–5 February 1988, 21.

5 Sruthi Radhakrisnan, 'Jayalalithaa vs Janaki: The last succession battle,' *The Hindu*, 10 February 2017. Accessed 17 March 2020, https://www.

thehindu.com/news/national/tamil-nadu/Jayalalithaa-vs-Janaki-The-last-succession-battle/article17284902.ece.

6   *Tamil Nadu Legislative Assembly (Eighth Assembly) Review: 1985–88*, (Madras: Legislative Assembly Secretariat, 1991), 13–17. Accessed 1 July 2019, https://assembly.tn.gov.in/archive/8th_1985/8threview_85-88.pdf; S.H. Venkataramani, 'Tamil Nadu: Janaki Ramachandran is chief minister but can she survive?,' *India Today*, 31 January 1988. Accessed 22 February 2019, https://www.indiatoday.in/magazine/indiascope/story/19880131-tamil-nadu-janaki-ramachandran-is-chief-minister-but-can-she-survive-769001-2013-11-21.

7   *Murasoli*, 21 January 1988, 1.

8   *Murasoli*, 29 January 1988, 1–3; *Tamil Nadu Legislative Assembly (Eighth Assembly) Review*, supra note 6, 43; 'No opportunistic decisions,' supra note 1, 98.

9   C. Raghavan, 'After MGR,' *Frontline*, 19 February 1988, 4–8.

10 A blow-by-blow account can be found in: S.H. Venkataramani, Prabhu Chawla, 'Tamil Nadu: Janaki Government's foundations cave in,' *India Today*, 15 February 1988. Accessed 22 March 2019, https://www.indiatoday.in/magazine/indiascope/story/19880215-tamil-nadu-janaki-governments-foundations-cave-in-796937-1988-02-15;.   T.S. Subramanian, 'No opportunistic decisions', supra note 1.

11 *Murasoli*, 1 February 1988, 1.

12 Karunanidhi, *Nenjuku Needhi*, 3: 590.

13 V. Jayanth, 'A political charade,' *Frontline*, 6–19 February 1988, 9–11; Cho Ramaswamy, *Ivargalai*, 2: 314–42.

14 'AIADMK split in 1984'—Interview with S. Ramachandran, *Frontline*, 6–19 February 1988, 14–15.

15 *Murasoli*, 29 January 1988, 1.

16 'AIADMK split in 1984'—Interview with S. Ramachandran, supra note 14.

17 Cho Ramaswamy, *Ivargalai*, 2:314–42.

18 V. Jayanth, 'Tamil Nadu: move one,' *Frontline*, 20 February–4 March 1988, 121–26.

19 Karunanidhi, *Kadithangal*, 17: 257–61.

20 *Murasoli*, 20 February 1988, 1.

21 *Frontline*, 5–18 March 1988, 99.

22 *Murasoli*, 21 February 1988, 1.

23 T.S. Subramanian, '"I'm ready to meet any harassment"—Interview with M. Karunanidhi,' *Frontline*, 3 January 1992, 107.

24 T.S. Subramanian, 'No opportunistic decisions,' supra note 1.

25 Karunanidhi, *Kadithangal*, 17: 316.

26 Ibid., 361–66.

27 *Murasoli*, 8 June 1988, 4.

28 *Murasoli*, 27 April 1988, 1.

29 S.H. Venkataramani, Prabhu Chawla, 'AICC(I) session: Rajiv Gandhi emerges as a cult figure, party exudes unexpected confidence,' *India Today*, 15 May 1988. Accessed 21 May 2019, https://www.indiatoday.in/magazine/special-report/story/19880515-aicci-session-rajiv-gandhi-emerges-as-a-cult-figure-party-exudes-unexpected-confidence-797246-1988-05-15.

30 *Murasoli*, 27 April 1988, 1.

31 *Murasoli*, 14 May 1988, 1.

32 *Murasoli*, 19 May 1988, 4.

33 Karunanidhi, *Kadithangal*, 18: 51.

34 Prabhu Chawla, 'Jayalalitha under pressure as section of her party questions her political decisions,' *India Today*, 31 July 1998, https://www.indiatoday.in/magazine/indiascope/story/19880731-jayalalitha-under-pressure-as-section-of-her-party-questions-her-political-decisions-797510-1988-07-31.

35 Muralitharan Kasiviswanathan, 'Natarasan kurithu Jayalalithaa kooriadhu enna?' *BBC NEWS Tamil*, 20 March 2018. Accessed 1 March 2023, https://www.bbc.com/tamil/india-43470197.

36 *Murasoli*, 9 August 1988, 5.

37 *Murasoli*, 30 October 1987, 2.

38 Kavitha Shetty, 'General Elections 1989: Ruling DMK faces uphill task in Tamil Nadu,' *India Today*, 30 November 1989. Accessed 21 June 2019, https://www.indiatoday.in/magazine/cover-story/story/19891130-general-elections-1989-ruling-dmk-faces-uphill-task-in-tamil-nadu-816764-1989-11-30.

39 *Murasoli*, 8 August 1988, 1.

40 Karunanidhi, *Kadithangal*, 18: 93–130.

41 Prabhu Chawla, 'Seven party National Front formally launched in Madras,' *India Today*, 15 October 1988. Accessed 1 June 2019, https://www.indiatoday.in/magazine/special-report/story/19881015-seven-party-national-front-formally-launched-in-madras-797802-1988-10-15.

42 Karunandihi, *Kadithangal*, 18: 175.

43 Cho Ramaswamy, *Ivargalai*, 3: 55, 71.

44 'DMK is my enemy number one in Tamil Nadu: Jayalalitha,' *India Today*, 31 December 1988. Accessed 1 June 2019, https://www.indiatoday.in/ magazine/interview/story/19881231-dmk-is-my-enemy-number-one-in-tamil-nadu-jayalalitha-798107-1988-12-31.

45 Karunanidhi, *Kadithangal*, 8: 204–05.

46 Ibid., 18: 211.

47 *Murasoli*, 31 December 1988, 1.

48 *Frontline*, 7–20 January 1989, 116–17.

49 *Murasoli*, 28 December August 1988, 1.

50 'DMK is my enemy number one in Tamil Nadu: Jayalalitha.' *India Today*. Accessed 1 March 2023, https://www.indiatoday.in/magazine/ interview/story/19881231-dmk-is-my-enemy-number-one-in-tamil-nadu-jayalalitha-798107-1988-12-30.

51 *Murasoli*, 9 January 1989, 6.

52 Amarnath K. Menon, Prabhu Chawla, 'Tamil Nadu elections: Karunanidhi storms back to vanquish might of Rajiv-led Congress(I),' *India Today*, 15 February 1989. Accessed 21 August 2019, https:// www.indiatoday.in/magazine/cover-story/story/19890215-tamil-nadu-elections-karunanidhi-storms-back-to-vanquish-might-of-rajiv-led-congressi-815764-1989-02-15.

53 *Murasoli*, 16 January 1989, 5.

54 Amarnath K. Menon, 'Tamil Nadu assembly elections: Four contenders for chief ministership,' *India Today*, 31 January 1989. Accessed 1 June 2019, https://www.indiatoday.in/magazine/special-report/story/ 19890131-tamil-nadu-assembly-elections-four-contenders-for-chief-ministership-815684-1989-01-31.

55 K. Raghunathan, '"We will win and form Government. DMK is main rival," The Jayalalitha view,' *The Hindu*, 13 December 1988, 8.

56 Mandira Moddie, 'A throwback to another battle for AIADMK's "Two Leaves" symbol,' *The Hindu*, 23 November 2017. Accessed 1 June 2019, https://www.thehindu.com/news/national/tamil-nadu/tn-politics-a-throwback-to-another-battle-for-the-two-leaves-symbol/ article20706468.ece.

57 Jo. Stalin, 'Aalum katchiyai aatam kaana vaitha idaitherthal! Sasikala Jayalalithaa udanpiravaa sohadhari aana kadhai.-34'. Accessed 1 June 2019, https://www.vikatan.com/government-and-politics/politics/85905-byelection-and-ruling-government-how-sasikala-became-bestie-of-jayalalithaa-34.

58   *Statistical Report on General Election, 1989 to the Legislative Assembly of Tamil Nadu*, New Delhi: Election Commission of India, 1989, 10. Accessed 1 June 2020, https://eci.gov.in/files/file/3333-tamil-nadu-1989/.

59   *Murasoli*, 5 February 1989, 1, 4.

Chapter 19: Exile Ends—Briefly

1   *Murasoli*, 28 January 1989, 1, 7.
2   *Murasoli*, 28 January 1989, 7; *Murasoli*, 10 February 1989, 6.
3   *Murasoli*, 10 February 1989, 1.
4   *Murasoli*, 10 May 1989, 1.
5   *Murasoli*, 26 November 1993, 1–3; Karunanidhi, *Nenjuku Needhi*, 4: 25–26.; *Murasoli*, 11 February 1989, 1, 8; *Murasoli*, 12 February 1989, 1; *Murasoli*, 29 February 1989, 1.
6   Ibid.
7   Veerapandi Arumugham, *Dravida*, 123.
8   *Murasoli*, 6 March 1989, 5.
9   *Murasoli*, 6 March 1989, 1.
10   *Murasoli*, 4 March 1989, 1.
11   Murasoli, 26 November 1993, 1–3.
12   India, *Parliamentary Debates*, House of the People, Murasoli Maran's 5 August 1998 speech on Rajiv Gandhi's 'DMK initiative.' 5: 37, col. 163. Accessed 2 February 2021, https://eparlib.nic.in/bitstream/123456789/759436/1/lsd_12_02_05-08-1998.pdf.
13   *Murasoli*, 12 June 1989, 1, 4.
14   S.K. Misra, *Flying in High Winds: A Memoir*, (New Delhi: Rupa Publications, 2016), 168.
15   Karunanidhi, *Nenjuku Needhi*, 4: 77–79.
16   P. Jayram, Prabhu Chawla, 'India rejects Sri Lankan President Premadasa's IPKF quit deadline,' *India Today*, 30 June 1989. Accessed 1 April 2019, https://www.indiatoday.in/magazine/neighbours/story/19890630-india-rejects-sri-lankan-president-premadasa-ipkf-quit-deadline-816213-1989-06-30; Robert C. Oberst, 'Political Decay in Sri Lanka,' *Current History* 88, No. 542, South Asia (December, 1989), 425–428, 448–449.
17   Karunanidhi, *Nenjuku Needhi*, 4: 101.
18   India, *Parliamentary Debates*, House of the People, 26 February 1991, cols. 391-92. Accessed 1 April 2019, https://eparlib.nic.in/

bitstream/123456789/811213/1/09_VII_26021991_p192_p242_PII.
pdf; Sukumar Muralidharan and N. Ram, 'Jain has just paraphrased the
Congress affidavit,' *Frontline*, 12 December 1997, 23.

19 *Murasoli*, 18 November 1997, 8.

20 *Murasoli*, 3 July 1989, 3; Karunanidhi, *Kadithangal*, 9: 358–60.

21 *Murasoli*, 18 February 1989, 1, 6, 8; *Murasoli*, 22 February 1989, 3.

22 Prabhu Chawla, 'I was bulldozed into joining politics, says Jayalalithaa,'
    India Today, 30 April 1989, https://www.indiatoday.in/magazine/
    interview/story/19890430-i-was-bulldozed-into-joining-politics-says-
    jayalalitha-816028-1989-04-30.

23 Karunanidhi, *Nenjuku Needhi*, 4: 33.

24 *Murasoli*, 20 February 1989, 1.

25 *Murasoli*, 23 February 1989, 3; *Murasoli*, 2 March 1989, 1.

26 Karunanidhi, *Nenjuku Needhi*, 4: 37–39.

27 *Murasoli*, 14 March 1989, 1–8; *Murasoli*, 17 March 1989, 8; *Murasoli*, 23
    April 1989, 1–4; *Murasoli*, 4 May 1989, 1, 7.

28 *Murasoli*, 15 March 1989, 6; *Murasoli*, 22 March 1989, 4.

29 Guha Prasad, 'Jayalalitha's "resignation" creates a ruckus in Tamil
    Nadu,' *India Today*, 15 April 1989. Accessed 1 April 2019, https://www.
    indiatoday.in/magazine/special-report/story/19890415-jayalalithas-
    resignation-creates-a-ruckus-in-tamil-nadu-815975-1989-04-14.

30 Ibid.

31 *Murasoli*, 20 March 1989, 1.

32 *Review of the work transacted by the ninth Tamil Nadu Legislative Assembly,
    1989–91*, (Legislative Assembly Secretariat, 1991) 72. Accessed 1 June
    2019, https://assembly.tn.gov.in/archive/9th_1989/9threview_89-91.pdf.

33 Mandira Moddie, 'A throwback to another battle for AIADMK's
    "Two Leaves" symbol,' *The Hindu*, 23 November 2017. Accessed 1
    June 2019, https://www.thehindu.com/news/national/tamil-nadu/tn-
    politics-a-throwback-to-another-battle-for-the-two-leaves-symbol/
    article20706468.ece.

34 Karunanidhi, *Kadithangal*, 18: 17.

35 Cho Ramaswamy, *Ivargal Solgiraaargal*, (Chennai: The Alliance
    Publication Company, 2019), 168–73; https://www.thenewsminute.
    com/article/dravidian-chronicles-march-1989-beginning-tamil-nadus-
    vendetta-politics-43286; Karunanidhi, *Nenjuku Needhi*, 4: 49.

36 *Murasoli*, 26 March 1992, 2.

37 Karunanidhi, *Kadithangal*, 18: 217.

38 *Murasoli*, 12 April 1989, 1, 5.

39   *Murasoli*, 26 March 1989, 9; *Murasoli*, 27 March 1989, 4; Cho Ramaswamy,
       Ivargal Solgiraaargal, (Chennai: The Alliance Publication Company), 168–
       73; Udhav Naig, 'Nothing can "beat" 1989 violence,' *The Hindu*, 18 February
       2017. Accessed 1 June 2018, https://www.thehindu.com/news/national/
       tamil-nadu/nothing-can-beat-1989-violence/article17326723.ece.

40   *Murasoli Pudhayal*, 19 April 1992, 3; J. Ramki, *Ammu mudhal Amma
       varai*, (Chennai: Kizhakku Pathippagam, 2008), 111.

41   *Murasoli*, 26 March 1989, 3, 12; *Murasoli*, 27 March 1989, 4–5.

42   *Murasoli*, 29 March 1989, 1, 8; *Murasoli*, 30 March 1989, 1.

43   'Sattamandrathil   Jayalalithaavin   aadai   kizhikapatta   vivagaram:
       nadanthadu enna? – duraimurugan vilakam,' *Thanthi TV*, 6 August 2018,
       YouTube, 7:37, https://www.youtube.com/watch?v=FsajioZf6PM.

44   '1989 sambahavam: J – Anbazhagan naeruku naer modhal,' One India
       Tamil, 5 March 2003. Accessed 1 June 2005, https://tamil.oneindia.
       com/news/2003/03/25/jaya.html?story=3.

45   *Murasoli*, 26 March 1989, 3, 12; *Murasoli*, 27 March 1989, 4–5.

46   'I was bulldozed into joining politics, says Jayalalithaa,' supra note 22.

47   *Murasoli*, 27 August 1989, 1, 4.

48   *Murasoli*, 8 September 1989, 7.

49   *Murasoli*, 9 October 1989, 1.

50   *Murasoli*, 19 October 1989, 1.

51   *Murasoli*, 23 October 1989, 1.

52   *Murasoli*, 18 October 1989, 1.

53   Guha Prasad, 'Tamil Nadu: Jayalalitha reasserts herself,' *India Today*,
       15 September 1989. Accessed 1 May 2019, https://www.indiatoday.in/
       magazine/indiascope/story/19890915-tamil-nadu-jayalalitha-reasserts-
       herself-816494-1989-09-15.

54   Karunanidhi, *Kadithangal*, 9: 402.

55   *Murasoli*, 10 November 1989, 1.

56   *Frontline*, 11–24 November 1989, 22; *Frontline*, 25 November–8
       December 1989, 21.

57   *Murasoli*, 19 November 1989, 1, 3.

58   Kavitha Shetty, 'General Elections 1989: Ruling DMK faces uphill task
       in Tamil Nadu,' India Today, 30 November 1989. Accessed 1 May 2020,
       https://www.indiatoday.in/magazine/cover-story/story/19891130-
       general-elections-1989-ruling-dmk-faces-uphill-task-in-tamil-
       nadu-816764-1989-11-30

59   *Murasoli*, 23 November 1989, 2.

60   *Murasoli*, 28 November 1989, 2.

61 *Murasoli*, 30 November 1989, 1.

62 General Election, 1989 (Vol I, II) - General Election Archive (1951–2004) – ECI. Accessed 21 May 2021, https://old.eci.gov.in/files/file/4120-general-election-1989-vol-i-ii/, 1: 123.

63 *Murasoli*, 1 December 1989, 1.

64 Mukerji, *Disruptor*, 317.

65 I.K. Gujral, *Matters of Discretion: An Autobiography*, (New Delhi, Hay House Publishers, 2017), 257.

66 Karunanidhi, *Nenjuku Needhi*, 4: 20.

67 Ibid., 109, 113.

68 T. Ramakrishnan, 'V.P. Singh's special connect with Tamil Nadu and Dravidian rule,' *The Hindu*, 24 November 2023, 4.

69 Ibid., 5: 824.

70 India, *Parliamentary Debates*, House of the People, Re. Alleged remarks made by Prime Minister about functioning of Tamil Nadu government, 11 January 1991, col. 8. Accessed 1 June 2019, https://eparlib.nic.in/bitstream/123456789/811653/1/09_VI_11-01-1991_p8_p20_PII.pdf.

71 https://sangam.org/sri-lanka-the-untold-story-chapter-42/, J.N. Dixit, 'The intelligence agencies said, Don't worry about the LTTE, they are our boys, they will not fight us,' *Rediff.com*, 24 March 2000. Accessed 1 July 2020, https://in.rediff.com/news/2000/mar/24lanka.htm/.

72 'Karunanidhi: is the Tamil Nadu Chief Minister becoming the LTTE's elder statesman?,' 17 April 1990, US consul general cable. Accessed 1 July 2019, https://wikileaks.org/plusd/cables/90MADRAS1249_a.html.

73 *Murasoli*, 12 December 1989, 1, 7.

74 *Murasoli*, 18 November 1997, 8.

75 *Murasoli*, 16 December 1989, 1; *Murasoli*, 17 December 1989, 1.

76 Adele Balasingham, *The Will to Freedom*, 252–53.

77 *Murasoli*, 21 December 1989, 2 *Murasoli*, 22 December 1989, 1, 7.

78 *Murasoli*, 5 January 1990, 2.

79 K.T. Rajasingham, 'Sri Lanka: The Untold Story, Chapter 42.' Accessed 1 July 2020, https://sangam.org/sri-lanka-the-untold-story-chapter-42/.

80 *Murasoli*, 12 February 1990, 1.

81 'Karunanidhi: is the Tamil Nadu Chief Minister becoming the LTTE's elder statesman?', supra note 72.

82 Ibid.

83 'Jain has just paraphrased the Congress affidavit,' *Frontline*, 29 November 1997. Accessed 1 March 2022, https://frontline.thehindu.com/other/article30160456.ece.

84 *Murasoli*, 31 March 1990, 1, 7; *Murasoli*, 3 April 1990, 8.

85 'Karunanidhi: is the Tamil Nadu Chief Minister becoming the LTTE's elder statesman?', supra note 72.

86 *Murasoli*, 21 April 1990, 1.

87 *Murasoli*, 9 May 1990, 1, 8.

88 T.S. Subramanian, 'Politics of allegations,' *Frontline*, 26 May–8 June 1990, 27–28.

89 Karunanidhi, *Nenjuku Needhi*, 4: 206–12; T.S. Subramanian, 'He stood by me,' *Frontline*, 12 February 2010. Accessed 1 January 2020, https://frontline.thehindu.com/other/article30179252.ece.

90 India, *Parliamentary Debates*, House of the People, Mandal Commission report, 6 September 1990, cols. 483–555. Accessed 1 January 2020, https://eparlib.nic.in/bitstream/123456789/813040/1/09_III_06-09-1990_p237_p283_PII.pdf.

91 M. Rahman, 'Devi Lal is just a politician with a different ideology: Pritish Nandy,' *India Today*, 31 August 1990. Accessed 1 May 2019, https://www.indiatoday.in/magazine/interview/story/19900831-devi-lal-is-just-a-politician-with-a-different-ideology-pritish-nandy-812933-1990-08-30.

92 India, *Parliamentary Debates*, House of the People, Statement by prime minister on Mandal Commission Report, 7 August 1990, cols. 560–62. Accessed 1 January 2020, https://eparlib.nic.in/bitstream/123456789/813002/1/09_III_07-08-1990_p301_p302_PII.pdf.

93 Gujral, *Matters*, 297.

94 B.D. Dua, 'The Prime Minister and the Federal System', in James Manor (ed.), *Nehru to the Nineties: The Changing Office of the Prime Minister of India*, (London: Hurst & Company, 1994), 41.

95 *Murasoli*, 28 October 1991, 1.

Chapter 20: Twice Bitten

1 Cho Ramaswamy, *Adhirshtam*, 420.

2 India, *Parliamentary Debates*, The House of the People, 7 November 1990, col. 127. Accessed 7 November 2020, https://eparlib.nic.in/bitstream/123456789/800832/1/CM_09_04_07-11-1990.pdf, *Murasoli*, 9 November 1990, 8.

3 *Murasoli*, 9 November 1990, 1.

4 Prabhu Chawla, 'Exclusive! Jain Commission Revelations: Damning the DMK,' *India Today*, March 1996. Accessed 1 June 2021, http://media1.intoday.in/indiatoday/images/JainCommissionReport.pdf.

5   *Murasoli*, 17 November 1990, 1, 8.

6   India, *Parliamentary Debates*, The House of the People, Motion of confidence in the council of ministers, 16 November 1990, 149. Accessed 1 June 2020, https://eparlib.nic.in/bitstream/123456789/800831/1/CM_09_05_16-11-1990.pdf.

7   'I am prepared to face any probe, says Jayalalitha,' *The Hindu*, 3 July 1996, 15.

8   V. Jayanth, 'A sticky wicket in Tamil Nadu,' *Frontline*, 8–21 December 1990, 34–35.

9   Karunanidhi, *Nenjuku Needhi*, 4: 320.

10   *Murasoli*, 4 January 1991, 3.

11   *Murasoli*, 7 January 1991, 5.

12   India, *Parliamentary Debates*, The House of the People, Re. Reported nexus between Tamil Nadu, LTTE and deteriorating law and order situation in Tamil Nadu, 10 January 1991, cols. 572, 76, 80–81. Accessed 27 June 2020, https://eparlib.nic.in/bitstream/123456789/811002/1/09_VI_10011991_p291_p306_PII.pdf.

13   Ibid., cols. 587–89; 91.

14   Barbara Crosette, 'New Delhi Ousts Government of a Big State,' *New York Times*, 4 February 1991, A 5.

15   India, *Parliamentary Debates*, Council of the States, Reference to the prime minister's remarks on situation in Tamil Nadu, 11 January 1991, col. 8. Accessed 21 January 2020, https://rsdebate.nic.in/bitstream/123456789/243894/1/PD_156_11011991_10_p4_p16_8.pdf Cols; B. Muralidhar Reddy, 'A close call,' *Frontline*, 2–15 February 1991, 29–30; T.S. Subramanian, 'A blow to federalism,'—interview with Karunanidhi,' *Frontline*, 16 February–1 March 1991, 114–18.

16   *Murasoli*, 26 January 1991, 1–2.

17   *Murasoli*, 19 January 1991, 1–2.

18   *Murasoli*, 22 January 1991, 6.

19   Karunandihi, *Kadithangal*, 19: 172–73.

20   Delhi Sampath, *Delhiyil DMK., Anna, Kalaignar: En Parvaiyil*, (Chennai, Uyirmai Pathippagam, 2009), 216–19.

21   Karunanidhi, *Kadithangal*, 19: 236–37; T.S. Subramanian, 'A blow to federalism,' supra note 15.

22   *Murasoli*, 2 February 1991, 1.

23   T.S. Subramanian, 'A blow to federalism,' supra note 15.

24   India, *Parliamentary Debates*, The House of the People, Motion to approve the presidential proclamation on direct rule in relation to the

State of Tamil Nadu, 25 February 1991, col. 526. https://eparlib.nic. in/bitstream/123456789/811173/1/09_VII_25021991_p255_p270_PII. pdf.

25 Misra, *Flying*, 170.

26 Ibid., 171.

27 'Goebbelsian propaganda-Kafkaesque trial,' *Frontline*, 16 February–1 March 1991, 118–19.

28 'Supra note 15, 'A blow to federalism'—interview with Karunanidhi.

29 The House of the People, Motion to approve the presidential proclamation on direct rule concerning the State of Tamil Nadu, 25 February 1991, cols. 506–07, 512, 530.

30 *Murasoli*, 28 February 1991, 1.

31 *Murasoli*, 19 March 1991, 1.

32 Karunanidhi, *Kadithangal*, 19: 397–400.

33 V. Suresh, 'The DMK Debacle-Causes and Portents,' *EPW*, 27, No. 42, (17 October, 1992), 2313–321.

34 S.V. Rajadurai, 'Letters to Editor', *Indian Express*, 14 May 1991 and V. Suresh and D. Nagasaila, 'Stooping Very Low', the *Independent*, Bombay, 15 June 1991.

35 *Aside*, the Magazine of Madras, 15 March 1991, 3.

36 R. Rajaram, K. Nagaraj, 'A good beginning: on the campaign trail with M. Karunanidhi,' *Frontline*, 25 May–7 June 1991, 114–16.

37 *Murasoli*, 2 May 1991, 1.

38 *Murasoli*, 12 May 1991, 1.

39 'Does Sonia want to save the DMK and the TMC?'—the Rediff Political Interview/Vazhappadi Ramamurthy, 28 January 1998. Accessed 1 June 2020, https://www.rediff.com/news/1998/jan/28vkr.htm.

40 'The shock wave: the nation's response to the tragedy,' *Frontline*, 8–21 June 1991, 28.

41 *Murasoli*, 26 May 1991, 4.

42 K. Nagaraj, 'DMK Swamped by sympathy wave,' *Frontline*, 22 June–5 July 1991, 121–23; R. Manivannan, '1991 Tamil Nadu Elections,' *EPW* 27, No. 4 (25 January 1992), 164–70.

43 T.S. Subramanian, 'Tamil Nadu jousting,' *Frontline*, 11 September 1992, 32; R. Muthukumar, *Thamizhaga Arasiyal Varalaaru*, (Chennai: New Horizon Media Pvt Ltd, 2013), 2: 284.

44 Ibid., 2: 84–85.

45 *Murasoli*, 23 June 1991, 1; 'I'm ready to meet any harassment'—interview with M. Karunanidhi.

46 *Tamil Nadu Legislative Assembly (Tenth Assembly) Review 1991–96*, (Chennai: Legislative Assembly Department, 1996), 16, 18. Accessed 1 June 2010, https://assembly.tn.gov.in/archive/10th_1991/10threview_91_96.pdf.

47 N. Kalyanasundaram, 'The fallout: resentment in Tamil Nadu,' *Frontline*, 17–30 August 1991, 19–21.

48 S. Guhan, 'The Cauvery dispute: what next?' *Frontline*, 13 August 1993, 16.

49 *Murasoli*, 20 November 1991, 1.

50 *Murasoli*, 10 January 1992, 1, 3.

51 'Mahamaham Stampede Deaths in Tamil Nadu,' *EPW*, 27, No. 13, 28 March, 1992, 625–27; *Murasoli*, 20 February 1992, 1; 'An avoidable tragedy,' *The Hindu*, 17 July 2015. Accessed 1 June 2020, https://www.thehindu.com/opinion/editorial/An-avoidable-tragedy/article59782840.ece; Prakash M. Swamy, 'Mahamaham celebrations: Official callousness causes killer stampede in Kumbakonam,' *India Today*, 15 March 1992. Accessed 1 June 2020, https://www.indiatoday.in/magazine/indiascope/story/19920315-mahamaham-celebrations-official-callousness-causes-killer-stampede-in-kumbakonam-765991-2013-06-21.

52 India, *Parliamentary Debates*, Council of States, Statement Re: Declaration [RAJYA SABHA] of L.T.T.E. as unlawful association, 14 May 1992, cols. 475–92. Accessed 1 June 2020, https://rsdebate.nic.in/bitstream/123456789/225841/1/PD_163_14051992_13_p463_p493_18.pdf.

53 *Murasoli*, 15 May 1992, 1.

54 T.S. Subramanian, 'Terror tactics: AIADMK response to Subramanian Swamy,' *Frontline*, 16 January 1993, 26–27.

55 *Murasoli*, 15 August 1992, 1.

56 *Murasoli*, 17 September 1992, 1–5.

57 Dr Subramanian Swamy vs J. Jayalalitha And Ors. on 15 November, 1993, (1994) 1 MLJ 314; T.S. Subramanian, 'Target Jayalalitha: Subramanian Swamy's campaign,' *Frontline*, 6 November 1992, 34–36.

58 'Terror tactics: AIADMK response to Subramanian Swamy.'

59 T.S. Subramanian, 'Failure on many fronts,' *Frontline*, 18 June 1993, 6.

60 John F. Burns, 'For Indian Politicians, An Opulent Wedding Means Political Bliss,' *New York Times*, 10 September 1995, Section 1, 8.

61 T.S. Subramanian, 'L'affaire Nagarajan,' *Frontline*, 20 December 1991, 115–16.

62 'The leaked report does not feature my testimony before the Jain panel, but before another court'—the Rediff Interview/R. Nagarajan,' Rediff.

com, 17 November 1997. Accessed 1 June 2020, https://www.rediff. com/news/nov/17naga.htm.

63 *Dinamani*, 24 November 1992, cited in Karunanidhi, *Nenjuku Needhi*, 4: 455.

64 Karunanidhi, *Nenjuku Needhi*, 4: 459.

65 Ibid., 465; G.C. Shekar, 'Congress's Sudden Love For Ram Catches DMK Off Guard In Tamil Nadu,' *Outlook*, 5 August 2020. Accessed 1 June 2021, https://www.outlookindia.com/website/story/india-news-congresss-sudden-love-for-ram-catches-dmk-off-guard-in-tamil-nadu/358014.

66 T.S. Subramanian, Asha Krishnakumar, 'Burning the bridges,' *Frontline*, 23 April 1993, 114–15.

67 *Murasoli Pudhayal*, 14 March 1993, 2–3.

68 Girish Nikam, 'Jayalalitha announces withdrawal of AIADMK support to Congress(I),' *India Today*, 31 March 1993. Accessed 1 June 2020, https://www.indiatoday.in/magazine/special-report/story/19930331-jayalalitha-announces-withdrawal-of-aiadmk-support-to-congressi-810880-1993-03-30.

69 Madras City Wine Merchants . . . vs State Of Tamil Nadu And Anr. on 27 July 1994. Accessed 1 January 2020, https://indiankanoon.org/doc/141187345/.

70 S. Rai, P.M. Swamy, 'Jayalalitha exploits Tamil insecurity,' *India Today*, 15 August 1993. Accessed 22 June 2020, https://www.indiatoday.in/magazine/indiascope/story/19930815-jayalalitha-exploits-tamil-insecurity-811413-1993-08-14.

71 *Murasoli*, 22 July 1993, 1.

72 S. Rai, P.M. Swamy, 'Jayalalitha exploits Tamil insecurity,' supra note 71.

73 T.S. Subramanian, 'The southern test: by-elections unnerve the ruling party,' *Frontline*, 7 May 1993, 20–21.

74 T.S. Subramanian, S.V. Balasubramanian, 'Double victory: The AIADMK proves a point,' *Frontline*, 22 October 1993, 42–44; T.S. Subramanian and S. Viswnathan, 'DMK is still strong'—interview with Karunanidhi,' *Frontline*, 14 January 1994, 31.

Chapter 21: Fourth Split

1 *Murasoli*, 26 March 1993, 1.

2 *Murasoli*, 27 March 1993, 3–4.

3 R. Muthukumar, *Thamizhaga*, 2: 302.

4   T.S. Subramanian, 'Tussles for power: Tamil Nadu's troubled political scene,' *Frontline*, 2 July 1993, 30.

5   *Murasoli*, 5 April 1993, 2.

6   *Murasoli*, 2 April 1993, 5.

7   *Murasoli*, 29 March 1993, 5.

8   *Murasoli*, 29 March 1993, 1, 6; *Murasoli*, 30 March 1993, 2.

9   *Murasoli*, 8 June 1993, 2.

10   *Murasoli*, 7 June 1993, 2, 6.

11   *Murasoli*, 10 June 1993, 5.

12   *Murasoli*, 18 June 1993, 5.

13   *Murasoli*, 24 June 1993, 6.

14   T.S. Subramanian, 'Tamil Nadu tantrums as Jayalalitha sits pretty,' *Frontline*, 30 July 1993, 100–02.

15   Ibid., K. Thirunavukarasu, *Thi.Mu.Ka.: Prachanaygalum Pilavugalum Marumalarchiyai Noaki* . . . (Chennai: Nakkeeran Pathippagam, 2022), 58–63.

16   *Murasoli*, 25 June 1993, 1.

17   *Murasoli*, 27 June 1993, 2.

18   *Murasoli*, 28 June 1993, 1.

19   *Murasoli*, 4 July 1993, 1.

20   *Murasoli*, 18 July 1993, 5.

21   T.S. Subramanian, 'Tamil Nadu tantrums as Jayalalitha sits pretty,' supra note 14.

22   *Murasoli*, 17 July 1993, 3.

23   *Murasoli*, 4 October 1993, 1.

24   *Murasoli*, 6 October 1993, 1.

25   *Murasoli*, 7 October 1993, 5.

26   *Murasoli*, 7 October 1993, 1.

27   Ibid.

28   *Murasoli*, 8 October 1993, 1.

29   Ibid.

30   *Murasoli*, 9 October 1993, 1; Kalaipuli S. Dhanu, 'Unmaigal Solven,' *Vikatan*, 23 December 2020. Accessed 1 January 2020, https://www.vikatan.com/news/general-news/series-by-kalaippuli-s-thanu-8.

31   *Murasoli*, 10 October 1993, 1, 6.

32   *Murasoli*, 13 October 1993, 1.

33   *Murasoli*, 16 October 1993, 1

34   *Murasoli*, 14 October 1993, 1

35   *Murasoli*, 17 October 1993, 1.

36   *Murasoli*, 20 October 1993, 1.

37   *Murasoli*, 23 October 1993, 1.

38   Muthukumar, *Thamizaga*, 2: 307–08.

39   *Murasoli*, 22 October 1993, 1.

40   *Murasoli*, 26 October 1993, 1.

41   Muthukumar, *Thamizaga*, 2: 309.

42   *Murasoli*, 27 October 1993, 1, 4.

43   *Murasoli*, 31 October 1993, 1.

44   *Murasoli*, 2 November 1993, 1, 4.

45   *Murasoli*, 1 November 1993, 1.

46   Murasoli, 3 November 1993, 5.

47   *Murasoli*, 7 November 1993, 8.

48   Karunandihi, *Kadithangal*, 42: 201.

49   Thirunavukarasu, *Thi.Mu.Ka.*, 48–52.

50   T.S. Subramanian, 'Leadership games in the DMK,' *Frontline*, 5 November 1993, 30–31.

51   *Murasoli*, 12 November 1993, 4–5.

52   *Murasoli*, 26 November 1993, 1–3.

53   *Murasoli*, 2 December 1993, 1.

54   *Murasoli*, 4 December 1993, 1

55   K. Anbazhagan vs M. Kannappan And 10 Ors. on 26 April, 1994, 1997 (2) CTC 47.

56   *Murasoli*, 30 December 1993, 3 wonder-5.

57   Supra note 51.

58   Karunanidhi, *Nenjuku Needhi*, 4: 500–05.

59   T.S. Subramanian, 'An upbeat meet: MDMK outlines ideology, identifies allies,' *Frontline*, 28 July 1995, 42–45.

Chapter 22: Veshti-Clad Tamils

1   Chakra, 'Naan "samooga needhi kaatha veeranganai aanadhu eppadi?" – J. Vilakam,' 23 July 2010. Accessed 1 May 2019, https://tamil.oneindia.com/news/2010/07/23/protected-69-reservation-tn-jayalalithaa.html?story=3.

2   T.S. Subramanian, 'Reservation ruckus: Tamil Nadu government in a fix,' *Frontline*, 15 July 1994, 32–34.

3   Ibid.

4   *Murasoli*, 24 January 1994, 3.

5   *Murasoli*, 20 June 1994, 1.

6 Ibid., A. Subramani, 'All accused in lawyer attack acquitted,' *Times of India*, 24 August 2012. Accessed 1 July 2019, https://timesofindia. indiatimes.com/city/chennai/all-accused-in-lawyer-attack-acquitted/ articleshow/15624970.cms.

7 'Supreme Court to examine plea against T.N.'s 69% quota in colleges, govt. jobs,' *The Hindu*, 2 February 2021. Accessed 1 July 2022, https://www. thehindu.com/news/national/tamil-nadu/supreme-court-to-examine- plea-against-tns-69-quota-in-colleges-govt-jobs/article33727741.ece.

8 *Murasoli*, 4 September 1994, 7.

9 *Murasoli*, 10 September 1994, 8.

10 T.N. Seshan, Chief Election . . . vs Dr M. Karunanidhi, President Of . . . on 22 August 1995, 1995 (3) ALT 108.

11 'During His Stint As EC, Seshan Faced The Wrath Of Dravidian Parties For Insinuating That Annadurai Was A CIA Asset,' *Swarajya*, 11 November 2019. Accessed 1 July 2020, https://swarajyamag.com/news- brief/during-his-stint-as-ec-seshan-faced-the-wrath-of-dravidian- parties-for-insinuating-that-annadurai-was-a-cia-asset.

12 T.S. Subramanian, 'Jayalalithaa's Legacy,' *Frontline*, 6 January 2017, 13.

13 Dr J. Jayalalitha vs Dr M. Channa Reddy, Governor of Tamil Nadu on 27 April 1995, (1995) 2 MLJ 187.

14 John F. Burns, 'For Indian Politicians, An Opulent Wedding Means Political Bliss,' *New York Times*, 10 September 1995, 1: 8.

15 T.S. Subramanian, 'Jayalalithaa's Legacy,' supra note 12.

16 *Tamil Nadu Legislative Assembly (Tenth Assembly) Review*, 1991–96, 58.

17 Karunanidhi, *Kadithangal*, 31: 332–34.

18 T.S. Subramanian, 'The Tansi turn,' *Frontline*, 8 November 2002, 36.

19 T.S. Subramanian, 'Lifer for attack on lawyer,' *Frontline*, 29 November 1997. Accessed 1 July 2020, https://frontline.thehindu.com/other/ article30160466.ece.

20 John F. Burns, 'For Indian Politicians, An Opulent Wedding Means Political Bliss,' supra note 14.

21 R. Muthukumar, *Thamizhaga*, 338–39; T.S. Subramanian, 'Bomb culture: AIADMK's new gift to Tamil Nadu,' *Frontline*, 11 August 1995, 29–30.

22 Nandini Ramnath, 'A war for love: Mani Ratnam's "Bombay" explored an inter-faith marriage battered by bigotry,' *Scroll*, 1 December 2020. Accessed 1 September 2021, https://scroll.in/reel/979821/a-war-for- love-mani-ratnams-bombay-explored-an-inter-faith-marriage-battered- by-bigotry; S.A.M. Barakath Ali, 'R.M. Veerappanin padhaviyai paratha Rajiniyin pechu! Ivar vazhi . . . thani vazhia? Rajiniyin arasiyal route:

pagudhi 7,' *Vikatan*, 27 July 2017. Accessed 1 July 2018, https://www.vikatan.com/government-and-politics/politics/96903-rajini-speech-gives-trouble-to-rm-veerappan-rajinis-route-to-politics-part-7.

23 *Murasoli*, 5 September 1995, 1, 3.

24 Tha. Kathiravan, Ka. Balaji, '"MGRai paaratinaa mattum thaan pidikuma?" veditha Jayalalithaa,' *Vikatan*, 23 September 2019. Accessed 1 September 2020, https://www.vikatan.com/news/politics/exclusive-interview-with-r-m-veerappan.

25 *Murasoli*, 28 September 1995, 3.

26 *Murasoli*, 6 March 1996, 1.

27 *Murasoli*, 14 January 1994, 3.

28 S.A.M. Barakath Ali, '"Jayalalithaa amarndhirundha medaiyil Rjainiyin aavesa pechu"– ivar vazhi . . . thani vazhiya?! Rajiniyin arasiyal route – paguthi 5,' *Vikatan*, 29 June 2017. Accessed 1 June 2018, https://www.vikatan.com/government-and-politics/politics/93717-rajini-anger-speech-in-jayalalithaa-s-stage-rajinis-route-to-politics-part-5.

29 S.A.M. Barakath Ali, 'Viral soduki Jayalalithaavai vimarsitha Rajini! – ivar vazhi . . . thani vazhiya?! Rajiniyin arasiyal route – paguthi 4,' *Vikatan*, 16 June 2017. Accessed 1 June 2018, https://www.vikatan.com/oddities/miscellaneous/92569-jayalalithaa-versus-rajini-rajinis-route-to-politics-part-4.

30 *Murasoli*, 22 July 1995, 1.

31 *Murasoli*, 25 December 1995, 5.

32 *Murasoli*, 20 February 1996, 1.

33 *Murasoli*, 30 January 1996, 4, 6.

34 *Murasoli*, 6 March 1996, 1.

35 Karunanidhi, *Nenjuku Needhi*, 4: 600.

36 *Murasoli*, 29 March 1996, 1.

37 John F. Burns, 'Political Pact With Ex-Film Star May Bring Down India's Premier,' *New York Times*, 3 May 1996, A 1; Vinay Sitapati, *Half Lion: How P.V. Narasimha Rao Transformed India*, (Gurgaon, Penguin Viking, 2015), 210.

38 'G.K. Vasan and TMC's history,' *The Hindu*, 3 November 2014. Accessed 1 November 2019, https://www.thehindu.com/news/resources/G.K.-Vasan-and-TMCs-history/article11004013.ece.

39 *Murasoli*, 2 April 1996, 7.

40 *Murasoli*, 2 April 1996, 1.

41 *Murasoli*, 23 April 1996, 1–2.

42 Ibid.

43 'Rajinikanth Regrets Backing DMK 1996, Hints At Joining Politics,' *Outlook*, 15 May 2017. Accessed 1 May 2018, https://www.outlookindia. com/website/story/rajinikanth-regrets-backing-dmk-1996-hints-at-joining-politics/298907.

44 Pradeep Kumar, 'Jayalalithaa lost 1996 election because of me, Rajinikanth says,' *Times of India*, 11 December 2016. Accessed 1 December 2018, https://timesofindia.indiatimes.com/city/chennai/jayalalithaa-lost-1996-election-because-of-me-rajinikanth-says/articleshow/55926960.cms.

45 *Murasoli*, 18 March 1996, 1, 6.

46 *Murasoli*, 1 April 1996, 5.

47 *Murasoli*, 3 April 1996, 1.

48 *Murasoli*, 8 April 1996, 6.

49 *Murasoli*, 3 April 1996, 1.

50 G.C. Shekhar, 'Elections 1996: Jayalalitha feels the heat as Karunanidhi goes all out in his bid for power,' *India Today*, 15 May 1996. Accessed 15 May 2020, https://www.indiatoday.in/magazine/cover-story/story/19960515-elections-1996-jayalalitha-feels-the-heat-as-karunanidhi-goes-all-out-in-his-bid-for-power-833177-1996-05-15.

51 Ibid.

52 *Murasoli*, 11 April 1996, 6.

53 *Murasoli*, 18 April 1996, 3.

54 *Murasoli*, 19 April 1996, 1.

55 'The Dravidian movement has got infected with Brahminism of the backward community'—The Rediff Interview/Dr K. Krishnaswamy, *Rediff*, 10 November 1998. Accessed 1 November 2019, https://www.rediff.com/news/1998/nov/10krish1.htm.

56 P. Sudhakar, 'An arid region with potential that is yet to be tapped,' *The Hindu*, 31 March 2021. Accessed 1 March 2022, https://www.thehindu.com/news/cities/Madurai/an-arid-region-with-potential-that-is-yet-to-be-tapped/article34208441.ece.

57 *Murasoli*, 9 May 1996, 1, 4.

58 T.S. Subramanian, S. Viswanathan, 'A powerful verdict: The sun sets on the AIADMK Government,' *Frontline*, 31 May 1996, 27.

59 Nirupama Subramanian, G.C. Shekhar, 'Elections 1996: AIADMK citadel crumbles as DMK-TMC alliance sweeps to power in Tamil Nadu,' *India Today*, 31 May 1996, Accessed 1 June 2019, https://www.indiatoday.in/magazine/cover-story/story/19960531-elections-1996-aiadmk-citadel-crumbles-as-dmk-tmc-alliance-sweeps-to-power-in-tamil-nadu-832999-1996-05-30.

60   *Murasoli*, 17 May 1996, 2.

61   'Karunanidhi doesn't have a good track record'—The Rediff Interview/ V.S. Chandralekha,' *Rediff*, 5 October 1996. Accessed 1 November 2020, https://m.rediff.com/news/1996/0510lek1.htm.

62   Nirupama Subramanian, G.C. Shekhar, 'Elections 1996: AIADMK citadel crumbles as DMK-TMC alliance sweeps to power in Tamil Nadu,' *India Today*, 31 May 1996. Accessed 1 June 2023, https://www. indiatoday.in/magazine/cover-story/story/19960531-elections-1996- aiadmk-citadel-crumbles-as-dmk-tmc-alliance-sweeps-to-power-in- tamil-nadu-832999-1996-05-30.

63   *Murasoli*, 25 May 1996, 1.

64   Sukumar Muralidharan, 'The fall,' *Frontline*, 14 June 1996, 3.

65   *Murasoli*, 14 May 1996, 3.

66   Karunanidhi, *Nenjuku Needhi*, 5: 27.

Chapter 23: 1996–2001: Momentous Years

1   *Murasoli*, 11 December 1996, 1.

2   *Murasoli*, 21 May 1996, 1.

3   See, Yogendra Yadav, 'Electoral Politics in the Time of Change: India's Third Electoral System, 1989–99', *EPW*, 21–28 August 1999, 2393–399.

4   *Murasoli*, 11 May 1996, 1.

5   *Murasoli*, 15 May 1996, 3; *Murasoli*, 20 May 1996, 3, 6.

6   L.K. Advani, *My Country My Life*, (New Delhi, Rupa Publications, 2010), 482.

7   Ibid.,

8   *Murasoli*, 14 May 1996, 3.

9   *Murasoli*, 19 May 1996, 6.

10   *Murasoli*, 20 May 1996, 6.

11   India, *Parliamentary Debates*, The House of the People, Murasoli Maran's speech, 27 May 1996, col. 95. Accessed 1 July 2018, https://eparlib.nic. in/bitstream/123456789/6036/1/11_I_27051996_p19_p53_t20.pdf.

12   *Murasoli*, 2 June 1996, 1.

13   Aditya Iyer, 'Setback for AIADMK chief Sasikala as 20-year-old case returns to haunt her,' *Hindustan Times*, 14 February 2017. Accessed 1 June 2018, https://www.hindustantimes.com/india-news/setback-for- aiadmk-chief-sasikala-as-20-year-old-case-returns-to-haunt-her/story- SJAJLQPPxKghiNpGE4neON.html.

14   *Murasoli*, 29 August 1996, 2; *Murasoli*, 2 September 1996, 5.

15 'I am prepared to face any probe, says Jayalalitha,' *The Hindu*, 3 July 1996, 15.

16 Lakshmi Subramaniam, 'My life with Jayalalithaa: V.K. Sasikala,' the *Week*, 18 July 2021. Accessed 1 July 2022, https://www.theweek.in/theweek/cover/2021/07/08/my-life-with-jayalalithaa-v-k-sasikala.html.

17 *Murasoli*, 16 September 1996, 3; *Murasoli*, 29 August 1996, 2; *Murasoli*, 2 September 1996, 5; T.S. Subramanian, 'War of statements,' *Frontline*, 23 August 1996, 40; T.S. Subramanian, 'Falling apart,' *Frontline*, 20 September 1996, 35, 37.

18 G.C. Shekhar, Amarnath Menon, 'Jayalalitha's arrest blows the lid off systematic loot of public money during her tenure,' *India Today*, 31 December 1996. Accessed 1 February 2019, https://www.indiatoday.in/magazine/cover-story/story/19961231-jayalalitha-arrest-reveals-systematic-loot-of-public-money-puts-political-future-at-risk-834258-1999-11-29.

19 *Murasoli*, 30 September 1996, 1, 5.

20 *Murasoli*, 24 May 1996, 3.

21 *Murasoli*, 15 September 1996, 1.

22 *Murasoli*, 17 September 1996, 7.

23 *Murasoli*, 25 September 1996, 2.

24 T.S. Subramanian, 'A threat in Chennai,' *Frontline*, 17 July 1998, 14–16.

25 *Murasoli*, 7 December 1996, 1, 3.

26 T.S. Subramanian, 'The law catches up with Jayalalitha,' *Frontline*, 27 December 1996, 10.

27 Suresh Nampath, 'We will not be cowed down: Jayalalitha,', 25 December 1996, 1; Suresh Nampath, 'Total loyalty: The cement that held AIADMK,' *The Hindu*, 2 October 2016. Accessed 1 May 2020, https://www.thehindu.com/news/national/tamil-nadu/In-her-they-trust-Jayalalithaa-built-the-party-on-loyalty/article60644119.ece.

28 Suresh Nampath, 'On verge of quitting politics, she bounced back stronger,' *The Hindu*, 6 December 2016. Accessed 1 May 2020, https://www.thehindu.com/news/national/tamil-nadu/On-verge-of-quitting-politics-she-bounced-back-stronger/article16761190.ece1.

29 *Murasoli*, 12 December 1996, 4.

30 India, *Parliamentary Debates*, Council of States, (Discussion on Jayalalithaa's arrest), col 275. Accessed 1 June 2020, https://eparlib.nic.in/bitstream/123456789/7129/1/11_III_09121996_p146_p161_t260.pdf.

31 *Murasoli*, 14 December 1996, 1.

32   Vaasanthi, 'Sonia Gandhi's turn to experience Jayalalitha after AIADMK chief squanders Vajpayee,' *India Today*, 12 April 1999. Accessed 1 May 2020, https://www.indiatoday.in/magazine/nation/story/19990412-sonia-gandhis-turn-to-experience-jayalalitha-after-aiadmk-chief-squanders-vajpayee-780631-1999-04-11; *Murasoli*, 8 December 1996, 1.

33   T.S. Subramanian, 'No respite,' *Frontline*, 26 December 1997, 41.

34   T.S Subramanian, 'Kannappan's turn,' *Frontline*, 10 January 1997, 31; T.S. Subramanian, 'Legal jolt,' *Frontline*, 17 October 2014, 11.

35   *Murasoli*, 14 February 1997, 1–2; T.S. Subramanian, 'DMK wins Pudukottai,' *Frontline*, 7 March 1997, 36.

36   Gujral, *Matters*, 383.

37   Advani, *My Country*, 483.

38   *Murasoli*, 17 December 1996, 3, 8; *Murasoli*, 28 December 1996, 1, 8.

39   Gujral, *Matters*, 386–87.

40   Ibid., 393.

41   *Murasoli*, 21 April 1997, 1,8.

42   V. Ramanathan, *Manbumigu Ulavuthurai* (Chennai: Tamil Puthagalayam, 2004), 167.

43   *Murasoli*, 22 April 1997, 1.

44   *Murasoli*, 22 April 1997, 1–2.

45   *Murasoli*, 2 May 1997, 3–4.

46   *Frontline*, 16 May 1997, 10.

47   *Murasoli*, 28 April 1997, 1, 8.

48   Venkitesh Ramakrishnan, Praveen Swami, N. Ram, 'The Making of the Prime Minister,' *Frontline*, 16 May 1997, 10, 15.

49   *Murasoli*, 29 April 1997, 2.

50   Venkitesh Ramakrishnan et al., 'The Making of the Prime Minister,' supra note 48, 34.

51   Janardan Thakur, *Prime Ministers: Nehru to Vajpayee*, (New Delhi, BPI India, 2002), 389; Karunanidhi, *Nenjuku Needhi*, 5: 367–77.

52   T.S. Subramanian, 'Divided ranks: the split in the AIADMK,' *Frontline*, 27 June 1997, 110–12.

53   Karunanidhi, *Nenjuku Needhi*, 5: 458–65; T.S. Subramanian, 'Low on content: DMK conference: in Salem,' *Frontline*, 25 July 1997, 108–11.

54   *Murasoli*, 2 July 1997, 2.

55   'Jain panel interim report indicts Karunanidhi, VP Singh, Chandra Shekhar,' *Rediff*, 8 November 1999. Accessed 1 May 2020, https://www.rediff.com/news/nov/08jain.htm.

56   https://eparlib.nic.in/bitstream/123456789/757047/1/532.pdf

57 'Tragi-comedy,' *Frontline*, 12 December 1997, 10–12.

58 Ibid., 14–17, 22–23.

59 India, *Parliamentary Debates*, The House of the People, 5 August 1998, (Motion for consideration of the final report of Jain Commission and Memorandum of Action Taken on the Report (Not Concluded). Accessed 1 June 2020, https://eparlib.nic.in/bitstream/123456789/757047/1/532. pdf.

60 Charu Lata Joshi, 'Jain panel report suggests deliberate attempt to tamper with Rajiv assassination evidence,' *India Today*, 28 February 1997. Accessed 1 June 2020, https://www.indiatoday.in/magazine/ nation/story/19970228-jain-panel-report-suggests-deliberate-attempt- to-tamper-with-rajiv-assassination-evidence-830192-1997-02-27.

61 Prabhu Chawla, 'Exclusive! Jain Commission Revelations: Damning the DMK.' *India Today*, March 1996, on file, *Murasoli*, 20 November 1997, 1.

62 Prabhu Chawla, 'Jain report not only scripted history but defined the future too,' *India Today*, 26 December 2005. Accessed 1 June 2020, https://www.indiatoday.in/magazine/cover-story/story/20051226- jain-report-not-only-scripted-history-but-defined-the-future- too-786408-2005-12-25.

63 *Murasoli*, 21 November 1997, 1.

64 *Murasoli*, 18 April 1998, 3.

65 Praveen Swami, Venkitesh Ramakrishnan, 'The politics of blackmail,' *Frontline*, 12 December 1997, 4–11.

66 R.S. Ramakrishnan and N. Ram, 'Karunanidhi hits back,' *Frontline*, 12 December 1997, 14–17.

67 Gujral, *Matters*, 444–53.

68 Karunanidhi, *Nenjuku Needhi*, 5: 573–74.

69 Ibid., 600.

70 *Murasoli*, 8 April 1998, 5; *Murasoli*, 17 April 1998, 8; *Murasoli*, 18 April 1998, 3.

71 *Murasoli*, 8 March 1998, 1.

72 *Murasoli*, 16 February 1998, 1; T.S. Subramanian, 'Behind the Coimbatore tragedy,' *Frontline*, 20 March 1998, 9.

73 *Murasoli*, 18 April 1998; 8; *Murasoli*, 24 April 1998, 2.

74 T.S. Subramanian, 'Tamil Nadu,' *Frontline*, 3 April 1998, 38.

75 P. Sainath, 'Stability is an 18-headed ostrich,' *Frontline*, 28 January 1998, 10–11.

76 The Rediff Political Interview/Vazhappadi Ramamurthy. Accessed 1 May 2021, https://m.rediff.com/news/1998/jan/28vrk1.htm.

77   Sanjay Ruparelia, *Divided We Govern* (Noida, Oxford University Press, 2015), 278.

78   Karunanidhi, *Nenjuku Needhi*, 5: 590–91; Ilangovan Rajasekaran, 'Our front faced many conspiracies'—interview with Thol. Thirumavalavan,' *Frontline*, 10 June 2016, 30; *Murasoli*, 18 April 1998, 3.

79   *Murasoli*, 9 February 1998, 2.

80   N. Sathiya Moorthy, 'Jaya confident, partymen confused as AIADMK hits campaign trail,' *Rediff*, 12 February 1998. Accessed 1 June 2021, https://www.rediff.com/news/1998/feb/13tn1.htm.

81   Venkatesh Athreya, 'Of polls and predictions: the electoral outcome in Tamil Nadu,' *Frontline*, 3 April 1998, 121–23.

82   Vaasanthi, Swapan Dasgupta, 'Jayalalitha plays key role in government formation, keeps BJP leadership dangling,' *India Today*, 23 March 1998. Accessed 1 June 2021, https://www.indiatoday.in/magazine/cover-story/story/19980323-jayalalitha-plays-key-role-in-government-formation-keeps-bjp-leadership-dangling-825984-1999-11-29.

83   T.S. Subramanian, 'Tamil Nadu,' supra note 75, 37–38.

84   'Of polls and predictions: the electoral outcome in Tamil Nadu,' supra note 82.

Chapter 24: Tail Wagging the Dog

1   Vinod Mehta, 'Vajpayee the liberal conservative or one who bent with the wind,' *Livemint*, 17 August 2018. Accessed 1 May 2019, https://www.livemint.com/Politics/Ux668Uxnoe2hdFz0fbEWBL/Vajpayeethe-liberal-conservative-or-the-one-who-bent-with-t.html.

2   Vaasanthi, Swapan Dasgupta, 'Jayalalitha plays key role in government formation, keeps BJP leadership dangling.'

3   'Sonia Gandhi's turn to experience Jayalalitha after AIADMK chief squanders Vajpayee,' *India Today*, 23 March 1998. Accessed 1 March 2021, https://www.indiatoday.in/magazine/cover-story/story/19980323-jayalalitha-plays-key-role-in-government-formation-keeps-bjp-leadership-dangling-825984-1999-11-29; Karunanidhi, *Nenjuku Needhi*, 5: 608–09.

4   *Murasoli*, 11 March 1998, 1, 5.

5   V. Venkatesan, 'Pulls and pressures,' *Frontline*, 17 April 1998, 119–20.

6   N. Sathiya Moorthy, 'Allies make Jaya toe the BJP line,' 14 March 1998. Accessed 1 March 2021, https://www.rediff.com/news/1998/mar/14jaya1.htm; T.S. Subramanian, 'On tenterhooks' *Frontline*, 17 April 1998, 121–23;

Murasoli, 21 April 1998, 2; K.M. Thomas, Govindan Kutty, 'AIADMK chief Jayalalitha's pressure tactics paralyse BJP-led Government,' *India Today*, 4 May 1998. Accessed 1 June 2020, https://www.indiatoday. in/magazine/cover-story/story/19980504-aiadmk-chief-jayalalithas-pressure-tactics-paralyses-bjp-led-government-826337-1999-11-29.

7   Cho Ramaswamy, *Anubhavangalum Abiprayangalum*, (Chennai, The Alliance Publication Company, 2019), 417–29.

8   N. Sathiya Moorthy, 'Jaya sent a clear message to BJP,' *Rediff*, 23 May 1998. Accessed 1 May 2019, https://inwww.rediff.com/news/1998/may/23jaya2.htm.

9   Shakthi Sinha, *The Years That Changed India: Vajpayee*, (Gurgaon, Vintage Books, 2021), 64–65.

10 T.S. Subramanian, 'On tenterhooks,' supra note 6.

11 R. Ramakrishnan, 'An aggressive campaigner for Tamil Nadu's water rights,' 6 December 2016, *The Hindu*. Accessed 22 June 2018, https://www.thehindu.com/news/national/tamil-nadu/An-aggressive-campaigner for Tamil Nadus water rights/article16762577.ece.

12 V. Venkatesan, 'Pulls and pressures,' supra note 5.

13 Sinha, *Vajpayee*, 65.

14 'Jaya repeats demand to sack Karunanidhi,' *Rediff*, 2 April 1998. Accessed 13 May 2018, https://specials.rediff.com/news/1998/apr/02jaya.htm; *Murasoli*, 4 April 1998, 2.

15 *Murasoli*, 17 April 1998, 2.

16 *Frontline*, 26 February 1999, 13; K.M. Thomas, 'Jayalalitha suffers serious setback as BJP govt forces Muthiah out of Union Cabinet,' *India Today*, 20 April 1998. Accessed 1 November 2018, https://www.indiatoday.in/magazine/states/story/19980420-jayalalitha-suffers-serious-setback-as-bjp-govt-forces-muthiah-out-of-union-cabinet-826209-1998-04-19; https://www.indiatoday.in/magazine/cover-story/story/19980504-aiadmk-chief-jayalalithas-pressure-tactics-paralyses-bjp-led-government-826337-1999-11-29.

17 *Murasoli*, 26 April 1998, 1, 8; T.S. Subramanian, 'Dealing with Jayalalitha,' *Frontline*, 9 May 1998. Accessed 1 May 2021, https://frontline.thehindu.com/cover-story/article30161356.ece.

18 *Murasoli*, 24 April 1998, 2; 'TN government presents white paper on Coimbatore blasts,' *Rediff*, 23 April 1998. Accessed 15 August 2020, https://www.rediff.com/news/1998/apr/23white.htm.

19 *Murasoli*, 26 April 1998, 2.

20 *Murasoli*, 26 April 1998, 4.

21 *Murasoli*, 27 May 1998, 1.

22 Karunanidhi, *Nenjuku Needhi*, 5: 641–42.

23 N. Sathiya Moorthy, 'Jaya charges BJP with winning her allies and influencing the DMK,' *Rediff*, 19 June 1998. Accessed 2 February 2018, https://www.rediff.com/news/1998/jun/19jaya.htm; Karunanidhi, *Nenjuku* 5: 642–43; *Murasoli*, 9 July 1998, 1.

24 'Jaya's latest: person who "has no concern for national security" is heading home ministry,' *Rediff*, 23 June 1998. Accessed 2 February 2018, https://www.rediff.com/news/1998/jun/23jaya.htm;   V.   Venkatesan, 'Coordination challenges,' *Frontline*, 17 July 1998, 11.

25 *Murasoli*, 1 July 1998, 8; T.S. Subramanian, 'A fragile truce,' *Frontline*, 31 July 1998, 123–24; N. Sathiya Moorthy, 'Jaya blows cold, BJP gets a breather,' *Rediff*, 4 July 1998. Accessed 22 February 2019, https://www.rediff.com/news/1998/jul/04jaya.htm.

26 'Karunanidhi, Jaya and allies call on PM to notify Cauvery award,' *Rediff*, 16 July 1998. Accessed 14 February 2018, https://www.rediff.com/news/1998/jul/16kaveri.htm.

27 N. Sathiya Moorthy, 'Jaya keeps off allies' meeting,' *Rediff*, 26 June 1998. Accessed 1 June 2018, https://www.rediff.com/news/1998/jun/26jaya.htm.

28 'I don't [see myself as prime minister], but anything is possible in politics'—the Rediff Interview/J Jayalalithaa, *Rediff*, 31 March 1999. Accessed 1 May 2018, https://www.rediff.com/news/1999/mar/31jaya2.htm.

29 'Centre warned against toppling DMK govt,' the *Tribune*, 2 August 1998. Accessed 12 May 2018, www.tribuneindia.com/1998/98aug02/head.htm.

30 T.S. Subramanian, 'Fallout in Tamil Nadu,' *Frontline*, 28 August 1998, 32; 'Karunanidhi accuses Centre of succumbing to "mindless pressure" on ATR,' *Rediff*, 31 July 1998. Accessed 7 February 2018, https://www.rediff.com/news/1998/aug/03jain.htm; N. Sathiya Moorthy, 'Jaya keeps off allies' meetings,' supra note 27.

31 'Jaya: Jain made charges against Karunanidhi,' the *Tribune*, 3 August 1998. Accessed 1 May 2018, https://www.tribuneindia.com/1998/98aug03/nation.htm#2; 'Jaya demands FIR, chargesheet against Karunanidhi over Jain's "indictment",' *Rediff*, 5 August 1998. Accessed 1 August 2018, https://www.rediff.com/news/1998/aug/05jain.htm.

32 Advani, *My Life*, 487–88.

33 'It is a victory of the people: Karunanidhi,' *Rediff*, 7 August 1998. Accessed 2 May 2018, https://www.rediff.com/news/1998/aug/07cauver.htm.

34 'Karunanidhi is irked by Chidambaram's comments on Cauvery dispute,' *Rediff*, 17 August 1998. Accessed 14 May 2018, https://www.rediff.com/news/1998/aug/17karu.htm.

35 N. Sathiya Moorthy, 'Jaya threatens BJP over Cauvery issue,' *Rediff*, 8 August 1998. Accessed 1 May 2018, https://www.rediff.com/news/1998/aug/10tn.htm.

36 'SC clears Cauvery scheme,' *Rediff*, 17 August 1998. Accessed 1 May 2018, https://www.rediff.com/news/1998/aug/17cauv.htm.

37 'Vajpayee, Karunanidhi sold Tamilians down the Cauvery: Jaya,' *Rediff*, 16 September 1998. Accessed 1 May 2018, https://www.rediff.com/news/1999/sep/16jaya.htm.

38 'Govt teeters as AIADMK-BJP talks fail', *Rediff*, 12 August 1998. Accessed 1 May 2018, https://www.rediff.com/news/1998/aug/12jaya.htm.

39 'Jayalalitha puts decision on hold,' *Rediff*, 13 August 1998. Accessed 1 May 2018, https://www.rediff.com/news/1998/aug/13jaya1.htm.

40 Ibid.

41 'PMO denies Jaya's charges of corruption,' *Rediff*, 17 August 1998. Accessed 1 May 2018, https://www.rediff.com/news/1998/aug/17jaya.htm.

42 Ibid.

43 *Murasoli*, 19 August 1998, 8.

44 'Mahajan dares Jaya to name him directly as bribe-taker' *Rediff*, 20 August 1998. Accessed 1 May 2018, https://www.rediff.com/news/1998/aug/20pramod.htm.

45 *Murasoli*, 25 August 1998, 1; T.S. Subramanian, 'Blow for blow,' *Frontline*, 11 September 1998, 12–13.

46 'Jaya threatens stir over Karunanidhi's Cauvery speech' *Rediff*, 24 August 1998. Accessed 1 May 2018, https://www.rediff.com/news/1998/aug/24jaya.htm.

47 *Murasoli*, 16 September 1998, 3–4.

48 Asha Krishnakumar, 'Alone but upbeat,' *Frontline*, 9 October 1998, 31–32.

49 Ibid.

50 'Vajpayee says he is ready for support from "any quarter",' *Rediff*, 16 September 1998. Accessed 1 May 2018, https://www.rediff.com/news/1998/sep/16abv.htm.

51 'Jaya hits out at Advani, "recalcitrant" allies' *Rediff*, 16 September 1998. Accessed 1 May 2018, https://www.rediff.com/news/1998/sep/16jaya.htm.

52   'Jaya will comment on DMK's support to BJP when it happens,' *Rediff*, 17 September 1998. Accessed 1 May 2018, https://www.rediff.com/news/1998/sep/17jaya.htm.

53   'Cabinet okays Rabri Devi's dismissal, all eyes on President,' *Rediff*, 22 September 1998. Accessed 3 May 2018, https://www.rediff.com/news/1998/sep/22bihar2.htm.

54   Ibid.

55   Harinder Baweja, Frazand Ahmed, 'K.R. Narayanan returns Cabinet resolution seeking imposition of President's rule in Bihar,' *India Today*, 5 October 1998. Accessed 1 October 2018, https://www.indiatoday.in/magazine/cover-story/story/19981005-kr-narayanan-returns-cabinet-resolution-seeking-imposition-of-presidents-rule-in-bihar-827153-1998-10-04.

56   'AIADMK invites BJP to tea party' *Rediff*, 8 October 1998. Accessed 3 May 2018, https://www.rediff.com/news/1998/oct/08jaya.htm.

57   Ibid.; Karunanidhi, *Nenjuku Needhi*, 5: 858–60.

58   'Jaya says she is with Vajpayee, despite support for Opposition strike,' *Rediff*, 9 December 1998. Accessed 3 May 2018, https://www.rediff.com/news/1998/dec/09jaya.htm.

59   Sinha, *Vajpayee*, 207.

60   'Karunanidhi accuses Centre of "double standards",' *Rediff*, 29 December 1998. Accessed 3 May 2018, https://www.rediff.com/news/1998/dec/29karu.htm.

61   T.S. Subramanian, 'Politics of corruption cases,' *Frontline*, 15 January 1999, 34–37.

62   Yashwant Sinha, *Confessions of a Swadeshi Reformer*, (Gurgaon, Viking, 2007), 226.

63   'Admiral Bhagwat was sacked in view of "security considerations",' *Rediff*, 1 January 1990. Accessed 4 May 2018, https://www.rediff.com/news/1999/jan/02navy.htm.

64   'Jaya demands inquiry into Bhagwat's dismissal,' *Rediff*, 2 January 1990. Accessed 4 May 2018, https://m.rediff.com/news/1999/jan/02navy1.htm.

65   'The Rediff Interview/Admiral Vishnu Bhagwat,' *Rediff*, 24 March 2001. Accessed 4 May 2018, https://www.rediff.com/news/2001/mar/24inter.htm.

66   'Beaming Jaya awaits Cabinet expansion,' *Rediff*, 9 January 1999. Accessed 4 May 2018, https://www.rediff.com/news/1999/jan/09jaya1.htm.

67   'Jaya promises not to withdraw support to Vajpayee' *Rediff*, 8 January
      1999. Accessed 4 May 2018, https://www.rediff.com/news/1999/
      jan/08jaya.htm.

68   'Jaya attacks Vajpayee for hike in cooking gas price' *Rediff*, 1 February
      1999. Accessed 4 May 2018, https://www.rediff.com/news/1999/
      feb/01jaya1.htm; 'Allies force withdrawal of price hike,' *Rediff*, 2 February
      1999. Accessed 4 May 2018, https://www.rediff.com/news/1999/
      feb/02cor1.htm; 'Jaya refuses to sign statement on price roll-back,'
      Rediff, 3 February 1999. Accessed 4 May 2018, https://www.rediff.com/
      news/1999/feb/03jaya.htm.

69   N. Sathiya Moorthy, 'Fernandes meets Jaya in effort to keep the BJP
      flock together,' *Rediff*, 5 February 1999. Accessed 4 May 2018, https://
      www.rediff.com/news/1999/feb/05tn.htm.

70   T.S. Subramanian, 'A judicial reprieve,' *Frontline*, 16 July 1999, 33;
      'Centre transfers corruption cases against Jaya,' *Rediff*, 8 February 1999.
      Accessed 5 May 2019, https://www.rediff.com/news/1999/feb/08jaya.
      htm.

71   V. Venkatesan, 'A judicial blow,' *Frontline*, 4 June 1999, 39–40.

72   N. Sathiya Moorthy, 'Bihar's developments rattle TN government,'
      Rediff, 13 February 1999. Accessed 5 May 2019, https://www.rediff.
      com/news/1999/feb/13tn.htm.

73   'AIADMK is hurt again,' *Rediff*, 22 February 1999. Accessed 5 May
      2019, https://www.rediff.com/news/1999/feb/22tn.htm.

74   'AIADMK backing for Vajpayee, not BJP, says Jayalalitha,' *Rediff*, 20
      February 1999. Accessed 5 May 2019, https://m.rediff.com/news/1999/
      feb/20jaya.htm.

75   Sinha, *Vajpayee*, 276.

76   George Iype, 'Coalition panel backs government against Bhagwat,'
      Rediff, 27 March 1999. Accessed 5 May 2019, https://www.rediff.com/
      news/1999/mar/27wrig.htm; T.V. Rajeswar, 'Dealing with Jayalalitha:
      Talk of political realignment,' the *Tribune*, 6 April 1999. Accessed 14
      February 2018, https://www.tribuneindia.com/1999/99apr06/edit.
      htm#4.

77   Swapan Dasgupta, 'Managing power not be a bed of roses for Congress
      unaccustomed to coalition politics,' *India Today*, 26 April 1999. Accessed
      13 February 2018, https://www.indiatoday.in/magazine/cover-story/
      story/19990426-managing-power-not-be-a-bed-of-roses-for-congress-
      unaccustomed-to-coalition-politics-780753-1999-04-25; George
      Iype, 'Jaya meets Sonia, warns of "political quake",' *Rediff*, 29 March

1999. Accessed 22 February 2018, https://m.rediff.com/news/1999/mar/29jaya3.htm.

78 R.D. Pradhan, *My Years with Rajiv and Sonia*, (New Delhi: Hay House, 2014), 237.

79 'BJP minister attacks Jayalalitha as undependable ally,' *Rediff*, 31 March 1999. Accessed 22 February 2018, https://www.rediff.com/news/1999/mar/31prk.htm.

80 'I don't [see myself as prime minister] but anything is possible in politics'—The Rediff Interview/J Jayalalithaa, *Rediff*, 31 March 1999. Accessed 22 February 2018, https://www.rediff.com/news/1999/mar/31jaya2.htm.

81 Cho Ramaswamy, *Anubhavangalum*, 442–43.

82 T.S. Subramanian, 'A hardening stand,' *Frontline*, 23 April 1999, 23.

83 The Rediff Interview/J Jayalalithaa, Part 1, supra note 80.

84 V. Venkatesan, 'The countdown to collapse,' *Frontline*, 7 May 1999, 16.

85 N. Sathiya Moorthy, 'AIADMK to vote for JPC in Lok Sabha,' *Rediff*, 3 April 1999. Accessed 22 February 2018, https://www.rediff.com/news/1999/apr/03admk1.htm; Suzanne Goldenberg, 'Minister attacks admiral in row that threatens India's coalition,' the *Guardian*, 6 April 1999. Accessed 13 February 1999, https://www.theguardian.com/world/1999/apr/07/suzannegoldenberg.

86 Sinha, *Vajpayee*, 277.

87 'Jaya asks AIADMK ministers to quit Union Cabinet,' *Rediff*, 5 April 1999. Accessed 22 February 2018, https://www.rediff.com/news/1999/apr/05admk.htm.

88 'The countdown to collapse.' *Frontline*, 7 May 1999, 17–18.

89 'Jaya extends stay in Delhi,' *Rediff*, 26 April 1999. Accessed 5 May 2018, https://www.rediff.com/news/1999/apr/26jaya1.htm.

90 'Jaya meets President, withdraws support,' *Rediff*, 14 April 1999. Accessed 5 May 2018, https://www.rediff.com/news/1999/apr/14jaya.htm.

91 Venkitesh Ramakrishnan, 'The numbers game,' *Frontline*, 7 May 1999, 11; T.S. Subramanian, 'The DMK's turnabout,' *Frontline*, 7 May 1999, 21–22.

92 Cho Ramaswamy, *Anubhavangalum* 453.

93 Pradhan, *My Years*, 245–46.

94 'Karunanidhi attacks Left parties,' *Rediff*, 15 April 1999. Accessed 1 June 2021, https://www.rediff.com/news/1999/apr/15tn.htm.

95   'The DMK's turnabout,'; V. Venkatesan, 'Holding Court,' *Frontline*, 7 May 1999, 20-22.

96   India, *Parliamentary Debates*, House of the People, (Discussion on the motion of Confidence moved by A.B. Vajpayee), 15 April 1999, cols. 13-14. Accessed 8 May 2018, https://eparlib.nic.in/bitstream/123456789/756556/1/1861.pdf.

97   T.S. Subramanian, 'Strange bedfellows,' *Frontline*, 21 May 1999, 17–19.

98   Surabhi Banerjee, 'The view the majority held was wrong. It was a historical blunder,' *Rediff*, 29 March 1997. Accessed 5 May 2018, https://www.rediff.com/news/1997/mar/29basu3.htm; 'Jaya mounts fresh attack on Sonia,' *Rediff*, 2 September 2002, Accessed 5 May 2018, https://www.rediff.com/news/2002/sep/02jaya.htm.

99   Pradhan, *My Years*, 249–50.

100   Cho Ramaswamy, *Anubhavangalum*, 449.

101   'Left had ditched Sonia in govt formation bid in 1999: Gujral,' *Hindustan Times*, 20 February 2011. Accessed 22 February 2019, https://www.hindustantimes.com/delhi/left-had-ditched-sonia-in-govt-formation-bid-in-1999-gujral/story-A7V9NWBkwlRYacwnWTPuoK.html.

102   *Murasoli*, 6 August 1999, 1.

103   Cho Ramaswamy, *Anubhavangalum*, 450–51.

104   'CPI-M agreed to make Basu PM, but Congress refused to extend support: Chatterjee,' *Rediff*, 26 April 1999. Accessed 1 March 2018, https://www.rediff.com/news/1999/apr/26cpim.htm; George Iype, 'Opposition roots for Basu, but Congress is not enthusiastic' *Rediff*, 24 April 1999. Accessed 1 March 2018, https://www.rediff.com/news/1999/apr/24iype.htm.

105   'Sonia's plan goes to pieces' *Rediff*, 21 April 1999. Accessed 1 March 2018, https://www.rediff.com/news/1999/apr/21pol.htm; Advani, *My Life*, 554–56.

106   'Jaya mum on fate of tie-up with Congress,' *Rediff*, 9 October 1999. Accessed 1 March 2018, https://www.rediff.com/election/1999/oct/09jaya.htm.

107   S. Viswanathan, 'Blaming the victims,' *Frontline*, 6 January 2001. Accessed 1 June 2018, https://frontline.thehindu.com/other/article30249644.ece.

108   *Murasoli*, 28 August 1999, 1, 8; S. Viswanathan, 'A consolidation of forces,' *Frontline*, 27 August 1999, 37–38.

109   S. Viswanathan, 'Blaming the victor,' *Frontline*, 19 January 2001, 42–44.

110   *Murasoli*, 17 August 1999, 1; Karunanidhi, *Kadithangal*, 34: 332.

111   Karunanidhi, *Nenjuku Needhi*, 5: 552–55.

112   Shanmughasundaram J, 'Samathuvapuram: An ideal that's far removed from reality,' *Times of India*, 8 November 2021. Accessed 20 February 2019, https://timesofindia.indiatimes.com/city/chennai/samathuvapuram-an-ideal-thats-far-removed-from-reality/articleshow/87580299.cms.

113   'PMK begins talks on alliance with DMK,' *Rediff*, 3 May 1999. Accessed 27 February 2018, https://www.rediff.com/news/1999/may/03pmk.htm; 'DMK reaches agreement with allies on seat-sharing,' *Rediff*, 2 August 1999. Accessed 27 February 2018, https://www.rediff.com/news/1999/aug/02tn.htm; *Murasoli*, 5 August 1999, 3.

114   *Murasoli*, 20 May 1999, 3.

115   Karunanidhi, *Nenjuku*, 5: 1024–28; *Murasoli*, 3 June 1999, 3; T.S. Subramanian, 'New alignments in Tamil Nadu,' *Frontline*, 2 July 1999, 35–36; T.S. Subramanian, 'Bombs and politics,' *Frontline*, 2 July 1999, 36–37.

116   'TMC, PT sign seat-sharing deal,' *Rediff*, 17 August 1999. Accessed 27 February 2018, https://www.rediff.com/election/1999/aug/17tmc.htm.

117   T.S. Subramanian, 'A front against communalism,' *Frontline*, 16 July 1999, 34.

118   *Murasoli*, 23 August 1999, 5–7.

119   *Murasoli*, 23 August 1999, 1, 3; 'PM hopeful of gains for NDA in State,' *The Hindu*, 22 August 1999, 1. 'Jaya wanted corruption cases withdrawn: Vajpayee,' *Rediff*, 21 August 1999. Accessed 27 February 2018, https://www.rediff.com/election/1999/aug/21madras.htm.

120   'Jaya vows to defeat "unholy" DMK-BJP combine,' *Rediff*, 6 August 1999. Accessed 27 February 2018, https://www.rediff.com/news/1999/aug/07jaya.htm; 'Vajpayee government failed on all fronts, says Jaya,' *Rediff*, 19 August 1999. Accessed 27 February 2018, https://www.rediff.com/election/1999/aug/19jaya.htm; T.S. Subramanian, 'Hurdles in Tamil Nadu,' *Frontline*, 27 August 1999, 18–19; Karunanidhi, *Kadithangal*, 37: 11. https://www.rediff.com/election/1999/aug/26jaya.htm; *Murasoli*, 26 August 1999, 2.

121   *The Hindu*, 31 July 1999, 1.

122   'Jaya's slight likely to leave Sonia smarting,' *Rediff*, 23 August 1999. Accessed 27 February 2018, https://www.rediff.com/news/2002/sep/05flip.htm.

123   *Murasoli*, 8 October 1999, 1.

124 'Jaya mum on fate of tie-up with Congress,' *Rediff,* 9 October 1999. Accessed 1 January 2022, https://m.rediff.com/election/1999/oct/09jaya. htm.

125 'The Union Council of Ministers,' *Rediff,* 13 October 1999. Accessed 27 February 2018, https://www.rediff.com/election/1999/oct/13portfo. htm.

126 'Though Karunanidhi launched Uzhavar Santhai, he did not claim for it,' *Times of India,* 9 August 2018. Accessed 2 March 2018. https:// timesofindia.indiatimes.com/city/madurai/though-karunanidhi-launched-uzhavar-santhai-he-did-not-claim-credit-for-it/ articleshow/65329622.cms; Karunanidhi, *Kadithangal,* 34: 332.

127 *Murasoli,* 2 January 2000, 1.

128 T.S. Subramanian, 'Karunanidhi on RSS,' *Frontline,* 3 March 2000, 37.

129 TMC joins hands with old foe AIADMK,' *Rediff,* 28 January 2000, Accessed 5 May 2018, https://www.rediff.com/news/2000/jan/28tn. htm; *Frontline,* 18 February 2000, 122–23.

130 T.S. Subramanian, 'The conviction of Jayalalitha,' *Frontline,* 3 March 2000, 38–40.

131 Ibid., 40.

132 *Murasoli,* 7 April 2000, 8.

133 'Karnataka govt paid Rs 300 million for Rajakumar's release: Jaya,' *Rediff,* 2 September 2002, Accessed 5 May 2018, https://www.rediff.com/ news/2002/sep/02jaya1.htm.

134 *Murasoli,* 6 March 2001, 3; 'Violence breaks out in TN as Karunanidhi sidelines son,' *Rediff,* 20 September 2002, Accessed 5 May 2018, https:// www.rediff.com/news/2000/sep/20tn.htm.

135 *Murasoli,* 20 September 2000, 3.

136 *Murasoli,* 23 September 2000, 8.

137 *Murasoli,* 26 September 2000, 1.

138 N. Sathiya Moorthy, '3 years RI for Jaya in Tansi case,' *Rediff,* 9 October 2000, Accessed 5 May 2018, https://www.rediff.com/news/2000/ oct/09jaya.htm; 'HC suspends sentences of Jayalalitha and five others,' *Rediff,* 31 October 2000. Accessed 5 May 2018, https://www.rediff.com/ news/2000/nov/03jaya.htm.

139 T.S. Subramanian, 'Can she or can't she?' *Frontline,* 11 May 2001, 32–33; N. Ram, 'Politics after disqualification,' *Frontline,* 25 May 2001, 4–9.

Chapter 25: Jayalalithaa Back in Power

1   *Murasoli*, 19 January 2001, 2.
2   *Murasoli*, 19 May 2001, 1, 8; *Murasoli*, 6 June 2001, 2.
3   Ibid.
4   T.S. Subramanian, 'Legal challenge,' *Frontline*, 4 August 2001. Accessed 29 March 2019, https://frontline.thehindu.com/other/article30251397. ece.
5   N. Sathiya Moorty, 'Karunanidhi awaits TMC response,' *Rediff*, 13 February 2001, Accessed 5 May 2018, https://www.rediff.com/ news/2001/feb/13tn.htm; 'DMK shuts door on TMC: PTI,' *Rediff*, 16 February 2001, Accessed 5 May 2018, https://www.rediff.com/ news/2001/feb/16dmk.htm; 'Shot in the arm for DMK-led front,' *Rediff*, 16 February 2001, Accessed 5 May 2018, https://www.rediff. com/news/2001/feb/16tn1.htm.
6   *Murasoli*, 6 March 2001, 7.
7   Karunanidhi, *Kadithangal*, 31: 209–12; *Murasoli*, 9 April 2001, 3.
8   *Murasoli*, 6 June 2001, 2.
9   *Murasoli*, 15 April 2001, 1.
10 'Maran to keep away from active politics,' *Rediff*, 16 February 2001, Accessed 5 May 2018, https://www.rediff.com/news/2001/apr/14tn1. htm; N. Sathiya Moorthy, 'Maran, a master strategist,' Rediff, 23 November 2003, Accessed 5 May 2018, https://www.rediff.com/ money/2003/nov/23maran1.htm.
11 Karunanidhi, *Kadithangal*, 31: 115.
12 *Murasoli*, 14 April 2001, 3–4.
13 'All Jayalalitha nominations rejected,' *Rediff*, 24 February 2001, Accessed 5 May 2018, https://www.rediff.com/news/2001/apr/24tn3.htm; 'Karunanidhi behind rejection of nominations: Jaya,' *Rediff*, 24 February 2001, Accessed 5 May 2018, https://www.rediff.com/news/2001/ apr/24jaya1.htm.
14 *Murasoli*, 25 April 2001, 3.
15 *Murasoli*, 9 May 2001, 7.
16 'DMK chief concedes defeat,' *Rediff*, 13 May 2001, Accessed 5 May 2018, https://www.rediff.com/news/2001/may/13dmk1.htm; T.S. Subramanian, 'The return of Jayalalitha,' https://frontline.thehindu. com/politics/article30250676.ece.
17 *Murasoli*, 14 May 2001, 1, 8.
18 *Murasoli*, 6 June 2001, 2.

19   *Murasoli*, 19 May 2001, 1, 8.

20   *Murasoli*, 16 May 2001, 1.

21   'Jaya determined to overcome hurdles to getting elected,' *Rediff*, 15 May 2001, Accessed 5 May 2018, https://www.rediff.com/news/2001/may/15jaya.htm.

22   *Murasoli*, 19 May 2001, 3.

23   'Mr. Karunanidhi Has Always Been a Man of Two Faces,' *Outlook*. Accessed 2 May 2019, https://www.outlookindia.com/website/story/mr-karunanidhi-has-always-been-a-man-of-two-faces/212591.

24   N. Sathiya Moorthy, 'Police restrain Sun TV,' 30 June 2001. Accessed 2 June 2021, https://www.rediff.com/news/2001/jun/30tn8.htm.

25   T.S. Subramanian, 'Tamil Nadu's shame,' *Frontline*, 7 July 2001. Accessed 2 February 2019, https://frontline.thehindu.com/cover-story/article30251114.ece.

26   T.S. Subramanian, 'After the storm,' *Frontline*, 21 July 2001. Accessed 2 February 2019, https://frontline.thehindu.com/the-nation/article30251277.ece.

27   T.S. Subramanian, 'Tamil Nadu's shame,' supra note 25.

28   Karunanidhi, *Kadithangal*, 32: 38.

29   'Personal agenda prevailed overrule of the law: Arun Jaitley' *Rediff*, 30 June 2001, Accessed 5 May 2018, https://www.rediff.com/news/2001/jun/30tn10.htm.

30   'TN governor asked to submit report' *Rediff*, 30 June 2001. Accessed 5 May 2018, https://m.rediff.com/news/2001/jun/30tn22.htm; Sheela Bhatt, 'PM condemns Karunanidhi arrest, seeks details,' *Rediff*, 30 June 2001. Accessed 5 May 2018, https://m.rediff.com/news/2001/jun/30tn6.htm.

31   T.S. Subramanian, supra note 25.

32   'NDA team to recommend President's rule,' the *Tribune*, 1 July 2001. Accessed 2 May 2019, https://www.tribuneindia.com/2001/20010702/main3.htm.

33   'Jayalalithaa in Guruvayur to offer calf elephant,' *Rediff*, 2 July 2001, Accessed 5 May 2018, https://www.rediff.com/news/2001/jul/02tn1.htm.

34   'Charges against Maran, Baalu dropped,' *Rediff*, 3 July 2001, Accessed 5 May 2018, https://m.rediff.com/news/2001/jul/03tn8.htm.

35   George Iype, '"They carried me out like a parcel": Maran,' *Rediff*, 3 July 2001, Accessed 5 May 2018, https://www.rediff.com/news/2001/jul/03tn9.htm.

36 'Karunanidhi breaks down at press conference' *Rediff*, 4 July 2001, Accessed 5 May 2018, https://www.rediff.com/news/2001/jul/04tn10. htm.

37 '"Police wanted to kill Karunanidhi": Maran,' *Rediff*, 4 July 2001, Accessed 5 May 2018, https://m.rediff.com/news/2001/jul/04tn6. htm.

38 Swati Das, 'Karunanidhi meets Vaiko in Vellore jail,' *Times of India*, 5 November 2002, https://timesofindia.indiatimes.com/india/karu%20 nanidhi-meets-vaiko-in-vellore-jail/articleshow/27399277.cms.

39 'Karunanidhi to boycott Raman's inquiry,' *Rediff*, 9 July 2001, Accessed 5 May 2018, https://www.rediff.com/news/2001/jul/09tn1.htm.

40 https://www.outlookindia.com/website/story/mr-karunanidhi-has-always-been-a-man-of-two-faces/212591.

41 'Maran, Baalu ought to be sacked: Jaya' *Rediff*, 10 July 2001, Accessed 5 May 2018, https://m.rediff.com/news/2001/jul/10tn2.htm.

42 Ibid.

43 'Jayalalithaa cleared in corruption cases' *Rediff*. 4 December 2001, Accessed 5 May 2018, https://www.rediff.com/news/2001/dec/04jaya. htm; 'DMK govt had fabricated cases against me: Jaya' *Rediff*, 4 December 2001, Accessed 5 May 2018, https://www.rediff.com/ news/2001/dec/04jaya3.htm.

44 'Jaya acquitted in coal import case' *Rediff*, 27 December 2001, Accessed 5 May 2018, https://www.rediff.com/news/2001/dec/27tn.htm.

45 Karunanidhi, *Kadithangal*, 44: 352.

46 Arun Ram, 'Andipatti by-elections: J. Jayalalithaa juggernaut rolls on.' *India Today*, 25 February 2002. Accessed 2 June 2019, https://www. indiatoday.in/magazine/nation/story/20020225-andipatti-by-elections-jayalalithaa-juggernaut-rolls-on-796713-2002-02-24.

47 Onkar Singh, 'SC acquits Jaya in Tansi land deal case,' *Rediff*, 24 November 2003, Accessed 5 May 2018, https://www.rediff.com/ news/2003/nov/24sc.htm.

48 S. Viswanathan, 'Controversy over a statue,' *Frontline*, 5 January 2002. Accessed 2 June 2019, https://frontline.thehindu.com/other/ article30243492.ece.

49 Jaya Menon, *Indian Express*, 6 June 2006 cited in 'Kannagi statue reinstated in Chennai Marina.' Accessed 2 June 2010, https://tamilnation. org/diaspora/tamilnadu/060606kannagi.htm.

50 Hannah Ellis Petersen, 'What is the BBC Modi documentary and why is it so controversial?,' the *Guardian*, 14 February 2023. Accessed

2 March 2023, https://www.theguardian.com/world/2023/feb/14/
why-is-bbc-report-on-narendra-modis-handling-of-sectarian-riots-
in-2002-socontroversial#:~:text=What%20is%20the%20BBC%20
documentary,in%20the%20UK%20in%20January.

51 Arun Ram, 'BJP, DMK drift apart in Tamil Nadu but alliance at
Centre holds,' *India Today*, 8 August 2002. Accessed 2 June 2020,
https://www.indiatoday.in/magazine/states/story/20020408-
bjp-dmk-drift-apart-in-tamil-nadu-but-alliance-at-centre-
holds-795463-2002-04-07.

52 'DMK to quit if temple gets nod,' the *Tribune*, 4 March 2002. Accessed
2 June 2018, https://www.tribuneindia.com/2002/20020304/nation.
htm#1; Karunanidhi, *Kadithangal*, 33: 33–36.

53 Prabhu Chawla, 'Jayalalithaa does not have leadership qualities: DMK
chief Karunanidhi,' *India Today*, 27 December 2004. Accessed 2 June
2018, https://www.indiatoday.in/magazine/interview/story/20041227-
jayalalithaa-does-not-have-leadership-qualities-dmk-chief-
karunanidhi-788842-2004-12-26.

54 Arun Ram, 'BJP, DMK drift apart in Tamil Nadu but alliance at Centre
holds,' *India Today*, 8 April 2002. Accessed 2 April 2021, https://www.
indiatoday.in/magazine/states/story/200204.08-bjp-dmk-drift-apart-
in-tamil-nadu-but-alliance-at-centre-holds-795463-2002-04-07.

55 'DMK snaps ties with BJP TN unit,' *Times of India*, 24 March 2002.
Accessed 2 June 2019, https://timesofindia.indiatimes.com/india/dmk-
snaps-ties-with-bjp-tn-unit/articleshow/4785564.cms; Karunanidhi,
Kadithangal, 33: 91–93.

56 K. Venkataramanan, 'Prabhakaran calls Rajiv Gandhi's assassination
tragic,' *Rediff*, 10 April 2002. Accessed 2 June 2018, https://www.rediff.
com/news/2002/apr/10ltte.htm; N. Sathiya Moorthy, 'Jaya refuses to
forget LTTE's past, seeks Prabhakaran's extradition,' *Rediff*, 11 April
2002. Accessed 2 June 2018, https://www.rediff.com/news/2002/
apr/11ltte4.htm.

57 'TN assembly urges Centre to seek Prabhakaran's extradition,' *Rediff*, 16
April 2002. Accessed 2 June 2018, https://www.rediff.com/news/2002/
apr/16tn.htm.

58 'TN police arrests MDMK leader Vaiko,' *Rediff*, 11 July 2002. Accessed
2 June 2018, https://www.rediff.com/news/2002/jul/11vaiko7.htm; N.
Sathiya Moorthy, 'Jayalalithaa threatens Vaiko with POTA,' *Rediff*, 3
July 2002. Accessed 2 June 2018, https://www.rediff.com/news/2002/
jul/03tn.htm.

59 'Vaiko's arrest is a case of POTA misuse: Karunanidhi,' *Times of India*, 11 July 2002. Accessed 2 July 2019, https://timesofindia. indiatimes.com/vaikos-arrest-is-a-case-of-pota-misuse-karunanidhi/ articleshow/15691524.cms.

60 'George visits Vaiko, deplores arrest,' *Times of India*, 19 July 2002. Accessed 2 July 2019, https://timesofindia.indiatimes.com/george-visits-vaiko-deplores-arrest/articleshow/16487767.cms; 'Opposition hits out at government over George meeting Vaiko,' *Rediff*, 30 July 2002. Accessed 2 June 2018, https://www.rediff.com/news/2002/jul/30vaiko.htm.

61 'Nedumaran arrested under POTA for pro-LTTE views,' *Rediff*, 1 August 2002. Accessed 2 June 2018, https://www.rediff.com/news/2002/ aug/01nedu.htm.

62 Karunanidhi, *Kadithangal*, 34: 194; 'Nedumaran's arrest another incidence of misuse of Pota: DMK,' *Zee News*, 2 August 2002. Accessed 2 July 2019, https://zeenews.india.com/news/nation/nedumarans-arrest-another-incidence-of-misuse-of-pota-dmk_52005.html.

63 'Karunanidhi meets Vaiko in jail,' *Times of India*, 2 November 2002. Accessed 2 July 2019, https://timesofindia.indiatimes.com/karunanidhi-meets-vaiko-in-jail/articleshow/27392163.cms.

64 Arun Ram, 'TMC merges with Congress, Sonia Gandhi looks to capture power in Tamil Nadu,' *India Today*, 26 August 2002. Accessed 3 July 2019, https://www.indiatoday.in/magazine/indiascope/story/20020826-tmc-merges-with-congress-sonia-gandhi-looks-to-capture-power-in-tamil-nadu-794499-2002-08-25; 'Sonia calls upon ex-Congressmen to return,' *Rediff*, 14 August 2002. Accessed 2 June 2018, https://www.rediff.com/news/2002/aug/14tn.htm.

65 'Jayalalithaa opposes Sonia as PM,' *Rediff*, 28 August 2002. Accessed 2 June 2018, https://www.rediff.com/news/2002/aug/28tn1.htm.

66 'Congress blames Jaya's "somersault" on political compulsions,' *Rediff*, 29 August 2002. Accessed 2 June 2018, https://www.rediff.com/news/2002/ aug/28cong.htm; Shahid Abbas, 'Congress releases Jaya's letter extending support to Sonia,' *Rediff*, 30 August 2002. Accessed 2 June 2018, https:// www.rediff.com/news/2002/aug/30shahid.htm; Purnima S. Tripathi, T.S. Subramanian, 'Seeing a foreign hand,' *Frontline*, 14 September 2002. Accessed 2 September 2020, https://frontline.thehindu.com/ politics/article30246088.ece.

67 N. Sathiya Moorthy, 'I supported Congress, not Sonia: Jaya,' *Rediff*, 31 August 2002. Accessed 2 June 2018, https://www.rediff.com/news/2002/ aug/31tn.htm.

68 'Jaya mounts fresh attack on Sonia,' *Rediff*, 2 September 2002. Accessed 2 June 2018, https://www.rediff.com/news/2002/sep/02jaya.htm.

69 N. Sathiya Moorthy, 'DMK reserves comment on Sonia's citizenship, Chandra Shekhar backs Jaya,' *Rediff*, 7 September 2002. Accessed 2 June 2018, https://www.rediff.com/news/2002/sep/07tn.htm,

70 'Tamil Nadu to approach Supreme Court on Cauvery issue,' *Rediff*, 21 June 2002. Accessed 3 June 2018, https://www.rediff.com/news/2002/jun/21tn1.htm; Karunanidhi, *Kadithangal*, 36: 201.

71 Karunanidhi, *Kadithangal*, 36: 234.

72 N. Sathiya Moorthy, 'TN moves Supreme Court on Cauvery row,' *Rediff*, 10 July 2002. Accessed 3 June 2018, https://www.rediff.com/news/2002/jul/10tn.htm.

73 Tara Shankar Sahay, 'Jayalalithaa walks out of talks on Cauvery issue,' *Rediff*, 27 August 2002. Accessed 3 June 2018, https://www.rediff.com/news/2002/aug/27tara.htm.

74 'SC orders Karnataka to release Cauvery water to Tamil Nadu,' *Rediff*, 3 September 2002. Accessed 3 June 2018, https://www.rediff.com/news/2002/sep/03cau.htm.

75 N. Sathiya Moorthy, 'Opposition failed to stand up for TN, says Jaya,' *Rediff*, 11 September 2002. Accessed 3 June 2018, https://www.rediff.com/news/2002/sep/11tn.htm.

76 Fakir Chand, 'Cauvery bandh logs out India's Silicon Valley,' *Rediff*, 12 September 2002. Accessed 3 June 2018, https://www.rediff.com/news/2002/sep/12cau.htm.

77 'Farmer may have been pushed into Kabini reservoir: Jaya,' *Rediff*, 19 September 2002. Accessed 3 June 2018, https://www.rediff.com/news/2002/sep/19cau1.htm.

78 'DMK to boycott all-party meeting in Tamil Nadu,' *Rediff*, 20 September 2002. Accessed 3 June 2018, https://www.rediff.com/news/2002/sep/20cau1.htm.

79 'Centre must take over dams across Cauvery: Jaya,' *Rediff*, 20 September 2002. Accessed 3 June 2018, https://www.rediff.com/news/2002/sep/20cau3.htm.

80 'Karnataka ignores PM's directive on Cauvery water,' *Rediff*, 23 September 2002. Accessed 3 June 2018, https://www.rediff.com/news/2002/sep/22cau.htm.

81 N. Sathiya Moorthy, 'Tamil Nadu to boycott Cauvery panel meet,' *Rediff*, 23 September 2002. Accessed 3 June 2018, https://www.rediff.com/news/2002/sep/23cau2.htm.

82 Sadananda R., 'Cauvery row: Rajakumar leads cine artists' protest rally,' *Rediff*, 26 September 2002. Accessed 3 June 2018, https://www.rediff.com/news/2002/sep/25cau1.htm.

83 Sadananda R, 'Karnataka farmers for rail roko agitation on September 29,' *Rediff*, 27 September 2002. Accessed 2 January 2019, https://www.rediff.com/news/2002/sep/27cau.htm.

84 Fakir Chand, 'Farmers lay siege to Kabini, KRS reservoirs,' *Rediff*, 6 October 2002. Accessed 2 January 2019, https://www.rediff.com/news/2002/oct/05cau7.htm; Sadananda R., 'Krishna to walk from Bangalore to KRS reservoir,' *Rediff*, 6 October 2002. Accessed 2 January 2019, https://www.rediff.com/news/2002/oct/06cau.htm.

85 N. Sathiya Moorthy, 'Jaya wants Karnataka government sacked,' Rediff, 6 October 2002. Accessed 2 June 2018, https://www.rediff.com/news/2002/oct/06cau1.htm; Fakir Chand, 'Karnataka, Tamil Nadu indulge in slanging match,' *Rediff*, 6 October 2002. Accessed 2 June 2018, https://www.rediff.com/news/2002/oct/06cau2.htm.

86 Fakir Chand, 'Tamil movies, TV channels banned in Karnataka,' *Rediff*, 6 October 2002. Accessed 2 June 2018, https://www.rediff.com/news/2002/oct/06cau3.htm.

87 'Karnataka chief minister begins "padayatra",' *Rediff*, 7 October 2002. Accessed 2 June 2018, https://www.rediff.com/news/2002/oct/07cau.htm.

88 N. Sathiya Moorthy, 'DMK suggests bandh, boycotts all-party meeting,' *Rediff*, 7 October 2002. Accessed 2 June 2018, https://www.rediff.com/news/2002/oct/07cau1.htm.

89 N. Sathiya Moorthy, 'Rajni distances himself from Tamil filmdom on Cauvery issue,' *Rediff*, 9 October 2002. Accessed 2 June 2018, https://www.rediff.com/news/2002/oct/09cau3.htm.

90 N. Sathiya Moorthy, 'Faceoff avoided, Rajinikanth puts off fast by a day' *Rediff*, 11 October 2002. Accessed 2 June 2018, https://www.rediff.com/news/2002/oct/11cau1.htm; 'Rajinikanth fasts for Cauvery waters,' *Rediff*, 13 October 2002. Accessed 2 June 2018, https://www.rediff.com/news/2002/oct/13cau2.htm.

91 'Rajinikanth fasts for Cauvery waters,'; 'Tamil film artistes stage anti-Karnataka rally in Neyveli,' *Rediff*, 12 October 2002. Accessed 2 June 2018, https://www.rediff.com/news/2002/oct/12cau4.htm.

92 'SC asks Karnataka to immediately release "some water",' *Rediff*, 17 October 2002. Accessed 2 June 2018, https://www.rediff.com/news/2002/oct/24cau1.htm; 'SC flays Karnataka for disobeying its

order,' *Rediff*, 17 October 2002. Accessed 2 June 2018, https://www. rediff.com/news/2002/oct/24cau.htm.

93 'Krishna tenders unconditional apology to Supreme Court,' *Rediff*, 28 October 2002. Accessed 2 June 2018, https://www.rediff.com/ news/2002/oct/28cau1.htm.

94 Karunanidhi, *Kadithangal*, 37: 110; Karunanidhi, *Kadithangal*, 44: 197.

95 Swati Das, 'Jaya to enforce ban on animal sacrifice,' *Times of India*, 28 August 2003. Accessed 22 January 2019, https://timesofindia. indiatimes.com/jaya-to-enforce-ban-on-animal-sacrifice/articleshow/ 151237.cms

96 N. Sathiya Moorthy, 'Anti-conversion law kicks off row in TN,' *Rediff*, 8 October 2002. Accessed 2 June 2018, https://www.rediff.com/ news/2002/oct/08tn.htm.

97 'Hindu, a thief of sorts: Karunanidhi,' *Times of India*, 25 October 2002. Accessed 14 February 2019, https://timesofindia.indiatimes. com/hindu-a-thief-of-sorts-karunanidhi/articleshow/26292178.cms; N. Sathiya Moorthy, 'Erase untouchability, DMK tells government,' *Rediff*, 25 October 2002. Accessed 2 June 2018, https://www.rediff.com/ news/2002/oct/25tn.htm; Karunanidhi, *Kadithangal*, 34: 345–48.

98 'Karunanidhi definition of "Hindu" statement draws flak,' *India Today*, 11 November 2002. Accessed 14 February 2029, https://www.indiatoday. in/magazine/indiascope/story/20021111-karunanidhi-definition-of- hindu-statement-draws-flak-794357-2002-11-10; 'Hindu—a thief of sorts: Karunanidhi.'

99 'Jaya hints at bigger role in national politics,' *Rediff*, 18 December 2002. Accessed 2 May 2019, https://www.rediff.com/news/2002/dec/18jaya. htm.

100 'Karunanidhi disapproves Aiyar's comments,' *Times of India*, 30 August 2004. Accessed 2 May 2019, https://timesofindia.indiatimes.com/ karunanidhi-disapproves-aiyars-comments/articleshow/832543.cms; Lakshmi Iyer, 'Cong pushed on backfoot as it comes to terms with Indira Gandhi's endorsement of Savarkar,' *India Today*, 10 May 2003. Accessed 20 May 2019, https://www.indiatoday.in/magazine/nation/ story/20030310-congress-pushed-on-backfoot-as-it-comes-to-terms- with-indira-gandhi-endorsement-of-savarkar-793244-2003-03-09.

101 Karunanidhi, *Kadithangal*, 35: 195–99.

102 N. Sathiya Moorthy, "Karunanidhi writes to PM over Azhagiri's arrest,' *Rediff*, 24 May 2003. Accessed 2 May 2019, https://www.rediff.com/ news/report/tn/20030524.htm.

103 https://www.rediff.com/news/2003/oct/10tn.htm; https://frontline. thehindu.com/other/article30217464.ece.

104 N. Sathiya Moorthy, 'M K Stalin rises up DMK ranks,' *Rediff*, 2 June 2003. Accessed 2 May 2019, https://www.rediff.com/news/2003/ jun/02tn.htm.

105 Karunanidhi, *Kadithangal*, 36: 166–70.

106 https://www.rediff.com/news/2003/jul/02tn1.htm; 'Tamil Nadu govt agrees to take back striking staff,' *Economic Times*, 24 July 2003. Accessed 1 May 2019, https://economictimes.indiatimes.com/tamil-nadu-govt-agrees-to-take-back-striking-staff/articleshow/93314.cms.

107 Karunanidhi, *Kadithangal*, 6: 44–49.

108 Karunanidhi, *Kadithangal*, 37: 120–23.

109 T.S. Subramanian, 'A secular front in the south,' *Frontline*, 30 January 2004. Accessed 2 May 2019, https://frontline.thehindu.com/other/ article30220906.ece.

110 'DMK pulls out from Vajpayee government,' *Rediff*, 20 December 2003. Accessed 1 May 2019; https://www.rediff.com/news/2003/ dec/20dmk.htm; 'Consensus must on strike says Vajpayee,' *Times of India*, 17 October 2003, https://timesofindia.indiatimes.com/india/ consensus-must-on-strike-says-vajpayee/articleshow/237346.cms; T.S. Subramanian, 'A parting of ways,' *Frontline*, 16 January 2004. Accessed 2 May 2019, https://frontline.thehindu.com/other/article30220678.ece.

111 Karunanidhi, *Kadithangal*, 42: 91.

112 Shoba Warrier, 'The Rajni Factor,' *Rediff*, 12 April 2004, Accessed 2 May 2019, https://www.rediff.com/election/2004/apr/12sld03.htm.

113 N. Sathiya Moorthy, 'Rajni fans miffed with PMK leader Ramadoss,' *Rediff*, 13 August 2002. Accessed 1 May 2019, https://www.rediff. com/news/2002/aug/13tn2.htm; R.D. Rati, 'To Rajni with love,' *Rediff*, 16 August 2002. Accessed 1 May 2019, https://www.rediff.com/ entertai/2002/aug/16baba.htm; 'Rajinikanth threatens to take Ramadoss to court,' *Times of India*, 17 August 2002. Accessed 2 May 2019; N. Sathiya Moorthy, 'Rajinikanth threatens to take Ramadoss to court,' *Rediff*, 17 August 2002. Accessed 2 May 2019, https://timesofindia. indiatimes.com/rajnikanth-threatens-to-take-ramadoss-to-court/ articleshow/19387900.cms; https://m.rediff.com/news/2002/aug/17tn1. htm.

114 'Karunanidhi caught in battle of words,' *Times of India*, 13 April 2004. Accessed 1 May 2019, https://timesofindia.indiatimes.com/karunanidhi-caught-in-battle-of-words/articleshow/613764.cms.

115 Karunanidhi, *Kadithangal*, 37: 102.

116 '29 new faces in AIADMK's list,' *Rediff*, 24 February 2004. Accessed 1 May 2019, https://www.rediff.com/election/2004/feb/24tn.htm.

117 'Vajpayee goes Tamil,' *Rediff*, 6 May 2004. Accessed 1 May 2019, https://www.rediff.com/election/2004/may/06web.htm?zcc=ar;   Karunanidhi, *Kadithangal*, 37: 212.

118 Arun Ram, 'Karunanidhi, Vaiko campaign against Jayalalithaa; Tamil Nadu CM targets Sonia,' *India Today*, 10 May 2004. Accessed 1 May 2019, https://www.indiatoday.in/magazine/cover-story/story/20040510-mkarunanidhi-vaiko-campaign-against-jayalalitha-tamil-nadu-polls-790158-2004-05-09.

119 'It is my duty to oppose the BJP,' *Rediff*, 12 May 2004, https://www.rediff.com/election/2004/may/12einter2.htm.

120 Karunanidhi, *Kadithangal*, 37: 209.

121 Advani, *My Country*, 769.

122 https://www.rediff.com/election/2004/may/06espec1.htm; 'Voters' fury against AIADMK,' *Frontline*, 4 June 2004, https://frontline.thehindu.com/the-nation/article30222798.ece.

123 'Verdict not against government: Jaya,' *Rediff*, 14 May 2004. Accessed 1 May 2019, https://www.rediff.com/election/2004/may/14jaya.htm

124 'Problem with Baalu, Palanimanikkam's portfolios,' *Rediff*, 24 May 2004. Accessed 1 May 2018, https://www.rediff.com/news/2004/may/24dmk.htm.

125 *Murasoli*, 25 May 2004, p. 6; Swati Das, 'Karuna to stand his ground over portfolio issue,' *Times of India*, 24 May 2004. Accessed 1 May 2018, https://timesofindia.indiatimes.com/karuna-to-stand-his-ground-over-portfolio-issue/articleshow/696156.cms?utm_source=contentofinterest&utm_medium=text&utm_campaign=cppst.

126 'DMK's continuation in ministry in PM's hands: Karunanidhi,' *Rediff*, 24 May 2004. https://www.rediff.com/news/2004/may/24dmk3.htm; Onkar Singh, 'Independent charge of revenue for DMK,' *Rediff*, 25 May 2004. Accessed 1 May 2019, https://www.rediff.com/news/2004/may/25dmk.htm.

127 Vinod Mehta, *Lucknow Boy: A Memoir*, (Gurgaon, Penguin Viking, 2011), 224.

128 Karunanidhi, *Kadithangal*, 37: 268.

129 *Murasoli*, 31 May 2004, 6.

130 Prabhu Chawla, 'Jayalalithaa does not have leadership qualities: DMK chief Karunanidhi,' *India Today*, 27 December 2004. Accessed 1 May

2021, https://www.indiatoday.in/magazine/interview/story/20041227-jayalalithaa-does-not-have-leadership-qualities-dmk-chief-karunanidhi-788842-2004-12-26.

131 'Tamil Nadu bags lion's share in ministry,' *Rediff*, 22 May 2004. Accessed 1 May 2019, https://in.rediff.com/election/2004/may/22tn.htm.

132 R.K. Radhakrishnan, 'Politicians' children, some acceptable and some not so, in the fray,' *Frontline*, 27 March 2019. Accessed 19 May 2019, https://frontline.thehindu.com/dispatches/article26652543.ece.

133 'Vijayakanth, Ramadoss bury their hatchet,' *Indiaglitz*, 29 June 2004. Accessed 19 February 2019, https://www.indiaglitz.com/vijayakanth-ramadoss-bury-their-hatchet-telugu--news-9636.

134 'Powerful speeches of late AIADMK supremo,' *New Indian Express*, 5 December 2016. Accessed 7 December 2018, https://www.newindianexpress.com/states/tamil-nadu/2016/dec/05/the-powerful-speeches-of-late-aiadmk-supremo-jayalalithaa-1545887.html.

135 Karunanidhi, *Kadithangal*, 38: 294.

136 T.S. Subramanian, 'A festival in Chennai,' *Frontline*, 19 November 2004. Accessed 7 May 2019, https://frontline.thehindu.com/cover-story/article30225520.ece.

137 S. Viswanathan, 'Controversial career,' *Frontline*, 3 December 2004. Accessed 7 May 2019, https://frontline.thehindu.com/cover-story/article30225715.ece; Karunanidhi, *Kadithangal*, 38: 53–56.

138 'DMK chief rallies behind Shankaracharya,' *Rediff*, 22 November 2004. Accessed 19 February 2019, https://www.rediff.com/news/2004/nov/22kanchi4.htm.

139 'Kanchi seer's arrest most painful decision: Jaya,' *Rediff*, 30 November 2004. Accessed 19 February 2019, https://www.rediff.com/news/2004/nov/30kanchi1.htm.

140 TVR Shenoy, 'It is my duty to oppose the BJP,' *Rediff*, 12 May 2004. Accessed 19 February 2019, https://www.rediff.com/election/2004/may/12einter2.htm.

141 TVR Shenoy, 'Will Jayalalithaa split the DMK alliance,' *Rediff*, 17 February 2006. Accessed 19 February 2019, https://www.rediff.com/news/2006/feb/18flip.htm.

142 'MDMK won't give up self-respect: Vaiko,' *Rediff*, 20 February 2006. Accessed 19 February 2019, https://www.rediff.com/news/2006/feb/20mdmk.htm.

143 Shoba Warrier, 'Ideology, electoral alliance separate,' *Rediff*, 29 March 2006. Accessed 1 November 2019, https://www.rediff.com/news/2006/mar/29inter1.htm.

144 Shoba Warrier, 'Let us forget the past,' *Rediff*, 24 March 2006. Accessed 21 June 2022, https://in.rediff.com/news/2006/mar/24inter.htm; 'Sun TV blacked me out: Vaiko,' *Rediff*, 27 March 2006. Accessed 1 November 2019, https://www.rediff.com/news/2006/mar/27inter.htm.

145 Shoba Warrier, 'DMK manifesto hero of 2006 election,' *Rediff*, 11 May 2006. Accessed 1 November 2019, https://www.rediff.com/election/2006/may/11shobha.htm.

146 'TN polls: DMK promises quota for minorities,' *Rediff*, 29 March 2006. Accessed 1 November 2019, https://www.rediff.com/news/2006/mar/29dmk.htm.

147 'Promises, promises: AIADMK releases manifesto,' *Rediff*, 28 March 2006. Accessed 1 November 2019, https://www.rediff.com/news/2006/mar/28tn.htm.

148 'DMK election manifesto 'hero of 2006': Chidambaram,' *One India*, 24 April 2006. Accessed 1 November 2019, https://www.oneindia.com/2006/04/24/dmk-election-manifesto-hero-of-2006-chidambaram-1145860527.html.

149 'DMK's poll promises may colour TN red: Jaya,' *Rediff*, 4 April 2006. Accessed 1 October 2019, https://www.rediff.com/news/2006/apr/04tn3.htm.

150 'TN: Jaya promises 10 kg of free rice,' *Rediff*, 17 April 2006, Accessed 11 October 2019, https://www.rediff.com/election/2006/apr/17ptn3.htm.

151 'I will not loot the people,'—The Rediff Interview/Vijayakanth, *Rediff*, 8 May 2006. Accessed 11 October 2019, https://www.rediff.com/election/2006/may/08pinter.htm.

152 'Promises Galore in DMK manifesto,' *The Hindu*, 30 March 2006.

Chapter 26: 'Thamizhinath Thalaivar'?

1 T.S. Subramanian, 'Promises to keep,' *Frontline*, 2 June 2006, 26–28.

2 Pa. Thirumavelan, 'Vaarthai virus thagudhi meerum thalai,' *Vikatan*, 1 September 2009. Accessed 2 September 2018, https://www.vikatan.com/government-and-politics/politics/41661--2.

3 'Karunanidhi launches Rs 2 per kg rice scheme,' *Rediff*, 3 June 20016. Accessed 1 June 2019, https://www.rediff.com/news/2006/jun/03tn.htm.

4 T.S. Subramanian, 'Farce in Chennai,' *Frontline*, 3 November 2006, 129–33; S. Viswanathan, 'President's plight,' *Frontline*, 18 May 2007, 38–39.

5 T.S. Subramanian, 'Muted elation,' *Frontline*, 23 February 2007, 8–15; T.S. Subramanian, 'Bitter allies,' *Frontline*, 18 July 2008. Accessed 2

June 2019, https://frontline.thehindu.com/cover-story/article30196736.ece.

6   *Murasoli*, 8 May 2007, 2.

7   Karunanidhi, *Kadithangal*, 41: 330–38.

8   Ibid.

9   *Murasoli*, 10 May 2007, 1, 3.

10   *Murasoli*, 14 May 2007, 3.

11   'Maran says Karunanidhi was misled,' *Rediff*, 14 May 2007. Accessed 1 June 2019, https://www.rediff.com/news/2007/may/14maran2.htm; 'DMK hangs up on Maran; dials in Raja,' *Rediff*, 19 May 2007. Accessed 1 June 2019, https://www.rediff.com/news/2007/may/19wk3.htm.

12   T.S. Subramanian, 'Mayhem in Madurai,' *Frontline*, 1 June 2007, 22–25.

13   Vinod Mehta, *Editor Unplugged: Media, Magnates, Netas And Me*, (Gurgaon, Penguin, 2015), 57–58; 61.

14   'Former IT Minister Maran Says India's Ruling Coalition In Trouble,' US consul general cable, 23 February 2008. Accessed 20 September 2020, https://wikileaks.org/plusd/cables/08CHENNAI69_a.html.

15   'Feud between Karunanidhi, Marans reaches point of no return,' *Rediff*, 21 November 2008. Accessed 1 June 2019, https://www.rediff.com/news/2008/nov/21tn-karunanidhi-maran-brothers-feud-worsens.htm; Karunanidhi, *Kadithangal*, 41: 330–38.

16   'Feud between Karunanidhi, Marans reaches point of no return,' *Rediff*, 21 November 2008. Accessed 1 June 2021, https://www.rediff.com/news/2008/nov/21tn-karunanidhi-maran-brothers-feud-worsens.htm.

17   *Murasoli*, 2 December 2008, 1.

18   Ajay Sukumaran and Vidya Sivaramakrishnan, 'Karunanidhi meets his grand nephews; ends feud,' *Livemint*, 3 December 2008. Accessed 1 June 2019, https://www.livemint.com/Politics/xX4EzfJK3UbQaGDRqWJSLO/Karunanidhi-meets-his-grandnephews-ends-feud.html.

19   Vinod K. Jose, 'The Last Lear,' *Caravan Magazine*, 31 March 2011. Accessed 21 May 2019, https://caravanmagazine.in/reportage/last-lear.

20   *Tamil Nadu Legislative Assembly (Thirteenth Assembly) Review 2006–2011*, (Chennai: Legislative Assembly Secretariat, 2015), 129. Accessed 1 June 2020, https://assembly.tn.gov.in/archive/13th_2006/13threview.pdf.

21   Sutirtho Patranobis, 'All eyes on TN, Lanka treads cautious path,' *Hindustan Times*, 15 October 2008. Accessed 1 June 2019, https://www.hindustantimes.com/world/all-eyes-on-tn-lanka-treads-cautious-path/story-wjzyWmasfpeQeDn2dPsneJ.html.

22   Tamil issue: 'Jaya dares Karunandihi to resign,' *One India*, 18 October 2008. Accessed 1 May 2019, https://www.oneindia.com/2008/10/18/tamil-issue-jaya-dares-karunandihi-resign.html?story=1.

23   'Maran called Karunanidhi's October 2008 resignation threat a 'diversionary drama,' *The Hindu*, 23 May 2011. Accessed 1 June 2019, https://www.thehindu.com/news/maran-called-karunanidhis-october-2008-resignation-threat-a-diversionary-drama/article2040647.ece.

24   'India opposition says Tamil quit threats a 'farce,' *Reuters*, 16 October 2008. Accessed 1 June 2019, https://www.reuters.com/article/india-politics-tamil-idINISL36813620081016.

25   'Lanka told to protect Tamils' rights,' *Times of India*, 22 October 2008. Accessed 2 June 2020, https://timesofindia.indiatimes.com/india/lanka-told-to-protect-tamils-rights-pranab/articleshow/3629293.cms.

26   'Director Seeman's fiery speech in Rameshwaram – 1/2,' 2008, 12:50. Accessed 1 June 2019, https://www.dailymotion.com/video/x76t2z; 'Director Seeman's fiery speech in Rameshwaram – 2/2,' 2008, 12:50, Accessed 1 June 2019, https://www.dailymotion.com/video/x76t3f.

27   S.D. Muni, 'India's Tamil Politics and the Sri Lankan Ethnic Conflict,' ISAS Brief No. 86 – Date: 6 November 2008, 1–4. Accessed 1 June 2019, https://www.files.ethz.ch/isn/93801/87.pdf.

28   *Murasoli*, 27 October 2008, 1, 2; 'Lankan Tamils issue: Karunanidhi assures UPA,' Rediff, 26 October 2008. https://www.rediff.com/news/2008/oct/26ltte.htm.

29   'India has constraints in intervening in Sri Lanka, says Karunanidhi,' *The Hindu*, 3 November 2008. Accessed 2 June 2018, https://eoi.gov.in/eoisearch/MyPrint.php?2259?000/0017.

30   'MK diverting public attention: Jayalalitha,' *New Indian Express*, 5 November 2008. Accessed 2 June 2018, https://www.newindianexpress.com/cities/chennai/2008/nov/05/mk-diverting-public-attention-jayalalitha-4473.html.

31   'Exclusive: Sri Lankan government selling the country, says ex-president Mahinda Rajapaksa,' *WION*, 17 April 2017. Accessed 2 June 2018, https://www.wionews.com/south-asia/exclusive-sri-lankan-government-selling-the-country-says-ex-president-mahinda-rajapaksa-14601.

32   '"India a relation for us, while other nations are friends": Sri Lanka PM Mahinda Rajapaksa,' *Hindustan Times*, 22 September 2020. Accessed 1 June 2021, https://www.hindustantimes.com/india-news/india-a-relation-for-sri-lanka-while-other-nations-are-friends-pm-rajapaksa/story-24wmRTAc4whwbpf3nHSCfI.html.

33   Karunanidhi, *Kadithangal*, 41: 320.

34   *Murasoli*, 7 November 2008, 1.

35   *Murasoli*, 28 November 2008, 2.

36   'Thirumavalavan drops fast, signals "change of strategy,"' *TamilNet*, 18 January 2009. Accessed 1 June 2018, https://www.tamilnet.com/art.html?catid=13&artid=28058.

37   Karunanidhi, *Kadithangal*, 42: 225–28.

38   Ibid., 30–31.

39   *Tamil Nadu Legislative Assembly (Thirteenth Assembly) Review 2006–2011*, supra note 20, 131–32; Karunanidhi, *Kadithangal*, 42: 73.

40   Karunanidhi, *Kadithangal*, 42: 106.

41   S. Senthil Kumar, 'Dravidian paranoia hurting DMK patriarch,' *India Today*, 31 January 2009. Accessed 21 June 2019, https://www.indiatoday.in/latest-headlines/story/dravidian-paranoia-hurting-dmk-patrirarch-38513-2009-01-31.

42   T.S. Subramanian, 'Political tension,' *Frontline*, 27 February 2009. Accessed 2 June 2020, https://frontline.thehindu.com/cover-story/article30183727.ece.

43   Karunanidhi, *Kadithangal*, 42: 130.

44   https://www.reuters.com/article/idINIndia-38416720090309; Karunanidhi, *Kadithangal*, 42: 10.

45   'Will press for separate Eelam: AIADMK manifesto,' *India Today*, 18 April 2009. Accessed 2 June 2018, https://www.indiatoday.in/elections-south/tamil-nadu/story/will-press-for-separate-eelam-aiadmk-manifesto-44726-2009-04-16; AIADMK manifesto: 2009 parliamentary elections. Accessed 2 June 2018, https://parliamentlibraryindia.nic.in/writereaddata/Library/E_Manifesto/AIADMK_Manifesto_2009.pdf.

46   'Jaya launches poll battle with Eelam war cry,' *New Indian Express*, 19 April 2009. Accessed 1 May 2019, https://www.newindianexpress.com/states/tamil-nadu/2009/apr/19/jaya-launches-poll-battle-with-eelam-war-cry-42245.html.

47   'Never said LTTE is not a terror group: Karuna,' *India Today*, 20 April 2009. Accessed 1 May 2019, https://www.indiatoday.in/latest-headlines/story/never-said-ltte-is-not-a-terror-group-karuna-44979-2009-04-19.

48   *Murasoli*, 22 April 2004, 1.

49   'War of words in TN over Lanka issue,' *Times of India*, 23 April 2009. Accessed 21 June 2019, https://timesofindia.indiatimes.com/india/war-of-words-in-tn-over-lanka-issue/articleshow/4437732.cms.

50 'Karunanidhi hits out at Jaya over Sri Lankan issue,' *India Today*, 23 April 2009. Accessed 15 September 2019, https://www.indiatoday.in/ elections-south/tamil-nadu/story/karunanidhi-hits-out-at-jaya-over-sri-lankan-issue-45389-2009-04-22.

51 Tamilaruvi Manian, *Oru Vazhipokanin Vazkaipayanam*, (Chennai: Karpagam Puthagalayam, 2000), 195–95.

52 *Frontline*, 22 May 2009, 22–23.

53 Karunanidhi, *Kadithangal*, 42: 268.

54 Karunanidhi, *Kadithangal*, 42: 276.

55 *Murasoli,* 29 March 2013, 1.

56 T.S. Subramanian, 'Tipping point,' *Frontline*, 19 April 2013, 19–24.

57 Karunanidhi, *Kadithangal*, 48: 90.

58 Shivshankar Menon, *Choices: Inside the Making of India's Foreign Policy (Geopolitics in the 21st Century)*, (Washington, D.C: Brookings Institution Press, 2016), 141–42.

59 'Chidambaram feels Tamil heat,' *Rediff*, 11 May 2009. Accessed 1 February 2019, http://election.rediff.com/report/2009/may/11/slide-show-1-kollywood-hits-out-at-congress-and-chidambaram-in-sivagangai.htm.

60 Ibid.

61 'Jayalalithaa slams DMK for its failures,' *New Indian Express*, 18 October 2010. Accessed 1 February 2019, https://www.newindianexpress. com/states/tamil-nadu/2010/oct/18/jayalalithaa-slams-dmk-for-its-failures-196200.html.

62 Karunanidhi, *Kadithangal*, Vol. 42: 222.

63 'Karunanidhi's poll strategy and maturity pay off,' *Economic Times*, 16 May 2009. Accessed 2 June 2019, https://economictimes.indiatimes. com/news/politics-and-nation/karunanidhis-poll-strategy-and-maturity-pay-off/articleshow/4540220.cms?from=mdr.

64 'Karunanidhi promises homeland for Lankan Tamils,' *Rediff*, 7 May 2009. Accessed 2 May 2019, http://election.rediff.com/report/2009/ may/07/loksabhapoll-karunanidhi-promises-homeland-for-lankan-tamils.htm.

65 'PM pooh-poohs Jaya's demand to send army to Lanka,' *Economic Times*, 9 May 20019. Accessed 2 May 2019, https://economictimes.indiatimes. com/news/politics-and-nation/pm-pooh-poohs-jayas-demand-to-send-army-to-lanka/articleshow/4503799.cms?from=mdr.

66 'Eelam: Jaya promises army action,' *India Today*, 30 April 2009. Accessed 2 May 2019, https://www.indiatoday.in/elections-south/tamil-nadu/ story/eelam-jaya-promises-army-action-46099-2009-04-29.

67   'Jayalalithaa calls Chidambaram's win in 2009 a fraud,' *Economic Times*, 15 June 2011. Accessed 1 March 2019.

68   Bharat ballot 09: Tamil Nadu analysis: Congress-DMK alliance stages a stunning victory, 15 June 2009, US consul general cable. Accessed 2 May 2019, https://wikileaks.org/plusd/cables/09CHENNAI185_a.html.

69   'Money power wins over democracy, says Jayalalithaa,' *Rediff*, 16 May 2009. Accessed 3 June 2019, https://www.rediff.com/election/2009/may/16loksabhapoll-money-power-wins-over-democracy-says-jayalalithaa.htm.

70   'U.N. panel says war crimes likely committed in Sri Lanka war,' *Reuters*, 18 April 2011. Accessed 3 June 2019, https://www.reuters.com/article/us-srilanka-un-idUSTRE73H2WI20110418; 'UN "failed Sri Lanka civilians", says internal probe,' *BBC*, 13 November 2012, Accessed 1 March 2019, ttps://www.bbc.com/news/world-asia-20308610/.

71   *Report of the Secretary-General's Panel of Experts on Accountability in Sri Lanka*, 31 March 2011, 41.

72   'Jaya says Rajapakse govt should address oppressed Tamilians,' *Times of India*, 22 May 2009. Accessed 2 June 2019, https://timesofindia.indiatimes.com/city/chennai/jaya-says-rajapakse-govt-should-address-oppressed-tamilians-grievances/articleshow/4562104.cms.

73   T.S. Subramanian, 'Tamil Nadu parties for U.N. role,' *Frontline*, 19 June 2009, 30–31.

74   'Sri Lanka: UN Rights Council Fails Victims,' HRW, 27 May 2009. Accessed 3 May 2019, https://www.hrw.org/news/2009/05/27/sri-lanka-un-rights-council-fails-victims.

75   'UN rejects calls for Sri Lanka war crimes inquiry,' the *Guardian*, 28 May 2009. Accessed 2 June 2019, https://www.theguardian.com/world/2009/may/28/sri-lanka-un-war-crimes-investigation.

76   'UN Rights Council: Sri Lanka Vote a Strong Message for Justice,' HRW, 22 March 2012. Accessed 3 June 2019, https://www.hrw.org/news/2012/03/22/un-rights-council-sri-lanka-vote-strong-message-justice.

77   Sutirtho Patranobis, 'By crushing Tamil Tigers, I fought India's war: Rajapaksa,' *Hindustan Times*, 29 May 2009. Accessed 14 May 2019, https://www.hindustantimes.com/india/by-crushing-tamil-tigers-i-fought-india-s-war-rajapaksa/story-ULicQz6xiFrICAgshQ3AOI.html.

78   'India won't tell Sri Lanka what to do,' *Tamil Guardian*, 23 June 2009, https://www.tamilguardian.com/content/india-won%E2%80%99t-tell-sri-lanka-what-do.

79 Lakshmi Subramanian, 'Gotabaya Rajapaksa interview: "This government is very complacent; I will run for president,' the *Week*, 14 May 2019. Accessed 20 June 2020, https://www.theweek.in/theweek/cover/2019/05/03/gotabaya-rajapaksa-interview-this-government-is-very-complacent-i-will-run-for-president.html; 'India won't tell Sri Lanka what to do.'

80 Pa. Thirumavelan, *Yaaraithaan Edhirkavillai?* (Chennai, Vikatan, Pirasuram, 2017), 91.

81 Ibid.

Chapter 27: Second UPA

1   *Murasoli*, 11 May 2009, 1–3.

2   Dhananjay Mahapatra, 'Cong to use '04 formula to allot berths,' *Times of India*, 22 May 2009. Accessed 1 March 2019, http://timesofindia.indiatimes.com/articleshow/4562509.cms?utm_source=contentofinterest&utm_medium=text&utm_campaign=cppst.

3   'DMK-Cong deadlock continues; Karunanidhi returns to Chennai,' *Hindustan Times*, 22 May 2009. Accessed 22 May 2019, https://www.hindustantimes.com/delhi/dmk-cong-dealock-continues-karunanidhi-returns-to-chennai/story-KU9qqjx0j4mtJkyUHnOGcK.html.

4   'DMK wants 8 posts, Cong offers 6,' *Economic Times*, 21 May 2009. Accessed 22 May 2019, https://economictimes.indiatimes.com/news/politics-and-nation/dmk-wants-8-posts-cong-offers-6/articleshow/4559162.cms?from=mdr' http://election.rediff.com/report/2009/may/22/loksabhapoll-rahul-gandhi-shut-the-door-on-dmk.htm.

5   'Karuna thanks PM for statement in favour of Baalu, Raja,' *Indian Express*, 23 May 20019. Accessed 21 May 2020, https://indianexpress.com/article/political-pulse/karuna-thanks-pm-for-statement-in-favour-of-baalu-raja/.

6   *Murasoli*, 30 May 2011, 3.

7   Thangavel Appachi, 'India cabinet minister breaks his parliamentary silence,' *BBC*, 6 August 2010. Accessed 1 May 2019, https://www.bbc.com/news/world-south-asia-10884125

8   'Not allowing Alagiri to speak Tamil is an insult: Jayalalithaa,' *The Hindu*, 14 September 2009. Accessed 17 November 2020, https://www.thehindu.com/news/cities/chennai/Not-allowing-Alagiri-to-speak-Tamil-is-an-insult-Jayalalithaa/article16881634.ece.

9   'Instances when late DMK chief Karunanidhi played hide n seek over his retirement from active politics,' *New Indian Express*, 7 August 2018. Accessed 20 May 2020, https://www.newindianexpress.com/states/tamil-nadu/2018/aug/07/instances-when-late-dmk-chief-karunanidhi-played-hide-n-seek-over-his-retirement-from-active-politic-1854617.html.

10   Ibid.

11   Ibid.

12   R. Arivanantham, 'DMK retains Pennagaram seat, AIADMK loses deposit,' *The Hindu*, 30 March 2010. Accessed 21 May 2019, https://www.thehindu.com/news/national/tamil-nadu/DMK-retains-Pennagaram-seat-AIADMK-loses-deposit/article16634621.ece.

13   'Alagiri theermaana paeti,' *Vikatan*, 27 March 2010. Accessed 20 May 2020, https://www.vikatan.com/government-and-politics/51714--2; Shekhar Iyer, 'Sidelined by father, Alagiri lets it all out,' *Hindustan Times*, 26 March 2010, https://www.hindustantimes.com/delhi/sidelined-by-father-alagiri-lets-it-all-out/story-I7Dv4TylDeKfTtQ46dedIO.html.

14   'Chronology of 2G scam case,' *Rediff*, 2 February 2012. Accessed 20 May 2019, https://www.rediff.com/money/slide-show/slide-show-1-chronology-of-2-g-scam-case/20120202.htm.

15   'Probe 2G spectrum allocation, demands Opposition,' *Times of India*, 24 July 2009. Accessed 22 May 2019, https://timesofindia.indiatimes.com/india/probe-2g-spectrum-allocation-demands-opposition/articleshow/4813080.cms.

16   'Raja is targeted because he is Dalit: Karunanidhi,' *Rediff*, 3 May 2010. Accessed 2 May 2019, https://www.rediff.com/news/report/raja-is-targeted-because-he-is-dalit-says-karunanidhi/20100503.htm.

17   'Karunanidhi playing Dalit card: Jayalalithaa,' *The Hindu*, 7 May 2010. Accessed 22 May 2019, https://www.thehindu.com/news/Karunanidhi-playing-Dalit-card-Jayalalithaa/article16298994.ece.

18   'Chronology of 2G scam case.'

19   'Karuna says "not guilty" but Cong set on replacing Raja,' *Times of India*, 13 November 2010. Accessed 22 May 2019, https://timesofindia.indiatimes.com/india/karuna-says-not-guilty-but-cong-set-on-replacing-raja/articleshow/6917292.cms

20   'Jayalalithaa demands detailed probe into 2G spectrum scam,' *Two Circles.net*, 15 November 2010. Accessed 22 May 2019, https://twocircles.net/2010nov15/jayalalithaa_demands_detailed_probe_2g_spectrum_scam.html.

21 'In resignation, Karunanidhi stands by Raja,' NDTV, 15 November 2010. Accessed 22 May 2019, https://www.ndtv.com/india-news/in-resignation-karunanidhi-stands-by-raja-439254.

22 T.S. Subramanian, 'Friends and foes,' *Frontline*, 11 March 2011, 9–10.

23 Karunanidhi, *Kadithangal*, 44: 335.

24 Subramanian Swamy v. A. Raja, 24 August 2012, 11 SCR 2012, 874-915. Accessed 2 June 2019, https://main.sci.gov.in/pdf/SupremeCourtReport/2012_v11_piv.pdf.

25 '2G scam: PAC summons Niira Radia, Ratan Tata on April 4,' *Economic Times*, 28 March 2011. Accessed 22 May 2020, https://economictimes.indiatimes.com/industry/telecom/2g-scam-pac-summons-niira-radia-ratan-tata-on-april-4/articleshow/7808117.cms?from=mdr.

26 'Karunanidhi slams media reports on Niira Radia tapes,' *India Today*, 20 December 2010. Accessed 20 May 2019, https://www.indiatoday.in/2g-scam/politics/story/karunanidhi-slams-media-reports-on-niira-radia-tapes-87271-2010-12-16.

27 M. Gunasekaran, 'Maran, Azhagiri and Raja set to join Cabinet,' *Times of India*, 25 May 2009. Accessed 22 May 2019, https://timesofindia.indiatimes.com/india/maran-azhagiri-and-raja-set-to-join-cabinet/articleshow/4572772.cms; Karunanidhi, *Kadithangal*, 4: 276-80.

28 Priyanka Mittal, Aditi Singh, '2G spectrum scam: A timeline of events,' *Livemint*, 21 December 2017. Accessed 22 May 2019, https://www.livemint.com/Politics/lhr4Lk37t2WooRRijoitxN/2G-spectrum-scam-verdict-A-timeline-of-events.html.

29 'Evidence! Part of OP Saini's 2G scam verdict borrowed from Bollywood hit Jolly LLB?' *India Today*, 18 January 2018. Accessed 2 May 2020, https://www.indiatoday.in/fyi/story/2g-scam-verdict-op-saini-accused-acquitted-a-raja-kanimozhi-1112388-2017-12-22.

30 'Manmohan Singh reacts on 2G scam verdict, alleges "vicious propaganda" against his government,' *India Today Television*, 21 December 2017. Accessed 22 May 2019, https://www.indiatoday.in/popular-now/video/2g-scam-case-manmohan-singh-a-raja-m-kanimozhi-congress-1114254-2017-12-21.

31 'Subramanian Swamy asks govt to challenge 2G scam verdict,' *Economic Times*, 21 December 2017. Accessed 22 May 2019, https://m.economictimes.com/news/politics-and-nation/subramanian-swamy-asks-govt-to-challenge-2g-scam-verdict/articleshow/62191260.cms.

32 T.S. Subramanian, 'Friends and foes,' *Frontline*, 11 March 2011. Accessed 22 May 2019, https://frontline.thehindu.com/cover-story/article30174653.ece.

33 'Kanimozhi arrested as bail plea rejected by CBI court in 2G scam,' *Hindustan Times*, 20 May 2011. Accessed 22 May 2020, https://economictimes.indiatimes.com/news/politics-and-nation/kanimozhi-arrested-as-bail-plea-rejected-by-cbi-court-in-2g-scam/articleshow/8463618.cms?utm_source=contentofinterest&utm_medium=text&utm_campaign=cppst

34 Krishnakumar Padmanabhan, 'TN: Greedy Congress upsets DMK, split imminent,' *Rediff*, 5 March 2011. Accessed 22 May 2019, https://www.rediff.com/news/report/tn-greedy-congress-upsets-dmk-split-imminent/20110305.htm.

35 M.C, Rajan, Kay Benedict, 'Tamil Nadu polls: Cong, DMK fight over "winnable" seats,' *India Today*, 10 March 2011. Accessed 22 May 2019, https://www.indiatoday.in/india/south/story/tamil-nadu-polls-congress-dmk-fight-over-winnable-seats-130033-2011-03-09; 'DMK yields, Cong gets 63 TN assembly seats in seat-sharing,' Governance Now, 8 March 2011. Accessed 2 May 2019, https://www.governancenow.com/news/regular-story/dmk-yields-cong-gets-63-tn-assembly-seats-seat-sharing.

36 'Naan kudikaaranaa? Jayvuku Vijayakanth kandanam,' *One India*, 24 October 2006. Accessed 2 May 2019, https://tamil.oneindia.com/news/2006/10/24/dmdk.html?story=1; 'Tamil Nadu: Vijayakanth and Jayalalithaa still do not see eye to eye,' *India Today*, 3 September 2011. Accessed 22 May 2019, https://www.indiatoday.in/magazine/nation/story/20110912-vijayakanth-and-jaya-still-do-not-see-eye-to-eye-747495-2011-09-02.

37 Shoba Warrier, 'Once a political tiger, now who cares?' *Rediff*, 22 March 2011. Accessed 22 May 2019, https://www.rediff.com/news/report/tamil-nadu-election-dmk-aiadmk-vaiko-dmdk/20110322.htm; S. Dorairaj, 'Troubles within,' *Frontline*, 22 April 2011, 115.

38 T.S. Subramanian, 'Troubled alliances,' *Frontline*, 8 April 2011, 126–28.

39 'Jaya unleashes war of sops to take on DMK,' *Times of India*, 25 March 2011. Accessed 20 May 2019, https://timesofindia.indiatimes.com/assembly-elections-2011/tamil-nadu/jaya-unleashes-war-of-sops-to-take-on-dmk/articleshow/7783839.cms; Karunanidhi, *Kadithangal*, 45: 392; 'DMK promises free wet grinder, 35 kg rice a month,' *The Hindu*, 29 March 2011. Accessed 1 May 2019, https://www.thehindu.com/news/national/tamil-nadu/DMK-promises-free-wet-grinder-35-kg-rice-a-month/article14953759.ece; 'State elections 2011: Tamil Nadu's freebie rage pushes up alcoholism,' *Economic Times*, 22 April 2011.

Accessed 2 May 2019, https://economictimes.indiatimes.com/news/
politics-and-nation/state-elections-2011-tamil-nadus-freebie-rage-
pushes-up-alcoholism/articleshow/8053615.cms?from=mdr;   Gladwin
Emmanuel, 'Eye on TN polls, Jaya offers gold to voters,' *Bangalore
Mirror*, 24 March 2011. Accessed 22 May 2019, https://bangaloremirror.
indiatimes.com/news/india/eye-on-tn-polls-jaya-offers-gold-to-voters/
articleshow/21645600.cms.

40 T.S. Subramanian, Clean sweep,' *Frontline*, 3 June 2011, 10–15.

41 Ibid., T.S. Subramanian, S. Dorairaj, 'Was there a wave?' *Frontline*, 6
    May 2011, 29–33.

42 R.K. Radhakrishnan, "Defeated by money power," *Frontline*, 22 July
    2016, 48.

43 '2G case: Ties with DMK will remain strong, says Congress,' *Economic
    Times*, 6 May 2011. Accessed 22 May 2019, https://economictimes.
    indiatimes.com/news/politics-and-nation/2g-case-ties-with-
    dmk-will-remain-strong-says-congress/articleshow/8176836.
    cms?from=mdr.

44 '2G chargesheet a publicity exercise: DMK,' *Rediff*, 26 April 2011.
    https://www.rediff.com/news/report/twog-chargesheet-a-publicity-
    exercise-says-dmk/20110426.htm

45 T.S. Subramanian, 'In a bind,' *Frontline*, 20 May 2011. Accessed 22 May
    2019, https://frontline.thehindu.com/politics/article30175559.ece.

46 '2G scam: Emotional Karunanidhi backs Kanimozhi,' *Moneylife*, 27
    April 2011. Accessed 2 May 2019, https://www.moneylife.in/article/2g-
    scam-emotional-karunanidhi-backs-kanimozhi/15910.html.

47 'Amma Jayalalitha and captain Vijayakanth quarrel in TN Assembly!!'
    (Jayalalithaa speech in the assembly criticizing Vijayakanth's conduct),
    YouTube, 7:20, https://www.youtube.com/watch?v=y-V8U19WN1E;
    Murasoli, 2 February 2012, 3.

48 R.K. Radhakrishnan, "I hope to unravel the truth one day'—Interview
    with Kanimozhi,' *Frontline*, 19 January 2018, 16.

49 *Murasoli*, 20 May 2011, 1.

50 'Karunanidhi blames Centre for Kanimozhi arrest,' *NDTV*, 6 June 2011.
    Accessed 1 June 2019, https://www.ndtv.com/india-news/karunanidhi-
    blames-centre-for-kanimozhi-arrest-457658.

51 Ibid.

52 Karunanidhi, *Kadithangal*, 45: 209–16; '2G Spectrum scam: Karunanidhi
    in Delhi to meet daughter Kanimozhi,' *Economic Times*, 23 May 2011.
    Accessed 2 June 2019, https://economictimes.indiatimes.com/news/

politics-and-nation/2g-spectrum-scam-karunanidhi-in-delhi-to-meet-daughter-kanimozhi/articleshow/8529405.cms?from=mdr.

53 *Murasoli*, 12 November 2011, 8.

54 Kaverre Bamzai, 'Karunanidhi fumes at reporters regarding daughter Kanimozhi arrest,' *India Today*, 27 June 2011. Accessed 2 June 2020, https://www.indiatoday.in/magazine/glass-house/story/20110627-karunanidhi-gets-angry-at-reporters-on-kanimozhi-arrest-746566-2011-06-17; Karunanidhi, *Kadithangal*, 45: 239–42.

55 V. Venkatesan, 'Clear confusion,' *Frontline*, 18 November 2011, 40.

56 Sarah Charlton, 'UN screens Channel 4 Sri Lanka war crimes film,' Channel 4 News, 3 June 2011. Accessed 1 June 2019, https://www.channel4.com/news/un-screens-channel-4-sri-lanka-war-crimes-film.

57 Brian Senewiratne, 'UK Channel 4 Videos on Sri Lanka: Background is essential,' *Sri Lanka Guardian*, 18 March 2012. Accessed 1 June 2019, http://www.srilankaguardian.org/2012/03/uk-channel-4-videos-on-sri-lanka.html.

58 'Tamil Nadu wants India to impose economic sanctions against Lanka,' *Indian Express*, 8 June 2011. Accessed 20 May 2020, https://indianexpress.com/article/india/regional/tamil-nadu-wants-india-to-impose-economic-sanctions-against-lanka/; 'Jaya faults DMK for death of Lankan Tamils,' *New Indian Express*, 9 June 2011. Accessed 1 June 2019, https://www.newindianexpress.com/states/tamil-nadu/2011/jun/09/jaya-faults-dmk-for-death-of-lankan-tamils-260917.html.

59 Venkatesh Chakravarthy, 'The star, the actor and the woman,' *Frontline*, 6 January 2017, 24–25.

60 'India should not support Sri Lanka at UNHRC hearing: Karunanidhi,' *Times of India*, 29 February 2012. Accessed 1 June 2020, https://timesofindia.indiatimes.com/india/india-should-not-support-sri-lanka-at-unhrc-hearing-karunanidhi/articleshow/12081095.cms.

61 'Support US-backed resolution at UN rights council: Jayalalithaa,' *The Hindu*, 7 March 2012. Accessed 1 June 2019, https://www.thehindu.com/news/national/tamil-nadu/support-usbacked-resolution-at-un-rights-council-jayalalithaa/article2967688.ece.

62 Ibid., 'PM's response to SL probe row not satisfying: Jaya,' *Rediff*, 14 March 2012. Accessed 1 June 2019, https://www.rediff.com/news/report/pms-response-to-sl-probe-row-not-satisfying-jaya/20120314.htm; 'Resolution against Sri Lanka: PM writes to Karunanidhi, hopes for "forward-looking outcome",' *India Today*, 14 March 2012. Accessed 1

May 2019, https://www.indiatoday.in/india/north/story/sri-lanka-war-crime-un-resolution-pm-karunanidhi-95855-2012-03-13.

63   'US seeks commitment from Lanka over reconciliation efforts,' *Rediff*, 14 September 2012. Accessed 1 May 2019, https://www.rediff.com/news/report/us-seeks-commitment-from-lanka-over-reconciliation-efforts/20120914.htm

64   'Jayalalithaa, Karunanidhi vie for credit on India's vote against Sri Lanka,' *Times of India*, 23 March 2012. Accessed 1 May 2019, https://timesofindia.indiatimes.com/india/jayalalithaa-karunanidhi-vie-for-credit-on-indias-vote-against-sri-lanka/articleshow/12375088.cms.

Chapter 28: Jayalalithaa Returns

1   'Sri Lanka raps Karunanidhi over Eelam call,' *Deccan Herald*, 21 April 2012. Accessed 1 May 2019, https://www.deccanherald.com/content/243724/sri-lanka-raps-karunanidhi-over.html.

2   'Karunanidhi grasps Eelam's last straw,' *New Indian Express*, 29 April 2012. Accessed 1 May 2019, https://www.newindianexpress.com/thesundaystandard/2012/apr/29/karunanidhi-grasps-eelams-last-straw-363076.html.

3   'Karunanidhi plays Eelam card, revives TESO,' *New Indian Express*, 1 May 2012. Accessed 1 April 2019, https://www.newindianexpress.com/states/tamil-nadu/2012/may/01/karunanidhi-plays-eelam-card-revives-teso-363833.html

4   Karthick S., 'Karunanidhi decides to drop Eelam agenda from TESO conference,' *Times of India*, 16 July 2012. Accessed 1 May 2019, https://timesofindia.indiatimes.com/india/karunanidhi-decides-to-drop-eelam-agenda-from-teso-conference/articleshow/14994104.cms.

5   'Eelam not an imaginary word: Karunanidhi,' *The Hindu*, 11 August 2012. Accessed 2 June 2020, https://www.thehindu.com/news/national/tamil-nadu/eelam-not-an-imaginary-word-karunanidhi/article3751284.ece.

6   'Centre withdraws its objection to the use of the term "Eelam",' *The Hindu*, 11 August 2012. Accessed 2 June 2020, https://www.thehindu.com/news/national/tamil-nadu/centre-withdraws-its-objection-to-the-use-of-the-term-eelam/article3754481.ece.

7   Pushpa Iyengar, 'In The Eelam's shade.' Accessed 1 May 2020, https://www.outlookindia.com/magazine/story/in-the-eelams-shade/281995; 'Karunanidhi seeks long and medium term solution,' *The Hindu*, 13

August 2012. Accessed 2 June 2020, https://www.thehindu.com/
news/national/tamil-nadu/karunanidhi-seeks-long-and-medium-term-
solution/article3758504.ece.

8   'TESO conference a deceitful drama,' *New Indian Express*, 28 August
2012. Accessed 2 June 2020, https://www.newindianexpress.com/cities/
chennai/2012/aug/28/teso-conference-a-deceitful-drama-400995.html.

9   *Murasoli*, 30 January 2013, 1.

10 *Murasoli*, 6 February 2013, 1–3; 'TESO calls for Indian resolution
on Lanka,' Colombo Gazette, 5 February 2013. Accessed 2 June
2020, https://colombogazette.com/2013/02/05/teso-calls-for-indian-
resolution-on-lanka/

11 T. S. Subramanian, 'Tipping point,' *Frontline*, 19 April 2013, 18–24.

12 *Murasoli*, 21 February 2013, 1.

13 *Murasoli*, 8 March 2013, 5.

14 *Murasoli*, 9 March 2013, 1.

15 *Murasoli*, 19 March 2013, 1; *Murasoli*, 20 March 2013, 1; Murasoli, 21
March 2013, 1; T.S. Subramanian, 'Tipping point,' supra note 11.

16 'India votes against Sri Lanka at UNHRC, DMK slams government
for diluting resolution,' *Times of India*, 21 March 2013. Accessed 22
March 2021, https://timesofindia.indiatimes.com/india/india-votes-
against-sri-lanka-at-unhrc-dmk-slams-govt-for-diluting-resolution/
articleshow/19109157.cms.

17 'Tipping point.' 'Congress, DMK meeting fails to make headway on
Sri Lanka,' *Rediff*, 19 March 2013. Accessed 1 May 2019, https://
www.rediff.com/news/report/congress-dmk-meeting-fails-to-make-
headway-on-sri-lanka/20130319.htm; 'India should back US move
against Sri Lanka, says Jayalalithaa,' *India Today*, 18 March 2013.
Accessed 1 May 2019, https://www.indiatoday.in/india/south/story/
sri-lankan-tamil-issue-jayalalithaa-aiadmk-chief-unhrc-geneva-us-
resolution-156478-2013-03-17.

18 Chaturanga Pradeep Samarawickrama, 'Stay away from Commonwealth
Heads meet: DMK,' Daily Mirror Online, 25 March 2013. Accessed
2 June 2019, https://www.dailymirror.lk/article/stay-away-from-
commonwealth-heads-meet-dmk-27196.html.

19 'Jayalalithaa accuses Karunanidhi of doublespeak on Tamils
issue,' *Economic Times*, 27 March 2013. Accessed 1 June 2019,
https://economictimes.indiatimes.com/news/politics-and-nation/
jayalalithaa-accuses-karunanidhi-of-doublespeak-on-tamils-issue/
articleshow/19240928.cms?from=mdr.

20   'India should boycott Commonwealth meet in Colombo: Tamil Eelam Supporters Organisation,' *Economic Times*, 16 July 2013. Accessed 1 July 2019, https://economictimes.indiatimes.com/news/politics-and-nation/india-should-boycott-commonwealth-meet-in-colombo-tamil-eelam-supporters-organisation/articleshow/21107504.cms?from=mdr.

21   *Tamil Nadu Legislative Assembly (Fourteenth Session) Review (2011–2016)*, 171–72. Accessed 1 July 2019, https://assembly.tn.gov.in/archive/14th_2011/14threview.pdf.

22   Matthias Williams, 'India PM likely to skip Sri Lanka summit amid war crimes row,' Reuters, 10 November 2013. Accessed 1 July 2019, https://www.reuters.com/article/india-sri-lanka-manmohan-idINDEE9A902E20131110.

23   *Murasoli*, 4 January 2013, 1.

24   'M.K. Alagiri Exclusive Interview In Puthiya Thalaimurai's Agni Paritchai - Part 3,' *Puthiyathalaimurai TV*, 5 January 2014, 9:21. Accessed 22 July 2019, 9:21, https://youtu.be/vBLcgiVh05M; 'M.K. Alagiri Exclusive Interview In Puthiya Thalaimurai's Agni Paritchai - Part 4,' *Puthiyathalaimurai TV*, 5 January 2014, 14:35. Accessed 22 July 2019, https://www.youtube.com/watch?v=t1E7wdWNxrU; '"I will accept no one except my father as party leader": M.K. Alagiri,' *The Hindu*, 6 January 2014. Accessed 2 July 2019, https://www.thehindu.com/news/national/tamil-nadu/i-will-accept-no-one-except-my-father-as-party-leader-mk-alagiri/article5542639.ece.

25   B. Kolappan, 'Alagiri's remarks against Vijayakant embarrass DMK,' *The Hindu*, 7 January 2014. Accessed 2 July 2019, https://www.thehindu.com/news/national/tamil-nadu/alagiris-remarks-against-vijayakant-embarrass-dmk/article5546161.ece.

26   'Karunanidhi warns rebel Alagiri, says anybody can be expelled from DMK,' *India Today*, 7 January 2014. Accessed 2 July 2019, https://www.indiatoday.in/india/south/story/karunanidhi-warns-rebel-alagiri-says-anybody-can-be-expelled-from-dmk-175910-2014-01-06.

27   *Murasoli*, 7 January 2013, 1.

28   *Frontline*, 8 February 2013, 47–49.

29   'Karunanidhi warns rebel Alagiri, says anybody can be expelled from DMK.'

30   R. Ramasubramanian, 'There will be bad blood: Bitter succession war between Alagiri and Stalin jeopardises the fading chances of DMK in the General Elections,' *India Today*, 10 February 2014. Accessed 2 July 2019, https://www.indiatoday.in/magazine/special-

report/story/20140210-mk-alagiri-dmk-chief-m-karunanidhi-stalin-800028-1999-11-29.

31   R. Ramasubramanian, 'Karunanidhi suspends elder son Alagiri from DMK,' *India Today*, 24 January 2014. Accessed 2 July 2019, https://www.indiatoday.in/india/south/story/karunanidhi-suspends-elder-son-alagiri-from-dmk-178189-2014-01-24.

32   T.S. Subramanian, 'Battle of brothers,' *Frontline*, 5 February 2014. Accessed 2 July 2019, https://frontline.thehindu.com/the-nation/battle-of-brothers/article5652552.ece.

33   *Murasoli*, 28 January 2014, 1; B. Kolappan, K. Radhakrishnan, 'Cruel remarks about Stalin broke my heart, says Karunanidhi,' *The Hindu*, 28 January 2014. Accessed 2 July 2019, https://www.thehindu.com/news/national/tamil-nadu/cruel-remarks-about-stalin-broke-my-heart-says-karunanidhi/article5626346.ece.

34   'Elections 2014: Vaiko meets Alagiri to seek support,' 23 March 2014, *Deccan Chronicle*, https://www.deccanchronicle.com/140324/nation-politics/article/elections-2014-vaiko-meets-alagiri-seek-support.

35   T.S. Subramanian, 'DMK and sons,' *Frontline*, 18 April 2014, 40.

36   N. Sathiya Moorthy, 'Jayalalithaa keeping her alliance options open?' *Rediff*, 28 February 2014. Accessed 2 July 2019, https://www.rediff.com/news/special/jayalalithaa-keeping-her-alliance-options-open/20140228.htm.

37   T.S. Subramanian, 'Interesting Contests,' *Frontline*, 2 April 2014. Accessed 2 July 2019, https://frontline.thehindu.com/politics/interesting-contests/article5854234.ece.

38   S. Vijay Kumar, 'AIADMK's election promises manifest national ambitions,' *The Hindu*, 25 February 2014. Accessed 22 July 2019, https://www.thehindu.com/news/national/tamil-nadu/aiadmks-election-promises-manifest-national-ambitions/article5725558.ece.

39   P. Ramasubramanian, 'In manifesto, DMK proposes abolition of death penalty,' *India Today*, 12 March 2014. Accessed 2 July 2019, https://www.indiatoday.in/elections/highlights/story/dmk-manifesto-m-karunanidhi-j-jayalalithaa-184467-2014-03-11.

40   T.S. Subramanian, 'Son-rise party,' *Frontline*, 2 May 2014, 47.

41   K. Annamalai (K. Annamalai), 'A gentle reminder to Thiru @mkstalin on what he spoke a few years back about the #CashForJobScam tainted Thiru Senthilbalaji. Are you going to refute this, Thiru @mkstalin?' Twitter, 14 June 2023, 1:51 am, https://twitter.com/i/status/1668858719365644288; Poulomi Ghosh, 'When Stalin spoke

about Senthilbalaji "corruption", Annamalai posts video,' *Hindustan Times*, 14 June 2023. Accessed 1 July 2023, https://www.hindustantimes.com/india-news/when-stalin-spoke-about-senthil-balajis-corruption-annamalai-posts-video-101686724912089.html; 'Old video surfaces of TN CM Stalin criticising Senthilbalaji "corruption, land grabbing",' *Indian Express*, 14 June 2023. Accessed 2 July 2023, https://www.newindianexpress.com/states/tamil-nadu/2023/jun/14/old-video-surfaces-of-tn-cm-stalin-criticising-senthil-balajis-corruption-land-grabbing-2585022.html.

42   T.S. Subramanian, 'AIADMK: Lone ranger,' *Frontline*, 16 April 2014, 36–37; 'Jayalalithaa ends campaigning, says she is better than Narendra Modi,' *India Today*, 22 April 2014. Accessed 1 July 2023, https://www.indiatoday.in/elections/tamil-nadu/story/jayalalithaa-says-she-is-better-than-narendra-modi-189943-2014-04-22

43   'Why decision to free Rajiv Gandhi killers is a political masterstroke,' *BBC*, 19 February 2014, Accessed 1 July 2023, https://www.bbc.com/news/world asia india 26252743.

44   Bhadra Sinha and Rajesh Ahuja, 'Supreme Court halts release of Rajiv Gandhi's killers,' *Hindustan Times*, 21 February 2014. Accessed 1 July 2023, https://www.hindustantimes.com/india/supreme-court-halts-release-of-rajiv-gandhi-s-killers/story-q6wSSKromeCSCGywabcMDL.html.

45   Rakhi Bose, 'Rajiv Gandhi Assassination: Who Were The Killers And Why Were They Released?', *Outlook*, 14 November 2022. Accessed 2 July 2023, https://www.outlookindia.com/national/rajiv-gandhi-assassination-who-were-the-killers-and-why-were-they-released--news-237411, 'Rajiv Gandhi Assassination To Release Of Convicts After 30 Years: A Timeline Of Events,' *Outlook*, 28 November 2022. Accessed 2 July 2023, https://www.outlookindia.com/national/rajiv-gandhi-assassination-to-release-of-convicts-after-30-years-a-timeline-of-events-news-240215.

46   Dhananjay Mahapatra, 'SC strikes down Kerala law on Mullaperiyar dam,' *Times of India*, 8 May 2014. Accessed 2 July 2019, https://timesofindia.indiatimes.com/india/sc-strikes-down-kerala-law-on-mullaperiyar-dam/articleshow/34795438.cms.

47   'Kerala seeks review of SC's 2014 verdict on Mullaperiyar dam by larger bench,' 17 February 2022, *New Indian Express*, 17 February 2022. Accessed 1 July 2022, https://www.newindianexpress.com/states/kerala/2022/feb/17/kerala-seeks-review-of-scs-2014-verdict-on-mullaperiyar-dam-by-larger-bench-2420711.html.

48   'Jayalalithaa wealth case: timeline of events,' *The Hindu*, 27 September 2014. Accessed 1 July 2019, https://www.thehindu.com/news/national/Jayalalithaa-wealth-case-timeline-of-events/article10887817.ece; *Frontline*, 17 October 2014, 4–17; *Frontline*, 31 October 2014, 26–36.

49   Sunil Khilnani, *Incarnations: A History of India in 50 Lives*, (Delhi: Penguin, 2016), 69–70.

50   V. Venkatesan, 'Qualified respite,' *Frontline*, 14 November 2014, 35–37; T.S. Subramanian, 'The game changer?' *Frontline*, 15 April 2016, 136–37.

51   T.S. Subramanian, 'The verdict in question,' *Frontline*, 12 June 2015, 125–38.

52   T.S. Subramanian, 'One sided contest,' *Frontline*, 26 June 2015, 34–35.

53   B. Kolappan, 'Karunanidhi promises total prohibition,' *The Hindu*, 21 July 2015. Accessed 1 July 2019, https://www.thehindu.com/news/national/tamil-nadu/Karunanidhi-promises-total-prohibition/article60334307.ece.

54   'DMK removed prohibition, 'ruined' generations: Ramadoss,' *The Hindu*, 21 July 2015. Accessed 1 July 2019, https://www.thehindu.com/news/national/tamil-nadu/Ramadoss-slams-Karunanidhis-remarks-on-prohibition/article60334316.ece.

55   B. Kolappan, 'DMK is not anti-Hindu: Stalin,' *The Hindu*, 17 October 2015. Accessed 1 July 2019, https://www.thehindu.com/news/cities/chennai/DMK-is-not-anti-Hindu-Stalin/article60235385.ece.

56   'Of nephews and sons-in-law,' *The Hindu*, 8 September 2014. Accessed 1 July 2019, https://www.thehindu.com/news/national/tamil-nadu/of-nephews-and-sonsinlaw/article6390202.ece.

57   Sandhya Ravishankar, 'Will Machiavelli and a makeover win MK Stalin the power he dreams of?' *Hindustan Times*, 13 May 2016. Accessed 1 July 2019, https://www.hindustantimes.com/assembly-elections/will-machiavelli-and-a-makeover-win-mk-stalin-the-power-he-dreams-of/story-6aH8kca3jcVG3y5nVC9fIK.html.

58   'DMK Leader MK Stalin Winds Up His "Successful" "Namakku Name" Campaign' *NDTV*, 12 February 2016. Accessed 1 July 2019, https://www.ndtv.com/tamil-nadu-news/dmk-leader-mk-stalin-winds-up-his-successful-namakku-name-campaign-1276767.

59   'Chinna payyanum appavin arasiyalum: Jayalalithaa sonna nammai naamae kutti kadhai,' *Hindu Tamil*, 10 February 2016. Accessed 2 February 2019, https://www.hindutamil.in/news/tamilnadu/185381-.html; Lakshmi Subramanian, 'Stalin to take charge of DMK today, 51 yrs after joining politics,' the *Week*, 28 August 2018. Accessed 1 July

2023, Lakshmi Subramanian, 'Stalin to take charge of DMK today, 51 yrs after joining politics,' the *Week*, 28 August 2018. Accessed 1 June 2019, 'https://www.theweek.in/news/india/2018/08/28/stalin-charge-dmk-today-51-joining-politics.html.

60   'People's Welfare Front will be a political alliance on October 5,' *The Hindu*, 3 October 2015. Accessed 1 July 2019, https://www.thehindu.com/news/national/tamil-nadu/peoples-welfare-front-will-be-a-political-alliance-on-october-5/article7720531.ece.

61   T.S. Subramanian, 'Battle Lines,' *Frontline*, 13 April 2016. Accessed 1 July 2022, https://frontline.thehindu.com/politics/battle-lines/article8465726.ece.

62   B. Kolappan, 'DMK promises smart phones in manifesto' *The Hindu*, 10 April 2016. Accessed 1 July 2019, https://www.thehindu.com/elections/tamilnadu2016/Tamil-Nadu-Assembly-elections-highlights-of-DMK-manifesto/article60513173.ece.

63   'En magano, marumagano arasiyaluku varamaatargal!- Mu Ka Stalin,' *Tamil One India*, 9 May 2016. Accessed 1 July 2019, https://tamil.oneindia.com/news/tamilnadu/no-more-political-heir-from-my-family-mk-stalin-253186.html?story=1.

64   'Stalin Can Be Chief Minister If Something Happens To Me, Says Karunanidhi,' *NDTV*, 12 May 2016. Accessed 1 July 2019, https://www.ndtv.com/video/news/news/stalin-can-be-chief-minister-if-something-happens-to-me-says-karunanidhi-415697.

65   R.K. Radhakrishnan, 'We pay, you vote,' *Frontline*, 22 July 2016, 41–52.

66   T.S. Subramanian, 'Bucking the trend,' *Frontline*, 25 May 2016. Accessed 1 July 2022, https://frontline.thehindu.com/cover-story/bucking-the-trend/article8644520.ece.

67   L. Saravanan, 'Breakfast scheme awaits chief minister Jayalalithaa's nod,' *Times of India*, 1 June 2016. Accessed 1 July 2022, https://timesofindia.indiatimes.com/city/madurai/breakfast-scheme-awaits-chief-minister-jayalalithaas-nod/articleshow/52531438.cms.

Chapter 29: The Titans Are Gone

1   B. Kolappan, 'Stalin elected as working president of DMK,' *Times of India*, 4 January 2018. Accessed 1 July 2022, https://www.thehindu.com/news/national/tamil-nadu/Stalin-elected-as-working-president-of-DMK/article16986783.ece.

2   R.K. Radhakrishnan, 'Chief Minister in hospital,' *Frontline*, 28 October 2016, 34–40.

3   'Jayalalitha's Interview to BBC World's HARDtalk India,' *BBC Tamil. com*, 30 September 2004. Accessed 22 July 2019, https://www.bbc.com/ tamil/highlights/story/2004/09/printable/040930_jayainterview.

4   'Exoneration of Sekar Reddy BJP's gift to AIADMK: DMK chief Stalin,' *Deccan Chronicle*, 29 September 2020. Accessed 22 July 2021, https://www.deccanherald.com/india/exoneration-of-sekar-reddy-bjp-s-gift-to-aiadmk-dmk-chief-stalin-894791.html.

5   'I was under house arrest, Tamil Nadu's ex-chief secretary blasts Centre,' *Times of India*, 27 December 2016. Accessed 1 July 2020, https://timesofindia.indiatimes.com/india/i-was-under-house-arrest-it-raids-were-unconstitutional-assault-on-me-former-tamil-nadu-chief-secretary-p-rama-mohana-rao/articleshow/56196136.cms.

6   'Sekhar Reddy diary: Stalin demands resignation of OPS, ministers; CBI probe,' *Indian Express*, 9 December 2017, Accessed 1 July 2020, https://indianexpress.com/article/india/m-k-stalin-demands-resignation-of-o-panneerselvam-ministers-cbi-probe-4974628/; 'OPS denies links with tainted businessman Sekhar Reddy,' 7 August 2017, *Times of India*, 7 August 2017, Accessed 1 July 2020, https://timesofindia.indiatimes.com/city/madurai/ive-nothing-to-do-with-sekhar-reddy-ops/articleshow/59946555.cms?frmapp=yes&from=mdr.

7   'Sekhar Reddy diary: Stalin demands resignation of OPS, ministers; CBI probe,', *Indian Express*, 9 December 2017. Accessed 1 July 2020, https://indianexpress.com/article/india/m-k-stalin-demands-resignation-of-o-panneerselvam-ministers-cbi-probe-4974628/.

8   N. Sathiya Moorthy, 'Reading the signals from the TN tax raids,' *Rediff*, 22 December 2016. Accessed 1 June 2019, https://www.rediff.com/news/column/were-tn-tax-raids-warning-to-sasikala-aiadmk/20161222.htm; Kumar Chellappan, 'I-T raid on TN Chief Secy's house, office,' the *Pioneer*, 22 December 2016. Accessed 1 June 2019, https://www.dailypioneer.com/2016/india/i-t-raid-on-tn-chief-secys-house-office.html.

9   'Exoneration of Sekar Reddy BJP's gift to AIADMK: DMK chief Stalin,' *Deccan Chronicle*, 29 September 2020. Accessed 1 June 2019, https://www.deccanherald.com/india/exoneration-of-sekar-reddy-bjp-s-gift-to-aiadmk-dmk-chief-stalin-894791.html.

10   'Jallikattu: Thousands protest at India bullfighting ban,' *BBC*, 18 January 2017. Accessed 1 June 2019, https://www.bbc.com/news/world-asia-india-38660377; Kirti Bhargava, 'Jallikattu: An Ancient Sport Caught Between Culture And Law, Tradition And Modernity, Religion And

Morality,' *Outlook*, 29 December 2022. Accessed 1 June 2019, https://www.outlookindia.com/national/jallikattu-how-an-ancient-sport-is-caught-between-culture-and-law-tradition-and-modernity-religion-and-morality-news-249233.

11 'The end of a protest,' *The Hindu*, 25 January 2017. Accessed 1 May 2019, https://www.thehindu.com/opinion/editorial/The-end-of-a-protest/article17089429.ece; N. Sathiya Moorthy, 'How Jallikattu protests left the State on the backfoot,' *Rediff.com*, 25 January 2017. Accessed 1 June 2019, https://www.rediff.com/news/column/how-jallikattu-protests-left-the-state-on-the-backfoot/20170125.htm.

12 'MK Stalin says people have not accepted Sasikala as CM,' *Indian Express*, 8 February 2017. Accessed 1 May 2019, https://indianexpress.com/article/india/mk-stalin-says-people-have-not-accepted-sasikala-as-cm-4512899/.

13 'Sasikala convicted in DA case: Full text of the Supreme Court verdict,' *Indian Express*, 16 February 2016. Accessed 1 May 2019, https://indianexpress.com/article/india/sasikala-convicted-in-da-case-supreme-court-aiadmk-jayalalithaa-4524275/.

14 ETB Sivapriyan, 'AIADMK belongs to everyone, not one community: Sasikala attacks Palaniswami,' 15 June 2021. Accessed 21 May 2019, https://www.deccanherald.com/india/aiadmk-belongs-to-everyone-not-one-community-sasikala-attacks-palaniswami-997807.html.

15 'Who is Palaniswami and why is he Sasikala's pick for next CM?,' *Economic Times*, 16 February 2017. Accessed 1 May 2019, https://economictimes.indiatimes.com/nation-world/who-is-palaniswami-and-why-is-he-sasikalas-pick-for-next-cm/third-chief-minister-in-three-months/slideshow/57182788.cms.

16 'AIADMK's OPS Camp Meets President, Seeks Probe Into Jaya's Death,' The Quint, 28 February 2017. Accessed 1 May 2019, https://www.thequint.com/news/politics/aiadmk-ops-panneerslevam-camp-mp-meet-president-seek-probe-into-jayalalithaa-death.

17 'Revolt in AIADMK against Sasikala, some loyalists back her,' *MoneyControl*, 19 April 2017. Accessed 1 May 2019, https://www.moneycontrol.com/news/politics/revolt-in-aiadmk-against-sasikala-some-loyalists-back-her-2260947.html.

18 'Dhinakaran arrested by Delhi Police in cash-for-symbol case,' *Deccan Herald*, 25 April 2017. Accessed 1 May 2019, https://www.deccanherald.com/india/dhinakaran-arrested-by-delhi-police-in-cash-for-symbol-case-585522.html.

19 Akshaya Nath, 'Agreed to AIADMK merger on Modi's suggestion, says OPS, DMK slams BJP's "shadow government" in TN,' *India Today*, 17 February 2018. Accessed 1 May 2019, https://www.indiatoday.in/india/story/agreed-to-aiadmk-merger-on-modi-s-suggestion-says-ops-dmk-slams-bjp-s-shadow-government-in-tn-1171844-2018-02-17.

20 V. Shoba, 'Rajinikanth: Action! Finally,' *Open*, 11 December 2020. Accessed 1 May 2021, https://openthemagazine.com/feature/rajinikanth-action-finally/.

21 Abdullah Nurullah and D. Govardan, 'Rajinikanth to float party and contest next assembly polls,' *Times of India*, 31 December 2017. Accessed 1 June 2020, https://timesofindia.indiatimes.com/city/chennai/rajinikanth-to-float-party-and-contest-next-assembly-polls/articleshow/62313085.cms.

22 'Kamal Hassan finally floats his political party "Makkal Needhi Maiam",' Tehelka, 22 February 2018. Accessed 1 May 2019, 'http://tehelka.com/kamal-hassan-finally-floats-his-political-party-makkal-needhi-maiam/.

23 'Kamal Haasan launches Makkal Needhi Maiam, starts political journey,' 21 February 2018, *Economic Times*, 21 February 2018. Accessed 1 May 2019, https://economictimes.indiatimes.com/news/politics-and-nation/kamal-haasan-launches-makkal-needhi-mayyam-starts-political-journey/articleshow/63017097.cms?from=mdr.

24 Karunanidhi, *Kadithangal*, 44: 106–07; 'BJP govt introduced NEET after it came to power in 2014,' *Times of India*, 11 February 2022. Accessed 1 May 2022 https://timesofindia.indiatimes.com/city/erode/bjp-govt-introduced-neet-after-it-came-to-power-in-2014/articleshow/89492218.cms.

25 'Supreme Court quashes NEET, says no unified exam for medical courses,' *DNA*, 21 November 2023. Accessed 22 November 2023, https://www.dnaindia.com/india/report-supreme-court-quashes-neet-says-no-unified-exam-for-medical-courses-1862537.

26 'Jayalalithaa asks PM to drop proposal to reintroduce NEET,' *India Today*, 29 July 2013. Accessed 1 May 2019, https://www.indiatoday.in/india/south/story/jaya-asks-pm-not-to-re-introduce-neet-proposal-171973-2013-07-28.

27 'Supreme Court Recalls Its Controversial 2013 Verdict On Medical Entrance,' NDTV, 11 April 2016. Accessed 1 May 209, https://www.ndtv.com/india-news/supreme-court-recalls-its-controversial-2013-verdict-on-medical-entrance-1391658.

28   Pramod Madhav, 'Tamil Nadu girl Anitha who spearheaded fight against
      NEET commits suicide,' *India Today*, 1 September 2017. Accessed 1 May
      2019, https://www.indiatoday.in/india/story/anitha-tamil-nadu-neet-
      suicide-ariyalur-medical-entrance-1035916-2017-09-01; R. Rajaram,
      'Girl who filed case against NEET commits suicide,' 1 September
      2017, *The Hindu*, 1 September 2017. Accessed 1 May 2019, https://
      www.thehindu.com/news/national/tamil-nadu/dalit-girl-who-filed-
      case-against-neet-commits-suicide/article61857652.ece; Sureshkumar,
      'TN bills seeking exemption from NEET rejected by President: Centre
      informs Madras HC,' *Times of India*, 6 July 2019. Accessed 1 May
      2020, http://timesofindia.indiatimes.com/articleshow/70107721.
      cms?utm_source=contentofinterest&utm_medium=text&utm_
      campaign=cppst; B. Sivakumar, 'Ensure NEET is never forced on
      Tamil Nadu, Jayalalithaa writes to PM Modi,' *Times of India*, 25 May
      2016. Accessed 1 May 2019, http://timesofindia.indiatimes.com/
      articleshow/52428303.cms?utm_source=contentofinterest&utm_
      medium=text&utm_campaign=cppst.

29   'Stalin kicks off rally for Cauvery rights,' *The Hindu*, 7 April 2018.
      Accessed 1 May 2019, https://www.thehindu.com/news/national/tamil-
      nadu/stalin-kicks-off-rally-for-cauvery-rights/article23469085.ece.

30   'IPL In Chennai An Embarrassment When Cauvery Protests On:
      Rajinikanth,' *NDTV*, 8 April 2018. Accessed 1 May 2019, https://www.
      ndtv.com/tamil-nadu-news/in-chennai-top-tamil-actors-protest-over-
      delay-in-cauvery-boards-constitution-1834322.

31   'CM blames DMK for violence; Stalin says Tamil Nadu GO an
      eyewash,' *Times of India*, 30 May 2018. Accessed 1 May 2019,
      http://timesofindia.indiatimes.com/articleshow/64376811.cms?utm_
      source=contentofinterest&utm_medium=text&utm_campaign=
      cppst.

32   B. Sivakumar, 'I'd have died had Karunanidhi not been buried on
      Marina Beach, Stalin says,' *Times of India*, 14 August 2018. Accessed
      1 May 2019, https://timesofindia.indiatimes.com/city/chennai/id-have-
      died-had-karunanidhi-not-been-buried-on-marina-beach-stalin-says/
      articleshow/65399357.cms.

33   'Kaavi vannam adika thudikum mathiya arasuku paadam pugatuvom!
      Thi Mu Ka thalaivar Mu.Ka. Stalin kanni pechu! Muzhu urai,' 28
      August 2018, *Tamil Indian Express*, 28 August 2018. Accessed 1 May
      2019, https://tamil.indianexpress.com/tamilnadu/dmk-leader-stalin-
      full-speech/.

Chapter 30: M.K. Stalin in Power

1   'DMK urges Governor to remove Palaniswami over Kodanad Estate case,' 14 January 2019, The Quint, 14 January 2019. Accessed 1 May 2020, https://www.thequint.com/news/hot-news/dmk-urges-governor-to-remove-palaniswami-over-kodanad-estate-case.

2   'DMK scripted Kodanad "drama": Tamil Nadu CM Edappadi K Palaniswami,' *Times of India*, 19 January 2019. Accessed 1 May 2019, https://timesofindia.indiatimes.com/city/chennai/dmk-scripted-kodanad-drama-tamil-nadu-cm-edappadi-k-palaniswami/articleshow/67597150.cms.

3   Udhayanidhi Stalin (Udhaystalin), 'Let us resolve to work for the victory of the ideologies of Periyar, Anna, Kalaignar and Perasiriyar. Let Social Justice flourish forever,' X, 7 September 2023, 12:32 am, https://twitter.com/Udhaystalin/status/1699641875836383269/photo/2.

4   'Stalin rakes up Kodanad in Chennai campaign despite High Court gag,' *DT Next*, 15 April 2023. Accessed 1 May 2023, https://www.dtnext.in/tamilnadu/2019/04/15/stalin-rakes-up-kodanad-in-chennai-campaign-despite-high-court-gag.

5   'M K Stalin Proposes Rahul Gandhi As Next Prime Minister, Says He Has The Ability To Defeat Modi,' *Outlook*, 16 December 2018. Accessed 1 May 2019, https://www.outlookindia.com/website/story/m-k-stalin-proposes-rahul-gandhi-as-next-prime-minister-says-he-has-the-ability-to-defeat-modi/321844.

6   '"What's Wrong In It?": MK Stalin on Rahul Gandhi as PM Candidate,' NDTV, 23 December 2018. Accessed 1 May 2019, https://www.ndtv.com/tamil-nadu-news/whats-wrong-in-it-mk-stalin-on-rahul-gandhi-as-pm-candidate-1967068.

7   'The precarious life of 'Makkal Nala Paniyalargals,' *The Hindu*, 10 April 2022. Accessed 1 June 2023, https://www.thehindu.com/news/national/tamil-nadu/the-precarious-life-of-makkal-nala-paniyalargals/article65309214.ece.

8   'Focus On Poverty Eradication Scheme As AIADMK Releases Manifesto,' NDTV, 19 March 2019. Accessed 1 May 2020, https://www.ndtv.com/tamil-nadu-news/lok-sabha-elections-2019-focus-on-poverty-eradication-scheme-as-aiadmk-releases-manifesto-2009887.

9   'No Alliance with DMK and ADMK in Future – Ramadoss,' YouTube, 8 April, 2016, *Daily Thanthi*, 2:42, https://youtu.be/1qkbLRQbhfA; https://youtu.be/1qkbLRQbhfA Dr S. Ramadoss, 9 April 2018.

10 Nityanand Jayaraman, 'All You Need to Know About the Neduvasal Protests Against Hydrocarbon Extraction,' *The Wire*, 1 March 2017. Accessed 1 May 2019, https://thewire.in/environment/neduvasal-protest-oil-gas.

11 'Situation at Kathiramangalam village calm now: TN CM,' *Business Standard*, 3 July 2017. Accessed 1 May 2019, https://www.business-standard.com/article/pti-stories/situation-at-kathiramangalam-village-calm-now-tn-cm-117070300437_1.html; N. Vinoth Kumar, 'Tamil Nadu government slips both ways on hydrocarbon projects,' *The Federal*, 10 February 2020. Accessed 1 May 2021, https://thefederal.com/states/south/tamil-nadu/tamil-nadu-government-slips-both-ways-on-hydrocarbon-projects/.

12 'Tamil Nadu: Stalin Promises To Junk Salem-Chennai Eight-Lane Expressway Project If DMK Comes To Power,' *Swarajya*, 23 March 2019. Accessed 1 May 2020, https://swarajyamag.com/insta/tamil-nadu-stalin-promises-to-junk-salem-chennai-eight-lane-expressway-project-if-dmk-comes-to-power

13 'Results out, TN govt reverses stand, pushes for vexed road project in SC,' *The Federal*, 31 May 2019. Accessed 1 May 2020, https://thefederal.com/news/week-after-election-results-tn-govt-appeals-in-sc-over-hc-order-on-8-lane-project/?infinitescroll=1https://thefederal.com/news/week-after-election-results-tn-govt-appeals-in-sc-over-hc-order-on-8-lane-project/?infinitescroll=1.

14 Julie Mariappan, 'Tamil Nadu govt set to back greenfield corridor to Salem,' *Times of India*, 9 August 2022. Accessed 1 November 2023.

15 'It's official. Cauvery delta is protected agri zone now,' *New Indian Express*, 23 February 2020. Accessed 1 June 2020, https://www.newindianexpress.com/states/tamil-nadu/2020/feb/23/its-official-cauvery-delta-is-protected-agri-zone-now-2107209.html.

16 T. Muruganandham, '7.5% quota for govt school students in UG medical courses,' *New Indian Express*, 15 September 2020. Accessed 1 May 2021, https://www.newindianexpress.com/states/tamil-nadu/2020/sep/15/tn-assembly-unanimously-passes-75-quota-for-govt-school-students-in-ug-medical-courses-2197210.html.

17 'In manifesto, AIADMK promises to make Centre rethink CAA, BJP says law will not be scrapped,' *India Today*, 15 March 2021. Accessed 1 May 2021, https://www.indiatoday.in/elections/tamil-nadu-assembly-polls-2021/story/in-manifesto-aiadmk-promises-to-make-bjp-rethink-caa-ally-says-law-will-not-be-scrapped-1779337-2021-03-15.

18 'DMK misleading people on CAA: Edappadi Palaniswami,' *The Hindu*, 19 February 2020. Accessed 1 May 2020, https://www.thehindu.com/news/national/tamil-nadu/dmk-misleading-people-on-caa-edappadi-palaniswami/article30855515.ece.

19 Kumar Anshuman, 'TV, tablets, gold—what AIADMK and DMK manifestos offer,' *Economic Times*, 18 March 2021. Accessed 2 March 2022, https://economictimes.indiatimes.com/news/politics-and-nation/tv-tablets-goldyou-name-it-tn-parties-offering-it-free/articleshow/81537260.cms?from=mdr.

20 'Free bus travel scheme to be expanded: Min,' *Times of India*, 31 August 2023. Accessed 2 November 2023, https://timesofindia.indiatimes.com/city/chennai/free-bus-travel-scheme-to-be-expanded-min/articleshow/103226895.cms?from=mdr.

21 'DMK will form govt in Tamil Nadu, says Stalin,' *The Siasat Daily*, 2 January 2021. Accessed 2 November 2023, https://www.siasat.com/dmk-will-form-govt-in-tamil-nadu-says-stalin-2059121/.

22 J. Sam Daniel Stalin, 'Disproportionate Assets Case Against Ex-Minister After Raids In Tamil Nadu,' NDTV, 22 July 2021. Accessed 2 July 2022, https://www.ndtv.com/tamil-nadu-news/disproportionate-assets-case-against-ex-minister-mr-vijayabhaskar-after-raids-in-tamil-nadu-2492615.

23 'Ex-minister AIADMK SP Velumani raided, Rs 13 lakh, documents seized,' *New Indian Express*, 11 August 2021. Accessed 1 July 2022, https://www.newindianexpress.com/states/tamil-nadu/2021/aug/11/ex-ministeraiadmk-sp-velumani-raided-rs-13-lakh-documents-seized-2343052.html; Sahaya Novinston Lobo, 'DVAC raids 28 houses and buildings linked to former AIADMK minister KC Veeramani,' *New Indian Express*, 16 September 2021. Accessed 2 July 2022, https://www.newindianexpress.com/states/tamil-nadu/2021/sep/16/dvac-raids-28-houses-and-buildings-linked-to-former-aiadmk-minister-kc-veeramani-2359516.html; Arun Janardhanan, 'Tamil Nadu: Raid at 14 premises of ex-AIADMK minister, assets worth crores seized,' *Indian Express*, 16 December 2021. Accessed 2 June 2022, https://indianexpress.com/article/cities/chennai/dvac-conducts-searches-at-aiadmk-ex-ministers-premises-7673597/; 'DVAC raids 58 premises linked to former TN Minister, seizes unaccounted cash, gold,' *Deccan Chronicle*, 20 January 2022. Accessed 15 December 2022, https://www.deccanchronicle.com/nation/politics/200122/tamil-nadu-anti-corruption-body-raids-at-places-linked-to-ex-aiadmk-m.html.

24 'Political vendetta behind DVAC raids: AIADMK,' *Daijiworld.com*, 15 December 2021. Accessed 2 July 2022, https://www.daijiworld.com/news/newsDisplay?newsID=904664.

25 ETB Sivapriyan, 'DVAC raids two former AIADMK ministers in corruption cases,' *Deccan Chronicle*, 16 September 2022. Accessed 1 July 2023, https://www.deccanherald.com/india/dvac-raids-two-former-aiadmk-ministers-in-corruption-cases-1144785.html.

26 'DVAC raids aimed at diverting public attention, says Tamil Nadu former CM Edappadi K. Palaniswami,' *Times of India*, 14 September 2022. Accessed 2 July 2023, https://timesofindia.indiatimes.com/city/chennai/dvac-raids-aimed-at-diverting-public-attention-aiadmk/articleshow/94188645.cms.

27 'NEET will take Tamil Nadu to pre-independence days: AK Rajan committee,' *Indian Express*, 21 September 2021. Accessed 1 June 2022, https://indianexpress.com/article/cities/chennai/neet-take-tn-pre-independence-days-ak-rajan-committee-7523694/; Ritika Chopra, 'NEET skewed results in favour of English-medium, well-off, urban, CBSE students, Tamil Nadu panel finds,' *Indian Express*, 18 September 2021. Accessed 1 June 2022, https://indianexpress.com/article/education/neet-skewed-results-in-favour-of-english-medium-well-off-urban-cbse-kids-tamil-nadu-panel-finds-7511410/.

28 '20 reasons and 2 routes to eliminate NEET, Justice AK Rajan committee tells Tamil Nadu govt,' *Times of India*, 21 September 2021. Accessed 1 June 2022, https://timesofindia.indiatimes.com/city/chennai/20-reasons-and-two-routes-to-eliminate-neet-rajan-committee-tells-tn-govt/articleshow/86380019.cms.

29 'MK Stalin Writes To Chief Ministers Of 12 States Over NEET Opposition,' *NDTV*, 4 October 2021. Accessed 21 September 2022, https://www.ndtv.com/india-news/mk-stalin-writes-to-chief-ministers-of-12-states-over-neet-opposition-2563430.

30 Arun Janardhanan, 'Ravi reignites debate: Will never ever clear NEET exemption Bill,' *Indian Express*, 13 August 2023. Accessed 21 September 2023, https://indianexpress.com/article/india/ravi-reignites-debate-will-never-ever-clear-neet-exemption-bill-8889983/.

31 M.K. Stalin (mkstalin), 'Today, I've written this letter to 37 leaders of key political parties inviting them to be part of the All India Federation for Social Justice, I had announced on 26 January 2022,' 2 February 2022, 3:32 am, https://twitter.com/mkstalin/status/1488792486436696064?lang=en.

32   T. Muruganandham, 'One year in office: The name of my goal is Dravidian model, says Tamil Nadu CM Stalin,' *New Indian Express*, 7 May 2022. Accessed 2 May 2023, https://www.newindianexpress.com/states/tamil-nadu/2022/may/07/one-year-in-office-the-name-of-my-goal-is-dravidian-model-says-tamil-nadu-cm-stalin-2450961.html.

33   Jaya Menon, 'Tamil Nadu governor RN Ravi's exclusive interview with TOI: "DMK's ideology parochial, dead,"', *Times of India*, 4 May 2023. Accessed 5 June 2023, http://timesofindia.indiatimes.com/articleshow/99973832.cms?from=mdr&utm_source=contentofinterest&utm_medium=text&utm_campaign=cppst, '"Dravidian-Model – the governance formula for all states": Stalin's rejoinder to Governor Ravi,' *The Federal*, 4 May 2023. Accessed 21 May 2023, https://thefederal.com/states/south/tamil-nadu/dravidian-model-the-governance-formula-for-all-states-stalins-rejoinder-to-governor-ravi/.

34   'Stalin anguished by actions of some Ministers, DMK leaders,' *The Hindu*, 10 October 2022. Accessed 22 May 2023, https://www.thehindu.com/news/national/tamil-nadu/stalin-sleepless-over-actions-of-some-ministers-and-leaders/article65989142.ece' 'Two years of Stalin government in Tamil Nadu: Two steps forward,' *Times of India*, 6 May 2023. Accessed 1 June 2023, https://timesofindia.indiatimes.com/city/chennai/two-years-of-stalin-government-in-tamil-nadu-two-steps-forward/articleshow/100026091.cms?from=mdr.

35   J. Sam Daniel Stalin, 'BJP Releases Rs 1.34 Lakh Crore "DMK Files". "Joke", Says Ruling Party,' NDTV, 14 April 2023. Accessed 2 June 2023, https://www.ndtv.com/india-news/bjp-releases-rs-1-34-lakh-crore-dmk-files-joke-says-ruling-party-3947775.

36   Ibid.

37   'Ippadi pesi pesithaan Annamalai periya aalaagiraar,' EPS gaatamaana vimarsanam!,' *News 18 Tamil*, 16 April 2023. Accessed 5 April 2024, https://tamil.news18.com/live-updates/edappadi-palanisamy-angry-with-bjp-state-leader-annamalai-questions-942282.html; 'Cool mood Edappadi . . . war mood Annamalai . . . silent mood Panneer . . . ADMK-BJP adhakalam!', *Vikatan*, 22 April 2023. Accessed 5 April 2024, https://www.vikatan.com/government-and-politics/annamalai-edappadi-palanisamy-o-panneerselvam-political-activities; 'DMK Files | BJP leader Annamalai says he will approach CBI with plaint against TN CM Stalin for "tweaking" tender 13 years ago,' *The Hindu*, 14 April 2023, Accessed 5 April 2024, https://www.thehindu.com/news/national/tamil-nadu/bjp-leader-annamalai-says-he-will-approach-cbi-

with-plaint-against-tn-cm-stalin-for-tweaking-tender-13-years-ago/article66737474.ece.

38 'BJP will not spare anyone who is corrupt,' *Hindustan Times*, 17 April 2023. Accessed 5 April 2024, https://www.hindustantimes.com/india-news/tamil-nadu-bjp-chief-annamalai-vows-to-expose-corruption-ahead-of-2024-parliamentary-elections-101681715709147.html.

39 Vinodh Arulappan, 'Audio clip, allegedly of TN finance minister PTR, puts DMK in the dock,' *The South First*, 20 April 2023. Accessed 2 June 2023, https://thesouthfirst.com/tamilnadu/audio-clip-allegedly-of-tn-finance-minister-ptr-puts-dmk-in-the-dock/.

40 'BJP's Annamalai tweets audio clip purported to be of PTR,' *Times of India*, 21 April 2023. Accessed 1 June 2023, https://timesofindia.indiatimes.com/city/chennai/bjps-annamalai-tweets-audio-clip-purported-to-be-of-ptr/articleshow/99654258.cms?from=mdr.

41 'Annamalai hits back at PTR on audio clip issue, to seek independent audit of voice tape,' *Indian Express*, 23 April 2023. Accessed 1 May 2023, https://indianexpress.com/article/cities/chennai/annamalai-palanivel-thiaga-rajan-audio-clip-voice-tape-8571162/.

42 K. Annamalai (Annamalai_k), 'Listen to the DMK ecosystem crumbling from within. The 2nd tape of TN State FM Thiru @ptrmadurai.' 25 April 2023, 6:24 am, https://twitter.com/i/status/1650807871968526337.

43 'AIADMK, AMMK flay Udhayanidhi Stalin's induction in T.N. Cabinet,' *The Hindu*, 14 December 2022. Accessed 1 June 2023, https://www.thehindu.com/news/cities/Coimbatore/dmk-surpasses-congress-in-family-based-politics-alleges-sp-velumani/article66262244.ece.

44 'Tamil Nadu BJP Chief Seeks Governor's Intervention Over His "DMK Files",' NDTV, YouTube, 2:16, 27 July 2023, https://youtu.be/SWFRAeax35o.

45 'High court clears Edappadi K Palaniswami to be 6th general secretary of AIADMK,' *Times of India*, 29 March 2023. Accessed 2 June 2023, http://timesofindia.indiatimes.com/articleshow/99074005.cms?from=mdr&utm_source=contentofinterest&utm_medium=text&utm_campaign=cppst; Julie Mariappan, 'AIADMK drama: OPS has a "relationship" with DMK, EPS says,' *Times of India*, 11 July 2022. Accessed 1 June 2023, https://timesofindia.indiatimes.com/city/chennai/aiadmk-drama-opshas-a-relationship-with-dmk-eps-says/articleshow/92799298.cms.

46 Akshaya Nath, 'Former rivals OPS and Dhinakaran join hands against 'evil force' DMK, hope to 'unite' AIADMK,' ThePrint, 9 May 2023.

Accessed 1 June 2023, https://theprint.in/politics/former-rivals-ops-dinakaran-join-hands-against-evil-force-dmk-hope-to-unite-aiadmk/1563052/.

47 'O. Panneerselvam, T.T.V. Dhinakaran are 'B' team of DMK: Edappadi Palaniswami,' 15 May 2023, *The Hindu*, https://www.thehindu.com/news/cities/Tiruchirapalli/ops-dhinakaran-are-b-team-of-dmk-palaniswami/article66854164.ece.

48 Blessy Mathew Prasad, 'The Deadly Games,' *The Citizen*, 11 December 2022. Accessed 1 May 2023, https://www.thecitizen.in/in-depth/the-deadly-games-552573.

49 Pramod Madhav, '"Dictator Ravi" posters spotted in Chennai after Tamil CM MK Stalin's remark on Governor,' *India Today*, 8 April 2023. Accessed 1 May 2023, https://www.indiatoday.in/india/story/dictator-ravi-posters-chennai-after-tamil-cm-mk-stalin-remark-governor-rn-ravi-2357321-2023-04-08.

50 'TN Assembly adopts resolution over need for timeframe for governors to approve bills,' *India Today*, 10 April 2023. Accessed 1 May 2023, https://www.indiatoday.in/india/story/tn-assembly-adopts-resolution-over-need-for-timeframe-for-governors-to-approve-bills-2358095-2023-04-10.

51 'Tamil Nadu governor RN Ravi's exclusive interview with TOI,' supra note 33.

52 'Is Tamil Nadu burning like BJP-ruled Manipur: MK Stalin asks Governor Ravi,' 7 May 2023, *India Today*, 7 May 2023. Accessed 2 June 2023, https://www.indiatoday.in/india/story/is-tamil-nadu-burning-like-bjp-ruled-manipur-mk-stalin-governor-ravi-2376128-2023-05-07.

53 'Stalin nervous, says EPS; he's Mr Clean, says DMK'; *Times of India*, 17 June 2023. Accessed 2 July 2023, http://timesofindia.indiatimes.com/articleshow/101057254.cms?from=mdr&utm_source=contentofinterest&utm_medium=text&utm_campaign=cppst.

54 K. Annamalai (K. Annamalai), 'A gentle reminder to Thiru @mkstalin on what he spoke a few years back about the #CashForJobScam tainted Thiru Senthilbalaji. Are you going to refute this, Thiru @mkstalin?' Twitter, 14 June 2023, 1:51 am, https://twitter.com/i/status/1668858719365644288; S. Kumarasen and C. Shivakumar, 'An able organiser who party-hopped four times and rose up the ranks quickly,' *New Indian Express*, 15 June 2023. Accessed 1 July 2023, https://www.newindianexpress.com/states/tamil-nadu/2023/jun/15/an-able-organiser-who-party-hoppedfour-times-and-rose-up-the-ranks-quickly-2585155.html.

55 T. Muruganandham, 'Governor RN Ravi okays reallocation of Senthilbalaji's depts,' *Indian Express*, 17 June 2023. Accessed 1 July 2023, https://www.newindianexpress.com/states/tamil-nadu/2023/jun/17/governor-rn-ravi-okaysreallocation-of-senthil-balajis-depts-2585763.html.

56 B. Kolappan, 'M.K. Stalin interview: Rein in Governor or face Tamil Nadu's ire, Chief Minister tells Centre,' *The Hindu*, 2 July 2023. Accessed 4 July 2023, https://www.thehindu.com/news/national/tamil-nadu/mk-stalin-interview-rein-in-governor-or-face-tamil-nadus-ire-chief-minister-tells-centre/article67035065.ece.

57 Divya Chandrababu, 'Charge sheet filed against 3rd AIADMK leader R Kamaraj for corruption,' *Hindustan Times*, 11 July 2023. Accessed 1 August 2023, https://www.hindustantimes.com/india-news/charge-sheet-filed-against-3rd-aiadmk-leader-r-kamaraj-for-corruption-101689078429369.html.

58 https://twitter.com/mkstalin/status/1678013847557521409/photo/4.

59 Pon Vasanth B.A, 'Amit Shah flags off En Mann En Makkal yatra at Rameswaram; says CM Stalin should be ashamed of retaining Senthilbalaji as Minister,' *The Hindu*, 28 July 2023, 2.

60 'CM hits out at Amit Shah, says En Mann En Makkal yatra is to wash away sins,' *The Hindu*, 30 July, 2023, 6.

61 'It is DMK that has to absolve itself of sins, responds Annamalai,' *The Hindu*, 29 July 2023. Accessed 1 August 2023, https://www.thehindu.com/news/national/tamil-nadu/it-is-dmk-that-has-to-absolve-itself-of-sins-says-annamalai/article67136277.ece.

62 '"Genocidal call": Udhayanidhi Stalin's remarks against "Sanatana Dharma" draw BJP fire,' *Times of India*, 3 September 2023. Accessed 1 October 2023, https://timesofindia.indiatimes.com/india/genocidal-call-udhayanidhi-stalins-remarks-against-sanatana-dharma-draw-bjp-fire/articleshow/103325217.cms?from=mdr.

63 Shubhomoy Sikdar, 'Destroying Sanatana Dharma is the hidden agenda of INDIA bloc: PM Modi,' *The Hindu*, 14 September 2023. Accessed 1 November 2023, https://www.thehindu.com/news/national/pm-modi-lays-foundation-stone-of-projects-worth-over-50700-cr-in-mp/article67306413.ece.

64 'Sanatana Dharma's eradication will annihilate Rajasthan's culture: PM Modi in election rally,' *The Hindu*, 21 November 2023, 9.

65 'PM Modi taking my five-minute speech across India, says T.N. Minister Udhayanidhi Stalin,' *The Hindu*, 22 November 2023, 6.

66 'South Indian traditions of Hindu Dharma have opposed Sanatana Dharma for over 2000 years,' *ULLEKH NP*, 5 September 2023. Accessed 1 October 2023. https://ullekhnp.com/2023/09/05/b-jeyamohan-hindu-traditions-sanatana-dharma-shaivite/.

67 '"Sanatanam-l alla varnasramathil thaan prachanai! Udhaynithiku theiryuma?' - Tamilaruvi Manian,' *Tamil News*, YouTube, 38:09, 18 September 2023. https://youtu.be/ay2PDNEVhRQ?si=WL9AYTJNO hVmS88O; Mohamed Imranullah S., 'Sanatana Dharma row | Udhayanidhi Stalin, A. Raja statements "perverse, divisive", says Madras High Court,' *The Hindu*, 6 March 2024, 2.

68 Jaya Menon, '"DMK files part 2 will be out soon": Tamil Nadu BJP president K Annamalai,' *Times of India*, 12 June 2023. Accessed 1 July 2023, https://timesofindia.indiatimes.com/city/chennai/dmk-files-part-2-will-be-out-soon-tamil-nadu-bjp-president-k-annamalai/articleshow/100926923.cms?from=mdr.

69 Kavya Shanmugasundharam, ed., *Pasumpon Sarithiram*, (Chennai: Kavya, 3rd ed., 2022), 145; T. Ramakrishnan, 'What really happened in the 1956 Madurai event, involving C.N. Annadurai and Muthuramalinga Thevar,' *The Hindu*, 20 September 2023. Accessed 1 November 2023, https://www.theindu.com/news/national/tamil-nadu/what-really-happened-in-the-1956-madurai-event-involving-annadurai-and-muthuramalinga-thevar/article67327497.ece.

70 Krishnadas Rajagopal, 'T.N. moves SC against Governor Ravi over delay in clearing Bills,',' *The Hindu*, 1 November 2023, 1, 16.

71 Krishnadas Rajagopal, 'Supreme Court to hear Tamil Nadu, Kerala pleas against their Governors on November 20,' *The Hindu*, 19 November 2023, 12.

72 '"Matter of serious concern": Supreme Court's message to Punjab, Tamil Nadu governors over delay in assent to bills,' *Times of India*, 10 November 2023. Accessed 1 December 2023.

73 B. Kolappan, 'Tamil Nadu CM Stalin says Governor's act is illegal, anti-people and against sovereignty of Assembly,' *The Hindu*, 19 November 2023, 6.

74 J. Sam Daniel Stalin, '"What Was Governor Doing For 3 Years?" Supreme Court On Tamil Nadu Bills,' NDTV, 20 November 2023. Accessed 23 November 2023.

75 ETB Sivapriyan, 'TN Guv accords sanction to prosecute two ex-ministers from AIADMK,' *Deccan Chronicle*, 22 November 2023. Accessed 1 December 2023.

76   Krishnadas Rajagopal, 'Tamil Nadu Governor cannot refer re-enacted Bills to President, says Supreme Court,' *The Hindu*, 1 December 2023, 2, 12.

77   'Ravi meets Stalin, holds discussions,' *The Hindu*, 31 December 2023, 1, 10.

78   Arun Janardhanan, 'Madras HC reopens cases against two more DMK ministers, says 'something very rotten' in acquittal,' *Indian Express*, 23 August 2023. Accessed 2 November 2023, https://indianexpress.com/article/political-pulse/madras-hc-reopens-cases-against-two-more-dmk-ministers-8905228/.

79   S. Rajesh, '"DVAC Is Becoming A Chameleon," says Justice Anand Venkatesh Of Madras HC While Hearing Suo Moto Revision Of Case Against O Panneerselvam,' *Swarajya*, 31 August 2023. Accessed 1 November 2023, https://swarajyamag.com/tamil-nadu/dvac-is-becoming-a-chameleon-says-justice-anand-venkatesh-of-madras-hcwhile-hearing-suo-moto-revision-of-case-against-o-panneerselvam.

80   Arun Janardhanan, 'Justice Anand Venkatesh, the Madras HC judge who "opened can of worms" by revisiting cases against DMK leaders,' *Indian Express*, 19 September 2023. Accessed 1 October 2023, https://indianexpress.com/article/cities/chennai/venkatesh-madras-hc-judge-revisiting-cases-dmk-leaders-8945465/.

81   Mohamed Imranullah S., 'No bail for Senthilbalaji, Madras High Court dismisses his plea,' *The Hindu*, 28 February 2024, 2.

82   Mohamed Imranullah S., 'T.N. Minister Periyasamy suo moto revision | Madras High Court sets aside his discharge from irregular plot allotment case,' *The Hindu*, 28 February 2024, 2.

83   '"Won't allow DMK to loot public money," says PM Modi in Tamil Nadu,' the *Week*, 4 March 2024, https://www.theweek.in/news/india/2024/03/04/wont-allow-dmk-to-loot-public-money-says-pm-modi-in-tamil-nadu.html.

84   'Elections 2024,' *The Hindu*, 4 April 2024, 4.

85   C. Palanivel Rajan, '"DMK, Congress will never succeed in developing T.N., will only scam, loot public": PM Modi,' *The Hindu*, 15 March 2024, https://www.thehindu.com/news/national/tamil-nadu/dmk-congress-will-never-succeed-in-developing-tn-will-only-scam-loot-public-pm-modi/article67953991.ece.

86   'Poll Bonds Scheme A Himalayan Scam: CM,' *The Hindu*, 23 March 2024, 1, 8.

87   'Edappadi Palanisamy Campaigns,' 27 March 2024, YouTube, 3:03, https://youtu.be/4U-2C6xo_pA.

88 '"Tamils are educated, will not fall for roadshows", says Palaniswami in Pollachi,' *The Hindu*, 11 April 2024, 4.

89 DMK Election Manifesto, Lok Sabha Elections 2024. Accessed 27 March 2024, https://dmk.blob.core.windows.net/website/assets/DMK_Election_Manifesto_Eng_Karthi_33ac415568.

90 'AIADMK manifesto promises Rs 3,000 monthly assistance to women,' *Economic Times*, 19 March 2024. Accessed 20 March 2024, https://economictimes.indiatimes.com/news/elections/lok-sabha/tamil-nadu/aiadmk-manifesto-promises-rs-3000-monthly-assistance-to-women/articleshow/108713865.cms?from=mdr; 'AIADMK manifesto | Multiple avenues to boost State revenue, dual citizenship for Sri Lankan Tamils are among key proposals,' *The Hindu*, 22 March 2024.

91 Pon Vasanth, B.A, 'R.N. Ravi refuses to read Governor's address in T.N. Assembly,' *The Hindu*, 12 February 2024, 1, 10.

92 '"Electoral bonds are 'white-collar corruption' of the BJP": T.N. CM Stalin,' *The Hindu*, 17 March 2024, 2.

93 Soumyadip Sinha, 'Cartoonscape,' *The Hindu*, 4 April 2024, 11.

94 D. Suresh Kumar, 'Drugs, a money trail, and politics in Tamil Nadu,' *The Hindu*, 12 March 2024, 9.

95 'T.N. House passes resolutions against delimitation and 'One Nation, One Election' proposal,' *The Hindu*, 15 February 2024, 1, 6.

96 Narendra Modi (Narendra Modi), X, 31 March 2024, 9:46 am, https://twitter.com/narendramodi/status/1774289695821938823.

97 T. Ramakrishnan, 'Lok Sabha elections | Katchatheevu issue unlikely to have electoral impact in Tamil Nadu,' *The Hindu*, 1 April 2021. Accessed 2 April 2024, https://www.thehindu.com/elections/lok-sabha/lok-sabha-elections-katchatheevu-issue-unlikely-to-have-electoral-impact-in-tamil-nadu/article68016513.ece.

98 Narendra Modi (Narendra Modi), X, 1 April 2024, 8:44 am, https://twitter.com/narendramodi/status/1774636476506223045.

99 Katchatheevu row | 'Don't hide truth . . .' EAM Jaishankar sharp . . . YouTube, ANI News, 3 April 2024, 5:46.

100 P. Chidambaram (P. Chidambaram_IN), X, 1 April 2024, 6.06 pm, https://twitter.com/PChidambaram_IN/status/1774777899192647840?ref_src=twsrc%5Egoogle%7Ctwcamp%5Eserp%7Ctwgr%5Etweet.

101 'Did Modi raise Katchatheevu issue with Sri Lanka even once in the last 10 years, asks Stalin,' *The Hindu*, 3 April 2024. Accessed 5 April 2024, https://www.thehindu.com/elections/lok-sabha/did-modi-raise-katchatheevu-issue-with-sri-lanka-even-once-in-the-last-10-years-asks-stalin/article68021177.ece#:~:text=Jagathrakshakan%20

(Arakkonam)%2C%20Mr.,affected%20fishermen%20in%20Tamil%20 Nadu.

102 '"AIADMK will cease to exist": Annamalai's big claim at Edappadi Palaniswami's party,' *India Today*, 13 April 2024. Accessed 17 April 2024, https://www.indiatoday.in/elections/video/aiadmk-will-cease-to-exist-annamalais-big-claim-at-edappadi-palaniswamis party-2526782-2024-04-13?onetap=true.

Chapter 31: The Near Future

1   Kannan, *Anna*, 164–65.

2   S. Kumaresan, 'Viduthalai Chiruthaigal Katchi reshapes identity, appoints 17 non-Dalits as district secretaries,' *New Indian Express*, 14 August 2023. Accessed 1 September 2023, https://www.newindianexpress.com/states/tamil-nadu/2023/aug/14/viduthalai-chiruthaigal-katchi-reshapes-identity-appoints-17-non-dalits-as-district-secretaries-2605074.html.

3   'Tamil Nadu Uniformed Services Recruitment Board: Sub-inspector exam held to fill aspirants,' *Times of India*, 26 June 2022. Accessed 1 July 2022, https://timesofindia.indiatimes.com/city/chennai/sub-inspector-exam-held-to-fill-aspirants/articleshow/92465507.cms.

4   Employment Exchange Statistics 2023, Ministry of Labour and Employment, Directorate General of Employment, 8, 15, 23. Accessed 2 November 2023, https://dge.gov.in/dge/sites/default/files/2023-03/Employment_Exchange_2023.pdf.

5   'Tangedco's losses narrowed in fiscal 2023 after tariff revision, says ratings firm,' *The Hindu*, 11 June 2023. Accessed 1 July 2023, https://www.thehindu.com/news/national/tamil-nadu/tangedcos-losses-narrowed-in-fiscal-2023-after-tariff-revision-says-ratings-firm/article66958045.ece.

6   CAG Report 2021, Accessed 1 July 2023, https://cag.gov.in/uploads/download_audit_report/2021/Chapter%20-%20 1-062a07ef523c9c8.63909162.pdf

7   'Tamil Nadu fares poorly in green rankings, is at 21 among 29,' *Times of India*, 6 June 2023. Accessed 1 July 2023, https://timesofindia.indiatimes.com/city/chennai/tn-fares-poorly-in-green-rankings-is-at-21-among-29/articleshow/100780179.cms?from=mdr.

8   Milan Vaishnav and Jamie Hintson, 'India's Emerging Crisis of Representation,' Carnegie Endowment for International Peace, 14 March 2019. Accessed 1 July 2022, https://carnegieendowment.org/2019/03/14/india-s-emerging-crisis-of-representation-pub-78588.

Select Bibliography

Books

Advani, L.K. *My Country My Life*. New Delhi, Rupa Publications, 2010.

A. Govindasamy Oru Sagaptham. Centenary Souvenir, Villupuram, AGS Pathippagam, 2017.

Aiyar, Mani Shankar. *The Rajiv I Knew and Why He Was India's Most Misunderstood Prime Minister*. Juggernaut, New Delhi, 2024.

Anna Centenary Souvenir. Dinamani, 2009.

Anna Commemorative Issue. Ananda Vikatan, 30 March 1969.

Anna (C.N. Annadurai), Perarignar. *Thambiku Annavin Kadithangal*. 7 vols. Chennai, Poompuhar Pathippagam, 2002.

Anaimuthu, V. ed. *Periyar E.V.R. Sindhanaigal*, 3 vols. Tiruchi, Thinkers Forum, 1974.

Arulselvan, S. *Annavin Arasiyal Guru:'Sunday Observer' P. Balasubramaniam*. 2nd edn. Chennai, Vikatan Pirasuram, 2017.

Arumugham, Veerapandi. *Dravida Iyakka Varalaatril En Payanam*. Chennai, Seethai Pathippagam, 2019.

Ayyamuthu, Kovai. *Enadhu Ninaivugal*. Coimbatore, Vidiyal Pathippagam, 2010.

Bhaktavatsalam, M. *Enadhu Ninaivugal*. Chennai, Jananayaga Seva Sangam, 1971.

Bala, Ajayan, *Periyar*. Chennai, Vikatan Pirasuram, 2009.

Balasingham, Anton. *Liberation*. Mitcham, Fairmax Publishing Ltd. 2003.

Chokkan, *Annaandhu Paar*. Chennai, Vikatan Pirasuram, 2009.

Dheenadayalan, P. *MGR*. Chennai, Sixth Sense Publications, 2014.

Dixit, J.N. *Assignment Colombo*. New Delhi, Konark Publishers, 1998.

Silver Jubilee Souvenir. Chennai, DMK, 1975.

Dravida Nadu. First Anniversary Issue, 24 September 1950.

Gopannaa, A. ed. *Periyarum Perundhalaivarum*. Chennai, Nava India Pathippagam, 2007.

------------. *Kamaraj Oru Sagaptham*. Chennai, Nava India Pathippagam, 2001.

Gowthaman, Pasu. ed. *Periyar E.V. Ramasamy: Naan Sonnaal Unakku Yaen Kobam Vara Vendum?* 5 vols. Chennai, New Century Book House, 2017.

Gunaratna, Rohan. *Indian Intervention in Sri Lanka: The Role of India's Intelligence Agencies*. Colombo, South Asian Network on Conflict Research, 1993.

Jayakar, Pupul. *Indira Gandhi*. Gurgaon, Penguin Random House, 2017.

Jayakanthan. *Oru Ilyakivadhiyin Arasial Anubhavangal*. Madurai, Meenakshi Puthaga Nilayam, 1974.

-------------------------. *Manavaasam*. 13th edn. Chennai, Vanathi Pathippagam, 2000.

-------------------------. *Vanavaasam*. 23rd edn. Chennai, Vanathi Pathippagam, 2000.

-------------------------. *Naan Paartha Arasiyal*. 11th edn. Chennai, Kannadhasan Pathippagam, 2007.

-------------------------. *Suyasaridham*. 22nd edn. Chennai, Kannadhasan Pathipipagam, 2007.

-------------------------. *Cinema Sandhayil Muppadhu Aandugal*. Chennai, Kannadhasan Pathippagam, 2013.

Karunanidhi, M. Kalaignar. *Nenjuku Needhi*. 6 vols. Chennai, Thamizhkani Pathippagam, 2020.

-------------------------------. *Kalaignarin Kadithangal*. 54 vols. Chennai, Seethai Pathippagam, 2023.

Kalaignarin Sattamandra Uraigal. 12 vols. Chennai, Poompuhar Pirasuram, 2008.

Karuppiah, Pala. *Ippadithaan Uruvaanen*. Chennai, Kizhakku Pathippagam, 2024.

Kannan, R. *Anna: The Life and Times of C.N. Annadurai*. 2nd edn. Gurgaon, Penguin Random House India, 2017.

-------------. *MGR: A Life*. Gurgaon, Penguin Random House India, 2017.

Karunanandam, Kavignar. *Anna Sila Ninaivugal*. Chennai, Poovazhagi Pathippagam, 1986.

Khilnani, Sunil. *Incarnations: A History of India in 50 Lives*. Delhi: Penguin, 2016.

Kripalani, J.B., *My Times: An Autobiography*. New Delhi: Rupa Publications, 2004.

Thavasu, M. *Latchiap Poraali L.G. (70th Birthday Souvenir)*. Thanjavur, Thanjaivaazh Kannanthangudi Makkal Munnetra Sangam, 2012.

Manian, Tamilaruvi. *Oru Vazhipokanin Vazkaipayanam*. Chennai, Karpagam Puthagalayam, 2000.

Manoharan, K. *Thamizhagath Thalaivar Kalaignar*, Chennai, Poompuhar Pathippagam, 1988.

Menon, Shivshankar. *Choices: Inside the Making of India's Foreign Policy (Geopolitics in the 21st Century)*. Washington, D.C., Brookings Institution Press, 2016.

Mukerji, Debashish. *The Disruptor: How Vishwanath Pratap Singh Shook India*. Gurgaon, HarperCollins, 2021.

Panneerselvan, A.S. *Karunanidhi*. Gurgaon, Viking, 2021.

Narayan, S. *The Dravidian Years: Politics and Welfare in Tamil Nadu*. Delhi, Oxford University Press, 2018.

Natarajan, Uttara. *Plain Speaking: A Sudra's Story*. New Delhi, Permanent Black, 2007.

Ramachandran, M.G. *Naan Yaen Pirandhen?* 2 vols. Chennai, Rajarajan Pathippagam, 2003.

Ramanathan, V. *Maanbimugu Ulavuthurai*. Chennai, Tamil Puthagalayam, 2008.

Ramesh, Thuglak. ed. *Enadhu Arasiyal Payanam*. Chennai, The Alliance Publication Company, 2021.

MGRin Sattamandra Uraigal, Chennai, Government of Tamil Nadu, 2017.

Muthukumar, R. *Thamizhaga Arasiyal Varalaaru*. Chennai, New Horizon Media Pvt Ltd, 2013.

--------------------. *Indhia Therdhal Varalaaru*. Chennai, Sixth Sense Publications, 2015.

--------------------. *Madhuvilaku: Arasiyalum, Varalaarum*. Chennai, Sixth Sense Publications, 2015.

Malarmannan. *Thi Mu Ka Uruvanadhu Yaen*. Chennai: Kizhakku Pathippagam, 2009.

Maperum Tamil Kanavu, Chennai, Tamil Thisai, 2019.

Mehta, Vinod. *Lucknow Boy: A Memoir*. Gurgaon, Penguin Viking, 2011.

----------------------. *Editor Unplugged: Media, Magnates, Netas and Me*. Gurgaon, Penguin, 2015.

Narayanan, Vellore. *Oru Mayorin Ninaivugal*. Chennai, Santha Pathippagam, 2006.

Nedunchezhian, Navalar. *Vaazhvil Naan Kandathum Ketathum*. Chennai, Navalar Nedunchezhian Pathippagam, 2000.

Neelamani, K.P. *Thanthai Periyar*. Chennai, CreateSpace Independent Publishing Platform, 2017.

Parthasarathy, T.M. *Thi. Mu. Ka. Varalaaru*. 7th edn. Chennai, Bharati Pathippagam, 1998.

Pradhan, R.D. *My Years with Rajiv and Sonia*. New Delhi, Hay House, 2014.

Rajaram, K. *Oru Saamaniyanin Ninaivugal*. Chennai, Nakkheeran Pathippagam, 2014.

Ramadoss, S. *Kazhagathin Kathai*. Chennai, Puthiya Arasiyal Pathippagam, 2017.

Ramaswamy, Cho. *Ivargalai Sandhithen*. Chennai, The Alliance Publication Company, 2016.

----------------------. *Adhirshtam Thanta Anubhavangal*. 6th edn. Chennai, The Alliance Publication Company, 2015.

----------------------. *Anubhavangalum Abiprayangalum*. Chennai, The Alliance Publication Company, 2019.

----------------------. *Ivargal Solgiraargal*. Chennai, The Alliance Publication Company, 2019.

Ramasamy, Kalyani. *Nadipisaipular K.R. Ramasamy Ninaivugal*. Chennai, Vasantha Pathippagam, 2014.

Sabanayagam, P. *Service to the Nation*. Chennai, Notion Press, 2019.

Saidai, Duraisamy. *Vergaluku Velicham*. 2nd edn. Chennai, Manidha Neyam Ilavasa I.A.S. Academy, 2018.

Sampath, Delhi. *Delhiyil DMK, Anna, Kalaignar: En Parvaiyil*. Chennai, Uyirmai Pathippagam, 2009.

Sinha, Shakthi. *The Years That Changed India: Vajpayee*. Gurgaon, Vintage Books, 2021.

Sinha, Yashwant. *Confessions of a Swadeshi Reformer*. Gurgaon, Viking, 2007.

Satyendran, Tiruchi. *Thanthai Periyarudanum Thalaivar Kalaigarudunum Car Payanangalil*. Chennai, Seethai Pathippagam, 2018.

-------------------------. *Ini Oru Periyarai Parpoma?* Chennai, Naam Thamizhar Pathippagam, 2009.

Mridula Mukherjee, ed. *Selected Works of Jawaharlal Nehru, Second Series*, New Delhi, Jawaharlal Nehru Memorial Fund, 2009.

Selvaraj, K.M. *Maamanidhar Mathiazhagan*. Chennai, Kaniur Pathippagam, 2004.

Senguttuvan, M. Kavikondal, *Nenjam Maravaa Nigazhchigal*. Chennai, Thamaraiselvi Pathippagam, 2002.

Senthilnathan, Aazhi, ed. *1974: Maanila Suyaatchi*. Chennai, Aazhi Publishers, 2022.

Sitapati, Vinay. *Half Lion: How P.V. Narasimha Rao Transformed India*. Gurgaon, Penguin Viking, 2015.

Sivagnanam, Ma. Po. *Enadhu Porattam*. Chennai, Poongodi Pathipppagam, 2018.

----------------. *MGRudan Enakirundha Thodarbu*, Chennai, Poongodi Pathippagam, 2018.

Solai. *MGR in Theerkatharisanam*. Chennai, Nakkheeran Publications, 2010.

------. *Netru-Indru-Naalai*. Chennai, Nakkheeran Publications, 2012.

Shanmugasundharam, Kavya, ed. *Pasumpon Kalanjiyam: Thevarin Sorpozhivugal*, Chennai: Kavya, 2nd ed., 2023.

------------------------, ed. *Pasumpon Sarithiram*, Chennai: Kavya, 3rd edn., 2022.

Stalin, Durga. *Avaraum Naanum*. Chennai, Uyirmai Pathippagam, 2018.

Stalin, M.K. *Ungalil Oruvan*. Chennai: Poompuhar Pathippagam, 2022.

Swaminathan, S. *Karunanidhi: Man of Destiny*. New Delhi, Affiliated East West Press, 2014.

Tamilvanan. *Thalaisirandha Kelvi Bathilgal*. 2nd edn., Chennai, Manimekalai Pirasuram, 1988.

Thakur, Janardan. *Prime Ministers: Nehru to Vajpayee*. New Delhi, BPI India, 2002.

--------------------. *All the Janata Men*. New Delhi, Vikas Publishing House, 1978.

Thangapandian, P. *Dravida Munnetra Kazhaga Therthal Arikkaigal*. Chennai, Nalanda Pathippagam, 2008.

Thennarasu, S.S. *Pennilaatha Oorinile*. Chennai, Thirumaran Nilayam, 1990.

Therkilirundhu Oru Suryian. Chennai, Tamil Thisai, 2015.

Thirunavukkarasu, K. *Thi. Mu. Ka: Prachanaygalum Pilavugalum Marumalarchiyai Noaki* . . . Chennai, Nakkeeran Pathippagam, 2022.

Thirumavelan, Pa. *Yaaraithaan Edhirkavillai?* Chennai, Vikatan, Pirasuram, 2017.

Thiruvidam, Ara. *Thiruvallikeni Mudhal Thiruvarur Varai*. Chennai, Gowra Pathippagam, 2018.

Veeramani, K. *'Periyar' Maraindhar: Periyar Vazhga*. Chennai, Dravidar Kazhagam.

Udayamurthi, Dr M.S. *Americargal Paarvayil Mudhalvar Anna Makkal Thilagam M.G.R.,* Chennai, Vidwan Pathippagam, 2003.

Varalaatru Suvadugal. Chennai, Daily Thanthi Publications, 2019.

Venkatachalam, M.S. *My Days With Anna.* Tiruchi, Tamil Kudil Pathippagam, 2010.

Velnambi, K. *Thamizhanai Uyarthiya Thalaimagan Uraigal.* 6th edn. Chennai, Seethai Pathippagam, 2018.

------------------. *Payanam.* 3 vols. 4th edn. Chennai, Seethai Pathippagam, 2017.

Venu, A.S. *Verdict.* Chennai, Kalai Mandram, 1953.

Vivekanandan, N., Iniyan Sampath and Kalpanadasan. ed. *E.V.K. Sampathum Dravida Iyakkamum.* Chennai, Iniyan Sampath Pathippagam, 2013.

Official Reports

Era Sezhian, Era. ed. *Shah Commission Report: Lost and Regained.* Chennai: Aazhi Publishers, 2011.

Sarkaria Commission of Inquiry, First Report, New Delhi, Ministry of Home Affairs, 1977.

Summary Record of Discussions of the National Development (NDC) Meetings: Five Decades of National Building (Fifty NDC Meetings).

President's Order, 1960, Copy of Notification No. 2/8/60-O.L. (Ministry of Home Affairs), dated 27 April 1960, Accessed 20 March 2020, https://rajbhasha.gov.in/en/presidents-order-1960.

Reserve Bank of India. *Gross State Domestic Product (Constant Prices).* New Delhi: RBI, 2022. Accessed 1 April 2023, https://rbi.org.in/Scripts/PublicationsView.aspx?id=21415.

Index

Scan QR code to access the
Penguin Random House India website